BOAT MECHANICAL SYSTEMS HANDBOOK

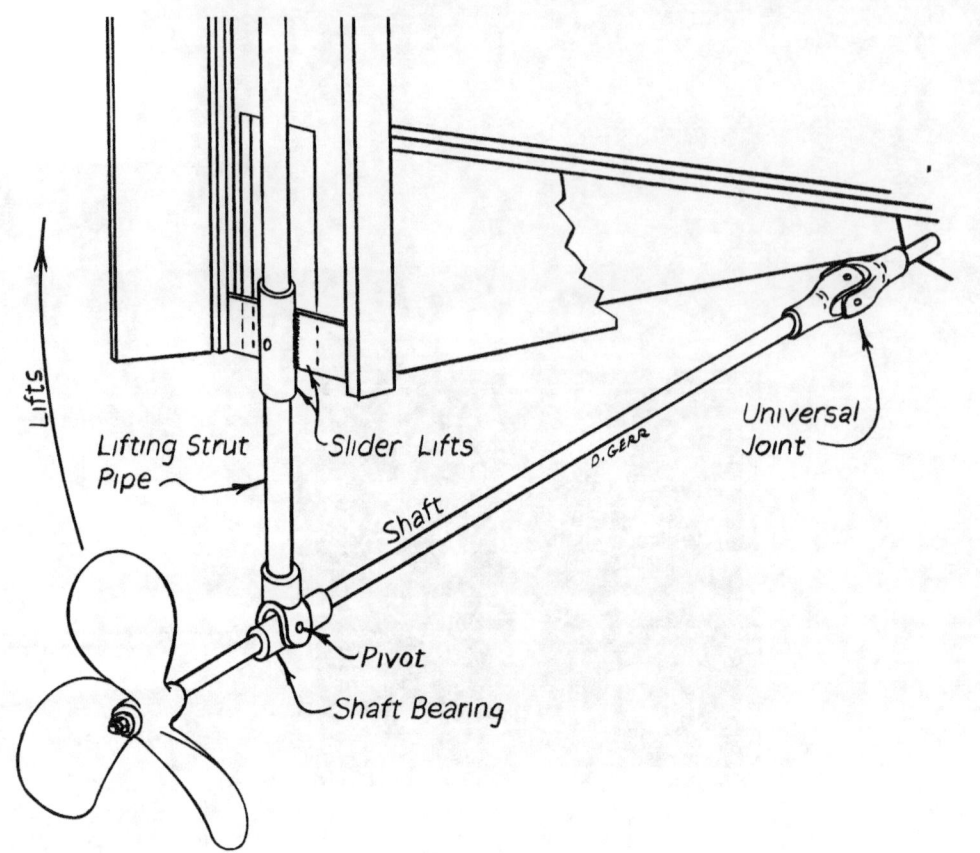

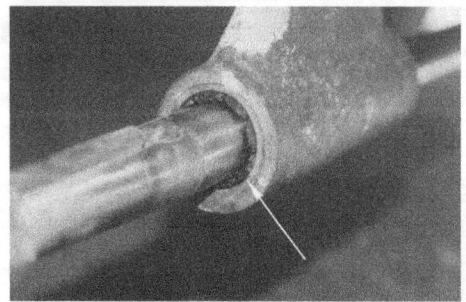

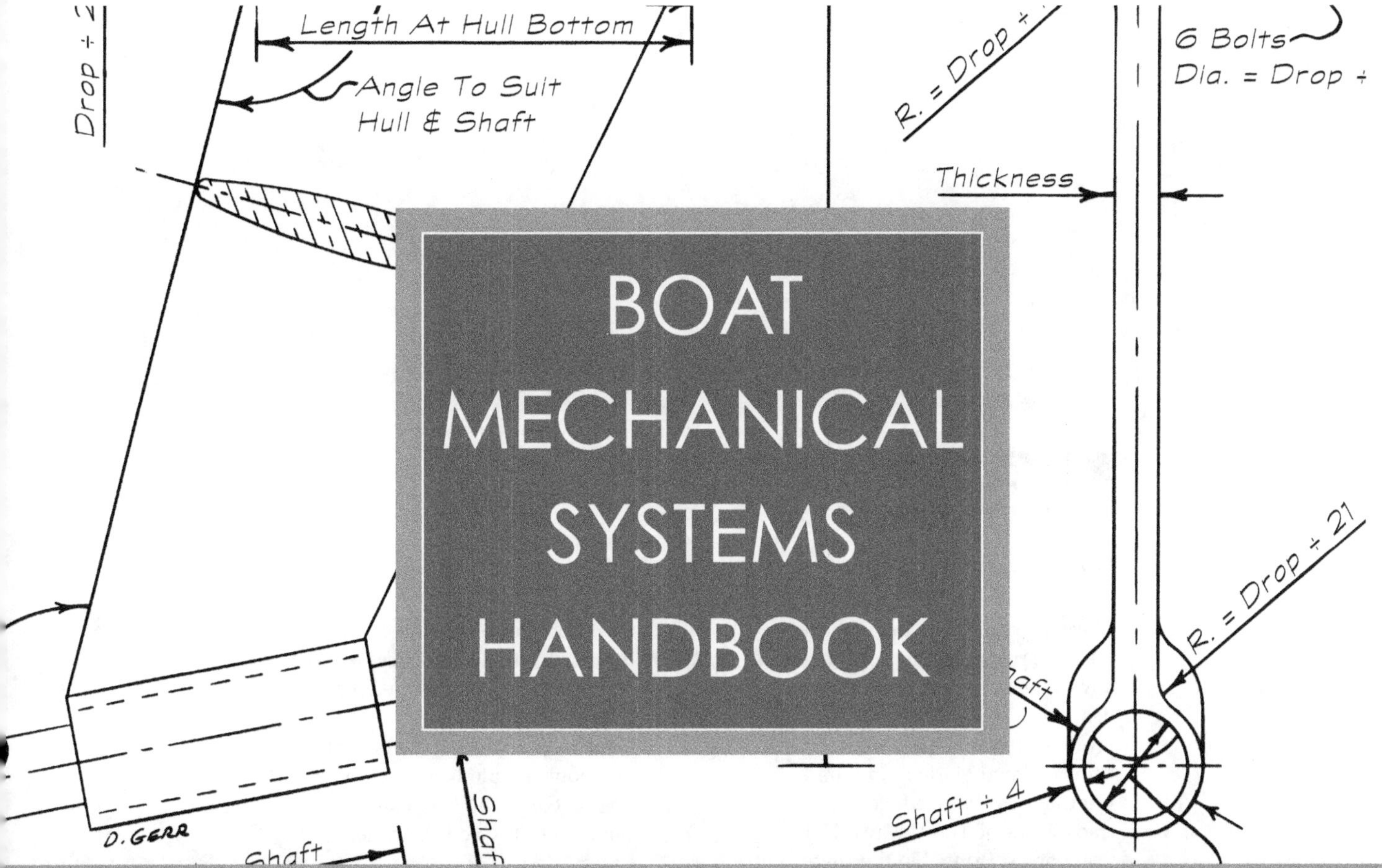

BOAT MECHANICAL SYSTEMS HANDBOOK

How to Design, Install, and Recognize Proper Systems in Boats

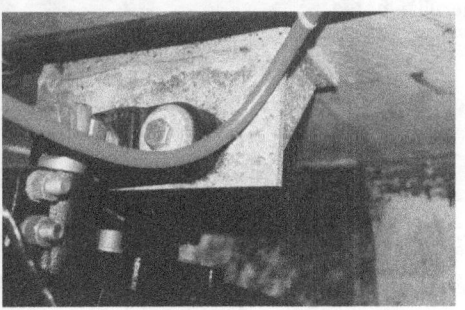

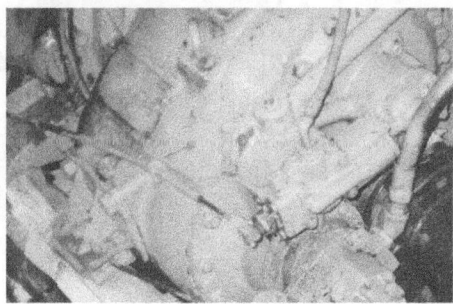

Dave Gerr

INTERNATIONAL MARINE / McGRAW-HILL

Camden, Maine • New York • Chicago • San Francisco • Lisbon • London • Madrid •
Mexico City • Milan • New Delhi • San Juan • Seoul • Singapore • Sydney • Toronto

The McGraw·Hill Companies

1 2 3 4 5 6 7 8 9 QPD QPD 0 9 8

© 2009 by Dave Gerr

All rights reserved. The publisher takes no responsibility for the use of any of the materials or methods described in this book, nor for the products thereof. The name "International Marine" and the International Marine logo are trademarks of The McGraw-Hill Companies. Printed in the United States of America.

Library of Congress Cataloging-in-Publication Data is on file at the Library of Congress.

ISBN 978-1-265-80722-1
MHID 1-26-580722-1

Questions regarding the content of this book should be addressed to www.internationalmarine.com

Questions regarding the ordering of this book should be addressed to
The McGraw-Hill Companies
Customer Service Department
P.O. Box 547
Blacklick, OH 43004
Retail customers: 1-800-262-4729
Bookstores: 1-800-722-4726

Photographs and illustrations by author unless otherwise noted.

In memory of my father, Raymond Gerr, the finest and smartest man I have ever known.

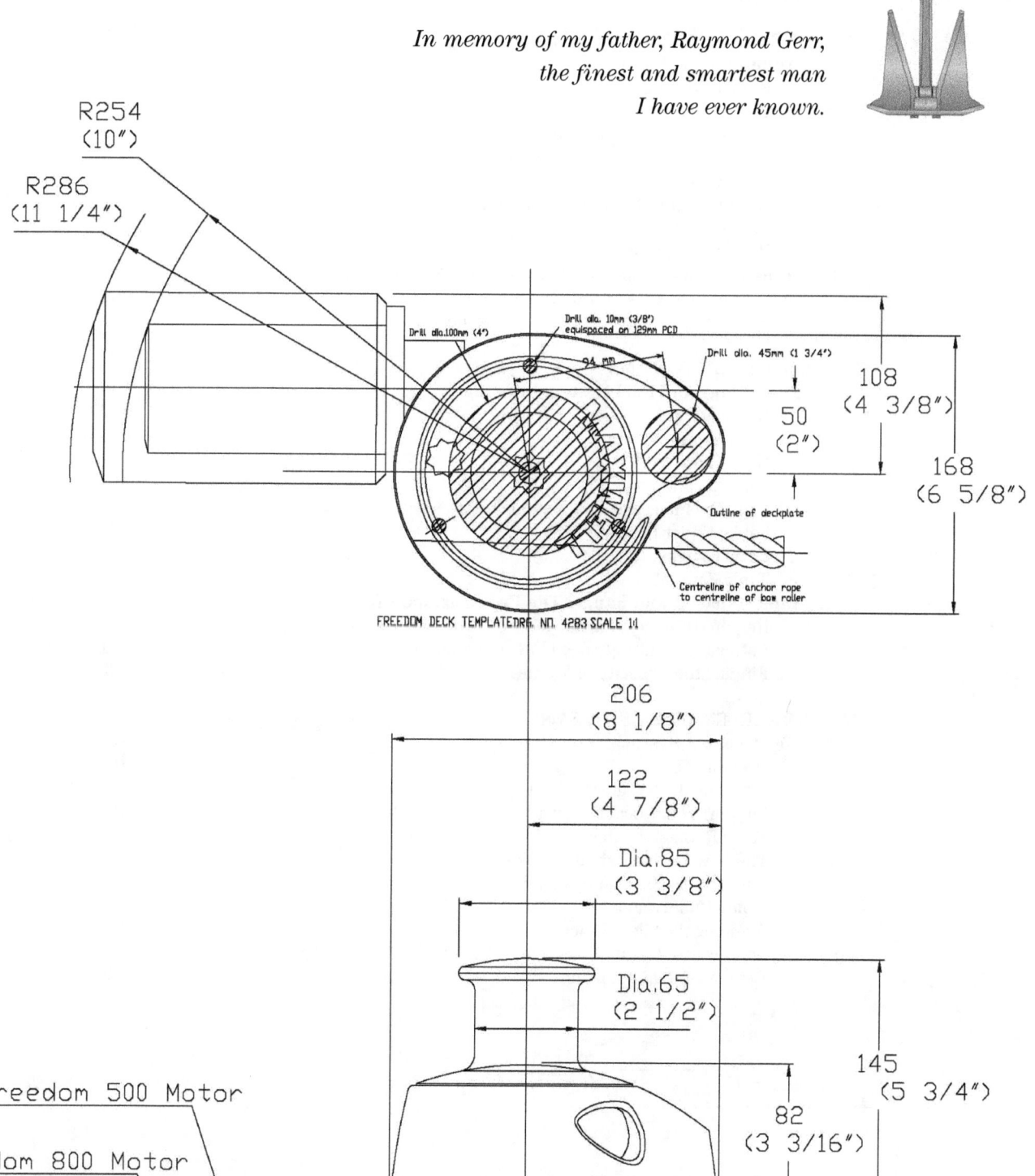

Contents

Lists of Figures, Tables, and Formula …… x
Acknowledgments …… xvii
Author's Notes …… xix
Introduction …… xxi

PART ONE. DRIVETRAIN INSTALLATIONS

1. Propellers and Shafts …… 1
  Proper Prop Nuts …… 1
  Blade Area …… 2
  Common Causes of Vibration and Noise …… 5
  Propeller Shafts: Diameter, Bearing Spacing, and Bearings …… 9
  Shaft Couplings and Keyways …… 15

2. Struts, Propeller Apertures, and Shaft Angle …… 18
  Propeller Struts …… 18
  Propeller Apertures and Shaft Angle …… 25

3. Transmission Geometry, CV Joints, Stuffing Boxes, and Engine Mounts and Beds …… 32
  Selecting Inboard Transmission Geometry …… 32

PART TWO. FUEL SYSTEMS

4. Fuel Piping and Fuel System Bonding …… 46
  Running Pipe …… 47

5. Fuel Tanks and Fittings …… 66
  Hold That Tank …… 66
  Tank Location …… 69
  Tank Openings and Penetrations …… 73
  Tanks Under Pressure …… 82
  Level Gauging …… 83
  Tank Materials …… 83

6. Tank Capacity and Range: The Free-Surface Effect …… 90
  Required Tankage for Range …… 90
  Estimating Cruising-Speed Fuel Consumption …… 91
  Finding the Capacity of a Tank …… 92

PART THREE. EXHAUST SYSTEMS

7. Wet Exhaust Systems …… 100
  Breathing Easy …… 101
  Watering the Exhaust …… 102
  Support Your Local Exhaust …… 106
  Make Room for Exhausts …… 108
  The Low-Engine Exhaust Problem …… 109
  The "Other" Exhaust Systems …… 114
  Going Underwater …… 119
  Avoiding the Silent Killer …… 125
  Summary of Requirements for a Reliable Wet Exhaust System …… 126
  Review of Requirements …… 126

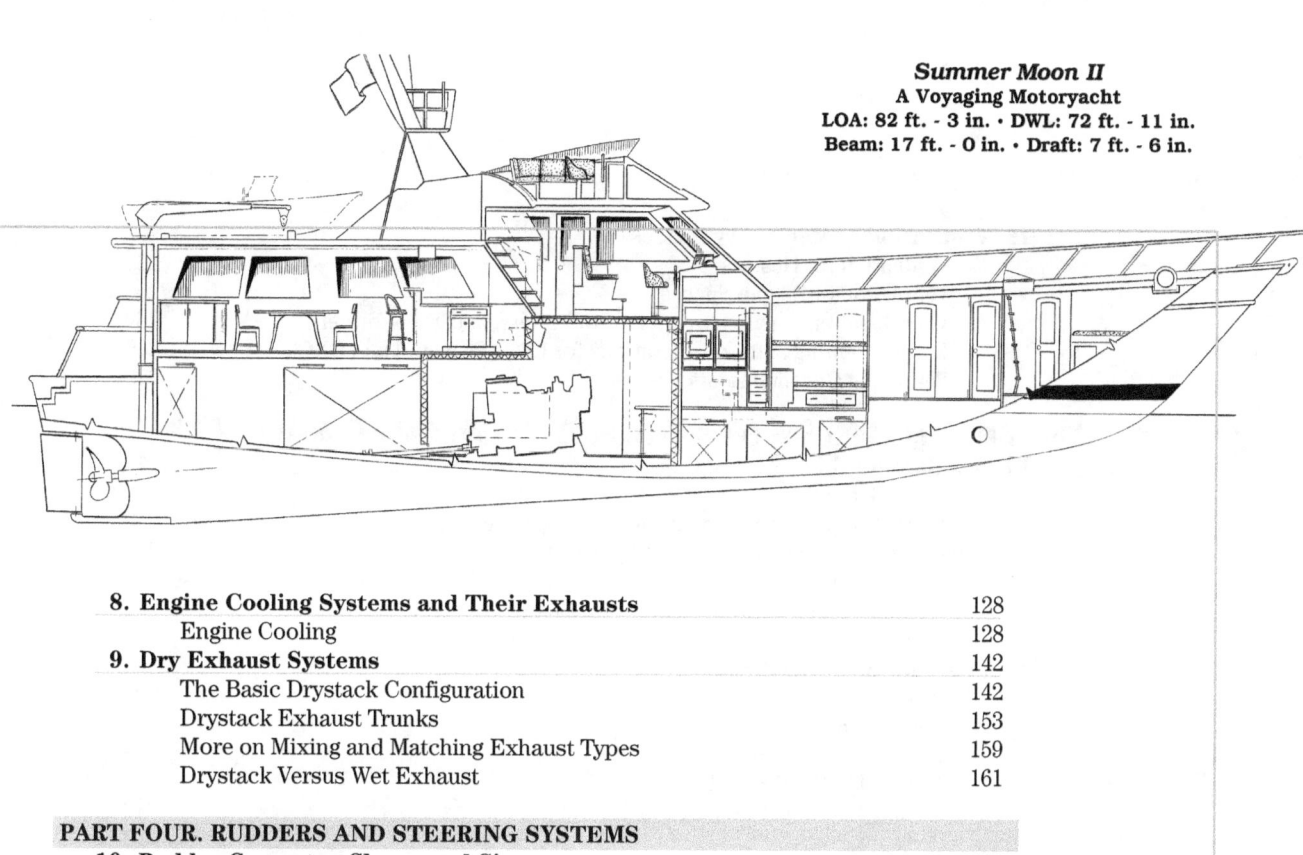

Summer Moon II
A Voyaging Motoryacht
LOA: 82 ft. - 3 in. • DWL: 72 ft. - 11 in.
Beam: 17 ft. - 0 in. • Draft: 7 ft. - 6 in.

8. Engine Cooling Systems and Their Exhausts	128
Engine Cooling	128
9. Dry Exhaust Systems	142
The Basic Drystack Configuration	142
Drystack Exhaust Trunks	153
More on Mixing and Matching Exhaust Types	159
Drystack Versus Wet Exhaust	161

PART FOUR. RUDDERS AND STEERING SYSTEMS

10. Rudder Geometry, Shape, and Size	163
Putting the Rudder to Work	163
Types of Rudders	165
Sizing Up the Rudder	168
The Rudder in Cross Section and Basic Scantlings	170
Rudder Profile or Planform	177
Boat Behavior in Turns	180
11. Rudder-Stock Size, Construction, and Bearing Specification	182
Rudder Stock, Bearing Calculations, and Construction	182
Rudder Bearings and Rudder Ports	189
Roller Bearings	194
12. Rudder-Stock Angle, Control, and Installation Considerations	197
Rudder-Stock Angle and Planing-Boat Rudder Configuration	197
Steering Systems: Controlling the Rudder	198
Fluid Power: Hydraulic Steering	202
Backup Steering Gear: Emergency Steering	208
Steering Refinements and Installation Considerations	211
Rudder Installation: Shaft and Propeller Removal	212
13. Unusual and Special Rudders: High-Lift Rudders	216
Ring-Form Rudders	216
High-Lift Rudders	219
Comparing Fishtail and Articulated Rudders (Flap Rudders)	226

PART FIVE. VENTILATION, AIR-CONDITIONING, AND HEATING

14. Ventilation of Passenger and Storage Areas	229
Ventilation of Passenger Compartments	231
Ventilation of Storage Spaces: Forepeak, Lazarette, Lockers	241
15. Air-Conditioning and Heating with Notes on Refrigeration	242
Air-Conditioning	242
Notes on Refrigeration	250
Cabin Heating	253
Thoughts on Heating and Air-Conditioning Installations	260

16. Ventilation of Machinery Spaces — 262
- Ventilation for Heaters — 262
- Ventilation of Engine Spaces — 263
- Vent Requirements for Inverters, Converters, and Transformers — 269
- Battery Venting and Considerations for LPG (Propane) and CNG — 270
- Venting of Gasoline Boats — 272

PART SIX. PLUMBING SYSTEMS WITH NOTES ON FIRE SUPPRESSION

17. Sea Suction — 278
- Seacocks — 278
- Hose Clamps, Sea Strainers, and Sharing Seacocks — 282

18. Bilge Systems, Fire Mains, and Fire Extinguishers — 288
- Bilge Systems — 288
- Thoughts and Recommendations on Bilge Systems for Boats — 295
- Fire Mains and Fire Suppression — 297

19. Selecting and Sizing Pumps — 302
- Types of Pumps — 302
- Understanding Head — 306
- Total Apparent Head — 309
- Acceptable Flow Speeds — 311
- Finding Required Pump Power — 312
- Pressure Drop — 313

20. Freshwater Systems — 314
- Freshwater Tanks and Water Tank Capacity — 315
- Freshwater Supply Piping — 316
- Freshwater Delivery Piping — 318
- Draining Away—Handling Gray Water — 319
- Running Pipe — 320

21. My Favorite Head: Thoughts and Recommendations on Marine Toilets and Installations — 322
- My Favorite Head—The Blakes Lavac Toilet — 323
- Head Installation Plumbing — 325
- Pumping Sludge—Handling Sewage — 326
- Types of Marine Toilets (Heads) — 327

PART SEVEN. ANCHORING SYSTEMS

22. Anchoring Systems, Anchor Types, and Anchor Selection — 331
- Anchoring Systems — 331
- Anchor Types — 332
- Anchor Size and Designation — 346
- Anchor Selection Recommendations — 346

23. Anchor Rode — 348
- Chain — 348
- Chain Fittings — 353
- Rope — 358
- Wire Anchor Rode — 363

24. Sizing the Anchor and Rode and Selecting Anchor-Handling Gear — 365
- Sizing the Anchor — 365
- Sizing the Rode — 366
- Selecting a Windlass — 370
- Anchor-Launching Considerations — 376
- Chain-Locker Requirements — 381
- Snubbing Up — 383

Appendix A. Calculating Areas of Plane Figures   386
Appendix B. International Pipe Standards and Pipe-Size Tables—Pipe-to-Hose Connections   388
     U.S. ISO Pipe Designations—DN Pipe Sizes   390
     U.S. Pipe Thread Standards   390
     Hose-to-Pipe Size Considerations   391
Appendix C. Measure and Unit Conversion Tables   396
Appendix D. Insulation Products and Sources   401
Bibliography   403
Index   405

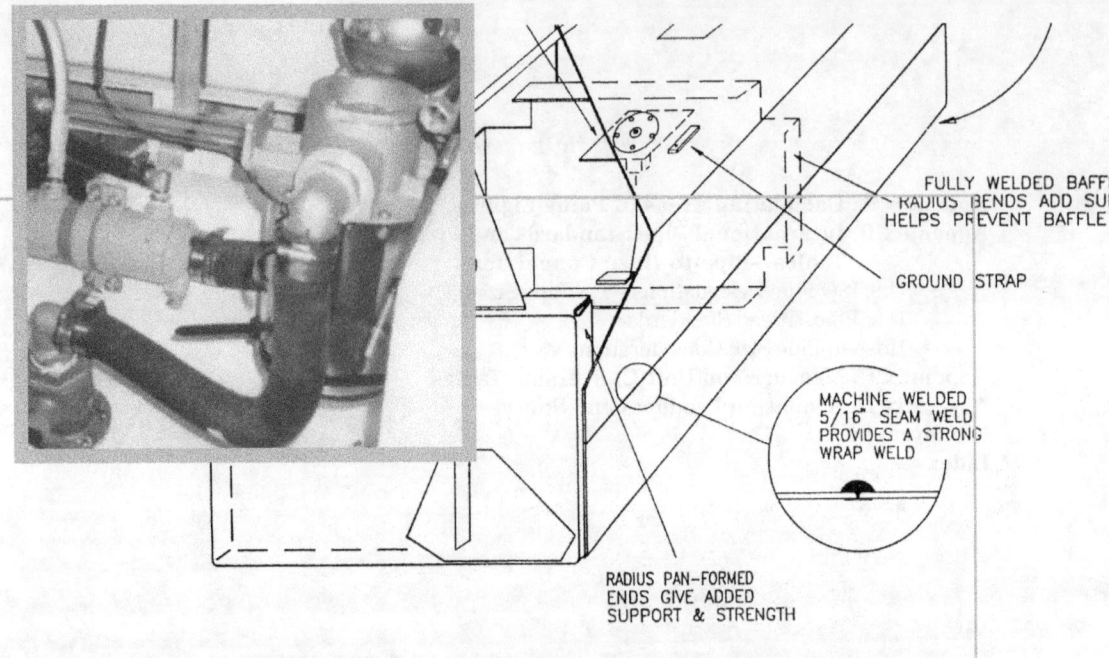

Lists of Figures, Tables, and Formula

Figure 1-1. Thread loading of a nut and locknut
Figure 1-2. A jam nut, applied under a large regular nut, is elastically deformed against bolt threads when the large nut is tightened
Figure 1-3. This segment of an SAE illustration clearly shows the smaller nut innermost
Figure 1-4. A standard 3-bladed prop and wide blade 5-bladed prop
Figure 1-5. Propeller clearances
Figure 1-6. Deep propeller tunnels
Figure 1-7. Recommended pocket proportions
Figure 1-8A and B. Pocket viewed from the stern (rear) and from starboard
Figure 1-9. Pocket or tunnel depth
Figure 1-10. V-section tunnel
Figure 1-11. Worn Cutless bearing
Figure 1-12. Pillow block
Figure 1-13. Intermediate strut bearing
Figure 1-14. Shaft coupling types
Figure 1-15. Tapered-bore coupling
Figure 1-16. Muff coupling
Figure 1-17. Keyway machining
Figure 1-18. Short hubs increase stress
Figure 2-1. I-strut dimensions
Figure 2-2. V-strut dimensions
Figure 2-3. Standard strut sections
Figure 2-4. Strut fastening
Figure 2-5. Metal hull strut construction: struts to girders
Figure 2-6. Metal hull strut construction: struts to floor or frame
Figure 2-7. Strut grounding skeg
Figure 2-8. Altering a keel to improve lobsterboat performance
Figure 2-9. Maximum shaft angle
Figure 2-10. Rotation of a right-hand wheel (viewed from astern)
Figure 2-11. Standard directions of rotation for twin screws (viewed from astern)
Figure 2-12. Different shaft placements compared
Figure 2-13. Single midships engine on centerline with angled shaft
Figure 2-14. Different shaft placements compared on twin-engine boats
Figure 3-1. Transmissions compared
Figure 3-2. Aquadrive system
Figure 3-3. CON-VEL CV joint
Figure 3-4. Flexible engine mount
Figure 3-5. Engine installed on rigid mounts
Figure 3-6. Jackshaft with universal joints
Figure 3-7. Retracting dory propeller
Figure 3-8. Cutaway view of retracting dory propeller box
Figure 3-9. Universal joint shaft configurations
Figure 3-10. Drivesaver-type coupling
Figure 3-11. Cutaway view of a rigid stuffing box
Figure 3-12. PSS shaft seal
Figure 3-13. Flexible stuffing box
Figure 3-14. Cracked transmission and hollow engine bed
Figure 3-15. Engine stringers
Figure 4-1. A fuel fire caused this boat to sink in minutes
Figure 4-2. Required fuel system access panels
Figure 4-3. Separ duplex fuel filter
Figure 4-4. Gasoline twin-tank piping
Figure 4-5. Diesel twin-tank piping
Figure 4-6. Fuel-piping or distribution manifold

Figure 4-7. Diesel day-tank fuel piping
Figure 4-8. Diesel day-tank fuel piping with common-rail manifolds
Figure 4-9. Common-rail fuel-feed manifold
Figure 4-10. Return oil cooler
Figure 4-11. Ball valve
Figure 4-12. Cutaway view of an open ball valve
Figure 4-13. A1 fuel hose
Figure 4-14. Recommended hose connectors
Figure 4-15. Hose clamp distance from hose end
Figure 4-16. A spring-type hose clamp is not acceptable for fuel lines
Figure 4-17. Twin fuel tank arrangement
Figure 5-1. Fuel tank installation
Figure 5-2. Tank hold-downs
Figure 5-3. Installed tank
Figure 5-4. *Kingfisher*
Figure 5-5. *Summer Moon II*
Figure 5-6. Fuel/air separators
Figure 5-7. Cutaway view of a Lifeguard fuel/air separator
Figure 5-8. Vent collection tank
Figure 5-9. ABYC's minimum clearance between ventilators and fuel tank fills
Figure 5-10. Splash-Stop installation
Figure 5-11. Splash-Stop
Figure 5-12. Seacurefill
Figure 5-13. Baffles in aluminum tank
Figure 5-14. Radius corner tank construction
Figure 5-15. Tank label
Figure 5-16. Painted aluminum wing tanks
Figure 6-1. Yanmar engine curves
Figure 6-2. Bow tank dimensions
Figure 6-3. Tank half-sections (in English units)
Figure 6-4. Tank half-sections (metric units)
Figure 6-5. ATL reticulated-foam bladder tanks
Figure 7-1. Exhaust system
Figure 7-2. Taking manometer readings
Figure 7-3. Exhaust line diameter as a function of engine power for gas and diesel engines
Figure 7-4. Water-jacketed exhaust riser
Figure 7-5. Water injection
Figure 7-6. Exhaust hose clamps
Figure 7-7. Exhaust tube glassed to transom—not a good idea
Figure 7-8. Malleable iron hose clamp
Figure 7-9. Note how much space the exhaust system requires
Figure 7-10. Inner workings of a waterlift muffler
Figure 7-11. Waterlift muffler installed
Figure 7-12. Standard waterlift muffler installation
Figure 7-13. Waterlift muffler above manifold exit
Figure 7-14. North Sea exhaust system with waterlift muffler
Figure 7-15. Forty-two foot *Summer Kyle/Belle Marie* with North Sea exhaust
Figure 7-16. Standpipe exhaust system
Figure 7-17. Details of a standpipe exhaust
Figure 7-18. Main engine raw-water piping
Figure 7-19. Profile of the exhaust system in a 72-foot schooner
Figure 7-20. Exhaust system continued (section view)
Figure 7-21. Schnell boat machinery and arrangement
Figure 7-22. Cape Dory 40 with underwater exhaust outlet
Figure 7-23. Inside view of the Cape Dory's underwater exhaust
Figure 7-24. Plan of the Cape Dory 40's underwater exhaust system
Figure 7-25. Inboard profile of the Cape Dory's underwater exhaust
Figure 7-26. Underwater exhaust nacelle on the Schnell boat
Figure 7-27. Exterior view of the Cape Dory's underwater exhaust system
Figure 7-28. Water-separator muffler
Figure 7-29. Waterlift versus water-separator muffler
Figure 7-30. The Centek VernaSep muffler
Figure 8-1. Raw-water cooling
Figure 8-2. Heat exchangers
Figure 8-3. Radiator cooling
Figure 8-4. Heat-exchanger cooling: jacket water aftercooled
Figure 8-5. Dual heat-exchanger cooling with a separate circuit for the aftercooler
Figure 8-6. Basic keel cooler
Figure 8-7. Keel cooler: jacket water aftercooled
Figure 8-8. Tank (or shell) cooler
Figure 8-9. Hull-side cooler recess
Figure 8-10. Dual keel cooler: aftercooler keel-cooler bypass
Figure 8-11. Keel cooler fairing
Figure 8-12. Box keel cooler
Figure 8-13. Walter keel coolers
Figure 9-1. Basic drystack exhaust
Figure 9-2. Section A through the funnel cover in Figure 9-1
Figure 9-3. Expansion slip joint
Figure 9-4. Slip joints or stainless bellows allow for expansion
Figure 9-5. Drain slots
Figure 9-6. Mounting for expansion
Figure 9-7. Standard pipe clamps/hangers
Figure 9-8. Hanging fixed-point insulated pipe hangers
Figure 9-9. Fixed-point insulated hanger on lagged exhaust pipe
Figure 9-10. Exhaust pipe stabilizers allow expansion
Figure 9-11. Flanged flexible bellows
Figure 9-12. Flexible bellows failure from stress corrosion

Figure 9-13. Welded-in flexible bellows
Figure 9-14. Flexible bellows with directional turbo liner
Figure 9-15. Flexible-steel dry exhaust hose
Figure 9-16. Alternate condensate drain
Figure 9-17. Well-insulated dry exhausts
Figure 9-18. Removable insulation cover with wire closure ties and hooks
Figure 9-19. Muffler/silencer insulation blanket
Figure 9-20. Fiberglass insulation cover
Figure 9-21. Wrapping an exhaust pipe
Figure 9-22. Alternate trunk insulation
Figure 9-23. Drystack exhaust trunk
Figure 9-24. To allow good airflow, 30 percent of the exhaust trunk (length x width) should be open
Figure 9-25. Exhaust-ejector ventilation: cone "jet" ejector
Figure 9-26. Exhaust-ejector ventilation: aft opening
Figure 9-27. Exhaust-ejector ventilation: transverse exit openings
Figure 9-28. Multiple-exhaust stacks
Figure 9-29. Water-jacketed exhaust pipe
Figure 9-30. Air-jacketed exhaust
Figure 9-31. Crewboat exhaust (section)
Figure 9-32. Crewboat exhaust water injection detail
Figure 10-1. Rudder plan geometry
Figure 10-2. Forces from a turn to port
Figure 10-3. Sailboat outboard rudders
Figure 10-4. Spade rudder with a 17 percent balance and a 2.32:1 aspect ratio
Figure 10-5. Overbalanced rudder
Figure 10-6. Low-speed rudder sections
Figure 10-7. High-speed rudder sections
Figure 10-8. Skeg- or keel-hung sailboat rudder sections
Figure 10-9. Basic flat-plate rudder
Figure 10-10. Barn-door rudder on a Marshall Catboat
Figure 10-11. Rudder width, or chord
Figure 10-12. Sailboat spade rudders
Figure 10-13. Stock cast rudders
Figure 10-14. Boats "skid" through turns
Figure 10-15. Effective rudder angles at different points during a turn
Figure 11-1. Powerboat spade rudder
Figure 11-2. Typical fabricated rudder port
Figure 11-3. Rudder bearing
Figure 11-4. Cross section of self-aligning rudder bearing
Figure 11-5. Assorted shaft collars
Figure 12-1. Planing boat rudder and prop configuration
Figure 12-2. Required tiller section
Figure 12-3. Cable steering
Figure 12-4. Hydraulic steering: 1 helm, 1 rudder
Figure 12-5. Hydraulic steering: 2 helms, 1 rudder
Figure 12-6. Hydraulic steering: 2 helms, 2 rudders
Figure 12-7. Hydraulic cylinder layout
Figure 12-8. Bronze tiller arm for a drag link or hydraulic cylinder
Figure 12-9. Drag-link assembly with jaws for clevis pins
Figure 12-10. Hydraulic steering with header tank
Figure 12-11. Hydraulic steering with power jog stick
Figure 12-12. Hydraulic power steering: 2 helms, 2 rudders
Figure 12-13. Minimum rudder rpm
Figure 12-14. High-aspect composite rudder and rudder stock with emergency tiller
Figure 12-15. Rudder stops
Figure 12-16. Bronze outboard rudder stop
Figure 12-17. Pull-pull or conduit-cable steering
Figure 12-18. Akermann steering for twin-screw boats
Figure 12-19. Rudder free-trailing angle in slipstream
Figure 12-20. Twin-screw rudder location (viewed from astern)
Figure 12-21. Single-screw rudder hole
Figure 12-22. Traditional sailboat rudder apertures
Figure 12-23. Rudder palm
Figure 13-1. Operation of the Kitchen rudder
Figure 13-2. Outboard Kitchen rudder
Figure 13-3. Harrison patent rudder
Figure 13-4. Steerable nozzle rudder
Figure 13-5. MacLear Thistle rudder
Figure 13-6. Thistle rudder sections
Figure 13-7. MacLear Thistle rudder with endplates
Figure 13-8. Flat-plate fishtail rudder section
Figure 13-9. Bulbous flap rudder
Figure 13-10. Deflector Rudder amidships
Figure 13-11. Deflector Rudder to starboard
Figure 13-12. Geometry of a Deflector Rudder
Figure 13-13. Double fixed-geometry high-lift rudders
Figure 13-14. Double fixed-geometry high-lift rudders with variable independent rotation
Figure 14-1. Classic cowl vent on dorade box
Figure 14-2. Water-trap cowl vent
Figure 14-3. Typical vent installations and airflow on a sailboat
Figure 14-4. Typical vent installations and airflow on a powerboat
Figure 14-5. Mushroom vent
Figure 14-6. Nearly every window on this motor cruiser can be opened
Figure 14-7. Open hatches and skylights provide plenty of vent area

Figure 14-8. Pilothouse of *Summer Kyle*
Figure 14-9. Solar mushroom vent
Figure 14-10. Squirrel-cage blower
Figure 14-11. Axial blower
Figure 14-12. The author on the foredeck of *Imagine*
Figure 14-13. Clamshell vent on a locker
Figure 15-1. Split direct-expansion air-conditioner
Figure 15-2. Single direct-expansion air-conditioner
Figure 15-3. Seawater pump serving two self-contained direct-expansion air-conditioning units
Figure 15-4. Typical air-conditioner ducting
Figure 15-5. Engine-driven holding-plate refrigeration: a 12-volt system with compressor driven off a 12-volt motor
Figure 15-6. Shipmate Skippy cabin heater
Figure 15-7. Smokehead with water-iron deck ring
Figure 15-8. Smokehead and water-iron deck ring
Figure 15-9. Diesel cabin heater
Figure 15-10. Typical central hot-air heating system
Figure 15-11. Hot-air heater
Figure 15-12. Typical hot-water heating system
Figure 15-13. Hydronic heater
Figure 16-1. Half-cowl side vent
Figure 16-2. Large axial blower in engine room
Figure 16-3. Vent plan for a ferry
Figure 16-4. LPG lockers
Figure 16-5. Exhaust ducts for blowers must extend down to the lower third of the compartment volume
Figure 16-6. Ventilated compartments
Figure 16-7. Minimum gasoline vent section area for 3 square inches (19.3 cm^2)
Figure 17-1. Correct and incorrect installation of seacocks
Figure 17-2. Marelon seacock
Figure 17-3. Safety seacock
Figure 17-4. Seacock service port schematic
Figure 17-5. Through-hull spool
Figure 17-6. Requirements for seacock locations on powerboats per ABYC H-27
Figure 17-7. Hull strainers
Figure 17-8. Sea strainer
Figure 17-9. Duplex sea strainer
Figure 17-10. Self-cleaning sea strainer
Figure 17-11. Sea chest seen from inside a motor cruiser
Figure 17-12. Sea chest seen from outside the motor cruiser
Figure 17-13. Sea chest profile
Figure 17-14. Sea chest section
Figure 17-15. One-sided sea chest section
Figure 18-1. Strum box
Figure 18-2. Bilge piping and fire main
Figure 18-3. Bilge-system vented-loop location
Figure 18-4. Submersible bilge pump
Figure 18-5. Float switch and cover guard
Figure 18-6. Fire station with hydrant, hose, and nozzle
Figure 18-7. Pumps suitable for fire mains
Figure 19-1. Diaphragm pump
Figure 19-2. Manual diaphragm pump
Figure 19-3. Flexible-impeller pump
Figure 19-4. Rotary vane pump
Figure 19-5. Centrifugal pump
Figure 19-6. Static head with negative suction head
Figure 19-7. Static head with positive suction head
Figure 19-8. Deck washdown plumbing
Figure 19-9. Flexible-impeller pump
Figure 20-1. Water casks
Figure 20-2. Freshwater supply piping
Figure 20-3. Freshwater delivery piping
Figure 20-4. Hose drain trap
Figure 20-5. PEX tubing and fittings
Figure 21-1. Blakes Lavac head
Figure 21-2. Head operation
Figure 21-3. Diaphragm pump
Figure 21-4. OdorSafe hose
Figure 21-5. Ideal head plumbing
Figure 21-6. Holding tank vent filter
Figure 21-7. T-pump
Figure 21-8. Plastic holding tanks
Figure 22-1. Parts of a standard anchor
Figure 22-2. Fisherman anchor
Figure 22-3. The Trotman anchor
Figure 22-4. Merriman-Herreshoff-type three-piece anchor
Figure 22-5. Herreshoff anchors stowed on deck
Figure 22-6. Comparison of anchor fluke patterns
Figure 22-7. Disassembled Luke anchor
Figure 22-8. Assorted stockless anchors
Figure 22-9. Parts of a stockless anchor
Figure 22-10. A navy stockless anchor in a hawsepipe
Figure 22-11. Typical Danforth anchor proportions
Figure 22-12. Fortress anchor
Figure 22-13. CQR anchor proportions
Figure 22-14. Delta anchor proportions
Figure 22-15. Bruce anchor proportions
Figure 22-16. Bruce anchor
Figure 22-17. A Northill anchor
Figure 22-18. Grapnel anchor
Figure 22-19. A folding grapnel anchor
Figure 22-20. Parts of a spade anchor
Figure 22-21. Spade anchor
Figure 22-22. Bugel anchor
Figure 22-23. Bulwagga anchor
Figure 23-1. Stud-link chain

Figure 23-2. 3B chain
Figure 23-3. Anchor or bow shackle
Figure 23-4. Chain or D-shackle
Figure 23-5. Assorted shackles
Figure 23-6. Anchor swivel
Figure 23-7. Anchor swivel with toggle
Figure 23-8. Ultra Swivel
Figure 23-9. A failed rope anchor rode
Figure 23-10. A broken chock and a failed anchor roller
Figure 23-11. A sharp chock
Figure 23-12. Yale Brait rope versus three-strand nylon rope
Figure 23-13. Tying an anchor bend
Figure 23-14. Devil's claw used as on-deck chain snubber
Figure 23-15. Rope spool
Figure 23-16. Wire-rope windlass
Figure 24-1. Tying the Carrick bend
Figure 24-2. Diagram of Maxwell Freedom 500 RC vertical windlass
Figure 24-3. Admiralty-pattern anchor lashed to bulwark under the anchor davit
Figure 24-4. Hoisting a yachtsman anchor from a spreader
Figure 24-5. Bent and broken anchor roller
Figure 24-6. Diagram of an anchor roller
Figure 24-7. Anchor roller in profile
Figure 24-8. Anchor roller sections
Figure 24-9. Double anchor roller
Figure 24-10. Bow-on view of the double anchor roller
Figure 24-11. Twin vertical windlasses and anchor rollers
Figure 24-12. Bow-on view of *Imagine*'s double anchor rollers
Figure 24-13. Diagram of a hawsepipe
Figure 24-14. Danforth anchor in a hawsepipe
Figure 24-15. Bobstay damaged from anchor chain
Figure 24-16. Anchors in hawsepipes
Figure 24-17. Ship windlass and hawsepipe
Figure 24-18. 75-foot (23 m) cutter with double vertical chain lockers
Figure 24-19. Close-up view of chain lockers
Figure 24-20. Chain stopper
Figure 24-21. Close-up view of chain stopper
Figure 24-22. Devil's claw
Figure 24-23. Devil's claw

Table 1-1. Recommended Divisors to Obtain Shaft Diameter from Prop Diameter
Table 1-2. Shaft Material Mechanical Properties
Table 2-1. Yield Strengths of Common Strut Materials
Table 5-1. Approximate Full-Tank Weights—Pounds
Table 5-2. Fuel Tank Materials and Thicknesses
Table 5-3. Minimum Wall Thicknesses for Fiberglass Fuel Tanks by Capacity
Table 6-1. Conversions for Liquid Volume and Liquid Measure
Table 6-2. Specific Gravity of Common Liquids
Table 7-1. Estimated Exhaust Manifold Service Life
Table 8-1. Keel-Cooler External Surface Area per Installed Power
Table 8-2. Keel-Cooler Tube Length (in./bhp)
Table 8-3. Keel-Cooler Tube Length (cm/bhp and cm/kW)
Table 8-4. Speed Comparisons Between Heat-Exchanger and Keel-Cooled Boats
Table 9-1. Drystack and Wet Exhaust System Comparison
Table 10-1. Foil-Thickness Form Dimensions
Table 11-1. Safety Factors
Table 11-2. Strengths and Densities of Standard Rudder-Stock Materials
Table 11-3. Allowable Bearing Stress
Table 11-4. Ultimate Shear Strength, USS
Table 12-1. Optimal Number of Helm Turns by Boat Type and Length
Table 12-2. Modulus, E
Table 13-1. MacLear Thistle Rudder
Table 14-1. Volume Change Rate (VCR) of Various Compartments
Table 14-2. Vent Requirements per Person
Table 14-3. Round Vent Areas
Table 14-4. ABYC Estimated Effect of Blower-System Components
Table 15-1. Required Heating Capacity
Table 16-1. Approximate Machinery Volumes
Table 16-2. Gasoline Blower Requirement Table (CFR 183.610)
Table 18-1. CFR 182.520(a) Bilge-Pump Table
Table 18-2. ABS Bilge-System Requirements
Table 18-3. CFR Fire-Main Power-Driven Pump/Capacity Requirements
Table 18-4. Fire-Extinguisher Classes and Sizes
Table 18-5. Minimum Number of Required Handheld Extinguishers
Table 18-6. ABYC A-4, Minimum Number of Required Handheld Extinguishers
Table 18-7. ABYC A-4 Extinguisher Capacity Versus Compartment Volume
Table 19-1. Pump Type Selection
Table 19-2. Equivalent Length of Pipe Fittings
Table 19-3. The Total Equivalent Length of Fittings per Table 19-2 for Figure 19-8
Table 19-4. Acceptable Flow Speeds, Water
Table 19-5. Flow Speed Versus Pipe Diameter
Table 20-1. Freshwater-Pump Capacity
Table 22-1. Three-Piece Yachtsman Anchor Dimensions (use with Figure 22-4)
Table 22-2. Danforth Anchor Dimensions (use with Figure 22-11)

Table 22-3. Recommended Sizes for Lightweight Danforth Anchors
Table 22-4. CQR Anchor Dimensions (use with Figure 22-13)
Table 22-5. Delta Anchor Dimensions (use with Figure 22-14)
Table 22-6. Bruce Anchor Dimensions (use with Figure 22-15)
Table 22-7. Recommended Anchors for Inshore and Cruising Boats of Various Sizes
Table 22-8. HMS *Victory*'s Standard Anchor Complement
Table 23-1. Grade 30—"Proof Coil" Chain Specifications
Table 23-2. BBB Chain Specifications
Table 23-3. Grade 40 or 43—"High Test" Chain Specifications
Table 23-4. ACCO 316 Stainless Chain Specifications
Table 23-5. Galvanized Screw-Pin Anchor "Bow" Shackle Specifications
Table 23-6. Galvanized Screw-Pin Chain or "D" Shackle Specifications
Table 23-7. Stainless Anchor "Bow" Shackle Specifications
Table 23-8. Galvanized Jaw-Eye Chain Swivel
Table 23-9. Stainless Anchor Swivel
Table 23-10. Ultra Swivel Specifications—Stainless Steel
Table 23-11. Three-Strand Nylon Rope
Table 23-12. Double-Braid Nylon Rope
Table 23-13. Yale Brait Nylon Rope
Table 23-14. 7 × 19 316 Stainless Wire Rope
Table 24-1. ABYC H40 Table 1—Design Loads for Sizing Deck Hardware
Table 24-2. ABYC H40 Table AP-1—Working Load Limit for Anchor Rodes
Table 24-3. Wire Gauges/Wire Size—AWG and Metric

Formula 1-1. Minimum Prop Diameter as a Function of Blade Area
Formula 1-2. Shaft Diameter
Formula 1-3. Maximum Shaft-Bearing Spacing (approximate)
Formula 1-4. Maximum Shaft-Bearing Spacing (precise)
Formula 1-5. Natural Whirling Frequency of a Propeller Shaft
Formula 2-1a. Required Section Modules for Silicon Bronze I-Struts
Formula 2-1b. Required Section Modules for Silicon Bronze V-Struts
Formula 2-1c. Required Strut Thickness for Silicon Bronze Strut with Half-Oval Section
Formula 2-2a. Strut Length (Any Section) at Hull Bottom
Formula 2-2b. Strut Length (Any Section) at Boss
Formula 2-3a. For a Rectangular Section with Rounded Ends
Formula 2-3b. For an NACA 16-Series Foil Section
Formula 2-3c. For the Flat Half-Oval Section with Rounded Ends
Formula 3-1. Thrust Loads
Formula 4-1a. Cross-Section Area in English Units
Formula 4-1b. Cross-Section Area in Metric Units
Formula 6-1. Fuel Consumption
Formula 6-2. Prismoidal Formula
Formula 6-3. Stability
Formula 6-4. Effective GM, or Metacentric Height
Formula 6-5a. Moment of Inertia of a Rectangular Plane Area (English)
Formula 6-5b. Moment of Inertia of a Rectangular Plane Area (Metric)
Formula 7-1. Water Volumes for Adequate Cooling
Formula 7-2. Volume in Canisters or Exhaust Lift Lines
Formula 7-3. Standard Minimum Diameter for a Waterlift Muffler with 3-inch (75 mm) Inlet
Formula 8-1. Circumference of a Circle
Formula 8-2. Converting Btu to hp or kW
Formula 8-3. Most Likely Water Flow (MLWF)
Formula 8-4. Flow Velocity (FV)
Formula 10-1. Aspect Ratio
Formula 10-2. Rudder Area for Displacement and Semidisplacement Powerboats
Formula 10-3. Rudder Area for Planing Powerboats
Formula 10-4. Rudder-Blade Thickness
Formula 10-5. FRP Rudder Shell Thickness for Standard Fiberglass Polyester Laminates
Formula 11-1. Precise Water Force on Rudder
Formula 11-2. Standard Calculation of Water Force on Rudder
Formula 11-3. Combined Twisting and Bending Moment (CM)
Formula 11-4. Diameter of Solid Rudder Stock
Formula 11-5. Weight per Lineal Foot of Selected Stock
Formula 11-6. Section Modulus of Required Solid Stock
Formula 11-7. Load on Rudder Bearings
Formula 11-8. Rudder-Bearing Clearance
Formula 11-9. UHMWPE Rudder-Port Allowance Thickness
Formula 12-1. Wheel Radius
Formula 12-2. Number of Turns Lock-to-Lock
Formula 12-3. Two-Pin-End-Column Moment of Inertia
Formula 12-4. Moment of Inertia for a Hollow, Round Section
Formula 12-5. Power for Power Steering
Formula 14-1. Required Airflow
Formula 14-2. Rod Stephens' Vent Rule

Formula 15-1. Preliminary Estimate of Required Btus of Air-Conditioning
Formula 15-2. Recommended Air-Conditioner Capacity
Formula 16-1. Determining Adequate Ventilation Area for Fuel-Burning Heaters
Formula 16-2. Minimum Engine Venting for Heat-Exchanger or Raw-Water Cooled Engines with Wet Exhaust
Formula 16-3. Minimum Engine Venting for Keel-Cooled Engines with Drystack Exhaust
Formula 16-4. Approximate Generator Engine Power
Formula 16-5. Minimum Allowable Cross-Section Area for Natural Ventilation
Formula 18-1. Minimum Internal Diameter of the Main Bilge-Suction Pipe
Formula 18-2. Minimum Internal Diameter of Branch or Submersible-Pump Lines
Formula 18-3. Flooding Rate from Hull Damage
Formula 18-4. Gerr's Bilge-Pump Rule: Minimum Pump Capacity
Formula 19-1. Friction Head
Formula 19-2. Flow Speed (Fluid Velocity)
Formula 19-3. Required Pump Power
Formula 23-1. Sizing Mooring and Docking Cleats
Formula 23-2. Rope Spool Size
Formula 24-1. Recommended Anchor Weight
Formula 24-2. Recommended Chain Size
Formula 24-3. Rope Anchor Rode Size
Formula 24-4. BBB Chain Weight
Formula 24-5. Copper Wire Size for a Given Voltage Drop
Formula 24-6. Recommended Chain-Locker Volume
Formula 24-7. Recommended Rope-Locker Volume

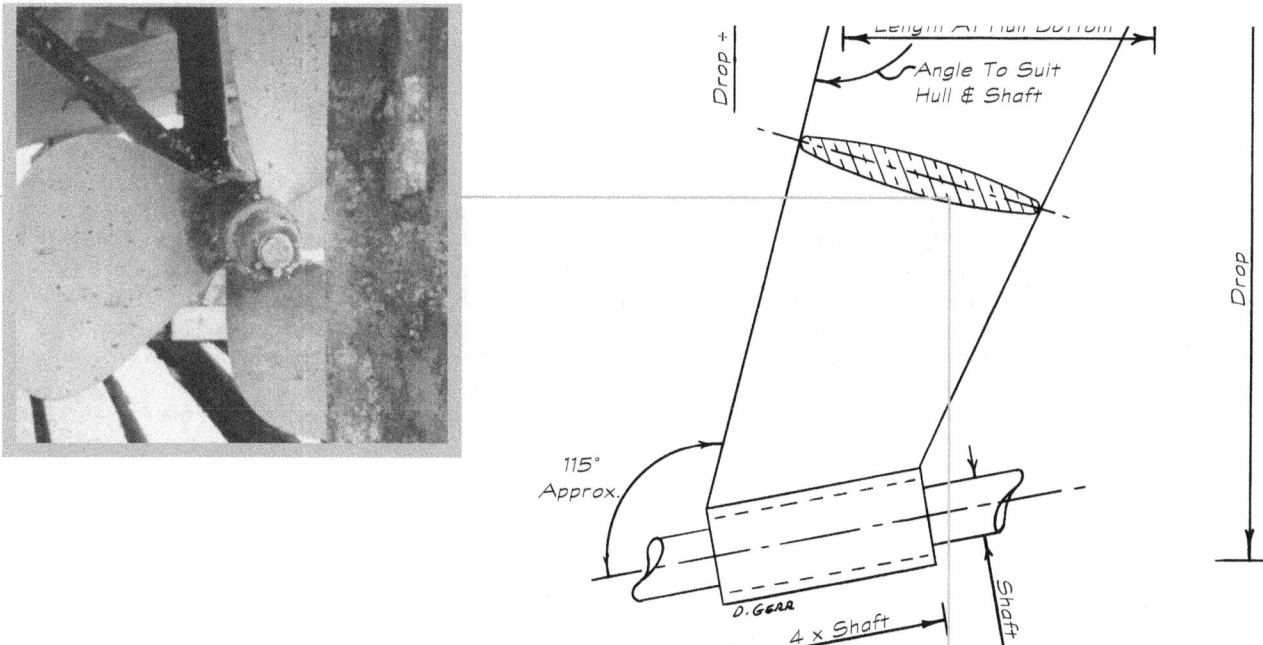

Acknowledgments

It would have been impossible to complete this book without the support of many, many other individuals and companies. Each gave generously of time and knowledge so that I could pass the information along.

Skip Burdon, John Adey, and the entire staff at the American Boat & Yacht Council—as ABYC has been doing for decades—not only supplied many of the backbone standards on which this book rests but never failed to go the extra mile to answer knotty questions and provide information on specialized topics. If they didn't know the answer, they pointed me to someone who did. As I've said elsewhere, ABYC remains the finest organization in the industry.

My thanks to Dana Hewson, Doug Teeson, Paul O'Pecko, and all the wonderful staff members of Mystic Seaport—where my Connecticut office is located—who tend so carefully to the vast store of information in their care. Whether it was the opportunity to inspect and photograph hardware and fittings on boats of earlier eras, or to study the original plans of some of the most successful designers in history, it was all there at Mystic Seaport.

My old friend Chris Wentz was always willing to drop what he was doing to grab a photo of some boat feature, or to send useful information, or to serve as a sounding board nonpareil. I'm deeply grateful. Norm Nudelman—who, years ago, was my instructor at Westlawn—still (as he always has) goes the extra mile to help find the answer to any question that crops up. David Applegate, of Applegate Industrial Materials, volunteered to send me an amazing amount of information on dry exhaust installations. Naval architect Chuck Neville was particularly generous in sharing knowledge he'd garnered through years of design.

Then there are the many dozens of individuals throughout the boating industry who interrupted their workdays to answer questions—frequently obscure or oddball. Most are employed by large corporations, including Caterpillar, Detroit Diesel, Yanmar, Groco, Forespar, Western Branch Metals, Northern Lights, and countless more. Others are independent designers, surveyors, and marine technicians. Their help might have been the answer to a single question or the forwarding of a flyer or brochure, but without their freely offered support, this book could not have been written.

The wonderful crew of *Professional Boatbuilder* magazine, including Carl Cramer, Paul Lazarus, Dan Spurr, Johanna Turnquist, and others made it possible for many of the chapters in this book to take shape in their first form. No other boating publication provides a venue for such in-depth articles on technical subjects.

Acknowledgments

David Brown undertook the truly daunting task of reading through and checking the entire book—formulas, recommendations, and procedures. To say I'm deeply appreciative of his diligent and watchful eye would be an understatement.

At International Marine, Ben McCanna was incredibly careful and conscientious in editing the manuscript, Shannon Swanson created the outstanding design, and Molly Mulhern presided carefully over production. Perhaps most important there's Jon Eaton of International Marine. His good advice and—above all—remarkable patience stand behind every word of this text.

To all my deep and sincere thanks.

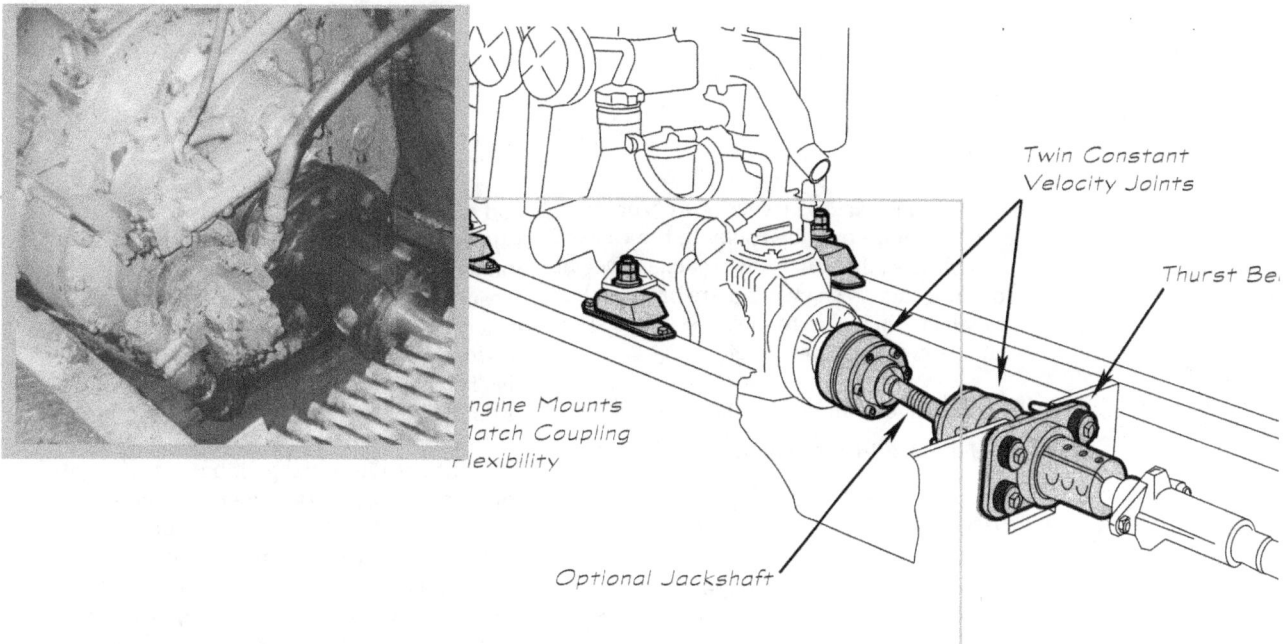

Author's Notes

USING DECIMAL EXPONENTS

Decimal exponents are used in a number of the formulas throughout this book. If you "don't like math," decimal exponents can seem a bit technical. Don't let them put you off, however. Decimal exponents are easy to master; it takes just a few moments. For instance, in the formula for BBB chain weight, Formula 24-4,

$$\text{BBB chain weight, lb./ft.} \approx 10.505 \times (\text{chain dia., in.})^{1.858}$$

1.858 is the decimal exponent.

It's quite easy to solve this on a pocket scientific calculator (an inexpensive one from any local stationery store or RadioShack), but it's important to understand what decimal exponents are

$X^{0.5}$ is the same as $X^{1/2}$ is the same as $\sqrt{X}$ or $\sqrt[2]{X}$, the square root of X

$X^{0.333}$ is the same as $X^{1/3}$ is the same as $\sqrt[3]{X}$ or the cube root of X

$X^{1.5}$ is the same as $X \times X^{1/2}$ is the same as $(X \times \sqrt{X})$ or X times the square root of X

$X^{2.333}$ is the same as $X^2 \times X^{1/3}$ is the same same as $(X^2 \times \sqrt[3]{X})$ or X squared times the cube root of X

and so on.

You can see that a decimal is just another way of writing a fraction and that it makes no difference whether you use a decimal or a fraction as the exponent. (The decimal, of course, is easier to enter in a calculator.)

You can also see that a decimal or fractional exponent is the same as taking the root of a number, and the root is always the same as the inverse (or reciprocal) of the decimal. Thus, raising a number to the 0.5 power is the same as taking the square root of that number. (The inverse or reciprocal of $0.5 = 1 \div 0.5 = 2$, and $\sqrt{X}$ is the same as $\sqrt[2]{X}$.) Raising a number to the 0.333 power is the same as taking the cube root of that number. (The reciprocal of $0.333 = 1 \div 0.333 = 3$, giving $\sqrt[3]{X}$.)

The nice thing about decimal exponents is that they allow quick manipulation of formulas with exponential relationships that don't happen to fall exactly on even powers or roots, such as square or cube roots. In the case of Formula 24-4, the data show that chain weight does not vary as an even square or cube, but as diameter in inches to the 1.858 power. This can be rewritten a number of ways:

$$(\text{chain dia. in.})^{1.858} \text{ is the same as}$$

$$((\text{chain dia. in.}) \times (\text{chain dia. in.})^{858/1{,}000}) \text{ is the same as}$$

$$(\text{chain dia. in.}) \times \sqrt[1{,}000]{(\text{chain dia. in.})^{858}}$$

Not only is the 1.858 exponent easier to enter into a calculator, it's easier to write by hand or to type as well.

Try it yourself. Take your calculator and punch in the number for chain diameter. Then hit the exponentiation key (usually the X^y key). Now enter the exponent, and finally press the equal key. That's it; there's your answer. For example, if you raise a chain diameter of 0.25 inch to the 1.858 power, the answer will be 0.076, while a chain diameter of 0.5 inch raised to the 1.858 power will equal 0.275.

THE ENGLISH SYSTEM OF MEASURE AND THE METRIC SYSTEM

Throughout this book I refer to *English* units and to *metric* units. These are the terms most often used in informal conversation in the United States and are easily understood. Though some fault the term *English units*, it is correct usage and refers specifically to the *English engineering system of units* or to the somewhat different *English gravitational system of units*, which employs the unit of mass known as the *slug* (see sidebar page 183), and so is internally more consistent than the English engineering system. Since much of the world has switched to the metric system, these "English units" are also less specifically called *United States customary units* or *U.S. customary units*. Whatever they are called, this is the foot/pound/second units system. It is similar to the British *imperial system of units* but is not the same. For instance, imperial units use imperial gallons, not U.S. gallons, as well as units of weight such as the *hundredweight* and the *stone*, which are not found in U.S. customary units. Accordingly, it is incorrect to refer to the English units in this book as imperial measure or imperial units. All liquid volumes in this book are based on U.S. gallons.

The *metric system* refers to one of two systems of units—the *cgs* and the *mks* systems. The cgs system is largely employed by chemists and physicists. Its base units are the centimeter, gram, and second. Most people and most engineers use the SI units system or mks system (*Système International d'Unités* or *International System of Units*). Its base units are meters, kilograms, and seconds. Where the term "metric units" or "metric" is used in this book, it refers to the SI (mks) system. There are two exceptions in my usage:

- The fundamental unit for temperature in the SI system is degrees Kelvin. This is virtually never employed in everyday work (though it is critical for some engineering calculations). Accordingly, I have used degrees centigrade (C°, also called degrees Celsius) for metric temperature unless otherwise noted.
- Also, the basic unit for angle in the SI system is the radian, not the more common degree (°). I have used angles in degrees throughout.

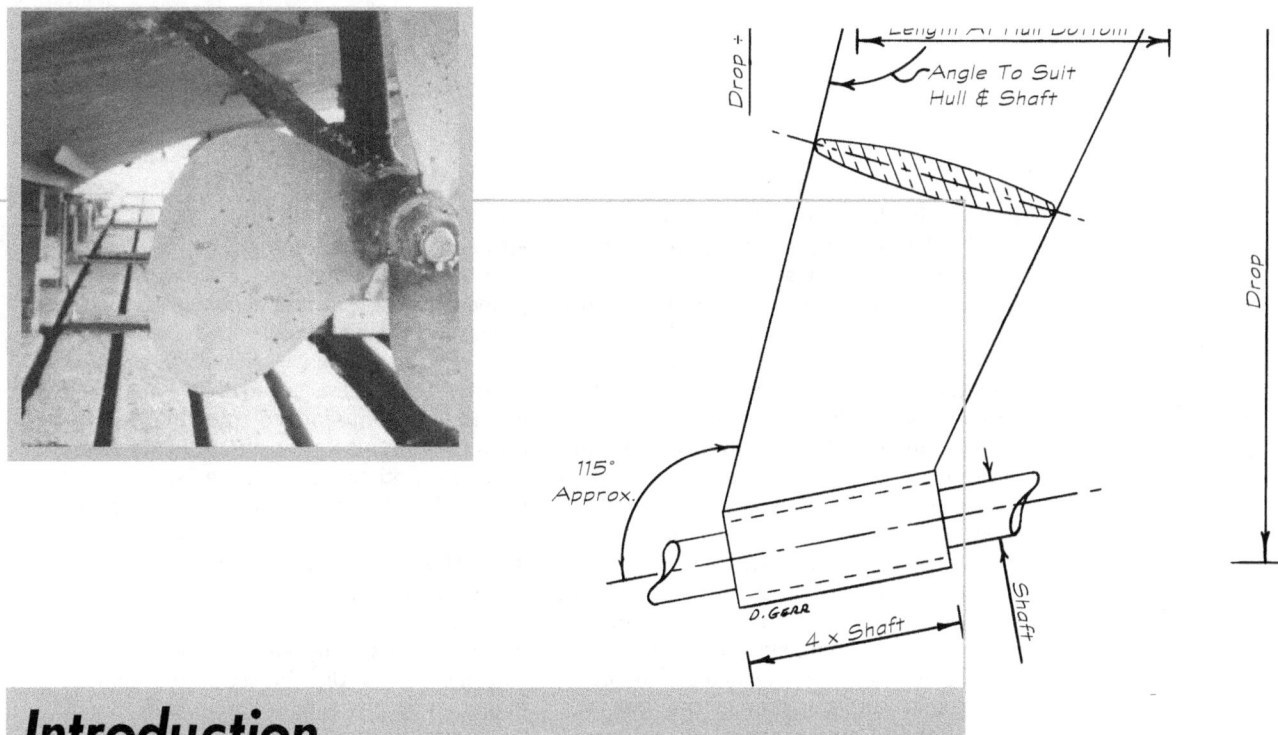

Introduction

We shook our heads in unison. One million for a 50-footer (15.2 m)! It wasn't that we weren't both proud of our custom creation. I had designed in all the features my client had asked for, and John's crew had done a fine job in building. Sea trials successfully completed, we were sharing a beer and talking boats. Complicated? You bet. Our new baby had every convenience. A voyaging motor cruiser, it was fitted not only with all the standard propulsion equipment and controls, and with hot-and-cold pressure water, but also with air-conditioning; central heating; bow thruster; autopilot; washer and dryer; gas range; microwave; fridge and freezer; two head compartments, each with shower and electric toilet; full double navigation electronics (wheelhouse and flybridge); and even a large heated Jacuzzi. And those were just the highlights.

"You know," I commented, "If it was my own boat, I would build it with virtually no systems beyond propulsion and navigation. I would have pressure water, two small cabin heaters, a few 12-volt fans—that would be it. Bet you could build it for $700,000."

"Probably less," John replied. He had just finished the construction, and the complexity was fresh in his mind.

"Three hundred thousand plus in savings!" I exclaimed. "Not to mention the maintenance and upkeep over the years, and for otherwise the same boat."

We drifted off into a discussion of my ideal cruiser . . . next year . . .

The fact is that boats are getting bigger and more complicated. It's not just size, of course. Even small to medium-size vessels carry far more in the way of systems than they did thirty or forty years ago. I have in front of me a brochure for the 35-foot (10.5 m) Allied *Seabreeze*, designed in the late 1960s by the first office I worked for—MacLear and Harris, Inc. (before my time, of course!). In those days, a 35-footer (10.5 m) was a big, serious voyaging boat. She sold for all of $20,000, back when. Systems? What systems? She came with—and I quote:

> 12-Volt with 2 heavy-duty batteries complete with safety switch and fuse panel, engine room exhaust blower, navigation lights, 6 screw-type cabin lights.
> Fuel tank: 30 gallons [110 L] Monel, under cockpit sole; Fresh water: 60 gallon [225 L] tank under cabin sole; Propeller shaft: 7/8" [22 mm] Tobin bronze; Propeller: Type E two-bladed 13 × 8 R.H. [330 × 203 mm]; Rudder: fiberglass-reinforced plastic; Rudder stock: 1 1/2" [38 mm] Tobin Bronze; Engine: 25 hp Gray model SS 91, direct drive.

That was it! The *Seabreeze* had an icebox, not a fridge. Water was supplied by hand pumps, one at the galley sink and one in the head. A shower was an optional extra, as was the pressure-water system to go with it. There were no fans, heaters, air-conditioners, or generators. The single manual head pumped right overboard. Simpler times.

Roughing it? Perhaps by today's standards, but a lot of safe, pleasant ocean miles have slipped under the keels of the few hundred *Seabreeze*s built and the many thousands of equally simple craft of those days.

This is a book about the primary mechanical systems on boats. Unless it's a canoe, a rowboat, or a sailing skiff, every boat will have such systems; nevertheless, the fewer the systems and the simpler they are, the more cost-effective, reliable, and enjoyable the vessel will be. Take this as the bottom line. Whether you're searching for your next boat or upgrading your current one; whether you're managing a full-service yard, running a large-production boatbuilding operation, or designing custom boats, if you can keep the mechanical systems down to the minimum and as simple as possible, you—and everyone connected with the vessel—will have a better experience from day one.

Of course, some systems are indispensable (like the drivetrain and the fuel system). Other systems are legally required (like holding tanks and related plumbing), and still other systems some boaters simply won't want to do without—hot-and-cold pressure water and a cabin heater being two examples.

In this book we'll take a close look at the primary systems necessary on boats, noting what's required to install the principal mechanical systems so they are reliable and trouble-free. We'll also look at some less common alternatives for some systems (e.g., unusual rudders), and at some of the ways you can identify and correct problems that may have been designed or built into an existing boat.

Mechanical systems on boats cover quite a range of possibilities, naturally. That 50-footer (15.2 m) John and I were discussing did have a Jacuzzi whirlpool. It had to be custom engineered. There was no way to carry enough fresh water (or make it) to fill the 300-gallon (1,100 L) Jacuzzi. Instead, it required a 120-volt, high-volume, raw-water pump to fill, along with intake seacock, sea strainer, and auto-shutoff. Then we had to heat the water: 12-volt circulation pump and propane flash-type water heater (with special arrangements made to deal with the salt water), with associated plumbing, strainer/filter, on/off controls, thermostat, and so on, and naturally, drains and their associated plumbing and fittings as well. All for a single tub! We won't cover installations like this here. What we will do is review the standard mechanical systems that form the backbone of operations and safety aboard most normal boats.

Mechanical systems on boats, are—more often than not—driven, controlled, or monitored using electricity. Most commonly this is 12-volt or 24-volt DC. On larger boats and for bigger, more powerful systems, it is 120- or 240-volt, 60-cycle AC (240-volt, 50-cycle in Europe). Except for the inescapable way the electric system may interface with the mechanical system, however, we won't be covering electric systems. Why not? Well, first, this is a book on mechanical systems, not electric systems. Second, electric systems are such an immense and complex subject that they would require their own dedicated book—a big one. If it's guidance on marine electric systems you're looking for, you'll need to seek elsewhere.

Similarly, there isn't any discussion of rigs and sail-handling systems here. Again, these aren't the mechanical systems that form the backbone of marine operations on all boats. An auxiliary sailboat needs the same general fuel, exhaust, and drivetrain systems as a powerboat, but only the sailboat would have things like hydraulic backstay adjusters or roller furling gear. Mast and rigging systems, too, are thus a subject for another book.

Of course, boat structure isn't in any sense a mechanical system; however, where appropriate, we will discuss whether a structure is strong enough to support a particular system's components.

What you will find here is sound guidance on the fundamental mechanical systems common to most boats. Follow these recommendations and keep things as simple as possible for the vessel you're working on, and you should have many years of trouble-free operation.

Finally, the central mechanical system in any boat could be considered the engine that provides the power to drive it. As with electric systems, however, this isn't a book about engines. What we'll start with, though, are the many mechanical systems that are required for the engine or engines to do their job properly—drivetrains, fuel systems, and exhaust systems. From there, we'll branch out.

The American Boat & Yacht Council (ABYC)

Throughout this book I make reference to appropriate standards from the American Bureau of Shipping (ABS), to the Code of Federal Regulations (CFR), to the National Fire Protection Association (NFPA), and so on. No standards are referred to or used more often than those of the American Boat & Yacht Council (ABYC). I've been an ABYC member for more than twenty-five years now. I couldn't have done much of the work I do (designing, surveying, teaching, and writing) without ABYC's invaluable support and the tremendous amount of hard work and research that goes into creating each of the many ABYC standards.

Though there are International Standards Organization (ISO) standards in Europe, I personally find ABYC standards more straightforward, easier to use, and more sensible. ABYC standards form the backbone for understanding systems installation on all boats. If you're not an ABYC member, you should become one and get their full set of standards. Like any such collection of standards, these references are not exactly bedtime reading, but if you're serious about installing, inspecting, or servicing equipment and machinery on any boat—and doing it properly—ABYC standards are *the* essential guide. Even better, as an ABYC member you will get invaluable tech support and guidance should you need it.

Part One

DRIVETRAIN INSTALLATIONS

Propellers and Shafts — CHAPTER 1

An often overlooked aspect of small-craft engineering is the drivetrain: all the components aft of the transmission—the shaft, its bearings, the strut, and the propeller. Also, the drivetrain itself is affected by the support needed to hold things in place—the engine mounts and beds. It's important to understand how these many disparate elements should work, and work together—reliably and smoothly. Vibration and noise, poor performance, and even damaged transmission and broken engine beds can result from drivetrain problems.

In the following pages we'll take a practical look at these many elements and see how they should be configured, sized, and installed. We won't look specifically at the alignment process, which is a whole topic in itself. We will, however, see some examples of what happens when things aren't installed or sized correctly.

There are so many different components, that—to keep things in some sort of order—we'll very roughly begin at the propeller and work our way forward. Some jumping about, however, will be unavoidable.

PROPER PROP NUTS

We'll start with a minor and somewhat amusing controversy. Two nuts hold the propeller on the shaft—a full-height nut and half-height locknut (Figure 1-1). Which nut goes directly against the propeller hub?

The fact is most boats have it wrong, with the full-height nut against the prop. It seems intuitive that the larger nut against the prop would be doing most of the work and the smaller nut should go on second. Actually the smaller nut should always go against the load. This is because when the second, outer nut is installed and tightened, it deforms/compresses the lower nut a smidgen, at the same time rotating it a tiny fraction of a turn. This effectively unloads the threads of the lower nut and engages the threads of the upper nut. Thus the top or outer nut really takes all the load. No matter how many times I explain this, some folks still seem dubious. An illustration in *Engineering Drawing and Design* (Cecil H. Jensen and J. D. Helsel, 3rd ed., New York: McGraw-Hill, 1985) shows that this is standard practice for all locknuts (Figure 1-2), and an illustration from SAE standard J756 and J755, for propeller shafts, clearly shows that the half-height nut is against the hub (Figure 1-3).

If you go to any marina where boats are hauled for the winter, my guess is that 99 percent of the prop nuts will be on the wrong way. I wouldn't worry too much about the nuts being on backward—as they usually are—because the wrong way has proven sufficient. But now that you know, you might as well put the things on right the next time you install a prop.

Figure 1-1. Thread loading of a nut and locknut

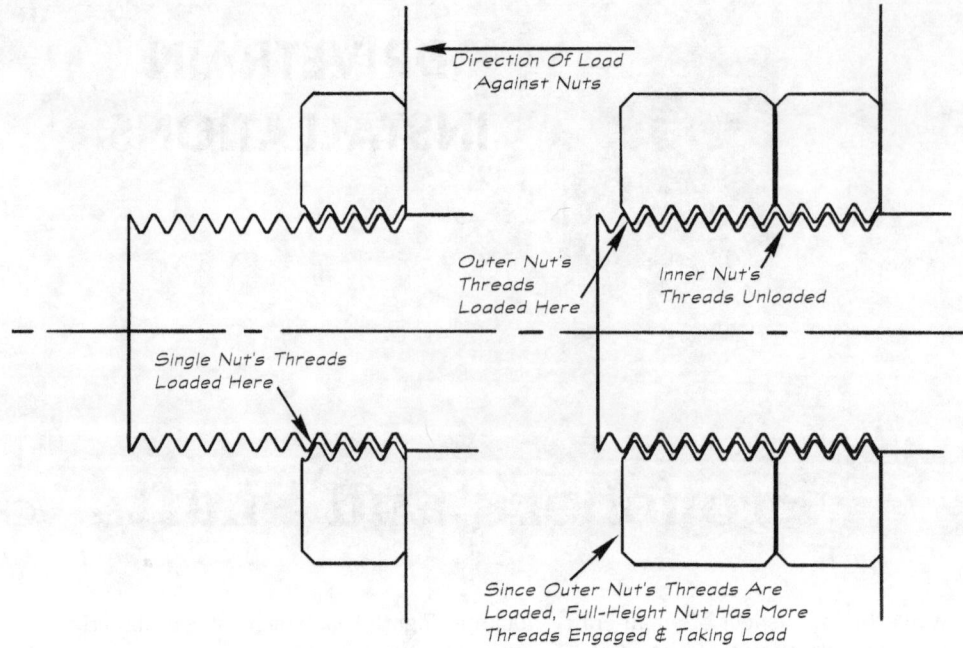

BLADE AREA

Naval architect Uffa Fox said:

"The final answer to all engineering effort in any vessel is in the propeller."

This is not an overstatement. You can build the most beautifully shaped hull and install the most magnificent and powerful new engines, but if the prop is wrong, the boat won't go. This isn't the place for a discussion of props, but a properly sized, properly balanced, and properly installed propeller is critical. One of the first things I check—whether I'm starting a new design or trying to solve a vibration problem—is the propeller. In this regard, the most overlooked aspect of propeller sizing is blade area. All too often just the diameter, the pitch, and the number of blades are specced. This is not enough information—blade area is critical. Too little blade area means the blades are overloaded (even if diameter and pitch are just right). Overloading leads to cavitation, which means loss in performance, possible blade erosion, and vibration.

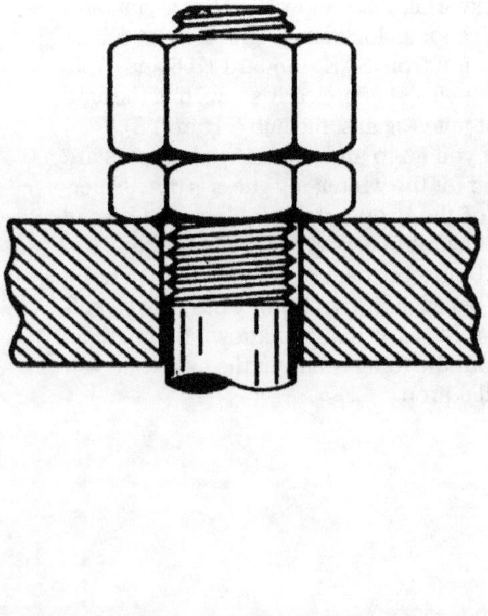

Disc Area Ratio

Blade area can be defined in terms of absolute area—so many square inches or square millimeters. But for propellers, it's usually more convenient to define blade area in terms of *disc area ratio* (also called *blade area ratio*)—DAR or BAR. This is the percentage of the area of all the prop's blades relative to a solid disc of the same diameter as the prop.

A standard 3-bladed propeller has a 50 percent DAR, and a wide-blade 5-blader has a DAR of about 120 percent. There's a huge difference in the power that these two props can absorb, even at the same diameter. By the way, a 120 percent DAR is about as close to the theoretical maximum as you can

Figure 1-2. A jam nut, applied under a large regular nut, is elastically deformed against bolt threads when the large nut is tightened

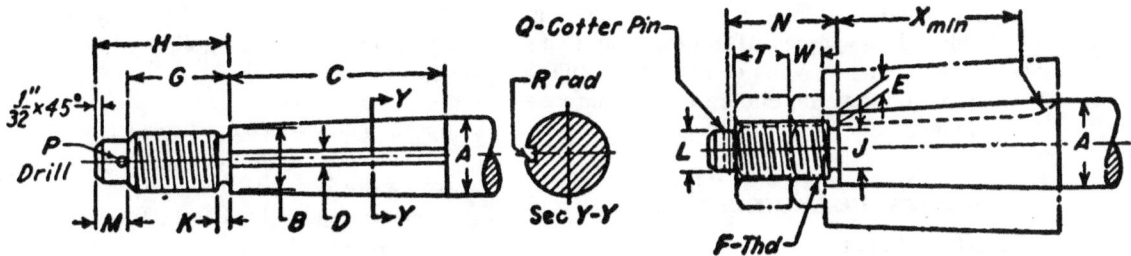

TAPER = 3/4 IN. ON DIAMETER PER FT = 1/16 IN. PER IN. = 3 DEG 34 MIN 47 SEC TOTAL INCLUDED ANGLE

Figure 1-3. This segment of an SAE illustration clearly shows the smaller nut innermost

Cavitation

Propellers drive a boat forward because their blades act as hydrofoils as they are rotated through the water by the torque and power of the shaft. Like all foils (aerofoil or hydrofoil) the blades generate a negative pressure—called *lift*—on their forward faces (termed the *blade backs*) and a positive pressure on the blades' rear-facing surfaces (termed the *blade faces*). The resulting force pushes the propeller forward, which in turn pushes on the shaft, which then pushes on the thrust bearing in the gearbox, which then transmits this thrust to the engine beds to drive the boat forward.

Cavitation results when the pressure around the blades is reduced below the local vapor pressure. Bubbles of vapor implode against the blades with enough impact to make considerable noise and vibration and to erode the blade surfaces. You can get a more complete explanation of cavitation from the relevant chapters in my books *The Nature of Boats* and *Propeller Handbook*.

A full understanding of cavitation still eludes science. It is a fascinating area of inquiry and connected with such truly odd phenomena as sonoluminescence. In theory, the force of the implosion of a cavitation bubble is nearly infinite at the point of impact (though, of course, in reality, the force is not infinite). It was this property of cavitation that led to the fantastic "cold-fusion" claims of professors Pons and Fleischmann a few years back.

In any case, even if we don't fully understand cavitation, we do largely know how to predict its onset and to minimize it.

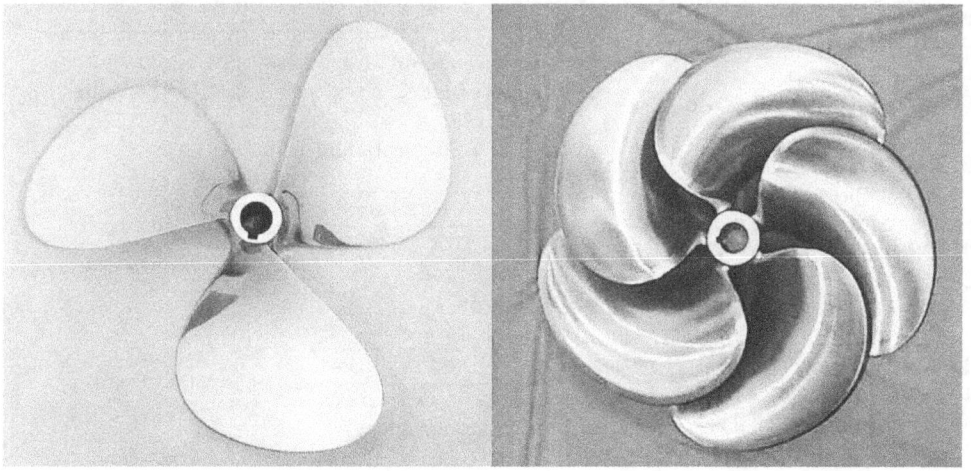

Figure 1-4. A standard 3-bladed prop and wide blade 5-bladed prop (Michigan Wheel; Paul Bremer)

get. There are some sources for custom 6-bladed, 140 percent DAR props, but that's truly the max. If you need still more blade area, you have no choice but to increase diameter.

Minimum Diameter and Blade Area

What's needed is an easy way to check blade area and relate it to diameter using the DAR. I've worked out a formula that will allow a quick estimate of the minimum diameter required for either displacement or planing hulls.

Formula 1-1. Minimum Prop Diameter as a Function of Blade Area

$$\text{Min. Prop. Dia., in. (Displacement Hulls)} = \sqrt{\frac{125 \times \text{hp}}{\text{DAR} \times \text{kts} \times \sqrt{\text{kts}}}}$$

NOTE: $\text{kts} \times \sqrt{\text{kts}}$ is the same as $\text{kts}^{1.5}$

$$\text{Min. Prop. Dia., in. (Planing Hulls)} = \sqrt{\frac{160 \times \text{hp}}{\text{DAR} \times \text{kts} \times \sqrt{\text{kts}}}}$$

or

$$\text{Min. Prop. Dia., cm (Displacement Hulls)} = \sqrt{\frac{1081.5 \times \text{kW}}{\text{DAR} \times \text{kts} \times \sqrt{\text{kts}}}}$$

$$\text{Min. Prop. Dia., cm (Planing Hulls)} = \sqrt{\frac{1384.2 \times \text{kW}}{\text{DAR} \times \text{kts} \times \sqrt{\text{kts}}}}$$

Where
hp = total brake horsepower for each engine
kW = total flywheel power for each engine
DAR = disc area ratio (or blade area ratio); expressed as a decimal
kts = maximum speed in knots
DARs FOR REPRESENTATIVE PROPS:
    2-Bladed Sailer = 0.24
    3-Bladed Standard = 0.50
    3-Bladed Wide Blade = 0.70
    4-Bladed Standard = 0.70
    4-Bladed Wide Blade = 0.95
    5-Bladed Standard = 0.95
    5-Bladed Extra-Wide Blade = 1.20

These formulas make a few simplifying assumptions, which apply quite well to most average boats:

    e = efficiency = 0.55 for displacement boats and 0.70 for planing boats
    wf = wake factor = 0.9
    propeller depth = 1 to 3 feet (30 to 90 cm) below the waterline

Full engine power is used in these formulas, not shaft power. The reduction for shaft losses has been incorporated into the formulas.

Using this formula, it's a quick job with a pocket calculator to see if a given boat is in the right ballpark for blade area.

Example: Say you have a 40-foot (12.2 m) sportfisherman powered with twin 400 hp (298 kW) diesels, and it has standard 3-bladed props, 24 inches (61 cm) in diameter. The boat gets a top speed of 30 knots. You would find.

$$\sqrt{\frac{160 \times 400 \text{ hp}}{0.50 \text{ DAR} \times 30 \text{ kts} \times \sqrt{30 \text{ kts}}}} = 27.9 \text{ in. Min. Prop. Dia.}$$

or

$$\sqrt{\frac{1384.2 \times 298 \text{ kW}}{0.50 \text{ DAR} \times 30 \text{ kts} \times \sqrt{30 \text{ kts}}}} = 70.8 \text{ cm Min. Prop. Dia.}$$

In other words, the 24-inch (61 cm), 3-bladed prop is too small in diameter to have adequate blade area and is likely to cavitate.

Given enough clearance and the right reduction gear, you could go to a 28-inch (71 cm), 3-bladed wheel. A more practical solution—in most instances—is to go to more blades, a wide-blade-pattern propeller, or both.

Trying a standard 4-blader gives

$$\sqrt{\frac{160 \times 400 \text{ hp}}{0.70 \text{ DAR} \times 30 \text{ kts} \times \sqrt{30 \text{ kts}}}} = 23.5 \text{ in. Min. Prop. Dia.}$$

or

$$\sqrt{\frac{1384.2 \times 298 \text{ kW}}{0.70 \text{ DAR} \times 30 \text{ kts} \times \sqrt{30 \text{ kts}}}} = 59.9 \text{ cm Min. Prop. Dia.}$$

which is spot on.

COMMON CAUSES OF VIBRATION AND NOISE

Cavitation due to inadequate blade area is—as we've just seen—one common cause of vibration. Two other common culprits are

- propeller tip noise
- shaft noise from poor alignment and from bearings

Induced Drag and Tip Noise

Propeller tip noise comes principally from inadequate tip clearance. Figure 1-5 shows the minimum recommended dimensions for adequate tip clearances and proper water flow. Props don't really screw their way through the water as some useful, but simplified, propeller calculations indicate. Instead, the propeller blades are hydrofoils that generate lift like airplane wings, keels, or sails. This means that the blades generate vortices at each blade tip just as any hydrofoil or airfoil does. These vortices are termed *induced drag*. They represent wasted energy, so it's a shame we can't eliminate them, but they are unavoidable. The key here is that they are energy.

If there's enough distance between the prop's blade tips and the hull, the energy in these vortices largely dissipates and is swept aft in the wake before it can impinge on the hull hard enough to make noise. If you have too little clearance, though, these vortices can create a surprising amount of noise or vibration.

Frequency Testing

You can simply listen to a boat underway as you move about, and try to determine if an annoying noise is propeller-tip noise, shaft noise, or cavitation. (Cavitation often sounds like small bits of gravel being driven through

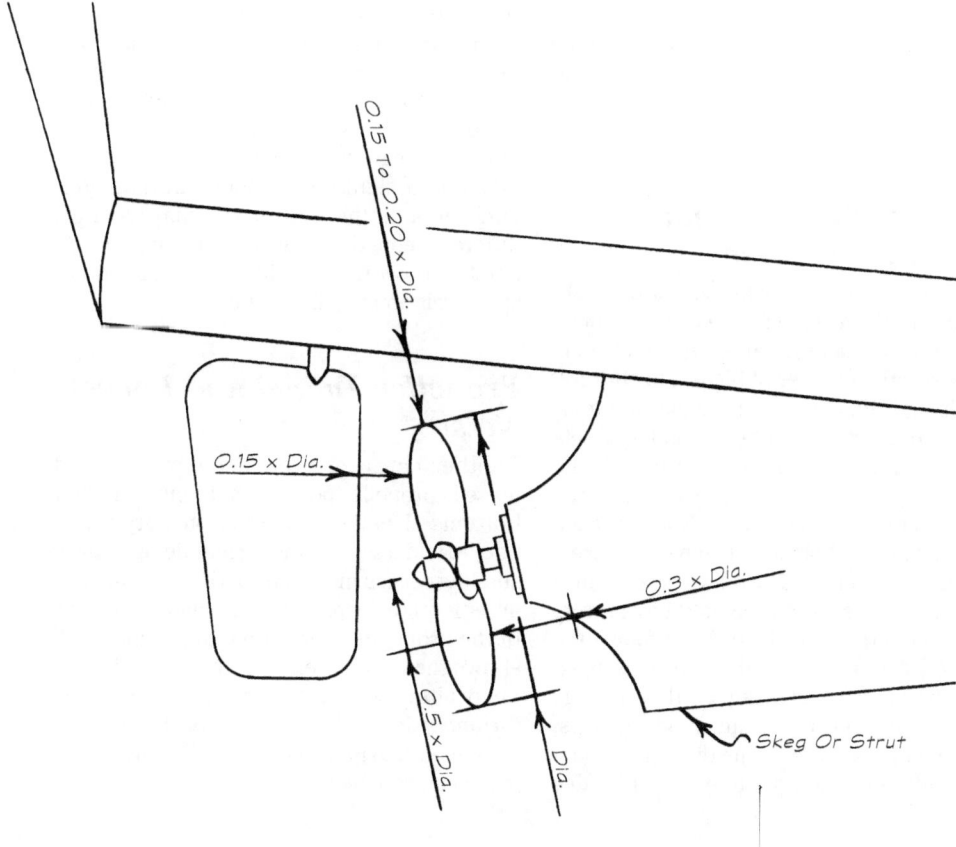

Figure 1-5. Propeller clearances

the prop.) A more accurate method is to record the vibration or noise on a small cassette recorder, using a contact mike capable of recording quite low frequencies. Play the cassette back into an oscilloscope or frequency analyzer, and you literally can get a better picture of what's happening. This sounds rather high-tech, but it's simple in principle.

Say the unwanted noise is occurring at 2,200 revolutions per minute (rpm), and the boat has a 2:1 gear and 3-bladed props. The frequency for shaft noise would simply be 2,200 rpm ÷ 2, or 1,100 shaft rpm, which would be 1,100 cycles per minute (cpm). Divide by 60 to get 18.33 cycles per second (cps), or hertz (Hz).

Propeller tip noise would be 1,100 rpm shaft speed × 3 blades = 3,300 cpm, or 55 cps or Hz.

You can see that there's a big difference in frequency, so usually it's fairly easy to distinguish between shaft or bearing and tip noise. The exception would be if one prop blade was damaged. Then the frequency for this vibration would be the same as shaft speed. Regardless, this isn't advanced electrical engineering. All you need is a simple shareware oscilloscope emulator program on a laptop computer.

Number of Blades and Curing Prop Noise

When you run into propeller vibration problems due to inadequate tip clearance or poor water flow to the prop, often the solution is to increase the number of blades, in addition to reducing diameter to increase tip clearance. Increasing the number of blades offsets the loss in blade area from the loss in diameter. Having more blades also reduces the vortex energy from each blade. Roughly, each tip vortex from a 4-blader will have just three-fourths the energy of a tip vortex from a 3-blader, while a 5-blader would have three-fifths the energy of a 3-blader and four-fifths the energy of a 4-blader in each tip vortex. Since the tip vortices dissipate their energy as the square of the distance from the tips, the combination of reducing diameter somewhat and increasing the number of blades can make a significant difference. In addition, more blades generate higher-frequency noise, which resonates in the hull structure less effectively.

Of course, the new propeller has to be fully calculated using standard methods. A reduction in diameter would mean a corresponding increase in pitch—in many cases, too much. In such instances, a new gear may be required. Actually, the calculations of propeller dimensions, including pitch, diameter, power, rpm, blade area, and boat speed, are all inextricably interrelated. The rough rule of thumb is that for every inch (25 mm) you decrease diameter, pitch should be increased by 2 inches (50 mm), and vice versa. If in an existing installation you reduce diameter by 2 inches (50 mm), this simple rule of thumb would indicate a 4-inch (100 mm) increase in pitch.

This, however, could very well increase the pitch ratio of the propeller (pitch divided by diameter) beyond what is suitable for the operational speed of the boat. In this case the blades would enter the water flow at too steep an angle of attack and therefore stall (cease to generate lift). This is exactly like an airplane wing stalling in too steep a climb. Accordingly—though pitch is not the subject we're dealing with here—you must keep in mind that the smaller-diameter propeller must be recalculated using standard methods, and a significant change in diameter, pitch, or both (they are related) may require a different reduction gear to keep the pitch, diameter, power, rpm, blade area, and boat-speed relationship in balance.

Propeller Tunnel and Pocket Noise

Another cause of propeller vibration and noise is propeller pockets and tunnels in hull bottoms. I make a distinction between a pocket and a tunnel, the former being a fairly shallow recess into an underbody, while the latter is quite deep, with more than 50 percent of the propeller tucked up into it. Figure 1-6 shows the exceptionally deep tunnels in one of my ultra-shoal tunnel-drive motor cruisers. *Twombly* draws just 22 inches on 42 feet LOA (56 cm on 12.8 m LOA) and is fully beachable, yet ocean capable.

Chapter 1: Propellers and Shafts

Figure 1-6. Deep propeller tunnels

Incorrect pockets can generate considerable noise. The most common problem is that the pockets are too short fore-and-aft, with an abrupt entry where they start forward. The result is interrupted water flow into the upper portion of the prop disk. In other words, the upper portions of the blades—when they reach the top of their rotation—momentarily see somewhat restricted water inflow compared with the rest of the blades. This causes uneven loading and thus vibration.

POCKET PROPORTION RECOMMENDATIONS When you are installing shallow pockets or are looking at vibration problems in a boat with pockets, review the pocket geometry. The pocket entry should probably be longer than you think. As a rough rule of thumb, I like at least a 7:1 slope on the entry. The pockets should retain their full depth about one prop diameter forward of the propeller before the taper starts (Figure 1-7). If the pocket is recessed into the hull about 9 inches (228 mm) at the prop, and the prop has a 25-inch (635 mm) diameter, then the pocket ought to remain constant in cross section until 25 inches (635 mm) forward of the prop. Then it should taper gradually through a distance of 63 inches (1.6 m) forward of that—9 in. × 7 = 63 in., or 228 mm × 7 = 1,596 mm (1.6 m). Pocket and tunnel design is a whole subject in itself, so this recommendation is just a rule-of-thumb guide. It is a reasonable marker for a possible problem, however.

Figures 1-8A and 1-8B show an aluminum ferry that required repowering work. This vessel had suffered from severe vibration because the pockets had been designed too short and with too little propeller tip clearance. The captain explained that the vibration had been so severe that welds had broken. Installing smaller-diameter propellers with higher DARs couldn't fully correct this built-in defect, but it did make a noticeable improvement.

SMALLER PROP DIAMETER AND MORE BLADE FOR POCKET PROBLEMS If you've got a problem caused by too short a pocket, one possible solution, again, is to go to a smaller-diameter prop with more blade area and wider blades. The additional blades will raise the frequency and smooth out the

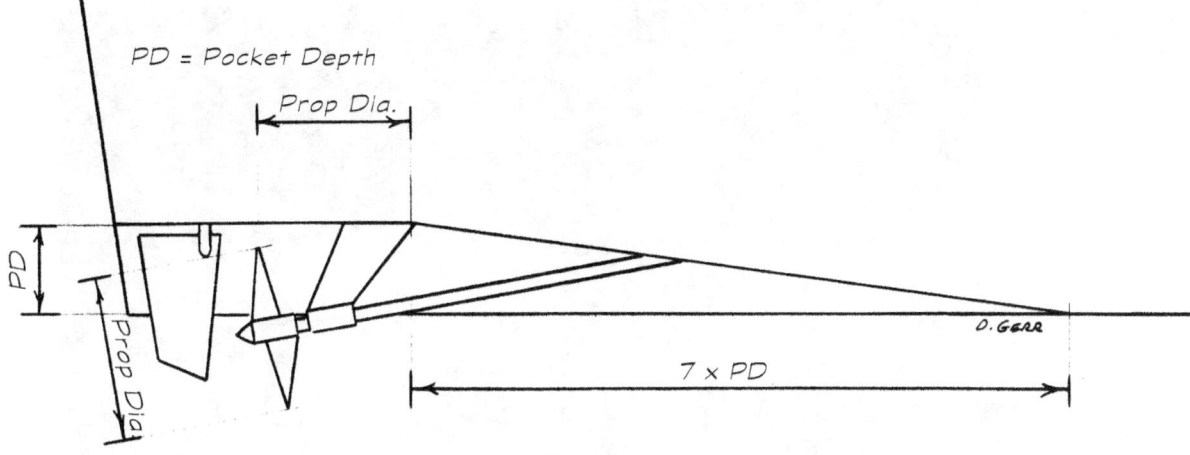

Figure 1-7. Recommended pocket proportions

Figure 1-8A. Pocket viewed from the stern (rear)

vibration, and the smaller diameter should reduce the portion of blades in interrupted water flow.

POCKET- OR TUNNEL-EDGE ALIGNMENT TO THE PROPELLER Another thing to check in a pocket or tunnel is the geometry in section. You want to ensure that two blades don't line up with the pocket or tunnel corners at the same time. For instance, if a prop were tucked up exactly halfway into a tunnel, you wouldn't want to use a 4-bladed wheel, because two blades would line up with the tunnel corners at the same time, which can cause vibration. Instead, use a 3- or 5-bladed prop (probably 5 for adequate blade area). Other vertical prop locations and tunnel configurations might line up with a 3-blader or a 5-blader. Such alignments should be avoided.

Some deep pockets with V-shaped cross sections pose another potential pitfall. The V shape can have the blades approach closest to the underbody (minimum tip clearance) twice instead of once (Figure 1-10). This doubles the potential tip noise. Once again, a smaller-diameter prop with more blades (maintaining adequate blade area) is the answer.

V-STRUTS AND POCKETS Still another difficulty with a pocket or tunnel is the strut. Keep in mind that the pocket or tunnel already restricts water flow, at least to some degree. For this reason, I don't like to use V-struts in pockets or tunnels; I prefer I-struts (also called P-struts). This introduces one less strut leg to further restrict water flow and cause vibration. Struts are discussed in Chapter 2.

Figure 1-8B. Pocket viewed from starboard. The arrow indicates the forward end of the tunnel, which is too short on this boat

Chapter 1: Propellers and Shafts

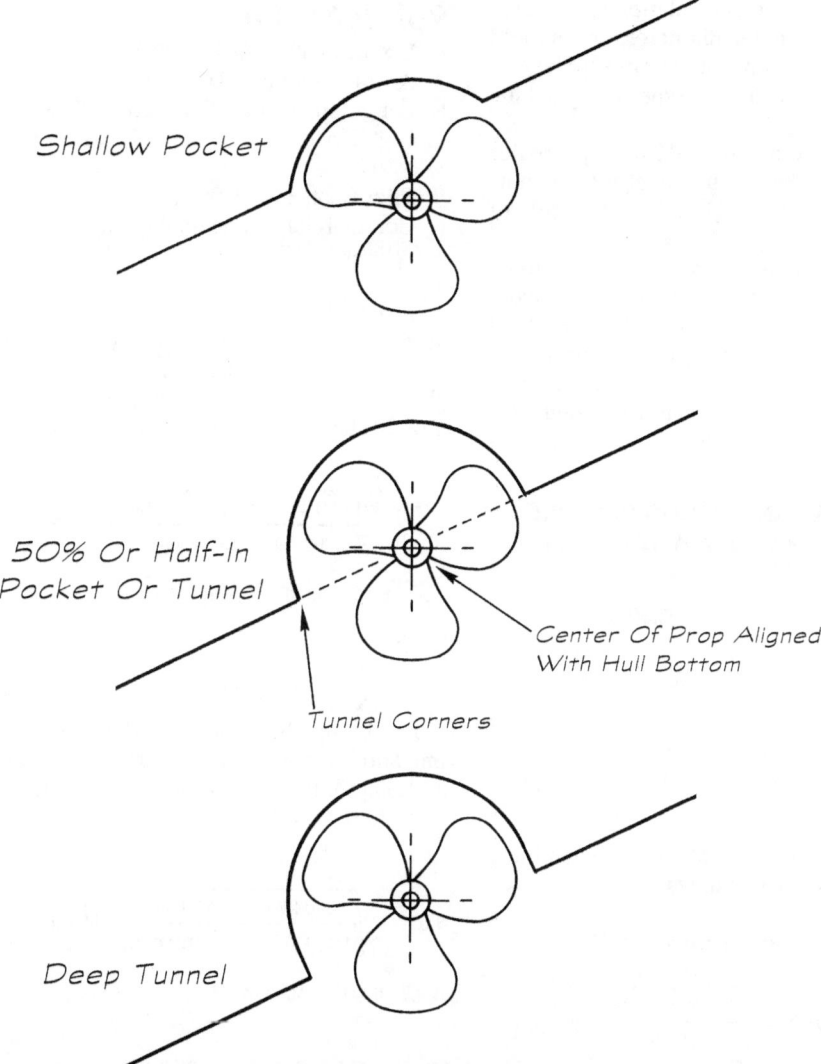

Figure 1-9. Pocket or tunnel depth

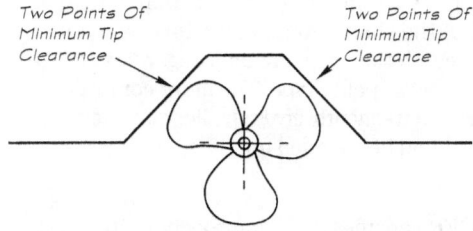

Figure 1-10. V-section tunnel

PROPELLER SHAFTS: DIAMETER, BEARING SPACING, AND BEARINGS

Of course, the propeller shaft itself has to be properly sized and supported. Too little diameter causes shaft whip and vibration, while too much diameter is waste. The simplest and roughest rule of thumb is that the shaft should be one-fourteenth the propeller diameter. In fact, this is pretty close—so much so that if more detailed calculations give you a significantly smaller diameter, you should check with the prop manufacturer to be certain that they don't have to specially machine the hub.

A 24-inch-diameter (610 mm) propeller should have a 1.71-inch-diameter (43.6 mm) shaft (use 1³⁄₄ in., or 44 mm) by this rule of thumb.

You can make a more exact estimate by dividing prop diameter by the factors from Table 1-1. Thus a 4-bladed, 30-inch wheel would use a 1.84-inch Aqualoy shaft (use 1⁷⁄₈ in. or 2 in. dia. Aqualoy). Or, a 4-bladed 762 mm prop would use a 46.7 mm diameter (use a 48 mm dia. Aqualoy).

TABLE 1-1. RECOMMENDED DIVISORS TO OBTAIN SHAFT DIAMETER FROM PROP DIAMETER

	Shaft Material	
	Tobin Bronze	Aqualoy SS or Monel
2-bladed propeller	14.5	18.1
3-bladed propeller	14.0	17.5
4-bladed propeller	13.1	16.3

The precise formula for determining shaft diameter is as follows.

Formula 1-2. Shaft Diameter

$$\text{Shaft Dia., in.} = \sqrt[3]{\frac{321{,}000 \times \text{shp} \times \text{SF}}{\text{St} \times \text{rpm}}}$$

or

$$\text{Shaft Dia., mm} = 3{,}651 \times \sqrt[3]{\frac{\text{kWshaft} \times \text{SF}}{\text{St} \times \text{rpm}}}$$

Where
- shp = shaft horsepower (assumed as 96 percent of rated brake horsepower)
- kWshaft = shaft power in kilowatts (assumed as 96 percent of rated kW at the flywheel)
- St = yield strength of shaft material in torsional shear, in psi or kPa (kilopascals; 1 kPa = 1,000 Pa)
- rpm = revolutions per minute at the shaft after the reduction gear
- SF = design safety factor

Safety Factors

Light Gasoline Yachts = 2.0
Average Yachts = 3.0
Long-Range Motor Cruisers = 3.5 to 4.0
High-Performance Racing Boats = 4.0 to 5.0
Pilot Boats and Patrol Boats = 5.0 to 6.0
Commercial Inspected Passenger Vessels = 7.5*

Example: For a vessel with an engine rated at 420 brake horsepower (403 shp) at 2,100 rpm, and fitted with a 2:1 reduction gear (giving 1,050 shaft rpm), the required Aqualoy 17 or 22 shaft would be

$$\sqrt[3]{\frac{321{,}000 \times 403 \text{ shp} \times 3.0 \text{ SF}}{70{,}000 \text{ psi} \times 1{,}050 \text{ rpm}}} = 1.74 \text{ in.,}$$

use 1³⁄₄ in. dia. Aqualoy

Or

For a vessel with an engine rated at 313 kilowatts, flywheel (300 kW, shaft) at 2,100 rpm, and fitted with a 2:1 reduction gear (giving 1,050 shaft rpm), the required Aqualoy 17 or 22 shaft would be

$$3{,}651 \times \sqrt[3]{\frac{300 \text{ kWshaft} \times 3.0 \text{ SF}}{482{,}000 \text{ kPa} \times 1{,}050 \text{ rpm}}} = 44.2 \text{ mm dia.,}$$

use 45 mm dia. Aqualoy

Real-World Shaft Diameter

I always do the precise calculation for every boat, but the fact is that the shaft sizes from Table 1-1 (after rounding off for standard sizes and fitting standard hubs) are usually so close that I often wonder if it's worth it. Indeed, ABYC P-6 currently has a flat recommendation that the shaft should never be less than one-fifteenth the prop diameter regardless of material or propeller type. The more complex full formula frequently gives smaller diameters, which would be rounded up.

*The CFR specifies a SF "approaching 10," which is usually taken to mean 7.5.

TABLE 1-2. SHAFT MATERIAL MECHANICAL PROPERTIES

Shaft	Torsional Shear*		Yield Strength Modulus of Elasticity (E)		Density	
Material	psi	kPa	psi	MPa	lb./cu. in.	g/cm³
Aqualoy 22	70,000	482,000	28,000,000	194,500	0.285	7.889
Aqualoy 19	60,000	414,000	28,800,000	200,100	0.281	7.778
Aqualoy 17	70,000	482,000	28,500,000	198,000	0.284	7.861
Monel 400	40,000	276,000	26,000,000	180,600	0.319	8.830
Monel K500	67,000	462,000	26,000,000	180,600	0.306	8.470
Tobin Bronze	20,000	138,000	16,000,000	111,200	0.304	8.415
Stainless Steel 304	20,000	138,000	28,000,000	194,500	0.286	7.916

* Yield strength in torsional shear generally taken as 66 percent of yield strength in tension.

Though one may follow ABYC's one-fifteenth rule, I have questions about it. For instance, given a 30-foot-waterline (9.14 m), 16,000-pound-displacement (7,259 kg) hull powered by a single 90 hp (67 kW) diesel running at 1,800 rpm, with a 2.86:1 gear (629.4 shaft rpm), standard prop calculations would indicate a 32-inch (813 mm) 3-bladed prop with a 0.50 DAR. Using Tobin bronze in the ABYC formula, we'd get a 1.87-inch (47.5 m) shaft (use 2-inch or 48 mm). This is 16 to 1, which—to meet the one-fifteenth rule—should be rounded up to $2\frac{1}{8}$- or $2\frac{1}{4}$-inch (55 mm), as available. If we took that exact same boat and gear and refitted it with a 5-bladed, 0.97 DAR prop, we'd get the same shaft diameter from the calculation, but prop diameter would be smaller—29 inches (736 mm). It would be delivering the same power, torque, and even a smidgen less thrust, but it would then pass the one-fifteenth rule at 14.5 to 1. This appears illogical to me. Though I can't state absolutely that shaft-diameter ratios smaller than one-fifteenth are safe, I believe that ABYC's one-fifteenth rule should apply only to 3-bladed propellers with Tobin bronze propeller shafts. I recommend that the diameters from Table 1-1 be considered the minimum instead of using the simple one-fifteenth rule.

Shaft-Bearing Spacing

The simplest rule of thumb for shaft-bearing spacing is that bearings should be no less than 20 times the shaft diameter apart and no more than 40 times the shaft diameter apart. By this rule, $1\frac{1}{2}$-inch (38 mm) shaft should have bearings spaced no less than 30 inches (760 mm) and no more than 60 inches (1,520 mm) apart. The reason for the minimum spacing is to avoid excessive rigidity, but this can be overcome in most boat installations by using a Drivesaver disk or equivalent.

Another rule-of-thumb formula follows.

Formula 1-3. Maximum Shaft-Bearing Spacing (approximate)

$$\text{Max. Bearing Spacing, ft.} = 4.6 \sqrt{\text{Shaft Dia., in.}}$$

or

$$\text{Max. Bearing Spacing, m} = \frac{\sqrt{\text{Shaft Dia., mm}}}{3.6}$$

For a $1\frac{1}{2}$-inch (38 mm) shaft, this gives

$$4.6 \sqrt{1.5 \text{ in. Shaft Dia.}} = 5.63 \text{ ft, or } 67.5 \text{ in.}$$

or

$$\frac{\sqrt{38 \text{ mm Shaft Dia.}}}{3.6} = 1.71 \text{ m, or } 1,712 \text{ mm}$$

The precise formula for maximum bearing spacing is as follows.

Formula 1-4. Maximum Shaft-Bearing Spacing (precise)

$$\text{Max. Bearing Spacing, ft.} = \sqrt{\frac{3.21 \times D_s}{\text{rpm}}} \times \sqrt[4]{\frac{E}{\text{Dens}}}$$

or

$$\text{Max. Bearing Spacing, m} = \sqrt{\frac{D_s}{85.4 \times \text{rpm}}} \times \sqrt[4]{\frac{3{,}984 \times E}{\text{Dens}}}$$

Where
D_s = shaft diameter, in. or mm
E = modulus of elasticity of shaft material, psi or MPa (megapascals; 1 MPa = 1,000,000 Pa) (see Table 1-2)
Dens = density of shaft material, lb./cu. in. or g/cm^3 (see Table 1-2)
rpm = shaft revolutions per minute

Example: For a 1^3/$_4$-in. (45 mm) Aqualoy 22 shaft rotating at 1,050 rpm, we would find

$$\sqrt{\frac{3.21 \times 1.75 \text{ in.}}{1{,}050 \text{ rpm}}} \times \sqrt[4]{\frac{28{,}000{,}000 \text{ psi}}{0.285 \text{ lb./cu.ft.}}} = 7.28 \text{ ft. or } 87.4 \text{ in. max. bearing spacing}$$

or

$$\sqrt{\frac{45 \text{ mm}}{85.4 \times 1{,}050 \text{ rpm}}} \times \sqrt[4]{\frac{3{,}984 \times 194{,}500 \text{ MPa}}{7.889 \text{ g/cm}^3}} = 2.23 \text{ m, } 2{,}230 \text{ mm max. bearing spacing}$$

The longer, more precise formula usually gives greater allowable bearing spacing, which is often helpful.

Alignment, Shaft Material, and Shaft-Bearing Wear

Once you're sure the bearings are properly spaced, you can go on to check alignment.

Figure 1-11. Worn Cutless bearing

The stern bearing can often be surprisingly worn by poor alignment, or a worn or damaged stern bearing can cause misalignment itself.

Properly installed Cutless bearings should last many years. When you grab the shaft or propeller and shake it vigorously, you should feel virtually no play or motion. The bearing itself should appear smooth—without cracks, low spots, dents, or tears. Any of these visual signs of wear or any wiggle in the shaft indicate a new bearing is required. Wear on one side or one end of the bearing indicates an alignment problem.

The standard rule is that a shaft should align with the couplings within 0.001 inch for every inch of coupling outside diameter, or 0.001 mm for every mm of coupling diameter, using a feeler gauge. Thus a 4-inch diameter coupling should be within 0.004 inch or within 1/250th of an inch, and a 100 mm diameter coupling should be within 0.10 mm.

I prefer Monel or Aqualoy stainless shafts. They can be a bit smaller in diameter and a bit lighter with similar shaft spacing than Tobin bronze, and they're less subject to corrosion. (Note that Aqualoy is a trade name for chromium/molybdenum stainless alloys fabricated and sold for shafting by Western Branch Metals. Similar alloys are available under the Aquamet trade name and others.)

Improper alignment of engine beds or bearings can cause incredible Cutless bearing wear. The arrow in Figure 1-11 shows a seriously degraded bearing.

Propeller-Shaft Overhang

Another source of shaft vibration is excessive overhang at the propeller. This is an odd one. On several occasions, I've examined boats that had several inches between the forward face of the prop hub and the aft face of the strut bearing housing. It ought to be obvious to anyone that this much overhang puts side-bending loads on the shaft, which leads to vibration—sometimes quite severe. Try not to have more than one shaft diameter in distance between the hub and the bearing housing. With spurs or similar rope cutters installed, this may have to be pushed up to one and one-half to two shaft diameters, but more than this is just asking for trouble.

Bent Shafts

Oh yes, shafts can be bent, too. If you suspect this, the simplest way to check is to back off the coupling from the transmission just enough to use a feeler gauge. Align as usual; then rotate the shaft in 90-degree increments. You should see no appreciable change in the feeler gauge clearances. If you do, either the shaft is bent or the coupling itself is skewed.

Shaft-Whirling Vibration

There is one final calculation that's worth doing on the shaft itself: check it for whirling vibration. Whirling vibration (also called lateral vibration) occurs when the shaft rpm matches the natural frequency of the beam that is the shaft. This natural frequency is largely controlled by the distance between bearings and by the shaft diameter.

All vibration analysis is complex. Vibration occurs in frequencies that have harmonics or modes. Small changes in mass and location of components can have large effects on the frequency (vibration period), so all such calculations—with the limited information available for most small craft—are approximations. Still, whirling vibration is a useful check.

An approximate formula for estimating the natural whirling frequency of solid, round steel shafts (which yields accurate enough results for all common shaft materials, including bronze) is as follows.

Formula 1-5. Natural Whirling Frequency of a Propeller Shaft

$$\text{Frequency, cpm} = C \times 10^6 \times \frac{\text{Shaft. Dia., in.}}{(\text{Bearing Spacing, in.})^2}$$

or

$$\text{Frequency, cpm} = C \times 10^6 \times \frac{25.4 \times \text{Shaft. Dia., mm}}{(\text{Bearing Spacing, mm})^2}$$

Where
cpm = cycles per minute
C = 4.78 for first mode
C = 19.2 for second mode
C = 43.2 for third mode

Example: In almost all cases, the frequency from the higher modes won't be relevant. We can quickly check the first-mode-vibration shaft-bearing spacing from our twin 450 hp (337 kW) sportsfisherman. Say its engines run at 2,800 rpm, and it has a 2:1 gear. Shaft speed is then 1,400 rpm, and it has an Aqualoy 22 shaft, 1¾ in. (45 mm) diameter.

Using the long form of the bearing-spacing formula, we find that we can place the bearings 75 inches apart. Checking this for whirling frequency, we find

$$4.78 \times 10^6 \times \frac{1.75 \text{ in.}}{(75 \text{ in. spacing})^2} = 1{,}487 \text{ rpm}$$

or

$$4.78 \times 10^6 \times \frac{25.4 \times 45 \text{ mm}}{(1{,}905 \text{ mm spacing})^2} = 1{,}505 \text{ rpm}$$

This is rather close to the 1,400 shaft rpm speed—a potential vibration problem. We can reduce the bearing spacing or increase the shaft diameter to increase the first-mode frequency and reduce the likelihood of whirling-frequency vibration. For example, if we decrease bearing separation to 68 inches:

$$4.78 \times 10^6 \times \frac{1.75 \text{ in.}}{(68 \text{ in. spacing})^2} = 1{,}809 \text{ rpm}$$

or

$$4.78 \times 10^6 \times \frac{25.4 \times 45 \text{ mm}}{(1{,}727 \text{ mm spacing})^2} = 1{,}831 \text{ rpm}$$

This no longer falls almost dead-on at top-speed rpm, and cruising rpms will produce lower frequency still, so this bearing spacing should be OK. Again, increasing shaft diameter to, say, 2 inches (50 mm) would also raise the natural frequency, though not as much as this decrease in bearing spacing.

Intermediate Shaft Bearings

What happens when the shaft is too long to be supported simply by the stern bearing at the end and by the engine (through the shaft coupling) forward? You have to install

Figure 1-12. Pillow block

additional *intermediate shaft bearings*. Their required locations are governed by the shaft-bearing spacing we just reviewed. There are three standard versions of intermediate bearings:

1. *Intermediate bearings housed entirely inside the boat* Intermediate bearings housed entirely inside the boat are also termed *pillow blocks* (Figure 1-12). They are relatively easy to install and to align, but require grease lubrication, often from a grease cup. Pillow blocks must be inspected and greased regularly, usually every 100 engine hours.
2. *A rigid stuffing box serving as an intermediate bearing* A rigid stuffing box serves as an intermediate shaft bearing (unlike a flexible or floating stuffing box on hose). Rigid stuffing boxes are somewhat more difficult to align than pillow blocks. Older rigid stuffing boxes sometimes used grease-cup lubrication. Today, it's standard to lubricate them with water injection. See the later discussion of stuffing boxes.
3. *An external intermediate bearing on a strut—an intermediate strut bearing* Intermediate strut bearings are external bearings, identical to the stern bearing and strut described in Chapter 2. The strut, of course, is shorter and closer to the hull bottom. These bearings can be the most difficult to align; however, they are water lubricated by water flowing through the bearing from ahead (as is the stern bearing in the main strut).

Intermediate strut bearings are usually I-struts (also called P-struts), because they are so much shorter than the longer stern strut. Sometimes, however—when they need to have a significant drop—they may be V-struts. Generally, these struts will have legs the same thickness and proportions as the main strut aft, even though they could be thinner due to the shorter drop. The intermediate strut shows at the arrow in Figure 1-13. Note that on this boat, the main struts aft are larger than recommended.

Figure 1-13. Intermediate strut bearing (Courtesy Chris Wentz)

You can use any combination of the preceding intermediate bearings as required or convenient to reduce the bearing spacing to the maximum allowable. I try to avoid intermediate strut bearings if possible, because they add external appendage drag. Often I'm able to arrange things so a rigid stuffing box will do this job without the extra external drag. The shaft runs from the engine coupling, through the rigid stuffing box, and then to the stern bearing in the propeller strut. There are situations, though, when an external intermediate strut bearing (occasionally two of them) is unavoidable. This is not a problem; it simply represents a bit more appendage drag.

SHAFT COUPLINGS AND KEYWAYS

Propeller-shaft couplings are available in several styles or types: there are tapered-bore, split straight-bore, straight-bore, and more (Figure 1-14). The straight-bore couplings are easier to machine, having no taper, but they are not my first choice for propeller shafts. It's not that they're weaker than tapered-bore couplings, but it can sometimes be quite a challenge to fit a shaft into a straight-bore coupling, even a split coupling, in a boat. It can also be nearly impossible to remove a straight-bore coupling that isn't split. By contrast, a tapered-bore coupling helps guide the shaft in during installation, and it breaks free more cleanly for disassembly.

I recommend only keyed tapered-bore couplings (Figure 1-15) for propeller shafting (unless an interference fit is used, as described later). Not only do these couplings make it easier to install and remove the shaft, but the nuts on the shaft ends, in the couplings, ensure that the shaft cannot pull out when the engine is reversed. Other forms of couplings rely on pressure/friction and the retaining power of setscrews to resist axial withdrawal during reverse operation. I've never felt secure with this. Nevertheless, straight-bore couplings of various types have been and are used successfully on many boats. There is no need to replace these with keyed tapered-bore couplings on existing installations. Most split straight-bore couplings have a machined hole on either side to install a retaining pin through the coupling and the shaft. This would effectively keep the shaft from pulling out in reverse, but I seldom see this installed. It is also more difficult to install the coupling with this pin.

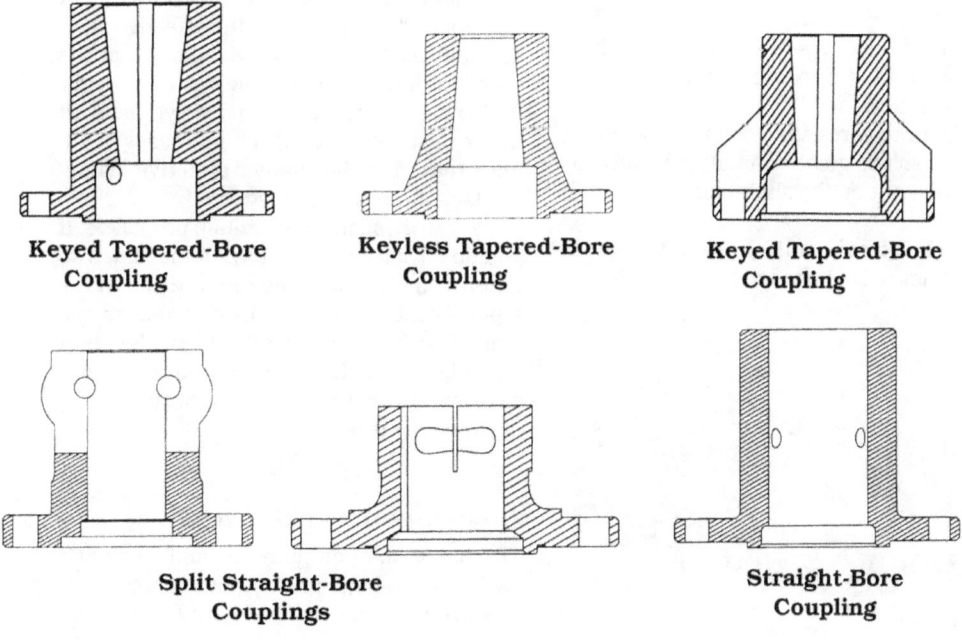

Figure 1-14. Shaft coupling types (Courtesy Marine Hardware, Inc.)

Figure 1-15. Tapered-bore coupling (Courtesy Marine Hardware, Inc.)

Muff Couplings and Intermediate and Tail Shafts

On large boats, dividing the propeller shaft into two sections can ease installation and transport considerations. The forward section (fastened to the transmission coupling) is the *intermediate shaft*, and the after section is the *tail shaft*. It is also less expensive to repair or replace only one portion of the shaft (usually the tail shaft) if it should be damaged.

When two short lengths of shaft are joined together inside the boat, they are best joined with keyed tapered-bore couplings. If the joint is outside the hull, a muff coupling should be used (also termed a sleeve coupling). Marine muff couplings (Figure 1-16) have rounded edges and are available in bronze, aluminum, or stainless. There are two drawbacks:

1. Even if the edges of the muff coupling are rounded, they create more resistance.
2. Withdrawal resistance in reverse operation isn't as great as a flanged coupling with a nut on the shaft end.

Nevertheless, muff couplings may be used if they solve installation problems.

Figure 1-16. Muff coupling

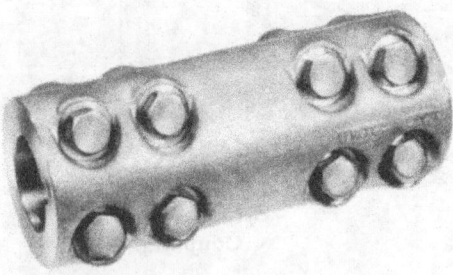

Keyways and Stress

Most propeller shaft failures occur all the way aft, at the forward face of the propeller hub. One reason for this is that the sharp corners resulting from the keyway create stress risers in this area. You should specify that the keyway be fabricated to SAE standards, which include a rounded forward edge. Then go the next step and specify that the corners of the slot (both the outer and inner corners) be radiused as shown in Figure 1-17.

A further precaution is to hollow out the keyway's forward end almost like a spoon. This removes the sharp corners there, eliminating stress risers.

Short-Hub Stress

Another source of stress at the end of the shaft is short propeller hubs (Figure 1-18). Getting propellers that have hubs shorter than the length of a standard shaft taper is more common than you would think. When this is the case—if the hub is bored and tapered to fit the aft end rather than the forward end of the taper—the propeller will snug up onto the taper on the shaft just fine. You can insert the key and tighten down the propeller nuts as usual. If you look closely at the forward face of the hub, however, you'll find that it stops short of the forward end of the taper. This means that the effective shaft diameter is reduced to the diameter at the point on the shaft taper where the hub ends. It also means that there's more overhang aft of the shaft bearing, which increases bending stress. And the smaller effective diameter itself increases local stress.

Try to avoid using short-hub propellers. If you do have to use one, have it machined so that it will seat up to the forward end of the taper. You then have to have a spacer machined to fit over the aft end of the shaft taper between the short hub and the propeller nuts; otherwise, the nuts won't tighten down on the propeller.

Interference-Fit Hubs

Though it isn't common on small craft and yachts (even large yachts), commercial vessels often use an *interference fit* between

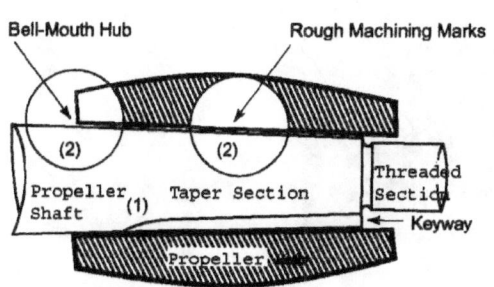
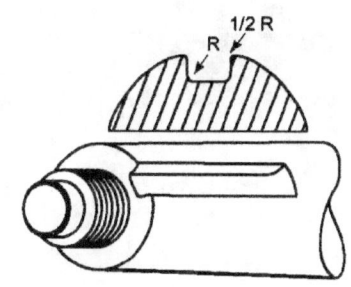

Poor Practice

Cross section showing (1) shortening of keyway sometimes minimizes stresses in shaft, and (2) types of corrosion-causing crevices.

Proper Rounding Of Corners

Sketches show sled-runner type end and filleted keyway recommended for maximum shaft life. Both top corners as well as bottom corners should be filleted.

Figure 1-17. Keyway machining (Courtesy Western Branch Metals)

the propeller hub and the shaft taper. In interference fit, the hub is machined to be slightly smaller in diameter than the taper on the shaft. The old method of installing these was to chill the shaft with ice and heat the propeller with a low-temperature torch (*never* a high-temperature torch, such as a welder's cutting torch). This caused the hub to expand enough (and the shaft to shrink enough) so the propeller could be slid on. By the time both components returned to normal temperature, the hub would have shrunk to an exceptionally reliable fit on the shaft, with no stress risers created by a machined keyway.

The modern method is to force the interference-fit propeller up onto the taper using hydraulic pressure. Most often this is accomplished with a Pilgrim nut from Mid Atlantic Pump and Equipment Company. This nut is set on the shaft aft of the prop, and hydraulic fluid is used to force the prop fully up onto the taper. This is common on large commercial and naval vessels.

Keeping the Shaft in the Boat

If a coupling lets go inside the hull, or if the shaft breaks inside, the shaft can pull right out of the boat. Though unlikely, such a problem not only can cause you to lose a costly shaft and prop, but also could sink the boat due to water entering through the now open shaft-log hole. Installing a shaft collar inside (a solid ring around the shaft, slid on and fastened with one or two setscrews) eliminates this possibility at virtually no cost. Even a hose clamp around the shaft inside will be better than nothing.

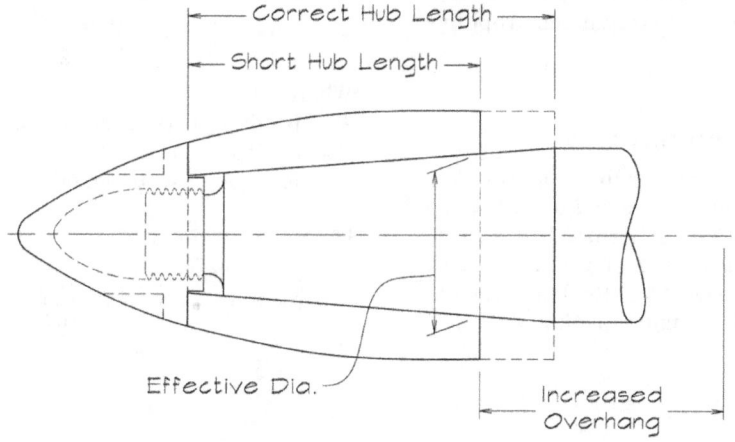

Figure 1-18. Short hubs increase stress

CHAPTER 2
Struts, Propeller Apertures, and Shaft Angle

PROPELLER STRUTS

You may spend hours selecting props and engines. You will carefully consider shafts and bearings, as you will engine mounts and engine controls. Struts, though—until you wipe one off by running aground—are often afterthoughts. This hardly makes sense. After all, the strut not only supports your propeller, but also affects the water flowing into the prop.

A strut that's too weak will whip under load, causing vibration that is often blamed on the prop itself. (Even worse, of course, the strut could break off entirely.) At the same time, a strut that's not well faired will cause whorls and eddies in the inflow to the prop. Not only does this turbulence cause vibration, it also reduces propeller efficiency.

Strut Dimensions

Figures 2-1 and 2-2 show the proportions of proper single-leg I-struts and diverging-leg V-struts of cast silicon bronze. These struts are strong enough not to whip and will cause minimal turbulence. Strut thickness for silicon bronze is determined as follows.

Formula 2-1a. Required Section Modulus for Silicon Bronze I-Struts

Z, in.^{3}, for I-Struts = (A ÷ B) × 6.41 (English)

Z, cm^3, for I-Struts = (A ÷ B) × 105 (Metric)

Formula 2-1b. Required Section Modulus for Silicon Bronze V-Struts

Z, in.^{3}, for V-Struts = (A ÷ B) × 3.21 (English)

Z, cm^3, for V-Struts = (A ÷ B) × 52.6 (Metric)

Formula 2-1c. Required Strut Thickness for Silicon Bronze Strut with Half-Oval Section

$$\text{Thickness, in.} = \sqrt[3]{\frac{Z}{0.572}}$$

Where
A = hp × drop, in. (Use full engine power.)
B = shaft rpm × propeller dia. in.
Z = the required section modulus in in.^{3}

Or

$$\text{Thickness, mm} = 10 \times \sqrt[3]{\frac{Z}{0.572}}$$

Chapter 2: Struts, Propeller Apertures, and Shaft Angle

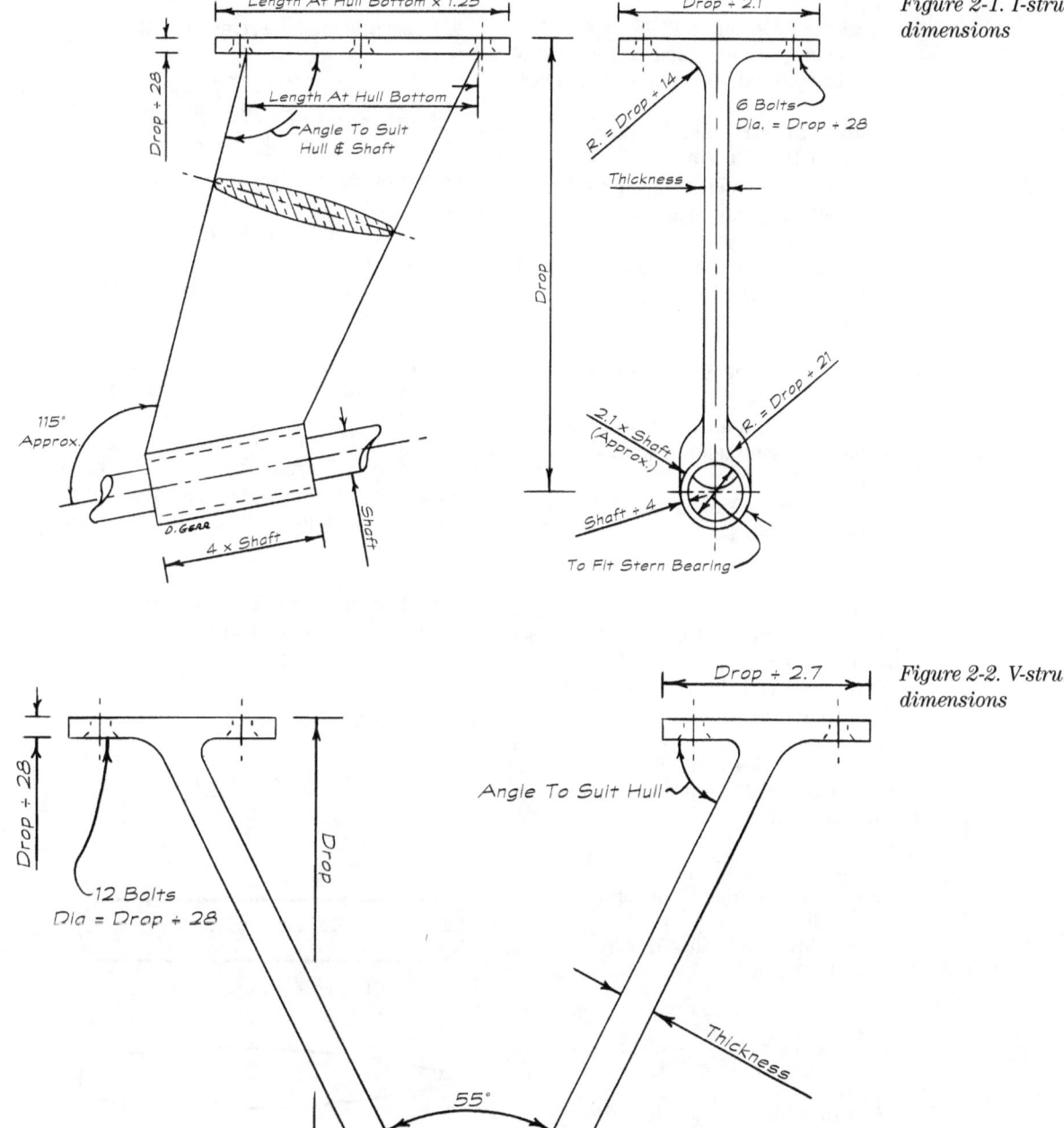

Figure 2-1. I-strut dimensions

Figure 2-2. V-strut dimensions

19

PART ONE: DRIVETRAIN INSTALLATIONS

Where
A = kW × drop, mm ÷ 18.95
B = shaft rpm × propeller dia. mm ÷ 25.4
Z = the required section modulus in in.^{3}

Formula 2-2a. Strut Length (Any Section) at Hull Bottom

Length, in., at hull bottom = 6.5 × thickness, but not less than 4 × shaft diameter (English)

Length, mm, at hull bottom (minimum) = 6.5 × thickness, but not less than 4 × shaft diameter (Metric)

Formula 2-2b. Strut Length (Any Section) at Boss

Length, in., at propeller-shaft boss (at bottom) = 4 × shaft diameter (English)

Length, mm, at propeller-shaft boss (at bottom) = 4 × shaft diameter (Metric)

Example: Say our boat has twin diesels delivering 300 hp (224 kW) each at 2,800 rpm. Its reduction gear is 1.51:1, so the shaft rpm is 1,854. Propellers are 20-inch (508 mm) diameter 4-blade on 1½-inch (38 mm) bronze shafts, and the strut drop is 15.5 inches (394 mm). We want silicon bronze struts with a half-oval section. We would then find:

A = 300 hp × 15.5 in. drop = 4,650
B = 1,854 shaft rpm × 20 in. prop. dia. = 37,080
Z for I-Struts = (4,650 ÷ 37,080) × 6.41 = 0.80 in.^{3}

Thickness, in. = $\sqrt[3]{\dfrac{0.80 \text{ in.}^3}{0.572}}$ = 1.118 in., use 1⅛ in.

Length at hull bottom = 6.5 × 1⅛ in. = 7.31; use 7⅜ in.
Length at propeller-shaft boss = 4 × 1½ in. shaft diameter = 6 in.

Or

A = 224 kW × 394 mm drop ÷ 18.95 = 4,657
B = 1,854 rpm × 508 mm prop. dia. ÷ 25.4 = 37,080

Z for I-Struts = (4,657 ÷ 37,080) × 105
(section modulus, cm^3) = 13.19 cm^3

Thickness, mm = $10 \times \sqrt[3]{\dfrac{13.19 \text{ cm}^3}{0.572}}$ = 28.46 mm;

use 29 or 30 mm

Length at hull bottom = 6.5 × 30 mm = 195 mm
Length at propeller-shaft boss = 4 × 38 mm shaft diameter = 152 mm

Note that the thickness obtained from Formula 2-1c is for the half-oval section shown in Figures 2-1 and 2-3. Three standard strut sections include, in addition to the half-oval section with rounded ends we've been discussing, a rectangular section with rounded ends and an NACA 16-series foil section.

Formula 2-3a. For a Rectangular Section with Rounded Ends

$$Z = 0.159 \times L \times T^2$$

Formula 2-3b. For an NACA 16-Series Foil Section

$$Z = 0.0891 \times L \times T^2$$

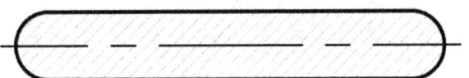

Flat With Round Ends

NACA Series 16 Foil

Half-Oval With Round Ends

Figure 2-3. Standard strut sections

Formula 2-3c. For the Flat Half-Oval Section with Rounded Ends

$$Z = 0.080 \times L \times T^2$$

Where
Z = the required section modulus from Formula 2-1a or 2-1b in in.^{3} or cm^3
L = length from Formula 2-2a and 2-2b, in. or cm
T = thickness to achieve the specified section modulus Z, in. or cm

NOTE: in metrics, for the preceding equations, enter dimensions here in centimeters, *not* millimeters.

You can enter different values of thickness and length in different combinations to get the required Z; however, proportions should follow Formulas 2-2a and 2-2b.

Using standard engineering references, you can use Z to find the required thickness and length for any other strut-section shape. You can also refer to ABYC standard P-6 for additional details.

Adjusting Strut Dimensions for Other Materials

The preceding calculations are for silicon bronze, which has a yield strength of 55,000 psi (379,000 kPa). If you use another alloy, you have to determine its yield strength and adjust Z proportionately. Say you use 316L stainless, which has a yield strength of 42,000 psi (289,500 kPa). Divide the yield strength of silicon bronze by the yield strength of stainless to get 1.309. Accordingly, you would increase Z by 1.309 times and then find the required dimensions. If you used 316L stainless for the half-oval-section struts in the earlier example, they would work out as

55,000 psi yield silicon bronze ÷ 42,000 psi yield 316L stainless = 1.309
Z for silicon bronze I-struts, you found, was 0.80 cu. in.
Z for 316L stainless I-struts = 0.80 cu. in. × 1.309 = 1.047 in.^{3}

$$\text{Thickness, in.} = \sqrt[3]{\frac{1.047 \text{ in.}^3}{0.572}} = 1.22 \text{ in; use } 1\tfrac{1}{4} \text{ in.}$$

Length at hull bottom = 6.5 × 1¼ in. = 8.125; use 8¼ in.
Length at propeller-shaft boss = 4 × 1½ in.
shaft diameter = 6 in.

Or

379,000 kPa yield silicon bronze ÷ 289,500 kPa yield 316L stainless = 1.309
Z for silicon bronze I-struts, you found, was 13.19 cm^3
Z for 316L stainless I-struts = 13.19^3 × 1.309 = 17.26 cm^3

$$\text{Thickness, mm} = 10 \times \sqrt[3]{\frac{17.26 \text{ cm}^3}{0.572}} = 31.13; \text{ use } 32 \text{ mm}$$

Length at hull bottom = 6.5 × 32 mm = 208 mm
Length at propeller-shaft boss = 4 × 38 mm
shaft diameter = 152 mm

TABLE 2-1. YIELD STRENGTHS OF COMMON STRUT MATERIALS

Alloy	Yield, psi	Yield, kPa
Commercial bronze	37,000	255,000
Manganese bronze, SAE No. 43	65,000	448,000
Manganese bronze, SAE No. 430 (GrA)	90,000	620,500
Manganese bronze, SAE No. 430 (GrB)	110,000	758,400
Silicon bronze	55,000	379,000
Phosphor bronze	55,000	379,000
Aluminum bronze	55,000	379,000
Stainless steel 304	35,000	241,000
Stainless steel 316	42,000	289,500
Stainless steel 316L	42,000	289,500
Aluminum 5000 series	34,000	234,400
Aluminum 5000 series as welded	14,000	96,500

Discussion of Strut Alloys

The longest-lasting alloys by far are silicon bronze or one of the phosphor or aluminum bronzes. All the other alloys are second best, even though the manganese bronzes have very high yield strengths. Of the steels, I would use only 316L stainless for struts, and then only if I had no other choice. Any other stainless is far too likely to suffer from pitting corrosion, especially at the welds. Even 316L suffers from this to some degree. Commercial bronze and manganese bronze are very common strut materials. They are strong, inexpensive, and cast easily. Though they're acceptable, both commercial and manganese bronzes are really brasses containing zinc—they're not bronzes, in spite of their name. (Bronze is copper alloyed with tin; brass is copper alloyed with zinc.) All brasses can suffer from a corrosion called dezincification and are not recommended for underwater work. If the struts are made of manganese or commercial bronze, you have to be careful to protect them with anodes.

Aluminum struts that are continuous through the bottom of the hull and are structurally welded to framing inside the hull (with welds at the hull shell only for watertightness) can use the full yield strength. If the aluminum strut welds directly to the bottom of the hull or to plates mounted to the bottom of the hull, you must use the as-welded yield strength.

Additional Strut Dimensions

The controlling dimensions for other aspects of the struts are either the drop (the vertical distance from hull bottom to shaft centerline) or the prop shaft diameter. Cutless bearings come in varying dimensions for the same prop shaft diameter, so the bearing must be selected before determining the bearing tube diameter. The bearing tube wall thickness should equal shaft diameter divided by 4, as shown in Figure 2-1, but should never be less than 3/16 inch (4.8 mm).

Note that the standard Cutless bearing length is four times the shaft diameter. If you can go less on high-speed boats, it will reduce wetted-surface drag. Thordon makes bearings that are designed at just two times the shaft diameter in length. These are well worth installing if the last ounce of speed is critical, and the previously shown struts can simply be trimmed down (tapered more) at their bottoms to match this shorter bearing length.

Strut Fastening and Mounting Considerations

Of course, sturdy struts alone do not necessarily make for strong support. The struts are no stiffer or stronger than their attachment to the boat. One 50-footer (15.2 m) that I was called in to fix had severe vibration problems. Her V-struts were massive, her props were new and carefully balanced, and her shaft alignment had been checked and rechecked. She was a new, twin-screw fiberglass boat.

When I clambered into her after bilge, I found that her V-struts were through-bolted to the fiberglass hull bottom with nothing more than individual backing plates of the same dimensions (footprint) as the V-strut bases below them. The resultant installation gave the illusion of being strong, but it wasn't. (Certainly, it fooled the boat's builder, who'd otherwise done a decent job on her.) Even though the bottom was a bit over 7/8-inch (22 mm) thick solid glass, it wasn't sufficiently stiff. The hull itself was flexing at the strut attachments—flexing enough to generate noticeable hairline cracks after only a few dozen operating hours.

Fiberglass is middling strong for its weight, in terms of pure tension, but it can only be described as weak in bending. (Its flexural modulus is low.) The stiffening for all fiberglass-reinforced plastic (FRP) hulls needs to be carefully thought out, with great attention to spreading loads and avoiding hard spots. It was relatively simple (though hard work for the repair yard) to fix this boat. The hull bottom was built up inside—around the struts—with another 1/4 inch to 3/8 inch (6.3 mm to 9.5 mm) of glass for about two feet square (60 cm squre). Then large backing blocks and backing plates were installed. This made all the difference.

Strut Backing Blocks

According to my experience, all FRP hulls require large backing blocks and plates behind the strut bolts (Figure 2-4). The wood, ply, or G-10 backing-block thickness should be at least 2 times the strut-bolt diameter, and the block's footprint should be 1.3 times the footprint dimensions of the strut base below it—more doesn't hurt. With

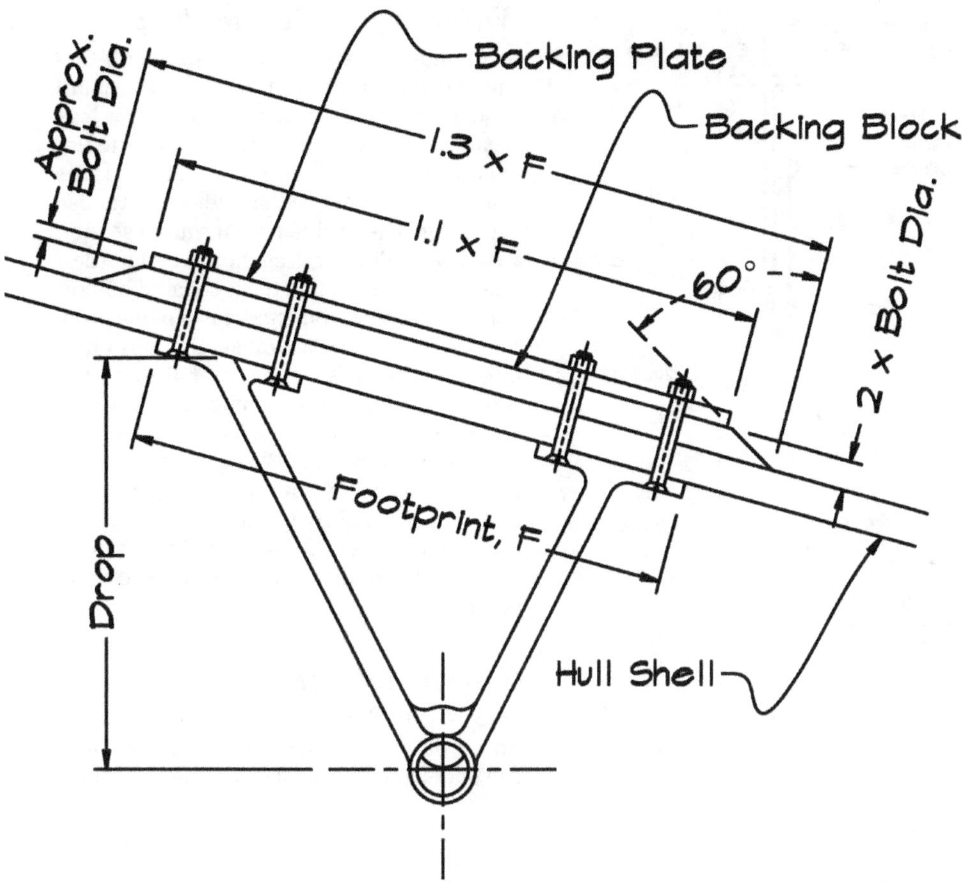

Figure 2-4. Strut fastening

V-struts, the backing block should span the width between its twin bases. The backing plate should have a footprint that is about 10 percent greater than the strut's base footprint outside. Don't forget to bevel the backing block edges and radius the corners as well. Cutting them off vertical and square can leave hard spots that aggravate stresses in the hull. If the backing block is wood, it must be very thoroughly saturated with epoxy—three coats minimum—with extra attention paid to sealing the end grain and bolt holes. Wooden hulls need similar careful attention to backing blocks and plates.

Strut Construction for Metal Hulls

For steel and aluminum boats, struts are usually best when fabricated of the same material as the hull itself. One method of fastening is to insert the strut legs through slots in the hull bottom and weld them to longitudinal girders inside the hull (Figure 2-5). Sometimes these girders are the same girders as the engine beds, but not always. The slot in the hull should be just a little bit long fore-and-aft. In this way the strut assembly can be inserted into the slots and slid around to get proper alignment before being tack welded in place. The doubler plates outside are installed as split plates around both sides of the strut legs and tack welded. Alignment is rechecked, and then the entire assembly is structurally welded in place.

An alternative method is to fasten the strut legs to a transverse floor or deep frame (Figure 2-6). In this case not only is the hull bottom slotted to accept the strut legs, but the floor or frame is notched as well.

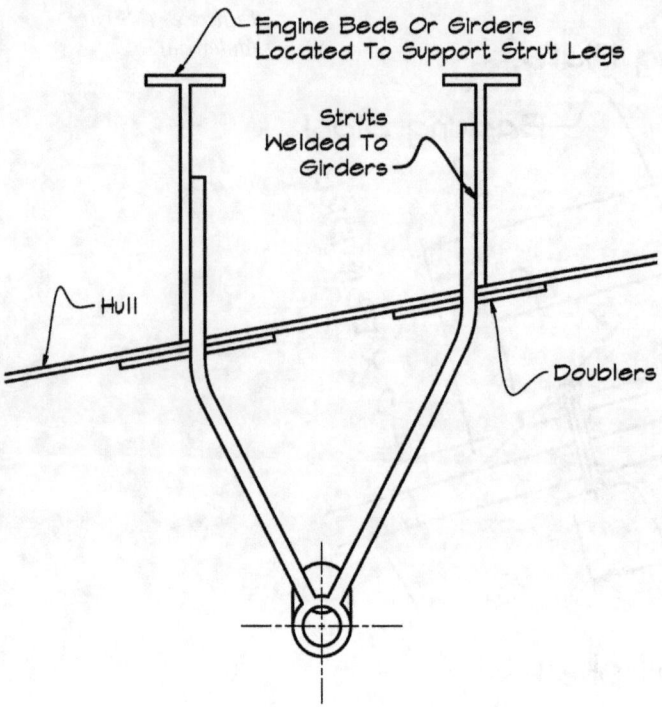

Figure 2-5. Metal hull strut construction: struts to girders

Water Inflow to the Prop

A common cost-cutting measure on off-the-shelf struts is to make the strut legs square in section. In fact, square-section strut legs create only slightly more drag than the flat oval section shown in Figure 2-3, and this leads many to believe that they compromise very little. The problem with square-section strut legs isn't their drag, however, but their effect on the propeller; these squared-off corners can create turbulence ahead of the prop. Theoretically, true airfoil-section strut legs interfere the least with water flow to the prop. In practice, the symmetrical flat-oval section shown in Figure 2-3 is nearly as good and is simpler to build. Boats operating under 20 knots can get by with flat and square strut legs that are slightly rounded at the leading and trailing edges, but these still won't be as quiet as the shaped strut section shown in Figure 2-3.

V-Strut Leg Angles

Since V-struts have two legs to impede water flow, you want to make sure that two legs can't line up with the blades at the same time.

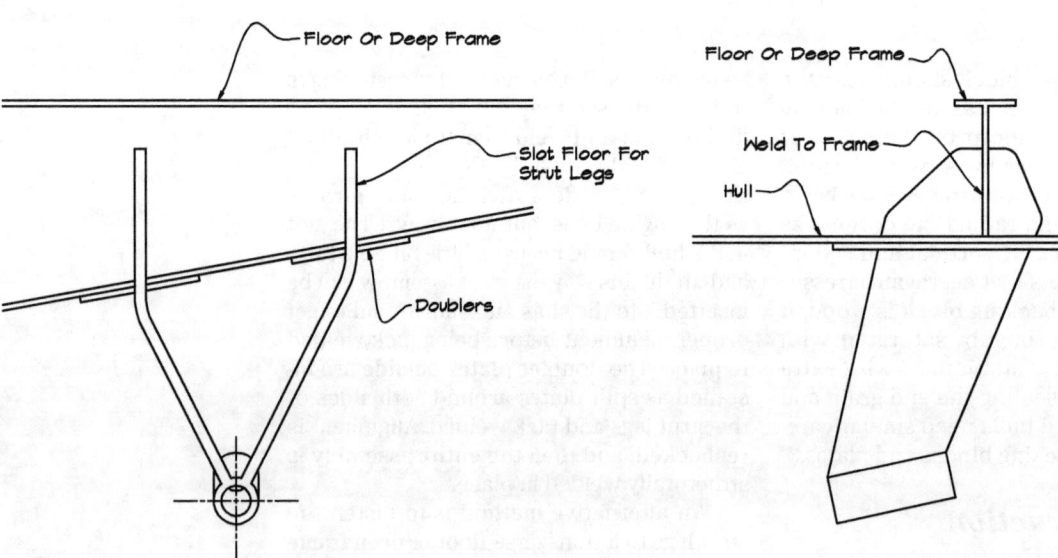

Figure 2-6. Metal hull strut construction: struts to floor or frame

This rules out the following angles between legs:

 3-bladed prop—120 degrees
 4-bladed prop—90 degrees
 5-bladed prop—72 degrees
 6-bladed prop—60 degrees

The standard V-strut angle is 55 degrees, which avoids all of the preceding angles.

Obviously, 120 degrees and 90 degrees aren't likely, but 72 degrees and 60 degrees can happen if you're not careful. I even saw 90 degrees once on an old wooden twin-screw boat. Someone had repowered her and installed a new I-strut, but—to make it "really strong"—they added a transverse strut leg that ran sideways to the keel at exactly 90 degrees. You guessed it, the boat had a 4-bladed prop.

Some V-struts have their legs so close together that the width between them is about the same as one prop-blade width. In this case, they form a perfect shadow for the upper blade every time it swings by. You can see that this was the case on the aluminum ferry with the short pocket (see Figure 1-8A), which obstructed water flow still more. No wonder this vessel vibrated so badly.

Strut Grounding Skegs

Behind the strut, the lower portion of the propeller is unprotected from the debris of grounding. Many cruising or workboats install V-struts with a grounding skeg projecting down in front of the propeller. The grounding strut isn't nearly as strong as a full keel, but it does protect the propeller better than having nothing in front of and below its lower half. Note in Figure 2-7 that it's important to sweep and curve back the leading edge of the grounding skeg as much as possible to avoid catching things and to clear the trailing edge of the grounding skeg as far as practical from the prop. The grounding skeg is usually made with the same thickness and section as the standard V-strut legs, with a similar section modified as necessary to fair it properly as the grounding skeg tapers toward the bottom. The drawback of a grounding skeg is more appendage drag.

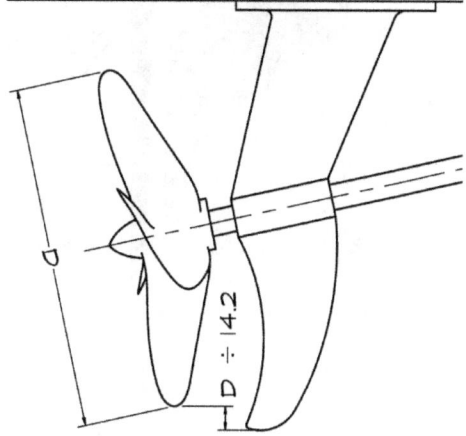

Figure 2-7. Strut grounding skeg

PROPELLER APERTURES AND SHAFT ANGLE

Strut in an Aperture

In Figure 2-8, you can see a typical strut in a full aperture. This provides good protection for the propeller. Such struts are usually standard I-struts with a rough mirror image of the upper strut leg below, fastened to the top of the skeg keel. Occasionally—when great strength to withstand frequent groundings is required—the strut is a V-strut with the extra leg on the bottom to form a Y, fastening to the top of the skeg. This is strong indeed, but again, it creates additional appendage drag.

Open Propeller Apertures in High-Speed Single-Screw Vessels

The faster the boat, the more important it is to concentrate on obtaining unobstructed inflow to the propeller. An example of a boat type that can have problems with inflow to the prop is a traditional Novi-type lobsterboat that has been powered to run at high speed—20 knots plus. Standard lobsterboats were originally displacement hulls. They're constructed with long, straight keels and a vertical deadwood just ahead of the prop. The stern bearing projects through the deadwood, and often this deadwood is not cut back or faired away ahead of the propeller at all. Frequently, the trailing edge of the

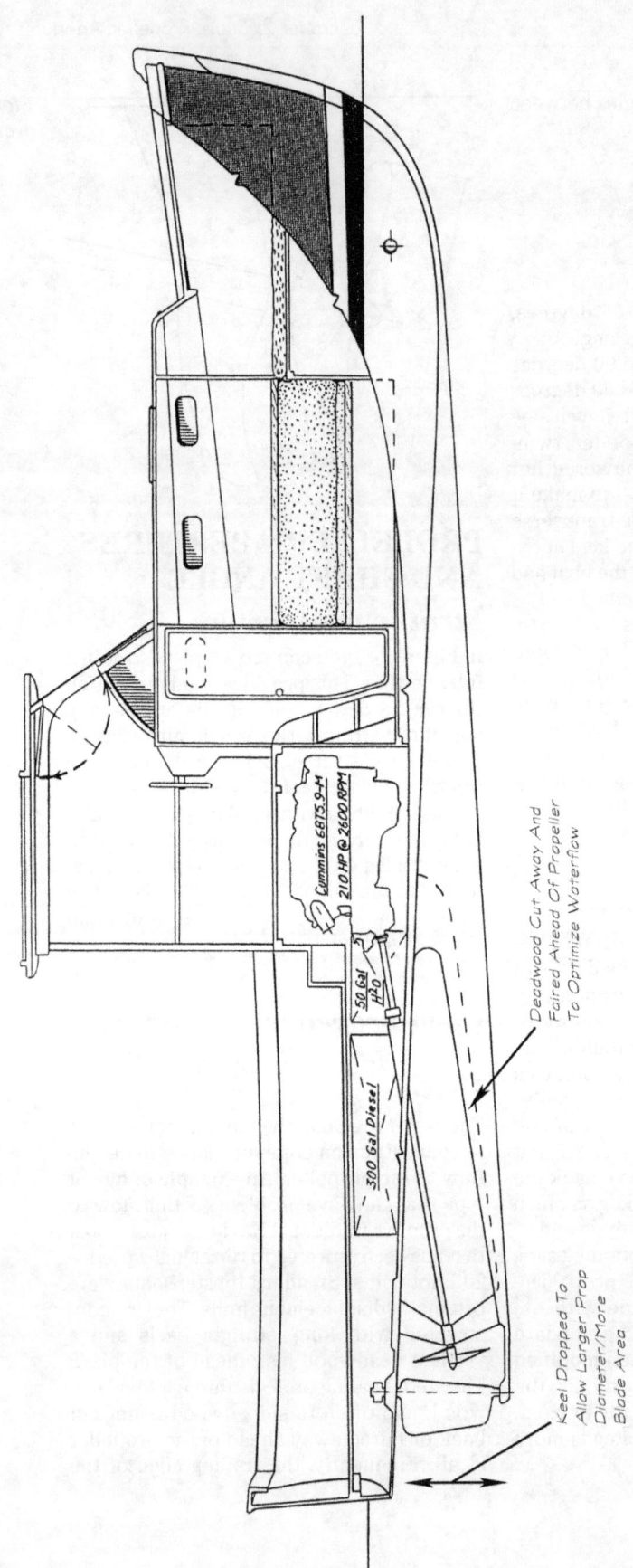

Figure 2-8. Altering a keel to improve lobsterboat performance

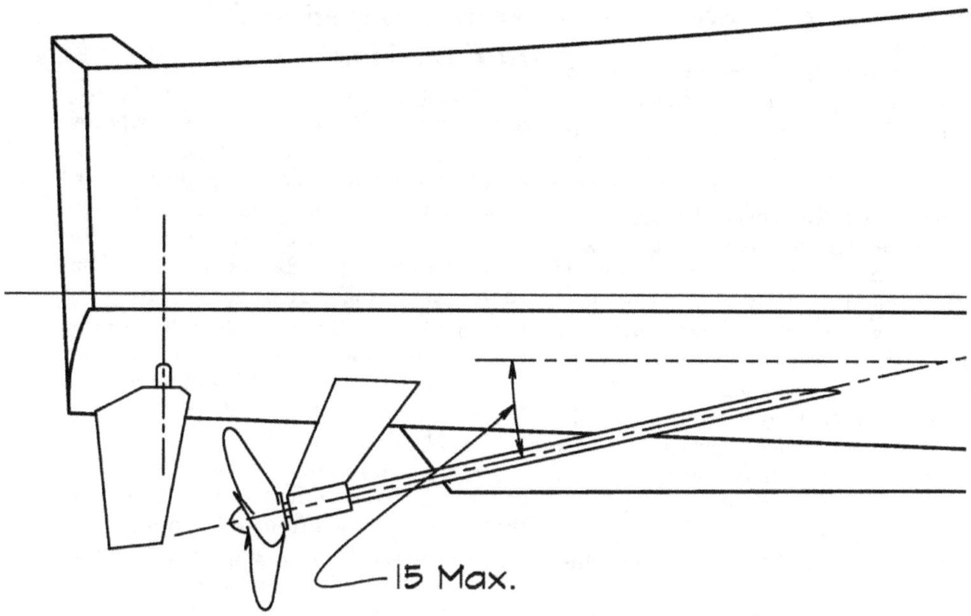

Figure 2-9. Maximum shaft angle

deadwood (ahead of the prop) doesn't even have its edges rounded off. At 12, 13, or 14 knots, or so, you can get by with such a setup (though it's less than ideal). But when you push such hulls faster, the propeller will be starved for water in the shadow of the heavy, blunt deadwood and keel just ahead.

Even though lobsterboats were originally displacement boats, as long as a lobsterboat's run is fairly broad and flat aft it can be made to go 25 or 30 knots or more—given the power—but you should provide the prop with room to breathe. The traditional full keel, ideally, should be cut away for 20 to 25 percent of the waterline length ahead of the prop, and the upper/trailing edge of the remaining keel/skeg should have a pronounced rounded taper to reduce turbulence (Figure 2-8). Additionally, the keel/skeg on these boats ought to be dropped aft to make room for a larger-diameter prop than fitted to traditional displacement-speed lobsterboats. Larger engines need additional blade area—as we've seen—to transmit their power, and greater diameter is the most efficient way to accomplish this.

Shaft Angle

The standard rule is that the propeller shaft angle should not be greater than 15 degrees from the horizontal. Further, the lower or flatter the shaft angle, the better. Broadly speaking, this is correct. On all ordinary designs, you should keep the shaft angle less than 15 degrees. There are two reasons for this. One is that with the propeller at a pronounced angle, the water flow into the propeller disk is uneven from top to bottom. This essentially changes the apparent pitch that the water "sees" at the top of the propeller from that at the bottom of the propeller. This in turn causes uneven blade loading, which can cause vibration. The other reason is that the thrust line will not be forward, but will be angled down, and so some efficiency is lost.

Another consideration is that almost all engines are designed to be installed at no more than 15 degrees. Fit them at a steeper angle, and the oil sump will collect a puddle in the lower aft corner, which won't be properly circulated. This can lead to a serious lubrication failure. In fact, the more level you can install the engine itself, the better for the lubrication system. Remember, if you have a planing hull with an engine and shaft installed at 13 degrees and the planing angle is 4 degrees, the real angle of the engine will be 17 degrees, which will cause these lubrication issues. The way around this is to install the engine with a down-angle gear or with a pair of CV or universal joints to get the engine more level than the shaft.

Having said all this, I recall how I once inherited the design project of a 40-foot (12.2 m) boat with a 17-degree shaft angle. It was a production vessel, and the tooling was too far along to change. So we kept the shaft angle and built around it. Though I had concerns, interestingly enough the boat ran flawlessly. Quite a few of these boats were produced. They all operated smoothly with no vibration, made exactly predicted speed (with no allowance for loss due to shaft angle), and were good sea boats. (A down-angle gear reduced the engine-installation angle to 7 degrees.) My feeling is that a bit too much emphasis is placed on getting flat shaft angles. My intuition tells me that the water flow entering the propeller disk is somewhat straightened out by the suction (lift) of the forward side of the propeller; so the water tends to enter the blades at closer to parallel to the propeller shaft than the shaft angle would indicate. It would be interesting to run systematic, real-world tests to see what is really happening in this complex flow pattern.

Regardless, I have never set out to design a boat that had more than a 15-degree shaft angle.

Shafts Angled or Offset in Plan View

Shafts, as previously discussed, are almost always angled in side or profile view; however, they can also be angled in plan view: i.e., angled in and out rather than higher forward and lower at the stern. This is not common, and it's generally best to arrange propeller shafts parallel to the boat's centerline, but shafts can be angled in or out to solve some installation problems. This practice was more common in the early days of powerboats and auxiliary sail. It's not unusual to find boat plans from the 1920s and '30s with shafts angled in plan.

The primary consideration with such installations—in single-screw boats—is that the turning effect of propeller be taken into account. In fact, one of the reasons old-time boats sometimes had angled shafts was to counteract this propeller effect. A right-hand wheel is the standard on single-screw craft. Such a propeller rotates clockwise as viewed from astern (Figure 2-10). It tends to turn the bow to port going ahead and the stern to port going astern. If you mount the shaft parallel to the centerline but off to port, then

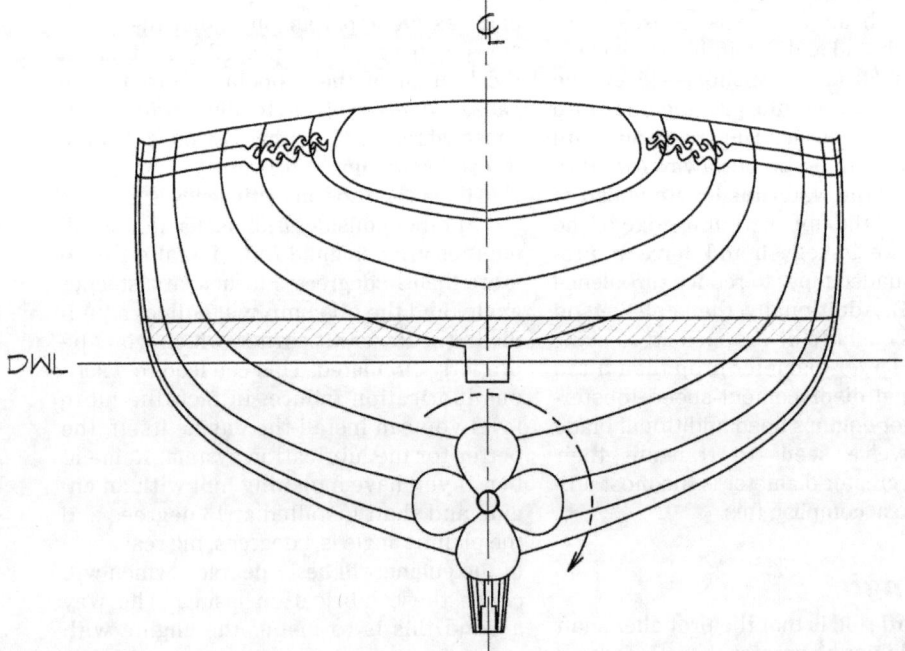

Figure 2-10. Rotation of a right-hand wheel (viewed from astern)

the force being off to that side will tend to push the bow to starboard going ahead and the stern to starboard going astern. Thus, installing a right-hand wheel off centerline to port helps cancel out the to-port tendency caused by the propeller. If instead you put the shaft off to the starboard side, it would increase the to-port tendency caused by the right-hand propeller, which would not be good. A left-hand wheel behaves exactly the opposite.

NOTE: On twin-screw boats, the starboard propeller is usually right-hand and the port propeller is left-hand (Figure 2-11).

Offset parallel propeller shafts are not uncommon on sailboats, where they help make more room on the side away from the engine and also avoid running the shaft through the structure of the keel on centerline (Figure 2-12). The offset distance shouldn't be more than about 8 percent of beam. Note that this offset puts the rudder out of the direct propeller slipstream, reducing steering response under power.

It is also not uncommon to angle the prop shaft so the propeller is still on the centerline, with the engine angled off to the port side on a right-hand wheel boat (Figure 2-12). This also counters the to-port tendency of a right-hand wheel. The maximum installed shaft angle in plan should be about 3 degrees. With this configuration, the rudder is still in the slipstream.

Occasionally, larger single-screw powerboats will use a similar configuration, with the prop on the centerline and the shaft angled up to 3 degrees to port on a right-hand wheel (opposite for left-hand). The primary advantage here is when the engine is at midships or forward (Figure 2-13). The shaft angle creates some added room on the starboard side of the engine. This might allow a passageway to starboard or some large item of machinery to be installed that otherwise wouldn't fit.

Twin-screw boats can also use shafts angled in plan. V-bottom hulls can angle the shafts out at the stern and in toward the

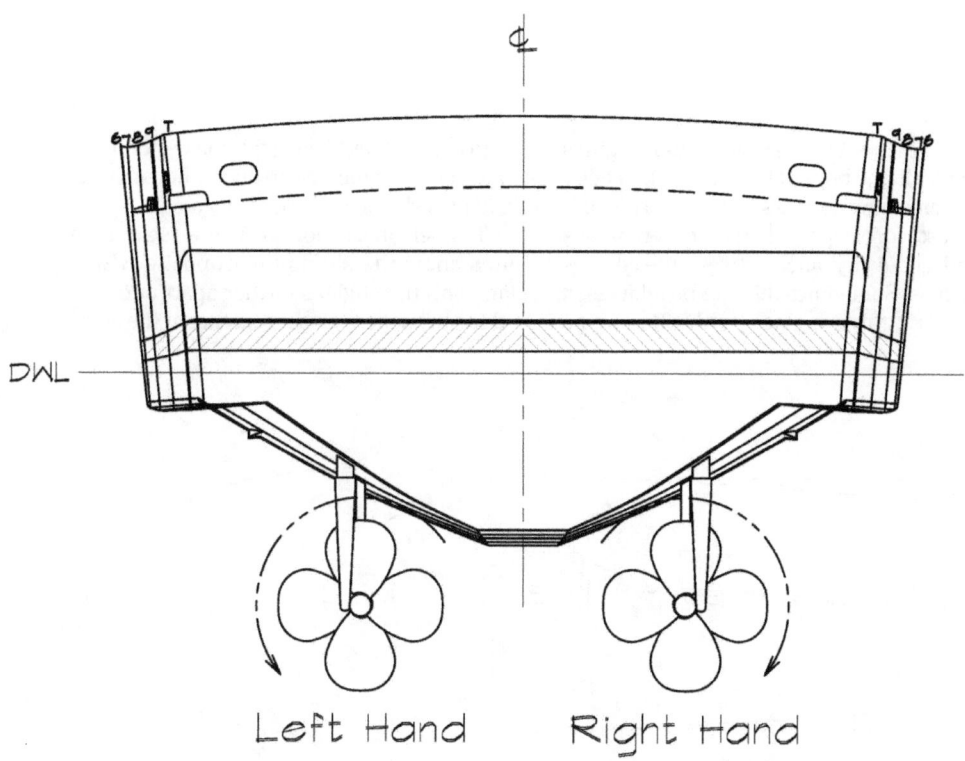

Figure 2-11. Standard direction of rotation for twin screws (viewed from astern)

PART ONE: DRIVETRAIN INSTALLATIONS

*Figure 2-12.
Different shaft
placements
compared*

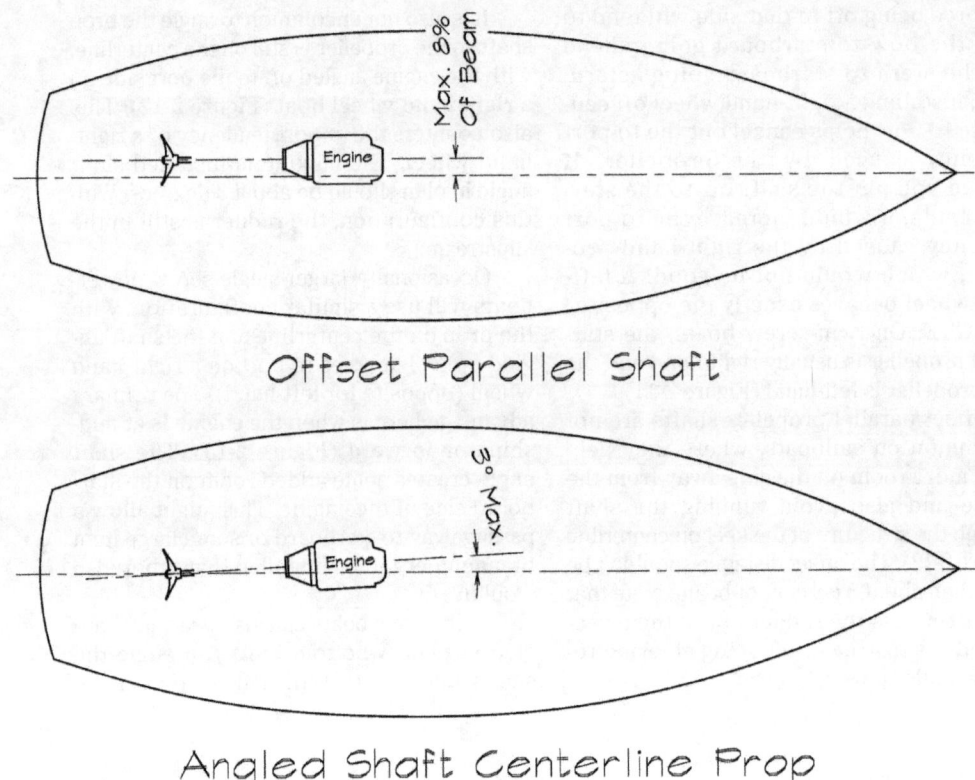

engines. The goal is to allow higher engines to fit lower in the bilge of the V of the hull body while maintaining normal separation of the propellers astern. Keep in mind that there needs to be adequate clearance between the engines at midships. Sometimes this can be addressed by staggering the engines, with one engine ahead of the other, though this makes for a long engine compartment. The maximum shaft angle in plan should be about 2 degrees.

Twin-engine, canoe-sterned vessels sometimes angle the shafts the opposite way in plan: with the engines farther apart midships and the propellers closer together at the stern.

*Figure 2-13.
Single midships
engine on center-
line with angled
shaft*

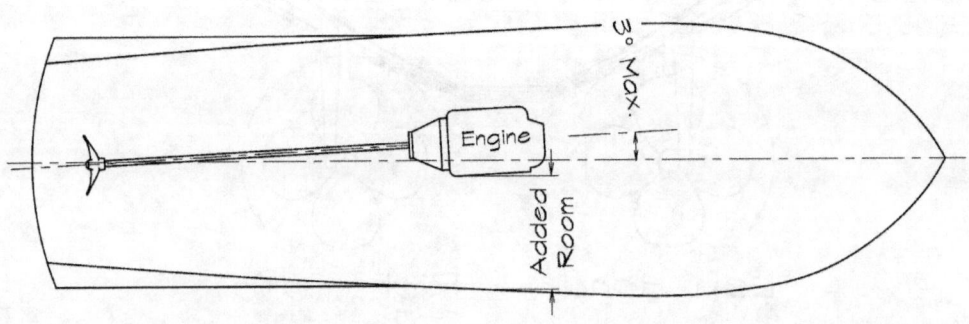

Chapter 2: Struts, Propeller Apertures, and Shaft Angle

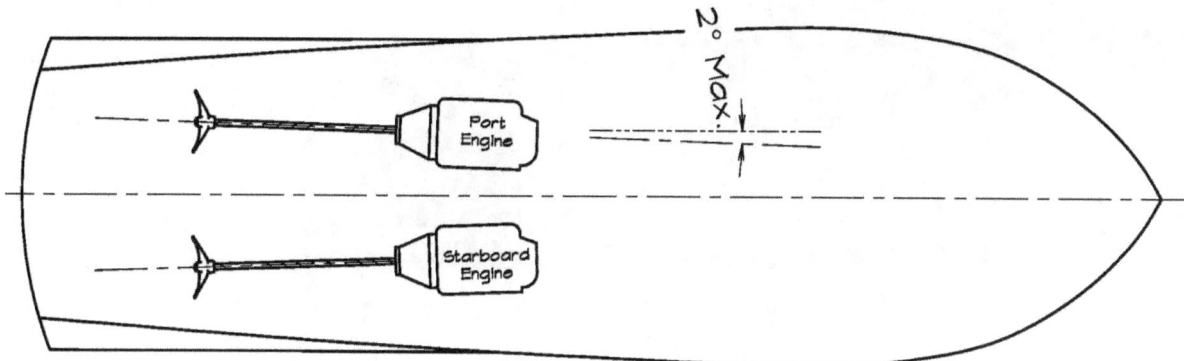

Twin-Screw Angled-Out Shafts
Gets Engines Lower In V-Bottom Hulls

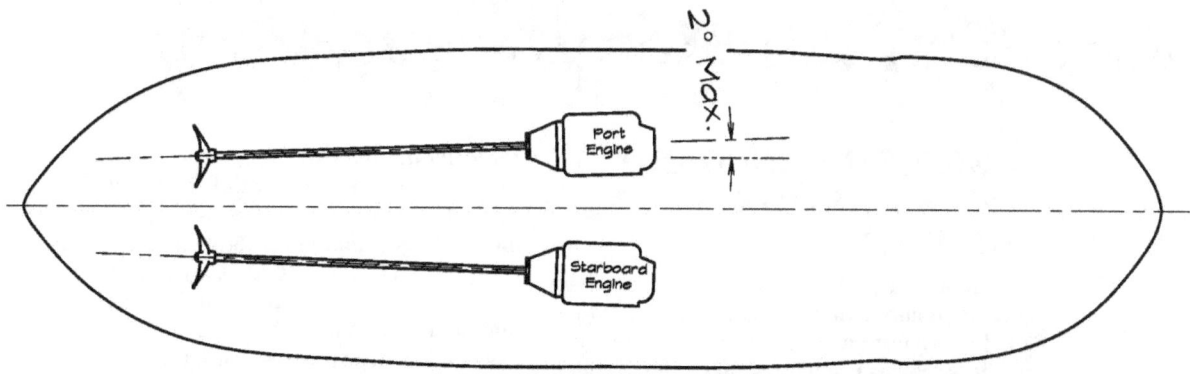

Twin-Screw Angled-In Shafts
More Width Between Engines
Props Closer Together For
Narrow Stern

Figure 2-14. Different shaft placements compared on twin-engine boats

This can be helpful on double-enders because the stern is pinched and the propellers and rudders may not fit properly too far apart. At the same time—particularly in deep-bodied, heavy double-enders—the engines can be farther apart near midships, which allows better access to the machinery space.

Keep in mind the possibility of shafts that are angled or offset in plan view. You may run across them in practice, or they may help solve some particularly difficult installation problem. In most instances, however, shafts parallel to the centerline are preferred.

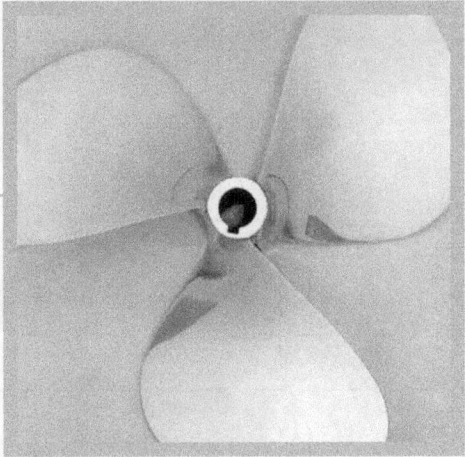

CHAPTER 3

Transmission Geometry, CV Joints, Stuffing Boxes, and Engine Mounts and Beds

SELECTING INBOARD TRANSMISSION GEOMETRY

Selecting the proper reduction ratio for a particular combination of boat, engine, and propeller is a critical part of propeller selection. This is really a propeller-sizing issue. Besides selecting the reduction ratio, however, you must also select a gear or transmission with the proper geometry to install the engine where you need it for arrangement-plan and weight-and-trim considerations, as well as to make the drivetrain fit properly in the boat.

There are several standard gear geometries (Figure 3-1):

In-line coaxial
The output shaft is in-line with and on the same axis as the engine driveshaft. This is usually the smallest and most compact gear configuration and is usually suited to shoal hulls with the engine near the hull bottom.

Parallel drop-shaft, shallow case
The output shaft is parallel to the engine driveshaft, but is offset down by a few inches. This is a common configuration that can help you raise an engine a bit to clear the bilge better. The shallow case means the drop isn't too great.

Parallel drop-shaft, deep case
The output shaft is parallel to the engine driveshaft, but is offset down by several inches. This common configuration can help you raise an engine significantly to clear the bilge better. You must have sufficient clearance over the engine to do this. The deep case means the drop is substantial. This is a common configuration for reduction gears over 3:1 in larger displacement vessels.

Down-angle gear
The output shaft angles down relative to the engine driveshaft. Angles are usually between 10 and 15 degrees. Down-angle gears permit installing a more level engine on a steep shaft. In doing this, they also lower the forward top corner of the engine, permitting a lower engine-compartment overhead or fitting a higher engine in a lower engine compartment.

Direct-mount V drive (also called UV drive or U drive)
The gear mounts directly on the engine bell housing as usual, with the output shaft reversed and angled down and under the engine in a V. Angles are usually available between 10 and 15 degrees. This permits keeping the engine well aft and facing backward. Direct-mount V drives are great

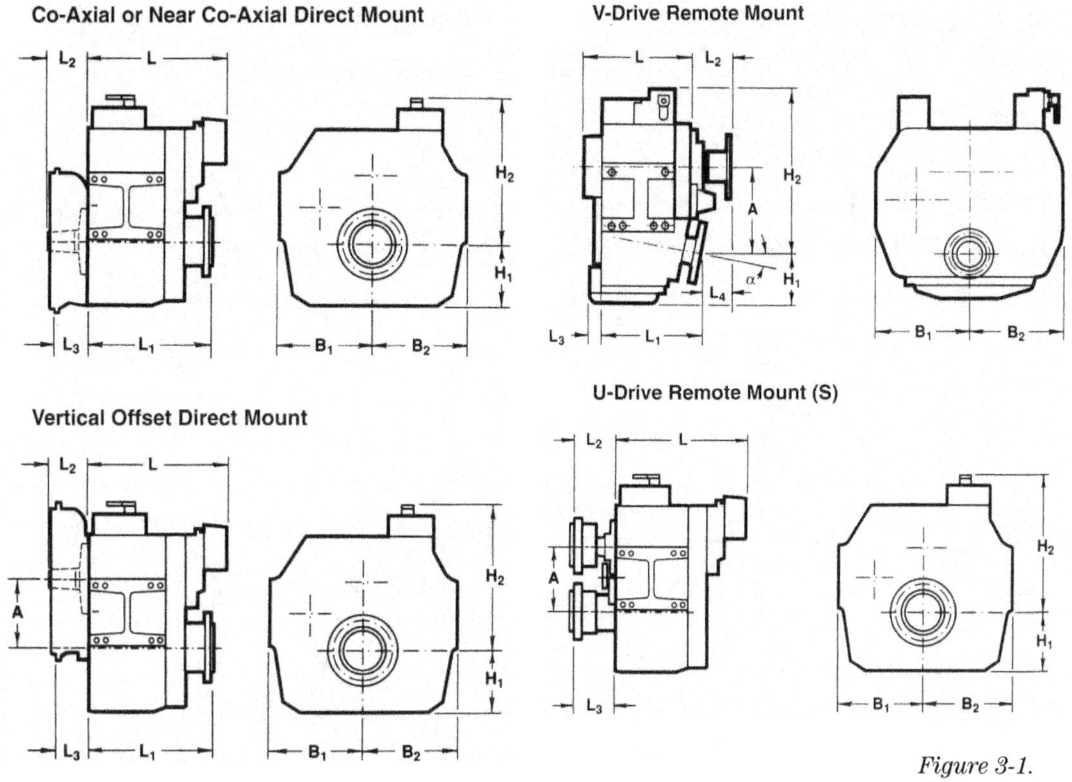

Figure 3-1. Transmissions compared (Courtesy ZF Marine)

space savers in some boats and can make it possible to fit more accommodations in the boat. The drawback to all V drives is that the additional gearing creates somewhat more power loss, and access to the stuffing box under the engine and behind the UV drive can be difficult and must be carefully considered during design.

Remote-mount V drive
The engine is installed facing backward and (usually) angled slightly down at the forward end. A jackshaft connects to the engine driveshaft and runs into the aft end of the V drive mounted some distance forward in the boat. The jackshaft is usually fitted with CV or universal joints at either end. (Figure 16-3 shows a remote-mount V drive.) Like the UV drive, the V drive changes output direction to reverse and runs aft and down at an angle. Angles are usually between 10 and 15 degrees. Remote V drives allow great flexibility in locating the engine. They do lose more power to gear friction than other drives. The remote V drive has its own independent lubrication system.

Unusual gears
There are gears with the output shaft offset to the side rather than down, and gears with outputs angled down and offset to the side. There are specialized gears that allow two side-by-side engines to drive one shaft, and gears that allow two engines (one in front of the gear and one aft) to drive the same shaft. Such gears are usually installed on craft with gas turbine engines. Gas turbines burn so much fuel that their vessels often fit diesels on one side of the gear and the gas turbine on the other. The diesel is termed the "loiter" engine, used for low to moderate speeds. The gas turbine is used for high-speed pursuit operation. All these unusual gears are intended for special design problems that don't apply to the vast majority of ordinary craft.

Regardless of the gear geometry you need, you must check with the manufacturer to confirm that the gear will mate with the bell housing on the engine (except for remote V drive); that the gear is rated for the engine's maximum torque, horsepower, and rpm; and that the gear will fit in the hull. It's

PART ONE: DRIVETRAIN INSTALLATIONS

Co-Axial or Vertical Offset Remote Mount

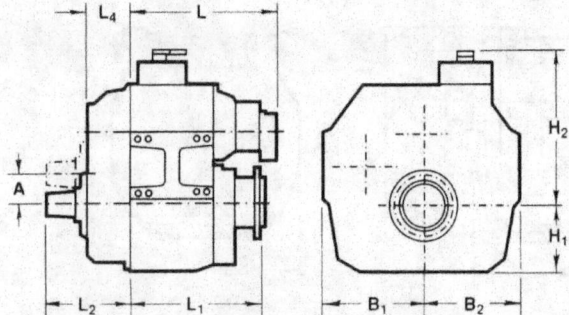

Diagonal Offset Remote Mount

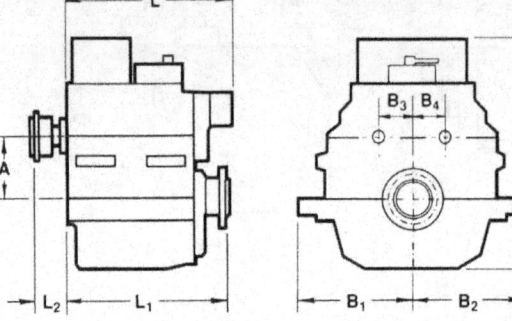

Horizontal Offset

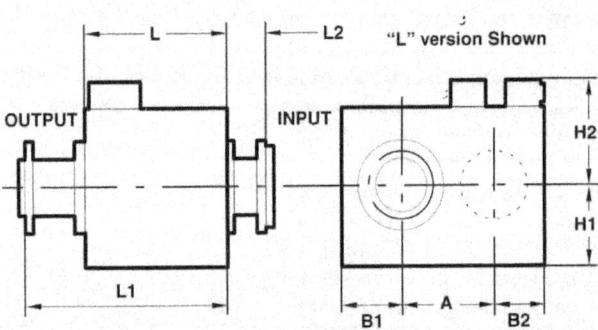

Vertical Offset

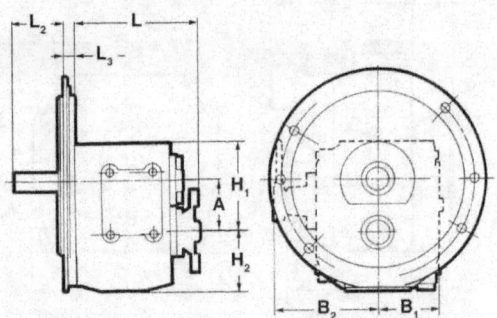

Down Angle

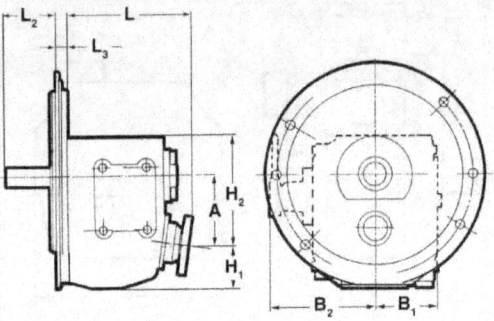

Hollow Shaft Integral V-Drive

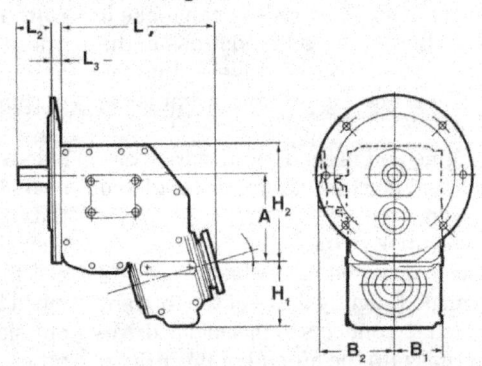

Figure 3-1. (Continued)

surprising how often I've learned of boats that had humplike protrusions molded into their bottoms as an afterthought to fit the proper gear. This is always bad and always wrong, and there's really no excuse for it if the design is done properly to begin with. I can usually find the gear configuration I want. Sometimes, however, even an exhaustive search shows that what I'm looking for just isn't available at the rpm, power, and torque ratings needed. If this happens, you have no choice but to go back to the drawing board. The most common instance of this occurs when you are looking for any form of gear with reduction ratios deeper than 3:1 on engines under 300 hp (224 kW). Such gears don't seem to be made. This is a shame—particularly on displacement-speed vessels—as larger reduction gears would allow larger and more efficient propellers. The resulting improvement in fuel economy (as well as low-speed oomph) would be highly beneficial.

Constant Velocity and Universal Joints

So far we've been talking about standard straight-shaft inboard installations. Being simple and rugged, they have much to recommend them. But when there is room enough and budget enough, I like to install double constant-velocity (CV) joints with an independent thrust bearing. Usually, I go with an off-the-shelf package like Aquadrive (Figure 3-2) or PYI's Python-Drive. Spicer and CON-VEL are two other sources for CV joints. Figure 3-3 shows the workings of a CON-VEL CV joint.

Using double CV joints has several pluses. They allow more flexibility (no pun intended) in engine location. They also accept what for straight-shaft systems would be unimaginable misalignment, so shaft-alignment problems are virtually unheard of.

In addition, because systems like Aquadrive allow so much flex, the engine can be "floated" on extremely soft mounts that further isolate engine vibration from the hull.

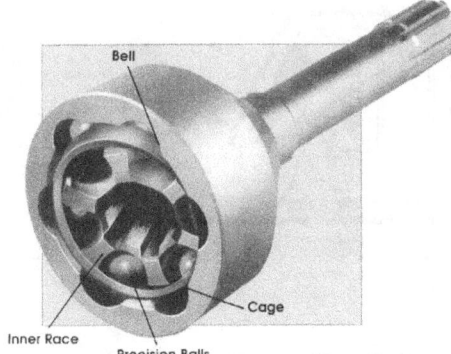

Figure 3-3. CON-VEL CV joint (Courtesy CON-VEL Inc.)

The Independent Thrust Bearing

It's important to remember that the independent thrust bearing in this system plays a big role in permitting such soft mounts. In standard straight-shaft installations, the thrust from the propeller is transmitted along the shaft and taken by a thrust bearing in the marine gear. (By the way, this is why you can't just use a car transmission in a boat; auto transmissions have

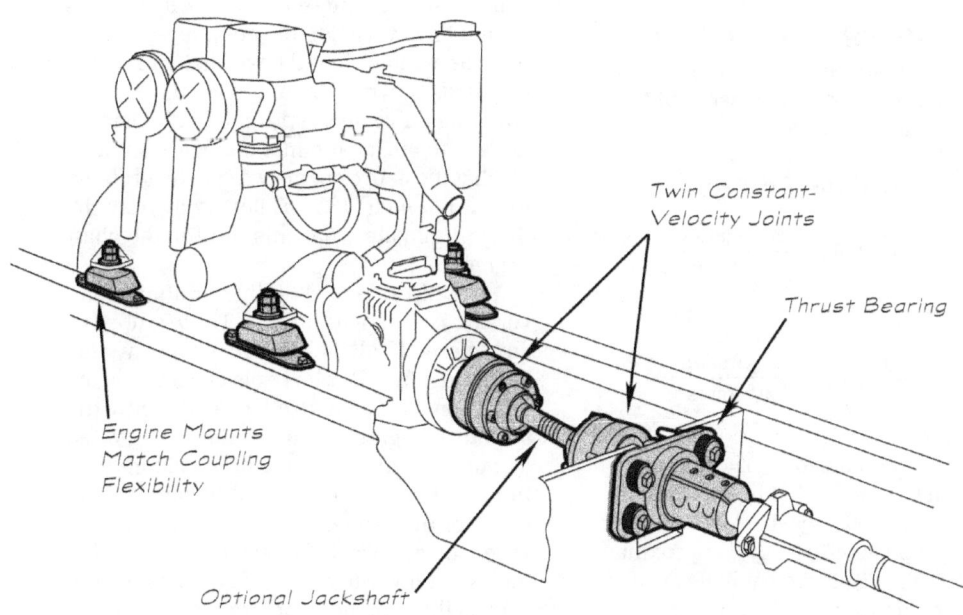

Figure 3-2. Aquadrive system (Courtesy Aquadrive)

PART ONE: DRIVETRAIN INSTALLATIONS

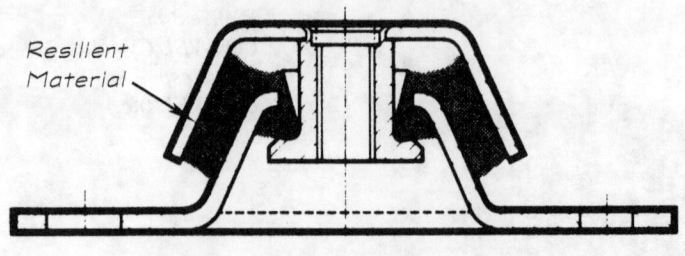

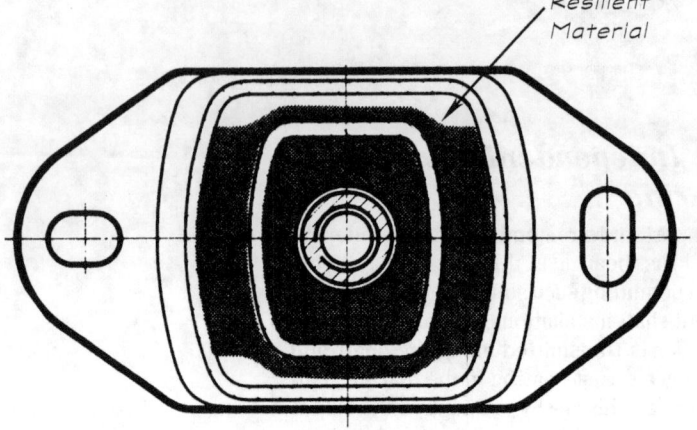

Figure 3-4. Flexible engine mount

no thrust bearings.) The thrust pushes the entire engine forward, and that drives the boat ahead through the engine mounts.

Calculating Thrust Loads

The thrust loads are large indeed. You can calculate the thrust load reasonably closely from the following formula.

Formula 3-1.

Formula 3-1. Thrust Loads

$$\text{Thrust, lb.} = \frac{326 \times \text{shp} \times e}{0.9 \times \text{knots}}$$

or

$$\text{Thrust, kg} = \frac{198.3 \times \text{kWshaft} \times e}{0.9 \times \text{knots}}$$

Where
shp = shaft horsepower = $0.96 \times$ bhp
kWshaft = power in kilowatts at the shaft = $0.96 \times$ flywheel kW
e = propeller efficiency—approximately 0.55 for displacement hulls and 0.70 for planing hulls

NOTE: The 0.9 is for an assumed wake factor to get Va (prop speed through the water in knots). Va will be less than boat speed because the boat drags a wake along with it as it travels. Making a 10% deduction for this provides a good-enough approximation.

Example: A 32-foot (9.7 m) express cruiser going 28 knots on twin 300 hp (224 kW) diesels will be subject to a thrust of 2,608 pounds (1,184 kg) along each shaft—well over a ton.

$$\text{Thrust} = \frac{326 \times 0.96 \times 300 \text{ hp} \times 0.70}{0.9 \times 28 \text{ knots}} = 2,608 \text{ lb.}$$

or

$$\text{Thrust} = \frac{198.3 \times 0.96 \times 224 \text{ kW} \times 0.70}{0.9 \times 28 \text{ knots}}$$

$$= 1,184 \text{ kg}$$

Engine Mounts, Thrust, and Couplings

It is absolutely vital that the engine mounts are able to transmit thrust load if you aren't using a system with a separate thrust bearing. It's thus equally vital that the shaft coupling match the engine mounts. Soft mounts should have very flexible couplings, slightly flexible mounts should have slightly flexible couplings, and rigid mounts should have rigid couplings. I've seen straight-shaft installations with engine mounts that were so flexible that the entire engine was pushed/rotated forward $1/2$ inch (13 mm) underway from the thrust. Imagine what this did for the shaft alignment!

The flip side of CV joints or double universals is the rigid mount. There's no give anywhere. If all is aligned properly, this works just fine. But it is noisier, as all engine vibration is transmitted directly into the structure. Figure 3-5 shows the engine of an aluminum ferry that had a fully rigid installation. The boat ran reasonably smoothly in terms of the propeller noise and was otherwise efficient. Welded metal hulls being what they are, however, every iota of engine noise carried through the structure.

Figure 3-5. Engine installed on rigid mounts

Universal Joints

Neither the standard old-fashioned universal joints (also called Cardan or Hooke's joints, Figure 3-6) nor modern CV joints can take thrust well, at least not much. Hence the separate thrust bearing. Before CV joints were available, some small fishing boats, like dories, actually used a single universal joint to make retractable propeller installations (Figure 3-7). You can get away with this on an old 10 or 20 hp (7 to 15 kW), one-lung, make-and-break engine, but not on anything much bigger.

Figures 3-7 and 3-8 show the old retracting propeller arrangement used for years by fishermen in Nova Scotia to allow them to beach their boats. Note that under load the universal joint is straight. It works well enough like this in small boats with limited torque and thrust, but I wouldn't try this on 300 hp (220 kW).

Double universal joints, by the way, must be installed with equal angles as shown in Figure 3-9 when used in pairs—as they should be. If the angles are mismatched you can actually rip the universals apart from torsional differences. CV joints don't have to follow this rule, but I like to lay them out this way if I can, just to be on the safe side.

To ensure that the balls in the bearing all rotate fully—for proper lubrication—Aquadrive

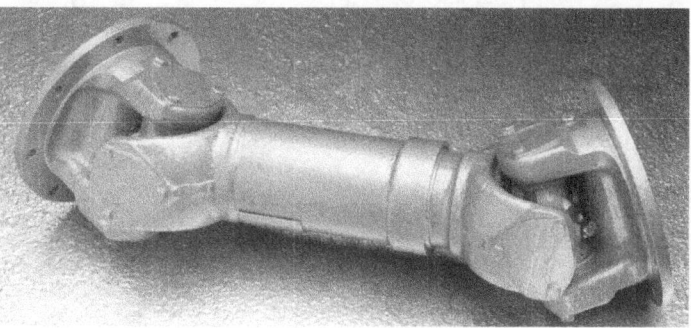

Figure 3-6. Jackshaft with universal joints. The proper term for this shaft is a "Cardan shaft," and the joints are "Hooke's joints," but many references use universal joint, Hooke's joint, and Cardan joint interchangeably to refer to a single one of these joints. (Courtesy Halyard Ltd.)

PART ONE: DRIVETRAIN INSTALLATIONS

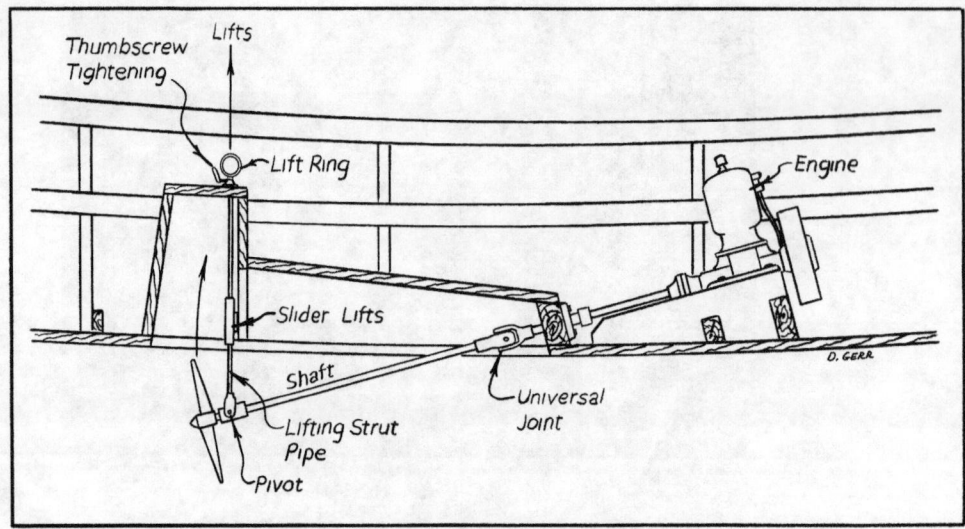

Figure 3-7.
Retracting dory propeller

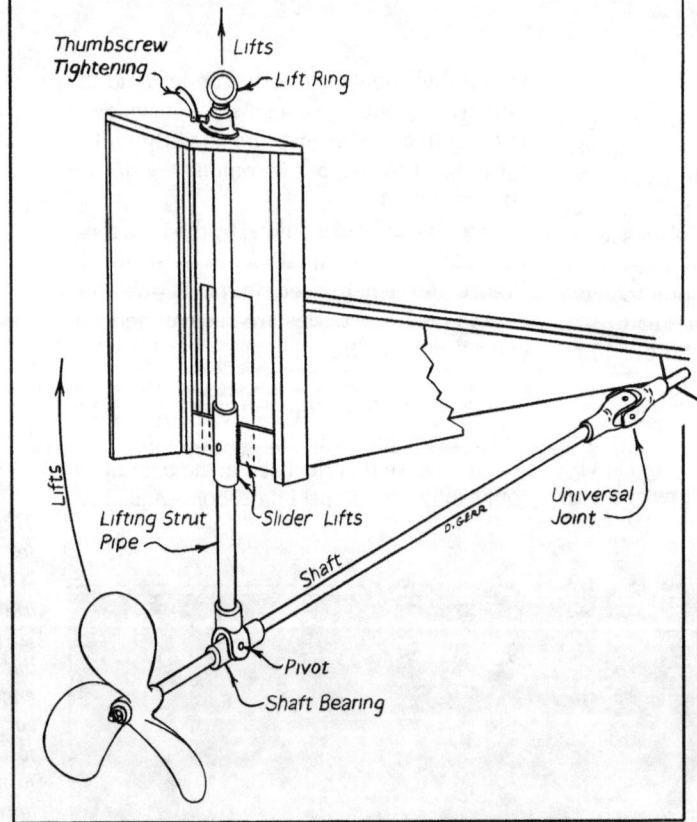

Figure 3-8.
Cutaway view of retracting dory propeller box

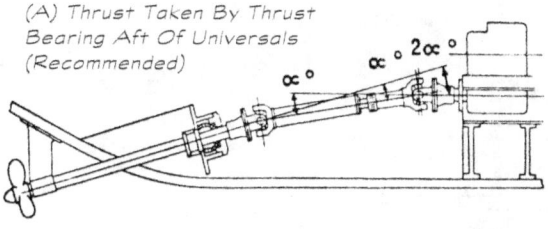

(A) Thrust Taken By Thrust Bearing Aft Of Universals (Recommended)

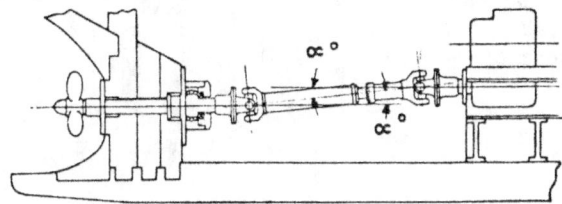

(D) Thrust Taken By Thrust Bearing Aft Of Universals (Recommended)

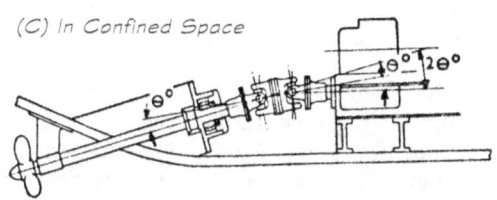

(B) Thrust Taken By Thrust Bearing In Gearbox, Forward Of Universals (Not Recommended)

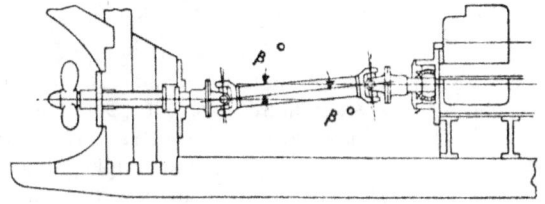

(E) Thrust Taken By Thrust Bearing In Gearbox, Forward Of Universals (Not Recommended)

(C) In Confined Space

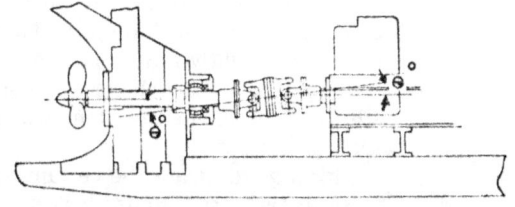

(F) In Confined Space

- Angles Indicated Must Be Equal
- With Independent Thrust Bearing, Shafts Or Close Couplings Should Be Splined/Telescoping To Allow Changes In Length

Figure 3-9. Universal joint shaft configurations

CVs (and most CV joints) should have a minimum 1/2-degree angle at each joint. Further, there are maximum installation angles for CV joints (and U-joints too). Be sure to follow the manufacturer's recommendations.

Whether using universal joints or modern CV joints, the shaft or the close coupling should be splined, enabling it to telescope, thus absorbing axial changes in length. This truly allows the engine to float, and it absorbs the changes in shaft length that universals, especially, can introduce at high angles. Instead of using a telescoping shaft, Aquadrive CVs have axial movement built into the CV joints themselves. The axial play ranges from approximately 1/4 inch (6 mm) on the small Aquadrive joints, to well over 1 inch (25 mm) on the larger models.

A practical example of the advantages of a modern CV joint occurred on a 60-foot (18.2 m) aluminum motor cruiser I designed. The builder did a fine job in general, but had installed the engine compartment overhead and insulation 4 inches (100 mm) lower than we had drawn. As a result the forward upper end of the engine was poking up through the overhead. It would have been costly to rework the overhead, so we cut down the aluminum engine mounts instead and installed the engine at a flatter angle. This could never have been done with a straight-shaft system, but we had already specced Aquadrive. Indeed, this couldn't even have been done with standard universal or Cardan joints as the carefully worked-out equal angles would have been ruined. With the modern double

Figure 3-10. Drivesaver-type coupling (Courtesy Globe Composite Solutions, Ltd.)

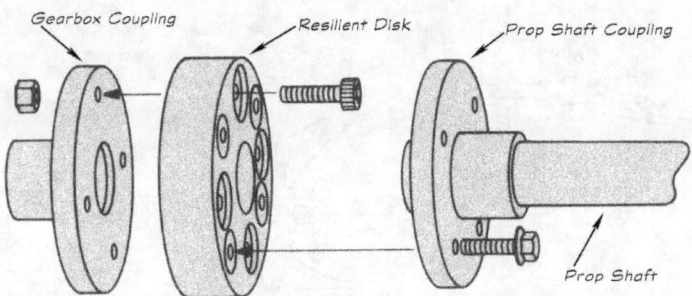

CV joints, there was no problem with this at all.

Drivesaver Disks

When there isn't room or budget for Aquadrive, I still prefer to build some flex into the drive system. In this case, I'll specify the Babbit or Globe Drivesaver disk. PYI also makes a rather different flexible shaft coupling that achieves similar results. Again, the engine mounts and the coupling should match. When installing a Drivesaver disk, I try to spec matching engine mounts from the same manufacturer.

These Drivesavers add just a small amount of flex, which helps isolate engine noise and slightly reduces potential alignment problems—though the entire drivetrain still must be aligned to standard straight-shaft tolerances.

It's a good idea to be certain to install these on shaft installations where the distance from the coupling to the stern bearing is less than 20 times the shaft diameter. Such a short distance can result in too much rigidity, which the Drivesaver disk reduces nicely.

Stuffing Boxes

It used to be that stuffing boxes were pretty much all the same: screw-down packing nuts around the shaft that compressed flax packing against the shaft (Figure 3-12). Of course, the flax had to be kept wet (lubricated) to keep it from burning up when the shaft spun. This meant backing off the compression nut just enough to allow a drip or two of water to flow every few hours at anchor and every 15 minutes or so underway.

These days, many of my clients are installing slip-ring-type stuffing boxes, with an elastic bellows that presses the slip-ring seals together. PSS Shaft Seal and Duramax are two brands that work fine. However, a problem occurs in conjunction with the Aquadrive. During maneuvering—when you go into reverse—the Aquadrive thrust bearing allows the shaft to pull aft roughly $3/8$ to $1/2$ inch (9 to 13 mm); then when you shift into "ahead," the shaft pushes forward again. In that instant, the pressure comes off the shaft seal and a perfect circular fan of water sprays

Figure 3-11. Cutaway view of a rigid stuffing box (Reprinted with permission from Boatowner's Mechanical and Electrical Manual, by Nigel Calder, 2005)

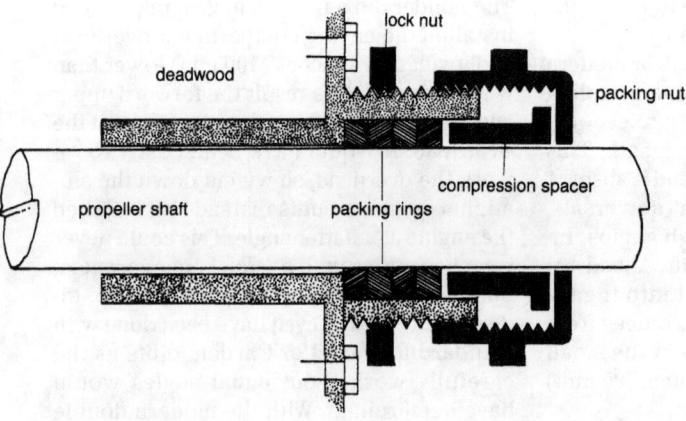

Chapter 3: Transmission Geometry, CV Joints, Stuffing Boxes, and Engine Mounts and Beds

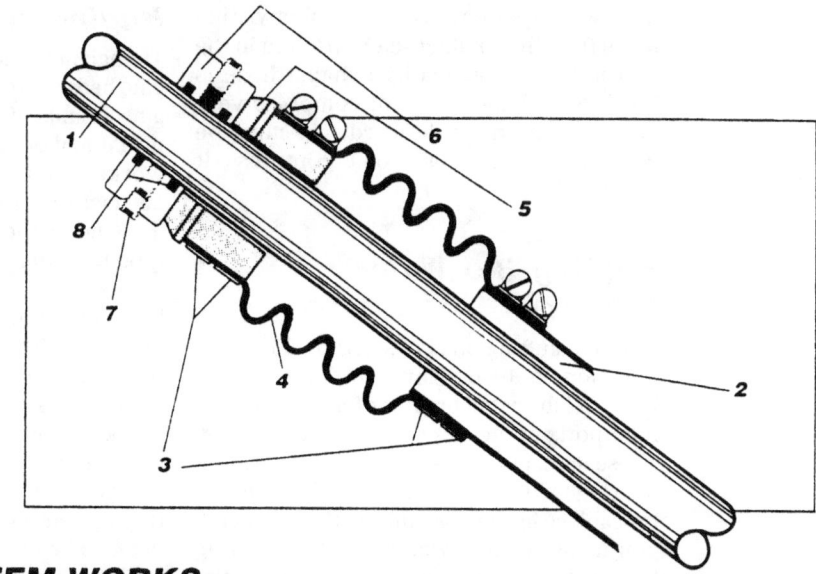

1. Prop Shaft
2. Shaft Log
3. Stainless Steel Hose Clamps
4. Reinforced Rubber Bellow
5. Carbon Flange
6. #316 Stainless Steel Rotor
7. Stainless Steel Set Screws
8. O-Rings

HOW THE PSS SYSTEM WORKS:

The reinforced rubber bellow (**4**) is secured at one end to the shaft log (**2**) and at the other to a high density carbon flange (**5**). The bellows, (slighty compressed at the time of installation) and the water pressure, force the carbon flange against a polished stainless steel rotor (**6**) which is mounted on the shaft and secured in place by a pair of double set screws (**7**). Two O-Rings (**8**) are used to prevent water from leaking between the shaft and the stainless steel rotor. When the shaft rotates, the stainless steel rotor turns against the carbon flange, the high polished carbon reduces friction to a minimum and elimates any possibility of leakage.

Figure 3-12. PSS shaft seal (Courtesy PYI, Inc.)

into the bilge. I'm not particularly crazy about this. This is neither a defect with Aquadrive nor a defect with the slip-ring shaft seals; it's simply the way these two mechanisms happen to function together.

In fact, I don't see much wrong with old-fashioned stuffing boxes, except for the hassle of replacing the flax periodically. My personal preference is a standard stuffing box with the new Teflon-impregnated packing material. This packing is virtually dripless and lasts many times longer than old flax.

Flexible Self-Aligning Stuffing Boxes

I also prefer to use the flexible (self-aligning) hose-type stuffing boxes (Figure 3-13). These

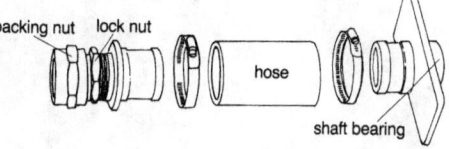

don't become a shaft bearing that has to be aligned. Of course, there may be circumstances where you want to have a bearing—an intermediate shaft bearing—at the stuffing box location, as we saw in Chapter 1. In this case, you would use a rigidly mounted stuffing box.

The hose on flexible or self-aligning stuffing boxes must be tough stuff. Use only heavy-wall, 5-ply minimum hose. Not only can you not afford any leaks here, but the

Figure 3-13. Flexible stuffing box (Reprinted with permission from Boatowner's Mechanical and Electrical Manual, Third Edition, by Nigel Calder, 2005)

hose will experience considerable twisting loads from the rotating shaft's friction in the stuffing box. Top-quality exhaust hose is ideal. Such hose does not compress very much, so the fit to the hardware must be close or the clamps won't compress it adequately.

Stuffing-Box Water Injection

Another stuffing-box consideration is water injection. In the old days, the Cutless bearing was lubricated by water forced into side inlet ports in the external bearing housing. These days, more often than not, the Cutless bearing is installed so that lubrication water can't be ingested by this method. Instead, you must install a water-injected stuffing box to get continuous water flow onto the rubber bearing. Water is taken off the main engine raw-water cooling circuit and injected into a port on the stuffing box; usually this port is $3/8$-inch (10 mm) diameter.

Note that water injection is below the waterline. A failure in the hose or piping is the same as a leak in the hull. You must use rugged, top-quality materials. A1 fuel hose is ideal. If more flexibility is needed, you can use B2 fuel hose.

Engine Beds

Though not strictly part of the drivetrain, engine beds are every bit as important as the engine mounts. If the beds are weak or flexible, no amount of careful alignment will help. I've worked on fixing several boats that had inadequate engine beds.

One of these boats was a twin 350 hp (260 kW) MerCruiser, gas-inboard craft. Its owner found a crack in the transmission housing at the starboard engine's starboard aft mount. The crack went right through to the transmission's interior and leaked fluid. He had the thing replaced. The new one cracked again. So he had it welded shut (not good practice, but he wanted to go cruising). It cracked again. Next season, he replaced the transmission once more. It cracked again. Then he called me in. It had always been the starboard engine that leaked, but I took a look at the port engine and found a crack beginning in the same place. The arrow in the first panel of Figure 3-14 points to the crack.

What I then found was that the apparently high, massive engine beds were in fact hollow, with a wall thickness of less than $7/16$ inch (11 mm). The engine mounts were bolted to small aluminum angles that were simply through-bolted to only the inboard

Figure 3-14. Cracked transmission and hollow engine bed

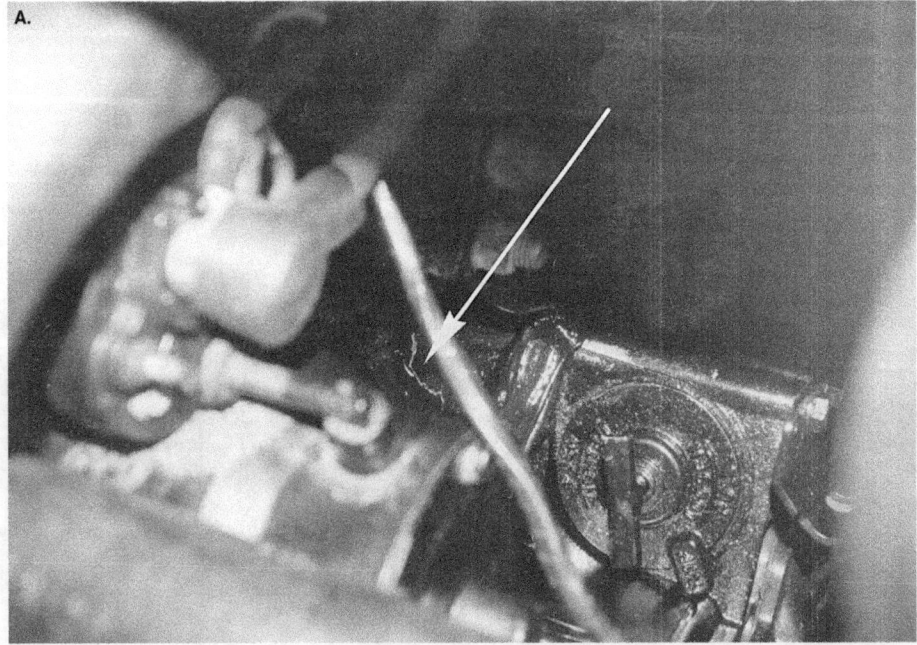

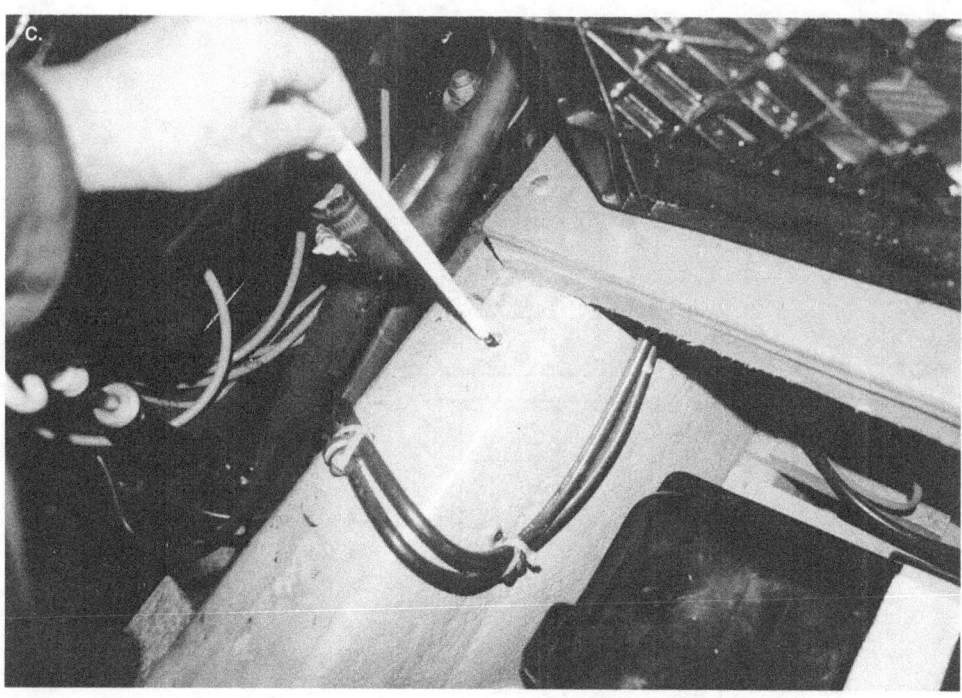

Figure 3-14. (Continued)

PART ONE: DRIVETRAIN INSTALLATIONS

Figure 3-14.
(Continued)

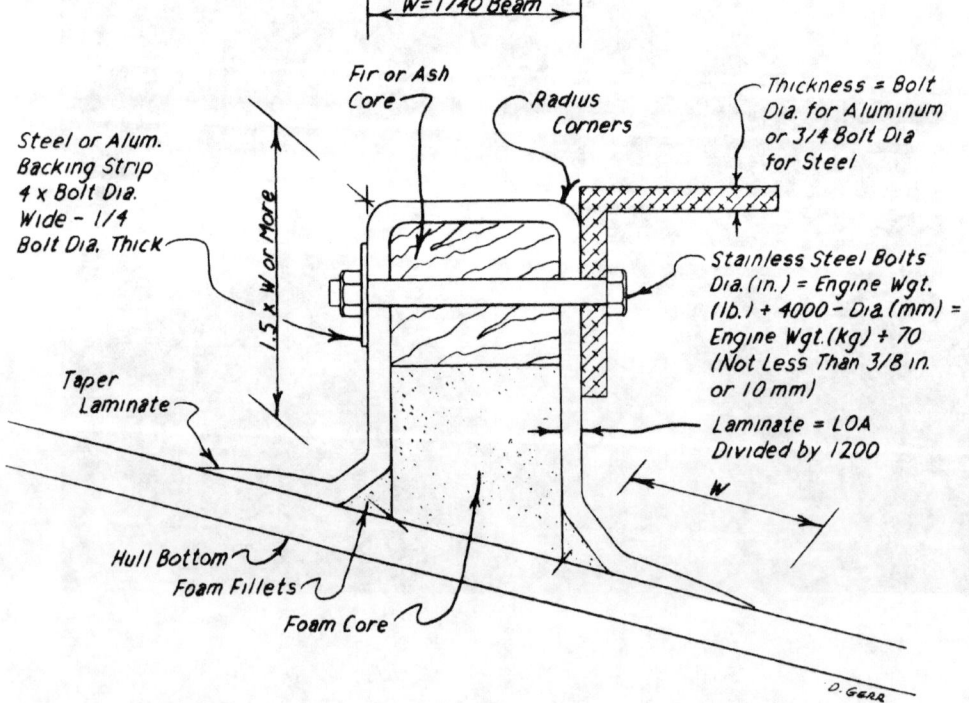

Figure 3-15.
Engine stringers

wall of the beds, with ordinary washers inside. Merely standing on the engine caused the side walls of these hollow beds to flex visibly. If the builder had only built in solid wood blocks in the engine bed and through-bolted the engine through both walls with a backing block on the other side, and used longer engine-mount-attachment angles, the installation would probably have been acceptably rigid.

Engine Bed Construction

Figure 3-15 shows simplified recommended dimensions for engine beds in fiberglass boats. You can get more detail about this, along with bed scantlings and construction as well as construction for other materials from my book *The Elements of Boat Strength*. If you're trying to track down a seemingly intractable vibration or alignment problem, don't forget the foundation itself: the engine beds.

Part Two

FUEL SYSTEMS

CHAPTER 4

Fuel Piping and Fuel System Bonding

Considering the potential dangers, it's odd that there are so few specific legal requirements governing boat fuel systems. This is serious business, and I'll start off with a bang. Figure 4-1 shows a 45-foot (13.7 m) express cruiser that burned and sank in minutes as a result of a fuel fire. This, by the way, was a diesel boat. Some folks act as if diesel were fireproof; it is anything but. In fact, diesel fuel contains more energy per unit volume or per unit weight than gasoline. Gasoline is much easier to ignite and can explode in the right (or wrong) conditions; however, once diesel starts burning, it's truly terrifying. Diesel or gas, we'll take a detailed look at the requirements for safe, reliable, and efficient fuel systems.

The only U.S. laws applying to yacht fuel systems are those dealing with gas-engine vessels under the Code of Federal Regulations (CFR). I'll call this the "CFR Yacht" from now on. To find U.S. legal requirements for diesel fuel systems, you have to look at passenger-vessel regulations under the CFR for T-, K-, and H-boats. T-boats (vessels under 100 gross tons and carrying fewer than 150 passengers) are the closest to recreational vessels, so I use the T-boat regulations as a guide for recreational fuel systems. This I'll refer to as "CFR Commercial." Though mandatory for passenger vessels, these rules are completely optional for pleasure craft.

The fundamental rulebook is the American Boat & Yacht Council (ABYC) standards on fuel systems: H-24 (for gasoline) and H-33 (for diesel). Though ABYC's standards are guidelines only, if you're building or repairing boats and don't comply fully with CFR Yacht and as completely as practical with ABYC H-24 or H-33, you're leaving yourself open to serious problems, including potential legal action.

Other standards for boat fuel systems are

The National Fire Protection Agency (NFPA), NFPA 302, *Fire Protection Standard for Pleasure and Commercial Motor Craft*

Equivalent to the ABYC standards for European Union countries are the ISO standards for fuel systems:

Figure 4-1. A fuel fire caused this boat to sink in minutes

ISO 10088, *Permanently Installed Fuel Systems and Fixed Fuel Tanks*
H-24, *Gasoline Fuel Systems*
DIS 21487, *Permanently Installed Petrol and Diesel Fuel Tanks*
H-33, *Diesel Fuel Systems*

ISO standards are available from several sources, including the American National Standards Institute (ANSI), www.ansi.org.

Using ABYC and the CFR as a starting point, we'll go through good practices in sound fuel systems, including details such as return oil coolers and piping manifolds, which aren't specifically covered in the CFR requirements or ABYC recommendations.

RUNNING PIPE

The piping schematics in this chapter show simple and reliable arrangements for twin-engine inboard vessels with twin tanks—diesel or gas. If the boat has no generator, just omit the generator piping. If the boat has two gen sets, draw in another branch for that. If the boat is single-engine, eliminate the valves and piping for the second "side." Small runabouts and day boats can be fitted with one fuel tank. Larger craft preferably should be equipped with at least two. It costs a bit more to do this, and some less expensive cruisers have only one tank, but it's not good practice. Why? With diesel, if the lone tank springs a leak or becomes contaminated, you're done—no more fuel. With twin tanks, you can almost always manage to motor home. Even with gas, you have a second chance should one tank become contaminated with dirt or water (though if even one tank springs a leak you will have to shut down both gas engines to avoid risk of explosion).

Accessibility of Fittings

Keep in mind when arranging fuel piping that you have to be able to get at important components. Under ABYC and CFR for gasoline, it's a primary requirement that all fittings, joints, connections, and valves be fully accessible for inspection, maintenance, removal, or repair without the removal of any permanent part of the boat structure. (ISO 10088 asks that all of the fuel pipe and hose be accessible as well.)

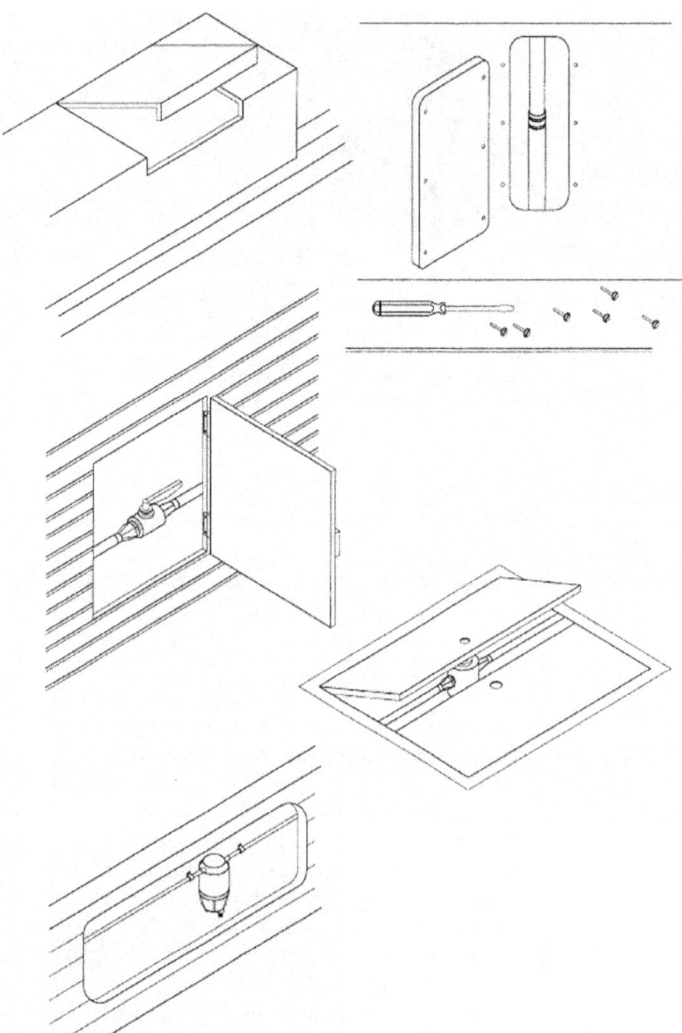

Where a fitting, joint, or piece of hardware is concealed behind a panel, liner, or similar structure, an access panel or deck plate must be installed to permit access.

If you're doing a survey, be sure to inspect all systems with this accessibility requirement in mind and to note any problem with access clearly in a report. If it's your own boat, be sure to correct the problem.

Figure 4-2. Required fuel system access panels (Courtesy ABYC)

Double Your Filters, Double Your Fun

The only slightly unusual feature of these fuel-piping schematics in this chapter is the

PART TWO: FUEL SYSTEMS

Figure 4-3. Separ duplex fuel filter

duplex fuel filters (see, for example, Fig. 4-3). Fuel tanks and fuel supplies are seldom as clean as they ought to be. A bad batch of fuel or some sludge getting into the fuel lines can clog a filter and stop an engine quickly. Invariably, this happens when a menacing squall is bearing down or during close-quarters maneuvering in harbor. The duplex system shown in Figure 4-3 permits switching to the second filter; removing, cleaning, and replacing the clogged filter; and continuing on without even slowing down. (On a gas-engine craft you wouldn't want to change the filter with the engine running, but you can still switch over and then clean or change the filter later.) You can make such a system using over-the-counter filters, valves, and piping components, or—much better—you can purchase a ready-made duplex system from companies like Racor and Separ. With a single-engine vessel, the duplex filters and fuel lines need only be large enough to handle the one engine.

Of course, duplex filters are optional. Most boats get along well enough with single filters. You can simply substitute a single filter for a duplex in the schematic if that's your preference. Considering the relatively small expense compared with the cost of an entire boat, however, I think it's penny-wise and pound-foolish not to install duplex filters on all but the smallest of day boats and runabouts.

Fuel-Filter Mounting and Location

Each fuel filter or fuel strainer must be mounted securely on the engine or the boat structure, independent from the fuel-line connection unless the fuel filter or strainer is inside a fuel tank. You must be able to access the filter easily and regularly to inspect the filter bowl and to drain when needed. This means having a clear space of at least 8 inches (20 cm) under the filter so you can put a cup or can under the filter drain valve to collect the discharge. You also need clearance above the filter to remove the top and pull the filter out vertically. This is usually at least 85 percent of the filter height above the top of the filter, but check the filter-element dimensions and the manufacturer's drawings for the filter. Then during installation, do a dry run. Remove the filter top, and draw out the element to make sure there's adequate clearance.

Sizing the Filters

You must be certain that each filter (whether operating solo or in a duplex) and all associated fuel lines are sized to handle maximum possible flow. For diesel, total fuel flow rate through the filter in gallons per minute (gpm) can be generously estimated as gpm = max. engine hp ÷ 360, or L/min. = max. engine kW ÷ 70.9. Note that this flow rate is considerably higher than actual engine fuel consumption; it includes the extra flow for injector cooling and lubrication—the extra taken off by the return line. The rule of thumb is that one-third of the fuel delivered will be burned and the remaining two-thirds is returned to the tank. (We can expect this ratio to increase to 20 percent: 80 percent in some new, very-high-power engines currently in development.) A vessel with twin 350 hp (261 kW) diesels would require a minimum of two 1.0 gpm (3.68 L/min.) filters (350 hp ÷ 360 = 0.97, say, 1.0 gpm; or 261 kW ÷ 70.9 = 3.68 L/min. Multiplying by 60 minutes—60 gph or 227 L/hr.). Greater capacity would do no harm. In the twin-duplex filter arrangement shown in this chapter's schematics, there would actually be four water filters/separators, a total of two for each engine.

Gasoline fuel flow is simply engine fuel consumption. The rule of thumb for flow is gpm = max. engine hp ÷ 600, or L/min. = max. engine kW ÷ 118. So a 140 hp (104 kW) gas engine would require a 0.23 gpm (0.88 L/min.) filter (14 gph or 55 L/hr.). These fuel-demand flow estimates are usually generous, but the engine manual is the final authority; don't fail to consult it. (Note that some fuel-injected gas engines have a return line just as diesel systems do. These engines will have higher fuel flow rates and will require diesel-like return piping.)

NOTE: All gallons are U.S. gallons. To convert U.S. gallons to imperial/UK gallons, divide U.S. gallons by 1.2. *Gasoline* in the United States is usually termed *petrol* in the United Kingdom.

To See Through or Not to See Through

Fuel filters, of course, are really fuel filters and water separators combined. To see the water level that has accumulated—as well as any sludge or sediment—fuel filters are available with clear glass or plastic bowls. On diesel installations, these see-through bowls are Coast Guard–approved only if they have a metal flame shield around the bottom of the bowl. (The shield enables the filter to pass the required 2½-minute burn test.) Gasoline inboards, however, cannot have any form of clear bowl; only solid metal bowls will pass muster. (See-through bowls are OK for outboard gas engines, presumably because any breakage would leak overboard.) Some classification society rules do not allow clear bowls on either gas or diesel installations. Such metal-bowl filters must be fitted with a water-probe indicator/alarm and with a vacuum gauge.

Filter Height and Location

It's poor practice for a filter to be at the highest point in the fuel system or even above the engine. If the filter is located high, air bubbles tend to collect in it or fuel can drain out, leaving an air bubble. Either way, this results in frequent and annoying bleeding of the system. If a filter must be located very high, then at least be sure to install a solenoid shutoff valve in the line to keep fuel from draining out. Ideally, filters should be about level with the fuel pump on the engine. The maximum lift (vertical height) from the takeoff at the tank to the inlet port on the engine is 48 inches (122 cm). Even that is a bit high. Less is always better. Lift heights approaching or more than 48 inches (122 cm) require installation of a booster pump.

Whenever the filter is above the tank level, a hand wobble pump (or similar) should be installed in the feed line so that the filter and the entire feed line can be purged of air and filled with a solid slug of fuel.

Fuel-Filter Micron Rating (Sieve Fineness)

Fuel filter elements come in various mesh or sieve sizes, or finenesses. The finer the filter, the finer the grit and sediment it will remove. Fineness is measured in microns—the nominal diameter of the minuscule openings in the filter element. A micron is roughly 40 millionths of an inch (one thousandth of a mm). The primary filter (the fuel/water separator with filter element; see Figures 4-3 and 4-10) should usually be fitted with a 30-micron filter. This catches the larger particles of sediment. Some prefer a 10-micron

---

Carburetors on Gasoline Engines

Under CFR Yacht and Commercial, each carburetor must leak no more than 5 cm³ (0.3 cu. in.) of fuel per second when
- the float valve is open
- the carburetor is at half throttle
- the engine is cranked without starting
- the fuel pump is delivering the maximum pressure specified by its manufacturer

Updraft and horizontal-draft carburetors must have a device that

- collects and holds fuel that flows out of the carburetor venturi section toward the air intake
- prevents collected fuel from being carried out of the carburetor assembly by the shock wave of a backfire or by reverse airflow
- returns collected fuel to the engine induction system after the engine starts

> ## Principal Differences Between ISO 10088 and ABYC Standards
>
> What we've been covering here is for compliance with ABYC guidelines. ISO 10088 is generally quite similar but has a few differences, most importantly,
>
> 1. ISO 10088 requires access not just to the fuel-line and tank fittings but to the entire fuel line as well.
> 2. ABYC requires 15 inches (381 mm) clearance between fill openings and any vents. ISO 10088 adds two additional clearance requirements:
>   a. The clearance between a gasoline tank and any part of the engine must be a minimum of 100 mm (4 in.).
>   b. The clearance between a dry exhaust and a gasoline fuel tank must be a minimum of 250 mm (10 in.).
>
>   NOTE: I agree with both of these as bare minimum clearances—more is better.
>
> 3. ABYC requires the minimum inside diameter of a fill pipe to be $1\frac{1}{8}$ in. (28.5 mm). ISO 10088 requires a minimum inside diameter of 31.5 mm ($1\frac{1}{4}$ in.).

primary filter, feeling it will ensure cleaner fuel to the engine. This is acceptable, but it will clog up more quickly unless the boat is using very clean fuel.

The best place for a 10-micron primary fuel filter would be in the duplex filter installed after a day tank (polishing tank). The filter from the wing fuel tanks to the day tank would have a 30-micron element, and the duplex filter after the day tank would have the 10-micron filter elements. This way, the coarser grit is removed before the day tank and then somewhat finer grit after the day tank. One drawback is the necessity of purchasing and keeping track of two different filter types. Using all 30-micron primary filters is fairly standard.

The secondary filter is the fine filter on the engine itself. The secondary filter removes the finest of remaining impurities. Secondary filters generally range from 2 to 7 microns. If in doubt, use 2 microns, but always refer to and follow the engine manufacturer's recommendations.

Gas-Engine Piping

Figure 4-4 shows a straightforward gas-engine fuel-piping arrangement for a twin gas-engine boat with twin tanks. In normal operation, the port tank feeds the port engine and the starboard tank the starboard engine. The cross-over valve is closed. If, however, you want to run off one tank only, you can shut the takeoff valves on the tank you don't wish to use and open the cross-over valve.

The generator feeds off either tank through a Y-valve, though you could eliminate the Y-valve and simply open and close the takeoff valves for the generator at each tank.

Diesel Return-Line Complications

Gas engines (with the exception of some fuel-injected gas engines, as noted above) simply run their fuel one way: from the tank to the carburetor. However, diesel engines use their fuel not only as fuel but also to lubricate and cool their injectors. The excess diesel—carrying off considerable unwanted heat—has to be piped back to the fuel tank. This makes diesel fuel runs twice as complicated as those for gasoline. It's straightforward enough, however, if the piping is set up as shown in Figure 4-5 or 4-7. The return line (sometimes termed the "spill") should enter the tank as far from the takeoff line as possible to prevent the drawing of foaming fuel into the pickup. The minimum workable distance is 15 inches (38 cm), but more is always better.

Chapter 4: Fuel Piping and Fuel System Bonding

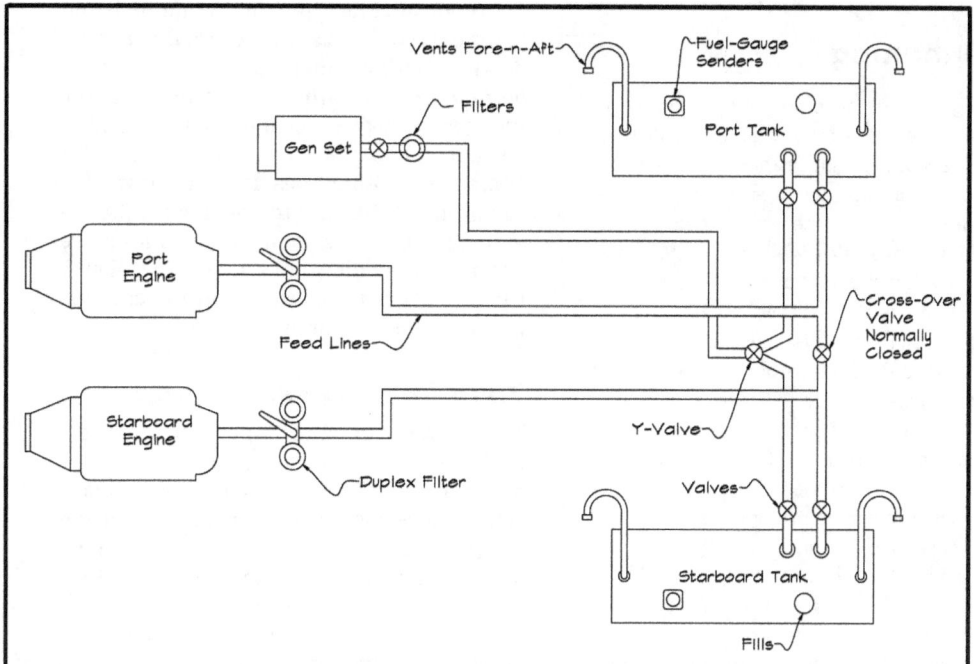

Figure 4-4. Gasoline twin-tank piping

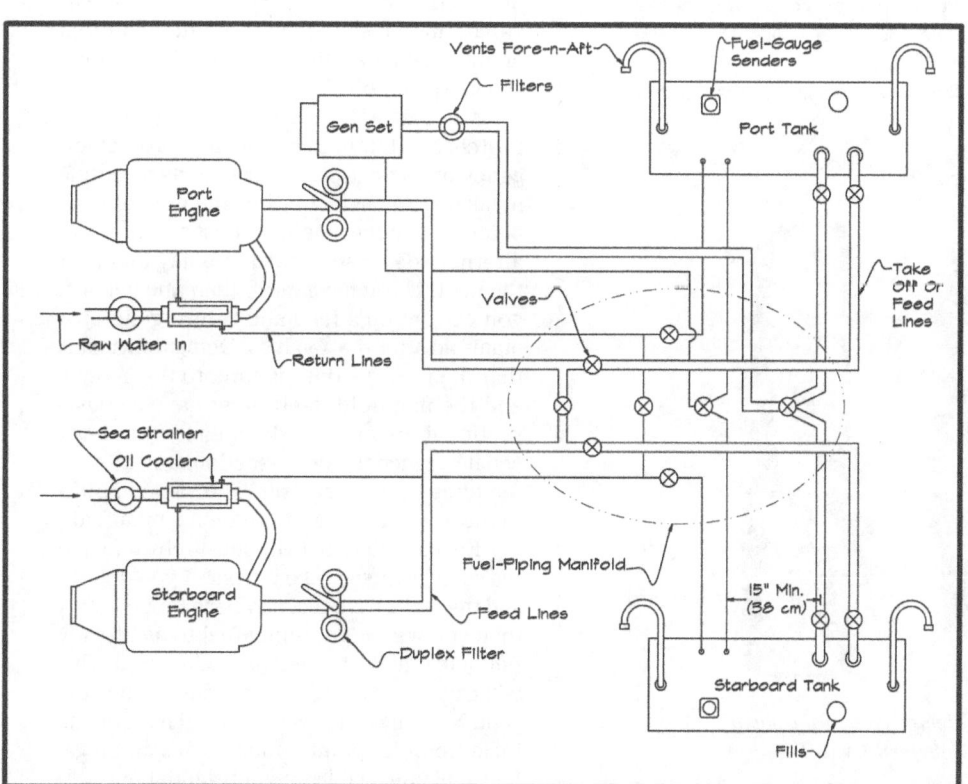

Figure 4-5. Diesel twin-tank piping

PART TWO: FUEL SYSTEMS

Gasoline Antisiphoning

Gasoline spills into the bilge are far more dangerous than diesel spills. Accordingly, all gas-engine craft must be equipped with antisiphon protection. John Eggers of EVM, Inc., explains that the purpose of the antisiphon protection is to prevent emptying the tank should someone, say, accidentally step on the fuel line near the engine and break it off. If the broken line were full of fuel and drooped down below the level of the fuel tank, it would literally siphon the tank contents into the boat—extremely hazardous!

Antisiphoning protection can be achieved by keeping all portions of the fuel lines—right up to the carburetor—above the tank top, using A1 hose, and securing the works so that it can't fall downward to create a siphon. Here, clearly, if the fuel line ruptures, the gas will simply run harmlessly back down into the tank. If this approach is taken, a standard shutoff valve at the tank takeoff is still required. It's often difficult or inconvenient to arrange the fuel system this way, in which case an inexpensive (usually $3 or less) antisiphon device must be installed in the fuel takeoff line right at the tank.

The most common antisiphon device is a ball check valve that prevents flow from the tank at low suction (as caused by a leak), but opens to allow flow at the higher suction created by the fuel pump. Alternatively, an electronically operated shutoff valve (a solenoid) can be installed at the tank takeoff and wired to the ignition. Since the antisiphon device prevents all flow from the tank unless the engine is running, no additional manual shutoff valve is required. Antisiphon fittings are longer than standard hose barb connectors. Inspect to see that these have in fact been installed.

Antisiphon device (left) and plain hose barb (Courtesy EVM, Inc.)

Some engines (like the Cummins B and C series) require that the return line extend down to within 1 inch (25 mm) of the tank *bottom*. This is so that air cannot enter the fuel system on these engines when the tank is partially full and the vessel is sitting idle for some time. Other diesels don't have this requirement. Be sure to check with the engine manufacturer about this detail before ordering or building tanks. If in doubt, simply run the return to the tank bottom, and this problem won't occur in any engine.

Twin-Tank Diesel Piping

The most common arrangement for diesel tanks on yachts is simply twin tanks. The schematic in Figure 4-5 shows a standard setup with a single gen set. In this system, the starboard tank feeds the starboard engine and the port tank feeds the port engine. During normal operation, the valves for both feed lines and both return lines are open, but the cross-over valves are closed, as they are in the gas fuel system earlier. If for some reason it were necessary to run both engines off one tank you would open the cross-over valves and close the valves in the manifold coming from or going to the tank you don't want to use (both feed and return).

The generator in this arrangement is switchable, but in this case, not as an emergency or backup procedure but as a routine measure. You select either the port or starboard tank at the manifold. Best practice is to alternate days: starboard one day and port the next. If you have more than one gen set, you can set up a feed and return generator manifold after the Y-valves. Doing this means that the piping from the tank to the Y-valve and the manifold itself must have a cross-sectional area (at inside diameter) at least equal to twice the cross-section area of each feed line to each gen set. The same applies to the generator-line return piping manifold.

Keep in mind that you must return fuel to the same tank you take it from. If you don't—and the tanks have recently been topped off—then you will be returning fuel to an already full tank that isn't otherwise being used. This will cause it to overflow and spill through the vent. Not only is this wasteful and hard on the local flounder population, but it's an illegal fuel spill punishable by a substantial fine.

Distribution Manifold

The distribution manifold shown in Figure 4-6 requires eight valves. You seldom need to open or close any but the generator valves (to equalize fuel usage), but it is not always apparent exactly which combination of valves to switch when you have an emergency or need to equalize tanks. All valves should be clearly labeled.

There should also be a clear diagram of the fuel system schematic mounted on a plastic placard right next to the fuel manifold. At the dock, you have plenty of time to ponder which combination of valves to open or close to make the correct selection, but underway—in an emergency or in heavy weather—it's another story altogether.

In addition, there should also be a warning placard reading:

"Always open valves in combination to takeoff and return to the same tank."

Of course, the required placard warning that oil discharge overboard is illegal must be posted as well.

Diesel Day-Tank Piping

Though the twin-tank diesel system is perfectly adequate, the day-tank system is superior for long-range cruising and all larger diesel craft. Here the main port and starboard fuel tanks (the "wing tanks") feed a single smaller, day tank. The engines and the generator draw off this day tank, and the return lines go to the day tank as well. Additionally, you can set up to have optional draw direct from the wing tanks; the piping is straightforward, though installing a placard of the piping schematic is still highly recommended.

For the serious voyager, routine filling of the day tank gives a good regular reckoning

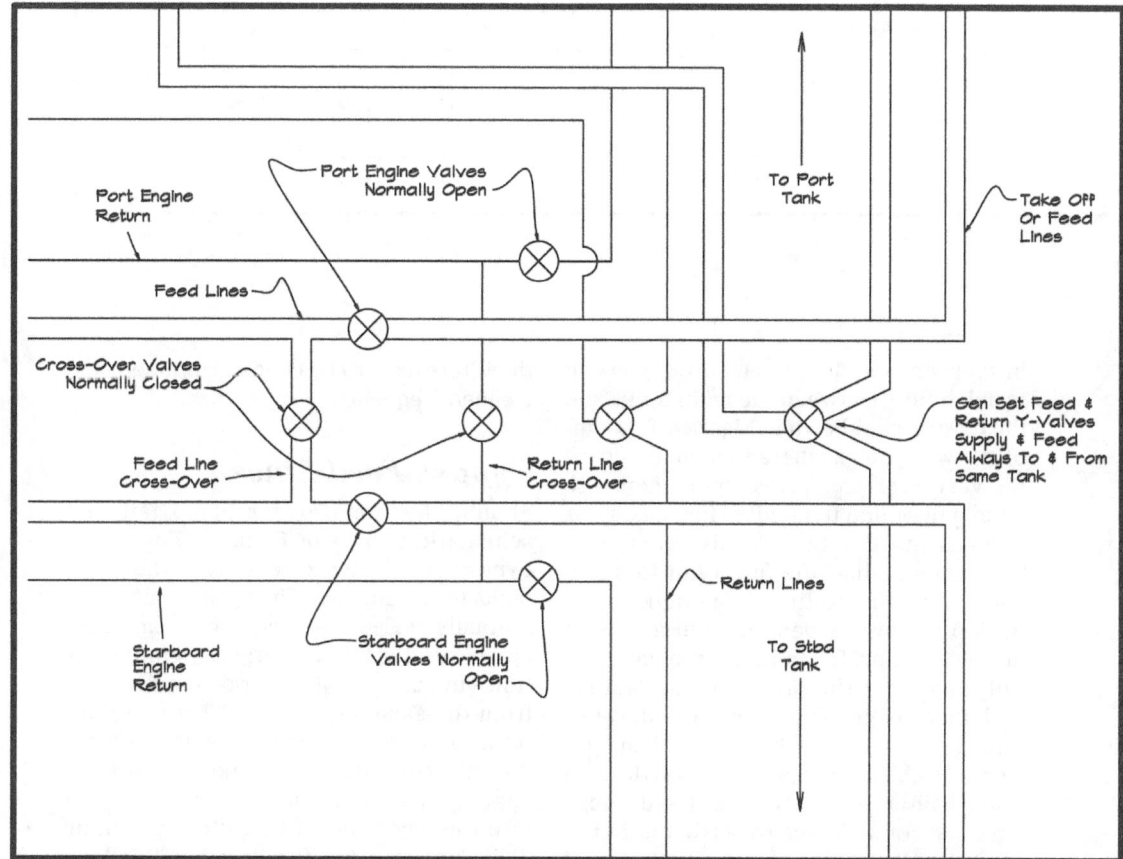

Figure 4-6. Fuel-piping or distribution manifold

PART TWO: FUEL SYSTEMS

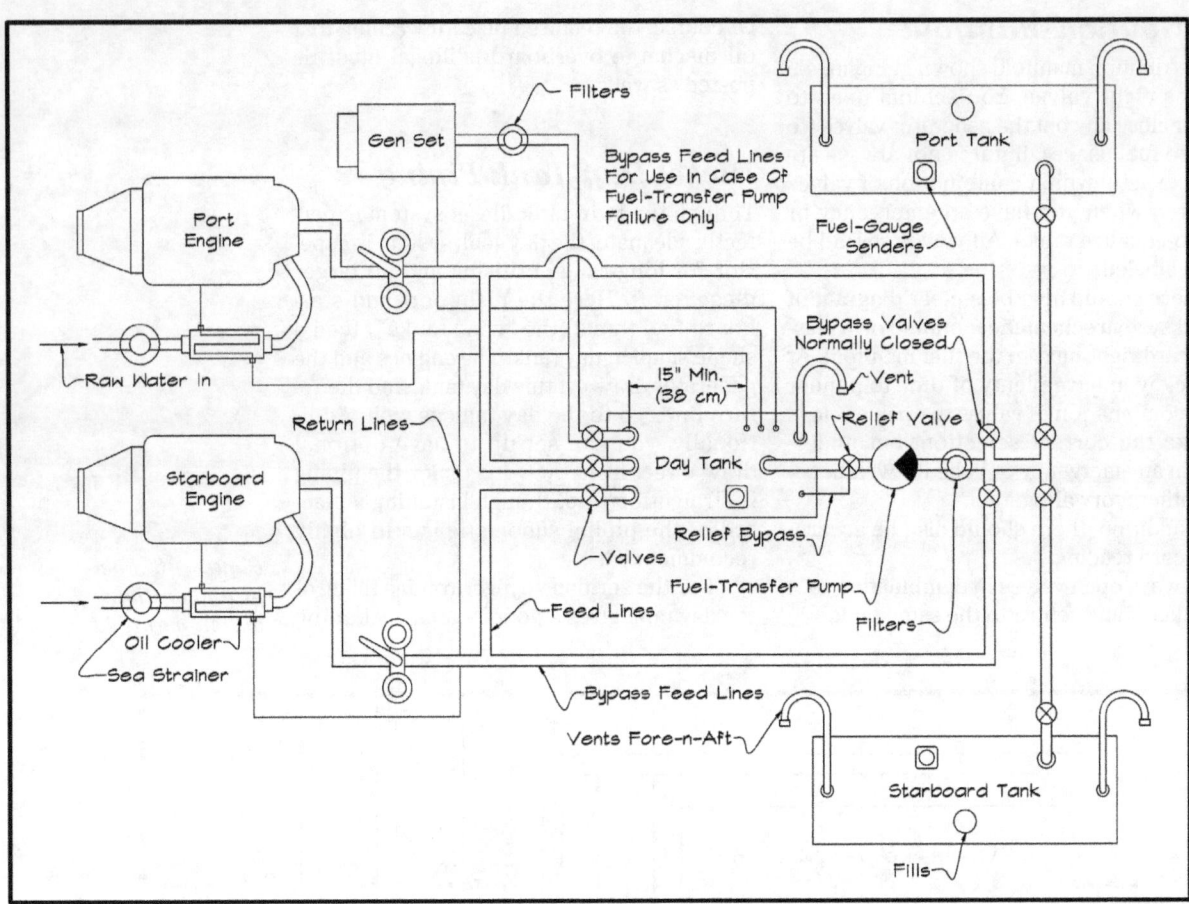

Figure 4-7. Diesel day-tank fuel piping

of fuel consumption. Even better, you can install a filter between the main tanks and the day tank as shown in Figure 4-7. In out-of-the-way places where fuel quality is often very poor, this gives you a chance to double filter and to monitor fuel quality as it feeds the day tank. (This practice is called "polishing" the fuel.) For this reason, I don't like to fit the day tank with a deck fill, though a vent, of course, is still necessary. I prefer to pump the day tank full only from the main onboard tanks. With this fuel polishing, you can safely use dirtier fuel—if you have to—than you would be able to with a single pass through a single filter. What's more, dirt and sludge have a second chance to settle out in the day tank. Obviously, in such situations, all the filters have to be checked, drained, and cleaned frequently.

Bypass Feed Lines

Should the fuel-transfer pump fail, the schematic shown in Figure 4-7 includes bypass feed lines direct from the wing tanks to the engines. The bypass valves are normally closed—opened only in emergencies. Note that this emergency configuration violates the always-take-and-return-from-the-same-tank rule. There are no return lines to the wing tanks. If you draw directly from the port tank to feed both engines, the return fuel will still be going into the day tank. At 60 gallons per hour (227 L/hr.) gross fuel flow, roughly 20 gallons per hour (76 L/hr.) fuel would be consumed and the remaining 40 gallons per hour (151 L/hr.) would spill back to the day tank. A 150-gallon (568 L) day tank would be topped off this way in 3 hours and 45 minutes. Accordingly—in an emergency like this—the crew would have to monitor the day-tank status and switch to draw off it rather than off the wing tank, when the day tank neared full. Another alternative is to install two transfer pumps in a switchable duplex arrangement. In this case only a full electric outage would require use of the bypass fuel lines, as it's highly unlikely that both transfer pumps would go down at the same time.

The Common-Rail Manifold

The term *manifold*, as applied to piping, literally means many parts or many paths or channels. Any systematic collection of pipes for directing fluid flow is a "manifold." The fuel-piping manifolds in Figures 4-6 and 4-7 are typical examples. There is a specific type of piping manifold that can offer added benefits in complex distribution systems. This is a piping manifold in which the source or the return branches from or into a single pipe. This single pipe is called the "common rail" or sometimes the "common bus." Common-rail manifolds can simplify and clarify distribution and control of piping and allow for easy installation of built-in spares for possible future equipment.

The day-tank piping schematic in Figure 4-7 can be arranged with a common-rail manifold on either the feed lines, on the return lines, or both. This schematic—with a common rail on both the feed and return lines—is arranged as in Figure 4-8.

Note that a valve is still required right at the tank takeoff, before the common rail. Notice how a spare branch pipe (or several spares) can easily be added to the common rail.

Figure 4-8. Diesel day-tank fuel piping with common-rail manifolds

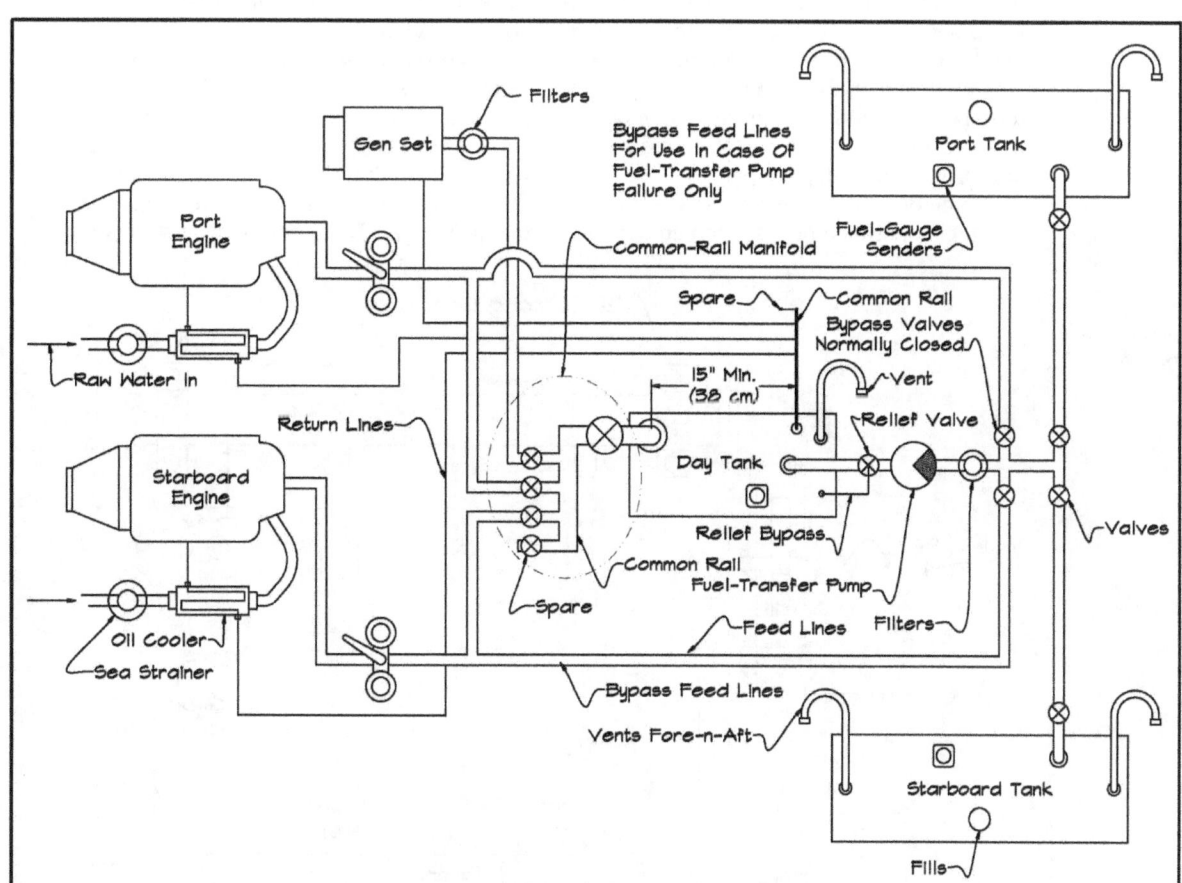

PART TWO: FUEL SYSTEMS

SPECIFYING THE COMMON RAIL The common rail—the single distribution line to the branches for each component (or from each return)—is usually made of pipe. It can be a single section with welded-on branch pipes, or several sections connected in line with T-connectors forming the branch pipes. Sometimes a solid block of metal is machined to form the common rail. In this case a long block—say, solid stainless—is bored along its center to form an internal common-rail channel. The end is drilled and tapped to accept the main inlet (or outlet) and the branch exits (or inlets) are drilled and tapped at right angles (into the side of the common-rail block). For most ordinary fuel-piping manifolds, however, plain pipe is the most cost-effective approach.

A mistake in setting up a common-rail manifold is making the common-rail pipe the same diameter as the branch pipes. If you stop to think about it, obviously the common rail has to handle the combined flow of *all* the branch pipes. There can also be some internal turbulence and flow restriction due to the sharp bends in flow required by the fluid inside the common-rail manifold. For this reason, the internal cross-section area of the common-rail pipe needs to be equal to the total cross-section area of all the branch pipes plus 10 percent, or

Common-rail pipe section area = total combined branch-pipe section area × 1.1

Say you have a common rail that needs to feed two large main engines and a gen set and the common rail is fitted with four standard-weight $3/4$ in. (or DIN 26.9×2.9) stainless branch pipes, including the spare. See Figure 4-9, which is also a detail view of the common-rail manifold in Figure 4-8.

Note in Figure 4-9 that the larger common-rail diameter must extend the full length of the pipe from the source. This means a large valve at the tank, which takes up space and requires a bigger takeoff pipe. This must be allowed for in design. The tank manufacturer has to install the large takeoff pipe leading from close to the bottom of the tank (see "Taking Off" on page 78) as well as a suitable valve or valve attachment. Note the brackets or supports required on the manifold piping to prevent flexing and cracking. Also note the screw-cap closure fitting on the spare branch pipe for added protection against accidental spills. The quarter-turn ball valves allow you to immediately see if a valve is open or closed.

The common-rail manifold could be used exactly as shown in Figure 4-9; however, space and installation requirements may make it necessary to locate the common rail, with its branch pipes and valves, much farther from the tank. This is fine as long as the piping is properly supported against bending

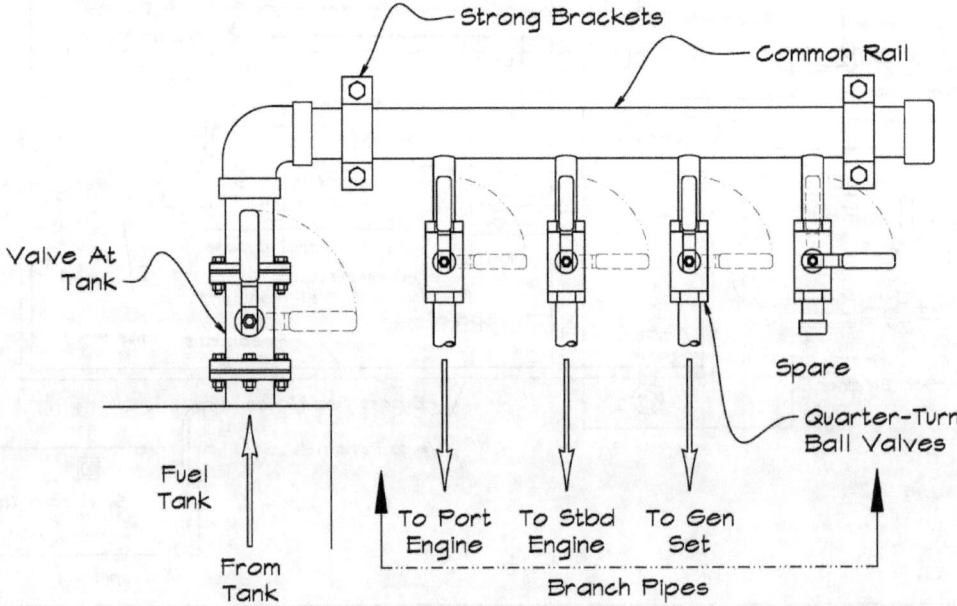

Figure 4-9. Common-rail fuel-feed manifold

and flexible hose is used to connect to the engine and any other vibrating or moving components.

ENGLISH-UNIT COMMON-RAIL SIZING Referring to the pipe tables (Appendix B), we see that the inside diameter of the Sched. 40, 3/4 in. branch pipes is 0.824 in. ID (inside diameter) each. Use the following formulas to find their cross-section areas.

Formula 4-1a. Cross-Section Area in English Units

$\pi(0.824 \text{ in. ID} \div 2)^2 = 0.53$ sq. in. $\pi \approx 3.14$
0.53 sq. in. $\times$ 4 branch pipes $\times$ 1.1 = 2.33 sq. in.
minimum common-rail section area

$$\text{required common-rail ID} = 2 \times \sqrt{\frac{\text{section area}}{\pi}}$$

$$\text{required common-rail ID} = 2 \times \sqrt{\frac{2.33 \text{ sq.in.}}{\pi}}$$

$$= 1.722 \text{ in.}$$

Referring to the pipe tables (Appendix B), we see that a 1½ in. Schedule 40 pipe has an ID of 1.610 in.—a bit too small. So we use the next size up: 2 in. Schedule 40, OD 2.375 in., ID 2.067 in., as pictured in Figure 4-9.

METRIC COMMON-RAIL SIZING The inside diameter of the 26.9 mm OD $\times$ 2.9 mm wall branch pipes is 26.9 mm – (2 $\times$ 2.9 mm wall) = 21.1 mm ID. Their cross-section area is then

Formula 4-1b. Cross-Section Area in Metric Units

$\pi(21.1 \text{ mm ID} \div 2)^2 = 349.7 \text{ mm}^2$ $\pi \approx 3.14$
349.7 mm^2 $\times$ 4 branch pipes $\times$ 1.1 = 1,538 mm^2
minimum common-rail section area

$$\text{required common-rail ID} = 2 \times \sqrt{\frac{\text{section area}}{\pi}}$$

$$\text{required common-rail ID} = 2 \times \sqrt{\frac{1,538 \text{ mm}^2}{\pi}}$$

$$= 44.2 \text{ mm}$$

We know that the outside diameter must be somewhat larger than 44.2 mm. Referring to the pipe tables (Appendix B), we calculate that a 51 x 3.2 pipe has an ID of 44.6, which will do nicely [51 mm – (2 x 3.2 mm) = 44.6 mm].

COMMON-RAIL MANIFOLDS HAVE MANY APPLICATIONS Note that common-rail manifolds are useful in many applications. You can employ them for freshwater systems, seawater intake (sea suction, see Chapter 17) either attached to a sea chest or to individual seacocks, or any other application with multiple pipes. Keep the common-rail manifold approach in mind for general use.

Fuel-Transfer Pumps

The fuel-transfer pump should be self-priming and have the flow capacity to fill the day tank in a reasonable period of time, say under 15 or 20 minutes. In real-world installations, pumps seldom deliver more than 70 percent of their rated flow. Thus for, say, an 80-gallon (303 L) day tank, you want about an 8 gpm-rated (30 L/min.) pump (80 gal. ÷ 0.70 = 114 gal., and 114 gal. ÷ 15 min. = 7.6, say, 8 gpm; or 303 L ÷ 0.70 = 433 L, and 433 L ÷ 15 min. = 28.8 L/min., say, 30 L/min.). Rotary sliding-vane pumps meet the criteria for self-priming (at least within 2 feet [60 cm] or so of lift, adequate for most boats), and they're available, rated for continuous use with diesel fuel. Though seldom critical, it's worth considering a reversible vane pump, which will enable you to empty the day tank back into one of the main tanks for cleaning or repair. Gear pumps are another good option, particularly for larger vessels requiring high transfer rates.

High-volume transfer pumps can generate high pressures should a blockage occur. In the worst case, this can lead to a fuel-line rupture and a horrendous fuel spill. Such pumps should be protected with a relief valve. Since you can't have the relief blowby spraying into the boat, the blowby should be plumbed through a bypass line into the nearest tank, usually the day tank. An alarm and an automatic pump shutoff on the relief valve complete the safety picture.

If the crew monitors the fuel transfer carefully, they can shut off the fuel transfer before overfilling. It is, however, too easy to forget. I recommend that a second tank-level sensor be installed in the day tank and dedicated to the transfer pump shutoff. It should be set up to automatically switch off the transfer pump at about 97 percent full. A one-time audible alarm (a few beeps, a momentary ring) alerts the crew.

Note that the fuel-transfer pump must also deliver fuel at a faster rate than maximum fuel consumption. For diesels this is the actual fuel consumed, and—regardless of manufacturer claims—it's almost always close to 0.054 gal./hp/hr., or 0.274 L/kW/hr. For twin 350 hp (261 kW) engines (700 hp [522 kW] total), this is 700 hp x 0.054 gal./hp/hr. = 37.8 gph. Dividing by 60 gives 0.63 gpm. Or 522 kW x 0.274 L/kW/hr. = 143 L/hr. Dividing by 60 gives 2.38 L/min. This is well under the rate of the transfer pump we just specced, but on large engines with comparatively small day tanks (really polishing tanks), the pump rate should be checked against actual fuel consumption.

For large vessels with sizable long-range tanks, you should install an additional fuel-transfer pump (or a manifold to the day-tank transfer pump) for shunting fuel between tanks. This allows moving fuel from tank to tank to adjust boat trim. Long-range cruisers may also want to add piping to allow drawing and returning directly from the wing tanks. This considerably complicates the fuel piping, however, and is gilding the lily for most boats in normal service. It may also require additional booster pumps to handle long fuel runs.

MULTIPLE TANK SYSTEMS Though best practice—even on the largest vessels—is to use no more than two wing tanks plus a day tank, the realities of fitting in machinery, accommodations, and the tankage required can make this impossible. In this case, added tanks can be installed. Fuel distribution to the day tank is controlled at the day-tank-feed manifold. The transfer pump for an installation like this must be reversible so you can use it to pump fuel from tank to tank to adjust trim. Since runs are long and gravity feed to the day tank probably won't be reliable or even achievable, you're relying on the transfer pump for operation. A backup transfer pump in a quick-operation, switchable, duplex configuration is mandatory.

Filling multiple tanks with multiple fills is inconvenient. On large boats, it's also a chore to pull the boat off the dock and turn the vessel around to fuel the opposite side. The best solution for this is to install identical fuel fills port and starboard, but manifold them and all tanks together so either the port or starboard fill can supply every tank on both sides. This is big-boat stuff, which is a good thing because it requires intelligent management during fueling. The fuel-fill manifold should have valves to close off each tank, so you fill each individually. In addition, there should be a tank-level gauge panel outside at each fueling station, port and starboard. This way one crewmember can monitor tank levels at the fill, while another shuts off and opens the appropriate tank valves belowdecks as instructed.

In laying out or modifying an existing installation for such manifolded fuel filling, keep in mind that the pipes are sizable—2 inches (50 mm) in diameter. It takes careful planning to fit such piping and its required valves and hangers into the confines of a boat.

PUMPS SUCK Whenever a pump is used to transfer fuel toward the engine, it should be located after the filter—that is, to work in suction. If the pump is located ahead of the filter, it mixes or emulsifies water and other impurities with the fuel so effectively that the filter/separator won't function adequately. Follow this principle of locating pumps for suction rather than for pressure throughout.

Cool Oil

As we've seen, the return diesel oil carries off excess heat from the injectors; the returned fuel can get quite hot. This will warm up the fuel in a tank considerably, even causing potential overflow through the

---

Gasoline Fuel Pumps

Under CFR Yacht and Commercial—with the exception of fuel-transfer pumps—gasoline fuel pumps must not operate unless the engine is running. Diaphragm gasoline tanks must not leak even if the primary diaphragm fails.

Except for fuel-transfer pumps, all gasoline fuel pumps must be mounted on the engine or within 12 inches (305 mm) of the engine.

tank vent in a full tank due to expansion. Further, hot fuel causes power loss, since it's less dense and thus packs less oomph per unit volume. I highly recommend return fuel oil coolers on all diesel engines. They are shown on the piping schematics. (Newer, high-output diesels often come with return oil coolers built in. Check this before ordering an unnecessary additional external oil cooler.)

Oil coolers are no more than simple heat exchangers. Raw seawater is drawn in for the main engine cooling (or heat-exchanger cooling) and passed through the sea strainer. (Figure 4-10 shows a seacock leading to the sea strainer, then to the Sen-Dure return oil cooler. A Racor clear-bowl fuel filter with a metal flame shield is located above the sea strainer.) The cool raw water is then routed down through the oil cooler and then to the water pump on the engine. You can see in Figures 4-5 and 4-7 that the return oil passes through coils in the oil cooler before traveling back to the fuel tank, now at lower temperature. (Duplex sea strainers—identical in concept to the duplex fuel filters—are also highly recommended.) See Chapter 17 regarding seawater intake.

Hot Oil

In cold climates—as anyone who has ever run a compression-ignition engine knows—diesels are hard starting. Fuel heating elements are available that fit into the fuel filter. Typically, they can raise fuel temperature from 0°F to 60°F (from –17°C to 15.5°C) in 5 minutes at under 10 amps. These units are switched on and off from the helm and automatically reduce current draw as the temperature increases. If you're building boats for Alaska, Newfoundland, or Baltic operation, late fall through winter and early spring, these heaters will make getting them going in the morning more pleasant.

Fuel-Line Valves

CFR Yacht, CFR Commercial, and the ABYC are strangely silent on recommended valve types for fuel systems. Technically, any valve is acceptable if it will withstand the required $2\frac{1}{2}$-minute burn test and has packing that won't break down from contact with the fuel. For example, some Detroit Diesel manuals recommend the use of gate valves for their lack of restriction on fuel flow. In fact, however, gate valves, as well as *any* valves with packing, are potential trouble. Even if the packing doesn't break down from the fuel, it will wear out eventually. Accordingly, no valves with packing for their primary seal should be used in fuel piping.

The two best alternatives are globe valves and quarter-turn ball valves. Globe valves are acceptable, but they cause restriction in fuel flow due to their construction. Also, you can't tell if they're open or closed simply by glancing at them. Two arguments in favor of globe valves are that

Figure 4-10. Return oil cooler

Figure 4-11. Ball valve (Courtesy Conbraco)

PART TWO: FUEL SYSTEMS

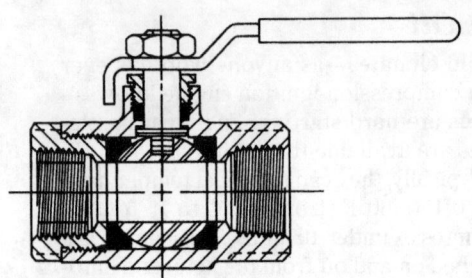

Figure 4-12.
Cutaway view of
an open ball valve
(Courtesy
Conbraco)

they screw up and down so they can't vibrate open or closed accidentally, and they permit adjustment for partial flow. Partial flow, however, isn't required for fuel shutoffs. In my opinion, quarter-turn ball valves are the hands-down best choice. They create no restriction in the fuel flow. Further, the position of their handle gives instant indication of whether they're open or closed. An added benefit: ball valves are relatively light and compact. Cheaply made ball valves have been known to vibrate themselves open or closed, but well-made ones don't engage in such hijinks.

Of course, you must make certain that the fuel-line diameter and valve size meet your engine manufacturer's requirements—the inlet port size on the engine. If the fuel-supply run is very long or has numerous bends and fittings, it's a good idea to go up one size to reduce friction.

Remote Fuel Shutoffs

Neither ABYC nor CFR Yacht require remote fuel shutoff valves outside the engine compartment. CFR Commercial and NFPA 302 do require this. Frankly, I think remote fuel shutoffs should be required on all boats over 28 feet (8.5 m) with inboard engines and cabin accommodations. The reason is both simple and frightening. The burning boat pictured at the beginning of this chapter had all the required fuel shutoff valves on the tanks. It also had fire extinguishers on board. A diesel fire like this is like a blowtorch, however. Cracking the engine hatches, the flames were so intense that the fire extinguishers were about as effective as spitting into a

Estimating Fuel-Line Diameter

Diesel Engines

Best practice is *always* to get the engine manufacturer's recommendation for fuel-line diameter, feed and return. Keep in mind that very long or complex fuel lines should go up a size in diameter. There will be instances, however, when you need to estimate fuel-line size, and you can use the following. Remember, err on the large size. You can always fit reducers, but you can't overcome the restriction of a pipe that is too small. The drawback to going too large is the extra cost, greater space used, and added weight of bigger plumbing. These considerations, too, are important, so don't simply specify huge piping.

Small diesel engines use about $1/4$-inch NPT (DN 8 mm) pipe minimum for feed and return, up to around 200 hp.

Diesels from 200 hp to about 350 hp use $3/8$-inch NPT (DN 10 mm) going to $1/2$ in. (DN 15 mm) at the upper end, feed and return.

Diesels from 350 hp to 650 hp use about $3/4$-inch NPT (DN 20 mm), feed and return.

Diesels from 650 hp to 1,200 hp use about 1-inch NPT (DN 25 mm), feed and return.

Again, the engine manufacturer should have the last word here. There is variation. For instance, a CAT 300 hp engine specs $1/4$-inch (DN 8 mm) feed pipe *and* return, while a GM 300 hp engine specs $3/8$-inch (DN 10 mm) feed and $1/4$-inch (DN 8 mm) return.

Gasoline Engines

Gasoline engines range from $1/8$-inch (6 mm) pipe or tube (different sizes) for 10 hp or 12 hp engines to $1/4$-inch NPT (DN 8 mm) pipe for 350 hp. Remember that many modern fuel-injected gasoline engines also have return lines. Check with the engine manufacturer.

furnace. If the crew could have got into the engine compartment to reach the shutoff valves first, they might well have stopped or at least slowed the fire. In reality, it was too hot to even think of getting close to the hatch. Entering the engine compartment would have been certain death. For this reason, I specify remote fuel shutoffs on all my boats. These are simple linkages (like throttle controls or push-pull cables) that allow you to turn off the fuel right at the tank without going near the engine compartment—cheap insurance.

Flex Connectors

Vibration causes the hull, piping, and machinery to work constantly. For this reason, connections to the firmly mounted tanks and all other components of the fuel system are best made with flexible hose. You can get away with rigid pipe connections to the tanks, if that's necessary, but you absolutely *must* use a flexible tubing or hose between the piping and the engine or gen set. Fail to do this, and you're certain to get cracks—major trouble! Good fuel-line hose isn't all that expensive; it doesn't make sense to scrimp. In some instances, other grades—like A2 or B1 hose—are permissible, but ideally you should use all Coast Guard A1-grade fuel-line hose. This hose meets SAE J1527 (ISO 7840) specifications for hose continuously filled with fuel and withstands a 2 1/2-minute burn test. I would replace anything else. Such hose is clearly labeled "A1" on the outside—there's no mistaking it.

SAE J1527 (ISO 7840) Marine Fuel Hose Types

A1 FUEL FEED HOSE Designed for having fuel in the hose all the time and with a fire-resistant cover.

A2 FUEL VENT HOSE Designed for applications with fuel not normally in the line and with a fire-resistant cover.

B1 FUEL FEED HOSE Designed for having fuel in the hose all the time but without a fire-resistant cover. Intended for nonenclosed engine spaces.

B2 FUEL VENT HOSE Designed for applications with fuel not normally in the line and without a fire-resistant cover. Intended for nonenclosed engine spaces.

A2 FUEL FILL HOSE Designed for applications with fuel not normally in the line and with a fire-resistant cover.

B2 FUEL FILL HOSE Designed for applications with fuel not normally in the line and without a fire-resistant cover.

Unfortunately, A1 hose is not generally available in sizes large enough for fuel fills. In such a case, use A2 fuel fill hose.

Holding Hose

Since you don't want these hoses coming loose, make sure there are marine-grade stainless steel hose clamps at each connection. Naturally, the hoses have to be supported with corrosion-resistant, chafe-free clips or hangers. Pay special attention wherever hoses pass through a bulkhead or panel. A rough edge here is certain to wear through the toughest material sooner or later. Protect the hose with soft ring grommets installed in the hole.

ABYC-recommended fuel-hose clamp widths are as follows:

Hose Outside Diameter	Clamp Width
$7/16$ in. and under	$1/4$ in.
$7/16$ in. to $13/16$ in.	$5/16$ in.
$13/16$ in. and over	$3/8$ in.

Hose Outside Diameter	Clamp Width
11 mm and under	6.3 mm
11 mm to 20.5 mm	8 mm
20.5 mm and over	9.5 mm

CFR Yacht and ABYC require *double* 1/2-inch-wide (12.7 mm) clamps on all large-diameter

Figure 4-13. A1 fuel hose

PART TWO: FUEL SYSTEMS

fuel hoses, such as fill pipes. All hose clamps should be of 100 percent 316 stainless.

Hose Connections

All fuel-line hose must fasten to proper barbed connectors specifically intended for hose. Such hose connections (hose barbs) must have annular rings, not spiral thread or crossed, knurled, or X grooves, all of which can form paths for fuel to leak.

The one exception to the requirement for barbed connectors is large-diameter hose-pipe connections, such as for fuel fills of $1\frac{1}{2}$-inch IPS (DN 40 mm) diameter or larger. In this case, double $\frac{1}{2}$-inch-wide (12.7 mm) hose clamps are required, with a minimum of $\frac{1}{2}$ inch (12.7 mm) between the end of the hose and the end hose clamp.

Acceptable Hose Clamps

In addition to the preceding hose-clamp size requirements, hose clamps must have a mechanical or deformation tightening mechanism. The clamp should be about one hose-clamp width from the end of the hose. Screw-type hose clamps of 316 stainless are strongly recommended. Hose clamps that use only spring tension cannot be used.

Fuel-Line Tubing

Older vessels used soft copper tubing with standard flare connectors for almost all fuel-line and vent piping. This is still acceptable according to CFR Yacht and CFR Commercial provided that a ring-spiral loop is built into the piping before each rigid component to absorb flex. These metal spirals, however, can harden and crack over time. Accordingly, A1 fuel-line hose is greatly preferable. Hose is also cheaper and easier to purchase and install. Copper, copper nickel, nickel copper, and stainless steel are the approved fuel piping metals. Minimum wall thicknesses for tubing should be as follows:

Tubing Outside Diameter	Wall Thickness
$\frac{1}{8}$ in. to $\frac{1}{4}$ in.	0.032 in.
$\frac{5}{16}$ in. to $\frac{3}{8}$ in.	0.035 in.
$\frac{7}{16}$ in. to $\frac{1}{2}$ in.	0.042 in.

Tubing Outside Diameter	Wall Thickness
3.2 mm to 6.3 mm	0.81 mm
8 mm to 9.5 mm	0.89 mm
11 mm to 12.7 mm	1.06 mm

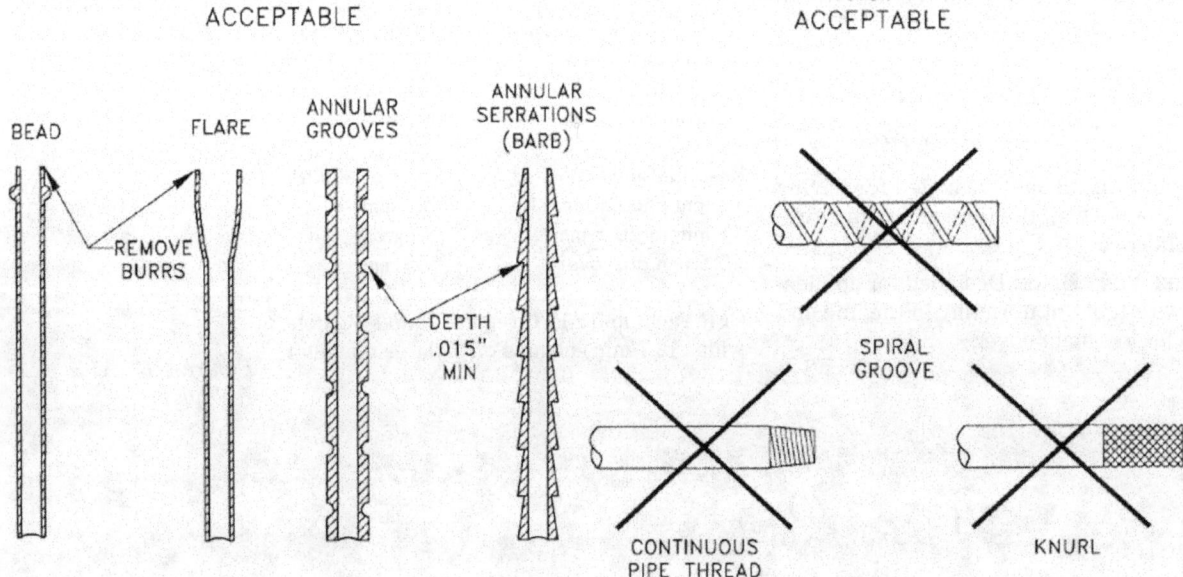

Figure 4-14. Recommended hose connectors (Courtesy ABYC)

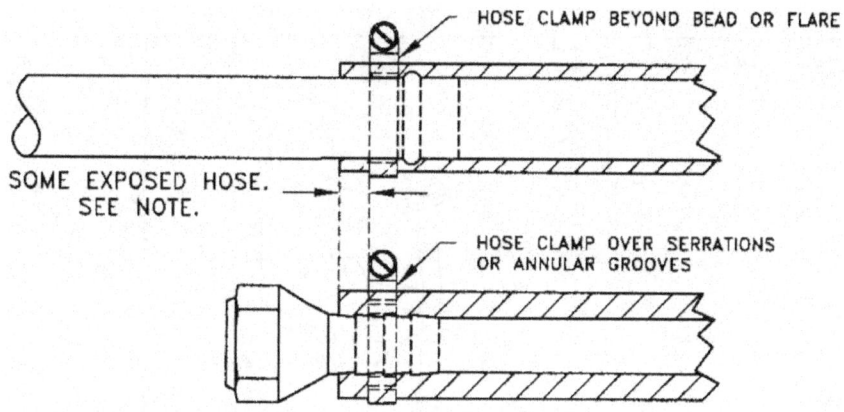

Figure 4-15. Hose clamp distance from hose end (Courtesy ABYC)

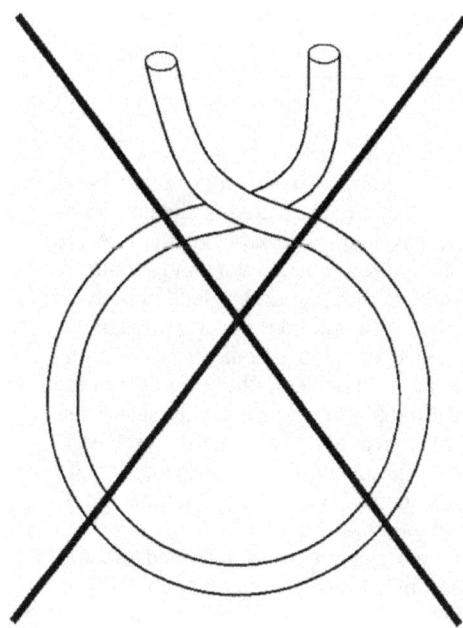

Figure 4-16. A spring-type hose clamp is not acceptable for fuel lines (Courtesy ABYC)

Aluminum Fuel Piping

CFR Commercial allows aluminum fuel piping on aluminum commercial vessels only. Though this makes no sense to me, it's the law. But you can go with aluminum on yachts of any material.

Schedule 40 (standard) marine aluminum pipe can in theory be used for noncommercial diesel, but CFR Commercial requires schedule 80 (double weight) for all aluminum fuel piping, and I recommend schedule 80 for recreational vessels as well. CFR Commercial does not allow hose for fuel piping and insists on all solid pipe or tube, except for a short length of hose at the engine or gen set. Though I follow the rules (there is no choice) for commercial craft, this one doesn't make sense to me for most yachts.

Note that on commercial craft, the Coast Guard is now sometimes requiring the next step up even from A1 hose: shielded hose, such as Aeroquip FC234. This meets SAE J 1942 (formerly USCG COMDTINST M16752.2) fire test criteria for type-A hose. My personal opinion is that this is overkill. It's cheaper just to comply than to argue the point. Remember that even if this hose is

PART TWO: FUEL SYSTEMS

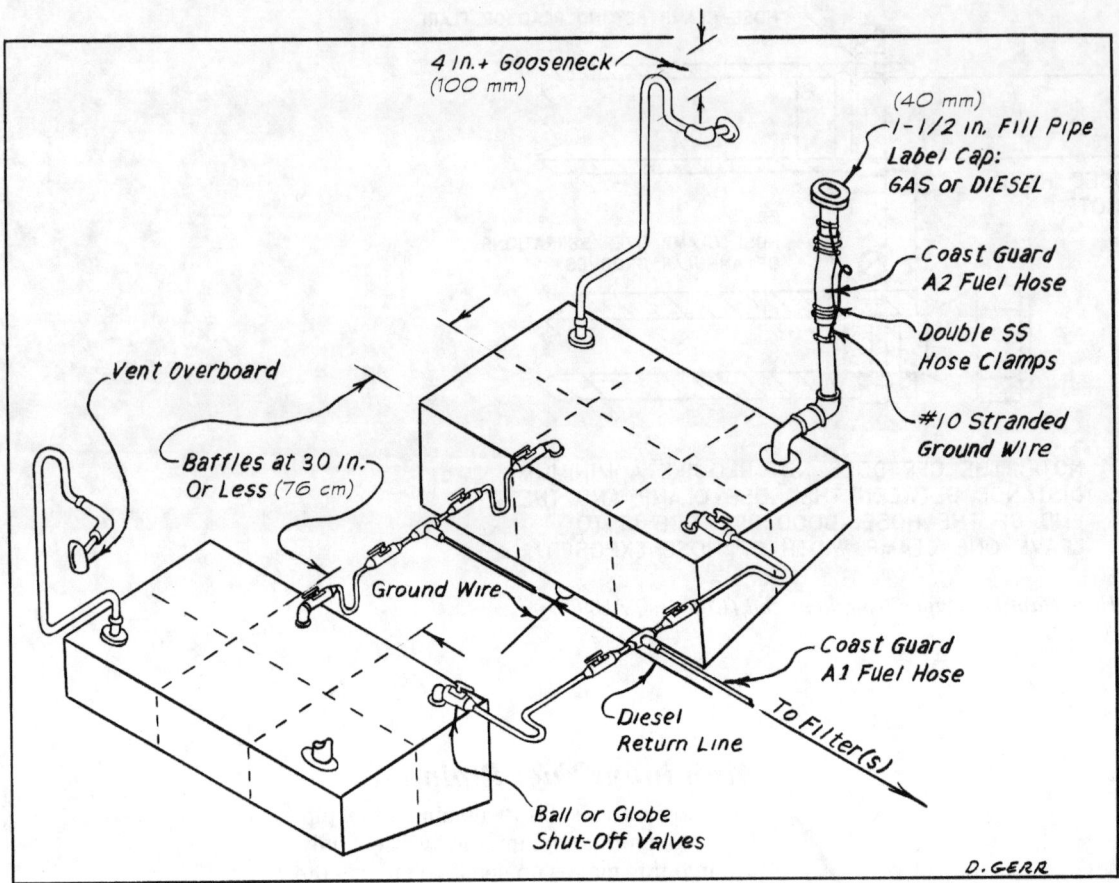

Figure 4-17. Twin fuel tank arrangement

much more expensive than A1, you only need a short lengths of it from the rigid piping to the engine or generator.

Of course, all rigid tubing or pipe must be well supported at regular intervals. There must be a support no more than 4 inches (100 mm) from either end, where it connects to flexible line. Although copper tubing spirals shouldn't be used to connect between components, there's no drawback to using tubing or pipe (of approved materials and type) for long fuel runs—if this is convenient—as long as flexible hose makes the connections at the engine and—better still—at either end.

Eliminating Sparks— Bonding

Sparks are always a potential problem around gasoline. To prevent static buildup, you must fit jumper ground wires across all the gaps between fill and tank created by the hose connections. The jumpers must be number 10 AWG (30-gauge metric) or larger wire and should be either soldered to and under dedicated hose clamps fastened around the pipes, or fastened to the hose clamp with a dedicated ring terminal and screw, not the double clamps around the hose itself. (Yes, I've actually seen this; you've got to wonder!) The tanks themselves, if metal, should also be grounded with 8 AWG (35-gauge metric) wire or larger connected to the boat's bonding system.

This wire may be soldered to a dedicated hose clamp fastened separately to the pipe or fill fitting, but this hose clamp can never be used for any other purpose, and no portion of this clamp or of the bonding conductor wire may run under the hose, where it could cause leaks.

(Note: *AWG* stands for American Wire Gauge. Larger numbers mean smaller conductor diameters. Metric wire gauge is 10 times the conductor diameter in mm: 30-gauge metric is 3 mm conductor diameter. In metric wire gauge, larger numbers are larger conductor sizes. See Table 24-3, page 340.)

Even though diesel won't ignite from a static spark, diesel tanks and piping should be grounded as well to control corrosion. Many small to mid-sized FRP and wood vessels are not equipped with a bonding system. Perhaps the best solution for such craft is to bond the tanks and fill pipes alone to an independent, through-bolted external zinc. You have to take *special* care not to accidentally cross-connect to any other part of the electrical system.

Don't Go Rubbery, and Don't Split!

A final thing to keep in mind is that rubber should never be used for gaskets, hoses, or padding on your tanks or fuel system. Petroleum-based products like gasoline and diesel break down the rubber, creating disastrous leaks. Neoprene is the proper gasket and padding material. And remember, split gaskets of any material aren't allowed. The split would be a potential path for a leak.

CHAPTER 5 Fuel Tanks and Fittings

HOLD THAT TANK

The fuel tank installation in Figure 5-1 shows the basic requirements for a standard inboard tank installation. Clearly, you don't want your tanks sliding around—not ever! They have to be extremely well secured. Wood or wood-cored-FRP chocks and blocks that are laminated, screwed, glued, or bolted in place or metal straps fastened with turnbuckles do the trick. Riser chocks—on which the tanks rest—should be 2 inches (50 mm) wide for tanks under 150 gallons (570 L) and 3 inches (75 mm) wide for tanks over 150 gallons (570 L). They should be about 1½ to 2 inches (38 to 50 mm) high (or higher as necessary to support the tank properly), spaced roughly on 15-inch (38 cm) centers and arranged to permit drainage of water and airflow for ventilation. Band-It bands and buckles of 316 stainless steel do a nice hold-down job. The breaking strength of the chocks, securing bands, fastening bolts, and screws must be 4 times the total combined weight of the tank and its contents, or more.

Aluminum-Strap Hold-Downs

Perhaps the simplest, least expensive, and most common tank hold-downs are made from aluminum flat bar ⅛ inch (3 mm) thick and 1½ inches (38 mm) wide (Figure 5-2). These straps are thin enough to bend to any required shape but wide enough to take fastenings and provide sufficient bearing on relatively thin tank walls. The effective strength of these hold-down straps is limited by the strength of the fasteners at either end. In wood chocks or wood or plywood-cored FRP chocks, use three No. 14 (6 mm) self-tapping stainless screws. (G-10 is an even better core material than wood for this application.) With a minimum bury of 1¼ inch (32 mm), this gives a breaking strength of around 1,400 pounds (635 kg) at each side of the strap—2,800 pounds (1,270 kg) total. If you were securing a 300-gallon (1,136 L) diesel tank, a look at Table 5-1 shows it would come in at 2,335 pounds (1,059 kg). Four times this is 9,340 pounds (4,236 kg), and 9,340 divided by 2,800 pounds per strap is 3.33 (4,236 kg ÷ 1,270 kg per strap = 3.33). Accordingly, you would use four straps—more wouldn't hurt.

NOTE: Some high-speed planing craft can expect to experience g-forces (accelerations from slamming) of 6 to 8 g's. Such boats need to give additional consideration to tank fastening. Tanks midships may not experience such high g's, but tanks and their hold-downs located farther forward may have to be designed to withstand the total expected acceleration, plus a safety factor of 3.

Chapter 5: Fuel Tanks and Fittings

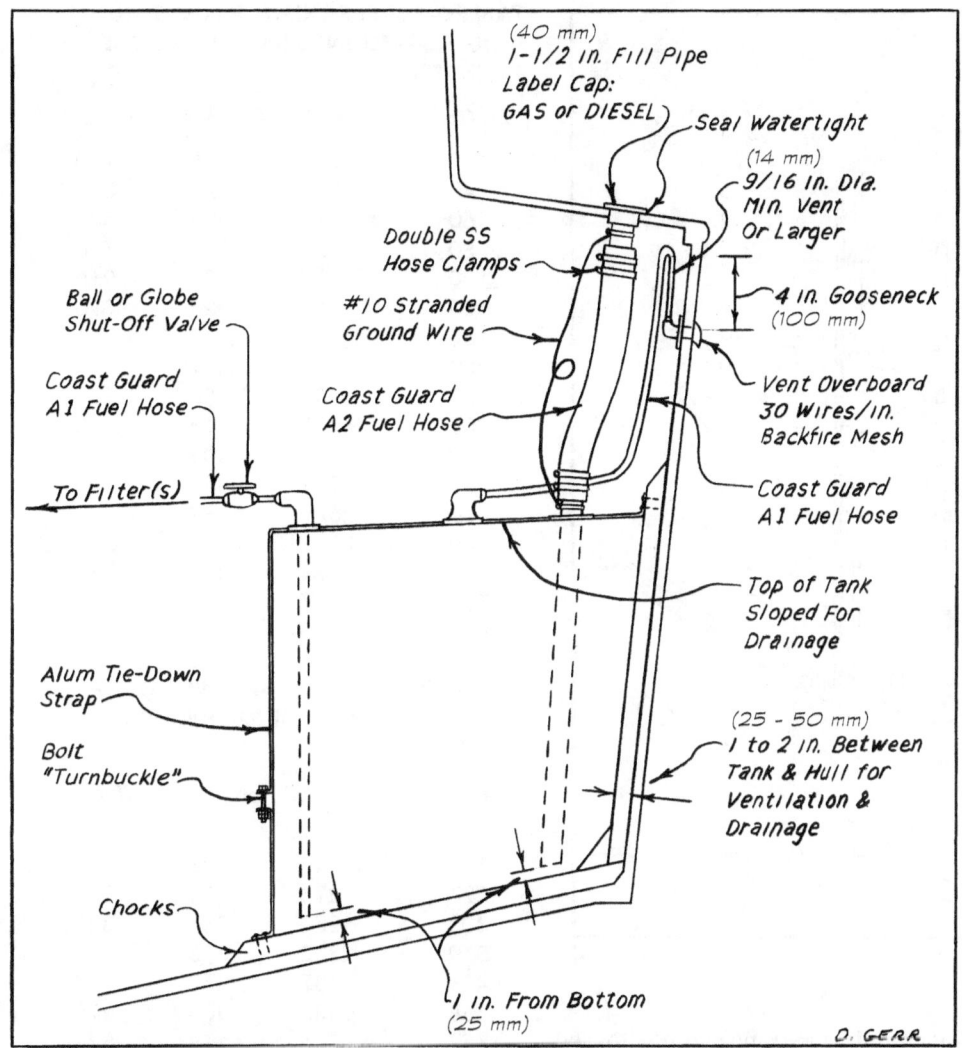

Figure 5-1. Fuel tank installation

G-10

G-10 or FR-4 epoxy is a thermosetting industrial laminate consisting of a continuous-filament glass cloth with an epoxy resin binder. First introduced in the 1950s, it has high strength, excellent electrical properties, and chemical resistance. These properties are maintained not only at room temperature but also under humid or moist conditions.

Today, what is called G-10 is usually FR-4, the flame-retardant version of G-10. The material FR-4 can usually be used where G-10 is specified; however, G-10 should not be used where FR-4 is specified. In structural applications on boats, this is not an issue, and either is fine.

The mechanical properties (strength) of G-10 or FR-4 exceed that of aluminum. With a density of 119 lb./cu.ft. (1,906 kg/m^3), it is only 70 percent the weight of aluminum, but it is about 3.7 times heavier than a solid plywood or fir core.

PART TWO: FUEL SYSTEMS

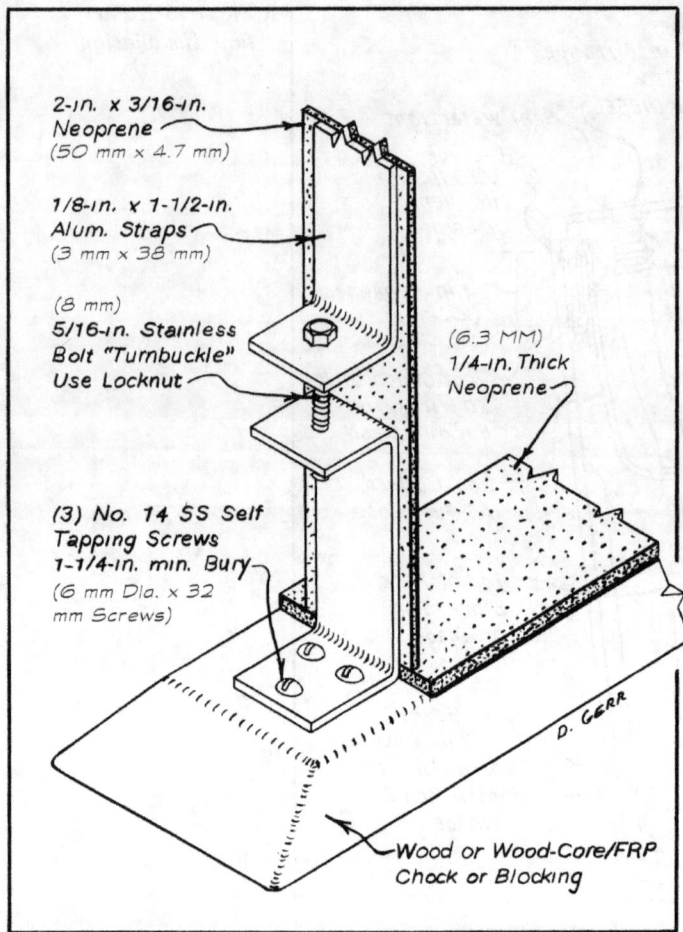

Figure 5-2. Tank hold-downs

TABLE 5-1. APPROXIMATE FULL-TANK WEIGHTS—POUNDS (INCLUDING THE TANK ITSELF)

U.S. Gallons	Diesel	Gasoline	Water
20	156	135	180
40	315	272	362
60	470	405	541
80	621	535	716
100	797	690	916
120	953	825	1,096
150	1,183	1,022	1,361
200	1,575	1,361	1,813
250	1,956	1,688	2,253
300	2,335	2,014	2,692
350	2,778	2,403	3,194
400	3,279	2,851	3,755
450	3,671	3,189	4,206
500	4,143	3,608	4,738
600	5,024	4,382	5,738
700	6,017	5,268	6,850
800	6,826	5,970	7,778

APPROXIMATE FULL-TANK WEIGHTS—KILOGRAMS (INCLUDING THE TANK ITSELF)

Liters	Diesel	Gasoline	Water
76	71	61	82
151	143	123	164
227	213	184	245
303	282	243	325
379	362	313	416
454	432	374	497
568	537	464	618
757	715	618	823
946	887	766	1,022
1,136	1,059	914	1,221
1,325	1,260	1,090	1,449
1,514	1,488	1,294	1,704
1,703	1,666	1,447	1,908
1,893	1,880	1,637	2,150
2,271	2,279	1,988	2,603
2,650	2,730	2,390	3,108
3,028	3,097	2,709	3,529

The hold-down straps can be bowsed tight by cutting them in half at a convenient, accessible flat section of the tank and bending over right-angle tongues at each half's end (Figure 5-2). Connect the two halves with a 5/16-inch (8 mm) diameter stainless bolt, through holes drilled in the tongues, and tighten the bolt down as a turnbuckle. Lock with a second lock nut. Adding a lock washer as well is a good extra precaution.

In addition to the straps, you should install substantial cleats fore and aft, at the bottom of the tank, so it can't slide.

Cushion Your Tank

To prevent chafe, tanks must never rest directly on the chocks or against hold-down straps anywhere; rather, they should be cushioned by some soft material. Tarred felt was the old standby; it is no longer acceptable. Hard Neoprene, 3/16 to 1/4 inch thick (4.5 to 6.5 mm), is the proper modern stuff (Figure 5-3). Moisture can collect under the Neoprene padding and cause corrosion.

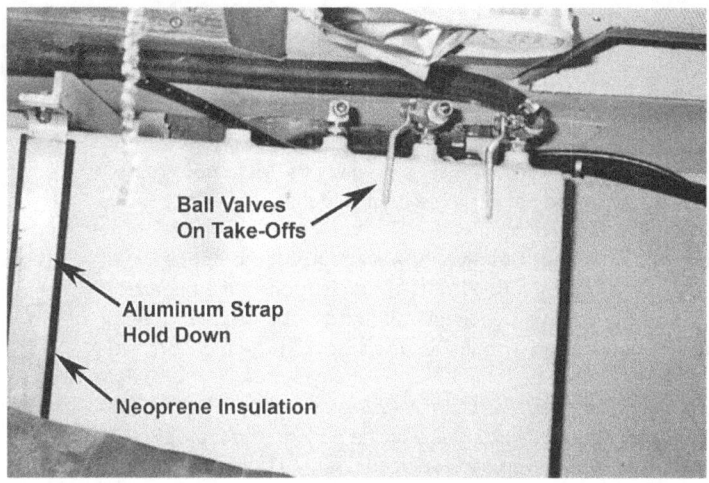

Figure 5-3. Installed tank. Note the Neoprene insulation under the hold-downs and the ball valves on the takeoffs.

To prevent this, use a good bedding compound between the tank and the Neoprene. A nonadhesive compound such as Woolsey Dolphinite or a silicone sealant is best. If you use an adhesive sealant like 3M 5200, you'll have to sand the pads off should you ever want to remove them. Whatever you do, don't use any padding that can hold water.

The following materials are *never* acceptable for use in padding or cushioning fuel tanks:

- cardboard
- carpeting
- unpainted wood
- felt (tarred or otherwise)
- canvas (tarred or otherwise)
- foams

All of these will absorb water and cause corrosion.

Other acceptable nonabsorbent materials for tank padding or cushioning are Teflon and high-density plastics (e.g., UHMWPE) that are not degraded by exposure to any petroleum fuel, water, or any standard boating cleaner or solvent.

Welded-on Tank Attachment

Metal tanks can also be secured by welding heavy bars or angles along the length of the tank corners (welded-on lugs). Again, the total weld strength must equal at least 4 times the total combined weight of the tank and its contents. The angles are drilled for through-bolts or lag bolts with UHMWPE (ultra-high-molecular-weight polyethylene) bushings to isolate the bolts from the tank material. The sheer or axial strength of the bolts (depending on how they're being loaded) has to equal at least 4 times the total combined weight of the tank and its contents (as does the bearing strength of the UHMWPE bushings and the wood or FRP structure). Of course, you need large-diameter heavy washers or backing plates under the nuts of all through-bolts where they contact wood or FRP. Tanks fastened with welded-on lugs don't require chocks or support stringers. Take care that tanks fastened that way don't make contact with any other material or object and that they have clear ventilation all around.

TANK LOCATION

Fuel tanks carry large variable loads. Proper location is critical to performance, stability, and proper boat trim. Diesel is 7.13 pounds per U.S. gallon (0.851 kg/L), and gasoline is 6.06 pounds per gallon (0.73 kg/L). A long-range motoryacht with 2,000 gallons (7,570 L) of diesel fuel will vary 6.3 tons between full and empty! A large, high-speed, twin-diesel

PART TWO: FUEL SYSTEMS

The Danger of Foam Burials

Many small production craft are built with aluminum fuel tanks installed buried in sprayed-in-place foam. This is permitted with an exact reading of CFR Yacht, but it is poor construction. You can't properly inspect such a tank for corrosion or leaks, you can't remove or replace the tank without major hull or deck surgery, and I've yet to hear of such an installation that didn't end up with at least some water accumulated between the foam and the tank surface—bad news! Over time, leaks, fires, and explosions on such craft are virtually guaranteed.

This book makes it clear that burying aluminum tanks in foam is poor practice; however, since this practice is permitted under the CFR, you will find aluminum tanks in many smaller production boats buried in foam in the bilge or in some other compartment. If you are surveying or working on a boat with such an installation, you need to do your best to inspect the tank for leaks. A pressure test may be the only option. You should also warn of potential corrosion problems in any survey or condition reports.

Note that no tank of any ferrous material may be buried in foam under any circumstances. If you can, test the tank with a magnet to determine if it is steel (though this will not identify stainless steel, which is no more acceptable than any other ferrous metal in this application). If it is, the tank must be removed and replaced.

Aluminum, plastic, and fiberglass are nonferrous. For this reason, tanks of these materials can be accepted if buried in foam (though, once again, not recommended). Note that fiberglass gasoline tanks are now suspect, as described in the sidebar on page 87.

The CFR terms the foam: "cellular plastic used to encase fuel tanks." Any such foam (cellular plastic) must not change volume by more than 5 percent or dissolve after being immersed in gasoline, diesel, or a 5 percent solution of trisodium phosphate in water, all for a 24-hour period. The foam cannot absorb more than 0.12 pound of water per square foot of cut surface (0.58 kg/sq.m of cut surface).

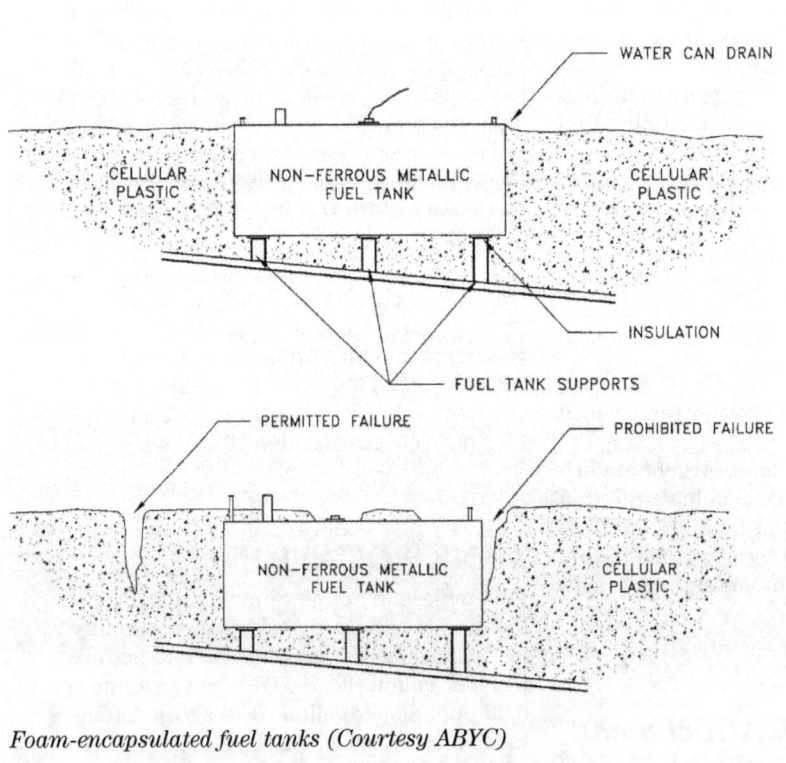

Foam-encapsulated fuel tanks (Courtesy ABYC)

> Any nonpolyurethane foam used to encase fuel tanks must have a compressive strength of 60 psi (413 kPa) at 10 percent deflection. And polyurethane foam must have a density of at least 2.0 lb/cu.ft. (32 kg/m^3).
>
> The foam must not be the sole support for a metallic tank. The metallic tank must be structurally supported independent of the surrounding foam.
>
> The summary of requirements for metallic gasoline tanks buried in foam (encapsulated in cellular plastic) is as follows:
>
> - The tank must be made from a nonferrous metal.
> - The tank must be structurally supported independent of the foam.
> - Water must drain freely from the tank's top surface.
> - The tank supports, chocks, and straps must be integral with the fuel tank or insulated from the fuel tank surface with non-moisture-absorbing material.
> - The tank must not support any other boat structure of any type.
> - The tank must be restrained from moving more than $1/4$ inch (6.3 mm) in any direction.
> - All connections, fittings, and labels must be accessible for inspection.
> - Failures in the foam or encasement material cannot occur at the joint to the surface of the fuel tank.
>
> There are still more requirements for foam used to encase fuel tanks. If you intend to build a boat with foam-encapsulated (cellular-plastic-encapsulated) foam—contrary to the recommendations of this book—you must carefully follow relevant portions of the CFR. You should use the *ABYC Compliance Guidelines* for fuel systems as a checklist for compliance.
>
> Again, though the practice is legally permitted if the preceding rules are followed, this book recommends *against* burying or encapsulating any tank in foam or cellular plastic.

cruiser might carry 1,200 gallons (4,540 L) to get adequate range—3.8 tons!

To convert lb./gal. to kg/L, multiply lb./gal. by 0.1198
To convert kg/L to lb./gal., divide kg/L by 0.1198

The optimum location for fuel tanks is over the boat's center of buoyancy. This way, there is no change in trim with varying tank levels, and the weight is kept out of the ends to reduce pitching.

On sailboats it is also important to locate tanks as low as possible to maximize sail-carrying power with full tanks, but this is not good practice for voyaging motor cruisers. Such motor cruisers are sometimes designed with huge fuel tanks built into double bottoms, but if the vessel is adequately stiff with empty tanks, then adding 6 tons or more of fuel this low down will make the vessel far too stiff—dangerously and uncomfortably so. Conversely, if the vessel relies on the weight of the fuel in the double bottom for proper stability, it will be dangerously tender when empty. The proper vertical location for big tanks on long-range cruisers is moderately high, with the tank's center of volume at or even just above the design waterline (DWL).

Planing hulls actually can benefit from tanks somewhat aft of the center of buoyancy. The goal is to have the vessel trim level when light and just a bit down by the stern when heavy. Again, the tanks should not be too low. Planing hull forms already have quick, snappy rolls. The vertical center of the tanks are, again, ideally at or just a bit above the waterline. The drawing in Figure 5-4 shows a 66-foot (20 m) express cruiser of my design that has the tanks located right over the longitudinal center of buoyancy (LCB) and at the optimum height. In this case we were able to make the tanks do double duty in blocking some engine noise from the accommodations.

Though the ideal is to have large tanks over the LCB, real-world considerations can make this impractical. This creates trim problems that must be addressed. One solution is multiple tanks and pumped distribution of fuel to maintain level trim. For long-range voyagers, another option is seawater trim-ballast tanks. Figure 5-5 shows an 82-footer (25 m) my office designed that has

PART TWO: FUEL SYSTEMS

Figure 5-4.
Kingfisher

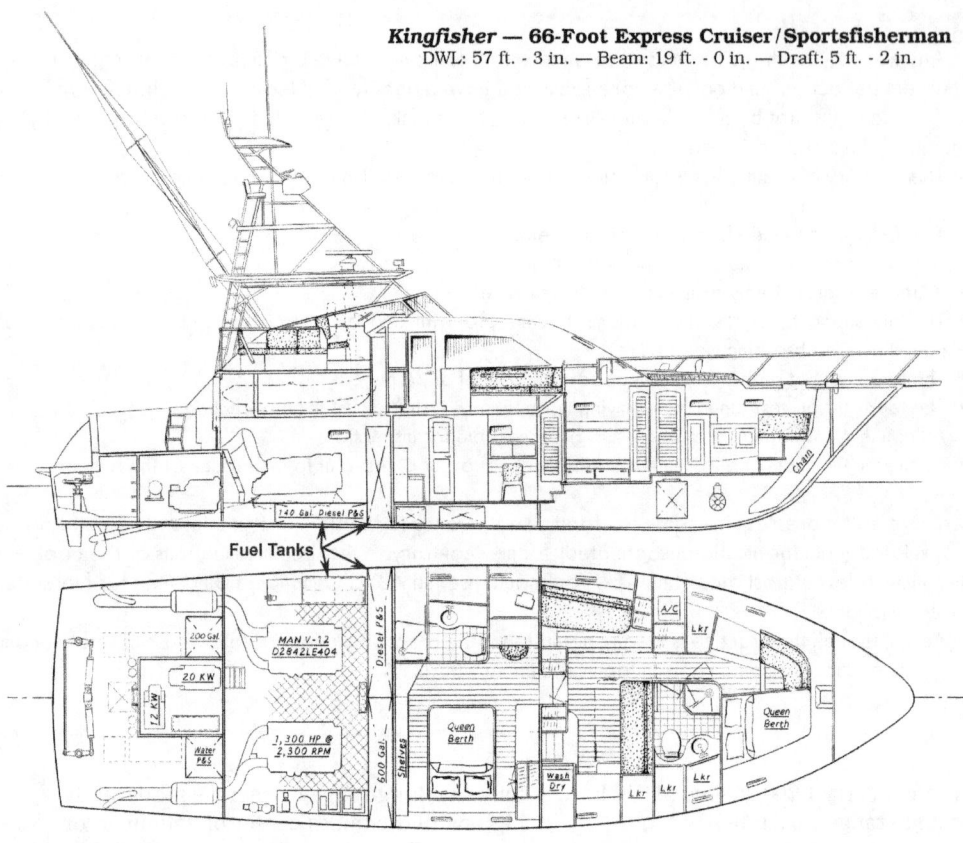

its 5,840 gallons (22,106 L) of tankage as near midships as possible and with the tank's vertical centers almost exactly at the waterline. Still, these tanks are aft of the LCB. The boat is designed to trim level with the tanks at 80 percent capacity. She's down just a bit by the stern at 100 percent. As the tanks empty below 75 percent, the aft seawater ballast tank is pumped up to compensate and maintain level trim.

Figure 5-5.
Summer Moon II

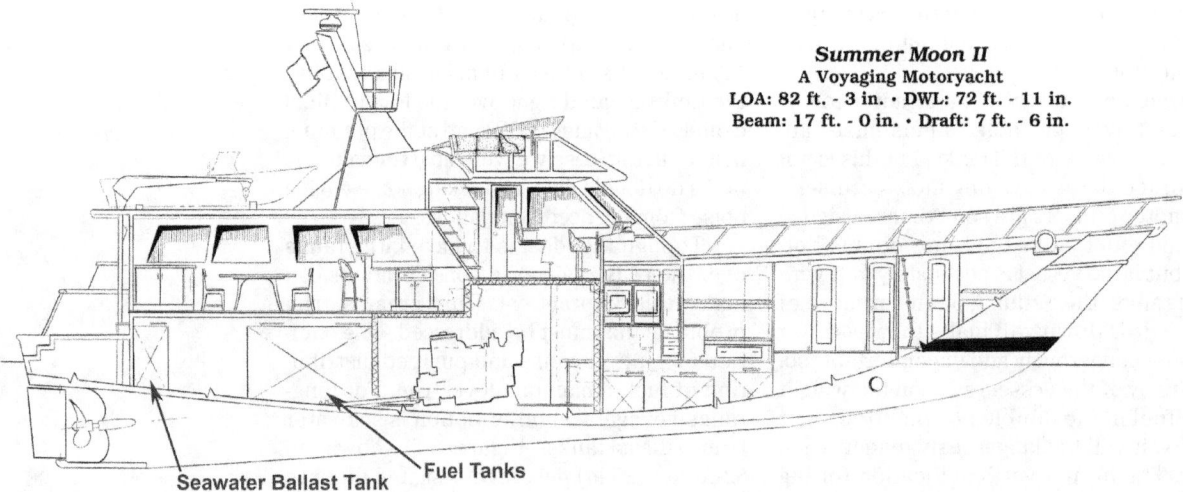

TANK OPENINGS AND PENETRATIONS

On gasoline tanks, all openings or penetrations (e.g., vents, fills, takeoffs, level gauges, cleanouts) *must* be on the top of the tank—*no exceptions*. Diesel tanks may have openings and penetrations on the tank sides, ends, or tops, but it's best to put most openings on the top to minimize chances of leaks. The exceptions are large cleanout manholes. Such cleanouts are highly recommended on tanks over 300 gallons (1,150 L) or so. For smaller craft and smaller tanks, it's difficult to justify the added expense of cleanout openings, and it's frequently impossible to locate them where they would be accessible, in any case.

Tank Drains

Diesel tanks can also fit tank drains at the lowest point of the tank. These are a good idea for cleaning convenience, but it's frequently not worth the effort, as access to these drains is usually very restricted in the boat. If you do fit tank drains, make sure that—in addition to the drain valve—there is a screw cap closure at the very end of the drainpipe. This way, even accidentally opening the drain valve won't empty the tank into the bilge. It also becomes possible to fit a screw-on hose fitting to pump out directly into a storage tank or barrel, which makes these drains much more practical.

Vent-a-Tank

Tank vents allow air to exit the tank so you can add liquid (which is our goal, after all). Vents (termed *breathers* in Europe) also protect against developing excessive pressure in the tank. It is best to recommend not topping off tanks 100 percent. On a hot summer day, the temperature in the underground storage tank can be 65°F (18°C), whereas the temperature in the engine compartment may be over 100°F (38°C). If the tank is topped off with cool fuel, the fuel can heat up and expand enough to spill 2 or 3 gallons (7 to 11 L) overboard through the vent. Yes, another illegal oil spill.

ABYC requires that the vent line should be at least 25 percent of the cross-section area of the fill pipe. For standard $1\frac{1}{4}$-inch (DN 32 mm) ID fills, this calls for a minimum of $9/16$-inch-diameter (15 mm) hose to match a $7/16$-inch-diameter (DN 11 mm) vent fitting. This is a requirement that I think could use some revision. Modern fuel docks pump at such a tremendous rate that these small vents are often inadequate. Further—though they are frequently configured in just this way—the vent opening on the tank shouldn't be near the fill. Instead, it should be at the opposite end of the tank. On one of my designs, a relatively long, narrow tank was fitted with the standard minimum vent and fill sizes previously specified and with the vent near the fill. The result was that even though we could feel air whooshing out of the vent, the pressure sensor on the fill nozzle would shut it off regularly. Then a moment later, a large bubble of air would burst out the fill pipe, spewing fuel over the deck. Installing a second vent near the fill helped, but it didn't fully eliminate the problem. Adding a vent at the tank end away from the fill was the cure.

Unfortunately, it's hard to find off-the-shelf vent fittings larger than $5/8$-inch diameter (18 mm). One solution is to install a $3/4$-inch NPT (DN 20 mm) pipe fitting in the tank (0.82-in. or 20.8 mm ID±) with a Y tee forking up to two standard $5/8$-inch (DN 18 mm) vents. On large or long tanks, you would install one of these at each end, running to $5/8$-inch (DN 18 mm) vent fittings—four vent fittings total for each tank.

CFR Commercial has a number of vent-size variables, but basically it requires a minimum vent cross-section area equal to $3/4$-inch (20 mm) OD tube with a 0.035-inch wall (20 gauge or 0.889 mm). This is 0.36 sq. in. (232 mm^2). The $3/4$-inch NPT (DN 20 mm) pipe fitting Y'ed to two $5/8$-inch (DN 18 mm) vent fittings meets this requirement.

Vent-Run Considerations

Fuel tanks must never vent into the hull; they must vent overboard as shown in Figures 4-17 and 5-1. Any other arrangement will dump vapors and spill into the bilge—a sure harbinger of a real blast! To keep water out, the vent should be as high as possible and equipped with the 4-inch (100 mm) or somewhat higher gooseneck or riser shown. Vent openings must be at least 15 inches (38 cm) away from

PART TWO: FUEL SYSTEMS

> ## New EPA Gasoline Vent Filter Requirements Proposed
>
> As of February 2008, the Environmental Protection Agency (EPA) is planning new regulations for gasoline fuel systems on boats. The anticipated changes are intended to reduce vapor escaping from the tank through the vent and also to reduce fuel spills. The most prominent feature of the new requirements will be a carbon-filled canister on the fuel vent line between the tank and the vent opening. A secondary feature is required to keep liquid gasoline overflow from entering this carbon-filled canister. This additional feature is a check valve to be installed in the vent line, as close to the tank as possible. The check valve will shut flow immediately if it senses liquid fuel, but will remain open for air and vapor. Other new features may include better pressure-sensor shutoff response on the fuel fill nozzle to further reduce spills. This may be integrated with the configurations of the check valve and fill pipe.
>
> Current plans are to phase in the carbon canister and its related check valve on gasoline vent lines for engines of 500 hp (373 kW) or higher starting in 2009, and for all gasoline engines as of 2010. Go to www.epa.gov for information on the latest developments. These changes will apply only to gasoline, not to diesel.

any opening into the hull. Fuel-tank vents also require a backfire flame mesh with 30 wires per inch (1.18 wires per mm) each way. This prevents flames from spreading down into the vent pipe, which seems prudent. CFR Yacht and ABYC require that the mesh be "cleanable." In practice, this means that the mesh or the vent unit with the mesh has to be removable. Presumably, if you can remove it, you can clean it.

Best practice is that each tank have a dedicated vent line. Essentially, all vents must rise continuously from the tank. There can be no sags or dips, which hold fluid or debris, in any vent line. If unavoidable, short horizontal runs (no more than 18 inches (45 cm) are acceptable, but such horizontal runs increase the chance of a potential clog in the vent line. As long as the vent run rises continuously, you can combine vents from different tanks into one line. You can do this only if the total cross-sectional area after joining is greater than the combined cross-sectional area of the individual lines. Such large-diameter vent lines won't fit off-the-shelf vent fittings.

Don't share vent lines with tanks containing other liquids, even if the shared cross-section area is adequate. For instance, if you shared a vent line from a diesel and a freshwater tank, the bad taste in the fresh water from migrating fuel-oil gases would be rather unpleasant. Microbes from black and gray water can exacerbate algae growth and contamination in fuel tanks.

Vents Under Pressure

Large vessels may be fueled under pressure rather than from a simple fuel-pump nozzle. This places still-higher demands on the vent lines. Clearly, if the vent lines were too small, internal tank pressure could build to a bursting point. For tanks filled under pressure, the vent lines must be the same diameter as the fill pipe or larger. My practice has been to install the two standard 3/4-inch (20 mm) vent lines described previously *plus* an additional vent line having the same ID as the fill or slightly larger.

Vent Spill Prevention

Several manufacturers offer inexpensive units to reduce fuel spills through the vent. Some devices whistle continuously as the tank is filled, changing pitch noticeably as it nears capacity. This warns you to ease back on the nozzle handle and top off the last few gallons slowly. Racor's Lifeguard fuel/air separator (Figure 5-6) traps small overflows in an enclosed plastic globe and routes them back to the tank (Figure 5-7). Larger overflows cause a ball-type check valve to seal the vent closed. If you wrap a rag around the fill nozzle, sealing it in the fill-pipe opening, the pressure buildup caused by the check valve closing shuts off the fill nozzle when the tank is full. Should something go wrong and the fill nozzle does not shut off, the check valve will open again as the pressure further increases, eliminating any chance of rupturing the tank.

Another option is to install a small, custom, overflow collection tank in the vent line (Figure 5-8). For space reasons, this may only be practical on larger vessels. Usually about 2 gallons (7.57 L) in capacity, the vent enters the bottom of the collection tank to one side. A horizontal baffle is built into the tank a quarter of the way above the bottom, but

Chapter 5: Fuel Tanks and Fittings

Figure 5-6. Fuel/air separators (Courtesy Racor)

sloping down about 5 degrees to drain. An opening about 3 square inches (20 sq cm) is in the baffle on the side away from the vent inlet. The vent line then exits the top of the tank—directly above the vent entry point below but shielded by the baffle—and runs overboard as usual. The baffle collects and deflects bubbles and foam. The tank can accept both foam and bubble overflow, as well as expansion overflow, simply returning the excess by gravity to the main tank.

Fill 'er Up

Standard fill pipes are nominal 1½-inch (DN 40 mm) pipe, with an ID of about 1½ inches (38 mm). On large yachts and commercial vessels, use 2-inch (DN 50 mm) pipe. The fill pipe should project down to within 1 inch (25 mm) of the tank bottom for 1½-inch (DN 40 mm) pipe and to within 1¼ inches (DN 32 mm) for 2-inch (DN 50 mm) pipe—no closer and not much higher. Effectively, this seals the vapors in the fill pipe from the vapors in the tank (as long as there's an inch or more of fuel in the bottom). With gasoline fuel, should a spark ignite the fill pipe vapors, the flame can't ignite the whole tank. You get, hopefully, no more than an impressive but relatively harmless bang. Extending the fill to

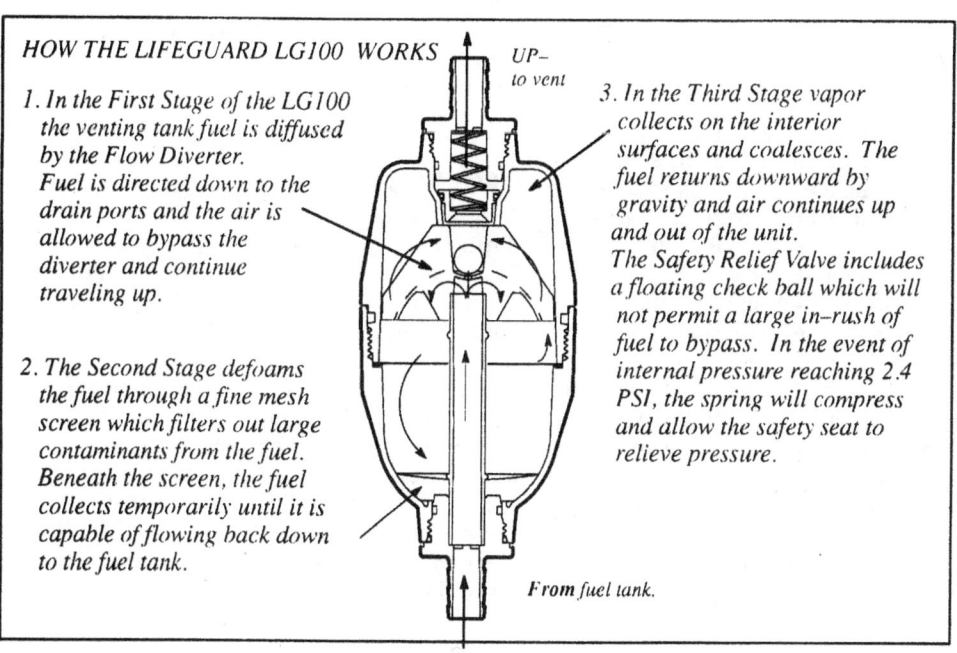

Figure 5-7. Cutaway view of a Lifeguard fuel/air separator (Courtesy Racor)

75

PART TWO: FUEL SYSTEMS

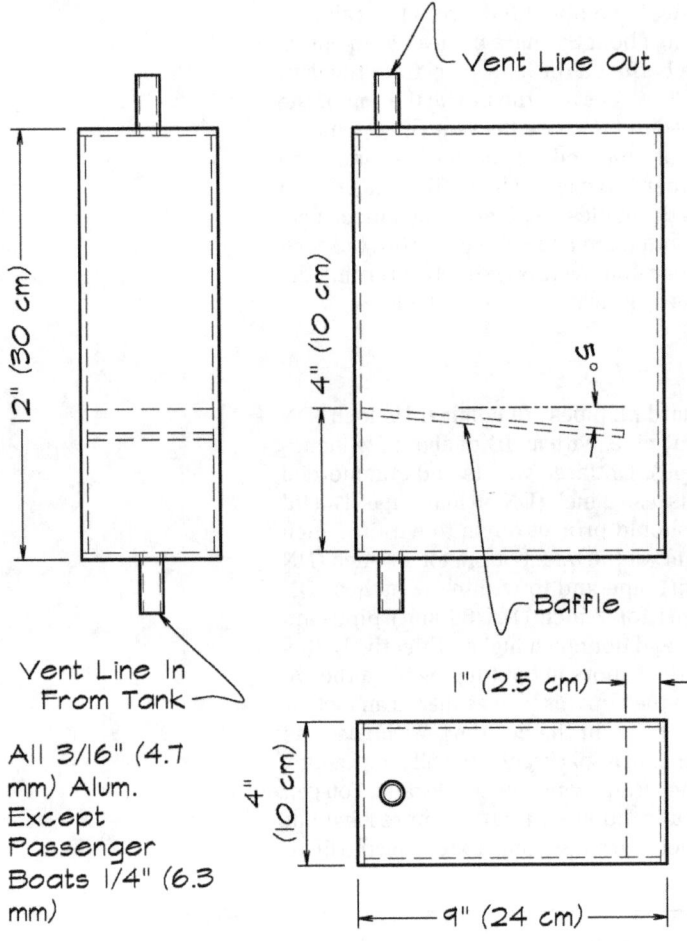

Figure 5-8. Vent collection tank (dimensions can be modified)

If you're installing hose from the deck-fill fitting to the tank, it's a good idea to have about 8 inches (200 mm) of pipe directly under the fill. This way, years of repeatedly jabbing the fill nozzle into the fill won't abrade the hose, yet another potential source of leaks over time.

Antipollution laws are a real poser with regard to minor fuel leaks. These laws forbid *any* oil or fuel spills into the water, while at the same time, safety regulations forbid any spills into the boat. (I wonder where they expect spills to go?) Obviously, some small spills and drips are unavoidable, and you can't have them run into the boat or you would have a very serious fire hazard. The only solution for the moment is to make certain that those few, unavoidable small spills do go overboard and hope that the policing agencies are reasonable. So far, I know of no cases of the Coast Guard or harbor police ticketing small, unintentional spills from boats, though it appears they could do so.

The Vetus Splash-Stop

Vetus offers its Splash-Stop unit (Figures 5-10 and 5-11), which is basically a vent collection tank combined into the fill-cap assembly. This gizmo addresses both the expansion and fill spill problems noted earlier, and it is available for both 1½-inch and 2-inch (40 and 50 mm) hose.

Seacurefill

Another approach to controlling spillage during fueling is Seacurefill (Figure 5-12). This unit is a vent assembly with a built-in fitting for a clear hose with a quick-connect device to the fill. During fueling, the vent and the fill are opened. The clear plastic hose is fastened into the vent fitting and led in a U down into the fill pipe next to the fill nozzle. When the tank tops off, the nozzle's pressure switch clicks off, and the clear hose fills with overflow that's directed back down into the tank. This is a clear warning of a full tank, and there are no spills.

near the tank bottom, once again, isn't necessary for a diesel tank, but it costs little and helps isolate the fuel in the tank and reduce foaming—both well worth doing. Fills extending this far down into the tank must be supported structurally at their lower end to prevent stress cracks from vibration.

Another common source of leaks, by the way, is at the joint between the fill cap flange and the deck. Vibration and weathering can destroy the sealant or bedding compound, allowing spills at fuel-up to find their way below. Check the boat carefully. You should also make sure that spills can run or drip overboard easily and absolutely cannot get down into the boat. Fills must be at least 15 inches (38 cm) away from any opening into the hull.

Chapter 5: Fuel Tanks and Fittings

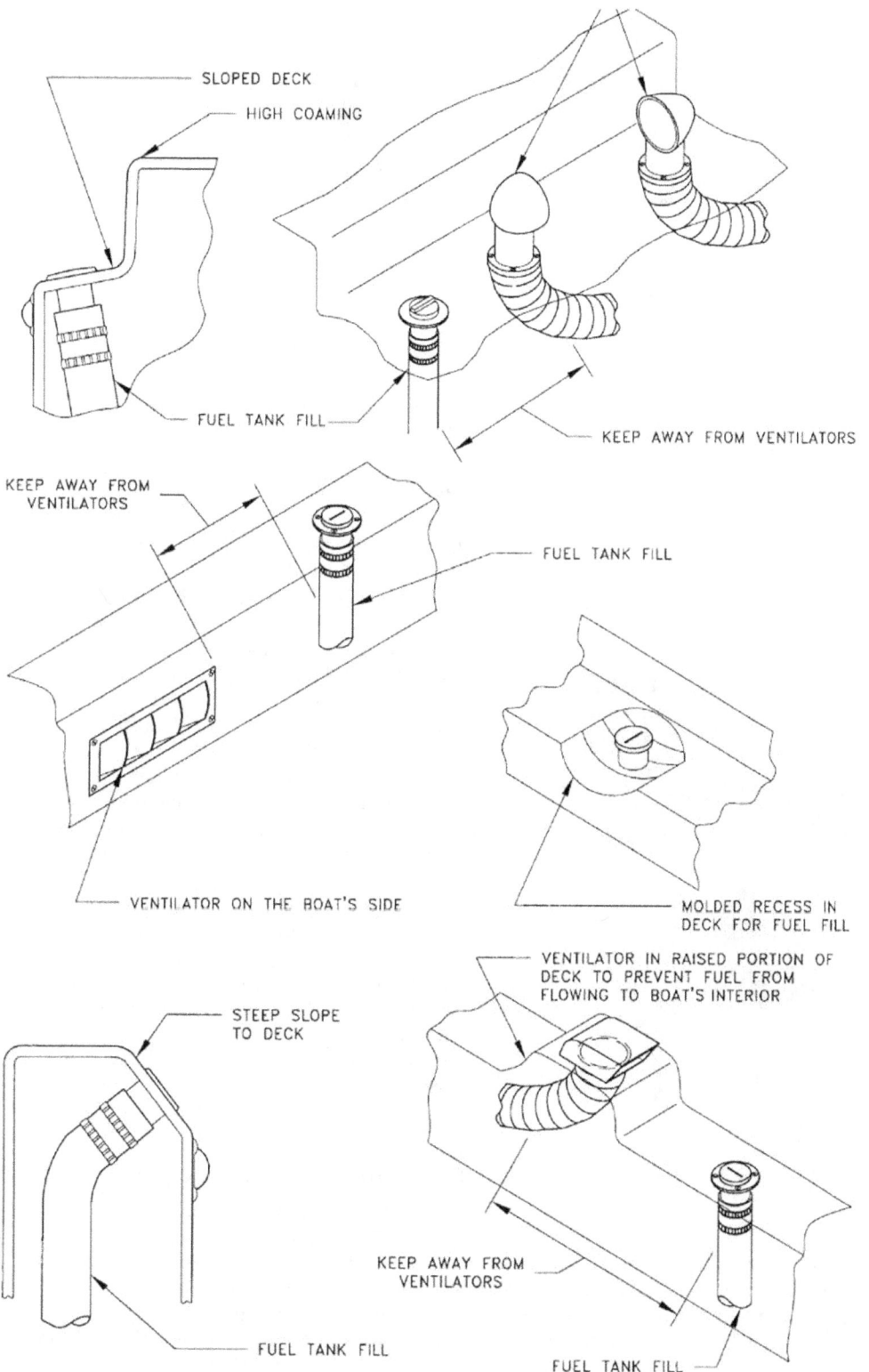

Figure 5-9. ABYC's minimum clearance between hull-compartment ventilators and fuel tank fills is 15 inches (38 cm). (See also Chapter 4 sidebar "Principal Differences Between ISO 10088 and ABYC Standards.") (Courtesy ABYC)

PART TWO: FUEL SYSTEMS

Figure 5-10. Splash-Stop installation (Courtesy Vetus)

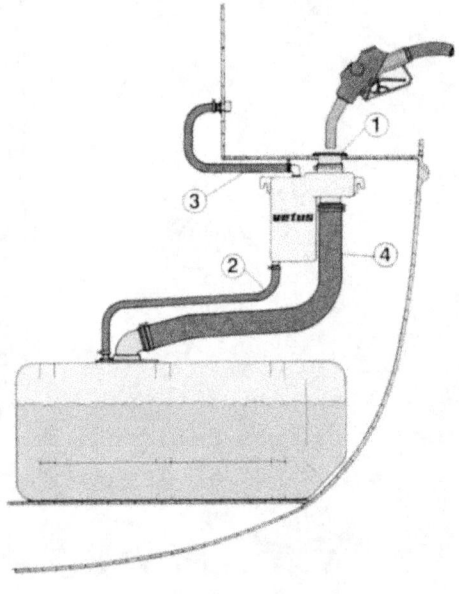

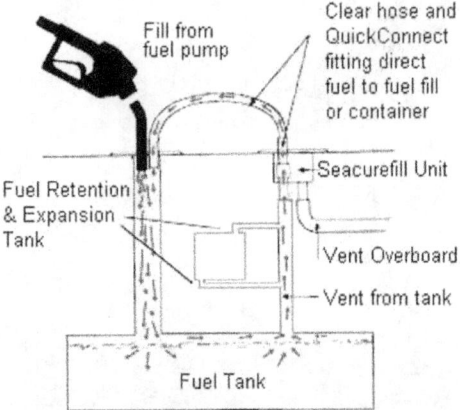

Figure 5-12. Seacurefill (Courtesy Seacurefill)

Taking Off

Of course, the takeoff pipe must reach well down into the tank if it's going to get all the fuel out. Again, 1 inch (25 mm) from the bottom is ideal. At this height the boat can draw off almost all the fuel, but it won't suck up the sludge and gunk swirling around the bottom of every tank. (The takeoff pipe must be structurally supported at the lower end to prevent stress cracks from vibration.) Shutoff valves (also termed "fuel-stop valves") must be fitted at each takeoff pipe right at the tank.

Additionally, if the fuel piping runs more than 12 feet (3.65 m) from tank to engine, another shutoff valve should be fitted near the connection to the engine or gen set.

NOTE: Some manufacturers install a filter at the bottom end of the takeoff pipe inside the tank. This is not good practice; if this filter clogs or corrodes, you can't get at it without draining the tank and withdrawing the takeoff pipe. The filters should be installed outside the tanks as described earlier. If you have such an installation, you should have the filter on the takeoff inside the tank removed.

Keeping Your Tanks Dry

Metal nonintegral tanks should have a 1- to 2-inch (25 to 50 mm) gap between the boat's hull and the tanks. This permits water to drain off and encourages the ventilation needed to prevent corrosion. Similarly, the tops of the tanks should be sloped or slightly rounded so water won't collect and sit on the top.

Figure 5-11. Splash-Stop (Courtesy Vetus)

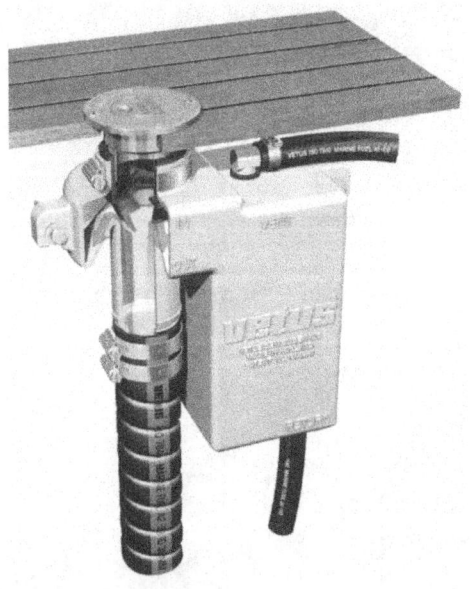

The pump-fill nozzle is then removed. The clear plastic hose is held vertically to drain back down into the tank and then is disconnected and stowed. Both the fill and Seacurefill vent caps are closed.

Chapter 5: Fuel Tanks and Fittings

CFR Yacht Test for Fuel-Fill Spill Compliance

Take care that the natural flow of any spilled or dripping fuel cannot run back into the boat through any path. Think through the locations carefully. If you are inspecting or surveying a boat and it appears that fuel spills potentially could enter the boat, be sure to note this as a problem that needs immediate correction.

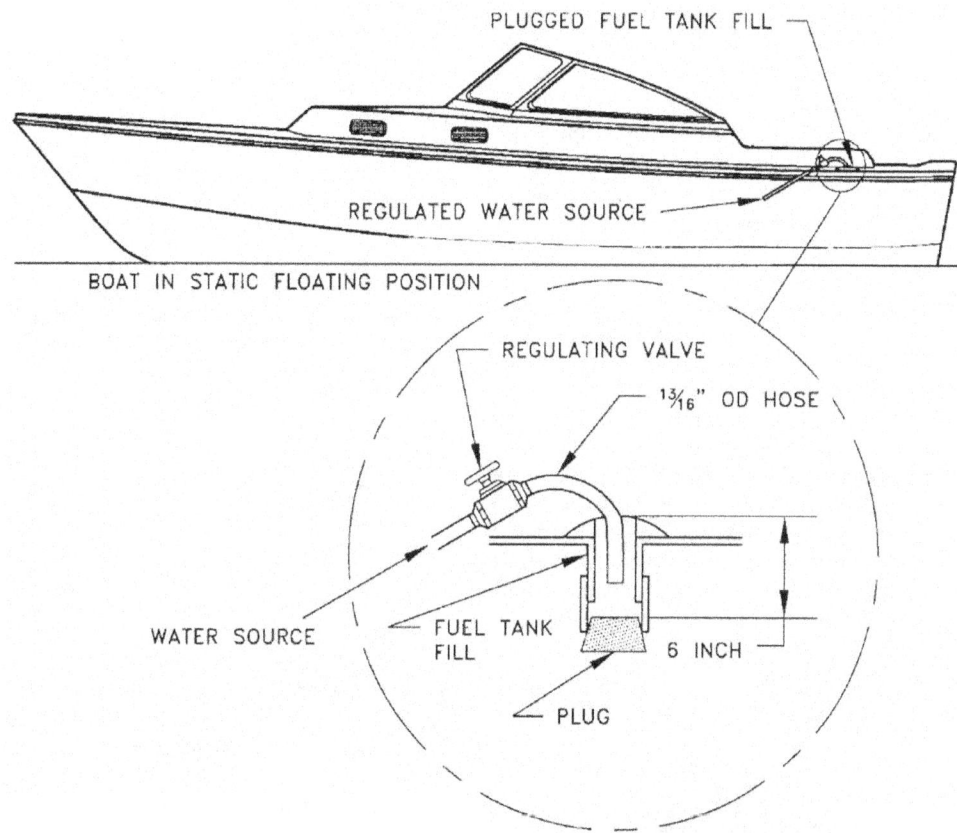

Fuel-fill spill test (Courtesy ABYC)

The required test under the CFR for fuel-fill spill compliance for gasoline boats is as follows (using water):

- Ensure the boat is in its normal static floating position.
- Plug the fuel-tank fill line at a distance at least 6 inches (152 mm) below the tank fill opening.
- Insert a 13/16-inch (20 mm) OD hose into the fill fitting.
- Discharge through the hose at the rate of 5 gpm (53.3 oz. in 5 sec.) or 19 L/min (0.147 L in 5 sec.).
- Fill until the pipe overflows. Time the overflowing water for 5 seconds, and turn off the flow.
- Inspect to determine if any of the overflowing water has made its way into the boat. No water is permitted at all. Any water entering the boat from this test indicates noncompliance and must be corrected. Overflow entering a self-bailing cockpit is considered entering the boat and does not comply.

NOTE: Though passing the preceding test is *required* for gasoline boats, it is strongly recommended for diesel vessels as well.

It's Baffling

CFR Yacht and ABYC do not set a fixed requirement for baffles on pleasure-craft tanks, and CFR Yacht doesn't cover diesel tanks. Nevertheless, baffles are essential in all tanks larger than a few gallons for proper stability and to reduce noise. CFR Commercial requires that all nonintegral tanks must be built with internal baffles spaced no more than 30 inches (76 cm), both athwartships and fore and aft. My strong recommendation is that tanks for yachts follow this 30-inch (76 cm) spacing in most instances. (Without proper baffles, tanks would fail the slosh and pressure-impulse tests, in any case.)

Still, 30 inches (76 cm) is a somewhat smaller distance than required to prevent excessive sloshing on larger craft. Such vessels can have their baffles spaced farther apart. A reasonable rule is to space baffles no more than 15 percent of beam, but never more than 44 inches (111 cm) apart. When using spacing greater than 30 inches (76 cm), the tank walls must be strengthened with stiffeners between the baffles, as structural calculations require. For metal tanks, these are standard angles or tees welded on as done on structural bulkheads. Tank strength must be calculated to meet the required head (pressure) over the wider panels with the larger distances between baffles, but including the added stiffeners. Note that CFR Commercial does not set requirements for baffles on integral tanks, only on nonintegral tanks.

Baffles must be fitted with large limber openings at all top and bottom corners to permit adequate fuel and air flow (Figure 5-13). The total opening area can't be more than 30 percent of the baffle—roughly 18 percent is a good average. On integral tanks, I try to center any cleanout access ports over a baffle with the baffle itself cut back in a half circle directly underneath. This way a single cleanout panel gives access to two or four baffle spaces. You can see these cutouts in the baffles in Figure 5-13. On nonintegral metal tanks, the baffles should be welded every 2½ inches (63 mm) with the weld one size smaller than the thinnest plate being welded to. Rivets can be used on internal baffle connections, but use only welds when connecting to the tank's walls.

You can't see inside your tank (unless it's large and fitted with cleanout ports), but it pays to be nosy and learn about the construction. Ask the manufacturer how they build and test their tanks. Though most tank fabricators are reliable and conscientious, I've occasionally seen bizarre things. Once, for instance, I was retained to "fix" a 54-foot (16.4 m) production diesel motor cruiser with a single 15-foot-long (4.6 m), 500-gallon (1,892 L) tank equipped with just two baffles! The result was some odd banging noises, some very peculiar trim problems, and a strange difficulty getting up on plane—but only some of the time! No one had thought to question the tank construction previously.

DON'T SHARE WALLS Speaking of baffles, it is tempting—to save space and simplify construction—to have integral water tanks and fuel tanks share a wall. This is not permissible. Any slight pinhole leak in the shared wall will contaminate both. Black- and graywater tanks are no exception. It is acceptable to have two fuel tanks (of the same fuel type) share a wall—basically a baffle with no openings in it. This is sometimes a convenient way to create a day tank inside a larger tank.

Round the Corner

Best practice for nonintegral sheet-metal tanks with walls 0.190 inch thick or less is not to weld them together at the corners. Corner

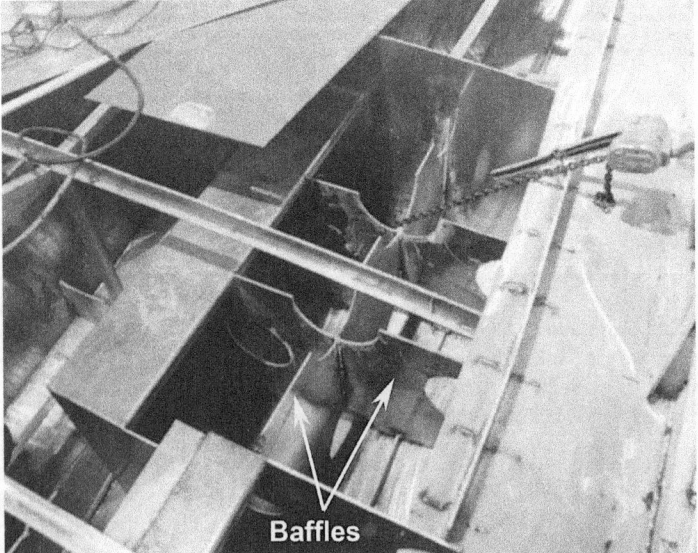

Figure 5-13. Baffles in aluminum tank

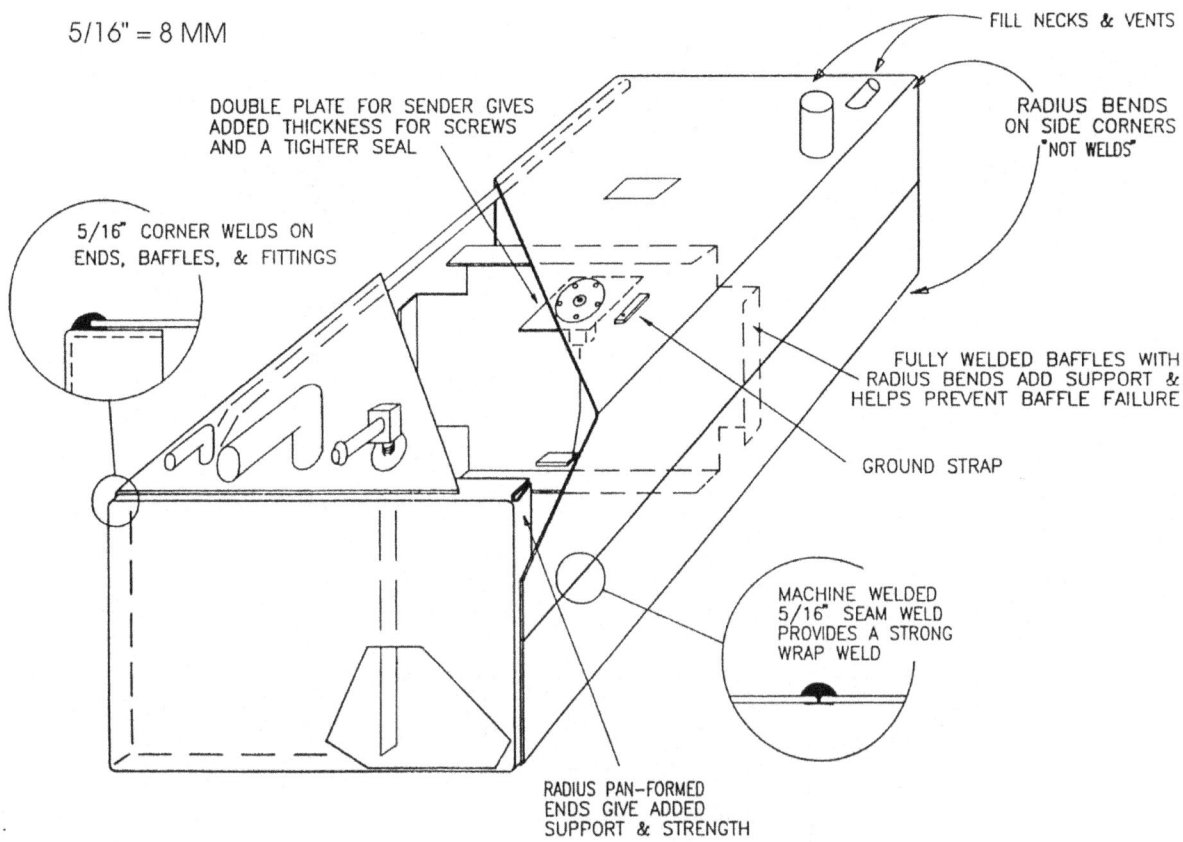

Figure 5-14. Radius corner tank construction

welds are subject to damage and corrosion. (One-quarter inch and thicker—the next standard size up after 0.190 inch, 4.82 mm—can't be bent to small radii and is thick enough to weld more effectively.) Sheet-metal tank walls should be wrapped around corners in a radius, with longitudinal butt-weld seams well away from the corners (Figure 5-14). On smaller, regularly shaped tanks, a single sheet can be wrapped all around and closed with just one longitudinal weld. Larger tanks or tanks with complex shapes must be made up of several wall sections requiring more than one seam. The tank's ends should be formed of flat plate or sheet with the edges bent inward to form a flange all around its perimeter. These bends should be radiused, and the tank walls should be welded to the flanges—not on the corners, but approximately $3/16$ inch (4.7 mm) in from the edge.

This construction is termed *lapped-corner construction* (sometimes *flanged-corner construction*). Though it is superior for metal tanks of small to medium size (it can't be used on plate over $3/16$ inch [4.7 mm] thick, because the thick plates won't take the bend), it is not acceptable under the CFR for commercial vessels. The reason for this is unclear. It may stem from the incorrect practice of fabricating with lapped *external* corners that could trap water (particularly on the top of the tank) leading to corrosion. Regardless, this is the regulation, and lapped-corner construction cannot be used on Coast Guard–inspected passenger vessels.

Tank Labels

Locating a tank's manufacturer shouldn't be difficult. The CFR and ABYC require that all tanks be labeled (Figure 5-15) with the

- manufacturer's name and address
- date of manufacture

Figure 5-15. Tank label

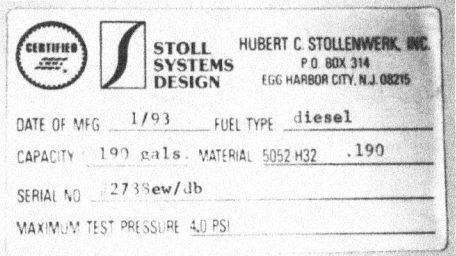

- intended fuel type
- capacity
- tank material and thickness
- serial number
- maximum test pressure

In addition, gasoline tanks must also contain the note

"This tank has been tested under 33 CFR 183.510(a)"

If the tank has been tested under 33 CFR 183.584 at less than 25g vertical accelerations, the statement that follows must be on the label:

"This tank must be installed aft of the boat's half length"

Metal gasoline tanks should be purchased from a qualified tank manufacturer with the facilities to conduct the full range of required tests.

All the lettering on a fuel tank label must be at least 1/16 inch (1.6 mm) high and clearly contrast with the background color of the label, or be clearly embossed on the label. Stamping, engraving, molding, and etching are all acceptable methods of lettering on the labels, as long as the result is clearly readable.

The label itself must be resistant to fading, corrosion, or damage by water, petroleum products, sunlight, or heat and cold. It cannot lose legibility over years of routine use, and it must be resistant to tampering or modification or show clear signs that it has been altered if tampered with.

TANKS UNDER PRESSURE

Several years back, I had a launching delayed by two weeks. The vessel seemed ready in all respects when the builder filled the tank only to find a steady leak—on the tank's bottom, of course. The only out was to remove the soft patch. (Happily—if it can be called that—I'd insisted one be built in, or we'd have had to chainsaw the deck.) Then we pulled the tank and returned it to the fabricator. That tank's maker claimed he'd run a pressure test, but somehow I doubt it.

Tank Pressure Ratings

ABYC and CFR Yacht both require that all fuel tanks in pleasure craft be able to withstand 3 psi (20.7 kPa) of pressure. This is substantially less than the CFR Commercial requirement of 5 psi (34.5 kPa). ABYC and CFR Yacht, however, also require additional tests such as slosh tests and pressure impulse tests for gasoline. These are not really practical for any but large commercial tank fabricators. Accordingly, on my custom designs, I always specify that the tanks be built to 5 psi (34.5 kPa) commercial or T-boat standards. This is the most cost-effective way to come close to ensuring that a custom or short-run production tank would meet the additional slosh and pressure impulse tests. Be careful in testing tanks, however. If you test a 3 psi (20.7 kPa) tank to 5 psi (34.5 kPa), you may well burst it! Check the tank label before running any pressure test, and if in doubt, test only to 3 psi (20.7 kPa), as no fuel tank on any boat should be accepted if it can't withstand this pressure.

When you're installing a new tank, it pays to perform the simple minimum pressure test required by the CFR—it's not difficult. A shop air compressor, standard hose fittings, and pressure gauge will do the job. Alternatively, attach a vertical standpipe to the fill opening (a watertight screw-in fit). Seal tight all other openings in the tank, and fill the tank and pipe with water to the top of the standpipe. A pipe 7 feet (213 cm) high gives 3 psi (20.7 kPa), and 11 feet, 6 inches (350 cm) gives 5 psi (34.5 kPa) of hydrostatic head. Leave everything to sit for 6 hours. The tank shouldn't leak a drop anywhere. If my builder had done this before installation, he would have saved himself a lot of work later on.

On larger vessels, an 11-foot, 6-inch (350 cm) standpipe might not be tall enough. The design pressure should be 1.5 times the pressure from the deepest drop from the highest vent opening. A 12-foot (366 cm) vent height would call for 12 ft. × 0.43 psi/ft. × 1.5 = 7.74 psi, or 3.66 m × 9.7 kPa/m × 1.5 = 53 kPa pressure. (One foot of standpipe height equals 0.43 psi of tank pressure—fresh water. One meter standpipe height equals 9.7 kPa of tank pressure—fresh water.)

Pressure Testing of the Entire Fuel System

The entire fuel system should be pressure tested to the same pressure as the tanks; however, the fuel tanks should be pressure tested separately first.

LEVEL GAUGING

In the "good ol' days," you would check the tank level by sliding a sounding stick down the fill pipe or down a dedicated sounding pipe. Withdrawing the sounding stick, you would read the level (like a car oil dipstick), though this isn't easy to do at night in a storm. These days, it's not unusual for tanks to be located where a direct fill run for a sounding rod is impossible. Still—if it'll fit—the sounding stick is *the* bulletproof backup for modern tank gauges, despite its inconvenience for regular use. For obvious reasons, you're required to have a level indicator, and any of the standard tank gauges will work if properly installed. (The sounding stick alone meets legal requirements.) Glass or plastic-tube sight gauges are too easily broken—they would cause a major spill. I don't recommend these in place of a proper marine tank level indicator system. Such sight gauges are illegal for gasoline in any case.

FloScan

In addition to level gauges, I like to install FloScan fuel-flow meters to provide the crew with accurate real-time information on fuel consumption. On twin-engine vessels—when possible—I prefer to install a single FloScan sender in the lines feeding and returning from both engines but separate from the line feeding the generator(s). This way, it's easy to get engine mile-per-gallon numbers. The generator consumption can be estimated adequately and added, or a separate FloScan can be installed on the generator feed and return lines. Be sure to install a FloScan meter that reads in the range of flow rate of your engine (or engines). Multiply total horsepower by 0.054 for gph, or multiply kilowatts by 0.274 for liters per hour. Twin 350 hp (261 kW) engines—monitored by a single FloScan—would burn about 37.8 gallons per hour (143 L/hr.) combined, at max. (For gasoline: gal./hr. = 0.10 × hp, or L/hr. = 0.508 × kW.)

TANK MATERIALS

Table 5-2 lists proper tank materials and thicknesses for nonintegral tanks with baffles spaced no more than 30 inches (76 cm). Tinned copper was the old standard for gasoline, but as the tanks aged, the tin reacted with the gas, creating a gum that fouled the carburetor. (There are fewer carburetor engines around every day, but I imagine the effect would be even worse on injectors.) Similarly, diesel tanks must never be galvanized inside. The zinc reacts with the fuel oil, ruining the diesel. Copper also reacts with the sulfur in diesel and can be eaten away. Plain old-fashioned marine aluminum, iron, or steel is the answer (Monel is the ultimate); however, iron and steel aren't acceptable for gas unless hot-dipped galvanized inside and out. A long time ago, terneplate steel (sheet iron or steel coated with an alloy of about 4 parts lead to 1 part tin) was a common inexpensive tank material. It isn't acceptable for any fuel tank, however. You'll often come across references to "black iron" tanks. I don't know where this term came from. Black iron tanks are simply ordinary mild steel.

Stainless steel tanks must be of only 316L or 317L ("L" for low carbon) and welded with the TIG process, per ABYC. An even better alloy (not ABYC approved) is 321 stainless (see sidebar). ABYC has now approved stainless steel for diesel, but *not* for gasoline fuel tanks. The one exception is that ABYC does permit stainless gasoline tanks if they are less than 20 gallons (75 L), are of cylindrical construction, and have domed ends. I personally can't see any reason to use such small stainless gas tanks. Polyethylene tanks are available in many shapes in this size range and are much superior for this application.

Except for integral tanks, no part of any fuel tank may be used for structural support or hull reinforcement.

TABLE 5-2. FUEL TANK MATERIALS AND THICKNESSES

Material	Specification	Capacity Gallons	Capacity Liters	Thickness Millimeters	Thickness Inches	Gauge
Nickel-Copper (Monel)	ASTM-B127 Class A	1–30	1–112	0.78	0.0310	22 U.S. std.
		30–80	112–300	0.94	0.0370	20 U.S. std.
		80–200	300–750	1.27	0.0500	18 U.S. std.
		200–400	750–1,500	1.57	0.0620	16 U.S. std.
Copper-Nickel	ASTM-B122	1–80	1–300	1.14	0.0450	17 AWG
		200–400	750–1,500	1.83	0.0720	13 AWG
Copper	ASTM-B152 Type E.T.P.	1–80	1–300	1.45	0.0570	15 AWG
		80–150	300–560	2.03	0.0800	12 AWG
Copper-Silicon	ASTM-B97 Type AB&G	1–80	1–300	1.27	0.0500	16 AWG
		80–200	300–750	1.62	0.0640	14 AWG
		200–400	750–1,500			
Sheet Steel	ASTM-A653/ A653M-07	1–80	1–300	1.89	0.0747	14 MSG*
Stainless Steel		80–200	300–750	2.66	0.1046	12 MSG*
Aluminized Steel	ASTM-463	1–80	1–300	1.89	0.0747	14 MSG*
		80–200	300–750	2.66	0.1046	12 MSG*
Aluminum	Alloy: 5052, 5053, or 5086	1–80	1–300	2.29	0.0900	
		50–80	190–300	2.54	0.1000	
		80–150	300–560	3.17	0.1250	
		150–300	560–1,100	4.83	0.1900	
		300–500	1,100–1,900	6.35	0.2500	

*MSG = Manufacturer's standard gauge for sheet steels.
NOTE: The thicknesses above occasionally need to be increased to achieve proper structural strength.

Stainless Steel Tanks

Stainless steel has been used successfully for fuel tanks, but it was not recommended by ABYC for many years. Dr. Harry Lipsitt, a professor of materials science, explains that it's because of corrosion at the welds, or "weld decay." Most common marine-grade stainless steels, 304 or 18-8 (containing 0.08 percent carbon), contain both chromium and carbon. When the metal is heated to over 1,000°F (538°C) for welding, the carbon is driven away and regions of chromium carbide form, with chromium-depleted areas immediately adjacent. These two "alloys" form a galvanic couple and can cause serious corrosion quickly.

The problem can be controlled by using a stainless steel with a strong carbide-forming material: titanium. This is available as type 321 stainless. Another alternative is to use a low-carbon alloy, with less than 0.03 percent carbon content. Type 316L or 317L meets this requirement. ABYC has recently accepted 316L and 317L tanks (for diesel) if welding is done according to very rigid specifications (see ABYC H-33).

Figure 5-16. Painted aluminum wing tanks

CFR Commercial requires that metal diesel tanks be made only of nickel-copper, steel or iron, aluminum, or fiberglass. Stainless is not accepted. Further, CFR Commercial insists that all aluminum tanks—even tanks of just 1 or 2 gallons (3 or 4 L) be a minimum 1/4 inch (6.35 mm) thick. This is considerable overkill for such small tanks, in my opinion; however, if you're building a crewed-charter or passenger vessel, you must comply.

Except for integral tanks, tanks cannot be used as part of the structure. You cannot mount or attach machinery to tanks.

Aluminum Tank Preservation

Marine aluminum tanks are probably the most common fuel tanks. They're relatively inexpensive to fabricate into custom shapes, and they are robust and fairly light. They have just one serious drawback: they can corrode. If aluminum tanks have been installed with proper ventilation all around, with sloped or rounded tops to drain water, and placed on proper chocks with Neoprene padding they'll last a long time. For really long life, however, aluminum tanks should be painted (on the outside *only*) with a good epoxy-based paint system (Figure 5-16): a prime coat plus at least two finish coats (three or four are better still). An aluminum tank built and installed like this will last a lifetime.

Glass Tanks and Integral Tanks

Interestingly, fiberglass tanks are not only acceptable, but also superior for diesel. (They were once superior for gasoline, too, but ethanol has changed this. See sidebar "Fiberglass Tanks and Ethanol.") FRP tanks have some great advantages: they don't corrode, they don't conduct electricity, they weigh less than metal tanks, and they can be molded to fit the hull more closely than any but the most expensive metal tanks, yielding greater tank capacity. Bertram and Hatteras are just two of the quality builders who install fiberglass tanks.

Though the CFR Yacht and Commercial rules permit integral fiberglass tanks (molded into and against the hull itself) for diesel, they aren't allowed for gas. Steel and aluminum diesel craft can have integral metal tanks under CFR Commercial; however, wood hulls cannot. (You can have integral wood-epoxy diesel tanks on yachts: tanks lined with fiberglass in epoxy.) Integral tanks provide the maximum fuel capacity at the lowest cost and volume. They're very slightly more prone to leak, though. This is the reason that integral tanks can't be used on gas-engine craft. Cored FRP hulls (under CFR Commercial) can also have integral tanks for diesel, but only if PVC foam is used as core in the hull or any of the tank walls, because there's been occasional trouble with sounding sticks penetrating the inner skin, causing the most interesting leaks. Regardless, care is required to ensure that leaks can't penetrate into the core. In addition, if sounding sticks are used, there must be a rugged metal strike plate fastened directly under the sounding hole on the hull inside the tank to prevent damaging the inner skin. Pleasure craft can and do use balsa core in FRP tank walls.

It's been found that ordinary orthopolyester resin will meet the 2½-minute burn test requirement. I recommend, though, that all fiberglass tanks be laid up with fire-retardant isopolyester resin to Milspec Mil-R-21607. Iso resins have slightly higher mechanical properties, greater resistance to blistering, and higher resistance to chemical attack than orthos. Using fire-retardant resins seems sensibly prudent for fuel tanks. Isos are more expensive than ortho resins, but on comparatively small components like tanks, the cost difference is negligible when compared to the cost of the entire boat.

Fiberglass Tank Construction

FRP tanks have to be laid up over a male mold to make the inside surface smooth and finished. All corner radiuses should be 1 inch (25 mm) or larger, and the inside 50 percent of the laminate should be all mat and slightly resin rich to eliminate any pinholes. Gelcoat shouldn't be used on the inside surface, but a heavy layer of resin 20 to 30 mils (0.020 to 0.030 in. [0.5 to 0.75 mm]) thick is necessary—again, to eliminate any chance of pinholes. (Though not required, the best interior finish employs 20 to 30 mils [0.5 to 0.75 mm] of vinylester resin, which has still higher resistance to chemical attack.) Outside of the interior mat layup, alternating layers of woven roving and mat are built up to meet the thickness called for on the table. Since FRP is bendy, the usual practice is to use a balsa or PVC core on the outside of the interior mat laminate (only PVC is acceptable for commercial craft)—finishing off the remaining mat-roving layup over that.

Fiberglass Tank-Wall Thicknesses

Tanks under 20 gallons (75 L) don't need core for stiffness. Half-inch core is good for tanks up to 120 gallons (454 L) or so, while ³⁄₄-inch (19 mm) should be used over 120 gallons (454 L). Large tanks, over 400 gallons (1,500 L), need to be carefully engineered, with baffle spacing, stiffeners (if required), core thickness, and laminate all calculated. Where fittings penetrate the tank, the laminate (with core removed) should be increased to 1.5 times the scheduled thickness for about twice the diameter or footprint of the fitting. One excellent method of attaching fittings—recommended by Lysle Gray of ABYC—is to use ordinary marine brass or bronze pipe fittings screwed down tight from inside and out before the top of the tank is added, and then glassed over from outside. Baffles and all other requirements are the same as for metal tanks. Baffles should be fiberglass, at least 80 percent of the tank-wall thickness, bonded to the inside of the tank with minimum 2-inch (50 mm) bonding angles laid on resin-rich 1.5 oz./sq. ft. (457 g/m^2) mat, and glassed over into place.

The Best Tank Material

Is there a "best" material for fuel tanks? I think so—it's polyethylene. This may be counterintuitive, as somehow plastic seems less robust and less fireproof than metal or even FRP, but polyethylene tanks have been

TABLE 5-3. MINIMUM WALL THICKNESSES FOR FIBERGLASS FUEL TANKS BY CAPACITY

Capacity—Gallons	Thickness—Inches
5–20	0.1
20–80	0.2
80–200	0.3
200–500	0.4
500–800	0.5

Capacity—Liters	Thickness—Millimeters
20–75	2.5
75–300	5.1
300–750	7.6
750–1,900	10.2
1,900–3,000	12.7

NOTE: All tanks have to have baffles spaced no more than 30 inches (76 cm) both athwartships and fore and aft.

NOTE: Use mat on the inner 50 percent of the layup, then alternating layers of woven roving and chopped-strand mat in isopolyester resin. The outermost layer should be woven roving.

proven and tested since the early 1970s—more than thirty years. A U.S. Coast Guard/ABYC study performed by an independent lab found no failures of any kind in polyethylene tanks. Former technical director of ABYC Tom Hale concluded that "polyethylene fuel tanks pose no risk at all." Further, polyethylene tanks have all the advantages of FRP—lower weight than metal tanks with *zero* possibility of corrosion.

Poly tanks do have two drawbacks. One is the difficulty of making them strong enough in sizes over 80 gallons (300 L), because baffles are nearly impossible to build in. The second is that poly tanks are available only in a limited range of sizes and shapes. Any form, of course, can be fabricated, but tooling up for a custom poly tank requires an investment of roughly $3,000 or more. Still, many off-the-shelf polyethylene tanks are made and will suit numerous applications at low cost. Whenever I can find an existing poly tank that will do the job, it's my first choice.

Another thing to keep in mind about polyethylene tanks is that they expand after their first fill-up by about 2 percent in all directions. You must allow for this in any tank installation and follow the manufacturer's mounting instructions carefully.

Fiberglass Tanks and Ethanol

Until a few years ago, fiberglass tanks were every bit as good for gasoline as for diesel. The introduction of ethanol into gasoline has changed this situation.

What Is Ethanol?

Ethanol is the common term for ethyl alcohol, also called "grain alcohol" (C_2H_6O). As you would expect, ethyl alcohol is commonly obtained by processing grain; though, almost any vegetable matter can be used to produce ethyl alcohol. It's the sugar or starch in plant matter that's distilled into alcohol. This is the same chemical that makes alcoholic beverages alcoholic; however, alcohol also burns and makes a moderately useful fuel. Since plants are grown as needed, they are a renewable energy source (unlike petroleum). This makes alcohol a useful potential alternative to petroleum-based fuels such as gasoline.

The word *alcohol* is used generically when speaking of ethanol, but keep in mind that there are other alcohols such as methanol (wood alcohol) and isopropyl alcohol (rubbing

(Continued)

(Continued from previous)

alcohol). Methanol or methyl alcohol (CH_3OH) is termed "wood alcohol" because originally it was distilled from wood. Rubbing alcohol (C_3H_8O) is used to rub sore muscles and as a medical disinfectant, an antifreeze, a solvent, and many other things. Neither methanol or rubbing alcohol is currently used in a mixture with gasoline as fuel, and both are poisons if ingested. Note that ethanol is also occasionally used as a rubbing alcohol.

Existing cars, trucks, and boats almost universally operate on gasoline or diesel fuel—both of which are petroleum products. Diesel engines—due to the way diesel engines function—can't burn alcohol in any form; however, almost all gasoline engines can safely run on the appropriate mixture of gasoline and ethyl alcohol. In this use, it's the mixture of gasoline and ethyl alcohol that's generally termed *ethanol*.

The role ethyl alcohol plays when mixed with gasoline is complex. It isn't simply burned, but it replaces MTBE (methyl tertbutyl ether), which in turn replaced tetraethyl lead to reduce lead emissions. The purpose of these various additives is primarily to increase the oxygen level in the fuel and so increase performance and reduce knocking—increasing octane level. Such additives are thus oxygenates.

Advantages of Ethanol

The alcohol in ethanol burns cleanly with low exhaust emissions, and it helps the gasoline burn more efficiently. As we've seen, ethyl alcohol is also renewable, and so—taken all together—it appears to be a green or environmentally friendly energy source. There is, however, some debate about the net gains from using ethyl alcohol to make ethanol gasoline. It can be argued that the energy required to produce and transport the raw material, distill it into ethyl alcohol, and properly blend it with gasoline—along with other practical factors—make the environmental gains less impressive or possibly a net loss.

Ethanol Fuel Mandates: The New Development

Regardless of any controversy that may exist about the merits of ethanol gasoline for the environment or for the economy, many states and the U.S. Congress have mandated ethanol's use as a fuel. In fact—since almost all gasoline engines can run well on gasoline with 10 percent ethyl alcohol blended in—such fuel is, all of a sudden, common. The concept of ethanol, however, has been around for decades and has been used as an actual fuel in quite limited distribution since the late 1970s. Until the recent legal mandates, though, ethanol was rare. Since 2006, it has become widespread.

Ten percent ethanol (the blend of 10 percent ethyl alcohol by volume and gasoline) is called E10, for ethyl alcohol 10 percent. E20 is a blend with 20 percent alcohol. E85 is 85 percent ethanol and 15 percent gasoline. It works well in gasoline engines, but only in engines and fuel systems specifically prepared to use it. In any case, the higher percentage blends are (as of 2006) less common because they are more likely to cause problems when used in existing, unmodified gasoline engines and fuel systems.

Ethanol Degrades Fiberglass Tanks

All of the preceding has led to a rather new (in 2006) and largely unforeseen problem with fiberglass gasoline fuel tanks. A spate of tank and fuel difficulties have developed. After research and testing arranged by BoatU.S. and several marine surveyors dealing with odd fuel-system failures, these problems have been traced back to the alcohol in ethanol gasoline reacting with and dissolving the resin in fiberglass fuel tank walls. The process is chemically similar to fiberglass osmotic blistering but more aggressive and more pervasive. In fact, it's been found that *all* standard fiberglass resins are attacked by ethanol. Tank walls have been seriously weakened, causing leaks. And styrene and related chemical by-products that have dissolved in or reacted with the ethanol have worked their way into the engine where they have caused serious fouling problems.

The least resistant resin has been found to be orthophthalic polyester (orthopolyester) followed by isophthalic polyester (isopolyester), which holds up a bit better. Epoxy resins are better still. (I know of no tests on vinylester so far.) Regardless, *every one* of these resins suffers noticeable degradation in contact with ethanol!

DO *NOT* USE FIBERGLASS GASOLINE FUEL TANKS

Until the advent of widely used ethanol, fiberglass gasoline fuel tanks were one of the best options possible. Many thousands of gasoline-powered boats are in service with fiberglass fuel tanks. This includes vessels from top builders. The new mandated usage of ethanol changes things. All these tanks are suspect, and *you should not design or build gasoline tanks of fiberglass.*

Resin vendors say that there are resin formulations that can be used safely with ethanol; however, these are not widely known in the boating industry and currently are not readily available. Before you could design and build a fiberglass tank for today's gasoline blends, you would need to consult the resin vendor, select a suitable resin, make a sample test panel, expose it for a long period of time to ethanol (months at least), and test the sample to ensure that it suffered no degradation of any type.

The process of developing fiberglass tanks safe for ethanol will probably be worked out over the next several years; until then, you should avoid fiberglass gasoline tanks in new construction. You must also be aware of this potential problem in existing vessels. When surveying, retrofitting, repairing, or simply owning or operating an older gasoline boat, be sure to determine its fuel-tank material. If fiberglass, the tanks need special attention to ensure they haven't suffered from ethanol degradation.

Diesel Fiberglass Tanks: Still a Top Choice

Diesel tanks are unaffected by this new development. There's no alcohol equivalent for any type for diesel. Biodiesel, which is the vegetable-based renewable energy source that can be blended with or even wholly replace petroleum diesel, is an oil, not an alcohol. Biodiesel does not degrade fiberglass resins. Fiberglass diesel fuel tanks are still an excellent choice, with all the previously described advantages of fiberglass tanks.

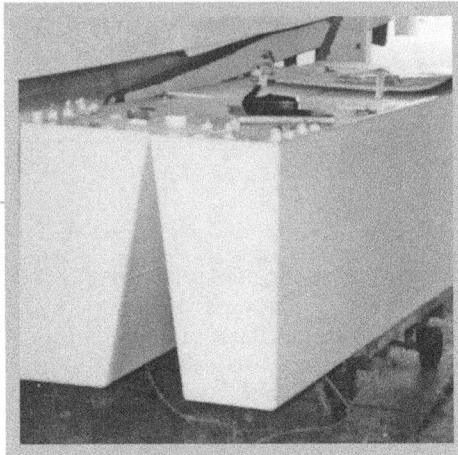

CHAPTER 6

Tank Capacity and Range: The Free-Surface Effect

REQUIRED TANKAGE FOR RANGE

We've looked at tank materials, tank fittings, and tank installation. For all boats—once the size of the engine(s) that will be installed to meet the desired speed has been established—you need to be able to determine how much fuel tankage is required to meet the range requirements.

For gasoline engines, fuel consumption can be estimated with the following formula.

Formula 6-1.

Formula 6-1. Fuel Consumption

$$\text{gal./hr.} = 0.10 \times \text{hp}$$

or

$$\text{L/hr.} = 0.508 \times \text{kWprop}$$

For diesel engines, fuel consumption can be estimated as

$$\text{gal./hr.} = 0.054 \times \text{hp}$$

or

$$\text{L/hr.} = 0.274 \times \text{kWprop}$$

Where
hp = propeller horsepower, from prop-hp curve
kWprop = kilowatts, from prop-power curve

Though performance curves from some engine manufacturers may indicate thriftier fuel consumption, experience shows that in the real world, the preceding numbers are usually about right. They are a bit conservative (normally, the preceding numbers slightly overestimate consumption). But this is good, as you want to ensure you have enough fuel on board to meet the range requirements.

Keep in mind that boats are not run constantly at full throttle. You can assume that diesels will be cruised at 80% of maximum rpm and gasoline engines at about 70% of maximum rpm. This is not 80% and 70% of power output. In fact, engine power falls off very quickly.

Look at the power curves for the 420 hp (313 kW) Yanmar diesel in Figure 6-1. You'll see there are two power curves—the engine power curve (with and without reduction gear in this case) and the propeller power curve. The propeller power curve is the one that indicates approximately how much power the propeller will be drawing at any given engine speed (assuming the propeller has been properly selected to allow the engine to reach maximum rated rpm). You can see from the propeller power curve that this engine delivers 420 hp (313 kW) at 2,700 rpm, but at 80 percent of max rpm (2,160), the propeller power curve shows that it's only delivering 217 hp (162 kW). This in fact would be the power for cruising speed. You need to

- know the speed the boat will go at this power (cruising speed)
- calculate the gallons per hour at this horsepower (at cruising horsepower)
- determine how many gallons you need to make the required range at this speed (cruising speed)

Example: Assume that this is a 30-foot (9 m) LOA, single-screw planing hull powered by the Yanmar diesel. The designer or engine manufacturer's speed calculations show that top speed (at full power) is 30.5 knots, at which speed consumption is

$$0.054 \times 420 \text{ bhp} = 22.7 \text{ gal./hr.}$$

or

$$0.274 \times 313 \text{ kWengine} = 85.7 \text{ L/hr.}$$

At cruise speed (2,160 rpm and 217 hp [162 kW]), speed will be 20.3 knots, and consumption is

$$0.054 \times 217 \text{ bhp} = 11.7 \text{ gal./hr.}$$

or

$$0.274 \times 162 \text{ kWengine} = 44.47 \text{ L/hr.}$$

Say you want a range of 750 nautical miles:

$$750 \text{ miles} \div 20.3 \text{ knots} = 36.9 \text{ hours running time}$$

$$36.9 \text{ hours} \times 11.7 \text{ gal./hr.} = 432 \text{ gal.}$$

Always add a 10% reserve:

$$432 \text{ gal.} \times 1.1 = 475 \text{ gal. diesel}$$

or

Say, you wanted a range of 750 nautical miles.

$$750 \text{ miles} \div 20.3 \text{ knots} = 36.9 \text{ hours running time}$$
$$36.9 \text{ hours} \times 44.4 \text{ L/hr.} = 1{,}638 \text{ L}$$

Always add a 10% reserve:

$$1{,}638 \text{ L} \times 1.1 = 1{,}802 \text{ L diesel}$$

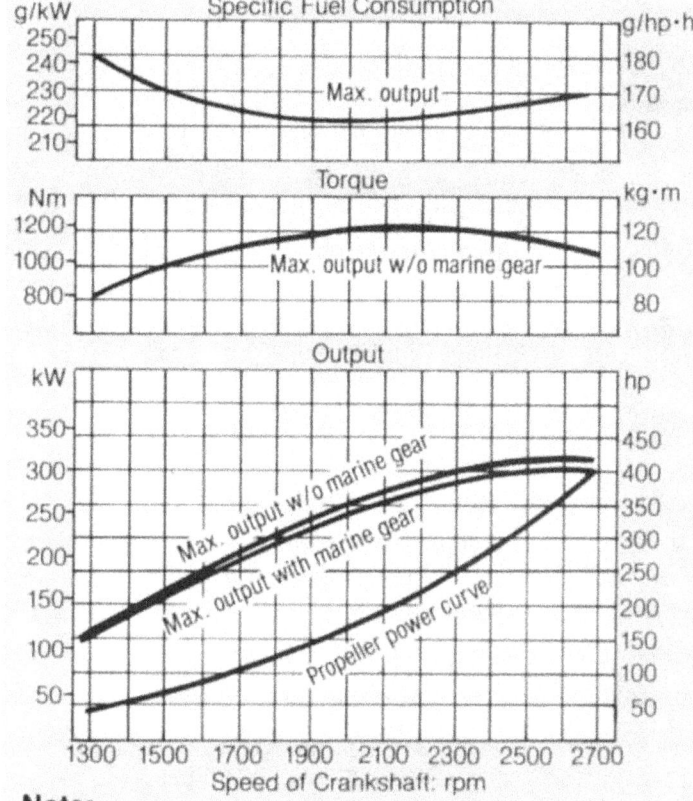

Note:
1. Above data are measured at crankshaft and show the average performance as tested at our laboratory.
2. Power loss of the marine gear YX70S is 3%.

On a boat of this size and type, the fuel would usually be carried in twin wing tanks of 238 gallons (900 L) each.

Figure 6-1. Yanmar engine curves (Courtesy Yanmar Marine)

ESTIMATING CRUISING-SPEED FUEL CONSUMPTION

If you don't have any engine curves available, you can estimate the propeller power used as follows:

80% Maximum rpm = About 52% Maximum-Rated Engine Power

70% Maximum rpm = About 40% Maximum-Rated Engine Power

(This assumes the propeller is properly matched to allow the engine to just reach full-rated rpms at maximum throttle.)

Generator Power and Fuel Consumption

Generator fuel consumption is best read from the manufacturer's data sheet. If you don't have the data sheets or specs for a generator or you are estimating for preliminary design, you can use the following:

Full-Load Engine bhp = 1.7 × Maximum-Rated Electric kW Output

Half-Load Engine bhp = 1.0 × Maximum-Rated Electric kW Output

or

Full-Load Engine kW = 1.27 × Maximum-Rated Electric kW Output

Half-Load Engine kW = 0.74 × Maximum-Rated Electric kW Output

Find fuel consumption using the same multiplier used for main-engine horsepower or kW output.

Calculating Tank Capacity: The Prismoidal Formula

Once you know how much tankage is required, you have to be able to determine the volumes or capacities of tanks. The same methods can be used to find the volume of other spaces such as locker volumes or compartment volumes. If the tank or other volume is a regular rectangle, cylinder, or some other simple shape, finding the volume is straightforward. Often, however, tanks will be rather odd shapes fitted under bunks or cabin soles and against the hull shell. One approach is to find the area of each of the tank's ends and the area of a section through the tank's middle. Add the three areas together, and divide by 3 to get the average area; then multiply by the overall tank length. This gives a pretty good calculation for volume.

A formula that gives more accurate results is the *prismoidal formula*. The prismoidal formula, in fact, automatically simplifies to the formula for a sphere, cone, cylinder, pyramid, and any common regular geometric shapes. It is the universal formula for finding volumes, as follows.

Formula 6-2. Prismoidal Formula

$$V = \left(\frac{B + 4M + T}{6}\right)H$$

Where (for vertical tanks)
V = volume
B = area of bottom
M = area of middle
T = area of top
H = height

or
Where (for horizontal tanks)
V = volume
B = area of one side
M = area of middle
T = area of opposite side
H = length

Sometimes a single tank has a particularly strange shape with an appendage built onto it. For instance, a standard wing tank fitted against the side of a hull may have a built-in protuberance from one end to add volume, to extend the lower portion of the tank under, say, a berth. When a tank has such odd shapes, you divide it into separate shapes (regions) that are simple to deal with, then add the volume of each region to get the total volume.

Knowing volume, you can find tank capacity in gallons and weight, when full, from the following tables.

FINDING THE CAPACITY OF A TANK

Say you have found an area in the boat that will fit a tank. You have mocked up the tank roughly with light plywood, doorskin, or

TABLE 6-1. CONVERSIONS FOR LIQUID VOLUME AND LIQUID MEASURE

U.S. Measure Liquid Volume

1 cu. ft. = 7.48 U.S. gal.
1 U.S. gal. = 0.134 cu. ft.
1 U.S. gal. = 231 cu. in.

Metric Measure Liquid Volume

1 m^3 = 1,000 L
1 L = 0.001 m^3
1 L = 1,000 cm^3

Liquid	English Units		Metric Units		Specific Gravity
	lb./cu. ft.	lb./gal.	kg/m^3	kg/L	
Seawater	64.00	8.56	1,025	1.025	1.03
Fresh Water	62.40	8.34	1,000	1.000	1.00
Fuel Oil	59.00	7.89	945	0.945	0.95
Lubricating Oil	57.50	7.69	921	0.921	0.92
Diesel Oil (Fuel)	53.30	7.13	854	0.854	0.85
Gasoline—Aviation	43.75	5.85	701	0.701	0.70
Gasoline—Marine	45.30	6.06	726	0.726	0.73
Alcohol	50.50	6.75	809	0.809	0.81
Kerosene	50.90	6.80	815	0.815	0.82

NOTE: In the metric system, specific gravity is the same as kg/L.

cardboard. Before you clean up and reinforce your tank mock-up for sending to the tank manufacturer to be fabricated, you have to determine if the capacity meets the requirements for the installation. Your proposed tank looks like the one shown in Figure 6-2.

Based on these measurements, you would determine the tank capacity as follows:

Step 1. Draw the shape of the sections at the front, middle, and back of the tank to a convenient scale. (On symmetrical tanks, it is usually easiest to draw half-section areas. On asymmetrical tanks, draw the full-section areas.)
Step 2. Calculate the area of each of the three shapes.
Step 3. Use the prismoidal formula to find the volume and the preceding tables to find the capacity in gallons or liters. (Don't forget to multiply by 2 to get total volume if you used the half-areas of the tank.)

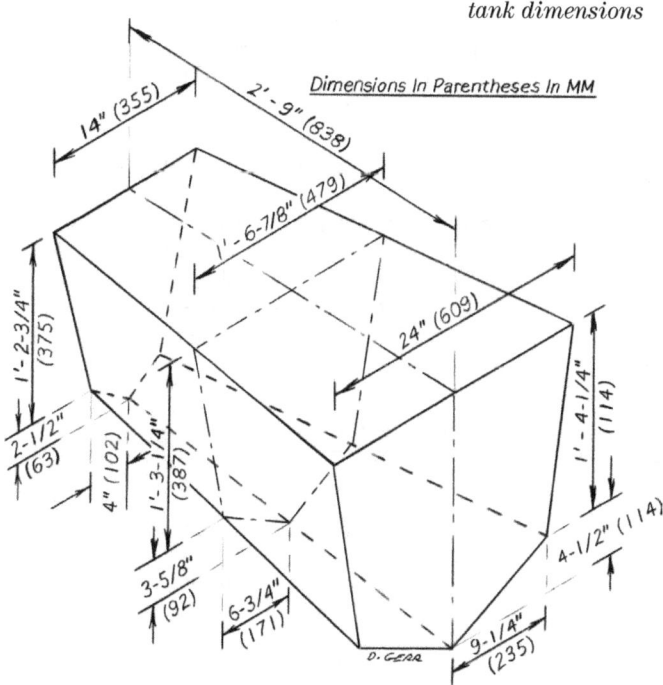

Figure 6-2. Bow tank dimensions

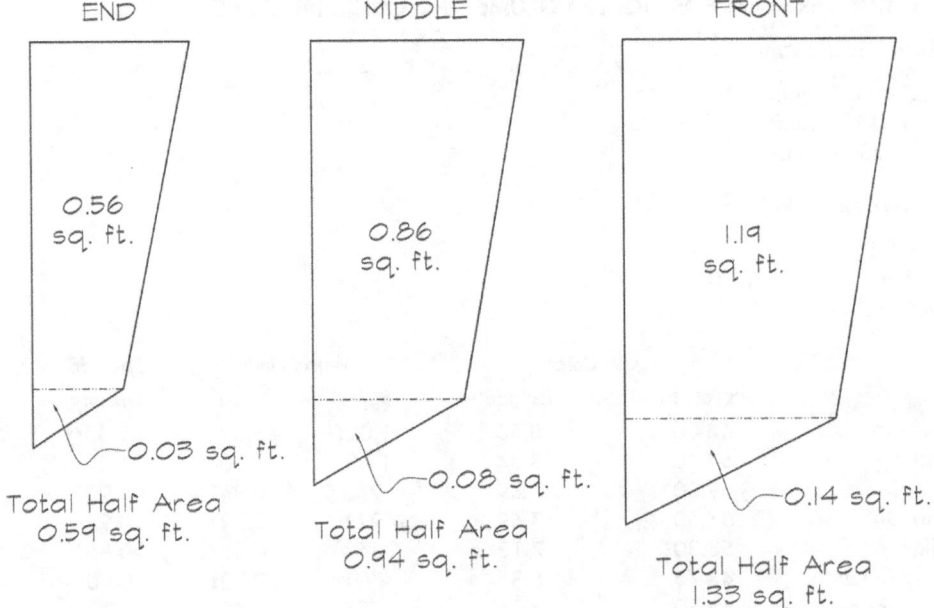

Figure 6-3. Tank half-sections (in English units)

Worked out in English units:

Step 1. Draw the half-areas of the front, middle, and back of the tank.

Taking the preceding measurements, we draw the three shapes (Figure 6-3).

Step 2. Calculate the area of each of the three shapes.

In this case, you divide each section into a regular trapezoid and a triangle. Using the formulas for plane areas (Appendix A), find the area of each and add to get the total area of each section (end, middle, and front).

Step 3. Use the prismoidal formula to find the volume and the preceding tables to find the capacity in gallons. (Don't forget to multiply by 2 to get total area, since you used the half-areas of the tank.)

V (one-half of tank) =

$$\left(\frac{0.59 \text{ sq. ft.} + (4 \times 0.94 \text{ sq. ft.}) + 1.33 \text{ sq. ft.}}{6}\right) \times 2.75 \text{ ft.} = 2.6 \text{ cu. ft.}$$

2.6 cu. ft. × 7.48 gal./cu. ft. × 2 sides = 38.9 gal.

Always deduct 2% for internal framing, baffles, and small air pockets:

38.9 gal. × 0.02 = 0.78 gal.

38.9 gal. − 0.78 gal. = 38.12 gal.

This is a 38-gallon tank.

Or

Worked out in metric units:

Step 1. Draw the half-areas of the front, middle, and back of the tank.

Taking the preceding measurements, we draw the three shapes (Figure. 6-4):

Step 2. Calculate the area of each of the three shapes.

In this case, you divide each section into a regular trapezoid and a triangle. Using the formulas for plane areas (Appendix A), find the area of each and add to get the total area of each section (end, middle, and front).

Step 3. Use the prismoidal formula to find the volume and the preceding tables to find the capacity in liters. (Don't forget to multiply by 2 to get total area, since you used the half-areas of the tank.)

V (one-half tank) =

$$\left(\frac{0.055 \text{ m}^2 + (4 \times 0.087 \text{ m}^2) + 0.123 \text{ m}^2}{6}\right) \times$$

0.838 m = 0.073 m^3

0.074 m^3 × 1,000 L/m^3 × 2 sides = 148 L

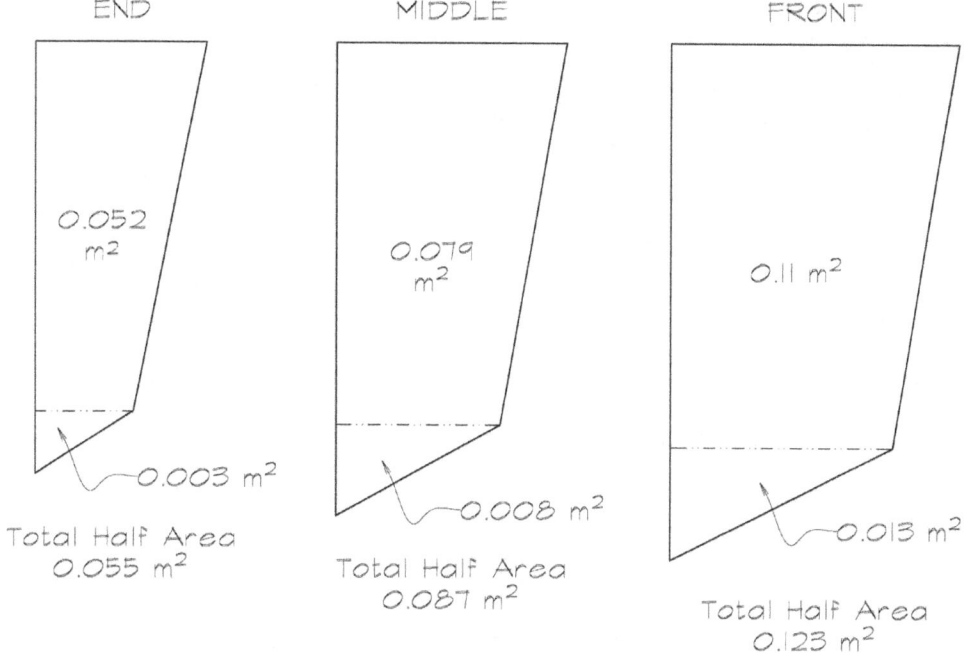

Figure 6-4. Tank half-sections (in metric units)

Always deduct 2% for internal framing, baffles, and small air pockets:

$$148 \text{ L} \times 0.02 = 2.96 \text{ L}$$

$$148 \text{ L} - 2.96 = 145.04 \text{ L}$$

This is a 145-liter tank.

Flexible Bladder Tanks

Another tank option is flexible bladder tanks. Basically sacks of reinforced rubberlike fabric, these are available in almost every size and shape imaginable, from 4 or 5 gallons (15 L) up to 10,000 gallons (38,000 L) or more. Two sources of marine bladder tanks in the United States are Imtra, which imports the Nauta line of bladder tanks manufactured by the French company Pennel, and Vetus den Ouden, Inc. Both companies also offer flexible portable gasoline tanks for outboard craft.

Standard sizes and shapes are available, as well as custom tanks on special order. Nauta tanks are fabricated of Neoprene nitrile, while Vetus uses Alcryn. Both are incredibly tough, puncture resistant, and abrasion resistant. Nevertheless, bladder fuel tanks are usually add-ons or replacements. Commercial fisherman or voyaging cruisers can use temporary deck-mounted bladder tanks to extend range. The tank is carefully secured on deck or in the cockpit; then it is fed into the built-in fuel tank's fills when the built-in is near empty. With the bladder tank drained, it can be rolled up and stowed out of the way.

Flexible bladder tanks can also be used to replace damaged built-in tanks. Rather than pull and replace old damaged fuel tanks, cut a hole or two in the original tank—large enough to get in and clean it out and smooth off any rough interior edges inside. Then insert a bladder tank. This is not a small undertaking, but it's less extensive than cutting out large portions of interior or deck to get an old tank out, as can be necessary on some boats.

As tough as bladder tank material is, it still must be protected against long-term chafe. The area where the tank is to be mounted must be carefully sanded smooth and all protrusions must be removed. Small tanks, usually less than 100 gallons or so, are fitted with corner grommets used to secure them. Larger tanks would place too much load on these grommets; so they are installed in a strong built-in box (almost a partial integral tank). Such large tanks may also be further restrained with netting wrapped over the entire tank and fastened to the hull.

As main "built-in" fuel tanks, standard bladder tanks are best suited for smaller sailboats. Their small size, light weight, and freedom from corrosion make installation easy and attractive.

The usual fill vent and takeoff lines are required for bladder tanks. (Yes, vents are required even for flexible bladder tanks.) Be sure to check with the manufacturer about the intended fuel. Some tanks are rated only for diesel, others for gasoline and diesel.

The ultimate in bladder tanks are bladder tanks completely filled with reticulated foam (Figure 6-5). These tanks aren't fully flexible but are held in their designed shape by their internal foam. The foam looks much like ordinary seat-cushion foam, but reticulated foam has had the walls between the individual foam cells chemically removed. This makes reticulated foam incredibly porous—so much so that the foam takes up a mere 2 to 3 percent of the volume of the tank. Reticulated-foam tanks require no baffles as the foam essentially divides the tank into millions of tiny chambers. There is no sloshing at all. For gasoline, these tanks are nonexplosive and—with the right high-end bladder material and external jacket—self-sealing and self-extinguishing. Because of this, reticulated-foam bladder tanks can be a good choice for very high-speed racing craft and for rescue and patrol boats. Ordinary level gauges won't function in reticulated-foam tanks. The manufacturer provides capacitance-gauge level indicators. As far as I'm aware, none of the bladder tanks have been approved for use on passenger vessels, not even reticulated foam.

Reticulated-foam bladder tank costs vary from somewhat higher than comparable custom aluminum tanks, to more than twice the price for ballistic, self-sealing tanks with an external flame shield. Of course, no aluminum tank is ballistic or self-sealing. Aluminum tanks are also heavier. Obviously—like fiberglass and poly tanks—all bladder tanks are immune to corrosion. ATL (Aero Tech Laboratories, Inc.) and Aircraft Rubber Manufacturing, Inc., both make reticulated-foam bladder tanks in stock or custom sizes. Aircraft Rubber also manufactures standard bladder tanks without the foam.

Wide Tanks Reduce Stability: The GM Reduction

Except when completely filled with absolutely no air in the tank at all—a condition termed "pressed up"—the fluid in all tanks of any size or shape reduces a boat's stability. This is because—even with baffles—the fluid in the tank moves from side to side as the vessel rolls. Both the shift in weight and

Figure 6-5. ATL reticulated-foam bladder tanks

the momentum of the sloshing liquid reduce stability due to "free-surface effect." The narrower a tank is in proportion to the beam of a boat, the less the reduction in stability—the less the free-surface effect. For this reason, tanks should generally be arranged to be as narrow as practical athwartships. Wide shallow tanks have the most free-surface effect for a given capacity and should be avoided if possible.

As a rule, if a tank's width is less than 20 percent of overall beam, and the capacity of the tank is less than 12 percent of displacement, you can neglect the free-surface effect for pleasure-craft work. Sometimes, however, wide tanks are desirable to meet specific design goals. If so, be sure to divide up the tanks into two or three separate tanks athwartships. An example of this is in the 66-foot (20 m) *Kingfisher* design shown Figure 5-4. Here it was advantageous to have the fuel tanks running full width athwartships aft of the master stateroom. In this case, the main diesel tanks are divided into two separate tanks at the centerline (with two additional smaller tanks low and outboard).

If you are doing a new design or a major modification to tank size, location, or capacity, whenever you have a tank wider than 20 percent of overall beam or with a capacity greater than 12 percent of displacement, you should calculate the reduction in stability and use that reduced stability in all your other stability work. (To be perfectly correct, you should do this for all tanks in all boats; but it generally isn't required if the tanks are narrow and of modest capacity.)

Stability is evaluated in terms of GZ (righting arm) and GM (distance to the metacenter M from the VCG (vertical center of gravity or G). If you know one, you can easily find the other for angles of heel up to 10 degrees using the following formula.

Formula 6-3. Stability

$$GZ = GM \times \sin\theta$$

or

$$GM = GZ \div \sin\theta$$

Where
  GZ = righting arm, ft. or m
  GM = metacentric height, ft. or m
  θ = the angle of heel in degrees (θ is the Greek letter called theta)

Free-surface effect is evaluated using the "free-surface GM correction" to find the actual GM known as "effective GM," after allowing for the tank free surface. To determine effective GM, calculate boat GZ and GM as usual, then apply the following formula.

Formula 6-4. Effective GM, or Metacentric Height

$$GM_{eff} = GM_s - GM_{redT}$$

$$GM_{red} = \left(\frac{I_L}{\nabla_s}\right)\left(\frac{\rho_L}{\rho_s}\right) \text{ (for each tank)}$$

$$GM_{redT} = \sum GM_{red} \text{ (of all tanks)}$$

Where
GMeff = GM effective, ft. or m
GMs = GM of the ship, prior to free-surface calculation, ft. or m
GMred = GM reduction for each tank, ft. or m
GMredT = total GM reduction for the sum of all tanks, ft. or m
IL = moment of inertia of the plan area of the surface of the tank about the tank's centerline, ft.^{4} or m^4
∇s = displacement of ship, cu. ft. or m^3
ρL = density of liquid in tank, lb./cu. ft. or kg/m^3, or specific gravity
ρs = density of the water boat floats in (usually seawater), lb./cu. ft. or kg/m^3, or specific gravity
(ρ is the lowercase Greek letter r called rho.)
($\sum$ is the uppercase Greek letter S called sigma. When used in a formula like this, it means "sum." So, in this case, the sum of all "GMred.")

NOTE:
The relationship $\left(\frac{\rho_L}{\rho_s}\right)$ is a ratio and can be in any units of density as long as the same units are used top and bottom.

Contrary to intuition, the total capacity of the tank does not affect stability with regard to free-surface effect, and neither does the tank location (again, with regard to free-surface effect). It doesn't matter how high or low, or how far inboard or outboard the tank is located. Only the tank's individual fluid surface area contributes to the free-surface effect. Separate and distinct from the free-surface effect is the effect of the total weight (mass) of the fluid in the tank and the vertical location of its center of gravity. High tanks will reduce stability when full, while low tanks will increase stability when full. This is the effect of the mass of the fluid and *not* free-surface effect, which is what we're dealing with here.

TABLE 6-2. SPECIFIC GRAVITY OF COMMON LIQUIDS

(At 60°F, 15.5°C)

Liquid	Specific Gravity
Diesel	0.852
Gasoline	0.727
Fresh Water	1.000
Salt Water	1.028
Lube Oil	0.921

Example: Say you have a boat with a calculated GM 1° of 3.58 ft. at a displacement of 2,156 cu. ft. (61.6 tons, 137,984 lb.) with half-full tanks. GZ 1°, for this load condition, is then 0.062 ft., and RM 1° is 0.062 ft. × 137,984 lb. = 8,555 ft. lb. The boat has four tanks—2 for diesel and 2 for fresh water. (The diesel and water tanks, in this case, are identical port and starboard.) You would find the effective GM by using the following formula (you can find the formula for other shapes in standard engineering texts).

Formula 6-5a. Moment of Inertia of a Rectangular Plane Area (English)

$$I = bh^3 \div 12$$

Where (for evaluating tank free surface)

b = the length of the tank fore-and-aft, ft.
h = the width of the tank athwartships, ft.

In our case, the diesel tanks are 9 feet long by 6.8 feet wide athwartships. Thus the moment of inertia of each tank is

$$I = 9 \text{ ft.} \times (6.8 \text{ ft.})^3 \div 12 = 235.8 \text{ ft.}^4$$

Then

$$GM_{red} = \left(\frac{235.8 \text{ ft.}^4}{2,156 \text{ ft.}^3}\right)\left(\frac{0.852}{1.028}\right) = 0.09 \text{ ft. (for each diesel tank)}$$

Multiply by 2 for both diesel tanks = 0.18 ft. GM_{red} (diesel)

The water tanks are 2.5 feet long and 6.5 feet wide athwartships. Thus the moment of inertia for each tank is

$$I = 2.5 \text{ ft.} \times (6.5 \text{ ft.})^3 \div 12 = 57.21 \text{ ft.}^4$$

Then

$$GM_{red} = \left(\frac{57.21 \text{ ft.}^4}{2,156 \text{ ft.}^3}\right)\left(\frac{1.000}{1.028}\right) = 0.026 \text{ ft.}$$

(for each water tank)

Multiply by 2 for both water tanks = 0.052 ft. GM_{red} (water)

Now

$$GM_{red}T = 0.18 \text{ ft. } GM_{red} \text{ (diesel)} + 0.052 \text{ ft.}$$
$$GM_{red} \text{ (water)} = 0.23 \text{ ft.}$$

and

$$GM_{eff} = 3.58 \text{ ft. } GM_s - 0.23 \text{ ft.}$$
$$GM_{red}T = 3.35 \text{ ft.}$$

This is the loss in stability due to free-surface effect and can be translated into reduced GZ or RM using the preceding relationship between GZ and GM.

In our case, stability after free-surface effect is

$$GZ \, 1° = 3.35 \text{ ft. } GM \times \sin 1° = 0.058 \text{ ft.}$$

$$RM \, 1° = 0.058 \text{ ft. } GZ \, 1° \times 137,984 \text{ lb.}$$

$$\text{Disp.} = 8,067 \text{ ft.lb.}$$

This is a reduction in righting moment of 6% due to free-surface effect.
Or
In metrics, this works out as follows:
Say you have a boat with a calculated GM 1° of 1.091 m at a displacement of 61.05 m³ (62.6 Mtons, 62,588 kg) with half-full tanks. GZ 1° for this load condition is then 0.0190 m, and RM 1° is 0.0190 m × 62,588 kg = 1,195 kgm. The boat has four tanks—2 for diesel and 2 for fresh water. (The diesel and water tanks, in this case, are identical port and starboard.) You would find the effective GM by using the following formula (you can find the formula for other shapes in standard engineering texts).

Formula 6-5b. Moment of Inertia of a Rectangular Plane Area (Metric)

$$I = bh^3 \div 12$$

Where (for evaluating tank free surface)
b = the length of the tank fore-and-aft, m
h = the width of the tank athwartships, m

In our case, the diesel tanks are 2.743 m long by 2.073 m wide athwartships. Thus the moment of inertia of each tank is

$$I = 2.743 \text{ m} \times (2.073 \text{ m})^3 \div 12 = 2.036 \text{ m}^4$$

Then

$$GMred = \left(\frac{2.036 \text{ m}^4}{61.05 \text{ m}^3}\right)\left(\frac{0.852}{1.028}\right) = 0.0276 \text{ m}$$

(for each diesel tank)

Multiply by 2 for both diesel tanks = 0.0552 m GMred (diesel)

The water tanks are 0.762 m long by 1.981 m wide athwartships. Thus the moment of inertia for each tank is

$$I = 0.762 \text{ m} \times (1.981 \text{ m})^3 \div 12 = 0.494 \text{ m}^4$$

Then

$$GMred = \left(\frac{0.494 \text{ m}^4}{61.05 \text{ m}^3}\right)\left(\frac{1.000}{1.028}\right) = 0.00787 \text{ m}$$

(for each water tank)

Multiply by 2 for both water tanks = 0.01574 m GMred (water)
Now

GMredT = 0.0552 m GMred (diesel)
+0.01574 m GMred (water) = 0.071 m

and

GMeff = 1.091 m GMs − 0.071 m GMredT = 1.02 m

This is the loss in stability due to free-surface effect and can be translated into reduced GZ or RM using the preceding relationship between GZ and GM.

In our case, stability after free-surface effect is

GZ 1° = 1.02 m GM × sin 1° = 0.0178 m

RM 1° = 0.0178 m GZ 1° × 62,588 kg
Disp. = 1,114 kgm

This is a reduction in righting moment of 6% due to free-surface effect.

Free-Surface Effect and Loading Conditions

Keep in mind that the free-surface reduction changes for various conditions of loading (for different displacements). Using boat displacement to the DWL (or to the expected flotation waterline at ²/₃ load) is adequate for most work on small craft; for commercial projects, however, carefully tabulated GMs for different loading conditions will be required. Performing stability calculations for all reasonable conditions of loading and flooding are detailed and time-consuming. Usually, these should be conducted using a software package, such as GHS, intended for this purpose; however, you need to understand the concept of free-surface effect to interpret the results correctly.

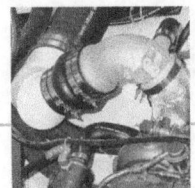

Part Three

EXHAUST SYSTEMS

CHAPTER 7 **Wet Exhaust Systems**

Imagine being able to breathe in, but not being able to breathe out. How long do you think you would last? Not long! The exhaust of your engine is quite literally its exhalation. Exhaust systems get rid of combustion by-product gases and a substantial amount of waste heat. Not only does the exhaust piping have to be properly designed and installed, but it also must be properly maintained. A poor exhaust system will rob a boat's engine of power and lead to excess and tiring noise, ruined engines, fires, and flooding—even sinking.

Whether you're drawing up a new boat or surveying an old one, installing a new engine or simply replacing a damaged or corroded part of an existing exhaust system, it's critical that you check to see that the exhaust system meets minimum requirements for safety and efficiency. In this chapter, we'll examine the fundamentals of standard and some not-so-standard wet exhaust installations to give you a good basis for either laying out a new system or evaluating or improving an existing one.

The basic system for a typical sportsfisherman or motor cruiser—one with the engine exhaust manifold well above the waterline—is shown in Figure 7-1. At first glance, it seems simple enough: you run a pipe aft from the exhaust manifold, stick a muffler somewhere in the middle, and that's that. If only it were so!

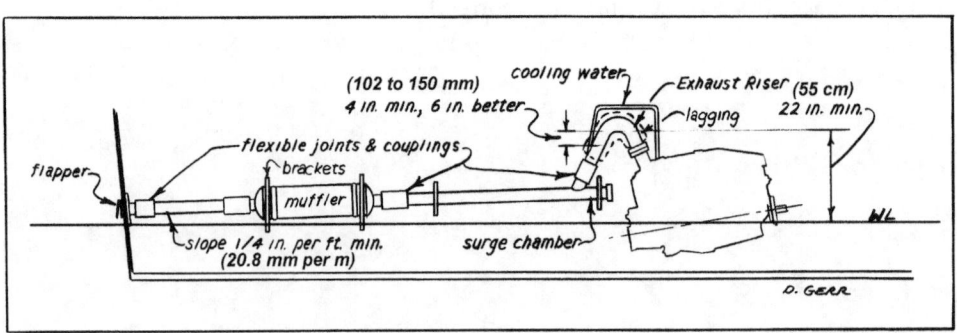

Figure 7-1. Exhaust system

BREATHING EASY

Principally, the engine needs to be able to breathe freely. If the exhaust line is too small in diameter, has too many bends, or is clogged, pressure called *back pressure* builds up and the engine has to use some of its power simply to expel the spent combustion gases—a real waste. After all, for the engine to run, it absolutely must make room for the next charge of fresh air being sucked into the cylinders.

Back-Pressure Guidelines

As a rough guide, exhaust back pressure shouldn't exceed 2.5 inches (63 mm) of mercury (Hg) for naturally aspirated engines and should be less than 2.0 inches (40 mm) Hg for turbocharged machines.

Specific engines have specific requirements, so consult the installation manual. The exhaust riser should be fitted with a tap for reading back pressure with a manometer (Figure 7-2; see also the accompany sidebar), and back pressure should be checked during major overhauls.

Generally, a wet exhaust system has about twice the back pressure as a dry system of the same diameter. To keep back pressure at acceptable levels, this means that the wet exhaust diameter should be 40 percent greater than the dry exhaust diameter for the same engine.

$$\text{Wet Exhaust Diameter} \approx 1.4 \times \text{Dry Exhaust Diameter (rule of thumb)}$$

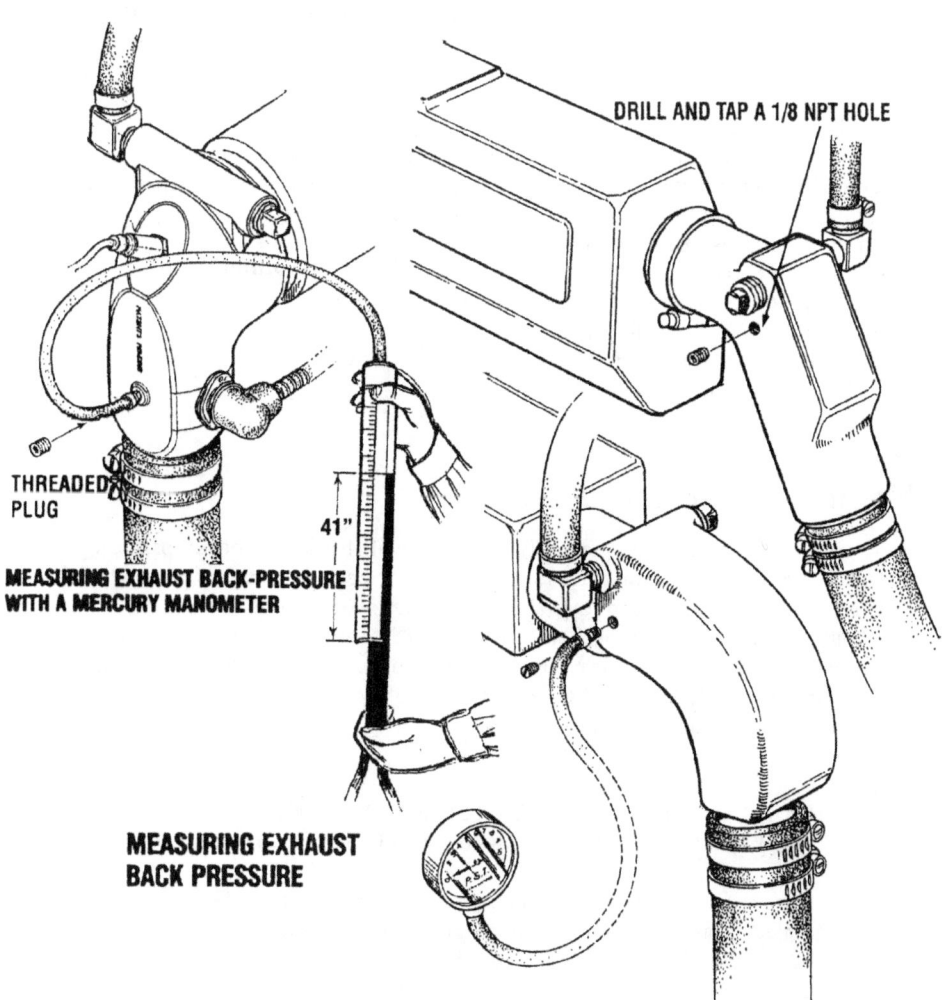

Figure 7-2. Taking manometer readings (Courtesy Westerbeke Corporation)

PART THREE: EXHAUST SYSTEMS

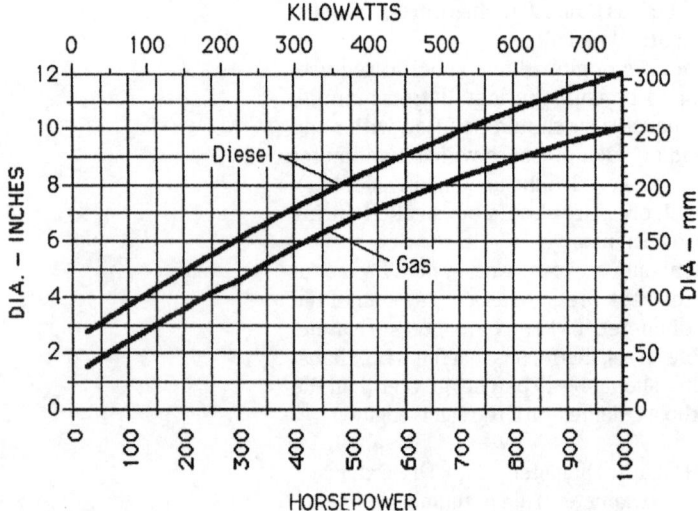

Figure 7-3. Exhaust line diameter as a function of engine power for gas and diesel engines

Formula 7-1.

There's nothing better than a large diameter and the fewest possible large-radius bends in an exhaust run to keep back pressure down. The exhaust line diameter chart in Figure 7-3 gives recommended preliminary design diameters for wet exhaust systems for engines of various horsepower, but you should confirm these dimensions with your manufacturer. Greater diameter doesn't hurt, but it is more expensive and more difficult to fit in the boat. A rough guide is that for every 12 feet (3.6 m) over the first 12 feet (3.6 m) of exhaust run, the exhaust diameter should be increased by ½ inch (12 mm).

WATERING THE EXHAUST

Of course, almost all yachts (and many small commercial vessels) have wet exhaust systems, which is our focus here. The engine cooling water is injected into the exhaust line just after the exhaust riser begins to drop. This serves two important functions. First, it cools the exhaust run tremendously. The dry sections of, say, a diesel exhaust reach 1,200°F (648°C). That's hot enough to start wood, oil, or cloth burning pretty quick! What's more, this heat is radiated into the engine compartment, reducing power potential. Cooling the exhaust with water eliminates these difficulties. The expansion of the cooling water into steam and the process of mixing with the exhaust also quiets the exhaust appreciably.

Formula 7-1 is a good guide to the volume of water needed for adequate cooling.

Formula 7-1. Water Volumes for Adequate Cooling

$$\text{GPM} = \text{cu. in.} \times \text{rpm} \div 66{,}000$$

The Meaning of Pressure

Atmospheric pressure, roughly 14.7 lb./sq. in. (psi) at sea level (101.3 kPa), envelops us all constantly. When engine pressures (or vacuums) are measured, they are measured *relative* to this surrounding air pressure, not added to it. This is known as *gauge pressure*. The instrument used is essentially a barometer, though in engineering work it's termed a *manometer*. Manometer and barometer readings are given in a number of different units, of which *psig* (pounds per square inch gauge), *in.* H_2O or *mm* H_2O (inches or mm of water), and *in. Hg* or *mm Hg* (inches or mm of mercury) are three of the most common.

Roughly
2.5 in. Hg = 34 in. H_2O = 1.2 psig = 63 mm Hg = 864 mm H_2O = 8.2 kPa
2.0 in. Hg = 27 in. H_2O = 1.0 psig = 51 mm Hg = 686 mm H_2O = 6.9 kPa

Although *psig* is the technically correct terminology, many references drop the *g* for *gauge* as it is taken for granted. In metric measure, pressure is given in kilopascals (kPa), which also should be *kPag*, but again the *g* for *gauge* is almost always omitted.

or

$$LPM = L \times rpm \div 285$$

Where
GPM = flow in gallons per minute
LPM = flow in liters per minute
cu. in. = engine displacement in cubic inches
L = engine displacement in liters
rpm = maximum engine rpm

Keeping the Water Where It Belongs

Although water injected into the exhaust cools it (and quiets it), the water also creates a new set of potential problems. Perhaps the most important of these is that you absolutely must prevent water—that is, *any* water at all—from working back up into the engine. Even small quantities of saltwater vapor in the turbo can seize it up fast. Water will also deteriorate the exhaust and valve mechanism of even a naturally aspirated engine. The consequences of a solid slug of water working back up past the manifold don't bear thinking about.

SLOPE AND RISE Figure 7-1 shows the principal features that should be built into an exhaust run to keep water out. The exhaust line should slope downward aft from the engine, ideally not less than ¼ inch for every foot of length (20.8 mm for every meter of length)—more is definitely better, and the bottom of the outlet pipe at the transom should be no more than 1 inch (25 mm) below the static waterline. (True underwater exhaust systems are viable options. We'll examine these later.)

The bottom inside surface of the highest bend in the exhaust riser should be at least 22 inches (55 cm) above the highest waterline on which the boat is likely to float. Indeed, it's so important to keep water out of the engine that some references call for the bottom inside wall of the exhaust riser pipe to be at least 24 inches (60 cm) above the highest expected waterline. This makes good sense. If you have an expensive turbocharged diesel engine sitting in a boat, and the boat's exhaust riser is less than 18 inches (45 cm) above the real flotation waterline, it would be a good investment to retrofit a higher riser in the off-season. This is assuming other internal-geometry constraints permit.

Risers: Water Jacketed or Dry?

The exhaust riser itself poses an interesting question: water jacketed or dry? A water-jacketed riser (Figure 7-4) consists of an inner

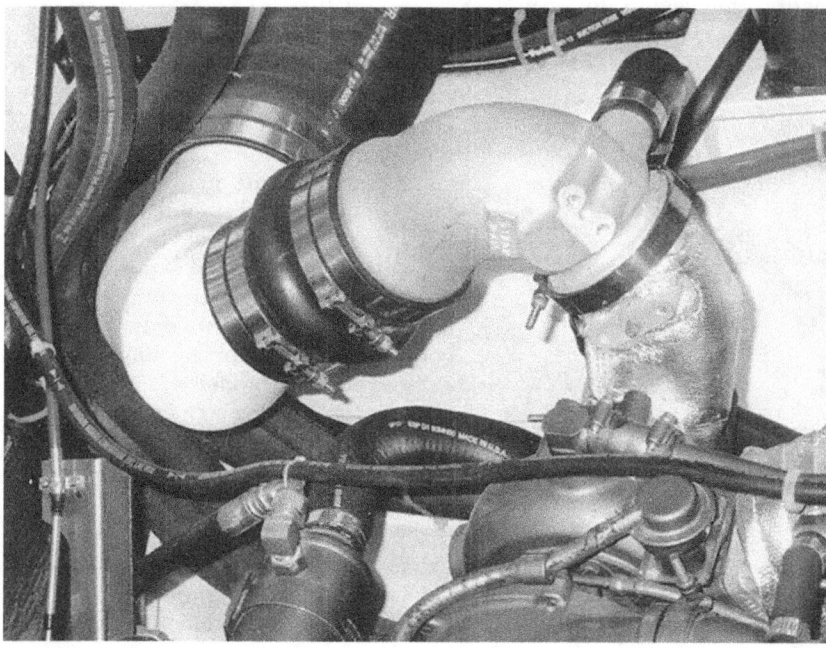

Figure 7-4. Water-jacketed exhaust riser

and outer pipe. The inner pipe carries the dry exhaust gas from the manifold. The outer pipe (the water jacket) is filled with engine cooling water injected through an outside tap. The advantage here is that the entire riser exterior is relatively cool to the touch. Also, it keeps less heat from radiating into the engine compartment. Cooling water sprays out into the exhaust gas proper through small holes at the aft lower end of the edge of the riser's water jacket, where the water mixes with and cools the hot gases directly.

There's only one drawback—a potential for corrosion inside the riser's jacket itself. For this reason, many commercial boats—and hard-worked sportfishermen—are fitted with dry exhaust risers. Here, the riser is simply a pipe elbow with a tap on top aft to inject cooling water directly into the gas flow (Figure 7-5). (The injection should angle down and aft, not at right angles to the riser pipe, which could lead to splashback into the turbo.) Even better, some manufacturers offer water-injection rings that fit on the end of the exhaust riser and disburse the injected water evenly around the periphery of the exhaust pipes.

Naturally, the hot riser has to be *well* insulated (lagged) all around the outside to prevent burns or chance of fire and to reduce radiated heat. (See Chapter 9 for more information on lagging.) Both water-jacketed and dry risers work fine, and both have their advocates. I lean toward the dry riser—carefully insulated—as it seems to have the least potential for long-range corrosion trouble.

Pyrometer Equals Thermometer

Just aft of the water injection point is where you should install an exhaust temperature *pyrometer*. (*Pyrometer* is a fancy term for a high-temperature thermometer.) This can be rigged to a simple idiot light and alarm—or better—to a temperature indicator dial with a programmable high-temperature alarm. In either case, the idea is to give ample warning if there is a reduction in cooling water. (A pyrometer in the dry exhaust rise ahead of the water injection is useful for tracking engine load. It's the best indicator of how hard an engine is working.)

A water-flow sensor can be installed in the injection line, just before entry into the exhaust riser. With the ignition on, it will sound an alarm if the flow to the injection point should stop. This is somewhat redundant with the pyrometer, and the alarm inserted into the exhaust system as described earlier; however, it may be used in lieu of the pyrometer.

Metal's Not So Hot

The metal parts of an exhaust system are attacked by acids created in the fuel-water mixture. Most stainless steels corrode in wet exhausts. Inconel and Hastelloy C (nickel-chrome-molybdenum alloys) are excellent, though costly. Type 316L stainless (the *L* stands for "low carbon"), which has some molybdenum, is acceptable; 18-8, 302, and 304 stainless alloys should be avoided. Copper, copper-nickel, nickel-copper, and Monel can be used if high temperatures and standing water can be prevented, but copper and copper alloys are for gasoline only—wet exhaust diesel by-products (among them sulfuric acid) attack the copper.

MANIFOLD CORROSION Dry exhaust risers, as we've seen, can virtually eliminate corrosion problems in the riser. One place where you really can't do much about corrosion in wet exhaust systems is the water-jacketed exhaust manifold. Just like a water-jacketed exhaust riser, the exhaust manifold is a

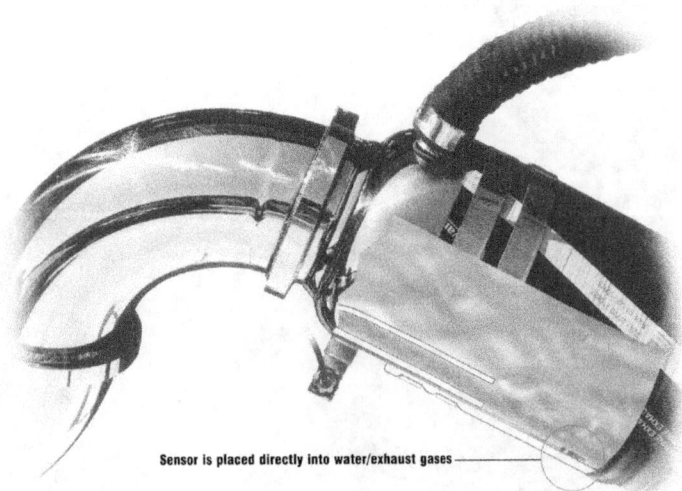

Figure 7-5. Water injection (Courtesy Vetus)

casting with the exhaust running inside channels that are surrounded by cooling water. Because the channels are usually of cast iron, corrosion will occur sooner or later in the water jacket of the manifold. Inspecting water-jacketed exhaust manifolds should be considered routine long-term maintenance. Table 7-1 presents tabulations by BoatU.S. for the probability of failure due to corrosion in exhaust manifolds.

TABLE 7-1. ESTIMATED EXHAUST MANIFOLD SERVICE LIFE

Years in Service	Probability of Failure
3	0.5 percent
4	25 percent
5	45 percent
6	65 percent
7	85 percent
8	90 percent
9+	100 percent

I think this is rather pessimistic. Also, it primarily applies to gasoline engines with raw-water cooling. Diesels with closed-circuit (heat-exchanger) cooling will experience far fewer problems with corrosion. Our office has had several such boats in service over a dozen years, with no sign of problems. Nevertheless, there will be some problems here eventually.

Injecting Low

Again, to keep water out of the engine, the water injection point must be at least 4 inches (102 mm) below the bottom inside surface of the highest bend in the exhaust riser—6 inches (150 mm) is better. Unless you're assembling your own exhaust piping from scratch, the injection location is already built into the riser. If, however, you have a choice during refits, during repairs, or for new construction, go for a riser with the larger 6-inch (150 mm) drop.

Surge Chambers and Flappers

You don't want some—or any—ocean water forced back up the line when backing down. Sportfishermen in particular jockey around, going back and forth in rough conditions while fighting fish. These boats need special protection from back surge. The surge chamber shown in Figure 7-1 absorbs a great deal of the force of a slug of water in what's essentially a compressed-air cushion. Fitting an external check-valve flap on the transom or an internal check valve is also a wise precaution. Indeed, if the bottom of your exhaust exits the transom lower than 6 inches (150 mm) above the static waterline, you should consider the combination of an external flapper or in-line check valve and a surge chamber. (Note that some engine manufacturers disapprove of transom flappers because they can block off the exhaust line completely during extended backing maneuvers.)

RUMRUNNER COVERS An interesting variation on the common external flapper valve was used on some rumrunners during Prohibition. Powered with twin World War I surplus aircraft engines—often producing in excess of 500 hp (373 kW) each—these craft fitted rubber clamshells over their transom exhausts. The rumrunners fabricated these gizmos from old car tires and attached them so the only opening was straight down, with just about an inch (25 mm) clearance above the waterline at rest. Needless to say, keeping away from the neighborhood Coast Guard cutter required stealth. Not only did these rubber clamshell covers help prevent back flooding, but the rubber itself appears to have flexed enough to absorb some engine noise. Much of the remaining racket seems to have been deflected down into the water.

The Best Exhaust Piping

Because it doesn't corrode, fiberglass exhaust tube and exhaust hose, meeting SAE J2006 standards, are the best for a trouble-free installation. The hose must withstand a minimum temperature of 280°F (138°C) and have no tendency to collapse. In the old days, this was called "steam hose." Today, there are hoses specifically manufactured for marine wet exhaust application. This is one of those rare cases where what's best is actually less expensive and lighter than metal.

There is, though, always the chance of a water pump failure. If this happens, your engine will seize up lickety-split. But in that bare lickety-split, 1,200°F (648°C) exhaust gases will momentarily be sprayed onto the hose and FRP tube. For this reason, I believe all fiberglass exhaust-line components (piping, mufflers, check valves, etc.) are best made of fire-retardant isopolyester resin to Milspec Mil-R-21607. Check with your manufacturer to see what they use. Built with this goop, the fiberglass exhaust tube or hose won't smoke or burst into flames should the water pump fail. And more than likely, the crew will have enough problems to worry about in such circumstances.

SUPPORT YOUR LOCAL EXHAUST

It's also important that the entire exhaust line be well supported with strong clamps and brackets. When filled with water, the exhaust piping can weigh a fair bit. When the vessel is jumping from wave crest to wave crest, resulting g-forces will break loose a flimsily supported line. Naturally, a cracked exhaust will admit not only noxious gases, but also all that water you've been pumping through the engine to keep it running cool. As many an insurance surveyor can attest, cracked exhaust lines are quite an effective way to sink a boat!

Where brackets support hot, dry portions of the exhaust system, the bracket must not only be able to withstand the heat, but also be insulated against transmitting the heat to the hull structure, and the bracket must allow for the expansion and contraction of the pipe from full-throttle hot to full-off cold (see Chapter 9).

Penetrating Bulkheads

Bulkheads frequently need to be penetrated by the exhaust line. This can actually be useful, and the bulkhead makes a fine support. You do have to be careful that there's no chafe and that there's room for expansion. For wet exhaust systems in wood and FRP bulkheads, the minimum clearance around the bulkhead is 2 inches (50 mm). On a number of boats, we've supported the exhaust pipe by cutting the hole in the bulkhead 2 inches (50 mm) oversize and then wrapping 2 inches (50 mm) of fiberglass sound insulation around the exhaust pipe where it went through. Stuffing this in and closing it off with an aluminum finish ring sealed the bulkhead for sound, eliminated transfer of vibration, and held the exhaust in place while allowing enough movement for expansion and contraction.

Dry exhaust pipes need much more clearance. Ten inches (250 mm) is the bare minimum. There should be insulation around the pipe (lagging) and around the bulkhead.

Tender Turbos

Turbochargers run at such high speeds and temperatures that it's critical not to place any external strain on their housings. Such strains can be enough to throw bearings out of whack and create nasty headaches. Make sure your exhaust piping—and anything else for that matter—isn't putting weight, a side load, or other strain on your turbo's case. Any piping here must be firmly supported by and fastened to the engine block itself, not by any portion of the turbo.

Supporting piping on the engine block at the turbo is OK, but common practice with larger boats is to isolate the dry riser pipe with the metal bellows, and the riser is supported by brackets to the vessel's structure, generally to the overhead (see Chapter 9).

Flexible Joints

To avoid cracks due to flexing, you must connect all the individual piping components with flexible connectors (Figure 7-6). If this isn't done, engine vibration combined with

Figure 7-6. Exhaust hose clamps

hull working—however slight—will be sure to open a seam somewhere. Exhaust hose is, again, the perfect solution, except where any dry, hot exhaust gases may be present. Here, you have to use flexible metal bellows of Inconel and Hastelloy C or—not quite as good, but the usually available standard—type 316L stainless. Accept no substitutes; get the alloy specs in writing before you buy. No other metals will stand up to the exhaust's high-temperature, corrosive, saltwater-hydrocarbon-sulfur-sulfuric-acid mix.

A related consideration here is that on FRP boats, it's tempting to glass a long length of rigid fiberglass exhaust tube right to the transom. Don't do it; it's likely to crack. One builder I worked with had been fabricating their own glass exhaust piping for sailboats and installing them this way for years. They'd lucked out and had no trouble. I specified that the exhaust tubing for the 420 hp (313 kW) diesel on a new powerboat be connected with flexible hose, but they persisted in doing it their old way. Well, after just a few hours of operation, the durn thing cracked big time, both at the transom and at a bulkhead. Luckily, someone noticed the water in the bilge immediately and they were able to limp home and retrofit with hose. I know there are successful boats out there with long fiberglass exhaust tubes glassed rigidly to the transom, but any boat fitted this way is playing a game of Russian roulette.

Metal boats with rigid metal exhaust pipes welded to bulkheads and the transom are OK, but they still are not ideal. The combination of corrosion and thermal expansion can cause cracking as well. Even on metal boats, FRP exhaust tube and exhaust hose are the best exhaust piping, and FRP piping must be flexibly connected at all rigid points. This, unfortunately, is not allowed under the CFR for metal T-boats (inspected passenger vessels, under 100 gross tons, and carrying less than 150 passengers). I distrust metal in wet exhaust systems, and I think the CFR requiring it in metal hulls is a shame.

Fiberglass exhaust tube through watertight bulkheads should consist of short FRP pipe fittings with flanges fastenerd to the bulkhead and the tube projecting on either side of the bulkhead. The flanges are bolted to the bulkhead and caulked. Exhaust hose connects to the pipe ends on both sides. Some class or government regulations may require a metal shutoff valve right at the bulkhead. In this case, all-metal piping is required.

Hose Clamps

As we've just seen, a leak into the boat from the wet exhaust piping can sink a boat fast. It can also spew deadly carbon monoxide into the accommodations. You must use the very finest quality all-316-stainless, T-bar hose clamps. Use double hose clamps, and be sure you can get at *all* of them for inspection and tightening. I once surveyed a 36-foot (11 m) lobster yacht that had its large aft cockpit sole glassed in permanently. Underneath was the exhaust run, with clamps but with no access at all. When I insisted that at least a cover plate be cut and installed over the exhaust hose where I could see (but not reach) a single hose clamp, there was considerable resistance. It was finally done, however, and I found that the single hose clamp had never been tightened!

Note that traditional exhaust hose clamps are of malleable iron (Figure 7-8). These usually were used singly, not in pairs. Malleable iron hose clamps are still available and still acceptable. I prefer double stainless steel, as they seem more secure and longer lasting.

Figure 7-7. Exhaust tube glassed to transom—not a good idea

PART THREE: EXHAUST SYSTEMS

Figure 7-8. Malleable iron hose clamp (Courtesy Buck Algonquin)

Keep It Down!

As we've seen, simple wet exhaust systems decrease engine exhaust noise considerably even without a muffler. Clearly, adding a muffler—if you don't already have one—will reduce noise still further. Most marine in-line mufflers (as opposed to waterlift mufflers) work by breaking the exhaust flow with baffles. These reflect the pulses (bangs) of the individual cylinders back and forth so they tend to cancel each other out. If you can find the space, a larger muffler for the same exhaust line will almost always give a quieter exhaust—it allows for more refractions to take place in the short time the exhaust travels through it. A little-known, extra step worth consideration for the very quietest boat is to wrap the muffler in 1 to 2 inches (25 to 50 mm) of fiberglass sound-absorbing insulation. In and of itself, it won't make the difference between a loud and a quiet boat, but it will reduce the racket one step more—and every step helps.

MAKE ROOM FOR EXHAUSTS

An often-overlooked aspect of exhaust system installations is the amount of volume they take up inside the boat (see Figure 7-9). A pair of 300 hp (224 kW) diesels will usually require 6-inch (150 mm) diameter wet exhaust systems. Standard in-line mufflers will be roughly 1.7 times this diameter, and that extra diameter will extend roughly 5.4 times the diameter. So for a 6-inch-diameter exhaust tube, the muffler will be about 10 to 11 inches in diameter and about 32 to 34 inches long; or for a 150 mm diameter exhaust tube, the muffler will be about 255 to 280 mm in diameter and about 810 to 870 mm long.

Add up the exhaust tube, surge chamber, muffler, brackets, and required access, and you realize just how much space you must allow. This can't be an afterthought. Indeed, if you're contemplating a repowering project,

Figure 7-9. Note how much space the exhaust system requires

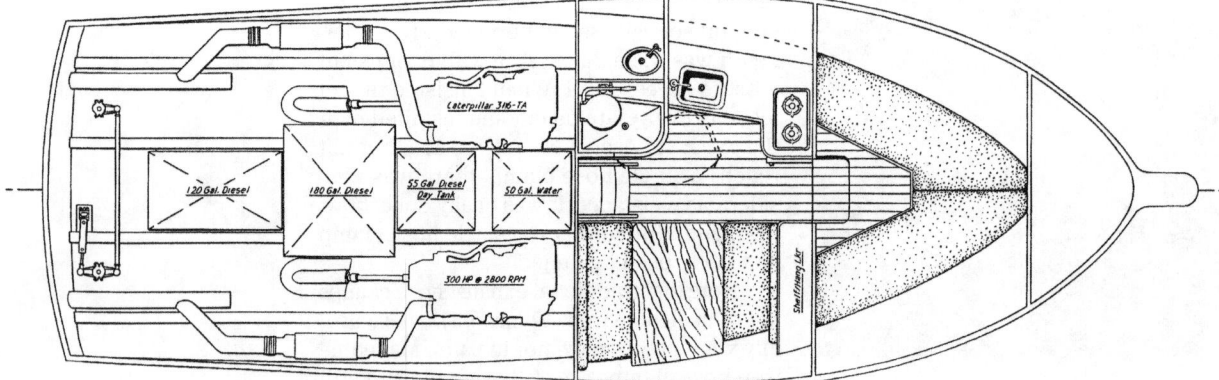

Gerr 34 Sportsfisherman

108

take a careful look at the diameter of the exhaust system. A switch from gas to diesel may up the diameter by a size or more (as might simply increasing power). Be sure you have the room to install the bigger piping.

Exhaust Lines Can't Share

Considering the space problems, it's tempting to combine twin-engine exhaust lines at some point into a single, large exit line. It would seem that if you just made sure the combined exhaust-line diameter was sufficient, this could solve a multitude of space problems. Unfortunately, you can't do it. Exhaust lines can't be shared, not between main engines and not between gen sets, compressors, or any combination of these. Why not? If you run on one engine with the other off for any period of time, the exhaust gases from the running engine will back up into the turbo and valves of the idle engine. This will cause unacceptable fouling. In addition, condensation can build up in the idle engine, which—combined with the carbon and other by-products in the engine and exhaust—can form acids that will damage seals and gaskets.

The only successful exception to this rule that I'm aware of is the current Coast Guard 47-foot (14.3 m) motor lifeboats, which do share the twin-engine exhausts. The design team did a careful study and calculated that the two engines would virtually always be run at the same time. In this case, there would be minimal exhaust back-fouling problems. These boats are operated with military precision and maintained the same way. Yachts and workboats aren't. I advise against sharing any exhaust lines on any vessel.

THE LOW-ENGINE EXHAUST PROBLEM

We've examined exhaust installations for standard powerboats, with the engine relatively high. Now we'll take a look at the exhaust systems that both powerboats and sailboats frequently have in common: exhaust systems that have to lift spent engine gases up and overboard from below the waterline. Powerboats frequently fit generators below or near the waterline, while sailboats almost invariably have their main engine low—real low—in the bilge. In the early days, such exhaust systems were simply dry pipes rising as close to vertical as possible—to well above the waterline—then with cooling water injected, sloping down and out a transom through-hull. There's still a place for these standpipe exhaust systems, and we'll discuss them shortly.

The Waterlift Answer

The usual modern solution to all this is the waterlift muffler (Figure 7-10). These gizmos are simplicity itself. The wet exhaust runs into the top or side of the muffler, which is no more than a large, empty cylinder. A second pipe, the outlet or lift pipe, runs up out of the top of the muffler canister. This pipe continues down to within a few inches or centimeters of the muffler-canister bottom. Since cooling water initially runs down into the cylinder (the waterlift muffler), it almost instantly fills about half full with water. The upper half of the muffler contains water vapor and exhaust gases that have nowhere to go. In a brief instant, gas pressure builds high enough to blow a mixed slug of water and exhaust gas down to the bottom of the muffler canister and up out of the exit pipe.

Waterlift Pluses

This system has several advantages. First, wet exhaust is safe and easy to deal with (as we've seen). Second, injecting the water in the first place quiets the exhaust (as well as cools it). Third, the process of expansion in the waterlift canister and forcing the gas/water mixture out quiets the exhaust even more. Fourth, the muffler cylinder itself—if properly configured—forms an excellent baffle against water working its way back up into the engine. A good case can be made for waterlift mufflers being the quietest of all mufflers.

The next step up from the simple waterlift, incidentally, is a dual-chamber waterlift. These have their canister divided internally into two sections (sometimes more). The process of forcing the air/water mixture through the dual chambers further reduces noise.

PART THREE: EXHAUST SYSTEMS

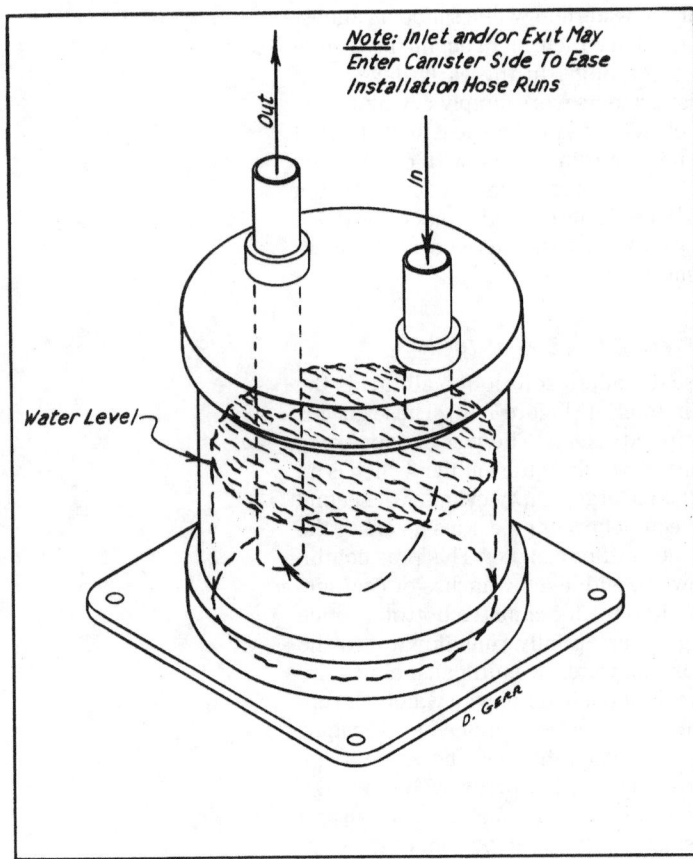

Figure 7-10. Inner workings of a waterlift muffler

Figure 7-11. Waterlift muffler installed

Doing It Right

As good as waterlift mufflers are, however, you can't simply jam one willy-nilly into the bilge, run some hose to it, and expect it to work properly. Like any exhaust installation, the waterlift muffler must be set up to minimize back pressure and to eliminate any possibility of water finding its way up into the exhaust manifold. Figures 7-12 and 7-13 show the two basic layouts: when the muffler is located below the motor exhaust outlet, and when the muffler is located above the exhaust outlet.

THE STANDARD LAYOUT When both the engine (or generator) and the muffler are installed below the waterline, you need a siphon break (also known as a vented loop, see Figure 7-12) to prevent siphoning water back into the engine. The loop should be at least 18 inches (45 cm) above the waterline, and sailboats need to be certain that the loop is at least 8 inches (21 cm) above the highest *heeled* waterline. Generally, if the loop is high and near the centerline, there's no problem here. If, however, the loop is way off to one side—on a sailboat—you'll just about have to run it up to the deck underside or higher still into the trunk cabin or cockpit coaming (see the sidebar on vented loops).

The inlet to the waterlift canister from the exhaust manifold has to be at least 12 inches (305 mm) below the water-injection point. There should be a downgrade of ½ inch for each foot of distance (41.5 mm for each meter) from the manifold outlet to the muffler inlet. Ideally, the lift pipe (usually just called the "lift") out from the muffler should be close to vertical, but this is often hard to accomplish. The important consideration here is to keep the lift height as low as practical to avoid excessive back pressure. For most installations, a maximum lift—from the bottom of the muffler canister to the top of the lift—should be 42 inches (106 cm).

The greater the lift, the greater the back pressure, so less lift or height is always better. The catch is that standard practice recommends that the center of the exhaust outlet be at least 6 inches (15 cm) above the waterline, and that, at the same time, there must be a drop of 12 inches (30 cm) from the high point of the lift pipe to the through-hull. The good news is that in practice I've had installations that exited the transom only an inch (25 mm) or so above

Chapter 7: Wet Exhaust Systems

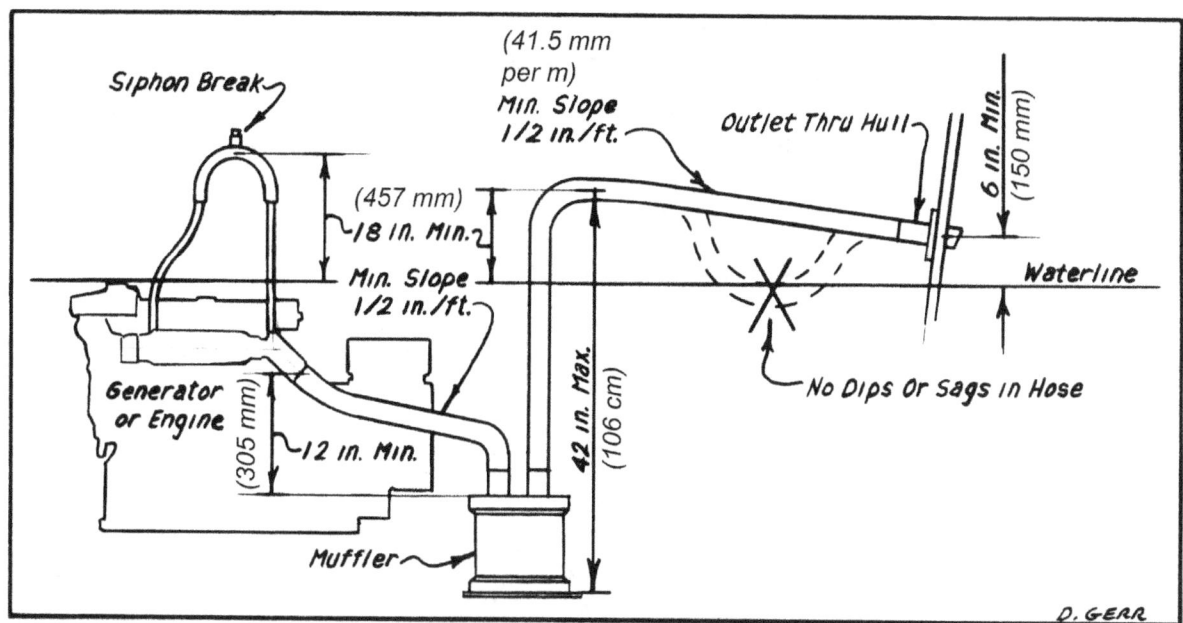

the waterline, or had the bottom edge of the exhaust pipe even an inch (25 mm) or so below, without a problem. You certainly can't immerse any standard exhaust more than this. At least 90 percent of the exhaust outlet area *must* be above the waterline, except for a true underwater exhaust, which we'll investigate shortly.

MUFFLER-ABOVE-MANIFOLD SETUP If you have to install the waterlift canister above the exhaust manifold, you need to lift the manifold to get the same 12-inch (305 mm) drop to the muffler inlet (Figure 7-13). How? Use an extended exhaust riser for small to moderate lifts or install an dry exhaust section—very

Figure 7-12. Standard waterlift muffler installation

Figure 7-13. Waterlift muffler above manifold exit

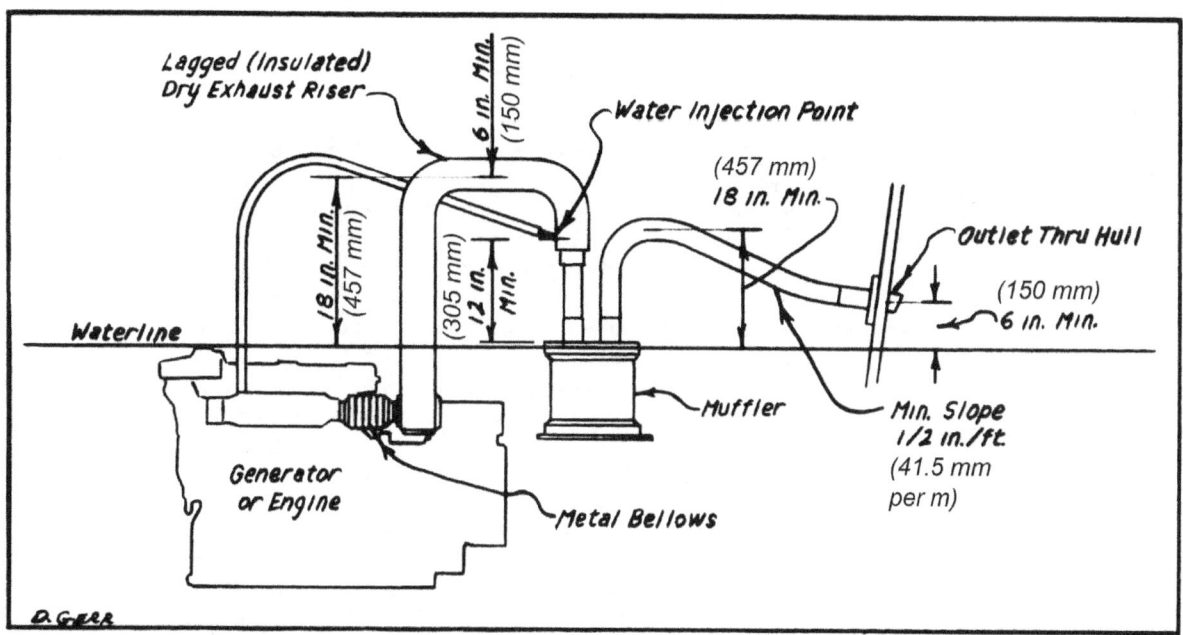

PART THREE: EXHAUST SYSTEMS

heavily insulated (lagged, see Chapter 9) and firmly fastened—which will raise the exhaust at least 18 inches (457 mm) above the waterline and the water injection point at least 12 inches (305 mm) above the inlet into the waterlift canister.

Deceptively Light

Keep in mind that one of the nicest things about waterlift mufflers is that they're light and easy to install. The waterlift canister is usually of fiberglass (metal ones are heavier, more expensive, and subject to corrosion), and almost

Vented Loops: Whys and Wherefores

Obviously, vented loops are important—but what exactly are they? Well, if you remember your high school science, a tube that's filled with a liquid will transfer that liquid from a higher-level container to a lower-level container even though the top of the tube may be far above the top of either container. Yes, a siphon. As long as the tube is closed to the atmosphere, the liquid "thinks" that the whole assembly—filled tube and two containers—is one. In our case, the inside of the bilge or engine is one container, seawater is the liquid, and the ocean is the second container—albeit an awfully big one!

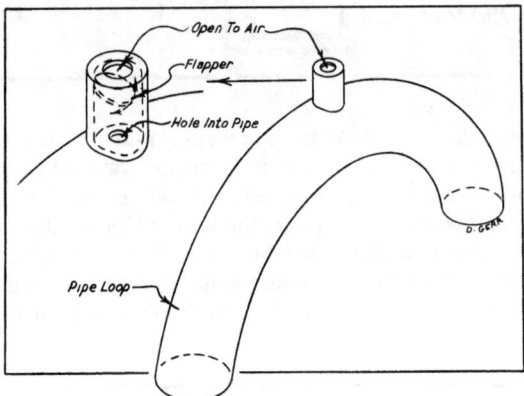

Vented loop or siphon break

To avoid siphoning, all you have to do is open the tube to the surrounding air (even a pinhole will do) and you have two separate containers—again, no flow and no siphon. Pictured here is a simple form of a vented loop. (There are other varieties, but they all work on the same principle.) The flapper is pushed up, sealing the vent opening by the pressure of water or gases flowing through the pipe. At engine shutdown, when flow and pressure stop, the flap opens, opening the line to the air and eliminating any chance of siphon backflow.

Sometimes these little siphon-break valves get salt encrusted and either jam open or jam closed. It pays to inspect them periodically and to wipe them clean with fresh water. On engine and generator installations, another option is to do away with the flapper or other valve mechanism and run a long tube vertically up from the break opening at the top of the U and into the cockpit. Without the flap, there is virtually no chance of clogging open or closed. The drawback is possibly an occasional slight weeping of sooty water into the cockpit.

Every through-hull that exits 6 inches (150 mm) above the water or lower and is attached to a hose or pipe leading down into the bilge—whether for engines, generators, heads, bilge pumps, or whatever—should be fitted with a metal or plastic pipe vented loop or siphon break to eliminate the chance of flooding (and sinking!) by siphon. Heads, though, ought not to be fitted with the open tube into the cockpit—unwanted odors would be interesting, to say the least!

all the plumbing can be of exhaust hose. Light as the muffler and hose components seem, they'll weigh more when filled with water. All these components must be very firmly fastened in place. As always, use only true exhaust hose and double stainless steel hose clamps at all hose connections. Be certain the hose is protected from chafing on other machinery, on the hull, or where it passes through bulkheads and panels. To keep the vertical clearances constant when a sailboat heels, you should try to mount the muffler on or close to the centerline. You mustn't have any sags or dips in the line where water can collect.

Canister Versus Lift-Line Size

When you shut off the engine or gen set, all the water in the exhaust lift will run back down into the muffler. Clearly, if there is too long a run and too small a waterlift canister, the water will overflow the canister and back up into the engine. This is a frequently overlooked pitfall. The safe rule of thumb is that the muffler canister should have 130 percent more volume than the entire lift line, from the canister to the highest point. (Aft of that point, the water will run out the transom.) How do you check this? Simple, as the following formula shows.

Formula 7-2. Volume in Canisters or Exhaust Lift Lines

> Canister Volume (cu. in.) = canister radius (in.) × canister radius (in.) × 3.14 × canister height (in.)
>
> Exhaust Lift-Line Volume (cu. in.) = hose radius (in.) × hose radius (in.) × 3.14 × length of lift run from muffler to highest point (in.)—both ways, from the manifold to the canister and from the canister out and up to the highest point aft of the canister

Or

> Canister Volume (cu. cm) = canister radius (cm) × canister radius (cm) × 3.14 × canister height (cm)
>
> Exhaust Lift-Line Volume (cu. cm) = hose radius (cm) × hose radius (cm) × 3.14 × length of lift run from muffler to highest point (cm)—both ways, from the manifold to the canister and from the canister out and up to the highest point aft of the canister

Divide the muffler canister volume by the exhaust lift-line volume. If the answer is 1.3 or larger, everything's OK. If the answer is less than 1.3, you need a larger-capacity waterlift muffler.

Standard Waterlift Muffler Dimensions

The standard minimum diameter for a waterlift muffler is 4 times the square root of the inlet pipe area. Height is usually equal to diameter or a bit more. Remember, this is the standard minimum. A larger muffler may be required as described above. Using this rule, a 3-inch (75 cm) wet exhaust inlet would require a 10.6-inch (266 mm) diameter canister about 11 to 12 inches (270–300 mm) high.

Formula 7-3. Standard Minimum Diameter for a Waterlift Muffler with 3-Inch (75 mm) Inlet

$$\text{Canister Dia.} = 4 \times \sqrt{\pi \left(\frac{3 \text{ in.}}{2}\right)^2} = 10.6 \text{ in.}$$

or

$$\text{Canister Dia.} = 4 \times \sqrt{\pi \left(\frac{75 \text{ mm}}{2}\right)^2} = 265.8;\ \text{use } 266 \text{ mm}$$

Greater diameter and/or height (more volume) never hurts.

It is also possible to flood the waterlift back up into the engine if an engine is hard starting. Repeated cranking will fill the waterlift canister with water, with no exhaust-gas pressure to push the water out the tail end. This is another good reason to fit the largest waterlift canister you can. It is also often worthwhile to have a drain cock on the bottom of the canister to draw off water should there ever be an engine problem with multiple crankings and no start.

Use Fat Hose in the Long Run

Very long lift runs increase back pressure. You should try to avoid lift-line runs greater than 30 times the exhaust-line diameter from the engine. If a boat has a 2½-inch (65 mm) exhaust-line diameter, the run shouldn't be over 75 inches, or 6 feet 3 inches (1.95 m), total length from the lift outlet to the through-hull. If the run must be longer, you should make the hose diameter larger. For lift runs up to 60 times exhaust-line diameter, increase the line size by 20 percent. With such a long run, a 2½-inch (65 mm) exhaust inlet muffler should be fitted with a 3-inch (80 mm) outlet. Still longer runs are possible, but you might have to increase diameter even more, and check with the engine manufacturer about the maximum acceptable back pressure. As with any exhaust system, you should use as few bends as possible with the largest radii possible; tight bends also increase back pressure.

NOTE: On waterlift installations, it is common and accepted to have a fairly tight 180-degree U at the top of the lift line. You can use this whenever needed; but it's still optimal not to, if possible.

Gasoline and Waterlifts Should Not Mix

Although waterlift mufflers have been used for years with both gasoline and diesel engines, I recommend against employing them for gas. There may be no problem for years, but just the right (or wrong) set of circumstances can fill the top half of the muffler canister with a mixture of gasoline vapor and air—an explosive combination. Though usually minor as such things go, there have been a few cases of explosions. Even if—taken as a whole—the odds against mishap are well in your favor, and even though such blasts haven't been catastrophic, I personally would sleep better on a gas-engine or gas-generator boat not equipped with a waterlift system.

THE "OTHER" EXHAUST SYSTEMS

So far, we've examined standard powerboat exhaust installations and waterlift mufflers. There are, though, other exhaust systems that are not only useful, but also date back to the first installation of internal-combustion engines in boats. These systems still can solve specific engine and interior-arrangement problems practically. One of the most interesting of these is the North Sea exhaust system. Strangely, this setup is little known and largely forgotten today. Indeed, I've employed it on several motor cruisers, yet some engine manufacturers' technical staffs had never seen it before. Being a suspicious lot—in spite of my assurances—they insisted on running their computer back-pressure analysis before giving their official go-ahead. They seemed genuinely surprised, when—after much number crunching—the old and tested North Sea arrangement proved to be as efficient.

A North Sea Problem Solver

The fact is the North Sea exhaust system solves one of the most common problems on many inboard cruisers: with engines roughly amidships, how do you get the exhaust out to the transom? Those long exhaust runs and their mufflers take up valuable space and are expensive to fit. With the North Sea exhaust system, the answer to the question is you don't take the exhaust to the transom. Instead, you run it out the sides of the hull—out *both* sides.

You can see how the system is arranged in Figure 7-14. This is a modern version using a waterlift muffler. The original North Sea configuration simply had the exhaust riser from the manifold make a large loop up and then drop down to the transverse pipe. (Sometimes a standpipe was used; more on this later.) Both methods work, but the waterlift muffler is quieter and makes installation even easier. Once the water exits up out of the waterlift canister, it doesn't care which direction you lead it, as long as there aren't sharp bends or numerous curves (back-pressure no-no's). On one boat, I ran the exhaust up from the canister and forward, then down to the transverse pipe.

The beauty of the North Sea exhaust system is that not only does it eliminate the long run to the transom, it also has twice the outlet-opening area. You can't ever get back-pressure problems (once the system is set up properly, that is). Naturally, when the boat rolls or when the sea slaps against one side, the other side is clear for full exhaust flow and for instant drainage. Because the outlets don't face aft, you're also free from worry about flooding when backing down hard.

In normal operation, the exhaust fumes exit the hull low enough so that they trail aft before they can rise to deck level, where they would create unpleasant smells. The North Sea exhaust system is so named because it

Chapter 7: Wet Exhaust Systems

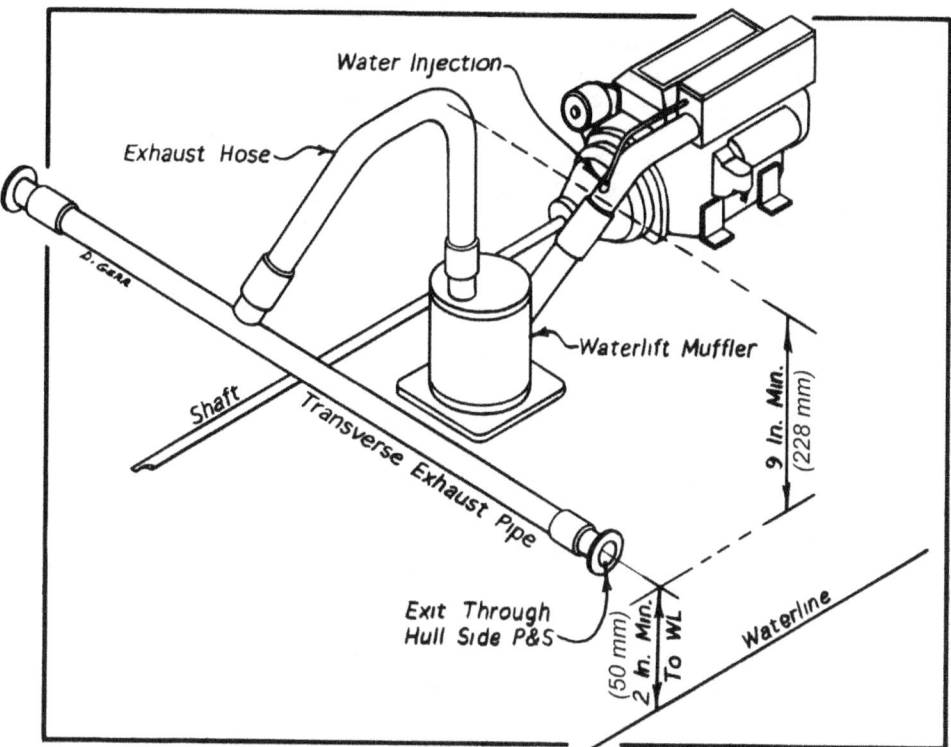

Figure 7-14. North Sea exhaust system with waterlift muffler

first became popular on the North Sea, a cold, rough bit of ocean. Everything on these boats had to work and work well, or they would be in for serious trouble. Figure 7-15 shows a 42-footer (12.8 m) my office designed with the North Sea exhaust system. You can just make out the puff of the exhaust a bit aft of midships at the waterline.

Figure 7-15. Forty-two-foot Summer Kyle/Belle Marie with North Sea exhaust (Courtesy Starke Jett)

I have to warn you that most of my clients haven't cared for the North Sea exhaust system, even though they have been very happy with their boats. They complained that they did get more exhaust smell aboard and that they had to wash soot off both sides of the boat instead of the transom. This has mystified me. I spent 16 days cruising on three different boats of my design with the North Sea exhaust system. I did not experience more exhaust smell (and possibly less) nor more cleaning of soot. When I asked the clients about this, they just shrugged—but they still complained while happily motoring along. It's a mystery to me. Regardless, though the North Sea exhaust may solve your installation problems, you should be aware of the operator reaction I've experienced, even if I can't explain it.

If you follow the height clearances shown in Figure 7-14 along with the engine manufacturer's standard wet-exhaust-line diameter recommendations, a North Sea exhaust will work fine. Remember, the maximum lift for a waterlift canister (from the bottom of the canister to the highest point on

115

PART THREE: EXHAUST SYSTEMS

the vertical pipe or hose exiting it) should be less than 42 inches (106 cm, see Figure 7-12) to keep back pressure within acceptable levels. The transverse exhaust pipe (and most of the rigid wet exhaust piping) can be ordinary fiberglass exhaust tube. Don't forget, however, to install flexible connectors between the pipe and anything rigid: the side outlets, the engine, and so on. This should be top-quality wet exhaust hose. If you connect to some dry exhaust section, however, you have to use flexible metal exhaust bellows.

An Exhaust Lift Solution

Another useful and these days often forgotten approach for getting the exhaust from a low engine installation high enough to run out the transom is the *standpipe exhaust system* (Figure 7-16). (This can be used in place of the waterlift muffler in a North Sea exhaust.)

In this configuration a dry exhaust line conducts the exhaust vertically upward from the exhaust manifold. This first portion of the run is dry and quite hot; it has to be very well and securely lagged (insulated) to prevent burns or fire. Don't forget a flexible metal bellows at the joint between the manifold and exhaust piping. Without the bellows, you'll get dangerous cracks surprisingly soon (see Chapter 9). The engine cooling water is injected into a large standpipe that caps the dry exhaust line. Here the water and gases mix, exiting the bottom of the standpipe to run out the transom.

STANDPIPES: OLD AND NEW Figure 7-17 shows the old and new versions of the standpipe. The old version works fine with two caveats, one being that the top of the standpipe gets very hot. Over several years' use, this arrangement has been known to cook the underside of a wooden deck until it looked as black as charcoal briquettes. The other caveat is that water lies in the bottom of the standpipe until you drain it manually—a corrosion headache. The new version injects water into the top of the standpipe. With a protective deflector cap to distribute the flow, the entire standpipe is kept cool and the water and gas mix more completely than in the old version. There's also little standing water in the bottom.

If you're repowering or designing a deep-bodied displacement hull, the dimensions given will allow you to fabricate a sound standpipe system. Again, you should use only the very best grade stainless, specifically 316L. Anything less is asking for corrosion problems down the line—a false economy. If you really want to do it perfectly, hunt around for Hastelloy C or Inconel. (This can be some hunt, but it is worth it even if quite expensive.) Whatever the alloy,

Figure 7-16. Standpipe exhaust system

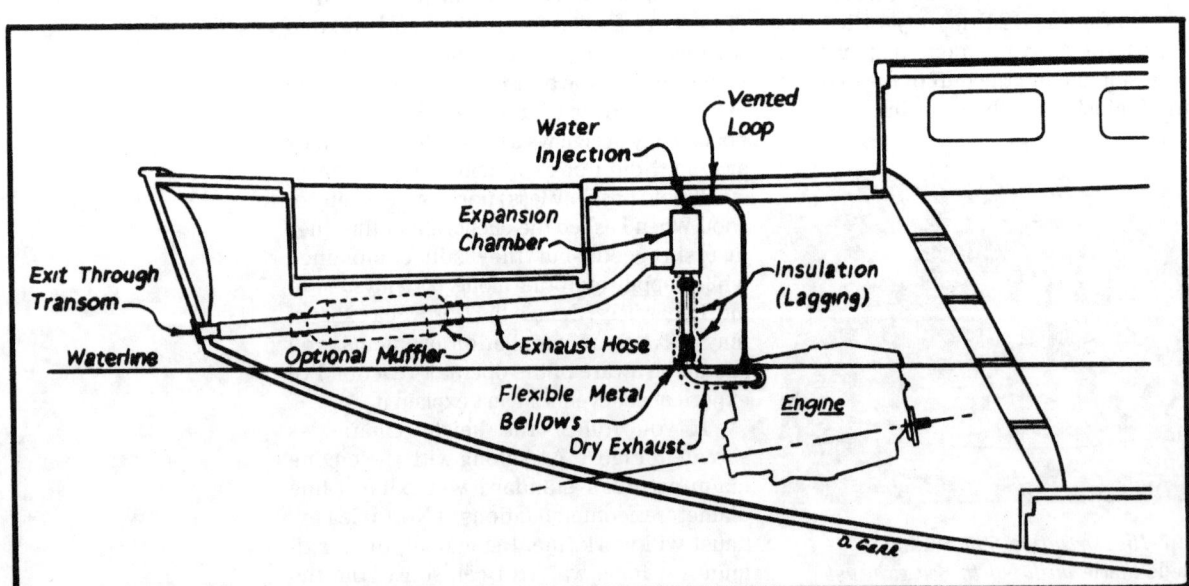

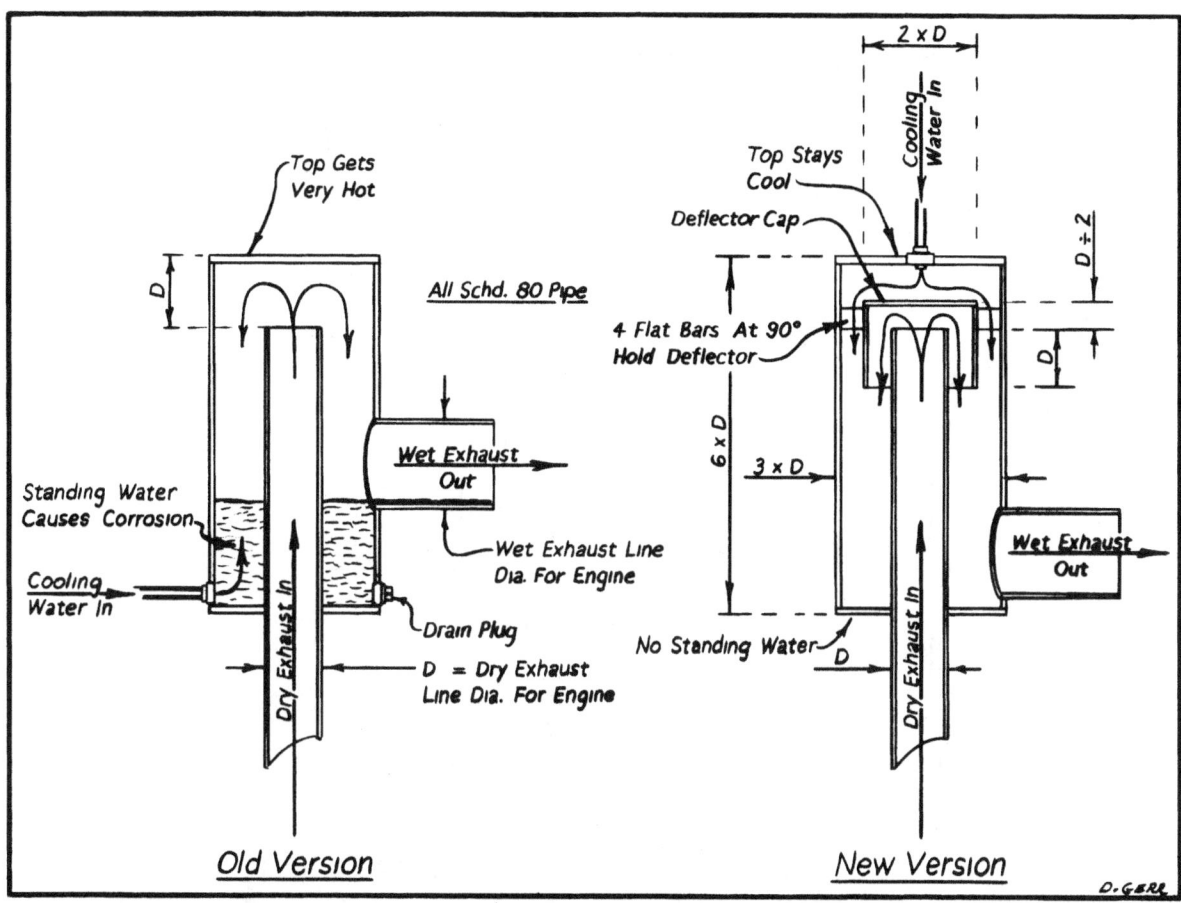

Figure 7-17. Details of a standpipe exhaust

all the metal piping should be from schedule 80 (double-weight) pipe. The plate caps and fittings should be as thick as or slightly thicker than the pipe wall they're fastened to.

THE MUFFLER OPTION By the way, some folks—on low-powered displacement vessels—don't bother with a muffler on a standpipe exhaust system. Again, the process of mixing water and exhaust gases in the standpipe—along with the expansion and cooling that take place there—makes it a pretty fair silencer in its own right. Nevertheless, if you want a really quiet boat, you won't regret installing a separate in-line muffler aft of the standpipe.

High-Powered Engines: Excess Water

Some large high-powered diesels are engineered to pump very large quantities of water through the system. The more cooling water available, the more you can use to cool intake air and fuel; the cooler the air and fuel are kept, the more efficiently the engine runs. This, however, poses a problem with exhaust runs. Where most small to midsize diesels can dump all their cooling water into the exhaust, such large engines may push so much raw water through the system that dumping it all into the exhaust would effectively clog it up, creating excess back pressure.

The solution is to T off a branch of the cooling water, directing, say, 60 percent into the exhaust system and the remainder directly overboard though a bypass line. The schematic in Figure 7-18 shows this installation on a design from my office with twin MTU, V-12 4000 diesels, rated at 2,300 hp (1,715 kW) each, and driving the props

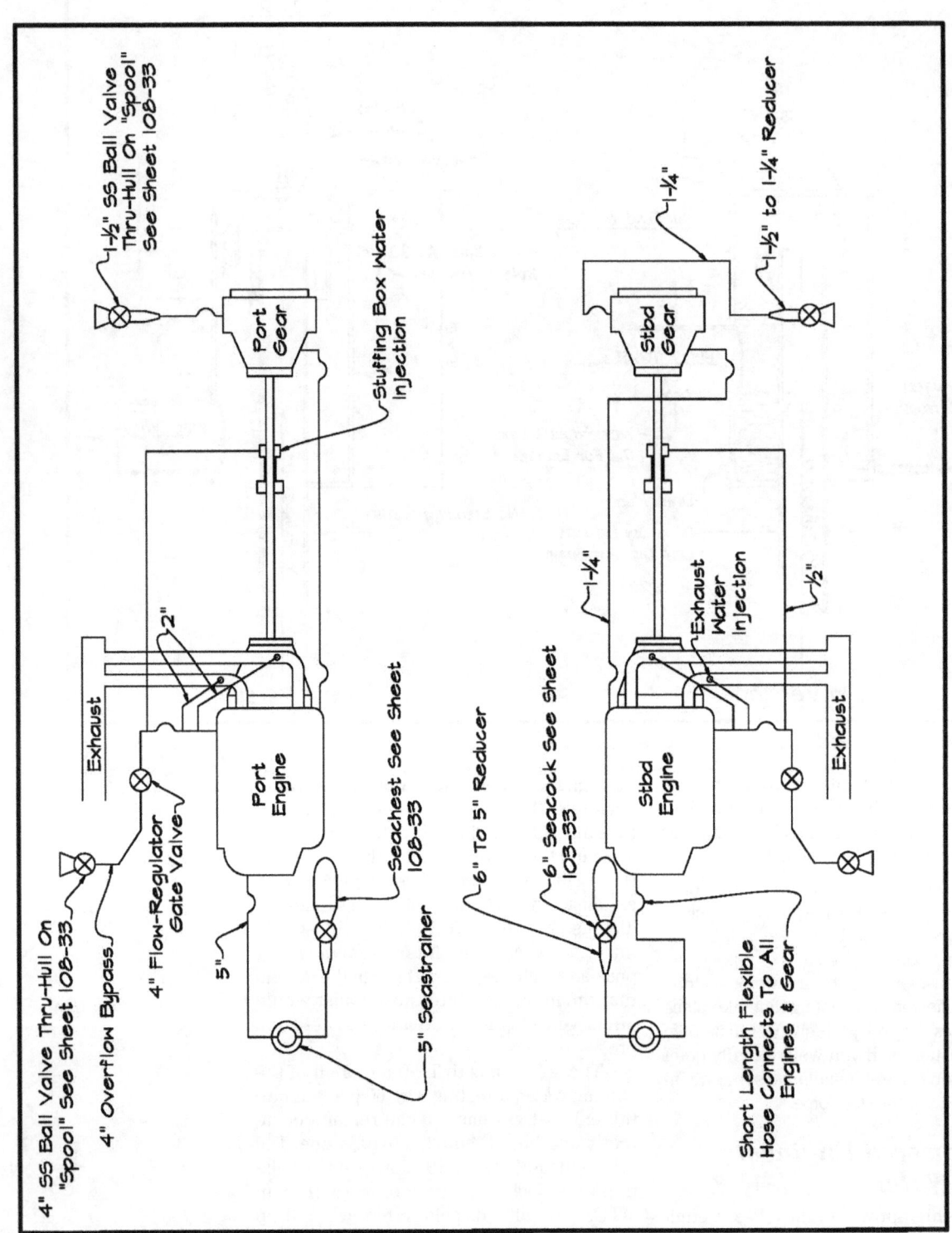

Figure 7-18. Main engine raw-water piping

through remote V-gears. The ratio of cooling water in the exhaust to that in the bypass line not only varies from engine to engine but with the same engine in different installations. You must consult the manufacturer, and even then it's a good idea to provide adjustment to the flow. A valve on the bypass line does this nicely.

Close the valve off, and 100 percent of the water will exit thorough the main exhaust piping. Open it completely and, if properly sized, 70 percent or more will exit via the bypass line. Somewhere in between is about right. The correct setting is found during sea trials with reference to the exhaust pyrometer and manometer. Once set to the right mix, the bypass-adjustment valve should be wired in place. A less expensive option is to insert variable-line reducers or plugs manually fitted into the bypass pipe. This is more difficult to adjust but is OK once the right combination is found, since the adjustment only needs to be done initially.

Mixing and Matching

Following the principles for each type of exhaust system, you can mix and match exhaust system types to solve specific installation problems. Figures 7-19 and 7-20 show profiles of the exhaust system of a 72-foot (22 m) schooner from my office. As often happens on sailboats, the engine installation was in a restricted space, and in this case the engine was reversed to drive a remote V drive. There was no room to shoot straight up with a conventional standpipe. Here I used a dry exhaust system running up and aft, with water injected at the end and then into a standard waterlift. (See Chapter 9 for details of dry exhaust installations.)

GOING UNDERWATER

So far, we've been discussing standard abovewater exhaust outlets. If you could exhaust underwater, then you would have no smell and minimal noise from the exhaust port. Even better, if you install an underwater outlet correctly, the motion of the water under the hull and past the outlet can generate a slight suction for a small additional "turbo" boost.

Underwater exhaust outlets have many potential pitfalls, however. There can be too much back pressure; exhaust gases can find their way into the propellers, causing ventilation and loss of thrust; exhaust gases can cause the rudders to ventilate; or exhaust gases can increase the likelihood of sucking air down under the hull and, on some planing hulls, lead to dynamic instability.

All these problems can be avoided, and underwater exhaust outlets can be quite successful. Figure 7-21 shows the underwater exhaust on the highly efficient, 40-knot, 116-foot (35 m) German Schnell boat from World War II (known to the Allies as "E-boats"). And Figure 7-22 shows the Cape Dory 40, which was fitted with a very successful underwater exhaust.

Requirements for Underwater Exhaust Systems

To avoid back pressure, there must be an idle bypass line forked off the after third of the main exhaust line. The rule of thumb is that the bypass line should be one-third the diameter of the standard wet exhaust line. At speed, there is no problem with back pressure, as the water rushing past the submerged outlet creates a suction. At low speed and at idle, however, the exhaust would have to push out against the static head of water, which would be far too much back pressure.

The idle bypass simply provides an exit for exhaust gases at low speed. There is less water pumped through at low speeds, and all or virtually all of the water will exit satisfactorily through the underwater outlet. It's best to branch the idle bypass at a distinctly sharp angle off the main exhaust line, and to run the bypass line upward. In fact, the idle bypass line on the Cape Dory 40 can be seen in Figures 7-23, 7-24, and 7-25 (as it can on the Schnell boat drawings). On the Cape Dory, the sole problem with the arrangement as drawn and installed was that at idle the bypass would sometimes spit a small trickle of black, sooty water, which was unsightly. If I did this again, I would probably raise the exit of the idle bypass somewhat higher to reduce this, even though the problem was minimal.

No valve is needed to control or close the idle bypass. The motion of the boat and

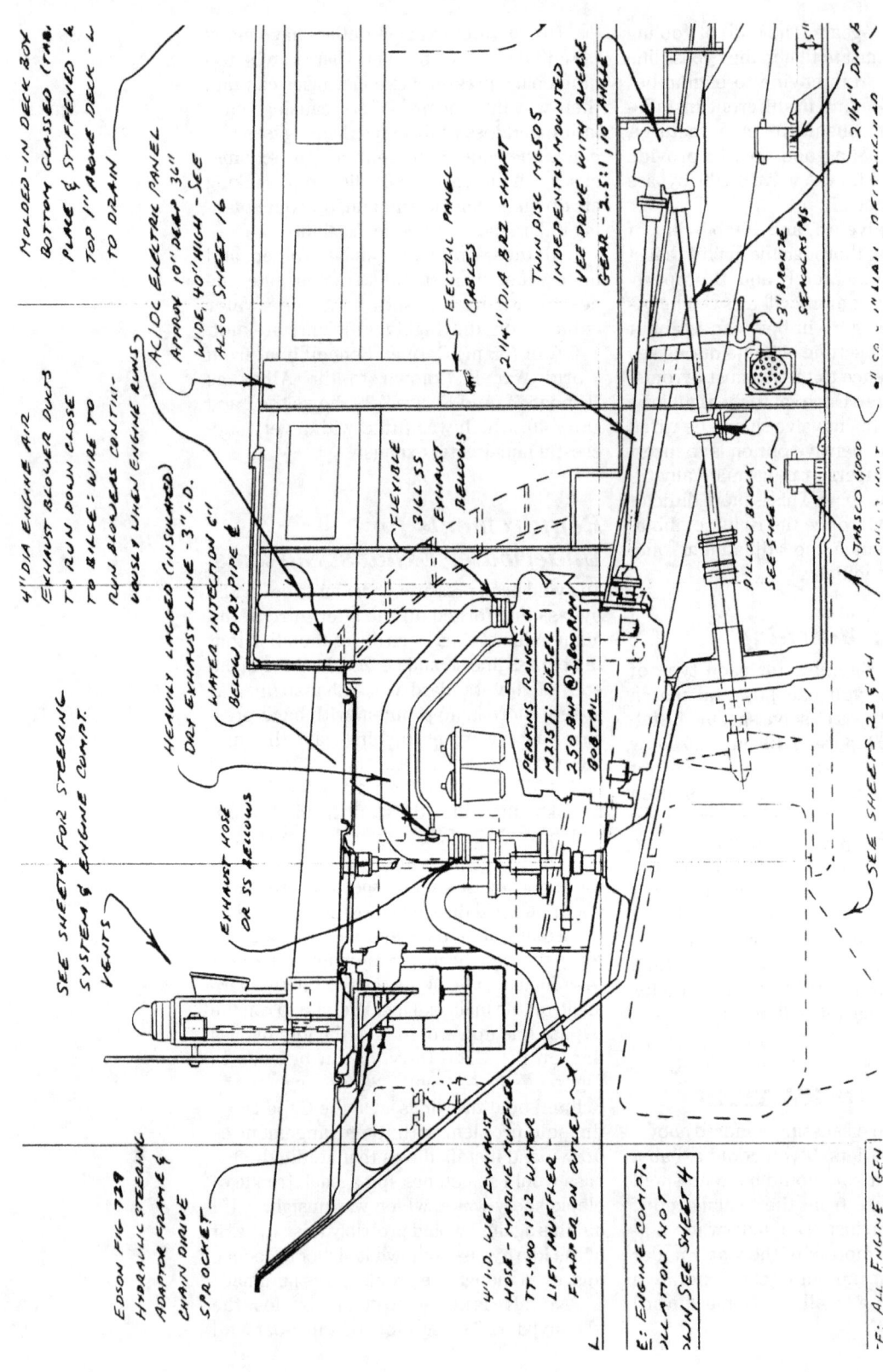

Figure 7-19. Profile of the exhaust system in a 72-foot schooner

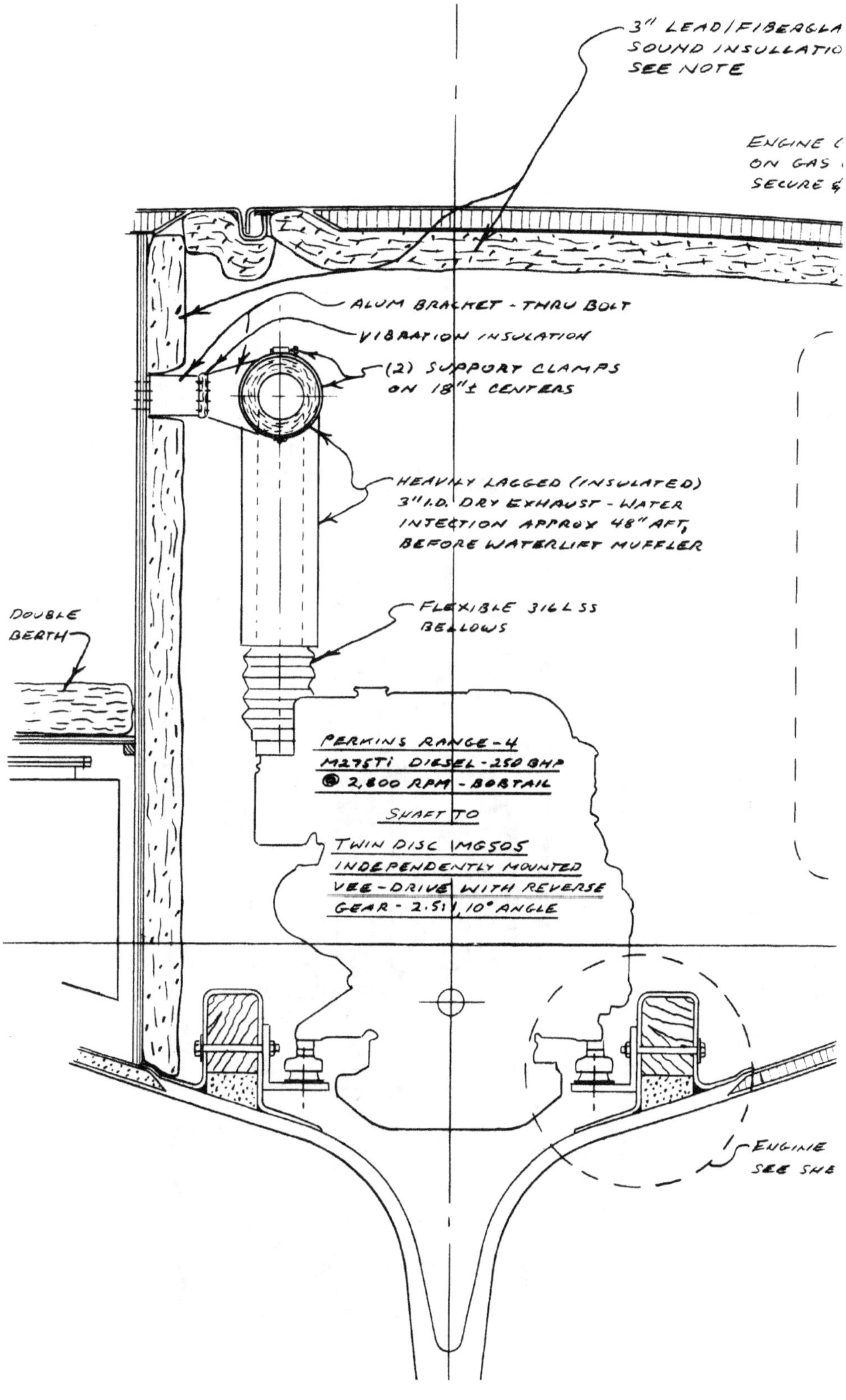

Figure 7-20. Exhaust system continued (section view)

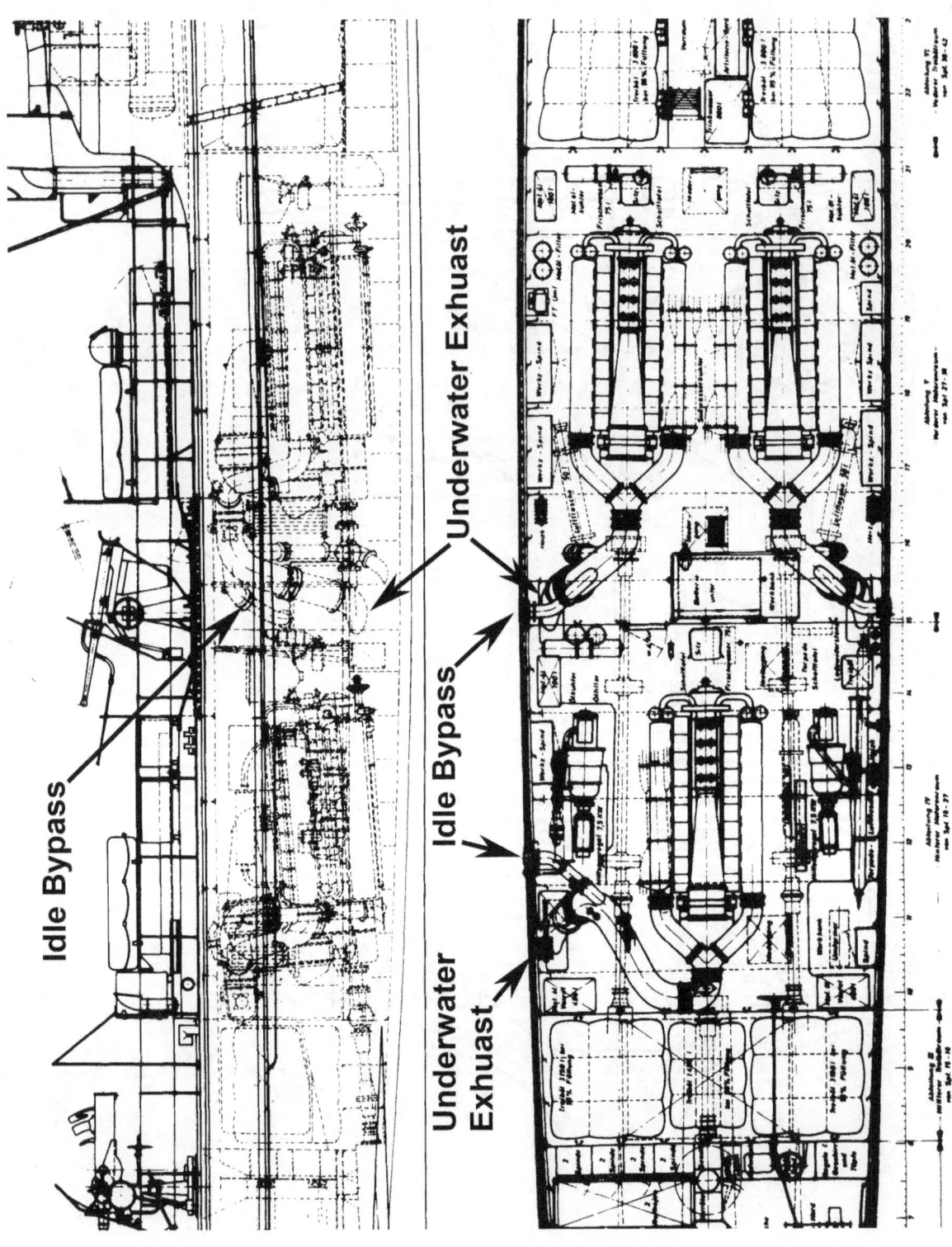

Figure 7-21. Schnell boat machinery and arrangement (Reprinted from Fast Fighing Boats, by Harald Fock)

Chapter 7: Wet Exhaust Systems

Figure 7-22. Cape Dory 40 with underwater exhaust outlet

resulting suction, combined with gravity, will ensure that all or almost all the exhaust exits underwater at speed.

Underwater Nacelles

The suction effect is enhanced by surrounding most of the main exhaust outlet's underwater exit with a fairing nacelle to generate suction through hydrodynamic lift. Figure 7-26 shows how this was done on the Schnell boats, which I think is ideal. On the Cape Dory 40, Figure 7-27 shows very large exhaust nacelles. These worked fine, and the boat handled well in all conditions, but I think I would cut these very large projecting nacelles down by two-thirds to more closely approximate the smaller Schnell boat nacelles.

Underwater Location

The Schnell boat's underwater exhausts exit near midships and well ahead of the

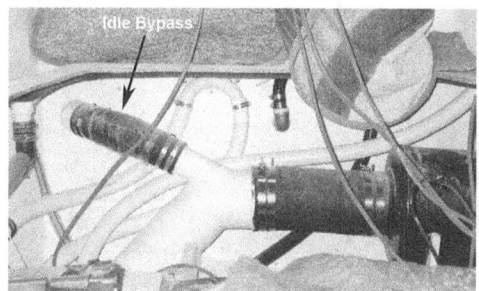

Figure 7-23. Inside view of the Cape Dory's underwater exhaust

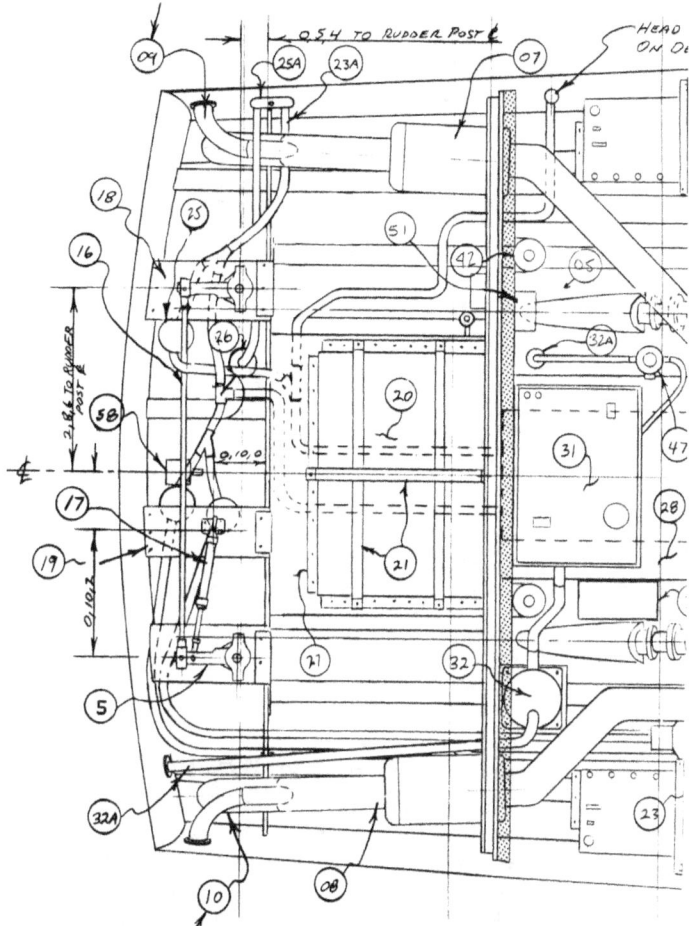

propellers. This is a potential source of trouble. It is possible that the exhaust gases can get trapped under the hull and flow back into the running gear. In the case of the Schnell boat, this configuration worked because the exhaust exits were well forward of the running gear, and the exits—though underwater—were up near the turn of the bilge on a round-bilge hull. This allowed the gases to escape up and outboard without being directed aft and down. On a hard-chine hull—with the exhaust exits under the chine—this might not work and could cause a problem.

The Cape Dory 40's exhausts exit as far aft and as far outboard as possible. All is aft of the running gear. This ensures that there is no possibility of the exhaust gases being trapped under the hull or ventilating propellers or rudders.

Figure 7-24. Plan of the Cape Dory 40's underwater exhaust system. Item #9 is the idle bypass, and #10 is the underwater exhaust.

123

PART THREE: EXHAUST SYSTEMS

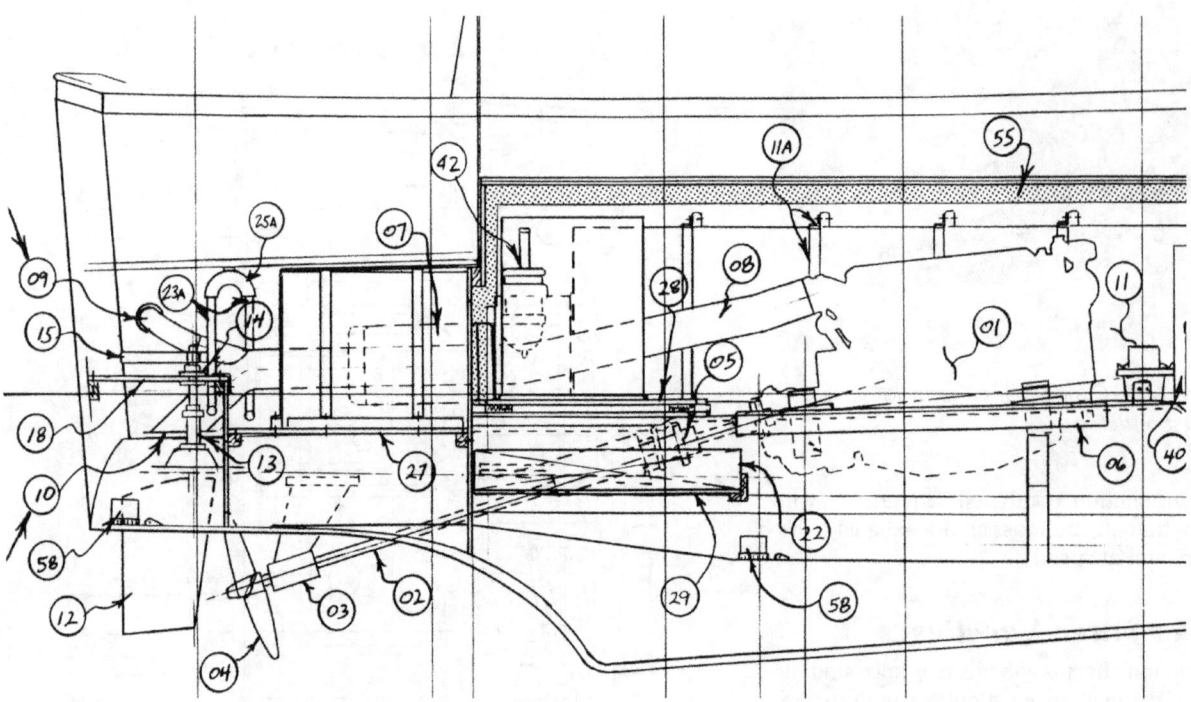

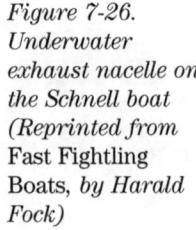

Figure 7-25. Inboard profile of the Cape Dory 40's underwater exhaust. Item #9 is the idle bypass, and #10 is the underwater exhaust.

Separating the Water

Still another exhaust option is mixing the water with the exhaust gases, as usual in a wet exhaust system, and then separating the water out again. Such water-separator mufflers (Figure 7-28) are, comparatively speaking, new, but they offer interesting advantages. First, the process of separating the water removes more energy from the exhaust, making it quieter. Second, the separated water can be dumped below the waterline, usually about 4 to 6 inches (100 to 150 mm) below, but no more. The tail-end, gas-line portion of the exhaust automatically acts as an idle bypass. Third, the tail-end gas line is now cool and a smaller diameter than the standard wet exhaust line. It's much easier to run this—usually as hose—for long distances and around weird corners without heat, noise, or back pressure problems. Like the North Sea exhaust system, water separators can assist greatly with engine installations near midships.

Figure 7-28 shows a Halyard water-separator exhaust on one of my boat designs,

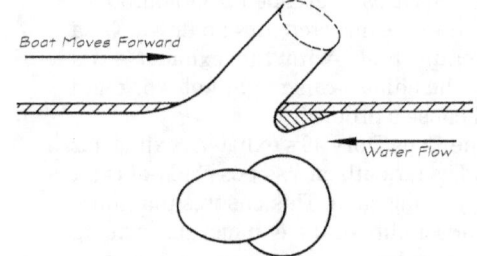

Figure 7-26. Underwater exhaust nacelle on the Schnell boat (Reprinted from Fast Fightling Boats, by Harald Fock)

Figure 7-27. Exterior view of the Cape Dory's underwater exhaust system

124

Chapter 7: Wet Exhaust Systems

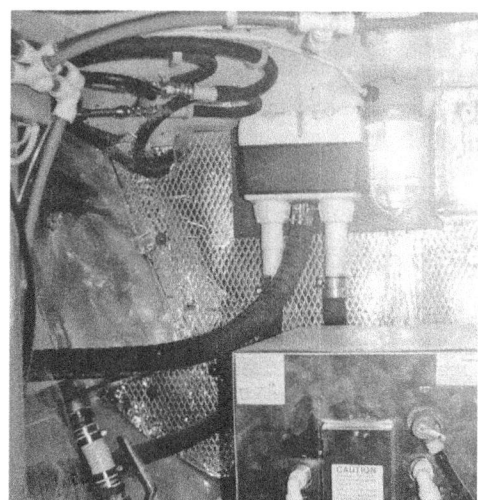

Figure 7-28. Water-separator muffler

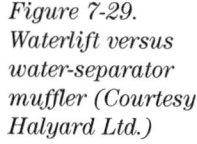

Figure 7-29. Waterlift versus water-separator muffler (Courtesy Halyard Ltd.)

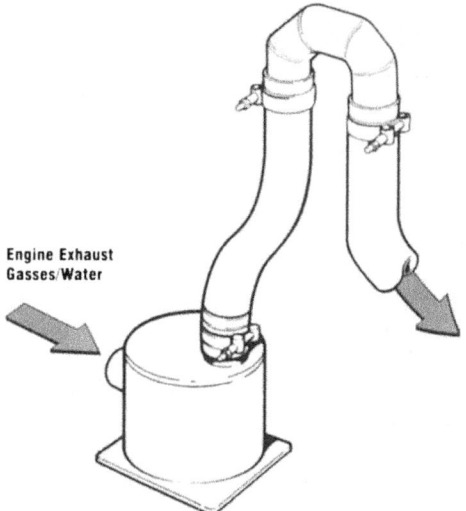

Standard Waterlift

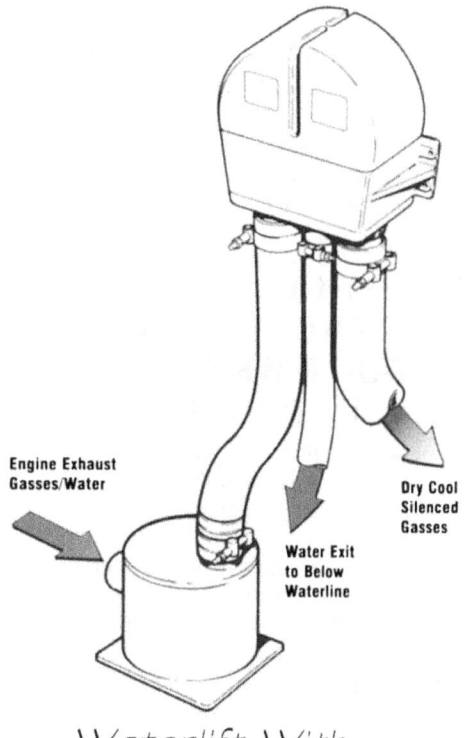

Waterlift With Water Separator

and the drawings (Figure 7-29) show the setup. This unit is designed to work with a waterlift muffler. The wet exhaust enters the bottom of the water separator through one hose, and the separated water and cooled gas each exit through their dedicated hoses.

Note: Avoid U-bends in the dry exhaust line. They can cause vapor locks, which may result in carbon monoxide backing up into the boat.

Other companies, such as Centek and Soundown, now offer an assortment of water-separator mufflers.

AVOIDING THE SILENT KILLER

A final and critical caution is needed. Carbon monoxide (CO) sickens or kills a number of boaters every year. CO is an inescapable by-product of burning fuel in an internal-combustion engine. CO poisoning is insidious and extremely dangerous. You must take great care to minimize the chance of CO (and other exhaust-gas by-products) from working its way back on board. Keep in mind that normal running conditions may well help disburse and dissipate CO, while lying against a dock (or another boat) with the engine idling or the gen set running may well

125

Figure 7-30. The Centek VernaSep muffler

create a dangerous situation that doesn't exist when you're underway. You should study both ABYC TH-22, *Educational Information about Carbon Monoxide*, and A-24, *Carbon Monoxide Detection Systems*. Use the information both to help work out your exhaust installation to minimize CO on board and to give early warning of a CO problem.

SUMMARY OF REQUIREMENTS FOR A RELIABLE WET EXHAUST SYSTEM

We can summarize the requirements for a reliable wet exhaust system, both for installation and for operation and maintenance:

1. ideally, raw-water intake from sea chest (best two-sided), see Chapter 17
2. seacock at water intakes, see Chapter 17
3. duplex sea strainer, see Chapter 17
4. quick access to raw-water pump
5. replacement impeller always ready; change every 6 months
6. regular change of heat-exchanger zincs
7. regular inspection and flushing of the heat exchanger
8. custom dry exhaust riser of Inconel or Hastelloy C
9. precautions against backflow of any water into the engine
10. all components in exhaust line should be hose or FRP

REVIEW OF REQUIREMENTS

We should go down the list to see what each item means.

1. WATER INTAKE FROM A SEA CHEST (BEST TWO-SIDED).

One potential problem with wet exhaust is sucking something into the raw-water intake and starving the engine and exhaust for water. Usually this is a plastic bag. Sometimes it can be seaweed or kelp. The optimal solution is a sea chest that opens on both sides of the keel with a flush grate on either side. With such a sea chest, you would have to have a plastic bag stuck against both sides of the keel to block water flow. This is virtually impossible. What's more—with the intake grates flush—the forward motion of the boat will sweep away any obstruction. I've never had such a sea chest blocked—ever. Not all boats have keel configurations that will allow such a two-sided sea chest, however. In this case even a single-sided sea chest with a flush grate is extremely unlikely to be clogged, because water flow will still sweep away any obstruction. There are many very successful vessels, though, without sea chests. Sea chests are not a requirement, but they are a plus when it's possible to install them. (See also Chapter 17.)

2. SEACOCK AT RAW-WATER INTAKE.

This is plain enough. It's a standard basic safety requirement. See Chapter 17.

3. DUPLEX SEA STRAINER.

These ensure that sand or mud—which can get past the sea chest grates—can't clog the raw-water intake lines or pump. The sea strainers should each be as large as possible and be switchable. This way, if one clogs up with silt at sea, you can switch over to the other without missing a stroke, and then clean out the gunk from the now-disconnected intake. See Chapter 17.

4. Quick access to the raw-water pump.
This is to ensure that you can clear any clog or breakage in the pump. Clogging is unlikely with the sea chest and duplex sea strainer. In fact, on my designs so equipped, it's never happened yet. It pays to be safe, though.

5. Replacement impeller always ready; change every 6 months.
The most common cause of raw-water pump failure is for one of its impeller vanes to break. With a spare always ready, a new one can be popped in quickly. This, too, is unlikely if you simply make a point of putting in a new impeller every 6 months. This also means you'll be familiar with the process of changing out the impeller should you ever need to do it in an emergency.

6. Regular change of heat-exchanger zinc.
Too often the zincs are forgotten or ignored. They play a vital role in protecting against corrosion. Be sure to have spares, check them regularly, and change them per the manufacturer's recommended schedule.

7. Regular inspection and flushing of the heat exchanger.
A standard schedule of flushing the raw-water heat-exchanger circuit with fresh water will greatly reduce the chance of corrosion and silting.

8. Custom dry exhaust riser of Inconel or Hastelloy C.
As we've seen, standard engine exhaust risers are water jacketed. This means the raw water from the exhaust manifold is injected into a double wall or exterior pipe that surrounds the exhaust pipe to cool it. Water-jacketed exhaust risers are a known source of corrosion. In most of the designs from my office we discard water-jacketed exhaust risers in favor of custom dry exhaust risers made of Inconel or Hastelloy C. These are exceptionally corrosion-resistant alloys. With no water jacket, the dry riser is insulated or lagged all around (it's fire hot) but is small enough not to put too much heat into the boat. At the end of the riser, the raw water is injected again to cool and quiet the exhaust, which then goes into the exhaust hose.

9. Precautions against backflow.
We've seen that these are simple and common sense. You don't want water backing up the exhaust line into the turbo or the manifold. A waterlift muffler is good protection in itself. Also use surge chambers and hinged flappers. Standard stuff, but vital.

10. All components in exhaust line should be hose or FRP.
By using only hose and FRP, you avoid corrosion problems in the exhaust line. No metal—even the best stainless—is fully corrosion resistant.

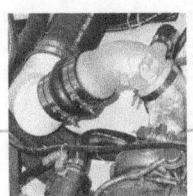

CHAPTER 8
Engine Cooling Systems and Their Exhausts

In the previous chapter we discussed the most common exhaust systems on boats: wet exhausts. As we saw, these exhausts are "wet" because engine cooling water is injected into the gases exiting the engine both to cool them and, through mixing and expansion, to make the exhaust quieter. Such exhaust systems have only a short dry portion prior to water injection. You can, however, have an all-dry exhaust system with no water injection at all. Such exhausts are, not surprisingly, termed *dry exhaust* or *drystack exhaust systems*.

The advantage of a drystack exhaust is that there is no seawater in the cooling system; it's 100 percent fresh water mixed with antifreeze. This reduces the likelihood of corrosion and eliminates any need for a seawater pump for cooling. We'll make a detailed comparison of the pros and cons of drystack versus wet exhausts at the end of the next chapter, but we'll begin by examining the engine cooling requirements particular to drystack installations.

NOTE: Some references call the dry section or dry line of a water-separator exhaust system (see Chapter 7) a "drystack." This is not strictly accurate. It should be termed the "dry leg of a water-separator exhaust system." When you see the term *drystack exhaust*, double-check which type of exhaust is being referred to.

ENGINE COOLING

First, we need to take a step back and think about engine cooling systems. All internal-combustion engines produce large amounts of waste heat that must be dissipated to avoid overheating. Maximum combustion temperatures range between 3,000° and 5,000°F (1,650° to 2,750°C). Very roughly, 30 to 35 percent of the total heat energy from the fuel is removed through the exhaust; 34 to 39 percent actually goes to propel the boat; and 30 to 35 percent has to be removed by actively cooling the engine itself. If engine cooling fails, the lubricating oil begins to break down at temperatures of 400°F (200°C); at around 500°F (260°C), the valve guides begin to score and the valve seats start to fail; and over 500°F (260°C), aluminum components lose strength and break.

Lubricating oil, fuel evaporating in the cylinders and manifold, and air around the engine do carry away about 10 percent of the excess heat. Largely radiated into the air immediately around the engine, this heat is important, and it is one reason for good ventilation. Removing only about 10 percent of the excess heat doesn't do the job, however. Accordingly, nearly all engines require a cooling system to keep them from literally melting and seizing up. Some small engines used outdoors—such as in lawn mowers, chainsaws, some older small cars (like the original VW Beetle), and even some airplane engines—are, indeed, simply air cooled. This means that the engine is specifically designed to be cooled entirely by air flowing over it. In fact, some small boats have used low-powered, air-cooled engines. This is simple and free from water-pump or corrosion problems, but—deep in the bilge—it's impractical to air-cool anything but diminutive engines, and it's not as efficient as using the much colder and denser seawater surrounding the hull for cooling.

Keep in mind that engines shouldn't run too cold, though. That's inefficient as well. In theory, the hotter an engine can run, the more efficient it is, but maximum possible operating temperatures are constrained by the limits of the lubricant and the structural materials we have to work with. Cooling-system thermostats on typical diesels are set to start to open (reduce coolant temperature) at around 160°F to 180°F (70°C to 82°C) and fully open at around 180°F to 200°F (82°C to 94°C), with maximum allowable water temperature just under freshwater boil, around 210°F (98°C). These are the optimum running temperatures for most standard-engine cooling systems. High-performance engines, running a 50/50 mixture of antifreeze and water under pressure, can run at coolant temperatures up to around 260°F (125°C). (Antifreeze is usually ethylene glycol or the newer propylene glycol.) The 50/50 mixture also protects against freezing down to about –40°F (which also happens to be –40°C).

There are three basic methods for using seawater to cool engines: *raw-water cooling*, *heat-exchanger cooling*, and *keel cooling*.

Raw-Water Cooling

The simplest water-cooled system ingests water from outside through a seacock and then a strainer to provide seawater directly to the engine. The usual path is from the strainer through the oil cooler, next through the exhaust manifold, then through the engine block, and finally injected into the exhaust and overboard. This is termed *raw-water cooling* or *direct cooling* (Figure 8-1). The advantage is that it is simple and light. The disadvantage is that the raw salt water (with algae, silt, pollutants, and other impurities) runs through the engine itself, where it can cause both corrosion and fouling ("silting") inside this most essential machine. A thermostat can and should be fitted. This switches some portion of the water flow from the water injection into the exhaust to recirculate through the raw-water pump and back into the engine, until the engine reaches the proper operating temperature.

Some raw-water systems aren't fitted with the thermostat and raw-water recirculation and so tend always to run cold, which is inefficient, as we've seen. Even with a thermostat and recirculation, the fluctuations in seawater temperature and the fact that this isn't a controlled closed circuit result in poorer engine temperature control. Raw-water

---

Central or Shared Cooling Systems

When two or more engines (or an engine and a generator) are installed, sharing a single cooling system (cooling circuit) can appear to simplify things. The advantage of apparent simplicity can be deceptive, however. Problems like the chance of unequal water flow are all too likely. External head pressures may be too great, and if there's a serious problem in the single cooling system, then you lose all engines. Troubleshooting is also complex. With two engines and a generator sharing a single, central cooling system, there are 162 possible operational permutations!

On a shared system there must be independent flow control through each engine; the heat exchanger or keel cooler must be able to deliver proper cooling at all engine loads. Balancing coolant flow through engines operating at different loads is difficult. An engine running at full throttle is pushing much more cooling water than one running at just over idle. For these reasons—though it can be done with very careful engineering and intelligent crew management—shared cooling systems aren't recommended.

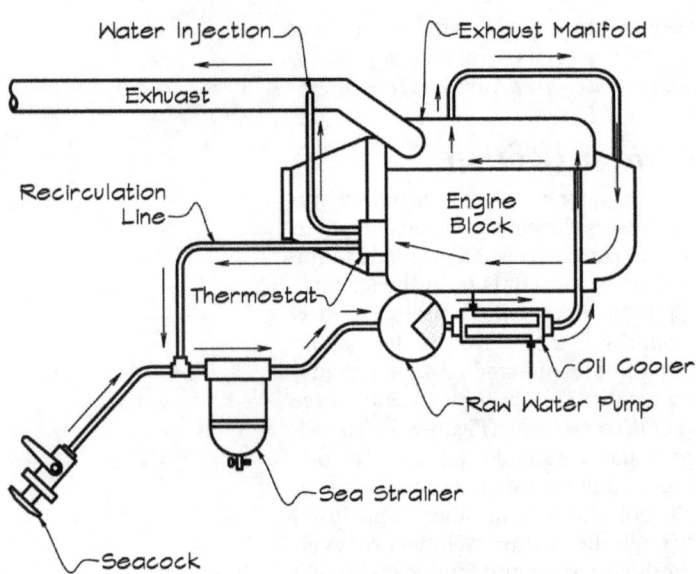

Figure 8-1. Raw-water cooling

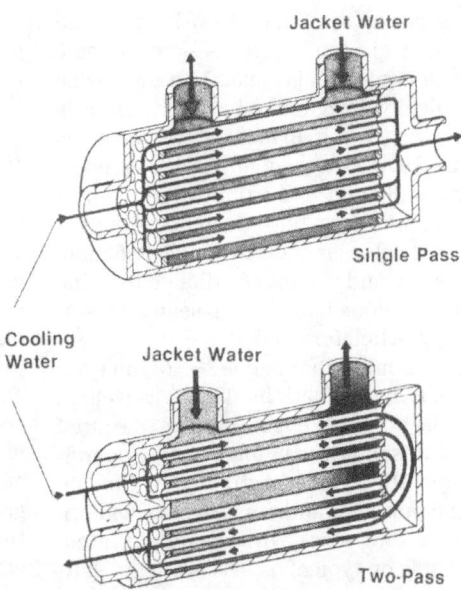

Figure 8-2. Heat exchangers (Courtesy Caterpillar, Inc.)

cooling is appropriate only for small, inexpensive runabouts and day boats, and only for vessels operated in temperatures well above freezing. For such craft, the savings in cost and some weight may be worth it. Corrosion and silting problems can be reduced somewhat by flushing the engine with fresh water after every run. This is accomplished by installing a valved T-fitting after the seacock on the raw-water intake. The seacock is closed after every run and a freshwater hose is connected to the T-fitting (see Chapter 17). The fresh water is turned on, and the engine is operated for several minutes at idle to flush the system.

Heat-Exchanger Cooling

Most boats use *heat-exchanger cooling* (also called *indirect cooling* or *closed cooling*; see Figure 8-2). This is similar to the cooling system of a standard car or truck, with one big exception. In cars, the water-cooling system is a closed loop. The cooling water is mixed with antifreeze to protect from freezing, reduce corrosion, and optimize operating temperature. The coolant path is similar to a raw-water system except that the water fills the system and part of a header tank (also called an expansion tank) and circulates round and round. (Note: The rule of thumb is that header tank capacity should be 10 percent of total cooling system coolant, but follow the manufacturer's recommendations.) In this circuit—in a car or truck—the hot coolant passes through a heat exchanger that is called the radiator (Figure 8-3). This literally radiates heat to the air, and it requires a fan to increase the airflow over the radiator's cooling surface.

Radiators won't work on a boat. Deep in the hull, there's no practical way to use an air-cooled radiator. Instead, a second cooling-water system is used to transfer heat away from a water-cooled heat exchanger rather than an air-cooled radiator (Figure 8-4). This is quite efficient because seawater is denser and often colder than air and is easily available from right outside the boat. The second raw-water cooling circuit enters the seacock, goes through a sea strainer, and then enters the raw-water pump (see Chapter 17). This circulates the raw water into the engine cooling heat exchanger. Most commonly, the raw water flows to the oil cooler and reduction-gear oil cooler prior to entering the engine heat exchanger or cooler. Finally the raw water—in the illustration, the raw water coming out of the heat exchanger—is injected into the exhaust and exits the boat, as we saw in the wet exhaust system in Chapter 7.

Chapter 8: Engine Cooling Systems and Their Exhausts

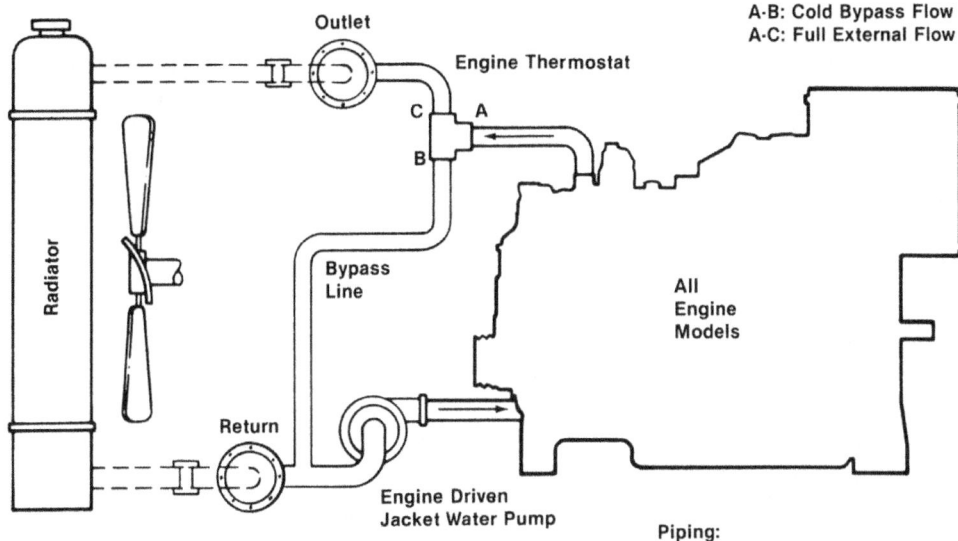

Figure 8-3. Radiator cooling (Courtesy Caterpillar, Inc.)

In this system, no raw water enters the engine block, only the antifreeze/freshwater coolant mixture. This closed system is efficiently temperature-controlled by the thermostat, and it keeps all raw water out of the engine. It does require two water pumps though: the water pump on the freshwater or closed-cooling circuit, and another pump on the raw-water circuit. Where there is an aftercooler or intercooler, separate heat exchangers are usually used for each (Figure 8-5).

Keel Cooling

Last, there is keel cooling. It is not new. In fact, steamboats in the 1840s used external condensers (effectively what we call keel coolers) mounted outside the hull. In keel cooling, there is no raw-water cooling circuit. Instead, the engine heat exchanger is placed outside the boat in contact with the sea. The seawater thus directly carries away the engine heat. This eliminates a raw-water pump and salt water in the boat, but you now have no raw water to cool the exhaust, which—as we've seen—is dangerously hot. The exhaust is now entirely a dry exhaust (or drystack exhaust), and it is at a very high temperature indeed. We'll cover the installation of these drystack systems in Chapter 9.

Before we move on to the exhaust piping itself, we need to look at the keel cooling that drystack exhausts require. Keel cooling is an integral part of a drystack exhaust system. Further, on heat-exchanger engines, most of the cooling package (minus some hose, a seacock, and raw-water strainer or sea strainer) comes as a package with the engine. In contrast, much of the keel-cooling

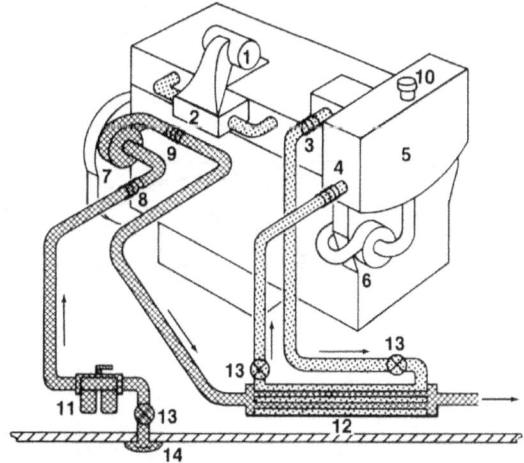

Figure 8-4. Heat-exchanger cooling: jacket water aftercooled (Courtesy Caterpillar, Inc.)

1. Turbocharger
2. Aftercooler, jacket water cooled
3. Jacket water outlet connection
4. Jacket water inlet connection
5. Expansion tank
6. Jacket water pump
7. Auxiliary pump, seawater
8. Seawater inlet connection
9. Seawater outlet connection
10. Pressure cap
11. Duplex full-flow strainer
12. Heat exchanger
13. Shut-off valve
14. Seawater intake

131

PART THREE: EXHAUST SYSTEMS

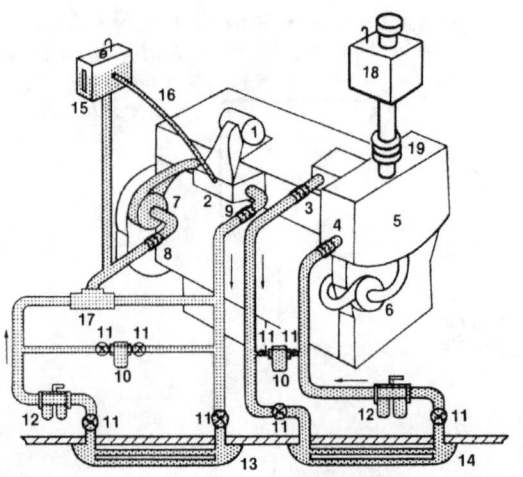

1. Turbocharger
2. Aftercooler, keel cooled
3. Jacket water outlet connection
4. Jacket water inlet connection
5. Expansion tank
6. Jacket water pump
7. Auxiliary fresh water pump
8. Auxiliary fresh water inlet connection
9. Aftercooler outlet connection
10. Bypass filter
11. Shut-off valve
12. Duplex full-flow strainer
13. Keel cooler for aftercooler
14. Keel cooler for jacket water
15. Expansion tank for aftercooler circuit
16. Vent line for aftercooler circuit
17. Bypass valve thermostatically controlled
18. Auxiliary expansion tank
19. Flexible connection

Figure 8-5. Dual heat-exchanger cooling with a separate circuit for the aftercooler (Courtesy Caterpillar, Inc.)

system components are either ordered or fabricated separately by the boatbuilder.

There are two basic types of keel coolers: hull-surface tanks (for metal hulls) and external tubing. A variant of external tubing is to run the cooling water though internal or external channels welded to a metal hull. When internal, these are sometimes part of the interior structural framing of a metal boat. Note that most of these coolers aren't usually in or on the keel proper, in spite of the common term *keel cooling*. (Note: Consult the pump manufacture for high-temperature pump vanes. Don't use raw-water plastic impeller pumps for a closed cooling circuit. The plastic vanes will fail in the hot water.)

TANK OR SHELL KEEL COOLING On metal boats, a flat shallow tank or pair of tanks can be welded to the inside of the hull. Coolant exits the engine and enters these tanks, where it circulates in contact with the exterior hull shell, dissipates the heat, and then is piped back to the engine. These tanks will be very warm, even hot, on the inside. You need to prevent that heat from radiating back into the boat by covering the inside surfaces of the tank with insulation.

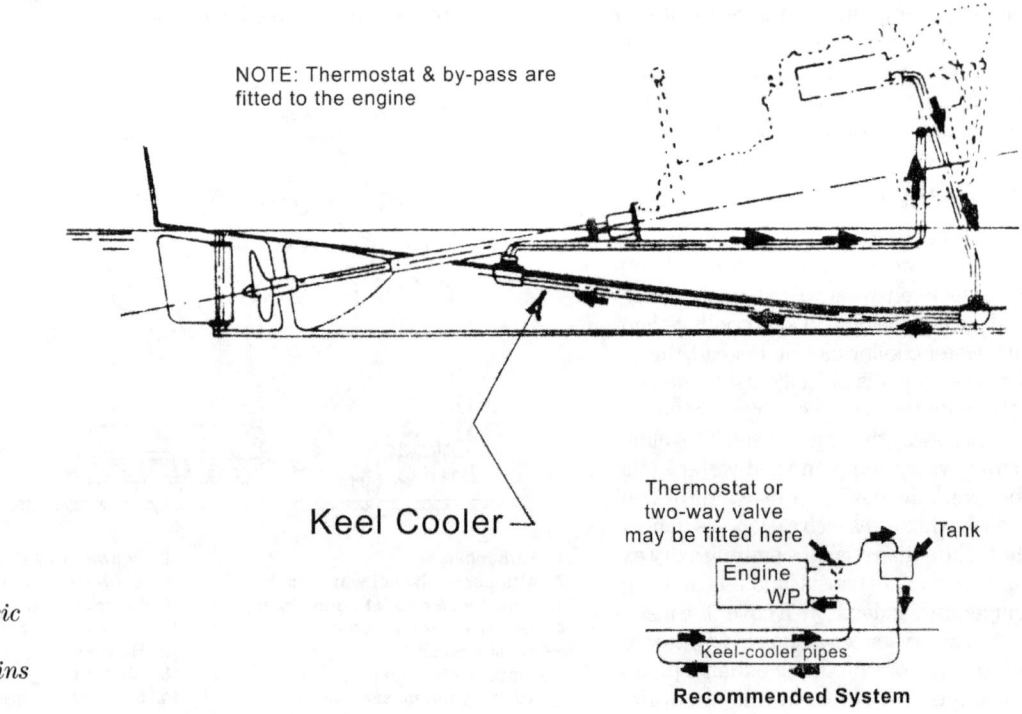

Figure 8-6. Basic keel cooler (Courtesy Perkins Engine Co.)

REQUIRED COOLING SURFACE AREA Regardless of configuration, this is a heat-transfer process, so the surface area required for adequate cooling (adequate heat transfer) will vary depending on the thermal conductivity of the material (steel, aluminum, copper), the material's wall thickness, the flow rate of water passing over the outside and through the inside of the cooler, and the outside seawater temperature. Paint reduces effective heat transfer, as does fouling from marine growth. On steel, rust and mill scale further reduce efficient heat transfer. Accordingly, painted steel requires more area than painted aluminum (including allowance for some fouling), while unpainted copper or copper-nickel tube requires less area than either steel or aluminum. Not only is the copper-nickel tube wall generally thinner than steel or aluminum hull plate or standard structural shapes, and not only does copper have the highest thermal conductivity, but both copper and copper-nickel are nonfouling and so require no paint.

Table 8-1 gives recommended external surface areas for keel coolers of various materials and at differing boat speeds.

LENGTH OF TUBING FOR REQUIRED SURFACE AREA Wood and fiberglass boats don't use integral tank keel coolers; rather, they use external tubing (which is most common on metal hulls as well). The length of round tubing or pipe required can be sized from Table 8-1 using the standard formula for the circumference of a circle.

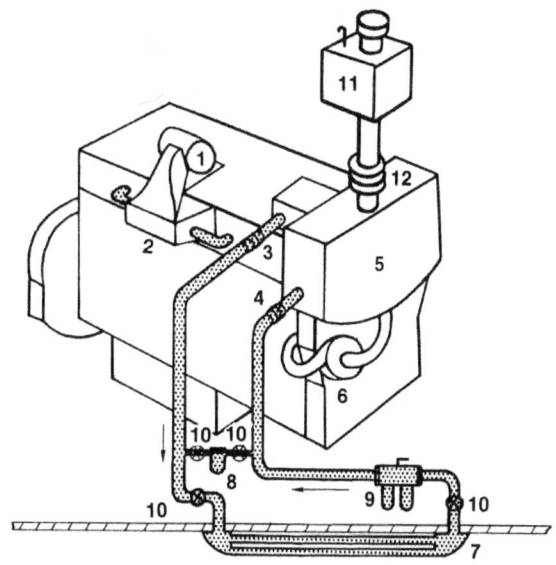

1. Turbocharger
2. Aftercooler, jacket water cooled
3. Jacket water outlet connection
4. Jacket water inlet connection
5. Expansion tank
6. Jacket water pump
7. Keel cooler
8. Bypass filter
9. Duplex full-flow strainer
10. Shut-off valve
11. Auxiliary Expansion Tank
12. Flexible connection

Figure 8-7. Keel cooler: jacket water aftercooled (Courtesy Caterpillar, Inc.)

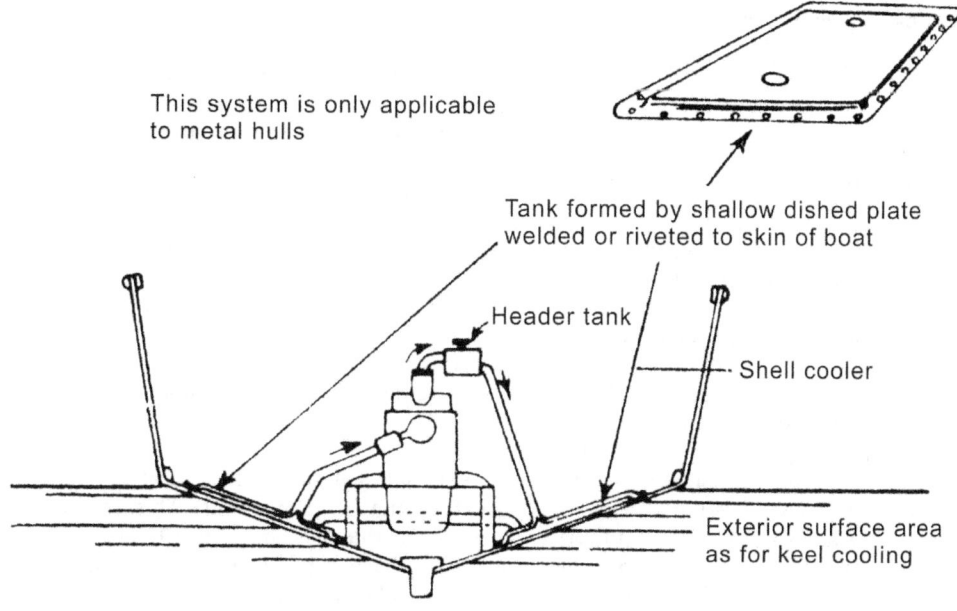

Figure 8-8. Tank (or shell) cooler (Courtesy Perkins Engine Co.)

TABLE 8-1. KEEL-COOLER EXTERNAL SURFACE AREA PER INSTALLED POWER UP TO 85°F (29.4°C) SEAWATER TEMPERATURE

STEEL, Painted—1/4 to 5/16 in. (6.3 to 8 mm) Thick

	Surface Area		
	sq. ft./bhp	m²/bhp	m²/kW
Generators and stationary vessels (dredges, etc.)	1.00	0.093	0.125
Slow-moving vessels (towboats, etc.)	0.50	0.046	0.062
Free-running vessels, under 8 knots	0.40	0.037	0.050
Fast free-running vessels, over 8 knots	0.34	0.032	0.042

ALUMINUM, Painted—1/4 to 5/16 in. (6.3 to 8 mm) Thick

	Surface Area		
	sq. ft./bhp	m²/bhp	m²/kW
Generators and stationary vessels (dredges, etc.)	0.60	0.056	0.075
Slow-moving vessels (towboats, etc.)	0.30	0.028	0.037
Free-running vessels, under 8 knots	0.24	0.022	0.030
Fast free-running vessels, over 8 knots	0.20	0.019	0.025

COPPER or COPPER NICKEL TUBE—Unpainted

	Surface Area		
	sq. ft./bhp	m²/bhp	m²/kW
Generators and stationary vessels (dredges, etc.)	0.21	0.020	0.0262
Slow-moving vessels (towboats, etc.)	0.15	0.014	0.0183
Free-running vessels, under 8 knots	0.12	0.011	0.0147
Fast free-running vessels, over 8 knots	0.10	0.009	0.0125

Formula 8-1.

Formula 8-1. Circumference of a Circle

$$\text{Circumference} = \pi \times \text{Dia.}$$

Where
$\pi = 3.14$
Dia. = tube outside diameter, in. or mm

Example: For instance, if we had a generator powered by a 12 bhp (8.95 kW) engine, and we wanted to use half-inch aluminum schedule 40 pipe for a keel cooler, how much would we need?

The aluminum has to be painted with bottom paint to minimize fouling. Generators are run not only underway but also when a boat is at the dock or at anchor, so the cooling area required has to be based on the worst case—zero external water flow—or stationary operation. Nominal 1/2-inch schedule 40 pipe has an OD of 0.840 inch. Wall thickness is 0.109 inch. This is less than the thickness in Table 8-1, meaning the area could be slightly less than indicated, but more cooling area is OK, so

We need 0.60 sq. ft./bhp from the table.

12 bhp × 0.60 sq. ft./bhp = 7.2 sq. ft.
Circumference = π × 0.840 in. = 2.638 in.
2.638 in. × 12 in. length = 31.656 sq. in. per lineal ft.
31.656 sq. in. ÷ 144 sq. in./sq. ft. = 0.219 sq. ft. per lineal ft. of pipe
7.2 sq. ft. required area ÷ 0.219 sq. ft. per lineal ft. = 32.9 ft. of pipe

Or

We could use DIN 2448 21.3 × 2 aluminum pipe (21.3 mm OD, 2 mm wall). This is less than the wall thickness in Table 8-1, meaning the area could be slightly less than indicated, but more cooling area never hurts, so

We need 0.075 m²/kW from the table.

$$8.95 \text{ kW} \times 0.075 \text{ m}^2/\text{kW} = 0.67 \text{ m}^2$$
$$\text{Circumference} = \pi \times 21.3 = 66.9 \text{ mm}$$
$$66.9 \text{ mm} \times 1{,}000 \text{ mm length} = 66{,}900 \text{ mm}^2$$
$$\text{per lineal m}$$
$$66{,}900 \text{ mm}^2 \div 1{,}000{,}000 \text{ mm}^2/\text{m}^2 = 0.067 \text{ m}^2$$
$$\text{per lineal m of pipe}$$
$$0.67 \text{ m}^2 \text{ required area} \div 0.067 \text{ m}^2 \text{ per lineal m}$$
$$= 10.0 \text{ m of pipe}$$

COPPER OR COPPER-NICKEL IS THE BEST TUBING MATERIAL Because it's nonfouling and has the highest heat conductivity, copper or copper-nickel makes a superior material for tubing, though care has to be taken to insulate it galvanically from a steel hull and it shouldn't be used on an aluminum hull. Copper-nickel is the first choice because it's considerably stronger than copper and also resists internal erosion from fluid flow better. For unpainted copper or copper-nickel tubing, you can use Table 8-2 or 8-3 to find the length of tube required. Note that in addition to being more efficient at conducting heat and being nonfouling, the wall thickness is less than for the steel or aluminum tables.

Don't use brass pipe or fittings! Brass is copper alloyed with zinc, and it will suffer from severe corrosion called dezincification.

KEEL-COOLER INSTALLATION CONSIDERATIONS Since keel coolers rely on seawater to cool them, they should be located as deeply as possible below the waterline. Too high up or too close to the waterline, and the cooler may roll out of the water or experience aerated water flow, both of which reduce heat-transfer (cooling) efficiency.

Keel coolers for stationary operation should be mounted on the side of the hull or the keel, not horizontally under the bottom of the hull. This is because—for a horizontal cooler when the boat isn't moving—warm water will not flow away by convection but will be trapped under the cooler, which will result in overheating. In addition, when hull-side-mounted keel coolers are recessed, the top of the recess should be angled to allow free convective flow from the top of the cooler (see Figure 8-9).

On tugs and towboats, the propulsion-engine keel cooler should be located aft in the underbody where the slipstream of the propeller will accelerate water past the cooler as much as possible.

When laying out the direction of water flow through the keel cooler, try to set things up so the flow runs from stern to bow. This increases the apparent velocity of the water flowing past the cooler relative to the water inside the cooler. Clearly, water in the cooler must flow in both directions in some configurations, but keep this principle in mind.

TABLE 8-2. KEEL-COOLER TUBE LENGTH (in./bhp) COPPER OR COPPER-NICKEL TUBE UP TO 85°F (29.4°C) SEAWATER TEMPERATURE ROUND TUBE, APPROX. 0.06 TO 0.10 in. THICK

Tube OD, in.		Generators & Stationary in./bhp	Slow-Moving in./bhp	Free-Running	
				Under 8 Knots in./bhp	Over 8 Knots in./bhp
1 1/8	1.13	8.56	5.99	4.79	4.07
1	1.00	9.63	6.74	5.39	4.58
7/8	0.88	11.00	7.70	6.16	5.24
3/4	0.75	12.83	8.98	7.19	6.11
5/8	0.63	15.40	10.78	8.62	7.33
1/2	0.50	19.25	13.48	10.78	9.17
3/8	0.38	25.67	17.97	14.37	12.22
5/16	0.31	30.80	21.56	17.25	14.67
1/4	0.25	38.50	26.95	21.56	18.33

NOTE: Tubes are mounted so seawater flows freely around the entire tube surface.
NOTE: Square tube may be 78 percent of the length of round tube.

Figure 8-9. Hull-side cooler recess (Courtesy R.W. Fernstrum & Co.)

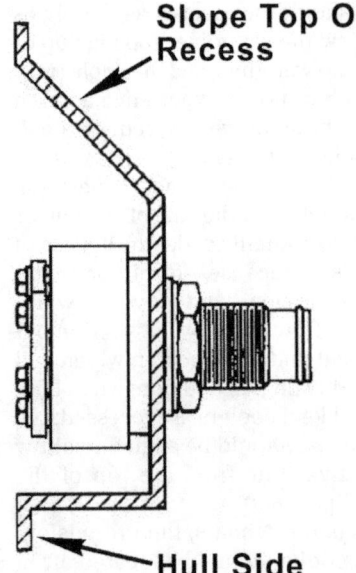

Formula 8-2.

Figure 8-10. Dual keel cooler: aftercooler keel-cooler bypass (Courtesy Caterpillar, Inc.)

INTERCOOLER, AFTERCOOLER, AND REDUCTION-GEAR KEEL COOLERS Most marine diesels have either intercoolers or aftercoolers (sometimes both) to further increase engine

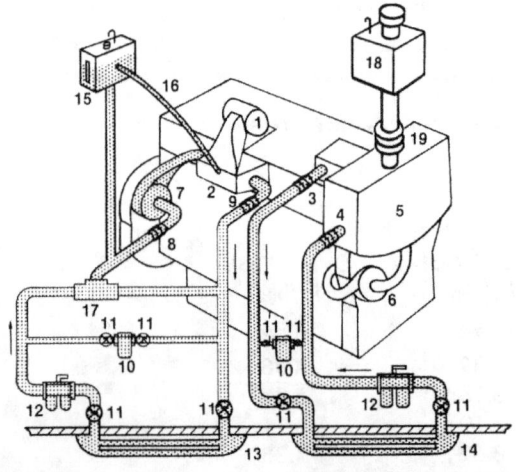

1. Turbocharger
2. Aftercooler, keel cooled
3. Jacket water outlet connection
4. Jacket water inlet connection
5. Expansion tank
6. Jacket water pump
7. Auxiliary fresh water pump
8. Auxiliary fresh water inlet connection
9. Aftercooler outlet connection
10. Bypass filter
11. Shut-off valve
12. Duplex full-flow strainer
13. Keel cooler for aftercooler
14. Keel cooler for jacket water
15. Expansion tank for aftercooler circuit
16. Vent line for aftercooler circuit
17. Bypass valve thermostatically controlled
18. Auxiliary expansion tank
19. Flexible connection

performance. Some intercoolers or aftercoolers are heat-exchanger cooled even when the primary engine cooling is via a keel cooler. Others are keel cooled. When the intercooler or aftercooler is keel cooled, their dedicated keel cooler should be located forward of the primary engine keel cooler.

The keel cooler for the aftercooler should be sized per the engine manufacturer's recommendation. You can also calculate the keel cooler based on the heat rejection of the aftercooler in Btu from the engine spec sheets. Convert Btu to hp or kW using Formula 8-2, and then use Tables 8-2 and 8-3.

Formula 8-2. Converting Btu to hp or kW

$hp \times 42.41 = Btu/min.$, or, $Btu/min. \div 42.41 = hp$
$kW \times 31.63 = Btu/min.$, or, $Btu/min. \div 31.63 = kW$

Reduction gears usually have their own cooler, which may be keel cooled as described. Consult the gear manufacturer for the heat rejection of the specific gear; however, you can estimate it based on between 95 and 97 percent efficiency. In other words—in almost all standard reduction gears—at least 95 percent of bhp is transmitted to the propeller shaft. Assuming 95 percent efficiency, on a 200 bhp (149 kW) engine, the heat rejection in the gear would be 5 percent (100% − 95% = 5%). Five percent of 200 bhp (149 kW) is 19 hp or 7.45 kW. The reduction-gear keel cooler would be sized for this power.

COOLANT-FLOW VELOCITY AND TUBE LENGTH SELECTION To avoid erosion of the piping (particularly at manifold exits and entrances and at sharp bends), coolant flow velocity (FV) should generally be less than 8 ft./sec. (2.45 m/sec.) At the same time—to avoid particulates and sediment settling out and gradually clogging the system—flow should be at least 2 ft./sec. (0.6 m/sec.).

Max. Flow Velocity ≤ 8 ft./sec., or 2.45 m/sec.
Min. Flow Velocity ≥ 2 ft./sec., or 0.6 m/sec.

Flow rate can be estimated by referring to the coolant pump specs from the engine manufacturer. It varies from a high at maximum rpm to a low at idle. Use the following procedure to find flow velocity (FV) in the cooler:

TABLE 8-3. KEEL-COOLER TUBE LENGTH (cm/bhp AND cm/kW) COPPER OR COPPER-NICKEL TUBE UP TO 85°F (29.4°C) SEAWATER TEMPERATURE ROUND TUBE, APPROX. 1.5 TO 2.5 mm THICK

Tube OD, mm	Generators & Stationary		Slow-Moving		Free-Running Under 8 Knots		Free-Running Over 8 Knots	
	cm/bhp	cm/kW	cm/bhp	cm/kW	cm/bhp	cm/kW	cm/bhp	cm/kW
28	10.6	22.2	29.7	15.5	20.8	12.4	16.7	10.6
27	11.0	23.0	30.8	16.1	21.6	12.9	17.3	11.0
26	11.4	23.9	32.0	16.7	22.4	13.4	17.9	11.4
25	11.8	24.8	33.3	17.4	23.3	13.9	18.7	11.8
24	12.3	25.9	34.7	18.1	24.3	14.5	19.4	12.3
23	12.9	27.0	36.2	18.9	25.3	15.1	20.3	12.9
22	13.4	28.2	37.9	19.8	26.5	15.8	21.2	13.4
21	14.1	29.6	39.7	20.7	27.8	16.6	22.2	14.1
20	14.8	31.0	41.6	21.7	29.1	17.4	23.3	14.8
19	15.6	32.7	43.8	22.9	30.7	18.3	24.5	15.6
18	16.4	34.5	46.3	24.1	32.4	19.3	25.9	16.4
17	17.4	36.5	49.0	25.6	34.3	20.5	27.4	17.4
16	18.5	38.8	52.0	27.2	36.4	21.7	29.1	18.5
15	19.7	41.4	55.5	29.0	38.9	23.2	31.1	19.7
14	21.1	44.4	59.5	31.0	41.6	24.8	33.3	21.1
13	22.7	47.8	64.1	33.4	44.8	26.8	35.9	22.7
12	24.6	51.7	69.4	36.2	48.6	29.0	38.9	24.6
11	26.9	56.5	75.7	39.5	53.0	31.6	42.4	26.9
10	29.6	62.1	83.3	43.5	58.3	34.8	46.6	29.6
9	32.9	69.0	92.5	48.3	64.8	38.6	51.8	32.9
8	37.0	77.6	104.1	54.3	72.9	43.5	58.3	37.0
7	42.2	88.7	119.0	62.1	83.3	49.7	66.6	42.2
6	49.3	103.5	138.8	72.4	97.2	58.0	77.7	49.3
5	59.1	124.2	166.6	86.9	116.6	69.6	93.3	59.1

NOTE: Tubes are mounted so seawater flows freely around the entire tube surface.

NOTE: Square tubes may be 78 percent of the length of round tubes.

Convert gallons per minute (gpm) to cu. ft./min., or liters per minute (L/min.) to m³/min.
Multiply gpm × 0.134 to get cu. ft./min.
Multiply L/min × 0.001 to get m³/min.

Find the minimum and maximum water flow in gpm or L/min. from the engine specs and convert to cu. ft./min. or m³/min.
Find most likely water flow (MLWF) using the following formula.

Formula 8-3. Most Likely Water Flow (MLWF)

MLWF = [0.67 × (max. flow − min. flow)] + min. flow

Where
max. flow = maximum water flow, cu. ft./min or m³/min.
min. flow = minimum water flow, cu. ft./min or m³/min.

Find the cross-section area of one keel-cooler channel, or one-channel area (1CA), in square feet or m².
Find flow velocity (FV) using the following formula.

Formula 8-4. Flow Velocity (FV)

FV = MLWF ÷ (1CA × no. channels × 60 sec./min.)

Where
MLWF = most likely water flow, cu. ft./min. or m³/min.
1CA = one channel cross-section area, sq. ft. or m²
no. channels = the number of channels from the keel-cooler inlet to the keel-cooler exit

NOTE: The number of channels are the tubes, pipes, or other shapes that run from the keel-cooler inlet to the outlet and then back to the engine. Two tubes running side by side with water entering aft and exiting forward on each are two channels. The same two tubes running side by side but with water entering aft, turning around at a U, and returning back through the other tube aft, comprise just one channel for these calculations.

Example: For our example 350 bhp (261 kW) engine, we can try using copper-nickel tubing 1-in. (25 mm) diameter. We'll try 5 tubes on each side of the keel, port and starboard (10 tubes or "channels" total), with flow running from the stern forward in each. We then get

max. flow = 97 gpm × 0.134
= 12.98 cu. ft./min.
min. flow = 61 gpm × 0.134 = 8.17 cu. ft./min.
MLWF = (0.67 × [12.98 cu. ft./min. − 8.17 cu. ft./min.]) + 8.17 cu. ft./min. = 11.4 cu. ft./min.

Inside diameter of 1-in. tube = 0.877 in. ID
Inside section area = π × (0.877 in. ID ÷ 2)²
= 0.60 sq. in.
0.60 sq. in. ÷ 144 = 0.0042 sq. ft. inside section area
FV = 11.4 cu. ft./min. ÷ (0.0042 sq. ft. × 10 channels × 60 sec./min.) = 4.5 ft./sec.

This falls in the desired range between 2 and 8 ft./sec. If the flow velocity (FV) had been over 8 ft./sec., you would have had to increase tube diameter, the number of tubes, or both. Had the flow velocity been less than 2 ft./sec., you would have had to reduce the tube diameter, the number of tubes, or both. Reducing diameter would require longer tube length exposed to the sea.

The required 1-in. copper-nickel tube length (for 350 bhp, over 8 knots) is 4.58 in./bhp, 1,603 in., or 133.6 ft., which divided by 10 tubes = 13.2 ft. length for each tube.

Or
max. flow = 367 L/min. × 0.001
= 0.37 m³/min.
min. flow = 231 L/min. × 0.001 = 0.23 m³/min.
MLWF = (0.67 × [0.37 m³/min. − 0.23 m³/min.]) + 0.23 m³/min.
= 0.32 m³/min.

Inside diameter of 25 mm tube = 21 mm ID
Inside section area = π × (21 mm ID ÷ 2)²
÷ 100 = 3.46 cm²
3.46 cm² ÷ 10,000 = 0.00035 m² inside section area

FV = 0.32 m³/min. ÷ (0.00035 m² × 10 channels × 60 sec./min.) = 1.52 m/sec.

This falls in the desired range between 0.6 m/sec. and 2.45 m/sec. If the flow velocity (FV) had been over 2.45 m/sec., you would have had to either increase tube diameter, the number of tubes, or both. Had the flow velocity been less than 0.6 m/sec. you would have had to reduce the tube diameter, the number of tubes, or both. Reducing diameter would require longer tube length exposed to the sea.

The required 25 mm copper-nickel tube length (for 261 kW, over 8 knots) is 11.8 cm/kW, 4,130 cm, or 41.3 m, which divided by 10 tubes = 4.1 m length for each tube.

REDUCING KEEL-COOLER LENGTH It is often desirable to reduce keel-cooler length. For our previous example, we could do this by doubling the number of tubes, returning the flow with a U at the end of each pair of tubes. With the flow rate under the maximum of 8 ft./sec. or 2.45 m/sec., we're not likely to have erosion problems at the U connections. Note that we have "doubled" the number of tubes but not the number of "channels" for flow, so the flow rate remains the same. Doing this will halve the length of the keel cooler from 13.2 to 6.6 feet (from 4.1 to 2.05 m).

As long as the tubes are arranged so that water can flow all around their exteriors, they can be packed fairly closely together to make a compact unit. Thus, a shorter, compact keel cooler can more readily be set flush into a recess built into the hull to reduce appendage drag—or, for the configuration in our example, into two recesses on either side of the hull.

Chapter 8: Engine Cooling Systems and Their Exhausts

INCREASING FLOW SPEED IN LARGE CHANNELS
If structural shapes like U channels are used to fabricate a keel cooler, you may find that flow speed is too low. This can be corrected by welding in right-angle partial "baffles" or plates that close off, say, two-thirds of the opening. The openings in the baffle plates will alternate from side to side so the flow follows a roughly zigzag pattern. Though this is a standard fix for builder-fabricated keel coolers, it almost always seems better to me to use a manufactured keel cooler, where such work-arounds aren't required.

KEEL-COOLER APPENDAGE DRAG AND FAIRING THE KEEL COOLER The keel-cooler piping outside the hull creates additional drag. On slower displacement vessels, this can be tolerated without fairing, but it's always better to fair the keel cooler (Figure 8-11). (The fairing also protects the cooler from damage.) If the cooler is mounted on the outside of the hull surface, it can be faired with tapered blocks or wedges to smooth the water flow over and around the front and back of the cooler.

It is even better to build a recess into the hull so the cooler can be mounted flush. The outer face of the cooler should be recessed about $1/2$ inch (12 mm) in from the outer surface of the hull and have a clearance of about $1 1/2$ inches (38 mm) around the sides of the recess.

Metal vessels with somewhat squarish midship sections can also install the keel cooler inside a walled-off box at the side of the hull near the turn of the bilge. This is functionally the same as being in a box keel, with openings to the sea at the bottom and sides of the box. This configuration is sometimes termed a *box cooler* (Figure 8-12).

On metal boats with box keels, the keel cooler can be built into the box keel itself. In this location, it's virtually invisible and creates no additional drag. The box keel must have numerous opening holes along its bottom and the sides at the top, so seawater can flow through them and around the keel-cooler tubes freely.

MANUFACTURED KEEL COOLERS Though builders can fabricate a keel cooler using the previous cooling-area guidelines, in most instances premanufactured keel coolers from companies like R. W. Fernstrum and Walter Machine Co. (Figure 8-13) are both more compact and more efficient. These are almost universally made of copper-nickel, and the manufacturer will provide sizing and installation guidance. Fernstrum also makes keel coolers of 5000-series aluminum. Only aluminum keel-cooler components should be used on aluminum hulls to avoid corrosion problems (though cleaning and painting with antifouling is a chore). Even on steel hulls, great attention must be paid to isolating the keel cooler and its piping from the steel. The manufacturer's installation kit and instructions cover this in detail.

SPECIAL KEEL-COOLER TUBE SHAPES Most commercially made keel coolers don't use simple, straight round tube. Instead, they use square tube, which has more surface area for a given inside cross-section area, or fluted or

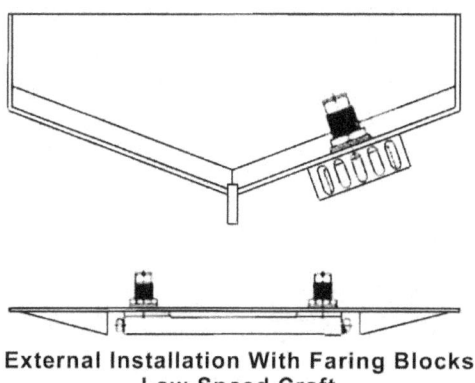
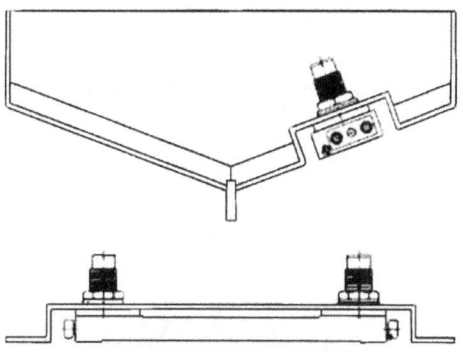

External Installation With Faring Blocks Low-Speed Craft

Recessed Installation High-Speed Craft

Figure 8-11. Keel cooler fairing (Courtesy R.W. Fernstrum & Co.)

PART THREE: EXHAUST SYSTEMS

Figure 8-12. Box keel cooler (Courtesy Caterpillar, Inc.)

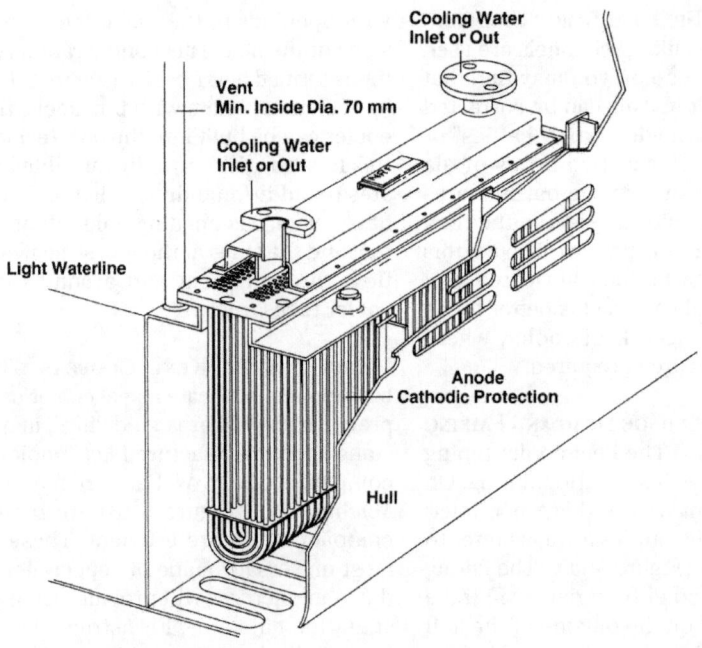

Figure 8-13. Walter keel coolers (Courtesy Walter Machine Co.)

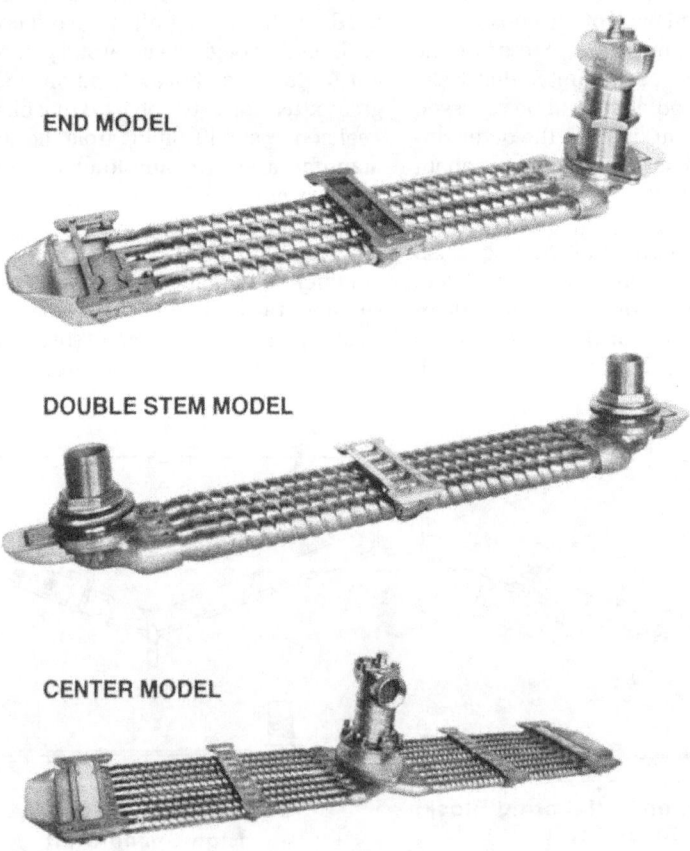

spiral-groove tubing such as Walter's "turbo tube." All these approaches increase surface area and cooling efficiency to make a more compact unit provide sufficient heat transfer.

FILTERS/STRAINERS ON KEEL COOLERS Regardless of the type of keel cooler, it's a good idea to install a standard water filter (sea strainer) in the piping at the exit from the cooler. This strainer collects any stray sediment, algae, or corrosion by-products that may accumulate in the system, and it thus protects the engine. The filter should be inspected and cleaned at regular intervals.

KEEL-COOLER APPENDAGE DRAG Though keel coolers aren't appropriate for really high-speed planing hulls, they can be used without too much appendage drag on semi-displacment and even low-speed planing hulls. Of course, such higher-speed vessels should have their keel coolers recessed to reduce drag.

Walter Machine Co. reports a test of a boat powered with twin V-8 gas engines of 200 bhp each (see Table 8-4).

TABLE 8-4. SPEED COMPARISONS BETWEEN HEAT-EXCHANGER AND KEEL-COOLED BOATS

RPM	Heat Exchanger	Keel Cooled
2,800	16.48 mph	16.40 mph
3,300	20.85 mph	20.62 mph
4,000	25.40 mph	25.25 mph

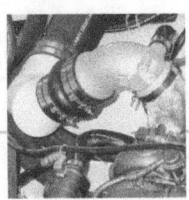

CHAPTER 9 — Dry Exhaust Systems

Once a keel-cooling system has been worked out, you can turn your attention to configuring a drystack exhaust to go with it. The fundamental concern is that a drystack gets exceptionally hot. As we saw in Chapter 7, the exhaust gas temperatures can reach around 1,200°F (648°C). Temperatures on the outside surface of uninsulated mufflers and exhaust pipe routinely reach between 400° and 900°F (200° and 480°C). Under insulation, these surface temperatures can exceed 1,000°F (540°C). Though it's fairly common and acceptable to use carbon steel mufflers and pipes, carbon steel starts to deteriorate and scale when temperatures reach 1,000°F (540°C). For this reason, stainless is superior for insulated piping and mufflers. This is even more important in the marine environment.

High temperatures create the two overriding considerations in drystack exhaust design:

1. Protect the hull structure, machinery, and crew from burns and heat damage.
2. Allow for the expansion and contraction of the exhaust piping to avoid cracking.

The other prime considerations—as with any exhaust—are ensuring that back pressure is not excessive and preventing noxious fumes from entering the boat. Following the engine manufacturer's recommended exhaust diameter is usually sufficient. If the exhaust run is particularly long, though, it may be necessary to increase diameter by one standard pipe size.

THE BASIC DRYSTACK CONFIGURATION

One of the common arguments in favor of drystack exhausts is their simplicity. As we'll see, this "simplicity" may be an illusion in proper installations. Nevertheless, the most basic drystack exhaust installation runs directly up from the engine and out the deck or cabin roof. Straightforward as this appears, however, the following standard components and considerations must be included or allowed for.

Requirements for Drystack Exhausts

1. Flexible stainless bellows (or flexible dry exhaust hose of stainless) connecting the exhaust pipe to the exhaust-exit flange on the engine to allow for expansion and contraction and to prevent cracking from engine vibration
2. Insulation or adequate clearance from the hull and other machinery
3. Pipe supports or hangers that allow for pipe expansion and that won't transmit heat to the boat's structure
4. Provisions to keep water out of the engine, both at the exhaust outlet and with a water trap at or near the bottom of the vertical exhaust exit pipe
5. Provisions for additional ventilation to carry away the extra heat from the hot exhaust piping and to cool the exhaust-pipe or exhaust-trunk area

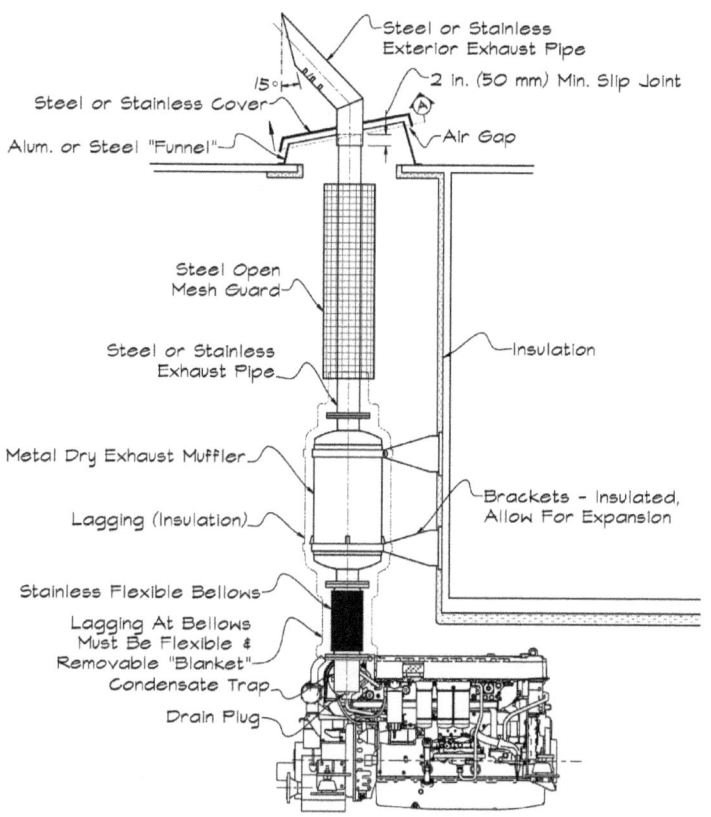

Figure 9-1. Basic drystack exhaust

6. The principal exit run of the exhaust should be as close to vertical as possible, and the system should have as few bends as practical.

Figure 9-1 illustrates all the components needed to meet the previous requirement when the exhaust rises straight up from the engine and exits the cabin roof immediately above. This exhaust run is entirely in a machinery space, so only the bottom portion of the exhaust and muffler is lagged (insulated), while the upper portion is shielded with a steel open-wire mesh or frame to protect the crew from accidental burns. Then the exhaust exits through a steel "funnel" (the bottom or side portion of which may be aluminum). The cap of this funnel has an air gap all around to provide for a generous flow of hot air out.

Figure 9-2 shows how the air gap is created all around. The exhaust outlet pipe is welded to the steel (or stainless) cover plate. The cover plate should be one standard plate

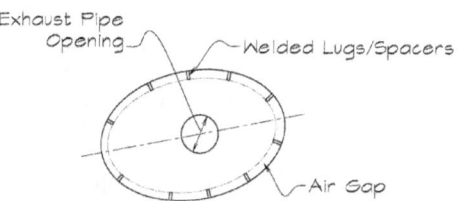

Figure 9-2. Section A through the funnel cover in Figure 9-1

size thicker than the wall thickness of the heaviest exhaust pipe. The lugs are the same thickness as the cover plate. If they attach to an aluminum funnel, they must be bent over at an angle and bolted (rather than welded) to the funnel. Since the pipe is rigidly attached to the cover plate, it must be free to expand below it, and this requires an expansion slip joint with—2-inches (50 mm) minimum travel. This may be fabricated as shown in Figure 9-3.

Exhaust pipe for marine drystack applications is of standard weight (schedule 40 or DIN 2448) in carbon steel and schedule 10 in

PART THREE: EXHAUST SYSTEMS

Figure 9-3. Expansion slip joint

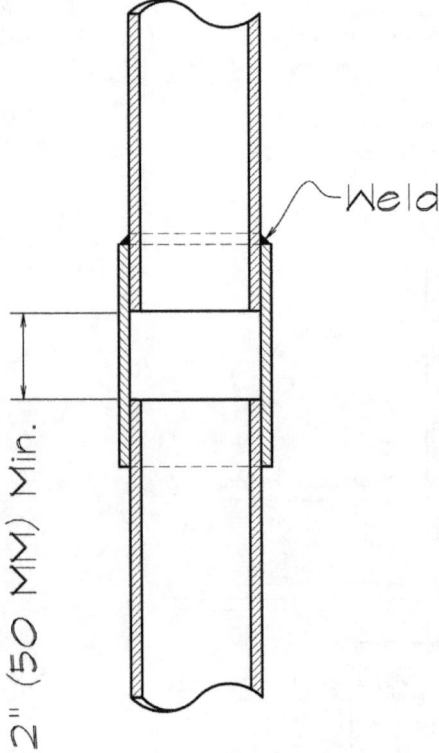

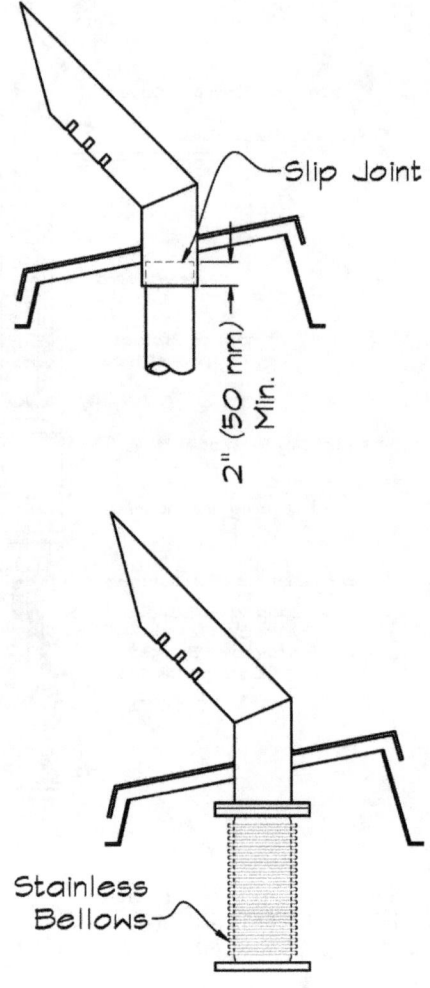

Figure 9-4. Slip joints or stainless bellows allow for expansion

stainless pipe of the diameter required to meet the engine manufacturer's specifications.

Alternatively, a flexible bellows may be used instead of the slip joint (Figure 9-4). Note that the expansion slip joint is not completely vapor tight. It should be used only in locations where the ventilation air will clear any possible fumes. This means high up on the exhaust stack. Lower down or in the boat hull and cabin spaces, bellows should be used.

Keeping Water Out

To keep rain and spray out, the open end of the exhaust outlet is cut off at approximately 15 degrees past vertical as shown in Figure 9-1 and equipped with the three drain slots as shown in Figure 9-5.

Fastening to Accept Expansion and Contraction

Keep in mind that the exhaust piping's temperature will vary from as cold as 10° or 20°F (–12° or –6°C) or less, to as hot as

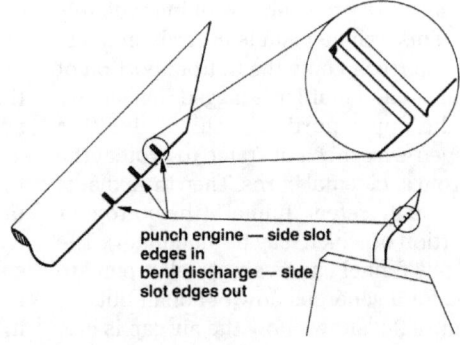

Figure 9-5. Drain slots (Courtesy Caterpillar, Inc.)

144

Chapter 9: Dry Exhaust Systems

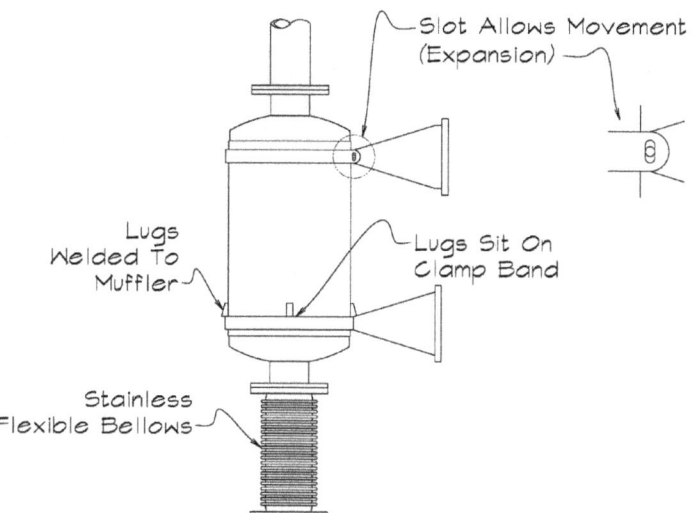

Figure 9-6.
Mounting for expansion

1,200°F (650°C). A single expansion slip joint at the outlet isn't enough to accommodate the substantial expansion and contraction cycles the exhaust will experience over and over throughout its service life. Careful thought must be given to mounting all piping so it can accept this expansion without damage. This can be accomplished using fairly standard pipe clamps and parts.

Figure 9-6 shows this principle applied to the muffler in the basic drystack exhaust system in Figure 9-1. You can see how the exhaust sits on the lower clamp band using lugs welded to the muffler. The upper clamp band is attached to the mounting bracket with bolts in a slot to ensure axial movement is not restrained. The flexible bellows below the muffler fastens to the engine and allows expansion here, as well as allowing for the engine's vibration.

You can apply this same approach to all the exhaust piping, using standard pipe clamps. Typical pipe clamps are shown in Figure 9-7. All these clamps (and clamps for mufflers) must have high-temperature insulating liners or pads to prevent the exhaust heat from being transmitted to the boat's structure.

An even better approach is to use premanufactured pipe hangers and fixed points specifically designed for such exhaust installations. Rubber Design B.V. (distributed through Soundown in the United States) manufacturers a complete series of insulated fixed points and stabilizers that are designed to insulate from heat and allow expansion (Figures 9-8, 9-9, and 9-10).

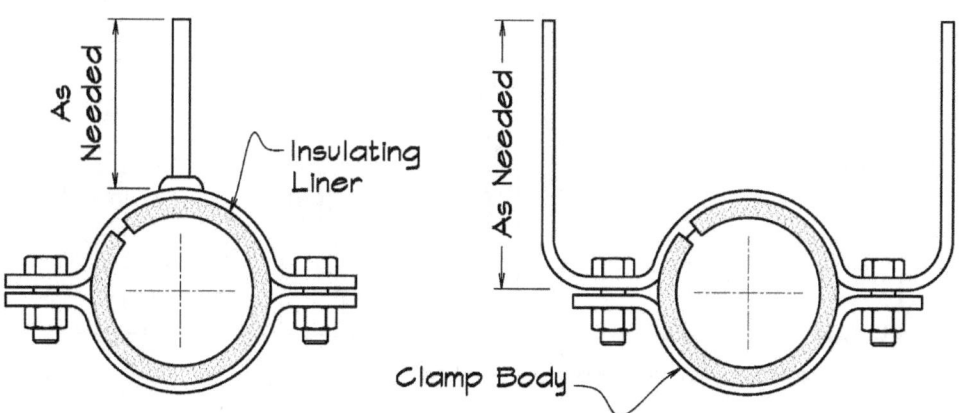

Figure 9-7.
Standard pipe clamps/hangers

145

Figure 9-8. Hanging fixed-point insulated pipe hangers (Courtesy Rubber Design B.V.)

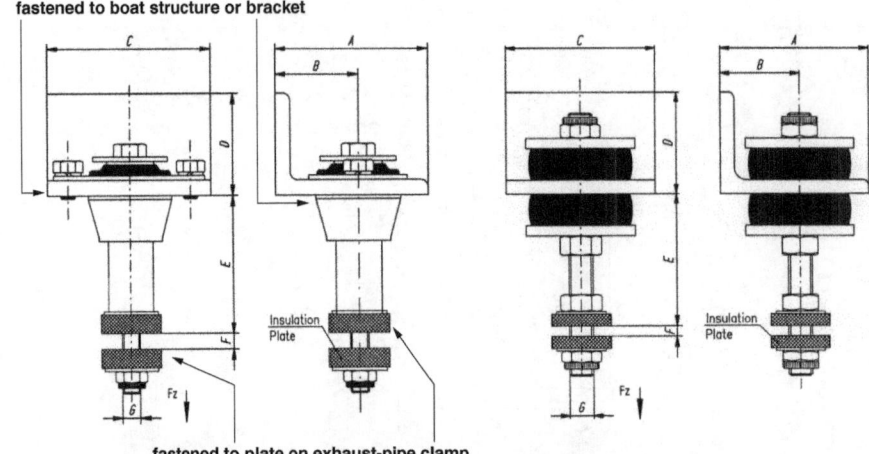

Figure 9-9. Fixed-point insulated hanger on lagged exhaust pipe (Courtesy Rubber Design B.V.)

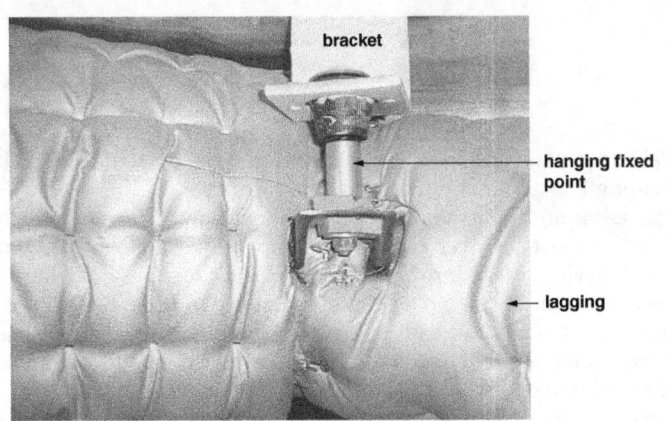

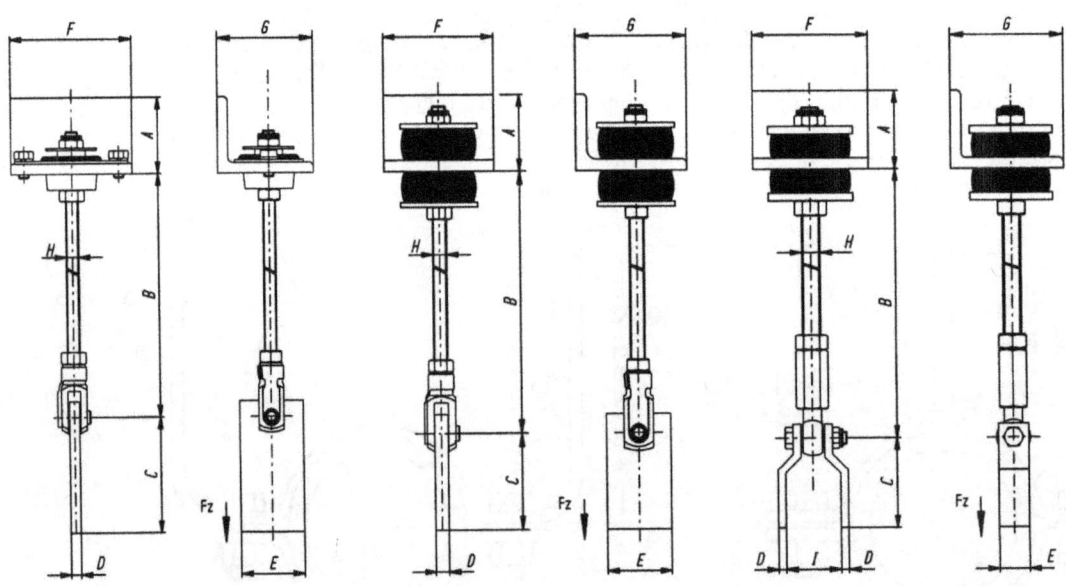

Figure 9-10. Exhaust pipe stabilizers allow expansion (Courtesy Rubber Design B.V.)

Chapter 9: Dry Exhaust Systems

Babying Flexible Bellows and Bellows with Turbo Liners

The stainless flexible bellows need careful attention during layout and installation (Figure 9-11). Remember, once installed and hidden behind their removable lagging boots, they are seldom inspected again—and almost never from their inside. Simple

Figure 9-12. Flexible bellows failure from stress corrosion (Courtesy Applegate Industrial Materials, Inc.)

Figure 9-11. Flanged flexible bellows (Courtesy Volvo Penta)

corrosion and stress corrosion (Figure 9-12) can result in spectacular failures, which can essentially stop you dead in the water. Weld spatter or even grease on the bellows can result in failure. Keep in mind that flexible bellows are of thin metal parts that are constantly moving, at temperatures around 1,000°F (540°C). The local temperature differential resulting from grease or weld spatter on their surface can result in a severe local breakdown.

The bellows need to be carefully installed at half their designated expansion, and they must not be twisted or torqued during installation. Twisting the bellows when tightening the flange bolts or welding them in place (Figure 9-13) will result in stress that will

Figure 9-13. Welded-in flexible bellows (Courtesy Applegate Industrial Materials, Inc.)

PART THREE: EXHAUST SYSTEMS

cause a failure. (The bellows are available in both weld-in and bolted-flange styles.) The bellows also cannot support any weight, neither axial nor transverse loads. You can see in Figures 9-1, 9-6, and 9-23 that the weight of the pipe or the muffler is taken by the brackets, not the bellows. These bellows really need to be babied on installation and to be well protected from dings, scratches, gouges, and foreign material during their installation and their service life.

In the old days of naturally aspirated engines, the flexible bellows were usually unlined. This is still acceptable for cabin-heater exhaust systems or for a naturally aspirated engine. Today, however, almost all engines and generators are turbocharged. All the bellows in the system must have an internal turbo liner or turbo shield. These are directional, as you can see in Figure 9-14. They are welded to the inside of the bellows at one end and open at the other so the bellows will remain flexible. This is why the bellows are directional. The welded-on, sealed end must be installed toward the engine. The result is a "shingle" effect as the exhaust gases pass through the bellows smoothly, without making direct contact with the inside of the exterior bellows itself. If you install the turbolined flexible bellows backward, it will cause turbulence, added back pressure, and ultimately a failure.

There's another important consideration here. You can see how close the clearance is between the interior turbo liner and the exterior bellows. This means that there is very little lateral (side-to-side) movement possible when using bellows with turbo liners. You have to line up the bellows as close to dead center on the exhaust pipe axis as possible. You cannot rely on the bellows with turbo liners to accept much side-to-side deflection or to make up for any misalignment at all.

Flexible Exhaust Hose for Dry Exhaust

Though bellows are most common for dry exhaust installations, the limitations just noted means that a very flexibly mounted engine (such as an engine on an Aquadrive installation) should use a length of flexible stainless, dry exhaust hose (Figure 9-15) between the engine-exhaust outlet and the exhaust pipe. This hose is a woven sleeve of stainless wire and flat strands. The flexible hose can absorb more motion in more directions than flexible bellows.

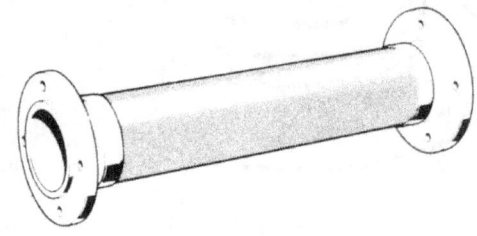

Figure 9-15. Flexible-steel dry exhaust hose (Courtesy Volvo Penta)

Figure 9-14. Flexible bellows with directional turbo liner (Courtesy Applegate Industrial Materials, Inc.)

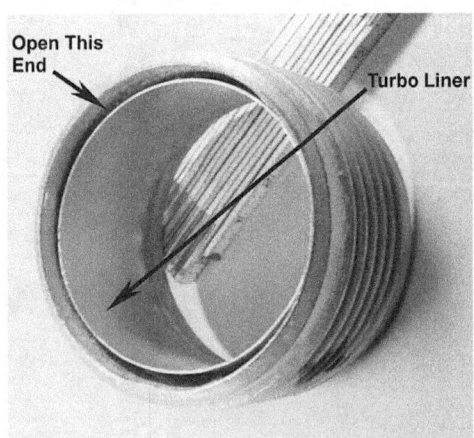
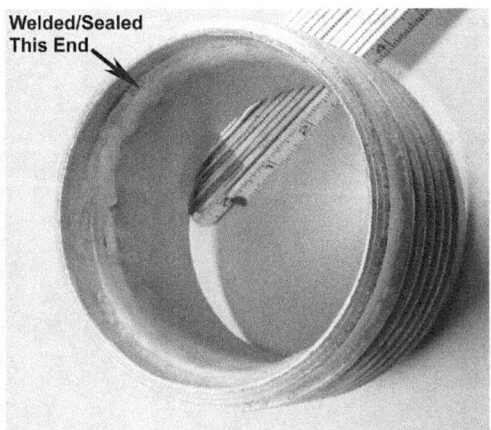

Collecting and Draining Spray and Condensation

Regardless of how high and how well installed the exhaust outlet opening is, some rain and spray may get in. Additionally, the long pipe has a considerable interior surface area that will generate condensation. All of this moisture must be kept from entering the engine, especially the turbo. For this reason a sump, or trap, should be installed at the lowest point in the vertical exhaust outlet pipe to collect spray and condensation, and it should be fitted with a drain plug to clear any standing water. You can see this in the basic drystack exhaust system illustrated in Figure 9-1. Note: A water sensor at the trap capable of withstanding high temperatures is recommended.

Alternatively some installations use a simple 90-degree elbow with a drain plug at the bottom (Figure 9-16). Though this has proved adequate in some installations, I recommend against it, as there really is no condensate sump to collect water.

Insulation or Lagging

Every bit as important is the insulation or lagging that protects the crew and the boat from burns and fire and reduces heat radiated into the vessel's interior. The terms *insulation* and *lagging* are used interchangeably in this application, but lagging is more specifically a semipermanent insulation wrapped around the piping, frequently sealed with a hard-coat surface. Insulation, in general, includes such lagging, but also includes moderately flexible and removable blankets, fabricated "boots," and pads, as well as the insulation installed on the boat structure itself.

Either hard-coat lagging or blanket-type insulation may be used as convenient. The exception is at the flexible bellows, where the insulation also must be flexible. Here, removable flexible insulation blankets (configured to wrap around and lace or hook closed) must be used (Figure 9-18). Similarly, care must be used at expansion slip joints, as well as at clamps and pipe hangers, to ensure that a hard-coat lagging doesn't restrain motion. Using removable blankets, wraps, or "boots" at these fittings also makes inspection, replacement, and repair much easier. Figure 9-17 shows a well-insulated pair of dry exhausts. You can see the removable blankets/boots over the flexible bellows and critical joints. The photo of the muffler/silencer insulation blanket in Figure 9-19 shows the components of such removable blankets.

High-temperature insulation used to be easy, as one material virtually did it all: asbestos. As a child, I can remember going with my father to the local hardware store and

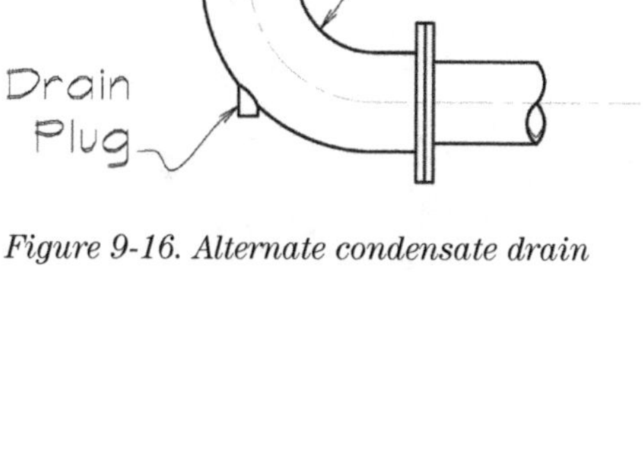

Figure 9-16. Alternate condensate drain

Figure 9-17. Well-insulated dry exhausts (Courtesy Detroit Diesel)

PART THREE: EXHAUST SYSTEMS

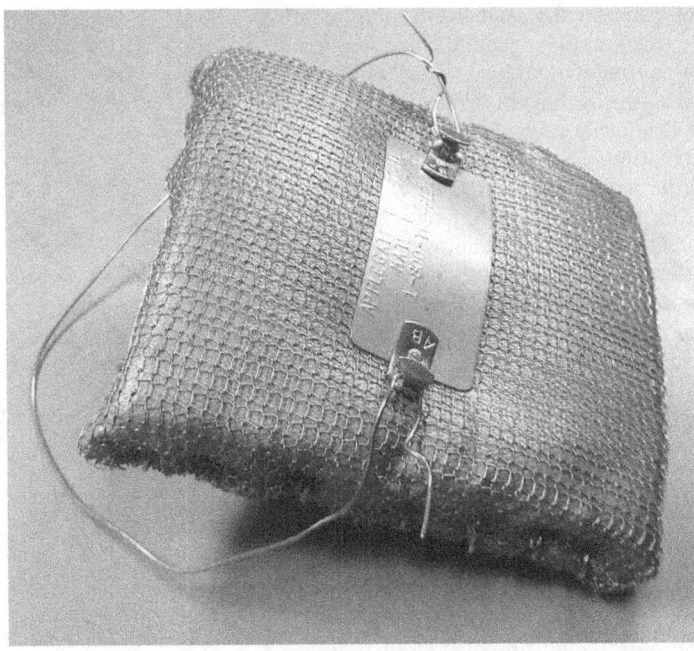

Figure 9-18. Removable insulation cover with wire closure ties and hooks (Courtesy Applegate Industrial Materials, Inc.)

Lagging supplies and kits are often available from engine manufacturers and from muffler manufacturers such as Nelson and Silex. You can also purchase lagging material independently.

LAGGING MATERIALS Without asbestos, the most common lagging and insulation materials for exhaust and fire installation are fiberglass, calcium silicate, and mineral wool. Depending on manufacturing details and secondary ingredients, fiberglass insulation (Figure 9-20) is usually serviceable to temperatures of around 1,000°F to 1,200°F (540°C to 650°C) and calcium silicate to about 1,800°F (980°C). Mineral wool is used as the name for two different products: slag wool from iron-ore blast-furnace slag, and rock wool from—as you would expect—rocks. They are good for maximum temperatures of about 1,500°F to 1,700°F (800°C to 930°C). All insulation should meet or exceed 46 CFR 164.009.

Calcium silicate, sometimes known under the trade name Thermo-12/Blue, is in fact hydrous calcium silicate. It is lightweight with good structural strength. It makes excellent insulation liners for pipe hangers and clamps as well as insulation pads and boards.

Even-higher-temperature insulation can be found in ceramic fiber boards, good for as much as 2,300°F (1,250°C) continuous and 3,000°F (1,650°C) intermittent, and amorphous silica, which is good for 2,000°F (1,100°C) continuous and 3,000°F (1,650°C) intermittent.

For most standard exhaust and muffler lagging, fiberglass insulation is quite adequate. Catalytic converters (so far, not found on

picking up a yard-wide (meter-wide) roll of the stuff about ⅜-inch (9.5 mm) thick. We cut it to shape with tin snips and nailed it to the wall of our cabin behind the coal stove's chimney. No respirators, not even a face mask. Indeed, look at any old text on plumbing, furnaces, kilns, or fire protection, and asbestos will be the primary ingredient for all high-temperature insulating needs. If you are working on a boat over 30 years old, it may well have asbestos lagging, possibly a lot of it. *Beware: we know now that inhaling or ingesting asbestos is a deadly health hazard.*

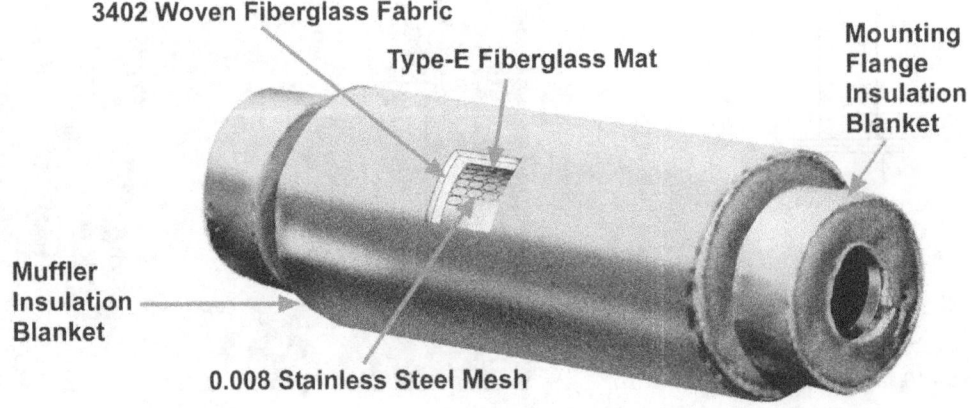

Figure 9-19. Muffler/silencer insulation blanket (Courtesy Nelson Silencer/Fleetguard, Inc.)

Chapter 9: Dry Exhaust Systems

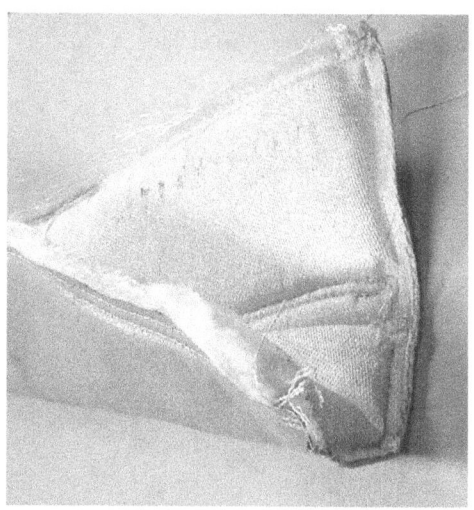

Figure 9-20. Fiberglass insulation cover (Courtesy Applegate Industrial Materials, Inc.)

boats) require insulation rated at continuous temperatures of 2,000°F (1,100°C). Also, the exhaust manifold on dry exhaust systems is seldom insulated. It's difficult to do so properly—that is, to make it stay in place and also retain good access to the engine for maintenance and repair. If used, however, insulation for exhaust manifolds should be rated for 2,000°F (1,100°C) continuous. (See Appendix D for insulation sources and products.)

Keep in mind that you need to insulate not only the exhaust piping itself but any nearby or overhead panels, particularly the inside of an exhaust trunk. The very best insulation method includes a layer of sound-deadening insulation (there is plenty of noise in the exhaust piping) outside a layer of heat insulation. Both may be fiberglass. A ¾-inch (19 mm) layer of fiberglass heat insulation backed by an inch of fiberglass sound insulation that is faced on the side toward the exhaust pipe with a 2-lb./sq. ft. (9.8 kg/m^2) mass-damping lead sheet makes a good combination. All, however, must be fiberglass (or one of the still more fire-resistant materials) and rated by the U.S. Coast Guard as acceptable fire-resistant insulation for marine use.

If space is a problem, a sheet of ½-inch (12.7 mm) Marinite board will serve to insulate the inside of the exhaust trunk, though somewhat thicker is preferable. This will not have the sound-deadening advantages of thicker, softer fiberglass insulation used with or without the mass-damping lead sheet.

Another option is to use ⅜-inch (9.5 mm) Marinite or Transite board against the inside surface of the exhaust trunk faced—on its exhaust-pipe side—with corrugated sheet aluminum or steel. (Aluminum is superior, as it's lighter and won't rust.) The key is that the corrugations must run vertically, opening at the top and bottom of the trunk. Natural convection drives cooler air up through these corrugation channels, forming a good insulating air cushion. Also, the metal reflects some heat back. The drawback to this method is poor sound deadening (Figure 9-22).

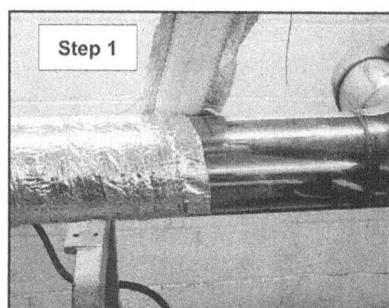 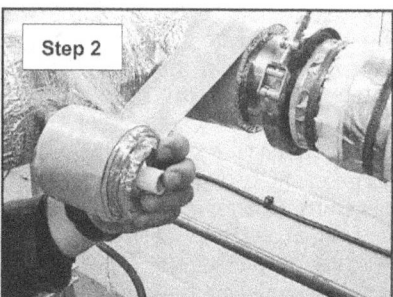 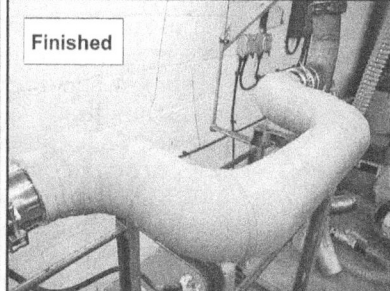

Figure 9-21. Wrapping an exhaust pipe (Courtesy Culimeta Textiglas Technologie GmbH & Co.)

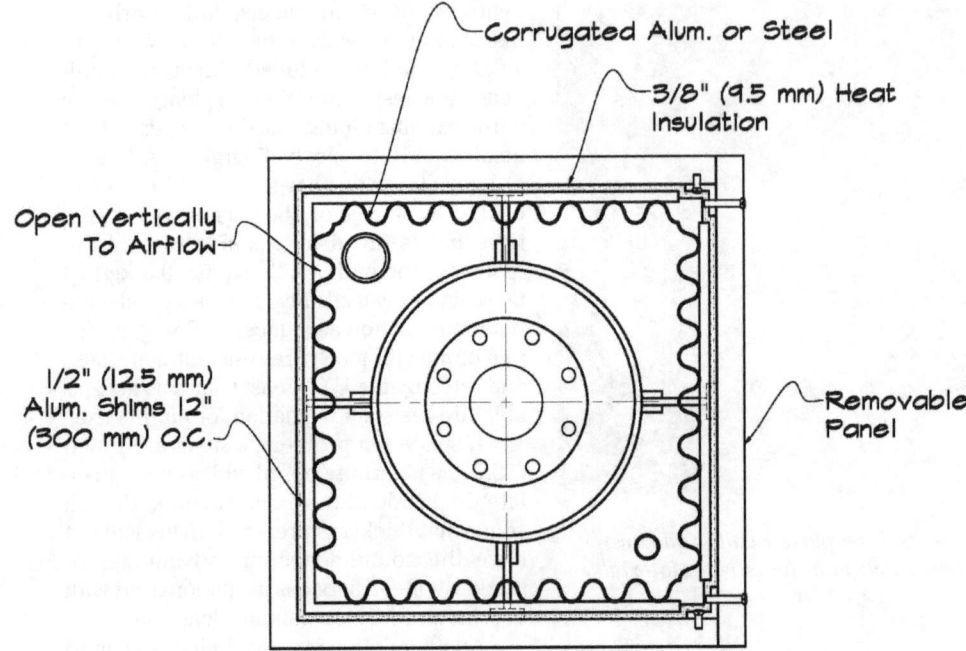

Figure 9-22.
Alternate trunk insulation

FIRE-RESISTANT (INTUMESCENT) PAINT

A relatively new (literally space-age) development is truly fire-resistant paint. This intumescent paint expands tremendously when exposed to the great heat caused by a fire. First created for use on Apollo spacecraft reentry vehicles, it is now available in a number of varieties from several paint manufacturers, such as International Paint/International Protective Coatings (Chartek). These paints are in common use on offshore oil platforms and in the machinery spaces of large ships. Paints such as these do *not* serve as insulation until there is a fire, but they add a considerable range of added safety should a fire occur.

In most average boats of steel or aluminum construction, an intumescent paint under the insulation of drystack exhaust systems (in exhaust trunks and such) is probably not justified. On fiberglass and wooden vessels, it will add a significant margin of safety to paint the inside of the exhaust trunk with an intumescent paint first before installing the usual and still required insulation. Again, such intumescent paint does *not* replace the usual required insulation or lagging, and it is not used on the exhaust pipe itself. It is for added protection of the structure.

Painting the Exhaust Pipe

If the exhaust pipe is polished stainless, it can be left unpainted, but a standard structural-steel exhaust pipe must be painted for protection as well as appearance (on the outside). International Paint's (International Marine Coatings) Intertherm 50 silicon aluminum paint is one good product for this application. It's rated to 1,000°F (540°C) and specifically listed for applications on exhaust stacks. It comes only in a silver/aluminum color.

POR-15, Inc., makes POR-20, a silver paint, and Factory Manifold Gray (gray, of course). Both are rated at 1,400°F (760°C). They also produce Black Velvet, rated at 1,200°F (650°C). All three are suitable for exhaust-stack-pipe paint. POR-15 also produces engine enamels in a wide assortment of colors suited to painting engine blocks, but not rated hot enough for exhaust pipes.

If you want a larger assortment of colors (and you aren't using polished stainless pipe) one source is automotive "header" paints, such as from VHT Paints (www.vhtpaints.com). These coatings come in many colors and are rated at over 1,300°F (700°C). VHT also makes manifold coatings rated as high as

2,000°F (1,090°C), as well as standard engine-block enamels in an assortment of colors rated around 550°F (288°C).

DRYSTACK EXHAUST TRUNKS

As we've seen, one of the supposed pluses of drystack exhaust installations is their simplicity. The basic drystack exhaust we've looked at so far isn't too complicated, but most boats have one or more generators, a cabin heater, and perhaps a water heater and compressor. If the main engine is drystack, these items are usually drystack as well. Such drystack systems run their exhausts up through a shared exhaust trunk. Even assuming just a single main engine, one gen set, and one cabin heater, you can see from the drawing in Figure 9-23 that laying such an exhaust trunk out correctly is not simple, and this isn't considering the keel-cooler installations required as well.

The exhaust trunk must be large enough to accommodate all the vertical dry exhaust components with room to spare. To ensure good airflow through the trunk (both for engine ventilation and cooling of the trunk and exhaust pipes themselves), about 30 percent or more of the cross-section area inside the trunk (after adding insulation) should be open for airflow (Figure 9-24).

The mounting of each muffler and each exhaust pipe must be worked out in detail. The pipe clearances and runs must be arranged so the pipes don't interfere with each other and have a clear run out of the stack. The walls of the trunk must be carefully lined—ideally with both sound and heat insulation—and there must be large removable access panels for most of the length of the trunk for inspection, maintenance, and repair. Simple this isn't.

Exhaust-Ejector Ventilation: Exhaust Trunk as a Ventilator

In many instances, it makes sense to specifically configure the exhaust trunk to double as a ventilator. The natural convection resulting from the hot air in the trunk can be used to pull more air out of the engine compartment. This is already the case, as shown in Figure 9-23, but it can be optimized further. Figures 9-25 through 9-27 show configurations and proportions for optimizing the exhaust trunk's ventilation capability. These use the energy in the convective flow of the hot air around the exhaust pipes to generate ejector ventilation.

These ejector-ventilator exhaust stacks work best on single-engine installations, because with multiple engines there can be unpredictable cross flow in the air circulation, particularly if one engine is running and the other is off.

Multiple-Exhaust "Stacks"

Often it's beneficial to raise the exhaust outlet high above the deck and superstructure. There may be a passenger deck too close to the exhaust, a high pilothouse forward of it, or similar considerations. In this case, the exhaust pipes can be run up into a multiple-exhaust "stack" left open at the aft end where the exhaust exits. These stacks can be designed as prominent decorative features, enhancing the vessel's appearance.

Figure 9-28 illustrates a typical example of multiple-exhaust stacks. The added height of the stack enhances the convective-ventilator effect. Note the large access panels on both sides—a detail too often overlooked. Note also that this stack sits on top of the exhaust trunk below, and the two must be worked out together.

Water-Jacketed and Air-Jacketed Exhaust Runs

To reduce the load on the insulation and lagging, you can use water jackets or air jackets to lower the external temperature of the dry exhaust piping. The drawing in Figure 9-29 depicts a typical installation. The OD of the water-jacket pipe is usually 1.45 times the OD of the exhaust pipe, or a bit more.

Water-jacketing of dry exhaust is common and acceptable, but I don't see great benefits from it. Yes, it reduces heat in the boat's interior, but it counters one of the fundamental advantages of a drystack exhaust: not having a second, separate raw-water pump and

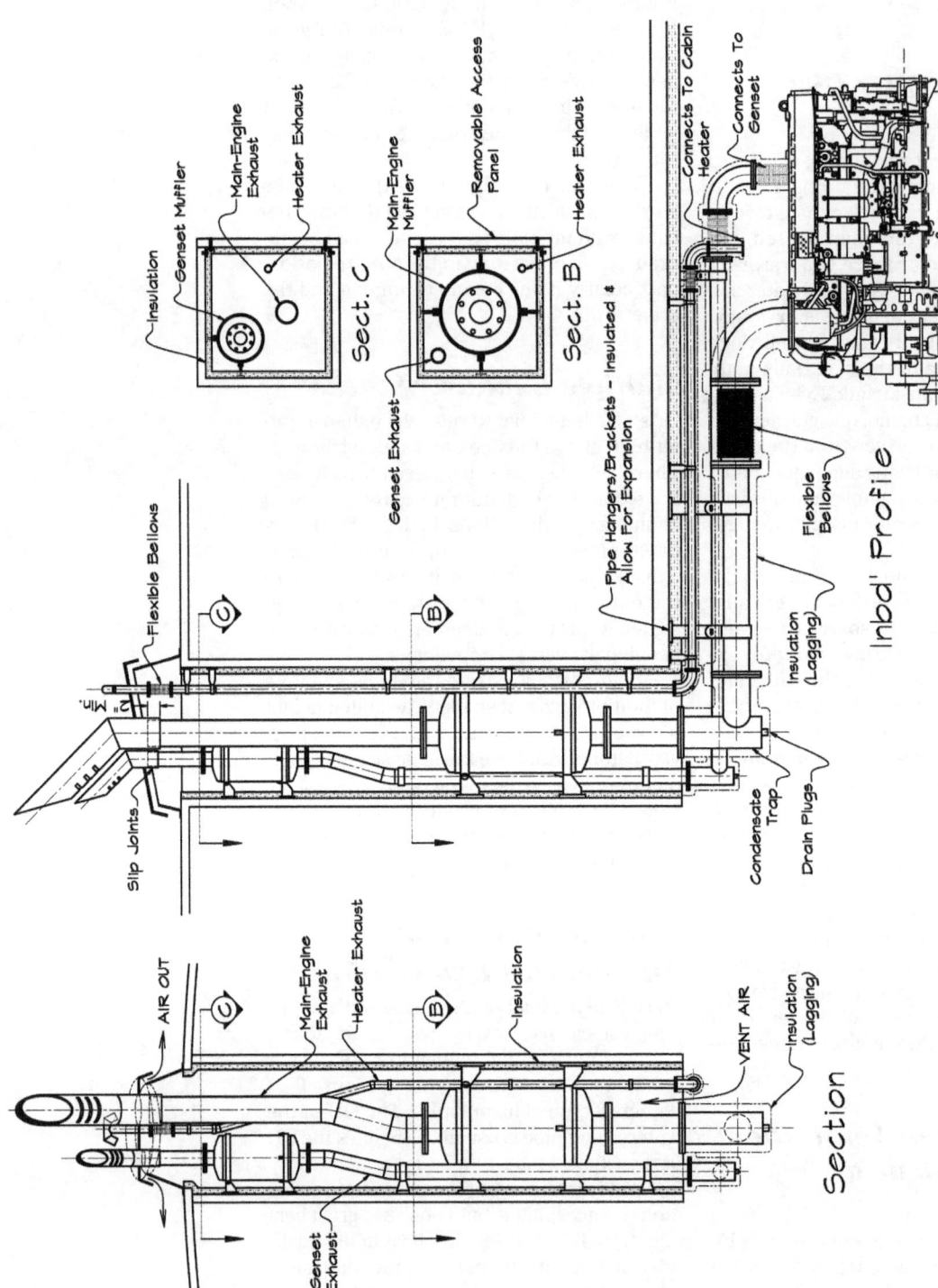

Figure 9-23. Drystack exhaust trunk

Chapter 9: Dry Exhaust Systems

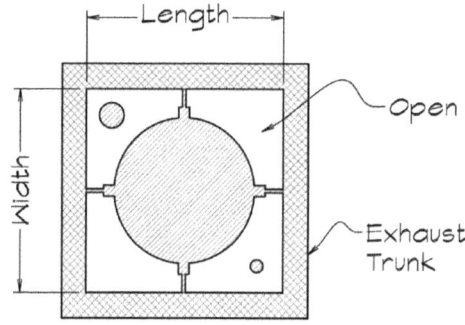

Figure 9-24. To allow good airflow, 30 percent of the exhaust trunk (length × width) should be open

not having seawater anywhere in the system to cause corrosion. To install a water-jacketed drystack exhaust, you must have this second raw-water pump and associated seacock and sea strainer (sea suction, see Chapter 17). In fact, one way to do this is to install a heat-exchanger-cooled engine with its full raw-water system (no keel cooler), but dump the raw water into the water jacket of a dry exhaust and from there overboard. It may be necessary to have a bypass leading overboard on the raw-water exit line, as the water-jacket flow may not be sufficient to handle all the raw water pumped through such a heat-exchanger-cooled engine. The seawater in the

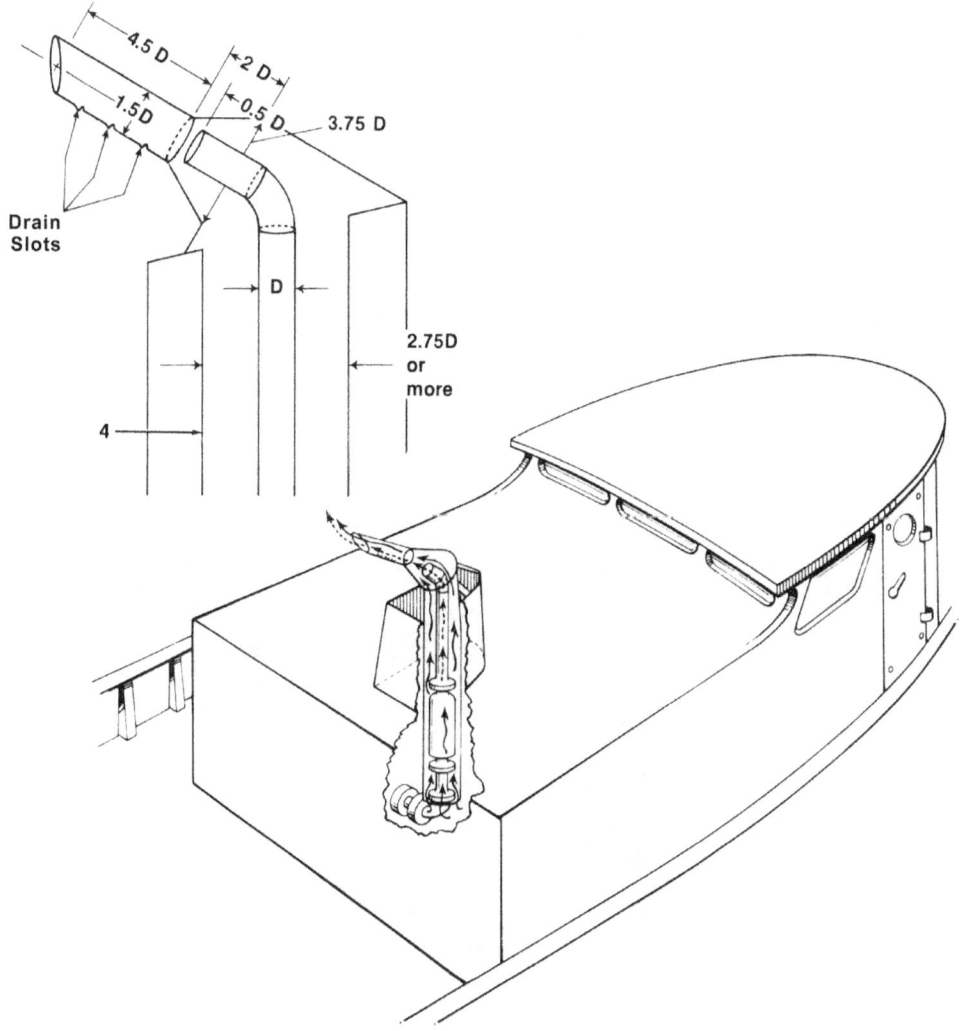

Figure 9-25. Exhaust-ejector ventilation: cone "jet" ejector (Courtesy Caterpillar, Inc.)

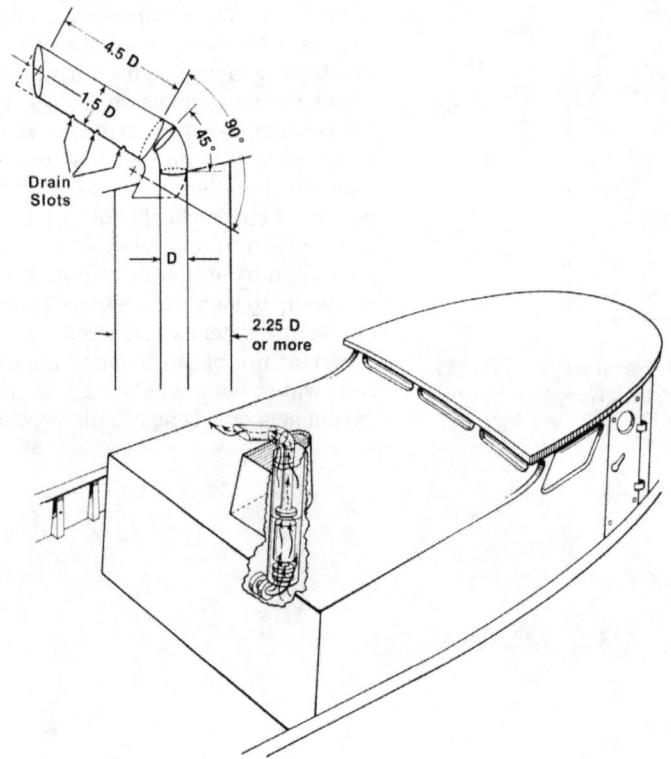

Figure 9-26. Exhaust-ejector ventilation: aft opening (Courtesy Caterpillar, Inc.)

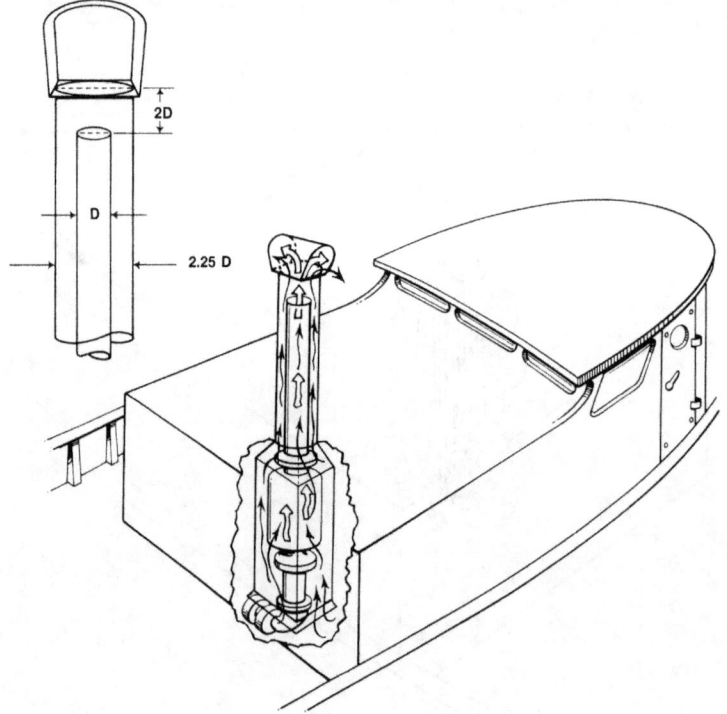

Figure 9-27. Exhaust-ejector ventilation: transverse exit openings (Courtesy Caterpillar, Inc.)

Chapter 9: Dry Exhaust Systems

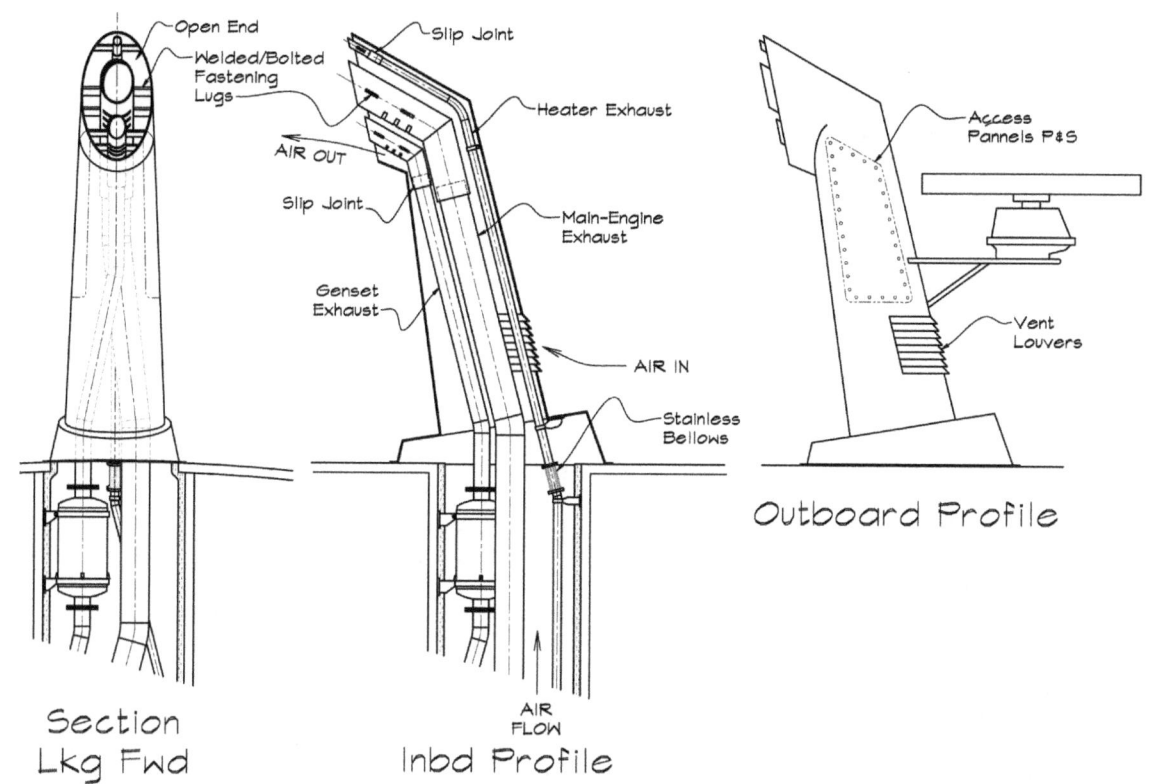

Figure 9-28.
Multiple-exhaust stacks

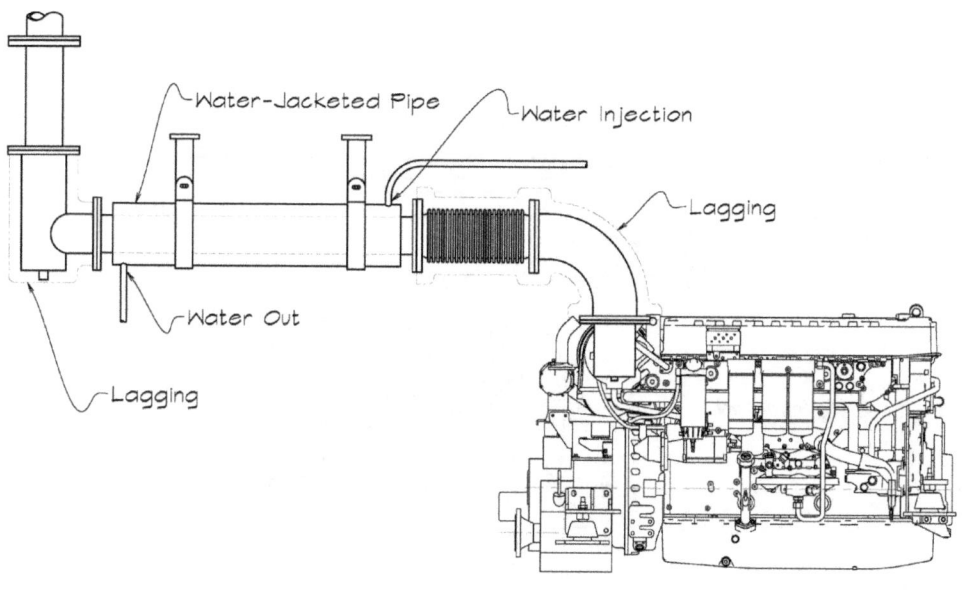

Figure 9-29.
Water-jacketed exhaust pipe

157

PART THREE: EXHAUST SYSTEMS

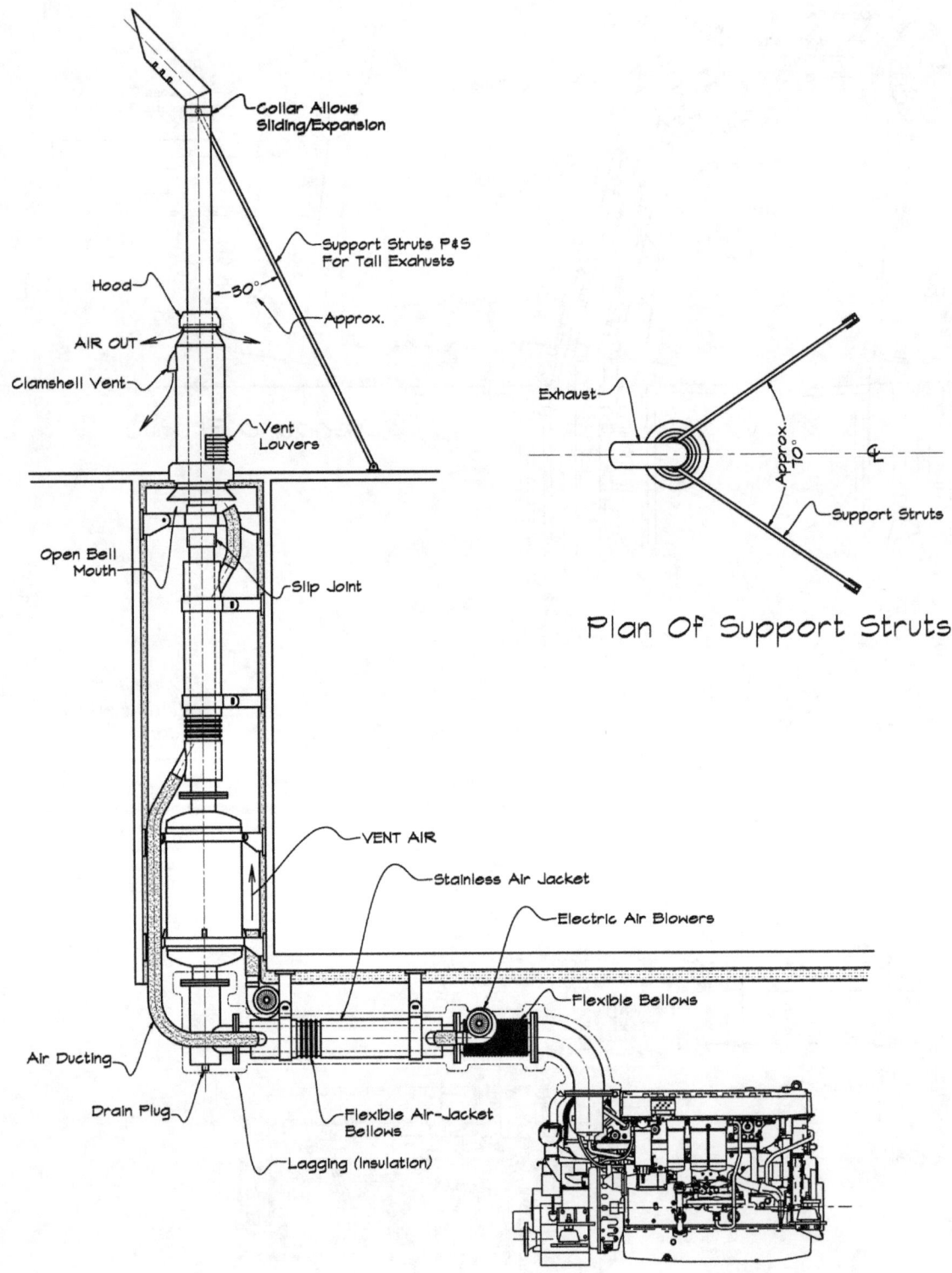

Figure 9-30. Air-jacketed exhaust

jacket can get fairly hot and will eventually lead to corrosion in the jacket (as we saw with water-jacketed exhaust manifolds). Finally, the water must exit the hull not through the exhaust (which, of course, is dry), but through yet another through-hull fitting.

Air-jacketed exhausts don't have raw-water pumps, any seawater, sea strainers, or the related potential for corrosion, but they require electric blowers to force cool air into the air jacket. The external air-jacket pipe must also be configured with flexible bellows (sometimes called wrinkle-tube) to allow for its expansion and contraction. (The air-jacket tube's OD is about 1.4 times the exhaust-pipe OD or a bit more.) Further, the air jacket does lower the surface temperature, but it doesn't lower it enough to avoid insulating any area with which the crew may come in contact. Thus, it still requires lagging, though this may be somewhat thinner than without air-jacketing. Finally, air-jacketed dry exhausts rely on the electric blowers to reduce the exhaust-pipe surface temperature. If there's an electric failure or a breakdown with the blowers, you have a serious exhaust problem.

Again, air-jacketed drystack exhaust installations are perfectly sound and acceptable, but they seem to get away from the rugged reliability that is a drystack installation's principal attraction.

Support Struts on High Exhaust Pipes

The drawing in Figure 9-30 shows another way to raise an exhaust pipe higher above the deck. In this case, it's not in a stack but is an individual pipe. When the height of the exhaust pipe is more than 7 times its diameter, it needs support, and you can see the struts installed for this purpose. The struts are lightweight pipe or heavy-wall tube with an outside diameter 1/50th of the strut length, pin center to pin center (or slightly more). A strut 100 inches (250 cm) long would be approximately 2-inch (50 mm) OD or a bit more. The fastening bolts at each end would be one-quarter the support strut's OD, or in this case, ½ inch (12.5 mm). Note that the support struts attach to the exhaust pipe at a sliding collar. This permits the exhaust pipe to expand and contract freely.

MORE ON MIXING AND MATCHING EXHAUST TYPES

As we saw previously, you can mix dry and wet exhaust components to solve installation problems. In Chapter 7 (page 119) we looked at a dry exhaust section used to fit an otherwise wet exhaust into a restricted space. In this chapter (page 155) we have seen how a heat-exchanger-cooled engine could use the raw water for engine cooling to also cool a water-jacketed drystack exhaust. In fact, you can have a heat-exchanger-cooled engine with an all-dry exhaust—without water-jacketing—and simply dump the cooling seawater directly overboard. With a sound understanding of both wet and dry exhaust systems, you can mix and match as needed to solve difficult installation problems.

Crewboat Exhaust

A mixed-exhaust installation is often used on crewboats and offshore supply boats, frequently with triple or quadruple engines mounted in an engine room aft. The engines are usually heat-exchanger cooled, but the exhaust run is very short and almost all dry. As you can see in Figure 9-31, the dry exhaust exits the engine into an exhaust bellows and dry muffler/silencer. The exhaust run is mostly horizontal—usually almost directly athwartships and out the side of the hull. (The exhaust rises from the engine to the muffler or horizontal exhaust pipe and runs athwartships to near the hull side, then down and out the side of the hull.) The raw engine-cooling water is injected at a custom fitting located just inside the hull, near the exit (Figure 9-32).

The advantage of this installation is that it is short, light, simple, and easy to repair. The disadvantage is that exhaust gas (and soot) exit the topsides where they can blow onboard and dirty the hull side and deck. This is acceptable on workboats but would be unacceptable on yachts or passenger vessels.

PART THREE: EXHAUST SYSTEMS

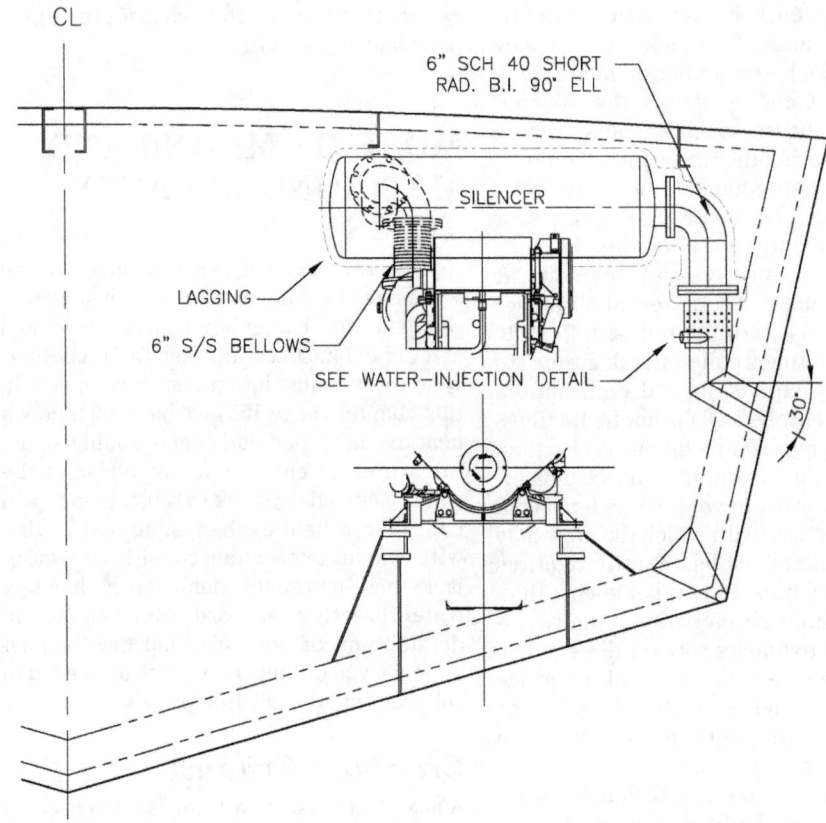

Figure 9-31.
Crewboat exhaust
(section)

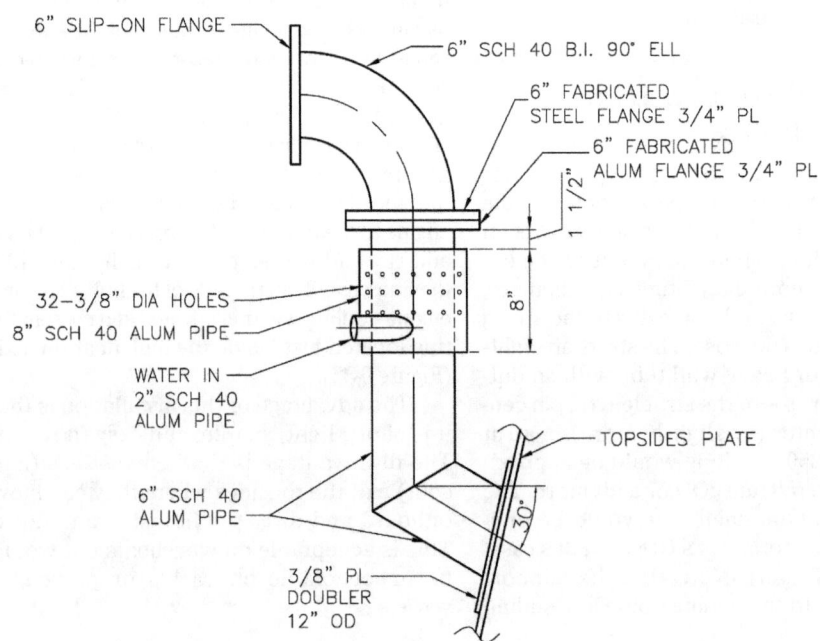

Figure 9-32.
Crewboat exhaust
water injection
detail

DRYSTACK VERSUS WET EXHAUST

Though wet exhaust systems are most common on boats, there appears to be an inclination to favor drystack exhaust systems for serious ocean cruising yachts as being somehow, well, "tougher." For almost all yachts and for most passenger vessels, however, I generally think a wet exhaust system is superior. It's important to keep in mind that this is most definitely not a question of right and wrong. Rather, it's a question of trade-offs. Both wet and dry exhaust systems have advantages and drawbacks. We can compare wet and drystack exhaust systems in Table 9-1.

We can examine these values item by item:

SEAWATER IN ENGINE COMPONENTS. Here the drystack system is the clear winner. There is simply no seawater in any engine component. Still, with a properly designed wet exhaust system, you can eliminate seawater in everything except the exhaust manifold itself.

HOLES BELOW THE WATERLINE. This is a bit deceptive. You would think that there would be no holes below the waterline with a drystack system, but as we've seen, drystack systems require external keel coolers. These usually necessitate two holes through the hull (though some are arranged to have just one). Alternatively, there's a complex set of internal or external metal channels for coolant flow, and these may develop pinholes or larger leaks. Thus there is only a slight improvement for drystack systems.

FIRE SAFETY. This is the drystack system's Achilles' heel. These things are really hot—dangerously so.

SIMPLICITY. We've seen that the drystack system's components—metal expansion bellows, expansion slip joints, safety cages, insulation/lagging, keel cooling, and so on—add up to a surprising amount of complexity on a well-designed system. The wet exhaust system is no more complex and possibly less so.

RELIABILITY. This is pretty close between the two systems. The only thing likely to go wrong with a properly designed wet exhaust system is a broken raw-water pump or (over the long haul) corrosion in the exhaust manifold. Drystack systems can have problems with expansion bellows, mounts, insulation, keel coolers, and so on.

PARTS TO INSPECT AND REPLACE. Wet exhaust systems have the raw-water impeller, quick and easy to take care of, and the heat-exchanger zinc, also fairly easy. Drystack systems require inspection of the insulation, bellows, mounts, and keel coolers.

TABLE 9-1. DRYSTACK AND WET EXHAUST SYSTEM COMPARISON

	Drystack	Wet Exhaust
Seawater in engine components	5	1
Holes below waterline	3	2
Fire safety	1	3
Simplicity	3	3
Reliability	4	3
Parts to inspect and replace	2	3
Ease of tracking and fixing leaks	2	3
Quiet	2	4
Corrosion of exhaust piping	3	5
Corrosion of manifold and heat exchanger	5	1
Can fit a return oil cooler	1	5
Space taken from accommodations	2	5
Unwanted interior heat in warm weather	2	4
Soot on deck	1	5
TOTAL	36	47

NOTE: Ratings are from 1 to 5, with 5 being best.

EASE OF TRACKING AND FIXING LEAKS. This, too, is a bit deceptive. The piping in a wet exhaust system is straightforward and generally visible. A drystack system's keel cooler is below the waterline and outside the hull. You can't get at it easily if it develops a pinhole, and it's hard to find the problem without a haulout. As we've seen, some drystack systems on metal hulls circulate cooling water though internal tanks or through channels of pipe welded to the inside or outside of the hull shell. Again, leaks in such piping or tanks can be difficult to locate.

QUIET. This is clearly the strong suit for wet exhaust systems. Even the best drystack "hospital" silencers can't equal the quiet from the combination of mixing cooling water with the exhaust, then running it through a muffler and exiting it through the hull topsides (or even underwater). Yachts, tour boats, and ferries usually want maximum comfort for the crew and passengers. A voyaging motor cruiser is a home. You don't want to hear the roar of your diesel endlessly—a soft purr would be nice.

CORROSION OF EXHAUST PIPING. Here we have another strong suit for wet exhaust systems. If the entire exhaust is hose and FRP exhaust pipe it can't corrode at all. Drystack exhaust systems are all metal and will experience corrosion over time.

CORROSION OF MANIFOLD AND HEAT EXCHANGER. This is a clear winner for drystack systems. There's no seawater in the manifold (it's not water jacketed), so there's no corrosion. Further, there is no heat exchanger with a raw-water circuit, which also can experience corrosion and silting and should be cleaned and inspected regularly. Wet exhaust manifolds have built-in water jackets. These will experience at least some corrosion eventually. Water-jacketed manifolds are much cooler and quieter, however.

CAN FIT A RETURN OIL COOLER. Only installations with raw-water intake can use a return oil cooler, which lowers fuel and engine room temperature. We've seen that you can have a mixed system with drystack exhaust and heat-exchanger engine cooling, but this would not be a pure drystack system.

SPACE TAKEN FROM ACCOMMODATIONS. It is amazing how much space drystack installations can require. On our 60-foot (18.3 m) *General*, with drystack, the exhaust trunk fills a column over 2.5 sq. ft. (0.2 m^2) in section right in the center of the arrangement. It is a real problem trying to work the accommodations around drystack installations.

UNWANTED INTERIOR HEAT IN WARM WEATHER. It's also surprising how much heat even a well-insulated drystack exhaust will give off. It can be quite uncomfortable and force you to run the air-conditioning more often than you would with a wet exhaust.

SOOT ON DECK. This is a special problem with drystack systems and one frequently overlooked. The fact is that all diesels produce black soot fairly regularly: at speed, only in small amounts; during acceleration and low-speed maneuvering, sometimes quite a bit. With wet exhaust systems, this soot is mixed with seawater and goes over the side, leaving nothing but a streak on the topsides—easily washed off. With dry exhaust, the soot comes out as a fine cloud that descends to the deck, gradually building up an unpleasant oily film of gray-black grime.

WET EXHAUST SYSTEMS ARE BETTER FOR YACHTS AND PASSENGER VESSELS Evaluating the preceding information, my preference is for wet exhausts on yachts and most small passenger vessels. Both wet and dry exhausts work well when properly configured, but I think that most boaters will be happier living with a wet exhaust.

Workboats Often Are Better with Drystack Systems

Particularly without water-jacketing or air-jacketing, drystack exhausts are somewhat more reliable for workboats, where more exhaust noise and additional soot on deck aren't such important considerations. Even so, many fast workboats—pilot boats, crewboats, supply boats, and such—are usually better off with wet exhausts.

A plus for drystack systems on boats that operate in very cold weather is that there is no problem with skim ice in sea strainers and sea chests. This is really a factor only in boats running in areas like the Bering Sea or Antarctica in winter, but in such weather, this is a notable added benefit for drystack systems. What's more, the extra heat from the dry exhaust will be welcome.

Part Four

RUDDERS AND STEERING SYSTEMS

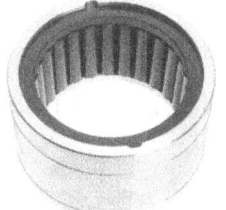

Rudder Geometry, Shape, and Size — CHAPTER 10

Rudders and the steering systems that control them make it possible for a boat to get where it's going. Crisp, responsive steering in all conditions and at all speeds make a vessel a pleasure to operate. Poor steering response (or worse, a broken steering system) is not only unpleasant but potentially dangerous. In this and the next three chapters we'll discuss the basics of rudders and steering systems for inboard boats: power and sail. We'll also review some important considerations that are often neglected, as well as look at a few special or unusual rudders.

PUTTING THE RUDDER TO WORK

Fundamentally, a rudder is no more than a board hung aft on the centerline of a boat such that it is free to pivot around hinges called *gudgeons and pintles* along its leading edge, or around a roughly vertical shaft called the *rudder post* or *rudder stock* (Figure 10-1). (On modern twin-screw craft, the rudders are hung just aft of each propeller on rudder stocks.)

If we deflect the rudder blade of a boat to one side—say to port—we increase the force of the water hitting the port, or left, side of the rudder, which in turn swings the boat's entire stern in the opposite direction, to the right, or starboard. Since we've used the force of water flowing past the rudder to kick the stern around to starboard, the bow has now been swung to port, and off we'll go to port—presumably what we had in mind when we put the helm over in the first place.

Describing the Rudder and Aspect Ratio

Rudders come in many shapes and sizes, so designers have adopted some airplane terminology to help describe them accurately. The depth or vertical height of a rudder is called its *span*. (Span is always measured vertically, and not along the length of an angled or swept-back rudder.) The fore-and-aft length of the rudder is referred to as its *chord*. Designers tend to visualize airplane wings and hydrofoils—like rudders or keels—as growing out of the fuselage or hull; this is, after all, where they are attached. Accordingly, the top of the rudder, near the hull underbody, is known as the *root*, and the fore-and-aft length at the root is the *root chord*. Similarly, the bottom end of the rudder—farthest from the hull—is named the *tip*, and the fore-and-aft length there is the *tip chord*. The average rudder length fore and aft is called the *mean chord* or the *midchord*, as it's usually at or near midspan (midheight).

163

PART FOUR: RUDDERS AND STEERING SYSTEMS

Figure 10-1.
Rudder plan
geometry

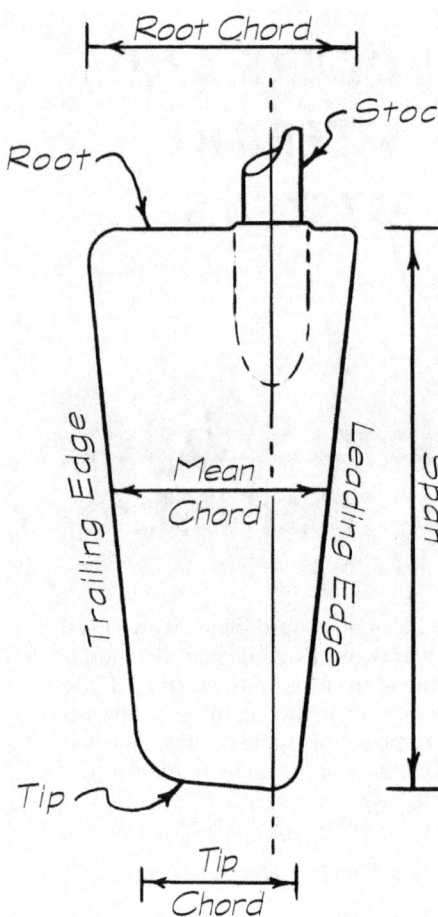

All hydrofoils—rudders are really hydrofoils, not simply "boards"—are more efficient if they are long and narrow rather than short and squat. It's important to be able to describe this feature clearly, as well. It is measured as *aspect ratio*, as shown in the following formula.

Formula 10-1.

Formula 10-1. Aspect Ratio

$$\text{Aspect Ratio} = \frac{(\text{Span})^2}{\text{Area}}$$

Where
Span = vertical height of rudder blade, ft. or m
Area = area of rudder blade, sq. ft. or m^2

(NOTE: This is sometimes referred to as the *geometric aspect ratio*, since the so-called mirroring effect of the hull above the rudder roughly doubles the *effective aspect ratio* in many cases. For our purposes, we'll stick with aspect ratio as simple geometric aspect ratio.)

The higher the aspect ratio, the deeper and narrower the rudder. To quickly estimate the area of the rudder, just measure its chord (fore-and-aft length) at midspan (height) and multiply by the span at midchord (the average height).

If our boat's rudder has an area of 1.9 square feet (0.176 m^2) and an average height or span of 2.1 feet (0.64 m), its aspect ratio is 2.32 to 1, or simply 2.32. The calculation looks like this: 2.1 ft. × 2.1 ft. ÷ 1.9 sq. ft. = 2.32:1, or 0.64 m × 0.64 m ÷ 0.176 m^2 = 2.32:1. This is a good, deep, narrow rudder for a powerboat. An aspect ratio higher than 2.4 or so gives a still more efficient rudder blade but adds excessive bending strain on the rudder stock. Such rather high-aspect ratios should generally be avoided on powerboats.

Sailboat-Rudder Aspect Ratio

Aspect ratios on sailboats are somewhat greater than the preceding. An aspect ratio somewhere between 2.2 and 3.5 is normal, tending to be higher for spade rudders on fin-keel boats. Very high-aspect rudders are becoming common on fin-keel performance sailboats with high-aspect fin keels. Such craft often have rudders with aspect ratios between 3.5 and 4.5. Even higher aspect rudders are found on some all-out race boats. Generally, I don't recommend aspect ratios over 4.5 as best practice; the bending loads on the deep rudder's stock are much higher, and improvement in rudder response becomes increasingly less as the aspect ratio gets very high.

Rudder and Hull Work Together

In turning, a boat pivots roughly around its combined center of gravity and the center of water pressure on the hull forward.

Chapter 10: Rudder Geometry, Shape, and Size

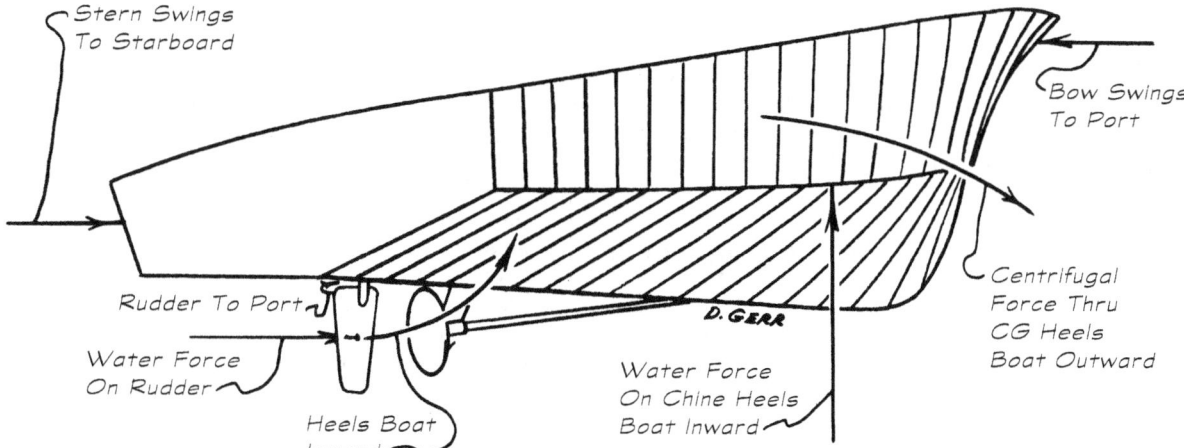

Figure 10-2. Forces from a turn to port

The greater the distance the rudder is aft of this combined center, the greater the lever arm it has with which to twist the boat around, and the more effective it can be. For the same steering effect, a smaller rudder can be used if it's farther aft. Similarly, a boat with a deep forefoot or a steering fin forward will respond more quickly to the helm than a boat without. This isn't of much importance on average craft, which generally have fairly good proportions for this purpose; however, long, shallow hulls or very high-speed, shallow-bodied planing hulls sometimes benefit from the addition of a small fixed steering or skid fin forward—around midships.

Sizing and Locating a Skid Fin

You have to be careful not to overdo a skid fin, as too much area forward makes a boat too quick on the helm. In rough seas, such a fin could broach a boat or cause it to trip over the forward fin and capsize. A rule of thumb is that the skid fin—when one is required at all—should be about 10 to 15 percent of the length of the waterline forward of the center of gravity, and that the area of the skid fin should be about 80 percent of the rudder area. (If you have no exact information, you can assume that the center of gravity of a high-speed planing hull is about 60 percent of the waterline length aft of the bow at the waterline.)

Aspect Ratio, Rudder Area, and Your Boat's Bank

A less-well-known consideration of rudder design is that the rudder's aspect ratio affects how your boat banks in a turn. When you put the helm over for a hard turn at high speed, centrifugal force acts on the boat's center of gravity, pulling outward. Since the center of gravity of almost all planing hulls—in fact, of most boats of any type—is well above the waterline, this tends to make the boat heel outward in a turn. The outward bank is uncomfortable, and decreasing it or getting an inward bank is ideal. The force of water pressure on the underside of a planing hull's outboard chine counteracts this outward heel considerably, but the water force acting on her rudder also helps. The deeper the rudder (i.e., the greater its aspect ratio) and the more area it has, the more effective it is in generating a sure-footed inward bank.

TYPES OF RUDDERS

Rudders come in two basic types—*inboard rudders*, or rudders that are mounted entirely under the hull, and *outboard rudders*, or rudders that are hung on the transom and thus project aft of the hull proper. These may each be divided again into *balanced* and *unbalanced* rudders. A balanced rudder has some of its area forward of its pivot or turning axis, whereas an unbalanced rudder pivots or

165

hinges entirely at its leading edge, with no area projecting forward at all. Finally, rudders may be *spade rudders*, with no bearing or support below the bottom of the rudder blade, or they may be rudders with bearings above and below the rudder blade.

Inboard Versus Outboard Rudders

For the same rudder shape and area, an inboard rudder is almost always more efficient than an outboard rudder. The hull traps the water rushing over the top portion of the blade, guiding the entire flow aft and forcing this water to do useful steering work. This is the important endplate effect, and it reduces induced drag, which is nothing more than the wasted energy caused by water roiling around the top or bottom edges of such a hydrofoil. Often, high-speed craft fitted with outboard rudders will have endplates (sometimes incorrectly called cavitation plates) fastened to them at the waterline or at the rudder's top edge. The proper term is either *endplate* or *ventilation plate*. These plates help noticeably, but such rudders still are not quite as efficient as a true inboard rudder.

The great advantage of outboard rudders—at least for larger rudders in low- to medium-speed craft—is their simplicity (Figure 10-3). It's comparatively inexpensive to attach the gudgeons and pintles outside the hull on the transom and to run the tiller to steering gear far above the waterline, where watertightness isn't a big consideration. By contrast, an inboard rudder usually requires a rudder port and stuffing box through the bottom of the hull—a potential source of leaks that should be inspected at the beginning and end of each season, as well as before and after any major passage. Further, the outboard rudder allows the propeller to be installed farther aft, which permits the shaft angle to be slightly lower (closer to parallel with the waterline) for slightly more efficient thrust. Outboard rudders on small planing hulls are available with premanufactured housings containing the tiller arm. The entire housing bolts to the bottom of the transom, with the tiller projecting through a hole forward into the hull or projecting over the top of the transom into the cockpit.

Balance and the Rudder

Balanced rudders move the center of the force of the water striking the rudder blade closer to the rudder's pivot axis than it would be on an unbalanced blade. Maximum water force occurs at maximum helm or rudder angle, which is about 35 degrees to either side of dead center—70 degrees from hard over to hard over. (At greater angles, ordinary rudders stall, lose effectiveness, and are strained by excessive water force. Internal stops should be fitted to keep rudders from turning farther. We'll look at special rudders designed for greater angles in Chapter 13.)

Because the water is striking the rudder blade from ahead, the leading edge does more work than the trailing edge. (This is true of

Figure 10-3. Sailboat outboard rudders

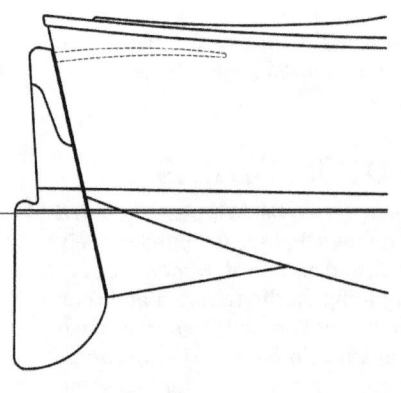

Outbord Rudder on Large Skeg
5 sq. ft., no balance, AR = 1.9

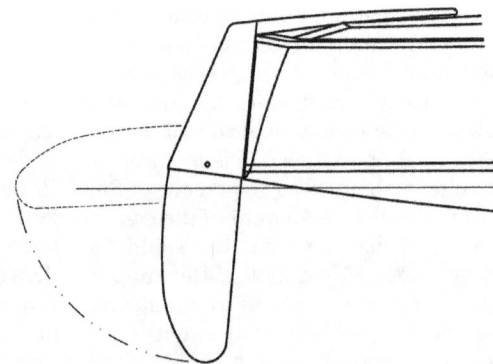

Kick-Up Rudder
5 sq. ft., no balance, AR = 2.4

all hydrofoils and of airfoils as well.) Accordingly, the center of water force doesn't fall at the geometric center of the rudder blade as viewed from the side, but forward of this. In fact, at a helm angle of 35 degrees, it usually falls somewhere between 30 and 40 percent of the fore-and-aft length of the rudder aft of the leading edge (see the sidebar to estimate the center of force at other rudder angles).

If a boat's rudder has a span—vertical height—of 2.1 feet (0.64 m) and a mean chord of 0.9 feet (274 mm), the center of water force will fall about 35 percent of the chord aft of the leading edge, or 0.31 feet (96 mm) aft. The unbalanced rudder—at a water force of 985 pounds (447 kg)—would thus generate a torque (a force multiplied by a lever arm) of 305 foot-pounds: 0.31 ft. × 985 lb. = 305 ft. lb., or 0.096 m × 447 kg = 42.9 kgm.

Fit this boat with a rudder of the same area and proportions but with a 17 percent balance, and the pivot point will be farther aft and closer to the center of water force—in this case, about 0.07 feet (21 mm) away. The balanced rudder will generate a torque of just 69 foot-pounds (9.4 kgm) less than a quarter as much! This results in much easier steering and lighter loads on the steering gear, autopilot, and not incidentally, on the helmsman.

Balance is determined by the percentage of rudder area forward and aft of the rudderpost axis. Figure 10-4 shows a rudder with 17 percent balance, which years of trial and error have demonstrated to be about ideal. Twenty percent balance is usually the absolute maximum. More balance than this can move the center of water force ahead of the pivot axis, making the rudder sheer wildly or lock up at hard over, causing uncomfortable steering.

Balanced rudders should not be installed directly behind a skeg or keel. Since the leading edge projects out from the hull centerline when the rudder is turned, such a balanced rudder would catch the water flow on the leading-edge side. This creates unwanted turbulence. For powerboats and racing sailboats with spade rudders, the advantage of a lighter and more responsive helm makes the balanced rudder hard to beat. For cruising sailboats, however, an unbalanced rudder with a skeg or keel immediately ahead of it offers better protection for the rudder and—depending on configuration—better tracking, particularly in a following sea.

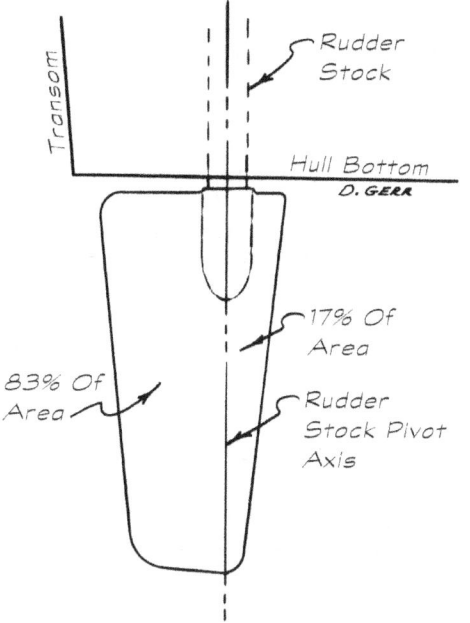

Figure 10-4. Spade rudder with a 17 percent balance and a 2.32:1 aspect ratio

Center of Water Force at Rudder Angles Other Than 35 Degrees

If a design project requires you to estimate the location of the center of water force on a rudder at helm angles other than the maximum 35 degrees, you can use the following approximate formula:

$$WFL\% = 0.195 + (0.305 \times \sin(\text{rudder angle}))$$

Where
WFL% = water-force location as percent of mean chord aft of leading edge
rudder angle = rudder angle, in degrees

This will give you a passable approximation for rudders of normal airfoil section shape and for angles up to 40 degrees. For wedge-section and parabolic rudders, add 14 percent to the formula result.

PART FOUR: RUDDERS AND STEERING SYSTEMS

Real-World Problem with Too Much Balance

An interesting example of a real problem created by too much balance is presented in Figure 10-5. This boat came into the service yard for repairs to the running gear after grounding, and the yard noted the sizable trim tab bolted to the rudder, as you can see in the photo. They asked the owner if the tab had been bent or straight, and the owner thought it had been straight. Repaired and relaunched, the boat steered so strongly to port that it was unmanageable. They hauled the boat again, and with a bit of experimentation the trim tab was bent 10 degrees to port. Then the steering was fine. The original construction yard or designer—not the service yard—had built in the problem and then had corrected for it by adding the tab and bending it over.

Looking at the photo, you can see the reason: there's too much balance (about 25 percent). A portion of the slipstream from the prop was catching the leading edge of the rudder in such a way that it swung the blade to port, which caused the boat to turn to port. Bending the tab to port counteracted the turning effect on the rudder, forcing the blade to starboard (back to center or "neutral"). In theory, you could also correct this effect by fairing away the leading edge, by grinding down the starboard side of the rudder at the leading edge, or by slightly bending the leading edge to starboard. In any case, you can see both why it's important not to have too much balance, and how you might correct the problem if you're faced with it. (Incidentally, there's also too much shaft overhang between the propeller and the stern bearing, and the propeller nut zinc is too large, which can cause turbulence. Also, the rudder has no shaft-pulling hole, so the entire rudder and probably the skeg below it would have to be unshipped to remove the propeller shaft.)

SIZING UP THE RUDDER

The big question regarding rudders is how large they should be. The smaller the rudder, the less drag it creates and the faster you can go. Further, smaller rudders require less steering force and are easier to manage. If the rudder is too small, however, you'll end up with insufficient steering control. Somehow, a happy medium has to be found.

The basic rule-of-thumb rudder area formulas are as follows:

Average Planing Boat Rudder Area = 0.018 × waterline length × draft (hull only)
Displacement Boat Rudder Area = 0.03 to 0.04 × waterline length × draft (including keel)
Deep Narrow Fin-Keel Sailboats = 0.045 × waterline length × draft (including keel)
Moderate (Modern Long Keel) Sailboats = 0.058 × waterline length × draft (including keel)
Traditional Full Long Keel Sailboats = 0.068 × waterline length × draft (including keel)

Or

The rule of thumb for planing hulls is that the total rudder area (all rudders) should be 2 percent of lateral plane. For displacement motor cruisers, the rule of thumb is between 3 and 4 percent of lateral plane.
These rules of thumb should be used for initial estimates and as a check. For the most accurate results, use the formulas below.

Displacement and Semidisplacement Powerboat Rudder-Area Formula

For displacement and semidisplacement powerboats, the following formula is useful for determining rudder area.

Figure 10-5. Overbalanced rudder (Courtesy Washburn's Boatyard)

Chapter 10: Rudder Geometry, Shape, and Size

Formula 10-2. Rudder Area for Displacement and Semidisplacement Powerboats

$$RA\% = 5.33 - (1.18 \times SL)$$
$$\text{Rudder Area} = RA\% \times WL \times \text{draft}$$

Where
RA% = rudder area percentage of WL length × draft
SL = speed-length ratio at *cruising* speed (not maximum boat speed)
Rudder Area = rudder area, sq. ft. or m²
WL = waterline length, ft. or m
Draft = draft, ft. or m
SL or speed-length ratio is

$$\text{SL ratio} = \frac{\text{Knots}}{\sqrt{WL, \text{ft.}}}$$

or

$$\text{SL ratio} = 0.552 \times \frac{\text{Knots}}{\sqrt{WL, \text{m}}}$$

Formula 10-2 should be used up to speed-length ratio speed 2.8 (cruising speed); higher than that you should switch to using Formula 10-3.

Example: If you had a boat that was 48 feet (14.6 m) WL and 5-foot (1.52 m) draft, with a top *cruising* speed of 9.5 knots, the rudder area would be

$$\text{SL ratio} = \frac{9.5 \text{ kts}}{\sqrt{48 \text{ ft.}}} = 1.37$$

or

$$\text{SL ratio} = 0.552 \times \frac{9.5 \text{ kts}}{\sqrt{14.6 \text{ m}}} = 1.37$$

$$RA\% = 5.33 - (1.18 \times 1.37) = 3.71$$

so

Rudder Area = 0.0371 × 48 ft. WL × 5 ft. draft = 8.9 sq. ft.

or

Rudder Area = 0.0371 × 14.6 m WL × 1.52 m draft = 0.82 m²

Planing Powerboat Rudder-Area Formula

For planing powerboats, rudder area is found from a variation of Skene's formula:

Formula 10-3. Rudder Area for Planing Powerboats

$$K = (WL, \text{ft.})^{1.5} \div 50$$

$$\text{Area} = K\sqrt{\frac{\sqrt{WL, \text{ft.}} \times \text{Disp., tons}}{100 \times \text{kts} \times (0.01 WL, \text{ft.})^3}}$$

or

$$Km = (WL, \text{m})^{1.5} \div 90.56$$

$$\text{Area} = Km\sqrt{\frac{\sqrt{WL, \text{m}} \times \text{Disp., tons}}{55.2 \times \text{kts} \times (0.0328 WL, \text{m})^3}}$$

Where
kts = max. speed in knots

A twin-screw planing 75-foot (22.8 m) motoryacht, 66.34 feet (20.22 m) WL and 77.85 tons, would work out as follows:

$$K = (66.34 \text{ ft. WL})^{1.5} \div 50 = 10.81$$

$$\text{Area} = 10.81\sqrt{\frac{\sqrt{66.34 \text{ ft. WL}} \times 77.85 \text{ tons, Disp.}}{100 \times 28 \text{ kts} \times (0.01 \times 66.34 \text{ ft. WLL})^3}} = 9.52 \text{ sq.ft.}$$

or

$$Km = (20.22 \text{ m WL})^{1.5} \div 90.56 = 1.004$$

$$\text{Area} = 1.004\sqrt{\frac{\sqrt{20.22 \text{ m WL}} \times 77.85 \text{ tons, Disp.}}{55.2 \times 28 \text{ kts} \times (0.0328 \times 20.22 \text{ m WLL})^3}} = 0.885 \text{ m})^3$$

Since this is a twin-screw boat, it has two rudders (one behind each prop) and each rudder would have 4.76 sq. ft. (0.442 m²) area, or a bit more.

Note that additional rudder area doesn't harm maneuvering, but it does add extra appendage drag and extra cost in larger steering gear. It doesn't make sense to use rudders much larger than required; however, boats that do a lot of low-speed maneuvering do well with 10 to 15 percent more area than indicated in the formula. Sportfishing boats and ferries fall into this category. There's some penalty in extra drag, but the quicker helm response at low speed will be worth this for such vessels.

High-Speed Displacement Power Catamaran Rudder Area

Many power catamarans reach high speeds without planing. Such craft are usually round-bilged with quite slender hulls and can be powered to go much faster than comparable displacement monohulls. Rather than determine rudder area directly, a good rule for each rudder (a rudder behind each hull, with a propeller directly ahead of each rudder) is that the rudder be entirely under the hull (not project beyond the transom), with clearance between the top of the rudder and the underside of the hull as close as practical. The rudder-blade span or height should be 90 to 95 percent of the maximum hull draft. The mean width of the rudder blade is then 60 percent of the height. It's common for such rudders to be nearly perfect rectangles; however, they can be trapezoidal, in which case the chord at the tip is usually roughly 60 to 65 percent of the chord at the root. Balance is 17 percent. For further rudder calculations (for the rudder stock, steering gear, etc.), you then calculate the area of the rudder you have drawn by multiplying the span times the mean chord.

Sailboat Rudder Area

For sailboats, rudder area should be between 8 and 10 percent of total lateral plane. The higher the aspect ratio and the farther aft the rudder, the lower the required area. Thus, if the rudder post is right at station 10 (at the aft end of the waterline) and the rudder is deep with a high aspect, you could even get sufficient steering response with 6 or 7 percent of lateral plane area (on a fin-keel sailboat).

Sailboat Rudders as Directional Stabilizing Fins

Though reducing the wetted surface with such a high-aspect rudder well-aft would seem to make sense, in practice it's seldom a good idea. This is because rudders on fin-keel sailboats perform a second function: they act as directional stabilizer fins, like the feathers on the trailing end of an arrow.

Common belief is that sailboats with deep and narrow (high-aspect) fin keels don't hold course well, and longer keels are needed for good directional stability. In fact, a high-aspect balanced spade rudder of sufficient area damps out or stabilizes directional oscillations well and can make a high-aspect fin-keel boat quite steady on the helm (though not as steady as a traditional long-keel design would be). For this reason, I usually use rudder areas of 9 percent of total lateral plane on all sailboats.

Indeed, with very high-aspect fin keels, the rudder additionally plays a larger role in resisting leeway, and a rudder area of 10 percent of lateral plane can give better upwind performance combined with better directional stability—a steadier helm.

Skegs on Sailboat Rudders

Sailboats with separate fin keels can have balanced spade rudders or unbalanced rudders on skegs. If the rudder is on a skeg, up to 12 percent of the rudder area can be assumed to be in the skeg. Thus if you need 10 sq. ft. (0.92 m^2) of rudder area (to get 9 percent of lateral plane), 12 percent of that 10 square feet (1.2 sq. ft. [1,115 cm^2]) could be counted as being in the skeg. If the skeg is larger, that's fine. The skeg will improve directional stability and further protect and strengthen the rudder, but the additional area (over 12 percent of the desired rudder area) should not be counted toward the effective rudder area.

If the skeg gets very large—if the skeg area is 80 percent of rudder area or more—this is closer to a rudder hung off the back of a traditional long keel, and none of the skeg should be counted as rudder area.

THE RUDDER IN CROSS SECTION, AND BASIC SCANTLINGS

There's a tendency to think of the rudder cross section (rudder sections) as being a classic airfoil shape: a rounded entry, maximum thickness roughly at 30 percent of chord aft of the leading edge, and a gently convex trailing section terminating at a point. In fact, for sailboats and displacement power cruisers, this is the ideal standard section shape. As vessels become faster, however, this section becomes less effective. Above 25 or 30 knots, the blunt rounded leading edge of a traditional airfoil section causes too much turbulence in front of the rudder.

At high speed, when the rudder is put over, this blunt leading edge virtually tears the water flow away from the blade, leaving a swirl of eddies along the blade surface. Such turbulent flow generates very little force or lift and is, in fact, a stall, just like the stalling of an airplane wing in too steep a climb. Accordingly, as boat speed increases, the leading edge of the rudder should be made sharper and sharper, and the point of maximum section thickness should be moved aft.

Airfoil Rudder Sections— Low to Medium Speed

Figure 10-6 shows typical sections that work well for rudders on sailboats and on displacement- and medium-speed powerboats (up to about 18 knots).

There is a variety of suitable airfoil sections for use on rudders, but the NACA 0010 section pictured in Figure 10-6 works well. Such a section has the theoretical minimum drag and highest lift in applications like this. Table 10-1 gives the proportionate half-breadths at various locations along the section's chord. At 30 percent of the chord length aft of the leading edge—the thickest point—the half-breadth is 5.002% of the chord length, and the rudder thickness will be twice the half-breadth.

The additional drag of a fat rudder stock (wider than the rudder-blade section) would be unacceptable. Accordingly, if the rudder stock has to be thicker than you can fit inside the 0010 section, make the section proportionally thicker by multiplying the half-breadths at each station by the required factor. For instance, if the 0010 section is 30 inches (76 cm) long (the chord) and the center of the rudder stock is at 17 percent chord, the half-breadths at the stock will be 1.38 inches and the thickness there will about 2.76 inches (69 mm). The rudder stock— to be completely inside the blade—would have to be no more than about 2.25 inches (55 mm) in diameter. You may, however, need a larger diameter. Say that your calculations indicate you need a 2¾-inch (70 mm) stock; then the rudder blade should be about 3¼ inches (81 mm) thick at the stock—at 17 percent chord. From that we can derive our required half-breadth multiplier as follows:

$$3.25 \text{ in.} \div 2.76 \text{ in. chord} = 1.17$$

or

$$81 \text{ mm} \div 69 \text{ mm chord} = 1.17$$

and

$$10\% \times 1.17 = 11.7\%$$

Thus you need to multiply all the section half-breadths (and the tip radius) by 1.17. The "10" in the "0010" indicates the basic section has a 10 percent ratio of thickness to chord. You would end up, in this case, with an 11.7 percent section, or a NACA 00–11.7 section. The fatter section will have more form drag than the 10 percent section; however, it will have less drag than a 10 percent section with a rudder stock projecting outside it.

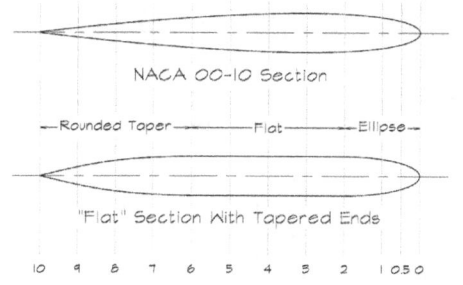

Figure 10-6. Low-speed rudder sections

> ## NACA Sections
>
> Objects designed to optimize lift in fluid flow (a gas or a liquid) are termed *foils*. This is the same as for airplane wings, and the standard source for rudder and keel-foil section shapes is the work of NACA (National Advisory Committee for Aeronautics). (NACA was subsequently replaced by NASA.) The complete selection of NACA foils can be found in *Theory of Wing Sections*, by Abbott and Doenhoff, published McGraw-Hill and then by Dover Publications, 1949, 1959.

PART FOUR: RUDDERS AND STEERING SYSTEMS

Flat Sections with Tapered Ends

Much is made of the optimum airfoil section. Such airfoil sections are best, assuming that budget and construction method permit. The fact is, however, that a simple flat section (thick enough to completely house the rudder stock) with the forward end rounded in an ellipse and the trailing edge tapered (as shown in Figure 10-6) works quite acceptably. The increased drag is slight, and there's little practical difference in steering response. Such rudders are much easier to fabricate of laminated ply (or laminated ply and foam) glassed on the outside. I have used this section on many designs.

Intermediate-Speed-Section Rudders

As speeds move higher than 18 knots, the airfoil section or flat section with tapered ends begins to stall too soon at modest helm angles. The effect can be accepted up to about 25 knots, but between 15 and 30 knots the intermediate-speed-section rudder is optimal (Figure 10-7). The sharp leading edge, the maximum thickness farther aft, and the square, thick trailing edge make the rudder work when cavitating at these higher speeds. This rudder shape is hard to find today and would usually have to be custom fabricated.

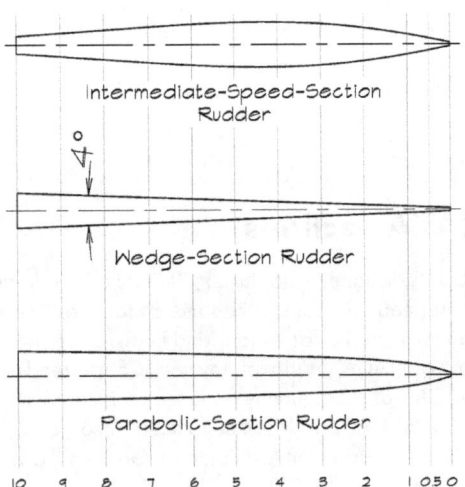

Figure 10-7. High-speed rudder sections

Wedge-Section Rudders for High Speed

Huckins—as in the famous Huckins PT boats—found that a true wedge-section rudder (Figure 10-7) gave the most reliable steering on most planing vessels cruising at 25 to 30 knots and higher. Such rudders come nearly to a true point at the leading edge—but with some slight thickness there for strength—and terminated in a wide, squared-off trailing edge. A wedge angle of about 4 degrees generally works best. Such wedge-section rudders incur somewhat more drag at dead center (going straight ahead) than do airfoil-section rudders, but they are much less prone to stalling and offer more positive steering control at high speeds. Also, assume the center of water force is at 40 percent of mean chord aft of the leading edge (at hard over).

Parabolic-Section Rudders for High Speed and Minimum Drag

The modern variant of the wedge-section rudder is the parabolic-section rudder (Figure 10-7). You can see that it is similar in concept to the wedge-section rudder; however, instead of having straight sides in section, its sides are curved in a gentle convex parabola. Parabolic-section rudders provide all the advantages of wedge-section rudders, but with less drag. The difference isn't large, but it is enough to be worthwhile where top speed or fuel economy is an important factor.

Real-World Comparison of Intermediate-Section and Parabolic-Section Rudders

Designer David Pugh reported the following results comparing the intermediate- and parabolic-section rudder shapes:

> I printed the page from your rudder drawings and enlarged it to the proper scale for our rudders. Then, I went out in the shop and had some extra blades modified.

We started with a simple wedge-shaped, transom-hung rudder from Marine Hardware. It is their stock rudder (OBRI 1.375 - B). We simply added fairing putty to one set of blades to achieve your Parabolic Section. On a second section, we ground down the trailing edge slightly and used fairing putty to achieve your Intermediate Section. The boat (our new 341-ft. inboard powered by twin 380 Cummins) topped out at 34.5 mph. There may have been a very slight improvement in speed with the Parabolic Section (0.1 mph). The Intermediate Section was equal to the Parabolic Section or perhaps slightly better (0.1 mph again). I say "perhaps" because I have found that even with a GPS, a 0.1 mph change in speed is usually not worth noting since so many variables can alter speed on each run. Load conditions, wind, and wave height were similar on each run. Most interesting to me was that I could not detect any difference in handling. The only difference was that the intermediate-speed rudder did have a very, very slight tendency to burble or cavitate at high angles at high speed, but this was negligible.

This indicates to me that though the intermediate-section rudder seems to be often overlooked, it is preferable at speeds up to about 30 or 32 knots.

Rudders for High-Speed Multihull Sailboats

Wedge-section and parabolic-section rudders are for use on powerboats. Such rudders create too much drag for racing or high-performance multihulls under sail, yet these boats can reach 30 knots or more. For such craft, airfoil-section rudders—as thin as practically achievable and with their maximum thickness farther aft—are best.

Skeg- or Keel-Hung Sailboat Rudders

On traditional sailboats, the rudder is fastened to the trailing edge of the keel. More modern sailboats may have the rudder running along the aft end of a large, full-height skeg. In either case, the optimum rudder section is the trailing portion of the standard airfoil section, starting with maximum thickness at the rudder stock, just aft of the keel or skeg. You can see this in Figure 10-8.

As with airfoil-section spade rudders, such skeg- or keel-hung rudders will be nearly as effective and with nearly as little drag if made flat with a rounded taper to the trailing edge as shown.

RUDDER-SECTION OFFSETS Table 10-1, "Foil-Thickness Form Dimensions," gives the offsets

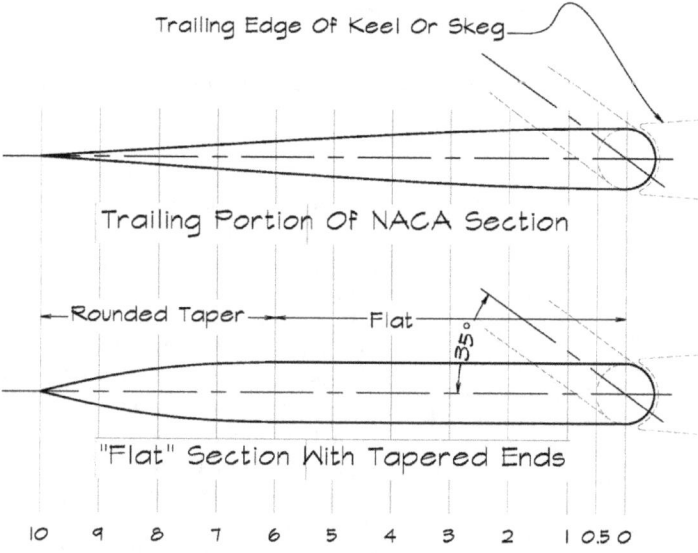

Figure 10-8. Skeg- or keel-hung sailboat rudder sections

PART FOUR: RUDDERS AND STEERING SYSTEMS

TABLE 10-1. FOIL-THICKNESS FORM DIMENSIONS

	Y as a Percent of Chord*		
% Chord**	00-10	Intermediate	Parabolic
Tip Radius	1.100	NA	NA
0.00	0.000	0.410	0.410
1.25	1.578	—	—
2.50	2.178	—	—
5.00	2.962	1.338	1.727
7.50	3.500	—	—
10.00	3.902	2.212	2.519
15.00	4.455	2.986	3.043
20.00	4.782	3.641	3.421
25.00	4.952	4.167	3.691
30.00	[5.002]	4.554	3.892
35.00	4.920	4.803	4.056
40.00	4.837	4.930	4.205
45.00	4.625	[4.948]	4.350
50.00	4.412	4.871	4.492
55.00	4.108	4.715	4.628
60.00	3.803	4.493	4.754
65.00	3.428	4.220	4.867
70.00	3.053	3.911	4.968
75.00	2.620	3.580	5.062
80.00	2.187	3.242	5.152
85.00	1.697	2.906	5.238
90.00	1.207	2.572	5.324
95.00	0.672	2.240	5.408
100.00	0.105	1.908	[5.492]

Boxes Indicate Region of Max. Thickness

* Y is the half-breadth thickness as a percentage of chord length at each location along the rudder-blade section. In a 00-10 section, the half-breadth at 30% chord length would be 5.002% × chord length. Thickness is twice the half-breadth.

** "% chord" refers to percentage of chord length back from the rudder's leading edge.

for the foil sections discussed above. Note that the section thicknesses are half-breadths.

Metal Flat-Plate Rudders

Many commercial vessels and some displacement motor cruisers are fitted with metal flat-plate rudders. Though these can work acceptably at low speed, I recommend against them. Flat plates are the least effective shape for generating lift (turning force) at all angles and at all speeds. This means more rudder angle for the same turn. It also means slower helm response and possibly a larger steering gear.

In addition, the round rudder stock runs outside down all or most of the height of the flat-plate rudder blade. This causes further turbulence and loss of steering effect.

Figure 10-9 shows a small and rather crude stainless steel flat-plate rudder (without stiffeners) on a single-screw lobster yacht. You can clearly see the erosion of the paint around the rudder stock from the turbulence. This rudder, though of adequate size, gave very unsatisfactory steering response. (Note also that there is too much overhang from the propeller hub to the stern bearing, and that the trailing edge of the rudder aperture isn't

Figure 10-9. Basic flat-plate rudder

well faired. Both can cause vibration and turbulence, and both can lead to loss of speed and reduced rudder response.)

The sole advantage of a flat-plate rudder is that it's cheap and easy to build. This is the reason they're so common on workboats. To my mind, this is false economy, as steering control is integral to the crew's experience of a boat during every moment of operation, and crisp, reliable helm control improves safety. Regardless, flat-plate rudders do work and are acceptable if cost-saving is important.

Rudder-blade thickness should be calculated per the following formula.

Formula 10-4. Rudder-Blade Thickness

$$\text{Plate Thickness, in.} = 0.1 + \frac{S \times \text{kts}}{666}$$

or

$$\text{Plate Thickness, mm} = 2.54 + \frac{S \times \text{kts}}{666}$$

Where

S = stiffener spacing, in. or mm

kts = boat speed, knots

Maximum allowable stiffener spacing is

Max. Stiffener Spacing, in., steel or stainless = 6 + (plate thickness, in. × 48)

or

Max. Stiffener Spacing, mm, steel or stainless = 152.4 + (plate thickness, mm × 48)

Max. Stiffener Spacing, in., aluminum = 4 + (plate thickness, in. × 32)

or

Max. Stiffener Spacing, mm, aluminum = 101.6 + (plate thickness, mm × 32)

Example: Let's say we have an 18-knot boat, with a steel flat-plate rudder:

Try ³⁄₈ in. (10 mm) plate. Then
6 + (0.375 in. × 48) = 24 in. maximum spacing

or

152.4 + (10 mm × 48) = 632 mm maximum spacing.

Try 10-inch (260 mm) stiffener spacing:

$$\text{Plate Thickness, in.} = 0.1 + \frac{10 \text{ in.} \times 18 \text{ kts}}{666}$$

$$= 0.37; \text{ use 3/8 in., OK}$$

or

$$\text{Plate Thickness, mm} = 2.54 + \frac{260 \text{ mm} \times 18 \text{ kts}}{666}$$

$$= 9.56 \text{ mm; use 10 mm, OK}$$

Stiffener thickness should be the same as the rudder-blade plate thickness.

Stiffener height (thickness athwartships) on either side of the rudder blade should be

0.6 × diameter of the rudder stock

or

0.06 × mean rudder chord
whichever is greater

Though the stiffeners are commonly of constant height from leading edge to trailing edge (rounded at the ends), they can be tapered. If tapered, the maximum height is centered at the rudder stock and continues for 15 percent of mean chord fore and aft. The stiffeners can then taper to 60 percent of maximum height at the leading and trailing edges.

Wood Outboard Rudder Thickness

Some traditional sailboats have what is essentially a wooden flat-plate rudder hung on gudgeons and pintles on the transom or behind the keel. Such rudders, as we've seen, are called *outboard rudders*. Particularly large outboard rudders on traditional craft are referred to as *barn-door rudders* (Figure 10-10). Traditionally, such rudders were of bolted-up solid timber. Modern wooden construction is of epoxy-laminated plywood sheathed in glass. In either case, the standard thickness is

$$\text{Thickness, in.} = 0.12 \times \text{immersed area, sq. ft.}$$

or

$$\text{Thickness, mm.} = 32.8 \times \text{immersed area, m}^2$$

$$\text{Thickness, in.} = \frac{\sqrt{\text{LOA, ft.}} + \text{Beam, ft.}}{12.66}$$

or

$$\text{Thickness, mm} = 3.63\sqrt{\text{LOA. m}} + (6.58 \times \text{Beam, m})$$

Use whichever is largest.

Example: Thus if we had a 26-foot (7.9 m) catboat, with 9.5-foot (2.89 m) beam, and a barn-door rudder hung on the transom of 5.5 sq. ft. (0.51 m²) immersed area, the thickness would be:

Thickness, in. = 0.12 × 5.5 sq. ft. = 0.66 in.
Thickness, mm = 32.8 × 0.51 m² = 16.8 mm

$$\text{Thickness, in.} = \frac{\sqrt{26 \text{ ft. LOA}} + 9.5 \text{ ft. Beam}}{12.66}$$

$$= 1.15 \text{ in.}$$

$$\text{Thickness, mm} = 3.63\sqrt{7.9 \text{ m LOA}} + (6.58 \times 2.89 \text{ m Beam}) = 29.2 \text{ mm}$$

Use the thicker measurement, and round to a standard size. In this case, use 1¼ inches (30 mm).

Foam-Core Fiberglass Rudder-Blade Shell Thickness

Many modern fiberglass rudders are hollow surfaced with a fiberglass shell and filled with a foam core. (In metal construction, this is often termed a *double-plate* rudder, though such rudders are empty inside except for metal stiffeners, and not filled with foam.) The FRP shell must be strong enough to resist water pressure and must also resist impact from debris. For standard fiberglass polyester laminates of woven roving and mat, with a tensile strength of 26,000 psi (180 MPa) or greater, use the following formula to determine the FRP shell thickness.

Formula 10-5. FRP Rudder Shell Thickness for Standard Fiberglass Polyester Laminates

$$\text{Thickness, in. or mm} = \frac{\text{kts} \times \text{Width, in. or mm}}{1{,}290}$$

Where
kts = boat speed in knots, but never less than 5 knots
Width = max. chord, or fore-and-aft width of the rudder blade, in. or mm
But not less than 0.09 in. (2.28 mm) thick.

Example: If we had a spade rudder with a maximum chord of 27.7 inches (703.6 mm) (Figure 10-11), on a boat with a maximum

Figure 10-10. Barn-door rudder on a Marshall Catboat

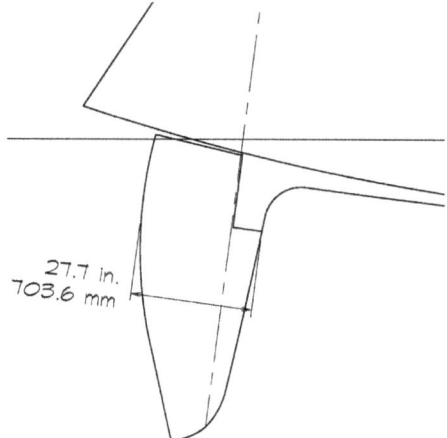

Figure 10-11. Rudder width, or chord

speed of 8.72 knots, the rudder laminate shell thickness should be as follows:

$$\text{Thickness, in.} = \frac{8.72 \text{ kts} \times 27.7 \text{ in.}}{1,290} = 0.187 \text{ in.}$$

or

$$\text{Thickness, mm} = \frac{8.72 \text{ kts} \times 703.6 \text{ mm}}{1,290}$$

$$= 4.76 \text{ mm}$$

The foam core at the central portion of the rudder blade—where the foam is between the rudder-frame support arms coming off the rudder stock and the inside of the FRP shell—should be at least 8.0 lb./cu. ft. (128 kg/m^3) density.

RUDDER PROFILE OR PLANFORM

The rudder profile or planform is the shape of the rudder viewed from the side. There has been an incredible variation in opinion regarding the planform shape that works best for different types of boats. To this day, there isn't wide agreement; however, certain fundamentals are important.

Sailboat-Rudder Planform

Earlier we saw what aspect ratio is and how it's calculated. On sailboats, the higher the aspect ratio (i.e., the longer/deeper and narrower the rudder), the more effective it is, within reason.

Rudder A in Figure 10-12 is a 20 sq. ft. (1.86 m^2) rudder with a span of 9.73 ft. (2.96 m). It has an aspect ratio of 4.73. The trade-off for a higher aspect ratio is that the bending moment on the rudder is greater and the stock is longer. This requires heavier, stronger stock and bearings, but the rudder blade itself is rather slender—hard to make really strong.

- Aspect ratios of 4 and over are high, and aspect ratios over 5 should generally be avoided.
- Aspect ratios between 3 and 3.5 are moderately high and are a good choice for most performance-oriented boats. Rudders B and C have aspect ratios of 3.2.
- Aspect ratios between 2.4 and 3 are moderate and work well on almost all normal sailboats. Rudder D has an aspect ratio of 2.6.

For the same rudder area and rudder-stock location, the higher the aspect ratio, the greater the turning force for a given helm angle. However, the difference isn't large. Identical boats fitted with rudder A or rudder B would have nearly the same steering response. Also, high-aspect rudders tend to stall more easily at high rudder angles.

Very high-aspect rudders, such as A, are only appropriate for sailboats with very high-aspect-ratio fin keels, which have been reduced to the minimum acceptable keel area. The deep, high-aspect-ratio rudder provides somewhat more resistance to leeway—it will be more effective as lateral plane generating lift. Such very high-aspect rudders thus effectively do double duty as additional keel area.

Rudders B and C have the same area and aspect ratio; however, B is curved and formed to have minimum area in the tip. This is to approximate the theoretical optimum elliptical planform—for minimum induced drag at the rudder tip. Rudder B would thus have slightly less drag than rudder C. Otherwise, the steering response of the two will be virtually identical. Rudder C is simpler and less expensive to build.

Rudder D will work quite well even though it has the lowest aspect ratio of all four and is roughly rectangular in section.

PART FOUR: RUDDERS AND STEERING SYSTEMS

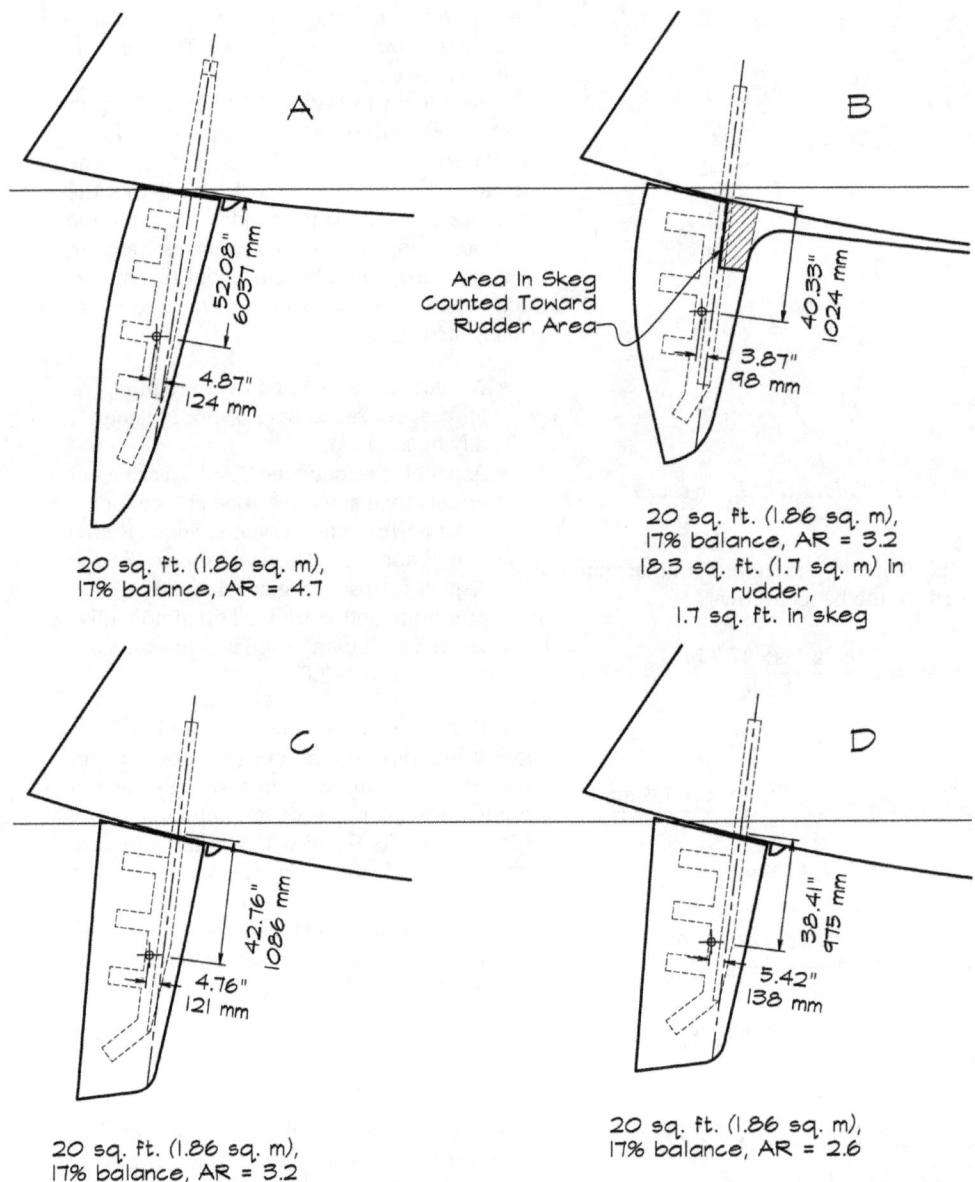

Figure 10-12. Sailboat spade rudders

As a practical matter, the difference in steering response between C and D won't be great. Rudder D will be the least expensive to build.

In the real world, my first choice for optimum performance would be rudder B. This is because it will have slightly less induced drag than the other rudders pictured, except for the extreme A. At the same time, rudder B is faired into the keel/skeg ahead of it. This makes for good tracking, and the area of the skeg immediately in front of rudder B counts as rudder area. So the rudder blade itself is of slightly less area to equal the total 20 sq. ft. This gives rudder B lighter helm feel by a small margin.

Both rudder B's shape and its faired-in skeg are more expensive than rudder C, however, and rudder C will give quite satisfactory results.

Spade rudders should have their leading edges angled slightly aft to shed debris—line, plastic bags, kelp, seaweed, nets, and so on. The forward lower corner should be somewhat rounded, not only to help shed debris but to reduce damage from minor impacts.

Antifouling Skeg

Note that the sailboat spade rudders shown all have a small antifouling skeg fastened to the hull just forward of the rudder's leading edge. This helps avoid line, plastic bags, seaweed, and so on from catching and jamming between the top of the rudder and the hull.

Traditional Sailboat Rudders

You can see a traditional sailboat rudder—hung on the back of the keel—in Figure 12-22, which shows rudder apertures. Another version is shown in the sailboat outboard rudder with skeg (Figure 10-3). On traditional or trailerable small craft, an outboard rudder is often made to kick up (as shown in the kick-up rudder drawing in Figure 10-3). The kick-up rudder blade is usually aluminum plate.

Powerboat Rudder Planforms

Single-screw displacement powerboats usually have balanced rudders on skegs immediately aft of the propeller. You can see one of good proportions in Figure 12-21. (Note: The *skeg* in this usage is the support for the lower rudder bearing projecting aft from the bottom of the keel, not a lateral-plane appendage forward of the rudder, as on sailboats.)

Generally, aspect ratios between 0.8 and 2.3 work well. A higher aspect ratio—as with sailboat rudders—improves response, but this is controlled by draft restrictions and propeller diameter. On some particularly shoal boats I've used rudders with aspect ratios as low as 0.6.

Usually, such rudders are better made roughly rectangular in planform. Over the years, though, almost every imaginable shape has been used, and all seem to work acceptably, so long as the area and balance are correct and the aspect ratio is reasonable.

Sometimes single-screw powerboat rudders are spade rudders (with no bearing at the bottom of the rudder blade). In this case, the rudder is better formed like a planing powerboat rudder, but no consideration has to be made for cropping the top corners for deadrise angle.

Planing powerboat rudders are a bit different. Such rudders are almost always spade rudders. Figure 10-13 shows standard, stock, cast-bronze powerboat boat rudders. And Figure 11-1 shows a custom-fabricated one in stainless. Current practice is to use trapezoidal-shaped rudders with sharp corners on high-speed boats, and rounded-corner, more-square rudders on medium- to low-speed boats. It's not clear that there's a great deal of difference in real-world steering response between these two planforms. Both will work well as long as the area and balance are correct and the rudder section shape is appropriate for the boat's speed.

Spade rudders for twin-screw boats, with out-turning props, are installed outboard of the shaft, aft of each propeller (see Figure 12-20). Since almost all planing hulls have considerable deadrise, the tops of the rudders (both forward and aft of the rudder stock) are cropped down at an angle so that the top corners don't hit the underside of the V-bottom hull when swung over. Out-turning propellers (viewed from aft, starboard props turns clockwise, port props counterclockwise) are standard. If the props turn in the

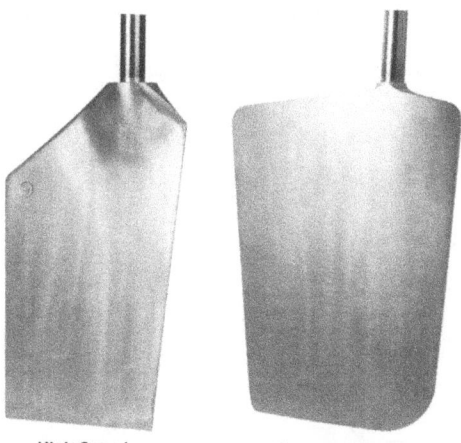

Figure 10-13. Stock cast rudders (Courtesy Marine Hardware, Inc.)

opposite direction, then the rudders are installed inboard of the shaft.

As with spade rudders, the leading edge of the rudder blade should be angled slightly aft to shed debris.

BOAT BEHAVIOR IN TURNS

At the beginning, we described rudders as acting like simple boards angled to the water flow. We then went on to explain that rudders are hydrofoils that generate hydrodynamic lift to create side force. Some references wax eloquent on determining the coefficient of lift (C_L) for a particular rudder-foil section shape and then calculating the resultant *normal force* (the force at right angles to the rudder blade) at the predicted angle of attack based on the C_L. Though these calculations give some engineers a feeling of comfort, this method isn't any more accurate than the method that follows. This is because there are so many unknowns:

- The water speed the rudder "sees" is difficult to calculate accurately as the rudder is partially in the wake of the hull, which reduces the apparent speed at the rudder. At the same time, the rudder is also in the slipstream of the propeller, which increases the apparent water speed at the rudder. Exactly how this balances out is impractical to calculate for most applications.
- The angle of attack that the water actually makes with the rudder is almost always less than the rudder angle. This is because the boat skids sideways as it turns, and the entire hull turns as the rudder turns. The magnitude of these effects will differ between boats, at different speeds on the same boat, with different loading and trim conditions, and in different sea conditions.
- Boat speed decreases during a turn.

Figure 10-14 shows the skidding effect and how it differs between different boats

Figure 10-14. Boats "skid" through turns

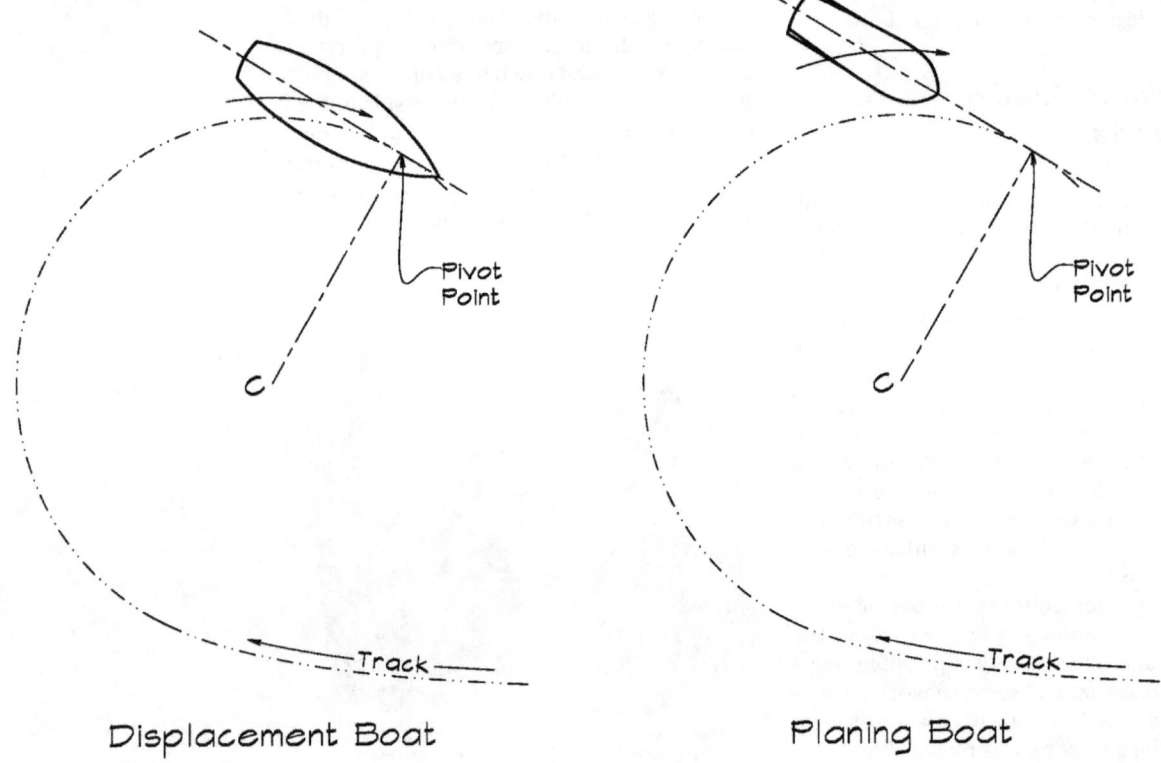

Displacement Boat

Planing Boat

Chapter 10: Rudder Geometry, Shape, and Size

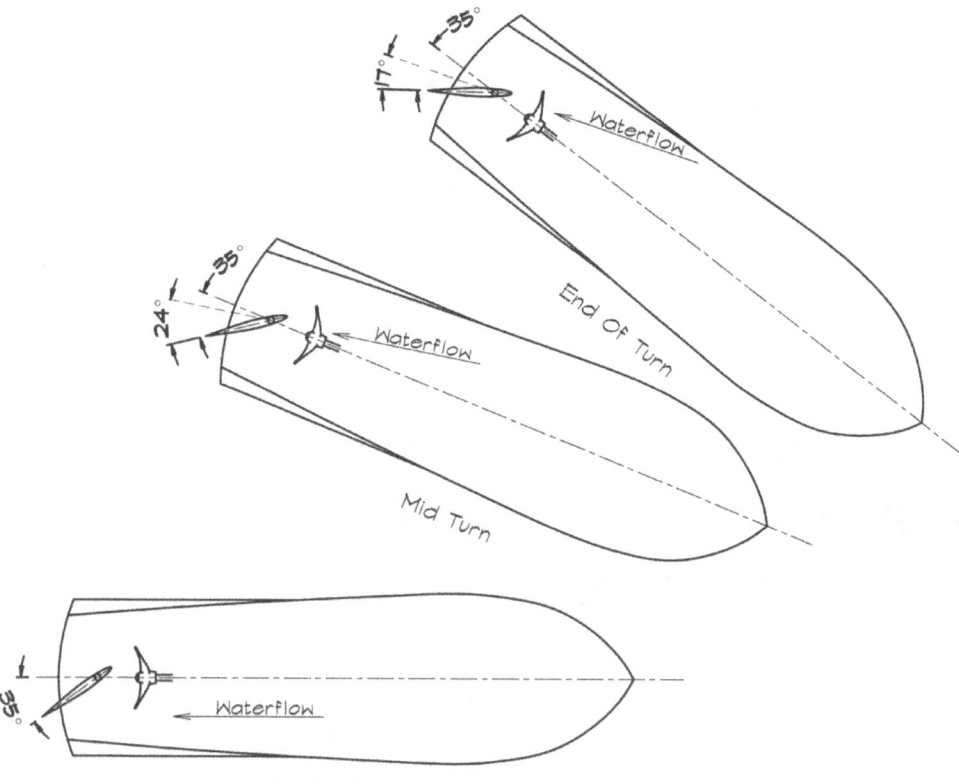

Figure 10-15. Effective rudder angles at different points during a turn

and at different speeds. In every case—as we discussed earlier—the rudder kicks the stern outboard (to make the turn), and the boat effectively pivots about a pivot point that is well ahead of the boat center. Indeed, on fast planing craft, the effective pivot point may be ahead of the boat itself. This puts the entire boat outside the nominal turning circle.

Figure 10-15 shows how the skid changes the effective rudder angle, even with the rudder actually held at the same absolute angle (in the case of the drawing, at hard over, 35 degrees).

Given these realities, the standard methods in Chapter 11 for calculating water force on the rudder are good practice and give conservative results.

181

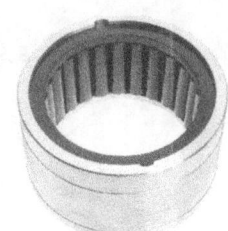

CHAPTER 11

Rudder-Stock Size, Construction, and Bearing Specification

Once you've determined the size, shape, and location of the rudder, you need to ensure that the rudder stock is strong enough to withstand any loads that may be placed on it in service. A broken rudder stock means total loss of steering control, which can even result in loss of the boat.

RUDDER STOCK, BEARING CALCULATIONS, AND CONSTRUCTION

Formula 11-2.

To calculate a required stock diameter, proceed as follows:

1. FIND THE WATER FORCE ON THE RUDDER BLADE AT 35 DEGREES, WHICH IS THE MAXIMUM RUDDER ANGLE.

Formula 11-1.

Formula 11-1. Precise Water Force on Rudder

$$\text{Force, lb.} = C_L \times \left(\frac{1}{2}\rho\right) V^2 \times A$$

Where
C_L = coefficient of lift for the rudder-blade section shape at the angle being investigated
ρ = mass density of water, 1.987 slugs/cu. ft. (see sidebar) or 1,025 kg/m³

A = rudder area, sq. ft. or m²
V = speed, ft./sec. or m/sec.

Since, as we've seen, the coefficient of lift isn't accurately known for most real-world rudders, and since we're interested in the maximum force, which occurs at maximum helm angle (almost always 35 degrees, or before this when the rudder stalls, in some instances), and since the mass density of water and acceleration of gravity are constant, this formula can simplified as follows.

Formula 11-2. Standard Calculation of Water Force on Rudder

$$\text{Force, lb.} = C_L \times (Pf \times \text{Speed, ft./sec.})^2 \times \text{Area, sq.ft.}$$

$$\text{Knots} \times 1.69 = \text{ft./sec.}$$

or

$$\text{Force, kg} = C_L \times (Pf \times \text{Speed, m./sec.})^2 \times \text{Area, m}^2 \times 52.55$$

$$\text{Knots} \times 0.514 = \text{m/sec.}$$

Where
C_L = coefficient of lift
0.5 for planing-powerboat rudders (see sidebar)
1.2 for all other rudders

Chapter 11: Rudder-Stock Size, Construction, and Bearing Specification

> ### Slug Units of Mass
>
> In the English system of units, *weight* is the *force* generated by the *mass* of an object, so
>
> Weight (or force due to mass) = mass × acceleration of gravity (32.2 ft./sec.^{2})
>
> This can be rewritten as
>
> Mass = weight (or force due to mass) ÷ 32.2 ft./sec.^{2}
>
> The density of seawater is 64 lb./cu. ft., therefore
>
> Mass density of seawater (ρ) = 64 lb./cu. ft. ÷ 32.2 ft./sec.^{2} = 1.987 slugs/cu. ft.
>
> This is so close to 2 that the mass density of seawater (ρ) is often given as 2. (ρ is the Greek letter rho.)
>
> *Slugs* are the English foot-pounds-seconds system (FPS system) units of mass, as opposed to the force created by the mass in Earth's gravity, which is the weight (confusingly though, weight in pounds is also mass).

> ### Lift Coefficient for Planing Powerboat Rudders
>
> A coefficient of lift (C_L) of 0.5 for planing powerboats has been found by practical experience to be not only appropriate but conservative for the rudder calculations shown. This ties in with the many unknowns discussed in Chapter 10, such as the real angle of attack and real water speed "seen" by the rudder, not to mention the complex effects of stall, ventilation, and cavitation. An excellent real-world example of this is found in Peter Du Cane's book *High Speed Small Craft*, where he works through the rudder-stock calculations of a Brave Class patrol boat (88 ft. [25.8 m] LOA; 75 tons, 8,500 hp, 52 knots) using a similar method to that of this chapter and using the same C_L of 0.5. The calculations result in a required stock diameter of 5.94 inches (151 mm). You would expect this to be rounded to 6.00 inches (155 mm) dia.; however, this is followed by the note:
>
> "In the "Brave" class F.P.B. stock diameter was actually 5 in. [127 mm] and in ten years no trouble occurred, so that even a $C_L = 0.5$ is unnecessarily large . . . ."

Pf = Propeller factor
  1.0 for boats where the propeller is more than 2.5 times propeller diameter forward of the rudder (usually sailboats)
  1.2 for all other boats

Example: If we had a 28-knot, twin-screw planing boat with two 5.28 sq. ft. (0.49 m^2) rudders, the maximum force on each rudder at 35 degrees would be

28 knots × 1.69 = 47.32 ft./sec.

Force = 0.5 × (1.2 × 47.32 ft./sec.)^2 × 5.28 sq. ft. = 8,512 lb.

or

28 knots × 0.514 = 14.39 m/sec.

Force = 0.5 × (1.2 × 14.39 m/sec.)^2 × 0.49 m^2 × 52.55 = 3,839 kg

NOTE: The total force on the surface of the rudder blade is more properly indicated by the symbol *kgf* for kilograms of force; however, the *f* is understood in this application.

2. LOCATE THE CENTER OF WATER FORCE ON THE RUDDER.

Refer to Figure 11-1 to locate the geometric center of area either by using a CAD program or by balancing a cardboard or stiff-paper cutout of the rudder blade.

Draw a horizontal line (a line parallel to the DWL) across the rudder through the

PART FOUR: RUDDERS AND STEERING SYSTEMS

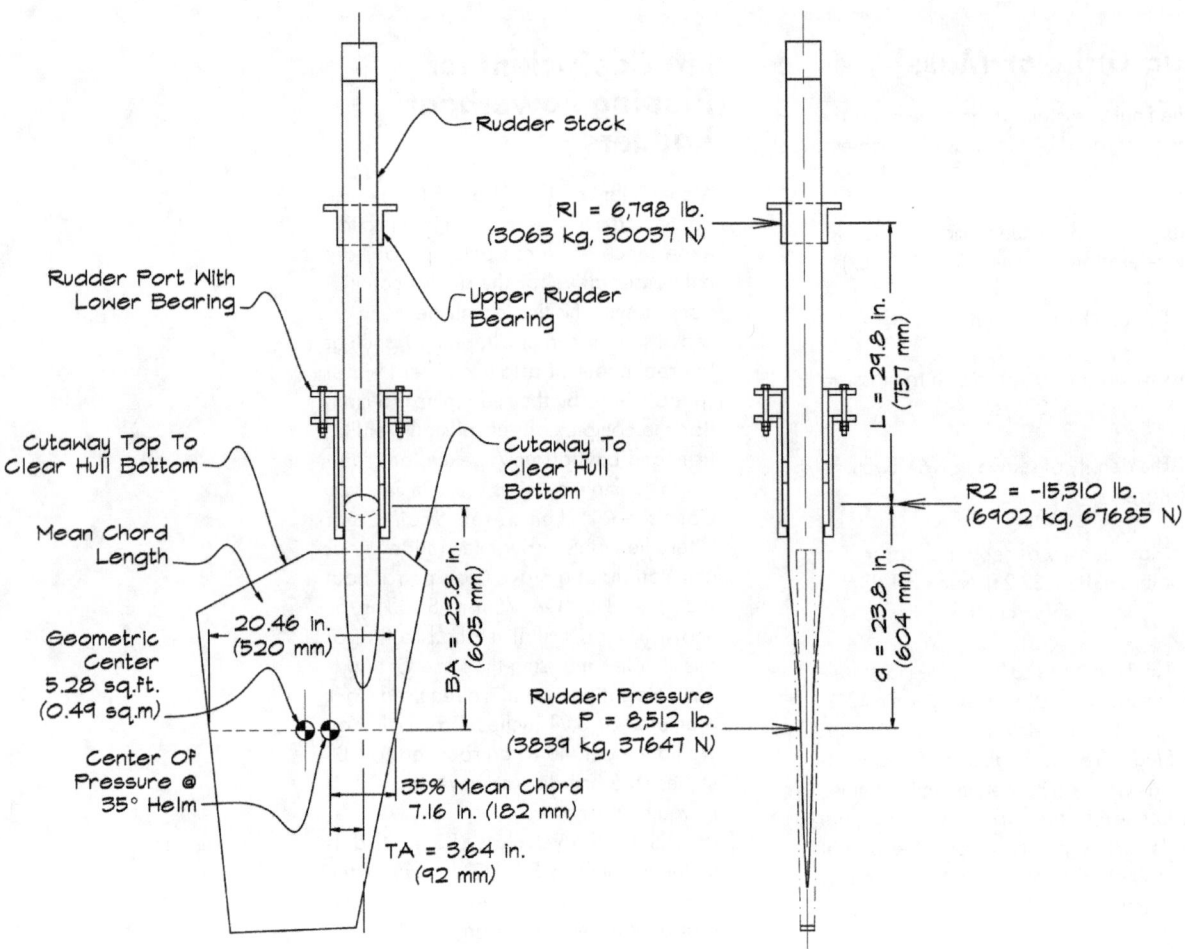

Figure 11-1. Powerboat spade rudder

geometric center point. This line is the effective mean chord. Measure 35 percent of the mean-chord length aft of the rudder's leading edge along this line to find the center of pressure. Use 40 percent aft on wedge-section or parabolic-section rudders. (See the Chapter 10 sidebar on page 167 to estimate the location of the center of pressure at rudder angles other than 35 degrees.)

3. FIND THE TWISTING ARM (TA).
Measure the distance at right angles from the center of water force (the center of pressure) on the rudder blade to the center of the rudder stock—the rudder-stock axis.

4. FIND THE BENDING ARM.
NOTE: If the rudder blade has bearings above and below it, then the bending arm is zero; see later in chapter.

Refer to Figure 11-1. The distance from the center of water force (or center of pressure) up to the middle of the lower rudder bearing in the hull (measured along the length of the rudder stock) is the bending arm.

5. FIND THE TWISTING MOMENT (TM) AND THE BENDING MOMENT (BM).

TM = rudder force (or pressure) center × twisting arm
BM = rudder force (or pressure) center × bending arm

Example: If the twisting arm for our example rudder is 3.64 inches (92 mm) and the bending arm is 23.8 inches (605 mm), then

TM = 8,512 lb. × 3.64 in. = 30,984 in.-lb.
BM = 8,512 lb. × 23.8 in. = 202,585 in.-lb.

or

TM = 3,839 kg × 0.092 m = 353 kgm
BM = 3,839 kg × 0.605 m = 2,322 kgm

6. Find the Combined Twisting and Bending Moment—Combined Moment (CM).

Formula 11-3. Combined Twisting and Bending Moment (CM)

$$CM = BM + \sqrt{BM^2 + TM^2}$$

Example: In our case

$$CM = 202{,}585 \text{ in.-lb.} + \sqrt{(202{,}585 \text{ in.-lb.})^2 + (30{,}984 \text{ in.-lb.})^2} = 407{,}525 \text{ in.-lb.}$$

or

$$CM = 2{,}322 \text{ kgm} + \sqrt{(2{,}322 \text{ kgm})^2 + (353 \text{ kgm})^2} = 4{,}671 \text{ kgm}$$

NOTE: Though the calculation for combined moment (CM) should be done as shown here, the result will consistently be close to twice BM. Use this check on your calculation. If the number is significantly different than 2 × BM, reexamine your work. In this case, 2 × 202,585 in.-lb. = 405,170; or 2 × 2,322 kgm = 4,644 kgm, which is nearly identical to our calculated CM.

7. Find the Diameter of a Solid Rudder Stock.

Formula 11-4. Diameter of Solid Rudder Stock

$$\text{Dia., in.} = \sqrt[3]{\frac{16 \times \text{Moment}}{\pi \left(\text{UTS} / \text{SF} \right)}}$$

Where

Moment = combined bending and twisting moment, in.-lb. or Newton-meters (Nm), for spade rudders

TABLE 11-1. RUDDER SAFETY FACTORS

	SF
Powerboat Spade Rudders	3.34
Racing-Powerboat and Patrol-Boat Spade Rudders	4.00
Power- and Sailboat Rudders, Bearings Above and Below Rudder Blade	4.00
Sailboat Spade Rudders	3.34

UTS = ultimate tensile strength of the material, psi or MPa (N/mm²); refer to Table 11-2.
SF = safety factor, refer to Table 11-1.

On metal spade rudders, there must be no welds from 1 shaft diameter below the top of the rudder blade up to 1 shaft diameter above the top of the lower rudder bearing. If welds are closer than this, then use the "As-Welded" strength from Table 11-2.

Because in spade-rudder configuration the bending moment will be vastly greater than the twisting moment, we use the ultimate tensile strength of the material from Table 11-2.

The rudder stock itself cannot be welded from separate pieces; it must be a continuous unwelded bar or tube.

Example: Our example has a fairly large rudder for this speed. We want to keep stock diameter down to reduce drag. Thus we'll go with a very high-strength chrome-molly stainless Aqualoy 22 HS.

$$\text{Dia.} = \sqrt[3]{\frac{16 \times 407{,}525 \text{ in.-lb.}}{\pi \left(\dfrac{130{,}000 \text{ psi}}{3.34 \text{ SF}} \right)}} = 3.76 \text{ in.,}$$

use 3¾-in. Aqualoy 22 HS

or

Metric structural calculations should be done using newtons, not kilograms. To convert kgm to Nm (kilogram-meters to newton-meters), multiply kgm by 9.8066.

so

4,761 kgm × 9.8066 = 46,699 Nm

$$\text{Dia., mm} = \sqrt[3]{\frac{16 \times 46{,}699 \text{ Nm} \times 1{,}000 \text{ mm/m}}{\pi \left(\dfrac{986 \text{ N/mm}^2}{3.34 \text{ SF}} \right)}}$$

= 93.05 mm, use 100 mm Aqualoy 22 HS

PART FOUR: RUDDERS AND STEERING SYSTEMS

TABLE 11-2. STRENGTHS AND DENSITIES OF STANDARD RUDDER-STOCK MATERIALS

MATERIAL	Ultimate Tensile Strength		As-Welded Tensile Strength[1]		Density	
	psi	MPa*	psi	MPa*	lb./cu. ft.	g/cm³
Aluminum 5000 series	34,000	234	16,000	110	168	2.69
Aluminum 6082[2]	45,000	310	20,000	137	168	2.69
Silicon Bronze	60,000	413	50,000	344	500	8.00
Stainless Steel (316L)[3]	85,000	586	70,000	482	505	8.09
Carbon Composite[4]	120,000	827	NA	NA	98	1.57
Aqualoy 22 HS[5]	130,000	986	105,000	724	508	8.14

*MPa = N/mm² (megapascals = newtons per millimeter squared)
[1] As-welded values for aluminum are the as-welded *yield* strength. Other as-welded values are as-welded ultimate tensile strength.
[2] Values are for 6082-T6 round bar between ¾ in. and 6 in. (20 to 150 mm).
[3] Use only 316L (L for *low carbon*) stainless to avoid pitting corrosion and weld-decay problems.
[4] Carbon composite requires expensive custom fabrication. Confirm mechanical properties and engineering details with the manufacturer.
[5] Aqualoy 22 HS is a chrome-molly alloy stainless from Western Branch Metals. Aquamet 22 from Marine Machining and Manufacturing is similar. Confirm alloy strength in the diameter specified.

Note that Nm has to be multiplied by 1,000 to get Nmm so that all the units are the same—mm in this case.

8. FIND THE WEIGHT PER LINEAL FOOT OF THE SELECTED STOCK.

Formula 11-5.

Formula 11-5. Weight per Lineal Foot of Selected Stock

$$\text{Section Area, sq. ft.} = \frac{\pi \left(\text{Dia., in.}/2\right)^2}{144}$$

or

Formula 11-6.

$$\text{Section Area, cm}^2 = \frac{\pi \left(\text{Dia., mm}/2\right)^2}{100}$$

Example: Thus

$$\text{Section Area} = \frac{\pi \left(3.75 \text{ in.}/2\right)^2}{144} = 0.076 \text{ sq. ft.}$$

0.076 sq. ft. × 508 lb./cu. ft. = 38.6 lb./lineal ft.

If this stock were 6 feet 2 inches (6.16 ft.) long, it would weigh 238 pounds—minus a bit for any tapering.

or

$$\text{Section Area, cm}^2 = \frac{\pi \left(100 \text{ mm}/2\right)^2}{100}$$

$$= 78.54 \text{ cm}^2$$

78.54 cm² × 8.14 g/cm³ = 639.3 g/lineal cm

If this stock were 1.87 m long, it would weigh 1.87 m × 100 cm/m × 639.3 g/lineal cm ÷ 1,000 g/kg = 119.5 kg

9. OPTIONAL: FIND THE SECTION MODULUS OF THE REQUIRED SOLID STOCK.

Formula 11-6. Section Modulus of Required Solid Stock

$$Z = \frac{\pi (\text{Dia.})^3}{32}$$

Where
Z = section modulus, in.³ or cm³
Dia. = rudder-stock diameter, in. or cm

Example: So

$$Z = \frac{\pi(3.76 \text{ in.})^3}{32} = 5.22 \text{ in.}^3$$

or

93.05 mm dia. = 9.305 cm dia.

$$Z = \frac{\pi(9.305 \text{ cm})^3}{32} = 79.1 \text{ cm}^3$$

10. OPTIONAL: SELECT A HOLLOW PIPE OR TUBE SECTION WITH THE EQUIVALENT SECTION MODULUS.
The pipe must be a minimum of schedule 80 or heavier wall.

Referring to the standard U.S. IPS pipe and tube-stock table in Appendix B, a 4.5-inch OD tube, with a ½-inch wall has a section modulus of 5.67 in^3. This weighs only 22.16 lb./lineal ft.

Or

Referring to a standard heavy-wall DIN-2448 pipe table (see Appendix B), a 114.3 mm OD pipe, with a 11 mm wall has a section modulus of 84.2 cm^3. This weighs only 28 kg/lineal m.

The section modulus of a hollow, round section can be found from the following:

$$Z = \left(\frac{\pi}{32}\right) \times \left(\frac{OD^4 - ID^4}{OD}\right)$$

For the metric DIN pipe, we get
114.3 mm OD − (2 × 11 mm wall) = 92.3 mm ID

$$Z = \left(\frac{\pi}{32}\right) \times \left(\frac{(11.43 \text{ cm OD})^4 - (9.23 \text{ cm ID})^4}{11.43 \text{ cm OD}}\right)$$

$$= 84.2 \text{ cm}^3$$

The larger diameter would create more drag. Further, the Aqualoy 22 HS alloy isn't available for this size tube, so we would have to redo the previous calculations for 316L stainless and find the pipe or tube size for the appropriate section modulus for that alloy.

About Welding to Rudder Stocks

The rudder stock itself cannot be welded from separate pieces; it must be a continuous, unwelded bar or tube. Any welds would be from welding external items to the stock. This might be a sleeve to "strengthen" the stock, as is sometimes mistakenly done. In fact—because of the loss of strength as welded and the increased tendency toward corrosion at welds—welded-on sleeves are generally a poor idea. The most common reason to have a weld in the critical zone is when welding on the top plate of an aluminum rudder blade to an aluminum rudder stock. In this case, the as-welded strength must be used.

In most instances, such an aluminum rudder blade on an aluminum rudder stock would be employed on a displacement boat with bearings above and below the rudder blade. This means that you would apply the calculations for this type of rudder (later in this chapter) using the shear strength based on the as-welded strength in Table 11-2. For aluminum, this would be the *as-welded yield shear strength* as noted on Table 11-2. For 5086 aluminum, that would be 60 percent of 16,000 psi (110 MPa) or 9,600 psi (66 MPa). For 6082, it would be 12,000 psi (82 MPa). It's customary with aluminum to round 5086 down to 9,000 psi (62 MPa) as-welded yield in shear as further insurance—and 11,000 psi (76 MPa) for 6082 aluminum.

Saving Weight in Sailboat Rudder Stocks

If a rudder is fitted to a strong skeg or to the back of a traditional long keel—with bearings above and below the rudder blade—sailboat rudder stocks aren't too large and heavy. On many modern fin-keel boats, however, balanced spade rudders can be both large and high aspect. A solid stainless, bronze, or even Aqualoy stock might well weigh over 500 pounds (225 kg) on a bigger boat. Such weight in the ends of the vessel is detrimental to performance—it increases pitching.

It makes good sense, in such instances, to go to heavy-walled stainless or bronze pipe or tube. Even though the rudder blade must be thicker to accommodate the greater stock diameter, the weight savings is well worth it. The more expensive alternative is a custom-fabricated, carbon-epoxy-composite stock. Another good option is a solid aluminum rudder stock of 6082 alloy. Some companies (like Jefa Rudder and Steering) specialize in custom fabricating and machining solid aluminum rudder stocks of 6082. These can be machined to any diameter desired and tapered as well. Weight can be close to that of carbon composite.

It is also worth considering whether such a high-aspect rudder really pays. The difference in performance between a rudder with an aspect ratio of 3 and one of 5 (of roughly equal area) isn't all that great. A lower aspect ratio reduces the bending arm, which reduces the bending moment, and so reduces the required stock diameter as well as the stock length, thereby reducing stock weight.

Checking Rudder-Stock Strength Going Astern

Because forward speed is so much higher than astern speed—for ordinary boats—simply checking the rudder-stock strength in the ahead condition is generally adequate. Some craft, however, may have rudder configurations that create greater loads when going astern. This is because when making sternway, the center of water force or center of pressure is about 20 percent of mean chord *forward of the trailing edge* (which, going backward, becomes the leading edge). This, in turn, significantly increases the length of the twisting arm, and so the twisting moment.

For displacement boats, use 70 percent of maximum ahead speed as speed for sternway calculations.

For planing hulls, use

Sternway, kts = (maximum forward speed, kts + 20) ÷ 3

If you're in doubt about the rudder-stock strength going astern, repeat all the previous rudder-stock calculations, using the sternway speed and locating the center of water force 20 percent of the mean chord forward of the trailing edge.

Rudders Stocks with Bearings Above and Below the Rudder Blade

A rudder that is supported with bearings both above and below the rudder blade, such as in Figure 12-21, is in nearly pure torsion with minimal bending. What bending exists is the result of the side force of the water, which is assumed to be distributed roughly evenly along the height of the rudder. This could be calculated as a "combined twisting and bending" similar to what we did earlier, but because the bending moment is such a small proportion of the total load, this can be taken care of simply by using the slightly larger safety factor of 4, rather than 3.34. You could then use Formula 11-3 above for combined twisting and bending with a zero entered for bending arm and therefore bending moment, but it's more straightforward to use torque alone as simply

TM = rudder pressure center × twisting arm
Along with a safety factor of 4 as in Table 11-1

In the combined twisting and bending of the spade rudder, bending dominated, so we used ultimate tensile strength (UTS). In the current case, however, *torsion* dominates. Accordingly, you need to use ultimate *shear* strength (USS), which can be taken as 60 percent of UTS.

If we assume for a moment that our previous rudder was supported by a lower rudder bearing on a strong skeg, then we would find the required stock diameter as follows:

From Step 5 above:

TM = 8,512 lb. × 3.64 in. = 30,984 in.-lb.

or

TM = 3,839 kg × 0.092 m = 353 kgm

From Step 7 above:

Since the resulting stock will be considerably smaller in this configuration, we'll use more standard 316L SS, with a UTS of 85,000 psi (586 MPa). Shear strength would then be

85,000 psi UTS × 0.60 = 51,000 psi USS

or

586 MPa UTS × 0.60 = 352 MPa USS

$$\text{Dia. in.} = \sqrt[3]{\frac{16 \times 30{,}984 \text{ in.-lb.}}{\pi \left(\frac{51{,}000 \text{ psi}}{4 \text{ SF}} \right)}} = 2.31 \text{ in.}$$, use

2⅜ in. or 2½ in. 316L stainless steel

or

353 kgm × 9.8066 = 3,462 Nm

$$\text{Dia., mm} = \sqrt[3]{\frac{16 \times 3{,}462 \text{ Nm} \times 1{,}000 \text{ mm/m}}{\pi \left(\dfrac{352 \text{ N/mm}^2}{4 \text{ SF}}\right)}}$$

= 58.5 mm, use 60 mm 316L stainless steel

NOTE: Nm has to be multiplied by 1,000 to get Nmm.

Silicon bronze would be superior for any boat that wasn't aluminum or steel. The silicon bronze would not have stainless steel's susceptibility to pitting corrosion. Using 60,000 psi (413 MPa) UTS for bronze, the USS is 36,000 psi (248 MPa). Entering this in the preceding formula would give a required diameter of 2.59 in.—use 2¾ in. (65.7 mm, use 70 mm) silicon bronze.

NOTE: For convenience, we assumed that this was a single-screw planing hull. In practice, this would be most uncommon for a boat of this size. Most (but not all) boats with bearings above and below their rudder blades are displacement or semidisplacement craft. In this case, the water force on the rudder would have to be calculated using a coefficient of lift (C_L) of 1.2, as indicated in Formula 11-2 for standard rudder water force—a significant increase in water force, but of course, at lower operational speed.

RUDDER BEARINGS AND RUDDER PORTS

Rudder Bearing Loads—Spade Rudders

All rudders must have at least two bearings—an upper bearing and a lower bearing (see Figures 11-1 and 11-2). Later we'll take a look at rudder bearings that are below the bottom of the rudder blade (see Figure 12-21). Here we'll examine the loads on the upper and lower bearings of a spade rudder. For such rudders, the lower bearing is just inside the hull bottom, while the upper bearing is well above this in the hull. Within practical limits, the higher the upper bearing can be in the hull the better, as this reduces the bearing loads.

Find loads (reaction forces) on rudder bearings by using the following formula.

Formula 11-7. Load on Rudder Bearings

Upper rudder bearing: $R1 = \dfrac{P \times a}{L}$

Lower rudder bearing: $R2 = -\dfrac{P}{L}(L + a)$

Where
P = water pressure on rudder blade, lb. or kg
L = distance from upper to lower bearing, in. or m
a = distance from center of water pressure to lower bearing, in. or m
R1 = reaction force on upper rudder bearing, lb. or kg
R2 = reaction force on lower rudder bearing, lb. or kg

NOTE: R2 is negative because it operates in the opposite direction of R1. R1 plus R2 must cancel out to equal –P.

Example: For our example spade rudder (Figure 11-1), we've already found that rudder pressure is 8,512 pounds (3,839 kg). Referring to the drawing, we see that a = 23.8 in. (604 mm) and L = 29.8 in. (757 mm). Then

$$R1 = \frac{8{,}512 \text{ lb.} \times 23.8 \text{ in.}}{29.8 \text{ in.}} = 6{,}798 \text{ lb.}$$

$$R2 = -\frac{8{,}512 \text{ lb.}}{29.8 \text{ in.}}(29.8 \text{ in.} + 23.8 \text{ in.}) = -15{,}310 \text{ lb.}$$

NOTE: –15,310 lb. + 6,789 lb. = –8,512 lb. The net reaction in the bearings equals the load (the rudder pressure) applied in the opposite direction.

Or

$$R1 = \frac{3{,}839 \text{ kg} \times 0.604 \text{ m}}{0.757 \text{ m}} = 3{,}063 \text{ kg}$$

$$R1 = 3{,}063 \text{ kg} \times 9.8066 = 30{,}037 \text{ N}$$

$$R2 = -\frac{3{,}839 \text{ kg}}{0.757 \text{ m}}(0.757 \text{ m} + 0.604 \text{ m}) = -6{,}902 \text{ kg}$$

$$R2 = -6{,}902 \text{ kg} \times 9.8066 = -67{,}685 \text{ N}$$

NOTE: –6,902 kg + 3,063 kg = –3,839 kg. The net reaction in the bearings equals the load (the rudder pressure) applied in the opposite direction.

TABLE 11-3. ALLOWABLE BEARING STRESS

Material	psi	MPa*
Lignum Vitae	360	2.48
Babbitt Bearing Metal (oil lubricated)	650	4.48
Plastic Bearing Material (UHMWPE, etc.)	800	5.51
Roller Bearings (alum. or stainless)	800	5.51
Roller Bearings (plastic)	350	2.41

*MPa = N/mm^2 (megapascals = newtons per millimeter squared)

Find bearings that have enough area to fall below the allowable stress (see Table 11-3).

Lignum vitae is a very hard, dense, oily wood traditionally used for bearings in marine applications (including propeller-shaft bearings). Though practical, lignum vitae is largely obsolete today. Babbitt bearing metal (or white bearing metal) should be oil lubricated and has been largely abandoned for use in rudder bearings. Of the hard, tough, slippery (low coefficients of friction) plastics, ultra-high-molecular-weight polyethylene (UHMWPE) is probably best for nonroller rudder bearings. Not only is it very strong and resistant to attack by chemicals, but it has virtually zero water absorption, so it doesn't expand after immersion, which would squeeze or bind the shaft.

Bearing area is shaft diameter times bearing height.

Maximum bearing height (length) is 1.75 times shaft diameter.
Minimum bearing height (length) is 1.0 times shaft diameter.

Example: For the lower bearing (of UHMWPE) we find

15,310 lb. ÷ 800 psi = 19.14 sq. in. required
19.14 sq. in. ÷ 3.75 in. shaft dia. = 5.1 in. high
Max. bearing height is 1.75 × 3.75 in. dia.
= 6.562 in.
Min. bearing height is 1.0 × 3.75 in. dia.
= 3.75 in.

Accordingly, a 5.1-inch-high bearing will do, but a bit more will reduce bearing stress; use 6 inches high.

For the upper bearing (of UHMWPE) we find

6,789 lb. ÷ 800 psi = 8.50 sq. in. required
8.50 sq. in. ÷ 3.75 in. shaft dia. = 2.27 in. high
Max. bearing height is 1.75 × 3.75 in. dia.
= 6.562 in.
Min. bearing height is 1.0 × 3.75 in. dia.
= 3.75 in.

Accordingly, a 3.75-inch-high bearing will do.

Or

For the lower bearing (of UHMWPE) we find

67,685 N ÷ 5.51 N/mm^2 = 12,284 mm^2 required
12,284 mm^2 ÷ 100 mm shaft dia. = 122.8 mm high
Max. bearing height is 1.75 × 100 mm dia.
= 175 mm
Min. bearing height is 1.0 × 100 mm dia.
= 100 mm

Accordingly, a 122.8 mm high bearing will do, but a bit more will reduce bearing stress; use 150 mm high.

For the upper bearing (of UHMWPE) we find

30,037 N ÷ N/mm^2 = 5,451 mm^2 required
5,451 mm^2 ÷ 100 mm shaft dia. = 54.5 mm high
Max. bearing height is 1.75 × 100 mm dia.
= 175 mm
Min. bearing height is 1.0 × 100 mm dia.
= 100 mm

Accordingly, a 100 mm high bearing will do.

If the rudder stock has been tapered at the upper bearing, the upper rudder bearing would have to be calculated, using the smaller (tapered) diameter.

The structure supporting the upper rudder bearing must be able to withstand the 6,798 lb. (3,063 kg) side load with a safety factor of 4. Similarly, the lower rudder-bearing structure must withstand 15,310 lb. (6,902 kg) with a safety factor of 4. When the lower rudder bearing is built into the keel structure, this isn't usually difficult to achieve, but keep the large loads in mind.

Chapter 11: Rudder-Stock Size, Construction, and Bearing Specification

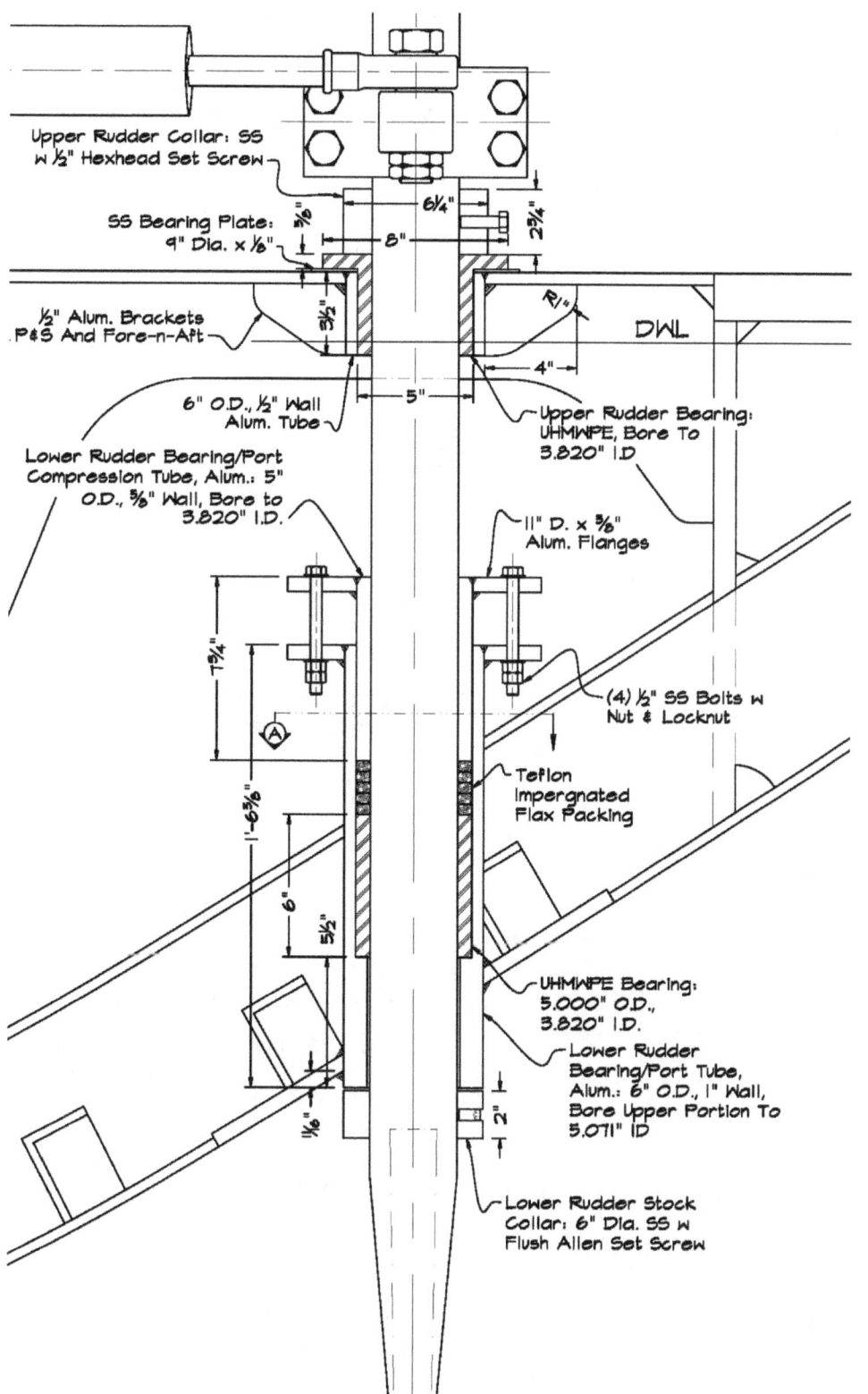

Figure 11-2.
Typical fabricated rudder port

PART FOUR: RUDDERS AND STEERING SYSTEMS

Rudder-Bearing Clearance

Because the rudder stock must be free to turn in the bearings, the bore (inside diameter, or ID) of the bearing must be slightly larger than the outside diameter (OD) of the shaft. The stock is almost always of standard, off-the-shelf diameter rod or pipe. You can't normally specify its diameter tolerances beyond what's commercially supplied. The bearing ID is thus specified to give proper clearance.

The difference between the shaft OD and the bearing ID is called *allowance*. The amount that the machinist can deviate from the specified ID with the allowance is the *tolerance*.

For low-speed (low RPM) heavy equipment (such as rudder bearings), use the following formula.

Formula 11-8. Rudder-Bearing Clearance

$$\text{Allowance} = 0.0025 \times (\text{dia., in.})^{0.67}$$
$$\text{Tolerance} = 0.0025 \times (\text{dia., in.})^{0.34}$$

or

$$\text{Allowance} = 0.0073 \times (\text{dia., mm})^{0.67}$$
$$\text{Tolerance} = 0.0211 \times (\text{dia., mm})^{0.34}$$

Where

dia. = shaft diameter

Example: Thus for our 3.75-inch shaft, we would call for a bearing ID of

$$\text{Allowance} = 0.0025 \times (3.75 \text{ in.})^{0.67} = 0.006 \text{ in.}$$
$$\text{Tolerance} = 0.0025 \times (3.75 \text{ in.})^{0.34} = 0.003 \text{ in.}$$

or

$$\text{Allowance} = 0.0073 \times (100 \text{ mm})^{0.67}$$
$$= 0.159 \text{ mm}$$
$$\text{Tolerance} = 0.0211 \times (100 \text{ mm})^{0.34}$$
$$= 0.101 \text{ mm}$$

So

Bearing ID = 3.756 in., +0.003 in., –0.000 in. (meaning the ID can't be smaller than 3.756 in. nor larger than 3.759 in.)

or

Bearing ID = 100.159 mm, +0.101 mm, –0.00 mm (meaning the ID can't be smaller than 100.159 mm nor larger than 100.260 mm)

UHMWPE-Bearing Wall Thickness

Minimum bearing wall thickness (for UHMWPE) should be 0.15 times nominal shaft diameter. Somewhat greater thickness is fine, to fit properly inside the bearing housing wall as needed.

Example: For our 3.75 inch (100 mm) shaft, the minimum wall would thus be 0.5625 in. (15 mm). Or the minimum bearing OD would be

$$2 \times 0.5625 \text{ in.} + 3.75 \text{ in.} = 4.875 \text{ in. OD}$$

or

$$2 \times 15 \text{ mm} + 100 \text{ mm} = 130 \text{ mm OD}$$

The inside wall of the lower portion of the rudder port (which houses the bearing) needs to be machined to be 4.875 in. (130 mm) ID, or somewhat larger inside diameter, as convenient.

The UHMWPE bearing is slid down into the rudder port, so it needs to be a close sliding fit. Use the following formula to determine the rudder-port allowance and diameter.

Formula 11-9. UHMWPE Rudder-Port Allowance Thickness

$$\text{Allowance} = 0.0014 \times (\text{dia., in.})^{0.67}$$
$$\text{Tolerance} = 0.0013 \times (\text{dia., in.})^{0.34}$$

or

$$\text{Allowance} = 0.0041 \times (\text{dia., mm})^{0.67}$$
$$\text{Tolerance} = 0.0101 \times (\text{dia., mm})^{0.34}$$

Where

dia. = bearing outside diameter

Example: Assume we select a 5-inch (130 mm) bearing OD. To size the rudder-port tube, proceed as follows:

$$\text{Allowance} = 0.0014 \times (5.00 \text{ in. dia.})^{0.67}$$
$$= 0.004 \text{ in.}$$
$$\text{Tolerance} = 0.0013 \times (5.00 \text{ in. dia.})^{0.34}$$
$$= 0.002 \text{ in.}$$

or

$$\text{Allowance} = 0.0041 \times (130 \text{ mm dia.})^{0.67}$$
$$= 0.107 \text{ mm}$$
$$\text{Tolerance} = 0.0101 \times (130 \text{ mm dia.})^{0.34}$$
$$= 0.053 \text{ mm}$$

So

Bearing OD = 5.000 in., +0.000 in., –0.002 in.
Rudder-Port Tube ID = 5.004 in., +0.002 in., –0.000 in.

or

Bearing OD = 130.000 mm, +0.000 mm, –0.053 mm
Rudder-Port Tube ID = 130.107 mm, +0.053 mm, –0.000 mm

The opening at the bottom of the rudder port should never make contact with the shaft, so this opening needs to be larger than the bearing diameter. Use twice the shaft allowance for the bearing ID, or a bit more. Thus for our 3.75-inch (100 mm) shaft, the ID of the opening in the rudder port (below the bearing) should be

0.006 in. × 2 = 0.012 in., and 0.012 in. + 3.75 in. = 3.762 in.

or

0.159 mm × 2 = 0.318 mm, and 0.318 mm + 100 mm = 100.318 mm

Rudder-Port Tube Wall Thickness

Aluminum = 0.13 × shaft dia., minimum
not less than ¼ in. (6.5 mm)
Steel, Stainless, Bronze = 0.08 × shaft dia., minimum
not less than 3/16 in. (4.7 mm)

Example: If we were building this rudder port into an aluminum boat, the rudder port would be of aluminum pipe or tube. Minimum diameter would be

Wall min. = 0.13 × 3.75 in. dia. shaft = 0.4875 in.
or
Wall min. = 0.13 × 100 mm dia. shaft = 13 mm

We selected a 5-inch (130 mm) OD rudder bearing, so the OD of the rudder port tube would be

0.4875 in. wall × 2 = 0.975 in. + 5.00 in. bearing = 5.975 in. OD; use 6.00 in. OD, or slightly greater as convenient for the lower rudder port tube.

or

13 mm wall × 2 = 26 mm + 130 mm bearing = 156 mm OD; use 160 mm OD, or slightly greater as convenient for the lower rudder port tube.

Rudder-Port Packing Gland

The lower rudder-port tube is fastened to the hull and houses the rudder bearing, the packing gland that makes the rudder port watertight, and the upper rudder-port compression tube, which squeezes down on the packing to make it watertight.

Generally, the packing for the gland is best made of standard flax packing. Even better is Teflon-impregnated flax packing. This has lower friction and longer life. (*Never use graphite-impregnated packing,* as the graphite/carbon will cause severe corrosion in seawater.)

The packing diameter should be approximately equal to the bearing wall thickness. The height of the uncompressed packing should be approximately 60 percent of shaft/stock diameter.

The rudder-port compression tube should be machined to have the same OD as the bearing below, and an ID with 50 percent greater allowance than the bearing.

Example: Our bearing allowance was 0.006 inch (0.159 mm).

0.006 in. × 1.5 = 0.009 in.
so
Compression-tube ID = 3.75 in. + 0.009 in. = 3.759 in. ID, +0.003 in., –0.000 in.

or

0.159 mm × 1.5 = 0.318 mm
so
Compression-tube ID = 100 mm + 0.318 mm = 100.318 mm ID, +0.101 mm, –0.000 mm

Compressing the Rudder-Port Compression Tube

For off-the-shelf machined bronze and stainless rudder ports, the compression to squeeze the compression tube down on the packing is usually generated by a screw-down nut threaded onto the top of the lower rudder-port tube.

On metal hulls, the entire rudder port is usually built into the hull, and the rudder-port compression tube is tightened down with four bolts through flanges on the upper and lower rudder-port tubes. The bolts should be of 316 stainless. Diameter should be 0.13 times rudder-stock diameter or larger, but never less than 3/16 in. (4.7 mm).

The flange thickness is

Aluminum: 0.18 × shaft diameter, or more
not less than 1/4 in. (6.3 mm)

Steel: 10.12 × shaft diameter, or more
not less than 3/16 in. (4.7 mm)

ROLLER BEARINGS

Delrin and other plastics that expand and degrade when immersed in water used to be used for rudder bearings. Since UHMWPE has become available, I've found solid UHMWPE has few problems and gives good service if installed as described above. The ultimate in rudder bearings, however, are stainless or aluminum roller bearings. Such rudder bearings have closer clearances for less "chatter" in the bearing and less "backlash." They also have the lowest friction for even better helm feel (Figure 11-3).

Initial dimensions for the bearing height can be estimated by using the allowable bearing loads for roller bearings (Formula 11-7), but

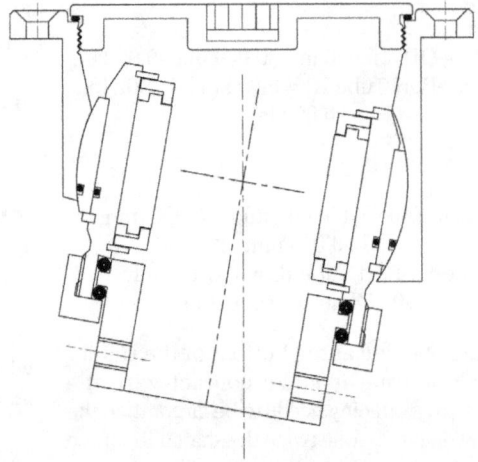

Figure 11-4. Cross section of self-aligning rudder bearing (Courtesy Jefa)

manufacturers provide tables giving the design loads for their bearings in different sizes and constructions.

Another advantage of manufactured roller bearings is that they are available in self-aligning configurations. This means that the bearing is free to rotate slightly to align with any flex of the rudder stock, thereby preventing binding, uneven wear, and excess friction. For performance sailboats with high-aspect spade rudders, self-aligning roller bearings are strongly recommended.

Premanufactured roller bearings are available with or without built-in bearing seals and in configurations suitable for installations in wood, fiberglass, aluminum, or steel hulls.

Rudder Bearing Loads—Rudder Bearings Top and Bottom of Rudder

All of the preceding applies to spade rudders with no bearing at the bottom of the rudder blade. On many single-screw boats (and some twin-screw vessels), the rudder is supported with a bearing in the hull just above the rudder blade, and with a lower bearing at the bottom of the rudder fastened to the keel or rudder skeg. In this case, the rudder stock experiences only modest bending loads; however,

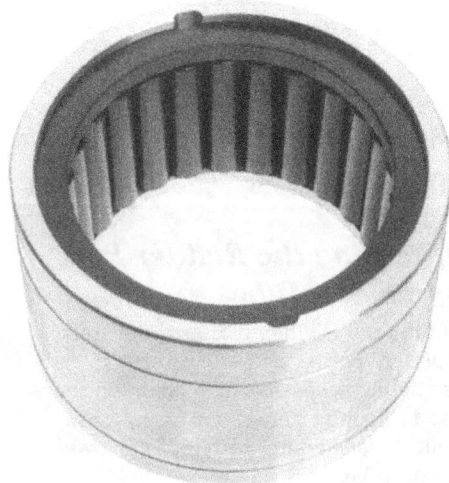

Figure 11-3. Rudder bearing (Courtesy Edson)

the stock and the bearing must resist the total side pressure of the water.

Example: If we assume that our 5.28 sq. ft. (0.49 m²) rudder were on a single-screw 28-knot boat, the force on the one rudder would be the same as we've already found: 8,512 lb. (3,839 kg, 37,647 N). Each bearing takes half this load, or 4,256 lb. (18,823 N).

You would find the required bearing size (for allowable bearing stress) as in Formula 11-7 above; however, it makes sense to turn down the lower end of the rudder stock to fit into a smaller, more streamlined bearing/skeg below, as that portion of the stock is taking only the shear resulting from the side load; it's not also transmitting the torque from the steering gear.

You are then forming a *pintle* for the lower rudder bearing. Generally, this should be approximately 44 percent of overall shaft diameter, but you need to check that it has adequate shear area to take the side load. Use a large safety factor of 5 to allow for the stress concentrations of abrupt change in shape between the main rudder stock and the lower pintle.

Example: Now for this rudder—with bearings top and bottom—the stock diameter will be considerably smaller, with no bending load. Working through the previous formulas (and using 316L stainless, instead of Aqualoy 22 HS), we found the stock diameter required was 2⅜- or 2½-inch 316L SS. We'll use 2½ inches as being more readily available and having a larger safety factor. For the metric shaft, we found 60 mm.

2.5 in. dia. × 0.44 = 1.1 in.; try 1 in. dia.

TABLE 11-4. ULTIMATE SHEAR STRENGTH, USS

Material	psi	MPa*
Aluminum 5000 Series	20,400	140
Aluminum 6082	27,600	190
Silicon Bronze	36,000	248
Stainless Steel (316L)	51,000	352
Carbon Composite	Not recommended in this application	
Aqualoy 22 HS	78,000	538

*MPa = N/mm² (megapascals = newtons per millimeter squared)

or

60 mm dia. × 0.44 = 26.4 mm; try 25 mm

Check shear stress (single shear):

Area = π(1.0 in. ÷ 2)² = 0.78 sq. in.
4,256 lb. ÷ 0.78 sq. in. = 5,456 psi
51,000 psi ÷ 5,456 psi = SF 9.3; this is well over 5 SF and so acceptable

or

Area = π(25 mm ÷ 2)² = 491 mm²
18,823 N ÷ 491 mm² = 38.3 N/mm²
352 N/mm² ÷ 38.3 N/mm² = SF 9.2; this is well over 5 SF and so acceptable

Gudgeon-and-Pintle Proportions

If this were a traditional rudder hung on several gudgeons and pintles instead of using a stock, the load is divided by the number of gudgeons and pintles. The pintle diameter can be as small as practical, as long as the safety factor in shear is greater than 5. Divide the side load by the number of pintles and gudgeons to get the load on each.

Pintle length in the gudgeon or bearing should be at least 1.2 times pintle diameter.

The pintle may be tapered at a ratio of approximately 1 to 6 from maximum diameter at the top, to minimum diameter at the bottom.

The height of the gudgeon housing the pintle must be at least 1.2 times pintle diameter.

The gudgeon wall thickness is to be 0.5 times the pintle diameter or more.

Fastening of the gudgeons into the hull or transom must take the side load from the pintle with a safety factor of 5. Check:

- fasteners in shear
- fasteners in tension
- fasteners in bearing in the hull, transom, or skeg as applicable

Axial Bearing Loads and Shaft Collars

Rudders have weight that pulls them down out of the boat. This axial load must be resisted with a shaft collar inside the boat at one of the bearings or by an axial bearing at the lower rudder bearing (Figure 11-5).

Where the lower rudder bearing is necked down to form a pintle, as described

Figure 11-5. Assorted shaft collars (Courtesy Marine Hardware, Inc.)

earlier, the shoulder that is formed works well as an axial-load bearing. A UHMWPE disk bushing/bearing can be placed under the main rudder stock here to take the axial load.

A spade rudder can also be struck from below and so knocked upward, damaging the steering gear. To prevent this, another shaft collar below one of the bearings should be installed.

On performance sailboats, roller-bearing shaft collars can be built into the upper or lower rudder bearing. These are sometimes termed *thrust bearings*. Such roller-bearing shaft collars give the smoothest helm feel and fingertip control.

Rudder-Stock Angle, Control, and Installation Considerations

CHAPTER 12

Armed with the proper rudder, rudder stock, and bearings, the next considerations are the rudder-stock angle and control of the rudder: the steering system. Installed rudder-stock angle can affect boat trim and performance, while without a reliable steering system, the best rudder still won't point the boat where it needs to go.

RUDDER-STOCK ANGLE AND PLANING-BOAT RUDDER CONFIGURATION

Fore-and-Aft Rudder-Stock Angle and Boat Trim

An often overlooked aspect of rudder installation is the rudder-stock angle. As viewed from the side, the stock can be dead vertical or angled either forward or aft. Keep the following in mind:

- A rudder stock angled/raked aft from top to bottom depresses the bow when the rudder is put over.
- A rudder stock angled/raked forward depresses the stern when the rudder is put over.

On contemporary sailboats, it's not unusual to have moderate aft rake to make the spade rudder more nearly perpendicular to the swept-up hull bottom aft. A moderate amount of aft rake is acceptable, but you should avoid raking rudders aft more than 9 degrees to vertical or forward more than 12 degrees. In fact, there's usually no reason for forward rake, except on transom-hung rudders. Traditional long-keel sailboats often have forward rake well over 12 degrees, but this is not best practice and there's no reason to do this on a modern boat.

On powerboats, rudders should always be vertical or nearly so.

Transverse Rudder-Stock Angle

On sailboats with twin rudders aft (such as the Open 60 class), it's normal to have the stocks roughly at right angles to the hull underbody. This splays the rudders out at an angle to the vertical plane when viewed from astern. On a wide-sterned sailboat that heels, this is a good thing. The lee rudder will be deeply immersed and at closer to vertical when heeled, and thus more effective on the wide underbody aft. Such hull forms roll a single, centerline rudder out of the water to a large degree when well heeled.

PART FOUR: RUDDERS AND STEERING SYSTEMS

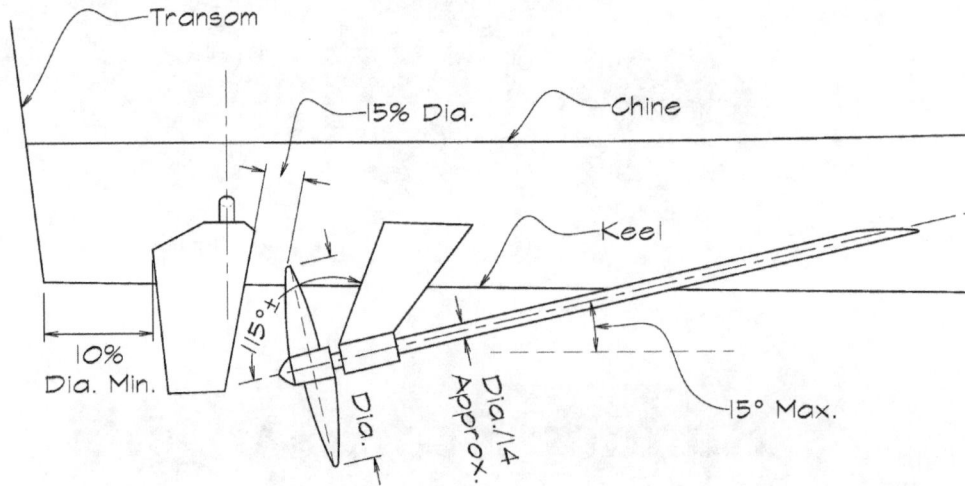

Figure 12-1. Planing boat rudder and prop configuration

On planing powerboats, twin rudders must always be dead vertical athwartships. It might look correct on a drawing to have the two rudders projecting out from the hull underbody (behind the propellers) at right angles to the hull shell, but on a deep-V boat, this would mean an athwartships rudder angle of 21 degrees or so to the vertical. Though it may *look* right, it is wrong. The angled rudders will act as diving planes or trim tabs—an effect that is aggravated further (and unpredictably) when the boat rolls.

Planing-Boat Rudder Configuration

Figure 12-1 shows the best proportions for rudders in relation to the hull, propeller, and shaft on twin-screw planing hulls. The leading edge of the rudder should be about 15 percent of propeller diameter aft of the propeller blades. Less is too close and can cause vibration or difficulty pulling the prop. A bit more is acceptable, but much more and the rudder is less effective, being farther aft in the slipstream. The aft edge of the rudder should ideally be 10 percent of propeller diameter forward of the transom's bottom edge, but a bit farther forward is OK if you meet all other criteria. Siting the prop and rudder farther aft allows a shallower prop shaft angle, but as the rudder blade nears the transom edge it experiences an increased chance of ventilation, being no longer shielded from surface air by the hull above. Of course, many boats do have their rudders farther aft, so the aft edge of the rudder is nearly at the transom. Most of the time, including on several of my designs, it works OK.

STEERING SYSTEMS: CONTROLLING THE RUDDER

Rudder Steering Torque

Having found the stock diameter, we have also found the maximum torque, or twisting moment (TM).

In our twin-screw planing boat example in the previous chapter, we found that the TM was 30,984 in.-lb. or 2,582 ft.-lb. (353 kgm or 3,462 Nm). IMPORTANT: *Don't forget to multiply total torque by the number of rudders.* This steering system, with two rudders, needs to handle 5,164 ft.-lb. (706 kgm, 6,924 Nm). This torque governs the size of the steering system, which we'll examine later.

So far, we've examined the rudder size, shape, and strength, but you need more than a properly sized and shaped strong rudder; it's every bit as important to be able to make it do what you want it to—all the time, every time. A modern wheel should have nearly fingertip control. Improperly designed steering systems and steering gear problems can

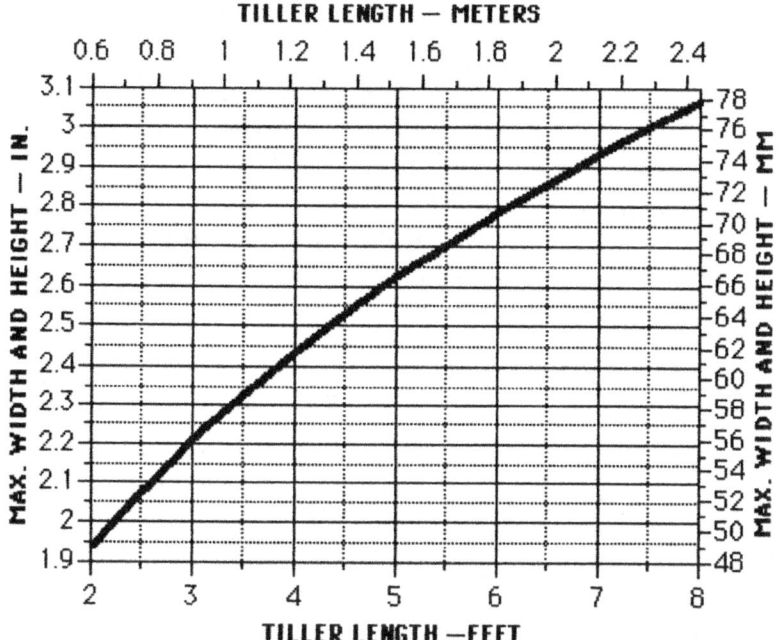

Figure 12-2.
Required tiller section

Stick It to 'Em: The Tiller

Small and medium-size sailboats have the simplest rudder control system there is—the tiller. Not much can go wrong: either the stick's strong enough or it isn't. Figure 12-2 gives the minimum height and width of square-section tillers at their widest part—at the rudder—for wood, handheld tillers of various lengths. The tiller should gradually taper from this square section to a round end 1¼ inches (30 mm) in diameter, the ideal size for a firm handgrip. A tiller with these proportions will not break even if a 200-pound (90 kg) man falls on it.

Tiller Limits

Tillers, unfortunately, have their limitations. You can use a tiller only from a location directly adjacent to the rudder, and there's also a limit to how large a rudder the tiller can manage without becoming too long.

Example: Say your sloop has a 10-square-foot (0.93 m²), airfoil-section, balanced rudder and cruises at about 7.7 knots. Using our rudder force formula (Formula 11-2), we find:

$$7.7 \text{ kts} \times 1.69 = 13 \text{ ft./sec.}$$

$$\text{Water Force} = 0.5 \times (13 \text{ ft./sec.})^2 \times 10 \text{ sq.ft.}$$

$$= 845 \text{ lb.}$$

or

$$7.7 \text{ knots} \times 0.514 = 3.96 \text{ m/sec.}$$

$$\text{Water Force} = 0.5 \times (3.96 \text{ m/sec.})^2 \times$$
$$0.93 \text{ m}^2 \times 52.55 = 383 \text{ kg}$$

The maximum water force on this rudder would thus be about 845 pounds (383 kg). As we saw in the previous chapter, this water force effectively acts through a center of pressure, which falls somewhere aft of the rudder post, creating a lever arm. The lever arm for the center of water force on a rudder—relative to the rudder-post axis at hard-over 35-degree helm—is found as described earlier.

Assuming that this is a balanced spade rudder with the center of water force or pressure 4.32 inches aft of the rudder-stock pivot point, the torque is 3,650 in.-lb. or 304 ft.-lb.—845 lb. × 4.32 in. = 3,650 in.-lb., and 3,650 in.-lb. ÷ 12 = 304 ft.-lb.

Or

Assuming that this is a balanced spade rudder, with the center of water force or pressure 110 mm aft of the rudder-stock pivot point, the torque is 42.1 kgm or 413 Nm—383 kg × 0.11 m = 42.1 kgm, and 42.1 kgm × 9.8066 = 413 Nm.

The 30-Pound (13.5 kg) Helm Limit

The greatest force the average person can exert comfortably on a wheel is about 30 pounds (13.5 kg, 122 N). This is really an upper limit, as holding the wheel against a continuous load like this will tire you out fast. However, maximum force occurs at hard over, and you'll seldom have the wheel over that far for more than an instant or two.

To find how long the tiller would have to be to keep the maximum hand force—the force you'll need to steer with—to under 30 pounds (13.5 kg), simply divide the maximum rudder torque by 30 pounds (13.5 kg). In our preceding example, we would get 10.13 feet (3.1 m). This is too long for many boats. In fact, on most boats longer than 40 feet (12.2 m) LOA, it becomes difficult to arrange a tiller long enough to give sufficient leverage or mechanical advantage—assuming that you didn't want to move the helm station somewhere else anyway.

Wheel-and-Cable Steering System

The solution is simple: use a steering wheel. Wheel steering systems have built-in mechanical advantage, and even better, they can be located wherever you happen to need them, rather than right aft at the rudder. In the proverbial good old days, there was only one way to get the power from the wheel to the rudder: rope or wire cables. This is still a simple, inexpensive, and reliable system; it is the standard for sailboats, and until quite recently it was common on powerboats. Cable steering systems, in fact, also offer the best helm feel.

Advantage Mechanical

The required component sizes to keep steering-wheel loads under 30 pounds (13.5 kg) can be found from the following formula.

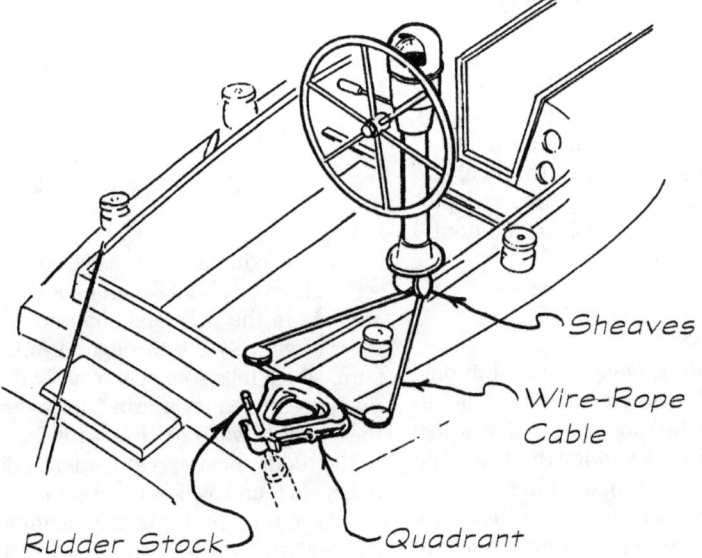

Figure 12-3. Cable steering (Courtesy Edson Corp.)

Formula 12-1. Wheel Radius

Wheel Radius, in. =

$$\frac{\text{Rudder Torque, in.-lb.} \times \text{Drum or Sprocket Radius, in.}}{30 \text{ lb. Hand Force} \times \text{Tiller Length or Quadrant Radius, in.}}$$

or

Wheel Radius, mm =

$$\frac{\text{Rudder Torque, kgm} \times 1{,}000 \text{ mm/m} \times \text{Drum or Sprocket Radius, mm}}{13.5 \text{ kg Hand Force} \times \text{Tiller Length or Quadrant Radius, mm}}$$

The drum or sprocket radius is the radius of the rope drum or chain sprocket, at the steering wheel, which accepts the steering cable. Drums can be any convenient radius (at least 16 times rope diameter) for rope. The smaller the drum or sprocket radius, the greater the mechanical advantage, but the harder it is on the rope or cable. Most modern wheel steerers use bronze or stainless steel roller chain over chain sprockets instead of a simple drum. For boats up to 35 or 40 feet (10 or 12 m), sprocket radiuses are usually 1.1 inches (27.94 mm), and for boats larger than 40 feet (12.2 m), 1.2 inches (30.48 mm).

Finding the Right Wheel

Trying a 12-inch (304.8 mm) quadrant radius on our example boat works out as follows:

Using a 1.1-inch sprocket you would get

$$\text{Wheel Radius, in.} = \frac{3{,}650 \text{ in.-lb.} \times 1.1 \text{ in.}}{30 \text{ lb.} \times 12 \text{ in.}}$$

$$= 11.15 \text{ in.}$$

Use a 22- or 24-inch diameter wheel.
Or
Using a 27.94 mm sprocket, you would get

$$\text{Wheel Radius, mm} = \frac{42.1 \text{ kgm} \times 1{,}000 \text{ mm/m} \times 27.94 \text{ mm}}{13.5 \text{ kg} \times 304.8 \text{ mm}} = 285.8 \text{ mm}$$

Use a 570 or 600 mm diameter wheel.

You could fit a 28- or 30-incher (700 or 750 mm) if you preferred—more mechanical advantage from a larger wheel never hurts. Larger boats frequently have to use larger wheels to increase the mechanical advantage. In fact, you can increase mechanical advantage by increasing wheel radius or quadrant radius (effectively tiller length) or both. Increasing quadrant radius also increases the number of turns it takes the wheel to swing the rudder, which brings us to helm quickness or helm speed.

Quick Turn? Helm Speed

There's another important consideration with wheel steering: How quick is the helm? If it takes, say, 30 turns of the wheel to swing our boat's rudder from hard-over port to hard-over starboard, the steering response is too slow—way too slow. On the other hand, if the rudder swings from hard over to hard over with just a half turn of the wheel, the steering response is too quick. You would tend to turn the wheel too far and every little jerk of your hand would cause a course change.

The ideal number of turns for different types of craft is shown in Table 12-1.

The number of turns from 35 degrees hard over to 35 degrees hard over—also

TABLE 12-1. OPTIMAL NUMBER OF HELM TURNS BY BOAT TYPE AND LENGTH

Type of Boat	LOA, ft.	LOA, m	Number of Turns
Runabouts and Small Power Cruisers	to 30	9	1.75 to 2
High-Speed Powerboats	all lengths	all lengths	1.75 to 2
Medium-Speed Power Cruisers	30 to 50	9 to 15	2.5 to 3.5
Medium-Speed Power Cruisers	over 50	over 15	3.5 to 4
Large-Displacement Power Cruisers*	over 50	over 15	as many as 14
Sailboats	16 to 30	4.8 to 9	1 to 2
Sailboats	30 to 45	9 to 15	2 to 3
Sailboats	over 45	over 15	3 to 5

*Traditional large-displacement power cruisers with cable steering can get by with a high number of turns; however, fewer turns (between 3.5 and 5) is preferable.

called *lock to lock*—is found by using the following formula.

Formula 12-2.

Formula 12-2. Number of Turns Lock-to-Lock

$$\text{Number of Turns Lock-to-Lock} = \frac{\text{Quadrant Radius}}{5.14 \times \text{Drum or Sprocket Radius}}$$

Where
Quadrant radius, in. or mm
Drum or sprocket radius, in. or mm

Wheel diameter doesn't appear here. It doesn't affect the helm quickness at all. Additional wheel diameter simply increases mechanical advantage or power.

Example: For our example boat, helm quickness works out as

$$\frac{12 \text{ in.}}{5.14 \times 1.1 \text{ in. Sprocket}} = 2.12 \text{ turns lock-to-lock}$$

or

$$\frac{304.8 \text{ mm}}{5.14 \times 27.94 \text{ mm}} = 2.12 \text{ turns lock-to-lock}$$

This is right for our boat, which is about 35 feet (11 m) LOA. Playing around with these formulas will enable you to pick the right combination of quadrant or tiller size and wheel and drum diameter for any boat.

Steering Cable Installation

Cable steering's drawback is the complexity of its installation. The cables take considerable loads for long periods of time. What's more, those loads oscillate back and forth. Further, the cable constantly runs over sheaves at about the same spots, which is the same as bending it back and forth. Flexing anything repeatedly will break it. To reduce this potential weakness, the cables must be run over large-diameter sheaves. Minimum sheave diameter is 16 times the wire diameter or greater—as large as 32 times wire diameter is excellent if you can fit it. All the sheaves and wire or rope runs must be carefully aligned to ensure smooth operation with firm cable tension. Often, if the wheel isn't close to the rudder stock in the cockpit, several sheaves will be required on each side to make the cable run correctly from the quadrant to the wheel. All must line up exactly. For example, you should be able to run a rigid dowel through the grooves of the quadrant to the turning sheaves on either side of the quadrant. The dowel must line up perfectly, with no bend or angle at all.

If the sheaves get out of line or the cable goes slack, the steering wire or rope can jump out of its grooves and jam—essentially a total steering failure. Clearly, this also means that the steering sheaves must be fastened very securely with heavy through-bolts and substantial backing blocks. If you're dealing with a boat that's fitted with cable steering, you should check to see that it's equipped with all the preceding components. There also must be hatches, panels, and so on to give access to all the steering-gear components: the sprocket or drum, cable sheaves, tensioning turnbuckles, and quadrant or tiller. If the boat is lacking in any of this, you've got a steering problem waiting to happen.

FLUID POWER: HYDRAULIC STEERING

These days cable steering is found less frequently on powerboats. Hydraulics have largely taken its place (Figures 12-4, 12-5, and 12-6). It's not that hydraulics are especially better; rather, they are easier to install, particularly with more than one helm station. Most sailboat skippers, in fact, don't care for

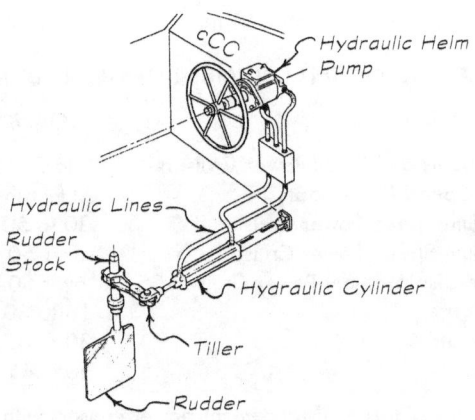

Figure 12-4. Hydraulic steering: 1 helm, 1 rudder (Courtesy Edson Corp.)

hydraulic steering because, compared with a well-set-up cable system, it gives a mushier helm feel. For power craft, however, this isn't much of a disadvantage. Indeed, it can be a plus; the slight mushiness damps out prop-wash vibrations at the rudder, which cable gear can transmit as a hum or jiggle to the wheel.

Easy Does It

Hydraulics are easy to install because—unlike the finicky alignment and tensioning required by cable systems—the hoses or pipes can literally be run any which way. (Kinks and abrasions must be avoided, of course, and the hoses must be well secured.) Though there are a few hydraulic systems with a rotary hydraulic driver (really a rotary pump acting in reverse) that fits right to the rudder stock, most are simple hydraulic cylinders attached to a short metal tiller arm that swings the rudder just as a traditional hand tiller does.

Hydraulic-Steering Torque

Since each cylinder model has a fixed throw or stroke, it's designed to work with a standard-length tiller arm. (Using a different length would give you either too much or too little rudder travel—more or less than 35 degrees hard over to hard over.) The cylinder force or power is also governed by the 30-pound (13.5 kg) limit you can deliver to the wheel and helm-pump unit at the bridge or helm station. (Power-assist or full-powered hydraulic steering is used on large vessels.) Accordingly, once again, you've got a force times a fixed distance—a torque—for each hydraulic cylinder configuration. Obviously, the cylinder/tiller system torque should equal or somewhat exceed the maximum rudder torque we found earlier. All you have to do is look through the steering-gear manufacturer's catalog and match their torque specifications to your rudder torque to get the correct cylinder and wheel-helm-pump combination (the two work together to generate the required mechanical advantage, torque, and helm speed).

Locating the Cylinder, and Keeping It There

It's important, however, to install the cylinder correctly. You'll sometimes find it's installed at right angles to the tiller when the rudder is amidships. This is not good. It puts the cylinder off angle at either end of its stroke. Instead, the cylinder must be installed so that it's at right angles to the amidships tiller location when the rudder is turned 35 degrees either way, as shown in the Figure 12-7.

Also, the forces on the cylinder mounts can be quite large. For our example boat, a typical hydraulic cylinder would be delivering around 280 pounds (127 kg) of force—back

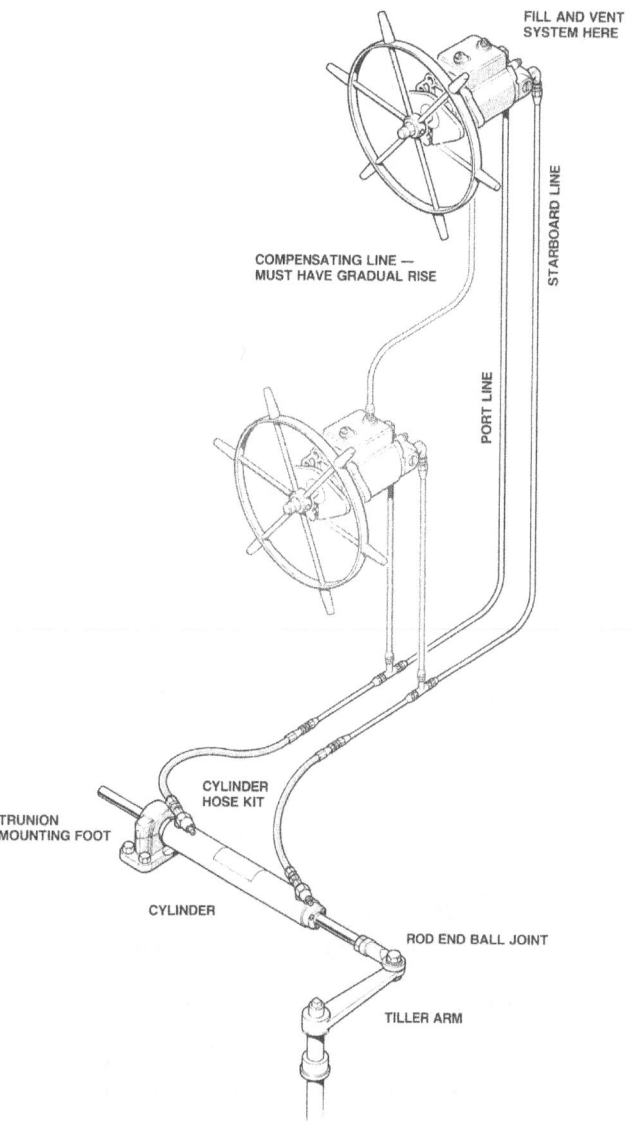

Figure 12-5. Hydraulic steering: 2 helms, 1 rudder (Courtesy Teleflex, Inc.)

203

PART FOUR: RUDDERS AND STEERING SYSTEMS

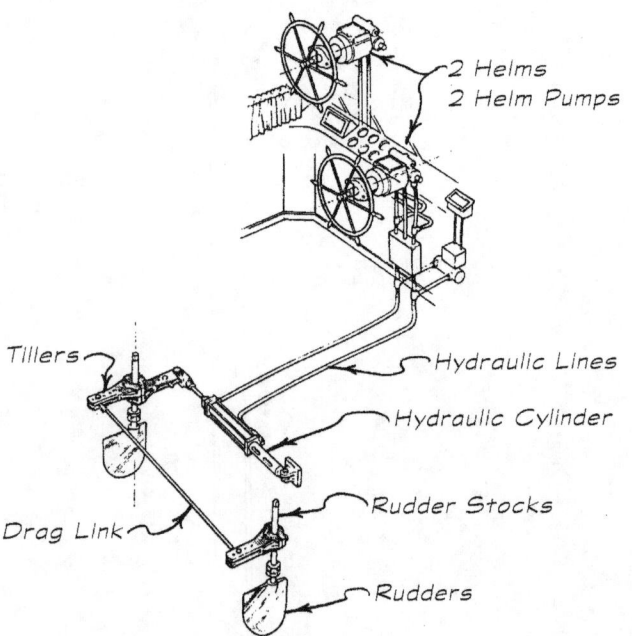

Figure 12-6. Hydraulic steering: 2 helms, 2 rudders (Courtesy Edson Corp.)

Figure 12-7. Hydraulic cylinder layout

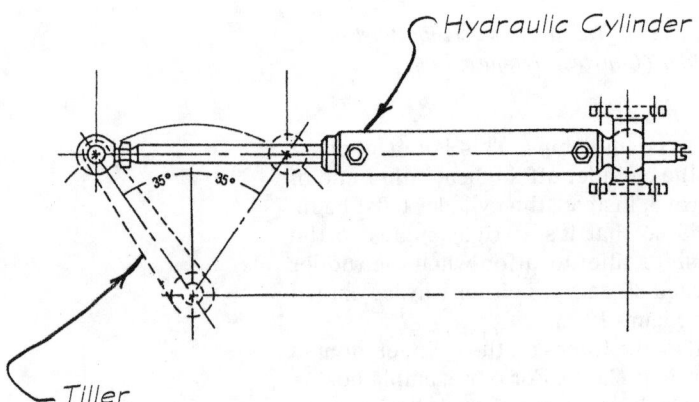

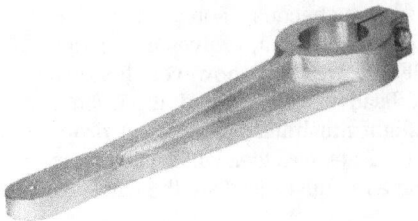

Figure 12-8. Bronze tiller arm for a drag link or hydraulic cylinder (Courtesy Marine Hardware, Inc.)

and forth, back and forth, over and over. This is like having an NFL linebacker jump up and down on it over and over for hours and days at a time! Hydraulics are much easier to install than cable systems, but the cylinder had better be mounted strongly.

Tiller-Arm Strength

The tiller or tiller arm (Figure 12-8) is usually fabricated and supplied by the hydraulic-steering manufacturer. If you need to design a custom tiller arm, the tiller is a cantilever in pure bending. The load at the cylinder-pin end is the rudder torque (as we found earlier) divided by the length of the tiller arm. You can then use standard beam theory to calculate the required section modulus and moment of inertia for the tiller. The safety factor should be 4 over ultimate tensile strength with an allowable deflection of 1:300 or less. The keyway and other details can be taken from the standard propeller-shaft dimensions for shafts of the same size.

Drag-Link Size

Tiller arms must be custom-designed only in special circumstances, but you will always need to specify the drag link that connects twin rudders inside the boat (Figure 12-9). The drag link is in pure compression with two pin ends. With the hydraulic cylinder or cylinders attached directly to the tiller arm or arms, the drag link is designed to withstand 60 percent of the total rudder torque (both rudders combined), with a safety factor of 4.

Take our example twin-engine boat from the last chapter. We found

TM = 8,512 lb. × 3.64 in. = 30,984 in.-lb.

or

TM = 3,839 kg × 0.092 m = 353 kgm

This is the torque from one rudder. The two rudders combined produce 61,968 in.-lb.

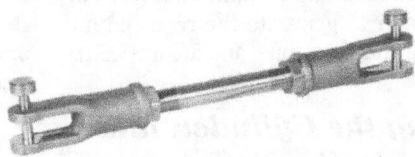

Figure 12-9. Drag-link assembly with jaws for clevis pins (Courtesy Marine Hardware, Inc.)

(706 kgm) of steering torque, 60 percent of which is 37,181 in.-lb. (424 kgm).

The tiller arm length that the drag link is fastened to on each rudder is 10.3 in. (262 mm). Thus the design compression load on the drag link from the rudder torque is 37,181 in.-lb. ÷ 10.3 in. = 3,610 lb., or 424 kgm ÷ 0.262 m = 1,618 kg.

The moment of inertia of the two-pin-end column (our drag link) required to accept the compression load without buckling is found with Formula 12-3.

Formula 12-3. Two-Pin-End-Column Moment of Inertia

$$I = \frac{SF \times PL^2}{\pi^2 E}$$

Where
I = moment of inertia, in.^{4} or cm^4
P = compression load, lb. or N
E = modulus of elasticity, psi or MPa (see Table 12-2)
L = drag-link length, pin center to pin center, in. or mm
SF = safety factor, use 4

Example: In our case, the length of the drag link from pin center to pin center is 116 inches (2,946 mm). You can use solid rod, but hollow pipe or tube is lighter, and the larger diameter required isn't a drawback. In fact, it's an advantage as it makes the drag link more resistant to being bent out of shape by someone leaning on it. You can use any material, but 6061 aluminum is usually best in this application and is highly corrosion resistant (unless there are bronze clevis end fittings, in which case stainless or bronze tube or pipe would be superior). Using aluminum, we find

$$I = \frac{4 \times 3{,}610 \text{ lb.} \times (116 \text{ in.})^2}{\pi^2 \times 10{,}400{,}000 \text{ psi}} = 1.89 \text{ in.}^4$$

Referring to a standard pipe table, we find that a nominal 2½-inch schedule 80 pipe has an I of 1.92 in.^{4} and is 2.875 inches OD, 0.276 inches wall. This section, or any pipe section with a greater moment of inertia, would serve. Don't use thinner wall than schedule 40 (standard weight).

Or

$$1{,}618 \text{ kg} \times 9.8066 = 15{,}867 \text{ N}$$

$$I = \frac{4 \times 15{,}867 \text{ N} \times (2{,}946 \text{ mm})^2}{10{,}000 \times \pi^2 \times 71{,}700 \text{ N/mm}^2} = 77.84 \text{ cm}^4$$

Note that the entered units were all mm. To convert to cm^4, we divided by 10,000 or by (10 mm/cm)^4.

Referring to a standard DIN 17172 pipe table, we find that a DIN 17172 76.1 × 6.3 aluminum pipe (76.1 mm OD, 6.3 mm wall) has a moment of inertia of 84.8 cm^4 (see Formula 12-4). Don't use thin-walled pipe or tube.

The moment of inertia of a hollow, round section can be found using Formula 12-4.

Formula 12-4. Moment of Inertia for a Hollow, Round Section

$$I = \left(\frac{\pi}{64}\right) \times (OD^4 - ID^4)$$

For the metric DIN pipe, we get:
76.1 mm OD − (2 × 6.3 mm wall) = 63.5 mm ID

$$I = \left(\frac{\pi}{64}\right) \times \left((7.61 \text{ cm OD})^4 - (6.35 \text{ cm ID})^4\right) = 84.8 \text{ cm}^4$$

Twin Rudders and No Drag Link?

There is a drawback to a drag link connecting twin rudders—it takes up space. Drag links

TABLE 12-2. MODULUS, E

	Modulus, E	
	psi	MPa*
Aluminum	10,400,000	71,700
Silicon Bronze	16,000,000	110,300
Steel and Stainless Steel	28,000,000	193,000

*MPa = N/mm² (megapascals = newtons per millimeter squared)

PART FOUR: RUDDERS AND STEERING SYSTEMS

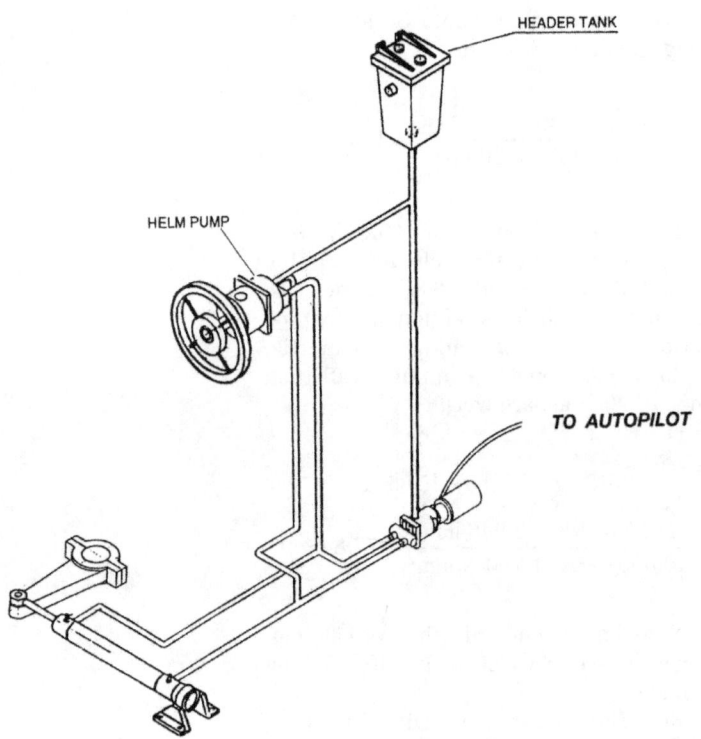

Figure 12-10. Hydraulic steering with header tank (Courtesy Kobelt Manufacturing Co., Ltd.)

Formula 12-5.

are the standard and most rugged method of arranging a twin-rudder setup. If extreme space considerations make it necessary, however, microprocessor-controlled systems can control separate cylinders on each rudder without a connecting drag link. Usually this solution is found on hydraulically steered catamarans, but it can be applied to monohulls if necessary. Kobelt is one manufacturer of these systems.

A Reservoir on High

A critical component for hydraulic installations—particularly those with power-assist or powered autopilots installed—is a reservoir tank (or *header* tank) built in at the highest point in the system (Figure 12-10). This will reduce the chance of air in the system and make bleeding and installation much easier.

Large-Vessel Hydraulic Steering

On larger boats, it becomes difficult to get the mechanical advantage required with a small enough number of turns for sufficiently quick steering. The solution is power-assisted hydraulic steering. For instance, the 28-knot twin-screw planing hull we used for our rudder-stock calculations earlier has a combined torque on the steering system of 5,164 ft.-lb. (706 kgm, 6,924 Nm). A review of the manufacturer's literature showed that we couldn't get down to four turns lock-to-lock on a manual hydraulic steering system and stay under 30 pounds (13.5 kg) at the wheel. Accordingly, we would go to a power-assist system. These systems use a hydraulic pump (driven with a power takeoff, or PTO, on a main engine) to amplify the power from the wheel. If the power system fails, you still have manual hydraulic steering, just slower than ideal. A jog stick can be fitted at the helm to directly activate the power helm pump for quick maneuvering in close quarters (Figure 12-11).

Power for Power Steering

Since larger vessels require power steering (Figure 12-12), you need to be able to estimate the power required by the steering gear. Minimum rudder rpm (rate of turn) for boats of varying displacement can be read off the graph in Figure 12-13. (Under International Maritime Organization [IMO] regulations for large ships, the minimum rudder speed is from 30 degrees port to 35 degrees starboard, and vice versa, in 28 seconds or less. This is 0.387 rpm.)

Formula 12-5. Power for Power Steering

$$hp = \frac{torque, ft.\text{-}lb. \times rpm}{5{,}250}$$

or

$$kW = \frac{torque, kgm \times rpm}{975.17}$$

Where
torque = total steering torque, ft.-lb. or kgm
rpm = revolutions per minute of rudder motion
hp = power required at the rudder stock(s)
kW = power required at the rudder stock(s)

Chapter 12: Rudder-Stock Angle, Control, and Installation Considerations

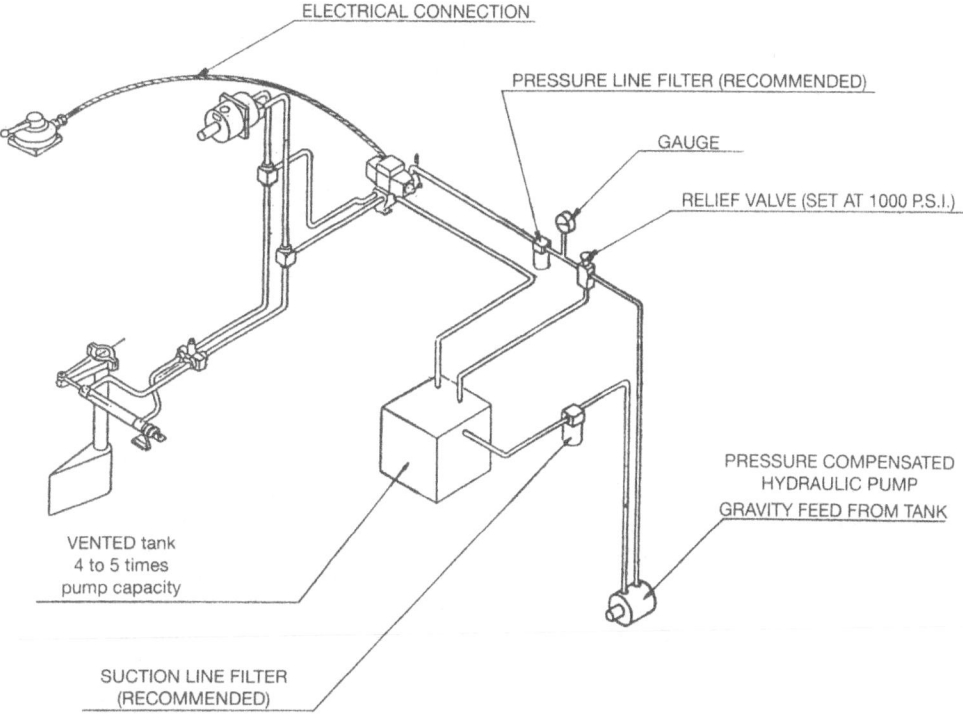

Figure 12-11. Hydraulic steering with power jog stick (Courtesy Kobelt Manufacturing Co. Ltd.)

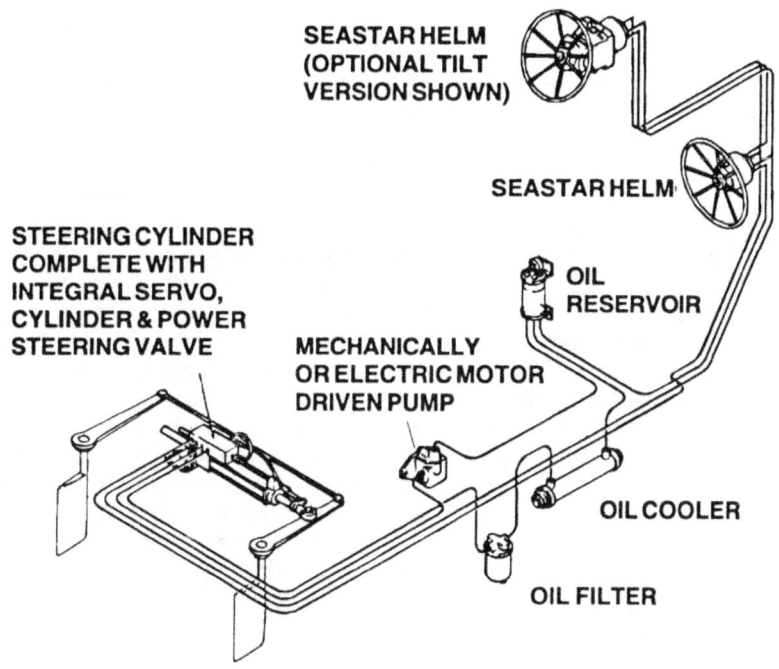

Figure 12-12. Hydraulic power steering: 2 helms, 2 rudders (Courtesy Teleflex, Inc.)

Figure 12-13. Minimum rudder rpm

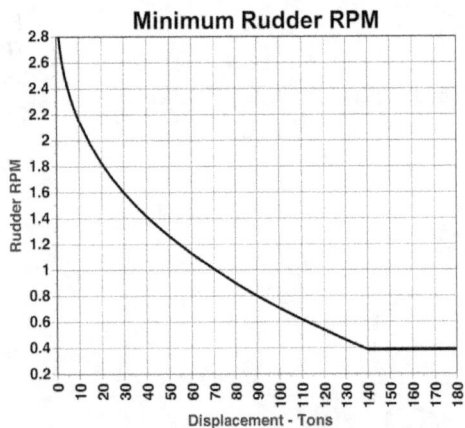

Example: Our example boat displaces 78 tons. From the chart, that indicates 0.9 rpm for the rudder. This is minimum rudder speed, so I usually round up slightly to ensure crisp response; use 1.0 rpm.

We found combined torque for the two rudders was

$$5{,}165 \text{ ft.-lb.}$$

or

$$706 \text{ kgm}$$

Then

$$hp = \frac{5{,}165 \text{ ft.-lb.} \times 1.0 \text{ rpm}}{5{,}250} = 0.98 \text{ hp}$$

or

$$kW = \frac{706 \text{ kgm} \times 1.0 \text{ rpm}}{975.17} = 0.72 \text{ kW}$$

This is the power required at the rudder stocks. If this were a hydraulic system, you could assume the hydraulic motor is about 75 percent efficient and the hydraulic ram (cylinder) is about 90 percent efficient—$0.75 \times 0.90 = 0.67$, or 67 percent efficiency. So

$$0.98 \text{ hp} \div 0.67 = 1.46 \text{ hp}$$

or

$$0.72 \text{ kW} \div 0.67 = 1.07 \text{ kW}$$

Add 15 percent to ensure the system always operates at somewhat less than maximum; you get 1.68 hp (1.23 kW). So you would need an engine or gen-set PTO or hydraulic power pack that delivered 1.68 hp, say 1.75 hp (1.3 kW). The final check would be with the steering-gear manufacturer.

BACKUP STEERING GEAR: EMERGENCY STEERING

All cruising or oceangoing vessels, which don't have direct tiller steering, should have emergency steering gear. On most average sailboats and displacement cruisers, this is usually best set up with an emergency tiller that sockets down onto a squared-off head on the rudder stock, accessed through a deck plate (Figure 12-14). Remember that the loads can be considerable. A pair of strong pad eyes and a pair of cleats should be permanently through-bolted in the cockpit or on deck where relieving tackle can be fastened to them and from there to the eyes at the end of the emergency tiller. This allows you to generate the mechanical advantage required to actually steer with the emergency gear. Because the loads are substantial, this all needs to be carefully engineered and rugged. The system also has to have clearance to swing—something surprisingly often overlooked.

Passenger vessels and larger offshore yachts with power steering require a completely separate backup steering system. The power source and all hose piping and related gear for the backup system need to be different and wholly separate. IMO regulations require only that the backup gear be capable of steering the boat at half normal speed or 7 knots, whichever is greater. The important exception to the backup steering requirement is for twin-screw craft that can be effectively steered by controlling the speed and direction of rotation of the two propellers. On such vessels, the twin-engines-and-propeller combination itself is considered to be the backup steering gear.

Chapter 12: Rudder-Stock Angle, Control, and Installation Considerations

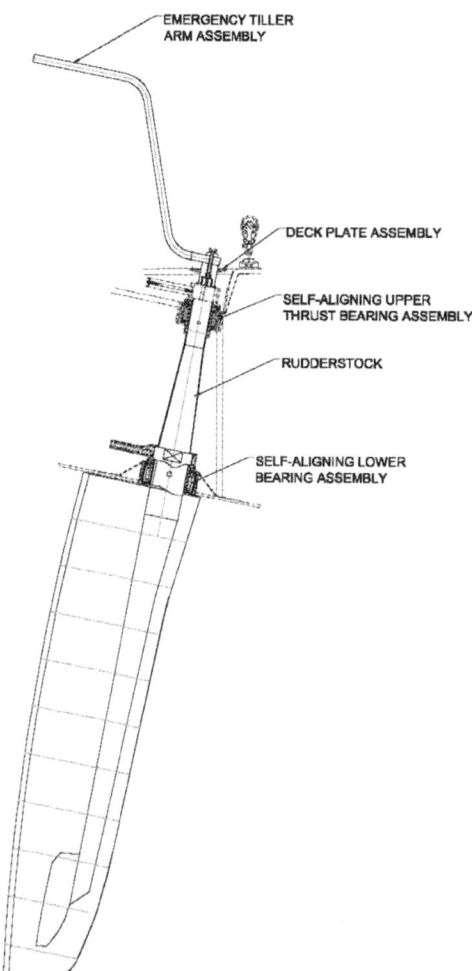

Figure 12-14. High-aspect composite rudder and rudder stock with emergency tiller (Courtesy Edson Corp.)

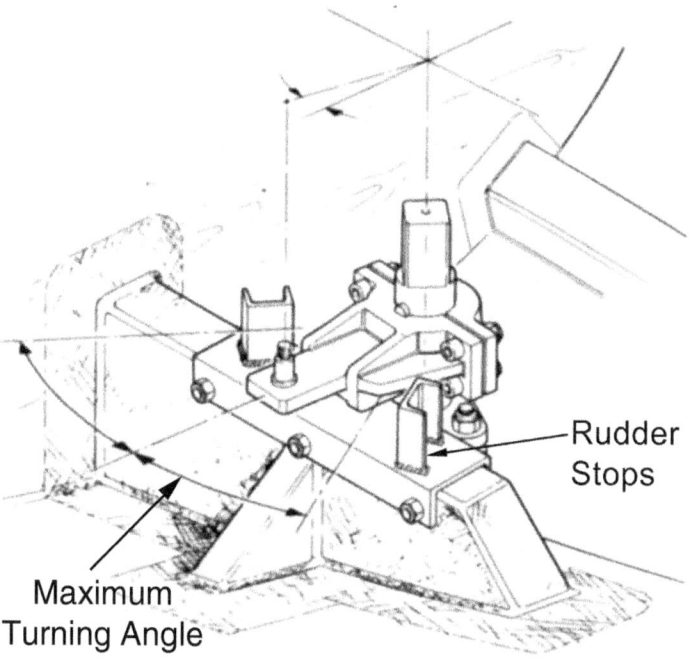

Figure 12-15. Rudder stops (Courtesy Lewmar/Whitlock)

Rudder Stops

All steering arrangements should have rudder stops installed (Figure 12-15). These block the rudder from rotating more than 35 degrees to either side. Without the stops, there can be serious problems when backing down or when lying a-hull in heavy seas. Usually, the stops are set up to block the motion of the quadrant on a cable-steering system or the tiller arm on a hydraulic system; however, the stops can be set up to block any of the moving parts of the system if some other component is more convenient and strong enough to accept the load from the stops. You need to be able to unbolt and remove the stops to rotate the rudder past 35 degrees on single-screw boats where the rudder must be rotated to 90 degrees to pull the prop shaft through a hole in the rudder (or remove or lift the tiller arm or quadrant for this purpose).

Rudder stops should also be fitted on outboard rudders. These can be made of wooden stop blocks (saturated with epoxy, painted, and bolted in place). Figure 12-16 shows a beautiful cast-bronze rudder stop for

Figure 12-16. Bronze outboard rudder stop

209

the outboard rudder of an old 23-foot (7 m) Speedway launch.

Rudder Feedback: Rudder Angle Indicators

Sailboats and powerboats with cable steering (and four or fewer turns lock-to-lock) can provide the helmsman with a reasonable indication of the rudder's position. This is done simply by marking the wheel (perhaps with a Turk's head) at rudder dead center. This indicator and a memory of how the wheel has been turned gives the helmsman a good feel for rudder position.

Larger boats and those with hydraulic steering should be fitted with rudder angle indicators at the helm. These come in a wide variety of sizes and types to give a precise, instant readout of the rudder angle port or starboard. A sender/sensor on the tiller arm or quadrant relays the angle information to the indicator display at the helm.

Autopilots require constant information on the exact rudder angle as well as course and speed. Feedback from the rudder angle is critical to proper autopilot operation. In most instances, the rudder angle sensor on the autopilot will also provide a readout to the helmsman.

Alternate Steering Gear

There are other steering systems besides simple cable and hydraulic systems. Wheels can be attached to rack-and-pinion steerers or worm-gear steerers. These are both solid machined units that give rugged service and the mechanical advantage needed for large rudder loads. Rack-and-pinion steerers provide positive helm feel or feedback from the rudder like cable steerers.

Worm-gear steerers are intended for larger vessels. They were, in fact, first common on large coasting schooners. Their advantage is that the wheel stays exactly where you leave it when you remove your hands—instant, automatic helm lashing, which can be quite convenient. The drawback, though, is that this eliminates all helm feel or feedback from the rudder. Both rack-and-pinion steerers and worm-gear steerers also have the same disadvantage as a tiller: they must be attached almost directly to the rudder stock aft.

A relatively recent twist on cable steering—not much more than 45 years old—is pull-pull or conduit-cable steering (Figure 12-17). It functions the same way as standard cable steering, but consists of cables sliding within flexible conduit instead of running over sheaves. This permits you, theoretically, to run the pull-pull cable any which way, as with hydraulics. In reality, there are limits. Pull-pull cable steering is a good solution for relatively small boats (under 35 feet or 10 m), in installations where bends can be kept to a minimum. Then you can run the pull-pull cables almost as easily as hydraulics. There's

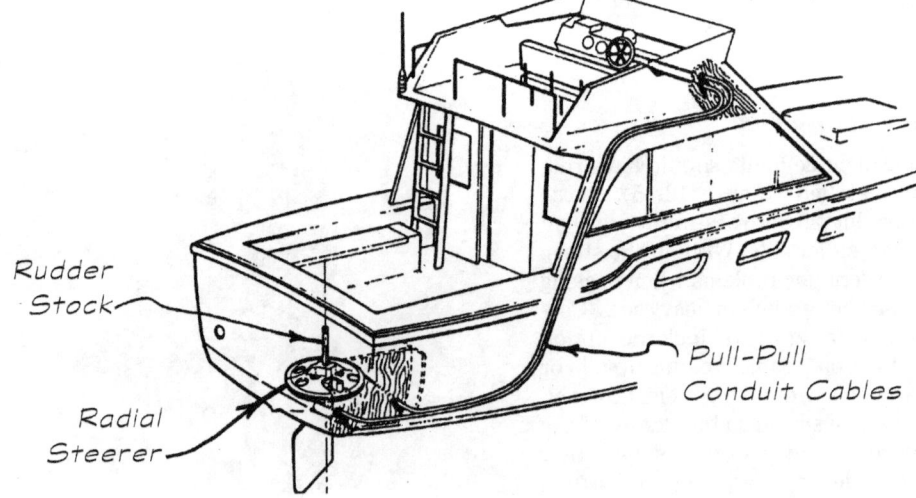

Figure 12-17. Pull-pull or conduit-cable steering (Courtesy Edson Corp.)

too much friction and play in these cables for larger boats or more complex runs, however.

Still other mechanical steering system linkages are available from companies such as Edson, Lewmar/Whitlock, and Jefa, among others.

STEERING REFINEMENTS AND INSTALLATION CONSIDERATIONS

We've reviewed the basics of sizing and selecting rudders, of the required strength of rudder stocks and bearings, and of selecting the steering gear itself. There are still other considerations for a good steering response.

A Problem with Buggies

Over a hundred years ago there was a problem with buggies—yep, as in horse and buggy. When one of these horse-drawn contraptions turned a corner, the two front wheels both pivoted to the same angle. So what's the problem? Well, since the buggy has width, the outside wheel was turning along a larger-radius circle than the inside wheel. To keep the wheels from skidding during a turn, the inside wheel really should pivot to a greater angle (to fit a tighter turning circle) than the outside wheel. Rising to the challenge, a fellow named Akermann realized that if the wheels were mounted on independent axles connected with a drag link to two arms with some in-angle (toe-in), you would get a buggy with front wheels that automatically adjust themselves. The Akermann steering geometry—in complex modern variants—is still used on all cars and trucks. Less well-known is that it's useful on twin-screw boats.

Akermann Steering

Figure 12-18 shows the Akermann steering setup for an average twin-engine vessel. The dotted lines show the two rudders with the helm midships. You can see that the tiller arms (connecting the two rudders through the drag link and also connected to the steering mechanism—not shown) are angled inboard at 10 degrees on both sides. When you put the helm over, the rudder on the outside

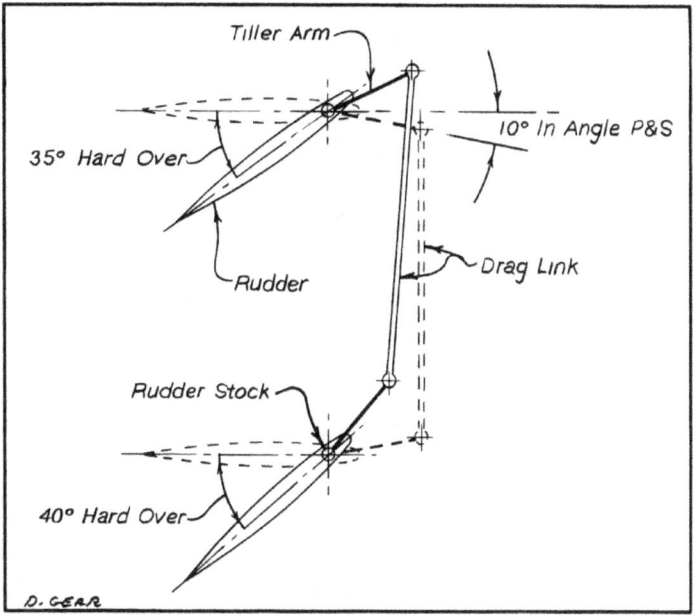

Figure 12-18. Akermann steering for twin-screw boats

of the turn will pivot to less of an angle than the inboard rudder. The solid lines show the steering system at hard over in a turn to starboard. Akermann's geometry puts the inboard rudder at 40 degrees, while the outboard rudder is only at 35. The whole thing's automatic and works the same—mirror image, of course—both port and starboard.

"AKERMANNIZE" YOUR BOAT? Of course, most boats—unlike all cars—don't have Akermann steering. Akermann steering is, however, worth considering. You don't notice the "skidding" of a boat's rudders (without Akermann geometry), because they're out of sight underwater. Nevertheless, when both rudders turn to the same angle, the outboard rudder's actually too far over and stalling somewhat (imposing excess drag), while the inboard rudder isn't over far enough (insufficient steering response).

If you retrofit or design a boat with Akermann steering, you'll find it will have a slightly quicker, more positive helm feel and higher speeds during maneuvering. Indeed, the principal reason most boats aren't fitted this way is that it slightly complicates initial machining and setup. Except for the initial machining, Akermann steering doesn't cost any more than the standard setup. The builder simply has to specify that the keyways on the rudder stocks be milled at the

PART FOUR: RUDDERS AND STEERING SYSTEMS

appropriate 10-degree in-angle. From then on, the same tiller arms, drag link, and steering cylinder, installed the same way, are used.

You can use a 7-degree tiller-arm in-angle for boats under a 10-foot (3 m) beam, and a 10-degree in-angle for boats over 10-foot (3 m) beam. Actually, if you know the actual turning radius, there's a geometric method for deriving a precise in-angle for each craft, but such a specific turning radius isn't accurately knowable; for most ordinary vessels, this 7- to 10-degree approximation will be close enough for practical purposes.

Free-Trailing Angle in the Slipstream

A further refinement is that rudders in the helical flow of the water in the slipstream don't trail straight aft but angle slightly (usually in) if disconnected from their linkage and left free. You can see a somewhat exaggerated drawing of this in Figure 12-19. If the rudders are held straight when the wheel is centered, the boat will go straight, but the rudders will create a bit of extra drag. One way to build this natural angle in is to disconnect the linkage of one rudder on a twin-screw boat when under way at cruising speed and going straight. Mark the angle the rudder takes naturally in the flow, and hook that rudder back up to the steering gear. Repeat the process for the other rudder.

Return to the dock, and adjust the drag link length and attachment so that the rudders are fixed at these free-trailing angles when the helm is at straight ahead (centered). This will provide the minimum resistance at speed. Combine this with the Akermann setup, and you would have minimum resistance at all speeds combined with maximum turning response.

RUDDER INSTALLATION: SHAFT AND PROPELLER REMOVAL

Shaft Removals, Anyone?

Two important practical rudder installation considerations are shaft and propeller removal. Many's the time that I've seen rudders installed just perfectly—just perfectly, that is, if you want to force the mechanic to remove the entire rudder every time he has to pull the shaft. Should you ever want to bone up on the latest nuances in sophisticated cussing, make a point of being around on such an occasion. Certainly, these are things you should look for when inspecting a boat: Has the builder arranged clearances for removing the prop shaft easily? Is there clearance to pull the prop?

Twin-Engine Shaft Pulling

On twin-screw inboard boats, there's a simple solution to pulling the shaft: place the rudder-post centerline slightly off to one side of the prop-shaft centerline so that the shaft can slide right past the rudder. This is plain enough, but you don't want the rudder to be too far from the prop center—you would be out of the slipstream and lose steering efficiency. A good rule is to place the rudder-stock centerline 2.2 prop-shaft diameters outboard of the shaft centerline, as shown in Figure 12-20. If our boat had 1½-inch-diameter (38 mm) shafts, its rudder stocks

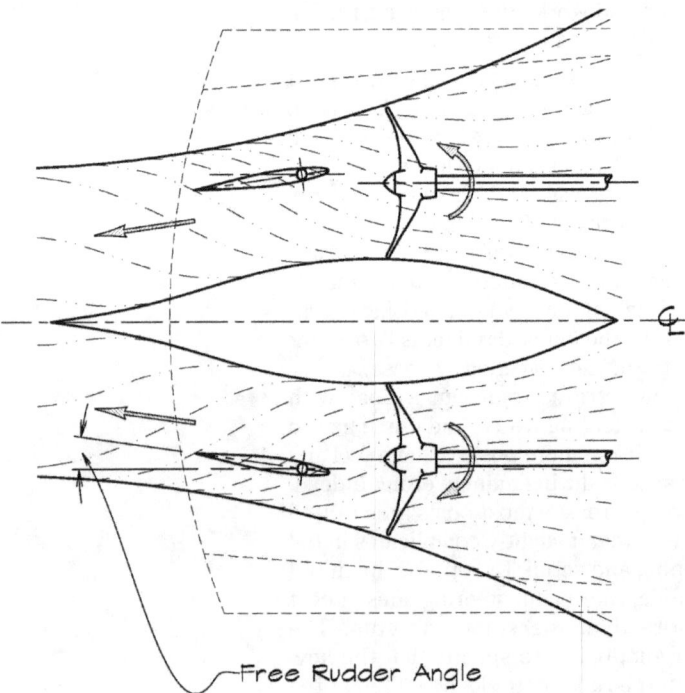

Figure 12-19. Rudder free-trailing angle in slipstream

Chapter 12: Rudder-Stock Angle, Control, and Installation Considerations

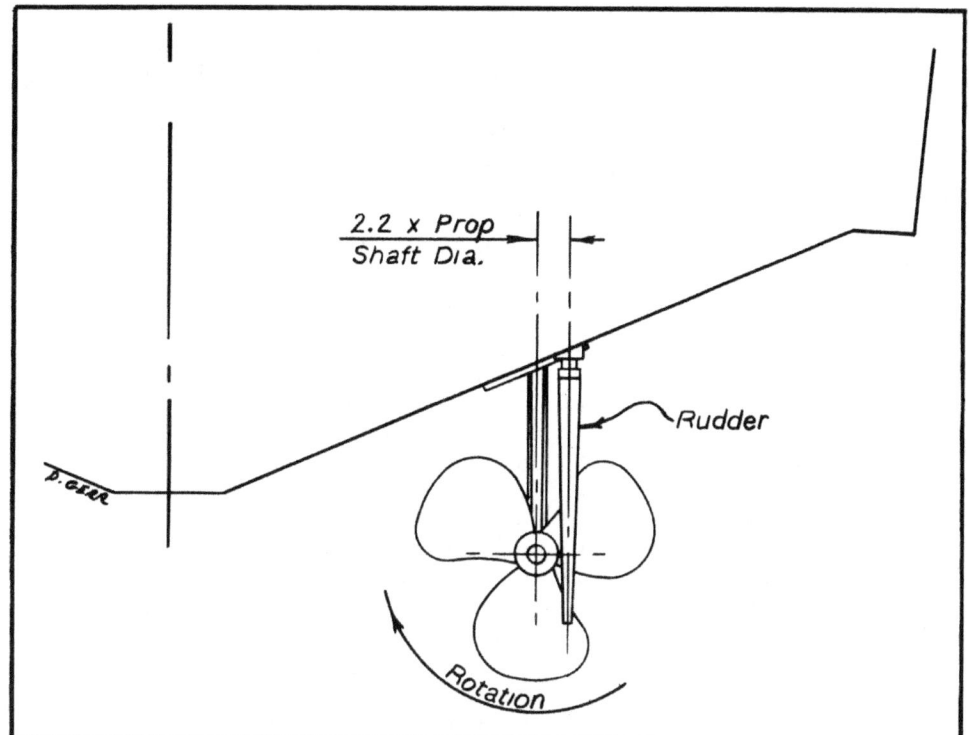

Figure 12-20. Twin-screw rudder location (viewed from astern)

should be 3.3, say, 3¼ inches (84 mm) outboard. This assumes that the boat's props are out-turning as viewed from astern. (This is the standard and usually the most efficient configuration.) If by some chance your props have the opposite rotation, then you would locate the rudder stock inboard by the same amount.

Pulling the Single-Screw Prop Shaft

On a single-screw vessel, you can't place the rudders off center. If you did, steering response would be different for port and starboard helm. The solution here for a standard balanced rudder is to install a hole in the rudder. If properly located, it will allow the mechanic simply to disconnect the rudder linkage and rudder stops inside the boat and pivot the rudder 90 degrees. If the hole has been drilled in the rudder blade at the location shown in Figure 12-21 (at the intersection of the extended prop-shaft centerline and the rudder-stock centerline), then the mechanic can draw the shaft out through the hole. Naturally, the hole has to be larger than the shaft, but not too large—that would create drag and reduce steering efficiency. Two to 2.5 times shaft diameter is a good compromise for the shaft-pulling hole diameter. Smaller gets to be too tight, and larger is just a waste. Also, very steep shaft angles may require a vertical oval slot.

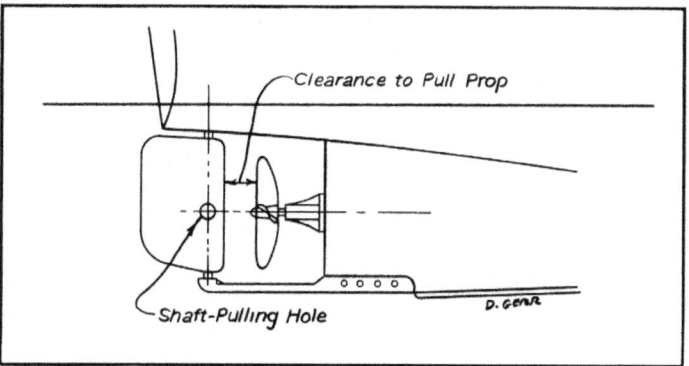

Figure 12-21. Single-screw rudder hole

213

PART FOUR: RUDDERS AND STEERING SYSTEMS

Wheel Removals

Sadly, as you've probably already learned the hard way, propellers have a fine propensity for locating and making contact with massive, usually jagged, hard objects. It's a rare boat that doesn't need its prop pulled and reconditioned at least once or twice. If having to pull a boat's rudder to remove the prop shaft can send a mechanic into the farthest reaches of imaginative swearing, I can assure you that having to do the same simply to remove a prop will transport him to a state just about indistinguishable from apoplexy.

Simply, the distance from the aftermost tip of the prop shaft to the face of the rudder blade has to be at least ½ inch (12 mm) greater than the fore-and-aft length of the propeller hub. As a rule, hub length, fore and aft, is 18 to 20 percent of diameter. So with a 20-inch (500 mm) wheel, you would need at least 4½ inches (112 mm) from the end of the shaft to the rudder blade. You should, however, check the hub length against the propeller manufacturer's specs.

Sail Rudder Refinements

Of course, not all single-screw craft have balanced rudders like that for single-screw powerboats. If the rudder post is right up at the leading edge of the rudder, then the leading edge should be curved or cut back slightly to permit pivoting the rudder over and sliding the shaft by it. This arrangement is shown in Figure 12-22. Indeed, this brings us to some of the considerations of propeller apertures in rudders for such craft. The left-hand figure of this drawing shows the ideal arrangement. It's clear that with the rudder over, you can pull both the shaft and the prop with ease. Less obvious is that this is the best—or nearly the best—configuration for steering. In this case, most of the rudder blade remains pretty much behind the propeller when the helm is put over.

A Sailing No-No

Now look at the center drawing in Figure 12-22, where the propeller aperture is cut almost entirely out of the rudder. This sort of configuration is amazingly common. Pulling the shaft and the prop is no problem here, but visualize what happens when the rudder is pivoted to one side: the blade is no longer behind the propeller. For good control under power, the prop wash simply must impinge directly on the rudder blade. Cutting the rudder away to make a prop aperture destroys any chance of this. Even worse, as you can see, the rudder area has been substantially reduced, making for poorer steering under sail as well.

A Removal-Proof Setup

The right-hand drawing in Figure 12-22 shows another propeller aperture configuration. Here steering is superb—it's the best configuration, even better (very slightly) than the left-hand drawing. In this arrangement, there's no loss of rudder area at all, and the rudder is always perfectly centered behind the wheel. The problem though—and it's a

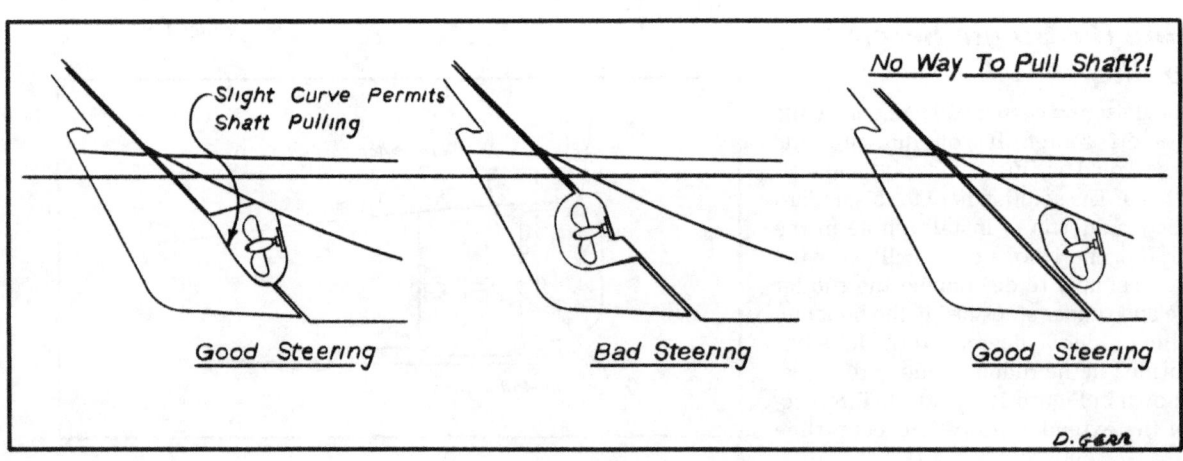

Figure 12-22. Traditional sailboat rudder apertures

doozy—is how to pull the shaft. Indeed, I've seen boats like this and wondered how the shaft was installed in the first place; clearly it was from inside before the engine was put in. This means that simply to change the shaft (or the propeller), you would have to unbolt and lift the entire engine out of the way! This situation would elevate a mechanic to the final stage: past swearing and apoplexy, all the way to sheer joy—joy from contemplating the size of his bill!

Removing Large Rudders

On large boats, rudders and their stocks may weigh over 300 pounds (140 kg). They are awkward shapes to handle, and dropping them could ruin steering alignment or worse. On most powerboats and even larger cruising sailboats, it's a good idea to install strong lifting eyes on either side of the rudder. If these are on the surface of the rudder blade, they should be aligned horizontally fore and aft to minimize turbulence. Alternately, flush screw-in deck plates can be fitted at a hole through the rudder blade, port and starboard. This way the deck plates can be removed and a padded hoist line run through to lift the heavy rudder. Be sure the lifting eyes are designed to take the full weight of the rudder, with a safety factor of 3.

Rudder Palms

Most boats have a continuous rudder stock running from inside the rudder up through the lower rudder bearing and into the hull. This is preferred because without a break, the stock is strongest, and with no external joint, it has the least water resistance. To remove rudders with continuous stocks, though, you have to raise the boat high enough above the ground to drop the full length of the rudder stock down through the bottom of the boat before the bottom of the rudder hits the ground. (You can also dig a pit under the boat for this purpose.) Clearly, this can be quite an undertaking on large boats.

For large vessels fitted with rudders—with bearings above and below the rudder blade, but *never spade rudders*—you can

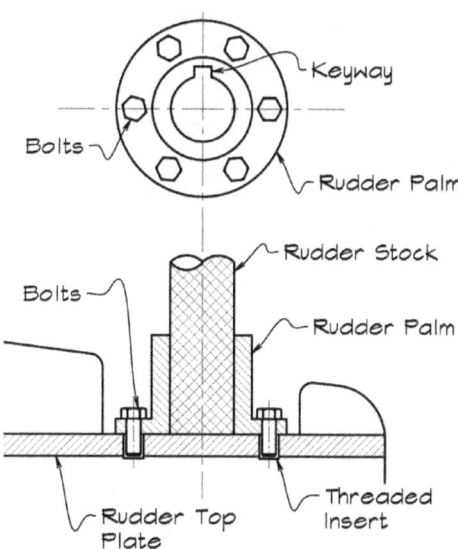

Figure 12-23. Rudder palm

eliminate this removal problem by cutting the rudder stock in half just below the bottom of the boat hull and joining the two halves of the stock together with a shaft coupling. Couplings used in this application are termed *rudder palms* (Figure 12-23).

Rudder palms are best sized from standard SAE Type I (internal-pilot) and Type II (external-pilot, straight-bore) propeller-shaft couplings. The dimensions can be found in Appendix C of my *Propeller Handbook* or in ABYC standard P-6. In this application the male-female protuberance around the center can be omitted. It is possible to have a true coupling fitting only at the upper part of the rudder-palm joint. It can make good sense to bolt this upper portion of the coupling directly to the top plate of a welded rudder. Be sure that this top plate is thick enough to accept the rudder-palm bolts properly (or use a doubler plate) and that it's wide enough to accept the full diameter of the upper half of the coupling fitting above it. Also, in steel or stainless rudders, which bolt into such a top plate, there should be stainless threaded (HeliCoil) inserts in the bolt holes in the rudder top plate. Without these, the bolts will seize over time and be nearly impossible to remove.

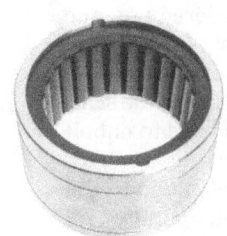

CHAPTER 13

Unusual and Special Rudders: High-Lift Rudders

In the preceding three chapters we've examined standard rudders in detail: how they are sized, their forms, the strengths of rudder and stock, installation considerations, steering systems, and considerations for optimizing performance.

Naturally—as you would expect with anything so vital—a host of inventors and gadgeteers have dreamed up all manner of spanking-new and improved steering gizmos. Some of these brainstorms were downright silly, but others—though they might seem peculiar—are worth a close look. Though conventional rudders will and usually should serve the needs of most average boats, we'll examine a few unusual and useful rudders here.

RING-FORM RUDDERS
Rudders from the Kitchen?

A long time ago a British admiral (Admiral John G. A. Kitchen, to be precise) sat down to design an improved rudder. He wanted vastly enhanced steering at low speed (maneuvering and docking) plus great simplicity. In fact, the rudder he came up with not only works but also completely eliminates the need for a reverse gear. The year Kitchen's patent was granted was 1916. You would expect—if it was so good—that you would be surrounded by Kitchen rudders by now. Instead, they've been virtually forgotten. Heck, I seldom meet someone who's even heard of them.

THE KITCHEN SETUP You can see from the illustrations in Figure 13-1 how the Kitchen rudder is set up. Basically, two half-circles (somewhat conically shaped) surround the prop in a ring (not unlike the Kort nozzles seen on some tugboats and trawlers). Instead of a single vertical rudder blade aft of the prop, the entire ring rotates in unison to steer. This actually slightly improves water flow into and out of the propeller disk, enhancing efficiency a bit. You can slow down by cutting back on the throttle in the usual way, but the Kitchen rudder offers another remarkable option: Each conical half-circle pivots aft, ultimately closing with its mate behind the prop. Half-closed, for instance—without touching the throttle—reflects about half the prop thrust forward (allowing half the wash still to flow aft) and effectively puts the boat in "neutral." Fully closed gives you a solid, reliable reverse—fully steerable. What's more, there's no unpredictable walk to port or to starboard. In reverse mode—at docking speeds—the Kitchen rudder acts like a true stern thruster.

In the late 1910s or early 1920s, the U.S. Navy performed trials on a 38-foot (11.6 m) launch fitted with a Kitchen rudder. They reported that from 10.4 knots, this vessel could

Chapter 13: Unusual and Special Rudders

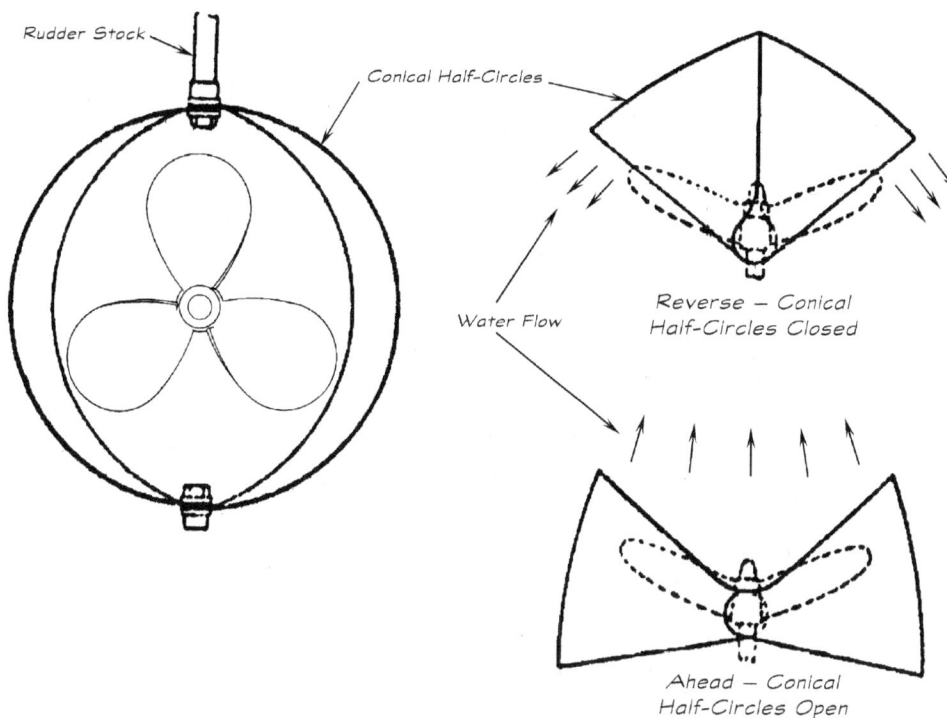

Figure 13-1. Operation of the Kitchen rudder

be stopped in just one boat length. Incredibly, they also reported that the Kitchen rudder enabled this launch to be pivoted around her own center—in other words, in place! You can't do better than that for low-speed, close-quarters maneuvering, period.

THE VANISHING KITCHEN MYSTERY Why the Kitchen rudder has been almost completely forgotten is one of those great mysteries. Manufactured by Kitchen's Reversing Rudder Co., Ltd., of Liverpool, England, Kitchen's rudder was extensively employed by the British

Figure 13-2. Outboard Kitchen rudder

and Canadian navies before World War II, and it won raves from those who used it. Sales and marketing here in the U.S.—under 1916 U.S. Patent No. 1,186,210—was spotty, though. The McNab Company—first of Bridgeport, Connecticut, and later of Yonkers, New York—had the American license. Though they made successful installations on everything from outboards (yes, outboard motors with Kitchen rudders) to large ships, all traces of it seem to have vanished.

KITCHEN STEERING MECHANISM One possible difficulty is the steering mechanism. The two halves of the rudder are steered in unison with a more-or-less conventional tiller, but that tiller is itself a worm-screw that controls the closing and opening of the two conical half-circles. This is reliable and apparently free from failures, but back in 1916 it required complex mechanical linkages to run controls to a remote helm station. Today, however, with modern hydraulics, such controls would be inexpensive and reliable to install. You would need only one standard hydraulic steering cylinder and one second half-circle closing (reversing) hydraulic cylinder—not a very powerful one at that. If you installed a Kitchen rudder, you would have to add the cost of fabricating the rudder and the second hydraulic cylinder. (You could subtract the cost and, not at all incidental, the weight of the reverse gear, if you could get a reduction gear only.) You would also have effectively added—at no extra cost or weight—a complete stern thruster for incredible maneuverability in harbor. For years I've been promising myself that the next motor cruiser I design will have a Kitchen rudder. Maybe one day it will.

The Kitchen rudder wouldn't be suitable for planing hulls or for most boats cruising at speed-length ratios over 1.5 or so, as the extra drag from the Kitchen rudder would be too great a drawback.

Harrison's Patent Rudder

Interestingly, another rudder shares a vague similarity with the Kitchen rudder. This is the Harrison patent rudder. Figure 13-3 shows a rudder that is a half-circle surrounding the top portion of the propeller. Mounted on a single rudder stock, these rudders were fitted to fast

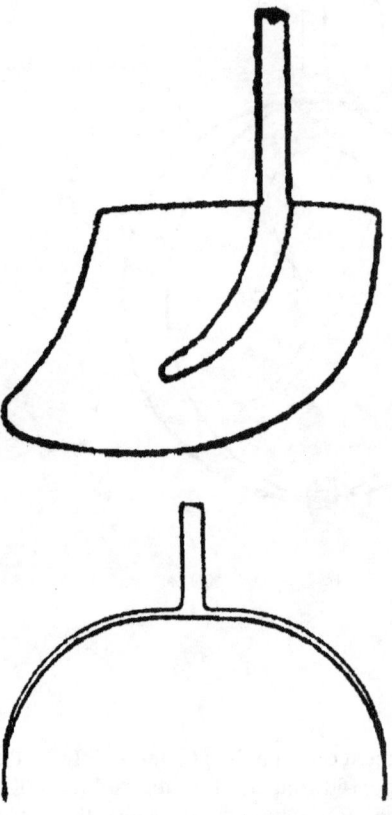

Figure 13-3. Harrison patent rudder

steam launches many, many years ago. The Harrison rudder worked well and gave slightly better water flow to and from the prop. Twin-screw vessels sometimes had two quarter-circle Harrison-type rudders installed, one on the outboard side of each rudder. This, too, worked well. Though effective and worth noting, the Harrison patent rudder didn't generate the broad array of advantages that the Kitchen rudder did and still does.

A very similar rudder is used on some surface-drive propeller installations with excellent results.

Steerable Kort Nozzles

A vaguely related ring-form rudder is the steerable Kort nozzle (Figure 13-4). This is the standard Kort nozzle most commonly used on tugs and trawlers to increase low-speed thrust. The common installation is to have the

Chapter 13: Unusual and Special Rudders

Figure 13-4. Steerable nozzle rudder (Courtesy Michigan Wheel Corp.)

nozzle fixed with a rudder immediately behind. The alternative, however, is to do away with the rudder behind and rotate the nozzle itself, just as the Kitchen rudder is steered. Usually, one (or a pair) of fixed "rudder" blades are bolted to the aft end of the nozzle, which thus turn along with the rotating nozzle to further enhance steering. This does not give the reversing effect of the Kitchen rudder, but it does give a very positive steering response. You do get the additional low-speed thrust (higher bollard pull) of the Kort nozzle, which a Kitchen rudder does not create.

HIGH-LIFT RUDDERS

Standard airfoil-section rudders stall and stop generating effective lift at rudder angles of 35 degrees or more. There are ways to modify the standard airfoil-section shape to induce the rudder blade to create useful lift (turning side force) at higher angles. This can be a fixed shape that doesn't change, often termed a *fishtail rudder* (more properly a *hydrodynamic fishtail rudder*), or it can be a rudder with a movable flap or some other variable-geometry *articulated rudder*. Fishtail high-lift rudders are also called *fixed-geometry high-lift rudders*. The Kitchen rudder is articulated, but it isn't in the form of a "blade" and so falls into a category of its own. In fact, the articulated rudders we're discussing here are more exactly termed *articulated flap rudders*. All such high-lift rudders can be thought of as *propeller slipstream diverters* since they get their low-speed, high-angle lift by radically changing the direction of the slipstream.

Fishtail Rudders

THE MACLEAR THISTLE RUDDER A good example of a fishtail rudder is the MacLear Thistle rudder (Figure 13-5). This rudder is substantially more recent than the Kitchen or Harrison rudders. It was invented by Frank

Figure 13-5. MacLear Thistle rudder

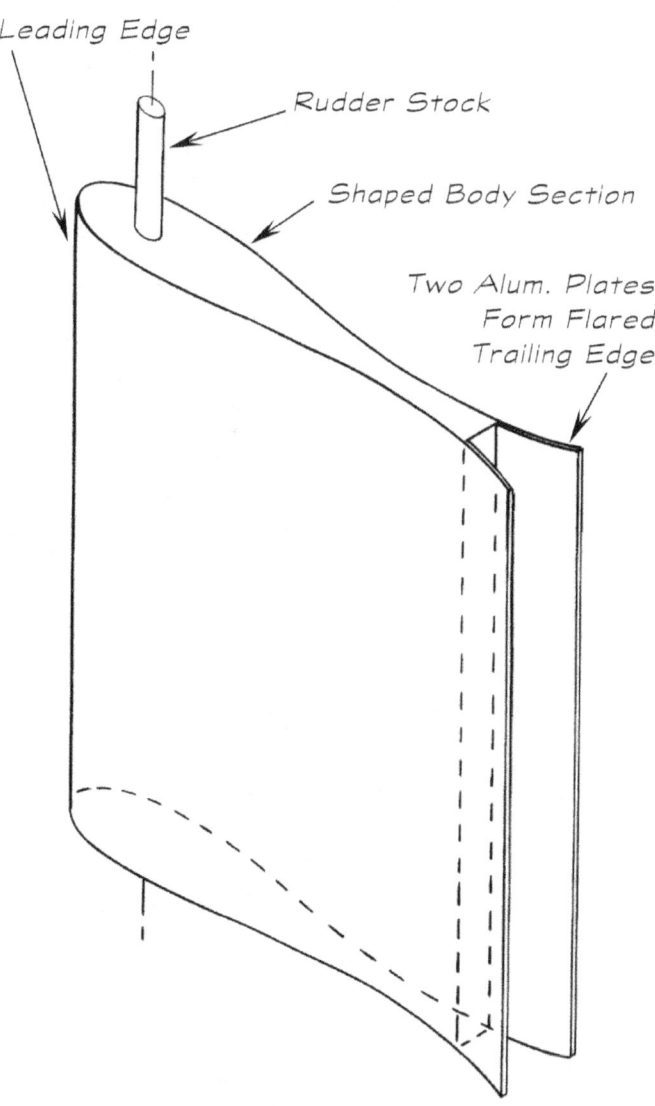

MacLear, president and chief naval architect of MacLear and Harris, Inc. (where I once worked). MacLear set out to improve low-speed maneuvering in close-quarters situations as well as enhance steering response at speed. It can ruin your whole day if you smash into your neighbor's boat while docking.

As we've seen in previous chapters, most ordinary rudders are ineffective when the helm is put over more than 35 degrees. Turn a normal rudder farther and it just acts like an unpredictable brake. It can even create eddies that throw the stern about randomly. But what if you could turn the helm to, say, 40 degrees and still get a controlled, positive helm response? Reasoning it through, MacLear came up with a new rudder-section shape. As you can see in the drawing, it starts off fattish and rounded, swelling as it runs aft, then tapering at the middle before flaring out again at the aft end. Indeed, the shape is much like the bulb of a thistle, hence the name. The shape is also basically a standard airfoil-rudder section flared to a fishtail at the trailing edge; thus it's a typical fishtail rudder.

What does all this shaping accomplish? At normal cruising speeds it doesn't change much, though it does increase steering response slightly at small course-keeping helm angles. But in low-speed maneuvering, you can turn the MacLear Thistle rudder over as much as 40 degrees. The water flow is guided around the leading edge and midsection by the rudder's section shape, and then the flared-out end makes water flow continue to do useful work at the higher angle. The result is that the rudder acts like a stern thruster, allowing tight turns at low speed. Another useful plus is that the MacLear Thistle rudder's trailing edges can be made of aluminum plate and—optionally—left open and not welded together at the trailing edge. These are precurved as you see in Figure 13-5; however, you can adjust them by grabbing them with Vise Grips or whatever and bending them in or out, either evenly from top to bottom, or to varying degrees from top to bottom and differently port and starboard. The rather clever advantage of this is that you can adjust the flare-out on each side by trial and error until your boat's handling is exactly predictable and as you want it. Having worked on the design of several boats fitted with the MacLear Thistle rudder, I can attest that it works precisely as advertised.

Figure 13-6 shows the section proportions (along with the optional endplates) and Table 13-1 gives the half-breadths as a percent of chord, and the tip radii. Note that as the center of pressure is a bit farther aft on the Thistle rudder, the rudder stock is at 20 percent chord, giving 20 percent balance.

On larger vessels, the entire rudder is usually fabricated from aluminum or steel. For smaller vessels you can make the forward three-quarters to seven-eighths of the rudder blade in the usual way, with a stainless steel or bronze stock through a wood/fiberglass blade. Then fabricate the

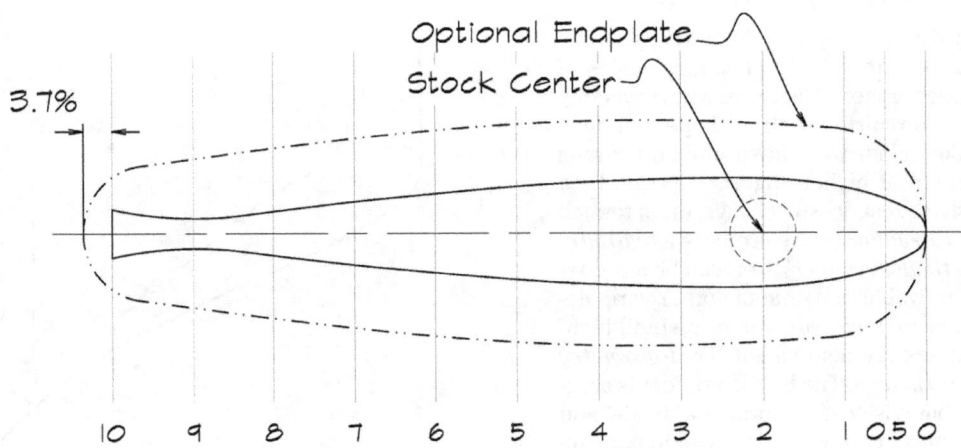

Figure 13-6. Thistle rudder sections

TABLE 13-1. MACLEAR THISTLE RUDDER

Foil Thickness Dimensions
Half-Breadth
as a Percent of Chord

% Chord	Rudder Blade	Optional Endplate
Tip Radius	2.676	12.49
5.00	3.977	9.995
10.00	5.353	12.240
20.00	6.424	12.955
30.00	6.424	13.347
40.00	6.103	13.337
50.00	5.532	12.938
60.00	4.675	12.219
70.00	3.746	11.248
80.00	2.600	10.094
90.00	1.785	8.826
100.00	2.860	6.676
Tip Radius	NA	8.030

flared-out trailing edges from curved aluminum plate, letting them in flush to the body of the rudder blade. You can retrofit almost any standard rudder installation this way. Even at the normal range (35 degrees hard over to hard over), steering is more precise and predictable. The only improvement I've made to the MacLear Thistle rudder is—where possible—to build on endplates over the top and bottom rudder edges (Figure 13-7). These

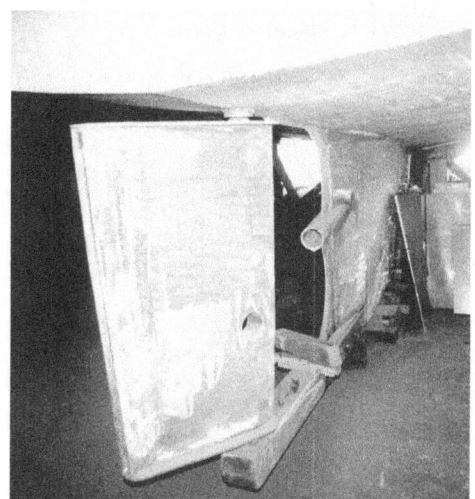

Figure 13-7. MacLear Thistle rudder with endplates

are fastened to the rudder blade but project aft over the flared ends, either attached or unattached. In this way you still get an endplate effect at the trailing edge while retaining adjustability. Such endplates further improve the MacLear Thistle rudder's already excellent helm response.

A rudder like this gives unusually positive steering, and my office has installed them on most of our single-screw displacement cruisers. Though you can turn the MacLear Thistle rudder to 40 degrees, all the installations I've done have only gone to the normal 35 degrees. At speed, somewhat less rudder angle is needed to get the same course correction you would achieve with a standard rudder. During low-speed maneuvering, these rudders really shine. Steering response is both crisp and predictable. You can very quickly kick the stern of your boat around to exactly where you want it.

Here's what the skipper of one of my designs, *Imagine*, had to say about the boat's handling with the Thistle rudder. This was in just his first week with the boat:

> *Imagine* is doing wonderfully! To date, my strongest impression is how easily she handles in close quarters. We've been staying at quaint, but small, marinas that are quite challenging for even a twin screw to maneuver in. Two nights ago I was even forced to dock stern-to. I gave the harbormaster my length, and he asked for my beam. I replied, "14 feet 6 inches," and he said, "Great. In that case, you can stay because I have one slip left with a 16-foot width." And then he told me I would have to follow marina custom and dock stern-to. I had 20 people watching, and I backed in with one try—*without using the bow thruster*. The response I got from the audience ranged from: "You must have been handling her for several years" to "Yep, I can always tell when a boat has twin screws." Needless to say, I'm flattered. *Imagine* backs down quite straight with very little prop walk.

Of course *Imagine* has a single screw. This Thistle rudder had endplates top and bottom (as you can see in Figure 13-7), but it was set up only for the standard 35 degree hard over. The one drawback to getting larger rudder angles is that the hydraulic steering

PART FOUR: RUDDERS AND STEERING SYSTEMS

gear needs to be somewhat customized to handle the added travel.

OTHER FISHTAIL RUDDERS Hydrodynamic fishtail rudders are commercially available for large vessels from companies such as Schilling (the Schilling rudder, which may predate the MacLear Thistle), Ulstein, and others. Many of these rudders have proportionately fatter (even bulbous) sections with more balance and a blunter, round leading edge than the MacLear Thistle rudder. These rudders are optimized for even better response at still higher rudder angles—as much as 65 degrees. Primarily intended for ships, these large-balance, fatter-section fishtail rudders pay a slightly higher penalty in drag at small rudder angles for nearly true stern-thruster response during maneuvering.

For both fishtail and articulated-flap rudders (see below), rudder-blade balances as high as 40 percent have been used, with 35 percent being common. This means that the rudder projects forward of the rudder stock more than on a standard balanced rudder, and adequate clearance must be checked and may require modifications on a retrofit. This larger balance is also one of the causes for sometimes problematic steering on high-speed boats with articulated rudders.

SIZING FISHTAIL RUDDERS The MacLear Thistle rudder, with 20 percent balance as indicated, should be sized according to the standard rudder area formula; however, many companies size fishtail rudders (and articulated-flap rudders) as rectangles, with their height slightly greater than propeller diameter, and the chord between 70 and 80 percent of propeller diameter. This should give good results as long as the propeller size and installation are within the normal range for a vessel of the type that it's driving.

FLAT-PLATE FISHTAIL RUDDERS In Chapter 10 we described the general construction of flat-plate rudders. Though we saw that flat-plate rudders are acceptable, we also found that they give less steering response and create more turbulence than any other rudder type. We learned that flat-plate rudders are really a cost-saving option.

There is a way to get flat-plate rudders to perform better. It is to weld a fishtail to their trailing edge. This is particularly effective when used in conjunction with endplates. There are a few advantages: The fishtail increases rudder response at higher angles than a standard flat-plate rudder could tolerate (as well as slightly improving course-keeping, low-angle rudder response). The endplate (as it does with any rudder foil form) increases the lift generated from a given rudder area. At the same time, both the fishtail and the endplates are fabricated of flat plates themselves, simply welded onto the flat-plate rudder blade, and so construction remains inexpensive. Such flat-plate fishtail rudders (Figure 13-8) are really only appropriate for displacement vessels, as the

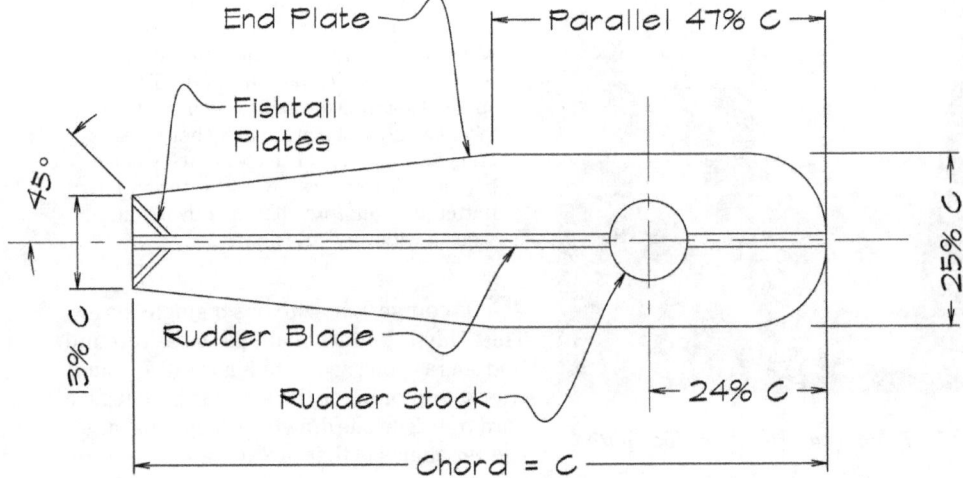

Figure 13-8. Flat-plate fishtail rudder section

additional drag of the flat-plate fishtail and endplates is too great at planing speeds.

The drawing shows a section through a typical flat-plate rudder with fishtail and endplates, courtesy of naval architect Charles Neville. The flat-plate blade thickness is determined using Formula 10-4 for flat-plate rudders, as are the stiffeners and the stiffener spacing. Alternately, you can use multiple endplates as stiffeners all along the height of the rudder blade (at the calculated stiffener spacing); however, endplates are only required at the top and bottom of the blade.

Note that where the MacLear Thistle rudder had the rudder stock at 20 percent of chord, the flat-plate fishtail rudder has the stock even farther back at 24 percent of chord. This can be done only with the angled fishplates installed. If they are not, such a high balance (about 24 percent) may cause the steering problems described earlier.

Endplate thickness = 75 percent of rudder-blade thickness
Angled fishtail plate thickness = 50 percent of rudder-blade thickness

Articulated-Flap Rudders

I'm partial to the MacLear Thistle rudder and related fishtail rudders because they are more effective (for displacement hulls) than conventional rudders, and they are also very simple—no moving parts. It is possible to get even more steering effect during low-speed maneuvering and even more pronounced stern-thruster effect (as good as the Kitchen rudder, though without reverse) with *articulated rudders* (articulated-flap rudders).

Instead of a single-piece blade, articulated-flap rudders have one or more movable flaps (sometimes rotating drums at their leading edge as well) to increase effectiveness at high rudder angles, at low speed. If you don't mind a bit more complexity (and these articulated systems can be quite rugged) and you have a displacement vessel that requires very precise handling at low speed, an articulated rudder may be the answer. (A Kitchen rudder is really a very different form of articulated rudder; however, the term *articulated rudder* usually refers to a rudder with flaps, so they're also termed *articulated-flap rudders*.)

It is possible to use articulated rudders on fast boats, but it takes very careful engineering and setup or there will be problems. An example of this was a commercial vessel, *Te Kouma*, chosen for use by the Royal New Zealand Yacht Squadron. This was a 25-knot boat and the following, from *NZ Professional Skipper* magazine, January/February 2004, is a typical experience for higher-speed craft:

Te Kouma was originally fitted with an articulated rudder for low-speed maneuverability. But this feature proved to be unmanageable, creating very tough steering on the hydraulics once she was up to her cruising speed. Had power steering been installed, this would not have been a problem. In trying to combat the stiff steering problem, [Harold] Bennett removed the articulator attachment to the rudder. On subsequent sea trials this has removed all the stiffness from the rudder operation, while maintaining good maneuverability at high speed, with little difference in her low-speed maneuverability.

Note that the trailing-edge flap on the articulated rudders moves the center of pressure considerably farther aft. For this reason, most such articulated rudders have well over 24 percent balance (unacceptable for standard rudders). Balance as high as 40 percent may be used, with 35 percent being common. This high balance can be one of the causes of potential problems for articulated rudders at high speed, though it can usually be tweaked to work. It's not clear, however, that the extra cost and complexity of an articulated rudder makes sense on a typical twin-screw planing hull, which has good maneuverability at low speed via backing and forthing the opposing propellers.

The idea behind articulated rudders is not new and has been around in one form or another since the 1890s. Since rudders are *foils* that generate lift in fluid flow, articulated rudders are also properly termed *variable-geometry foils*. They have been used not only on boats, but on airplanes as well. Some of the best-known manufacturers of articulated marine rudders are Rolls Royce/Ulstein (Figure 13-9), Hinze Becker Marine Systems (the Becker rudder), Wartsila Van der Velden Marine Systems' Barke rudder, and Jastram, which offers not

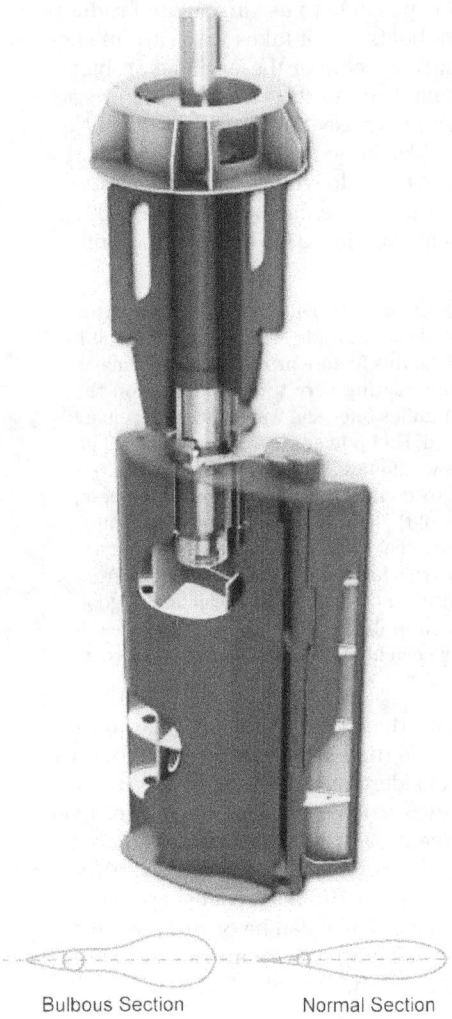

Figure 13-9. Bulbous flap rudder (Courtesy Ulstein Hinze FB/MH)

Figure 13-10. Deflector Rudder amidships

only articulated-flap rudders but rudders with rotating drums built into their leading edge. These companies primarily manufacturer rudders for ships.

The Deflector Rudder

A U.S.-fabricated articulated rudder is the Deflector Rudder, made by Deflector Marine Rudder of Naselle, WA. Figure 13-10 shows a stern view of the Deflector Rudder at dead center and Figure 13-11 shows a side view of the rudder in a starboard turn. The basic workings of the rudder are automatic and require no external power to move the flap (that's accomplished by the geometry of the flap linkage and pivot location alone). Like most flap rudders, the Deflector Rudder articulates to a total of 90 degrees. The main/forward rudder blade swings to 45 degrees, and the trailing-edge flap swings to twice that—so 90 degrees (Figure 13-12).

Double Fixed-Geometry High-Lift Rudder

Another unusual rudder configuration is the double fixed-geometry high-lift rudder. This is two balanced rudders (usually with endplates) acting in unison behind a single propeller. The twin rudders turn together but usually use differential steering (similar to the Ackermann steering described in the

Figure 13-11. Deflector Rudder to starboard

Chapter 13: Unusual and Special Rudders

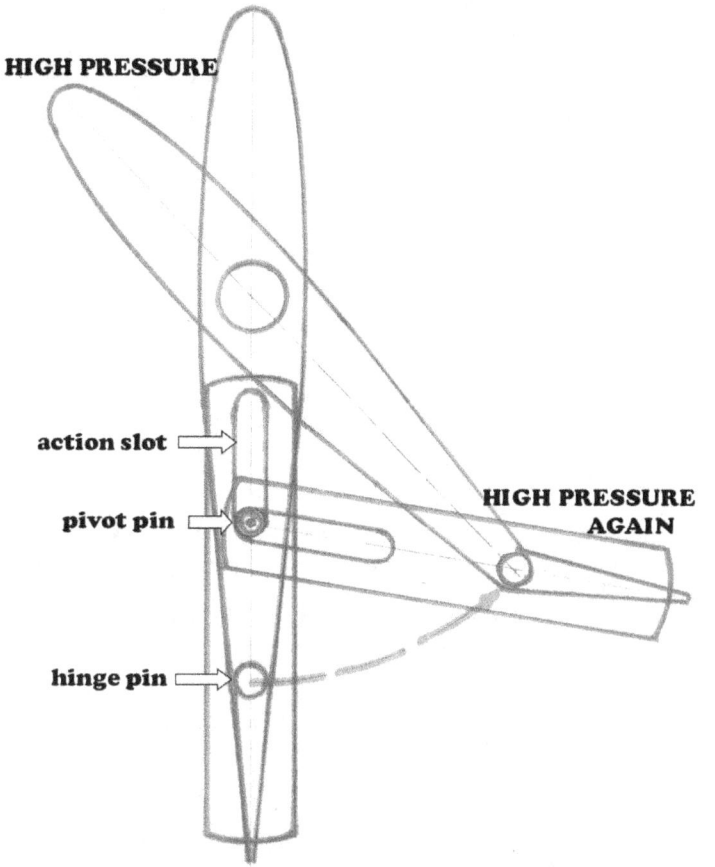

Figure 13-12.
Geometry of a
Deflector Rudder

previous chapter), so the rudder on the inside of the turn angles more than the outside rudder. In addition, because they are acting in tandem, these twin rudders can turn effectively to as much as 75 degrees on the inboard-turn rudder and 55 degrees on the outboard. To get such high angles, the rudders must have a half fishtail on the outside of each blade. You can see this if you study Figure 13-13 closely.

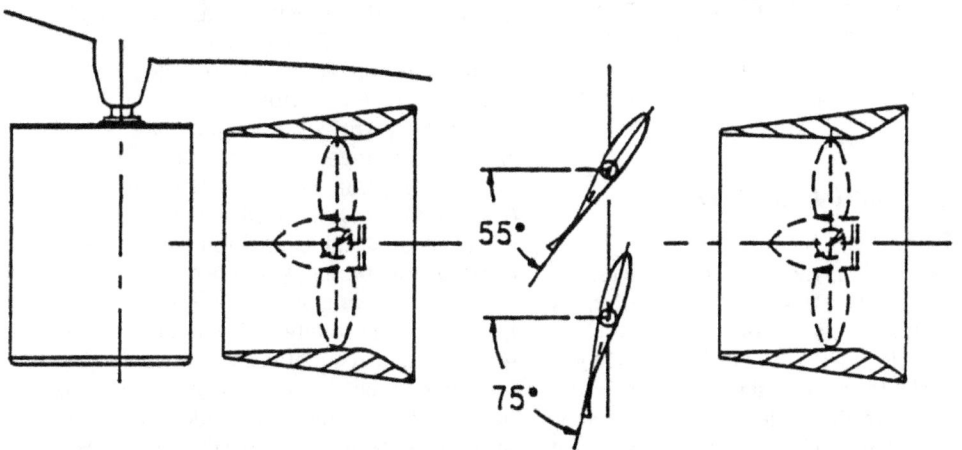

Figure 13-13.
Double fixed-geometry high-lift rudders (Courtesy Jastram Canada Ltd.)

225

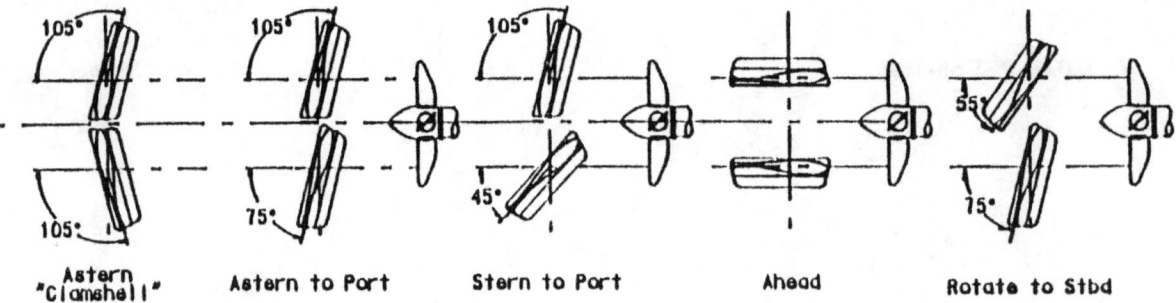

Figure 13-14. Double fixed-geometry high-lift rudders with variable independent rotation (Courtesy Jastram Canada Ltd.)

Variations of this twin-rudder configuration have been used for years. Computer-controlled systems can now articulate such twin rudders behind a single propeller, in the same or opposite directions and at varying different angles, with independent but related control. The result is handling similar to the Kitchen rudder; however, the Kitchen rudder doesn't require any computer controller to generate the correct combination of rudder angles needed for this twin-rudder configuration.

The Jastram Rotor-Rudder and T-Rudder

Rudders begin to stall at surprisingly small angles of attack. By building in a hydraulically driven rotating drum flush with and forming the leading edge of the rudder, flow separation can be delayed, and thus so can stall. This means that the rudder can be effective at higher angles (well over 45 degrees). Jastram manufactures this as the Rotor-Rudder. Even greater rudder angles can be achieved by adding an articulated flap to the trailing edge, combined with the rotor at the leading edge. This is Jastram's T-rudder, and it truly is equal to a powerful stern thruster.

Articulated Rudders for Boats

As noted earlier, the Jastram rudders, the Becker, and the Barke rudders are largely manufactured in sizes appropriate for ships and generally aren't suitable for boats. If you are looking for an articulated rudder for use on small craft, the Deflector Rudder fits the bill. It is a good option for those looking for the maximum possible low-speed maneuvering rudder response.

COMPARING FISHTAIL AND ARTICULATED RUDDERS (FLAP RUDDERS)

Both fishtail and articulated rudders have the same goal: to improve steering response. Is one better than the other? No. As with so many things, it's a question of trade-offs. Rudder function can be divided into two modes of operation: *course keeping* and *maneuvering*. We'll take a look at the pluses and minuses of each type of rudder in each mode of operation.

Course Keeping

When running at normal speed, the purpose of the rudder is to keep the vessel on course. Essentially, this means holding a straight course more than 95 percent of the time with minimum rudder action and minimum rudder drag. Course corrections will be small and should be positive and immediate. Occasional pronounced changes of heading will be required, but these are done gradually (compared with low-speed maneuvering) and again, minimal rudder angle and minimal rudder drag are optimal. With the correct rudder and steering gear installed, almost all course-keeping rudder angles will be under 10 degrees, with infrequent use of 15-degree helm for pronounced changes in heading. Seventy to 80 percent of the time, rudder angles during course keeping will be 5 degrees or less.

The optimal characteristics can be summarized as

- a good lift-drag ratio for minimum fuel consumption
- minimum drag with rudder at or close to zero angle, for minimum fuel consumption
- gradual and steady increase of lift at low to moderate helm angles (If the slope of the lift curve is too steep, it will cause oversteering. This results in an added small reverse course correction, which is hard on the helmsman or the autopilot and causes additional drag and increased fuel consumption.)

Course-Keeping Comparison

The lift-drag ratio at helm angles up to 10 degrees is similar for both types of rudders. Since the flap on the flap rudder moves to twice the rudder angle, the lift-drag ratio is a bit more than a fishtail rudder at angles over 5 degrees. Because the flap angle continues to be double the main rudder angle, it is more likely to generate an oversteer reaction at cruising speed, particularly at higher speeds.

The conclusion is that the fishtail rudder has a slight advantage over articulated or flap rudders in course keeping.

Maneuvering

At low speed in close quarters, such as during docking, anchoring, precise station keeping, and so on, large, quick, accurate changes in course are required.

The optimal characteristics for maneuvering can be summarized as

- maximum lift coefficient regardless of drag; fuel economy is not a factor
- the capability to redirect the flow from the propeller slipstream to the maximum angle possible, to get as close to true stern-thruster response as practical

Maneuvering Comparison

At maximum rudder angles, the articulated-flap rudder produces about 7 to 9 percent more lift than a fishtail rudder.

Articulated-flap rudders usually have a total rudder angle of 90 degrees (45-degree main blade, 90-degree flap). They thus work at nearly perpendicular to the slipstream. Fishtail rudders vary from 40 degrees for the MacLear Thistle rudder to as much as 65 degrees for the fatter-section rudders such as Schilling. Fishtail rudders thus cover up to 65 percent of the slipstream, while the articulated-flap rudder will cover almost 90 percent.

Note that both fishtail and flap rudders almost always have greater balance than standard balanced rudders.

Considering the preceding information, the articulated-flap rudder will be somewhat more effective for maneuvering.

Articulated Versus Fishtail Rudder Summary

Both the fishtail and articulated-flap rudders will result in a pronounced improvement in steering response. The fishtail rudder would generally be the best all-around rudder, as it has no moving parts and less drag during course keeping (95 percent of operation for most vessels), while at the same time giving very significant benefits in maneuvering.

Articulated-flap rudders give the maximum low-speed maneuvering response. For vessels that will be docking repeatedly in difficult conditions, boats that have very precise station-keeping requirements, or for craft whose great windage makes them difficult to handle, articulated-flap rudders have a slight edge over fishtail rudders.

There is one important exception: when going astern, articulated-flap rudders stall earlier than even conventional rudders. This is because the flap—at twice the main rudder blade angle—stalls in sternway conditions very quickly.

The difference between the two rudder types isn't large, however, and both accomplish nearly the same results.

A Hierarchy of High-Lift Rudders?

It is possible to very roughly create a hierarchy of high-lift rudders based on the relative size of the turning circles they make possible at maneuvering speeds. The following list

PART FOUR: RUDDERS AND STEERING SYSTEMS

is in order from largest turning circle to tightest turning circle. Remember there are many variables in the rudder installation and in the boat itself, so this is at best a rough guide:

- MacLear Thistle rudder
- Schilling rudder and articulated-flap rudder
- Rotor-Rudder, double fixed-geometry unison rudders
- T-rudder (Rotor-Rudder with articulated flap), Kitchen rudder, double fixed-geometry variable-control rudders

Again, very broadly speaking, the complexity and cost of the rudder increases as the turning circle decreases, and all of these rudder systems provide dramatically smaller turning circles and better low-speed control on displacement than standard rudder vessels.

Part Five

VENTILATION, AIR-CONDITIONING, AND HEATING

Ventilation of Passenger and Storage Areas

CHAPTER 14

If you live in the Northeast, you know that Florida is not a bad place to spend some time in February. As you can imagine, I wasn't at all disappointed to find I had to work the Miami Boat Show aboard a boat that my office designed. The weather exceeded expectations, and—except for a couple of days that actually reached 84°F (29°C)—conditions were flawless. One afternoon in particular stands out in my mind. It was about 72°F (22°C) and 35 percent humidity. A steady 15-knot breeze blew in from the northeast, and the blue sky was dotted with puffy clouds just dense enough to throw occasional welcome shadows in the brilliant sun. Aboard our boat we had all the windows open, and with the steady wind whistling through, it was even a bit chilly in the shade (just a bit).

Of course, one of the perks of having to do a boat show is getting to check out what other designers and builders are doing. When a couple of my crew returned aboard, I decided to steal a few hours and poke around some of the other vessels. A client of mine had mentioned that he had liked a few features on a 60-foot (18.3 m) high-speed production motor cruiser, so I set off for a look at it.

Air from Where?

Though this was a fairly conventional boat of its type, it certainly had some well-thought-out details. I clambered into the engine compartment, which was clean and open, and then up onto the flybridge, where visibility was good. Going below, I thought the builder had done a fine job on the joinerwork, though there were few access panels for

Figure 14-1. Classic cowl vent on dorade box

229

PART FIVE: VENTILATION, AIR-CONDITIONING, AND HEATING

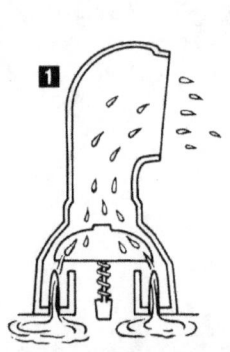
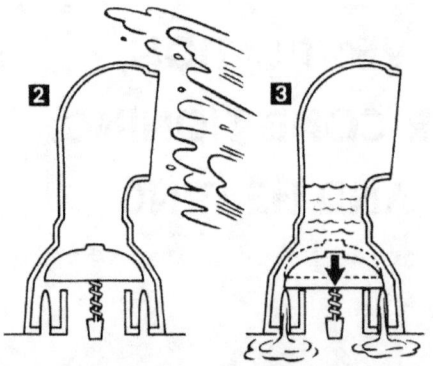

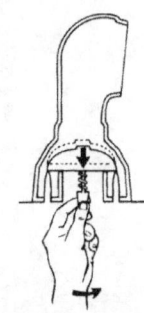

1. Rain and spray is directed away from deck opening where it drains out weep holes at bottom of trap.
2. In extreme conditions, a green water intrusion gives our new water trap a chance to shine.
3. The weight of the green water pushes down on the damper, shutting off the trap 100%. The green water drains off onto the deck through the four weep holes at the bottom of the water trap.
4. When the green water is gone, the damper pops up again and ventilation continues.
5. The damper can be shut-off from below by pulling down on damper arm and rotating it ¼ turn. This will shut off the water trap 100%.

Figure 14-2. Water-trap cowl vent (Courtesy Marinco/Nicro Ventilation Systems)

maintenance and repair—all too common on production boats. Ambling toward the bow, I found myself in the forward guest stateroom. It was bright, with large hanging lockers, and seemed a bit cool. "Incredible weather," I thought to myself, and then it hit me. It wasn't the weather; it was the boat's air-conditioning. In fact, even though this was a perfect, clear, almost-cool day outside, the air-conditioning was running full bore.

One glance around made the reason apparent. The forward stateroom (and all the staterooms below deck) had no opening windows. In fact, the forward stateroom windows couldn't have been made to open safely, because with the great flare at the bow, these windows (even though high up on the topsides) actually faced down toward the water at nearly a 40-degree angle. If there had been opening ports installed, and you forgot to close one underway, well, you would soon have given the accommodations a nice salt-water bath. As a result, with no other means of ventilation, the air-conditioner had to run all the time, even on a comfortable day like this one. "Imagine," I thought to myself, "what this boat would smell like after you had it closed up for a few weeks in the summer sun and came aboard for a cruise. Why, the combined smell of styrene and mildew would probably knock you flat." There wasn't even a hatch in the overhead, which could have been opened. (This, by the way, is bad for another reason, as there ought to be two avenues of escape from every compartment, and a hatch works as the second avenue.)

A Comfort Component

Ventilation is a key component in comfort aboard any boat, yet I doubt you spent much time considering it the last time you were looking to buy a boat, planning a new design, doing a retrofit, or conducting a survey. In fact, almost any boat will benefit from added ventilation. Really good ventilation doesn't just make life more comfortable aboard. It reduces rust, mildew, and decay, as well as lessens the likelihood of seasickness. It also means that you can run the air-conditioning less frequently, which is quieter, saves money, and saves our small planet some pollution.

Ventilation—that is, providing adequate airflow—has four primary jobs aboard any boat:

1. provide for the safety and comfort of the crew
2. minimize mildew, mold, rust, and decay
3. ensure efficient operation of internal-combustion engines and other machinery
4. dissipate any dangerous or undesirable gases or fumes

VENTILATION OF PASSENGER COMPARTMENTS

Ventilation Measure

Ventilation is a subject that can occupy a HVAC (heating, ventilation, and air-conditioning) engineer for a lifetime of study. Controlling temperature and humidity, reducing system noise, maximizing efficiency, laying out extensive duct systems, and more are complex subjects in themselves. A full discussion of ventilation includes heat and humidity control. For instance, when it gets cold you want less airflow through a compartment, but you can't seal the compartment airtight because you need to breathe. Humidity and air velocity combine to govern comfort, and in cargo ships, they can make the difference between a load arriving fresh or completely spoiled. For this discussion, however, we'll assume that our object is simply to keep things cool and comfortable using relatively simple systems, and that the crew will actively go around closing ventilators, hatches, and windows and turning off fans as the weather gets colder. We will review straightforward approaches to meeting basic ventilation requirements on boats.

The Volume Change Rate (VCR) or Air Changes Per Hour (ACH)

The amount of ventilation in a compartment can be evaluated as the number of air changes in the compartment in a given time (usually 1 hour)—say, 5 changes of air per hour for a bilge area, for example. This is the volume change rate (VCR) or air changes per hour (ACH).

As a practical matter, you need to find the airflow in cubic feet per minute (cfm) or cubic meters per hour (m³/hr) required to meet the VCR requirement for a given compartment.

Formula 14-1. Required Airflow

Required Airflow, cfm = VCR × vol ÷ 60 min./hr.

TABLE 14-1. VOLUME CHANGE RATE (VCR) OF VARIOUS COMPARTMENTS

Compartment	VCR per Hour	Time to Change Air (Minutes)
Galley	10 to 20	3 to 6
Lavatories and WCs	8 to 10	6 to 7
Sleeping Cabins	6 to 8	7 to 10
Saloons	5 to 10	6 to 12
Forepeak and Lazarette	5	12
Bilges	5	12
Storage Compartments	8 to 12	5 to 7
Engine Compartments	150 to 250*	0.24 to 0.4*
Battery Compartments	Covered separately, see below	

*See engine-vent section below.

Or

Required Airflow, m³/hr. = VCR × vol

Where:
VCR = volume change rate
vol = compartment volume, cu. ft. or m³

Example: Say you have a master stateroom that is 9.9 feet (3.02 meters) long by 8.8 feet (2.68 meters) wide. It has a head compartment in one corner that is 3.25 feet (1 meter) by 4.67 feet (1.43 meters) wide. Headroom is 6.5 feet (1.98 meters). Then

9.9 ft. × 8.8 ft. × 6.5 ft. headroom = 566 cu. ft.
3.25 ft. × 4.67 ft. × 6.5 ft. headroom = 98 cu. ft.
566 cu. ft. − 98 cu. ft. = 468 cu.ft.

VCR should be between 6 and 8 times per hour.

6 × 468 cu. ft. = 2,808 cu. ft./hr., or
2,808 cu. ft./hr. ÷ 60 min./hr. = 46.8 cfm
to
8 × 468 cu. ft. = 3,744 cu. ft./hr., or
3,744 cu. ft./hr. ÷ 60 min./hr. = 62.4 cfm

Formula 14-1.

Or

$$3.02 \text{ m} \times 2.68 \text{ m} \times 1.98 \text{ m headroom} = 16 \text{ m}^3$$
$$1 \text{ m} \times 1.43 \text{ m} \times 1.98 \text{ m headroom} = 2.8 \text{ m}^3$$
$$16 \text{ m}^3 - 2.8 \text{ m}^3 = 13.2 \text{ m}^3$$

VCR should be between 6 and 8 times per hour.

$$6 \times 13.2 \text{ m}^3 = 79 \text{ m}^3/\text{hr}.$$

to

$$8 \times 13.2 \text{ m}^3 = 106 \text{ m}^3/\text{hr}.$$

(NOTE: It's customary in passenger spaces to use gross compartment volume, as we have here. As we'll see, net compartment volume is employed for machinery spaces.)

We would need to install blowers or passive ventilators that provide this flow rate to meet our VCR requirement.

How Much Air per Person? For passenger spaces, you should also check the minimum amount of ventilation based on the amount of air required to keep each person comfortable in fairly warm weather. For reasonable comfort, each crewmember needs about 15 cubic feet of air per minute (cfm) or 25 m^3/hr. Obviously, a small passive vent delivers more air when it's blowing hard than when there's barely a breeze. What we need, however, is ventilation when it's hot and there is little wind. Accordingly, the boat should be fitted with vents that'll deliver 15 cfm (25 m^3/hr.) per person in light winds, say 4 knots. Table 14-2 gives the cross-sectional vent areas that will give the required flow in just 4 knots of breeze. It assumes a roughly standard cowl vent sitting on a water trap, or a good-quality mushroom vent.

Standard cowl and mushroom vents come in diameters ranging from 3 to 10 inches (7.6 to 25.4 cm) and have minimum opening cross sections per Table 14-3. (NOTE: Proper cowl vents should unscrew so they can be closed with screw-in deck plates in extreme weather conditions, and they are designed to rotate to face into or away from the wind as needed.)

Example: If a boat routinely carries six crew, you will read the required 90 cfm (153 m^3/hr.) off the table, which would be provided by 92 square inches (594 cm^2) of vent area per person in a summertime 4-knot wind. Table 14-3 shows that this would call for seven or eight 4-inch (10.2 cm) vents.

TABLE 14-2. VENT REQUIREMENTS PER PERSON

No. of Crew	cfm*	Area, sq. in.	m^3/hr.*	Area, cm^2
1	15	21	25	135
2	30	37	51	239
3	45	51	76	329
4	60	64	102	413
5	75	77	127	497
6	90	92	153	594
7	105	110	178	710
8	120	131	204	845
9	135	157	229	1,013
10	150	190	255	1,226
11	165	229	280	1,477
12	180	278	306	1,794
13	195	335	331	2,161
14	210	404	357	2,606
15	225	484	382	3,123
16	240	578	408	3,729
17	255	686	433	4,426
18	270	809	459	5,219
19	285	949	484	6,123

*Approximate vent flow for the specified vent area in a 4-knot breeze

(Seven 4-in. [10.2 cm] vents at 12.6 sq. in. [81.1 cm^2] each equals 88.2 sq. in. [568 cm^2].)

Few boats have this number, so it's no wonder that so many are uncomfortable below on hot days. In fact, although 3-inch (7.6 cm) vents are quite common, they're really too small to give enough ventilation. Three-inch (7.6 cm) vents should be used only for passenger-compartment ventilation on the tiniest craft, where you may have no option but to go this small. If hatches or windows can

TABLE 14-3. ROUND VENT AREAS

Dia., in.	Area, sq. in.	Dia., cm	Area, cm^2
3	7.1	7.6	45.6
4	12.6	10.2	81.1
5	19.6	12.7	126.7
6	28.3	15.2	182.4
7	38.5	17.8	248.3
8	50.2	20.3	324.3
9	63.6	22.9	410.4
10	78.5	25.4	506.7

Chapter 14: Ventilation of Passenger and Storage Areas

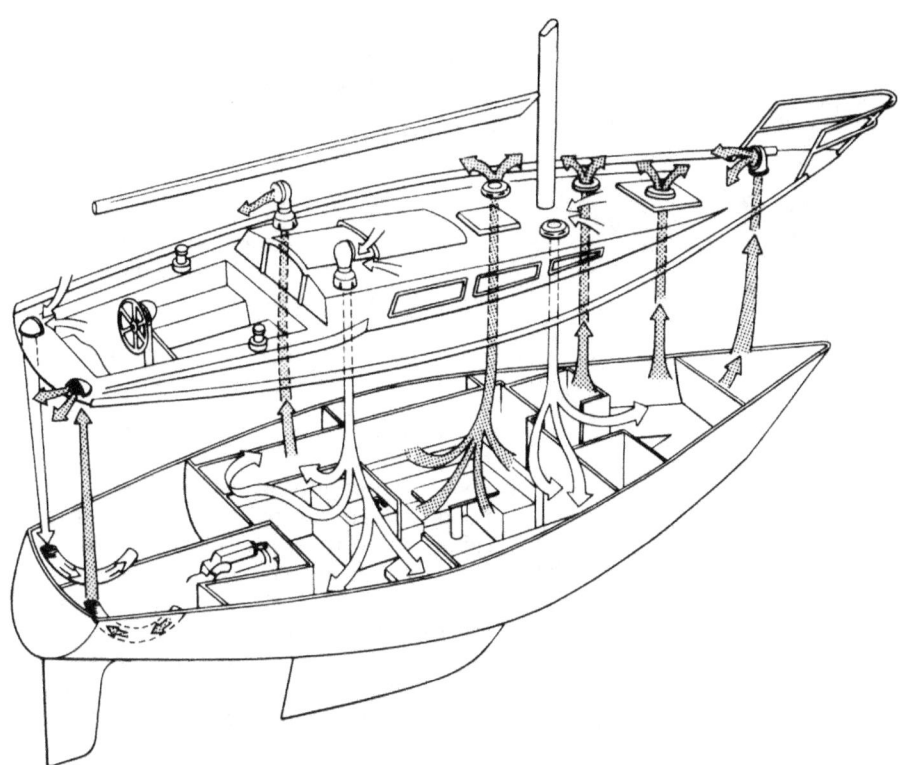

Figure 14-3. Typical vent installations and airflow on a sailboat (Courtesy Marinco/Nicro Ventilation Systems)

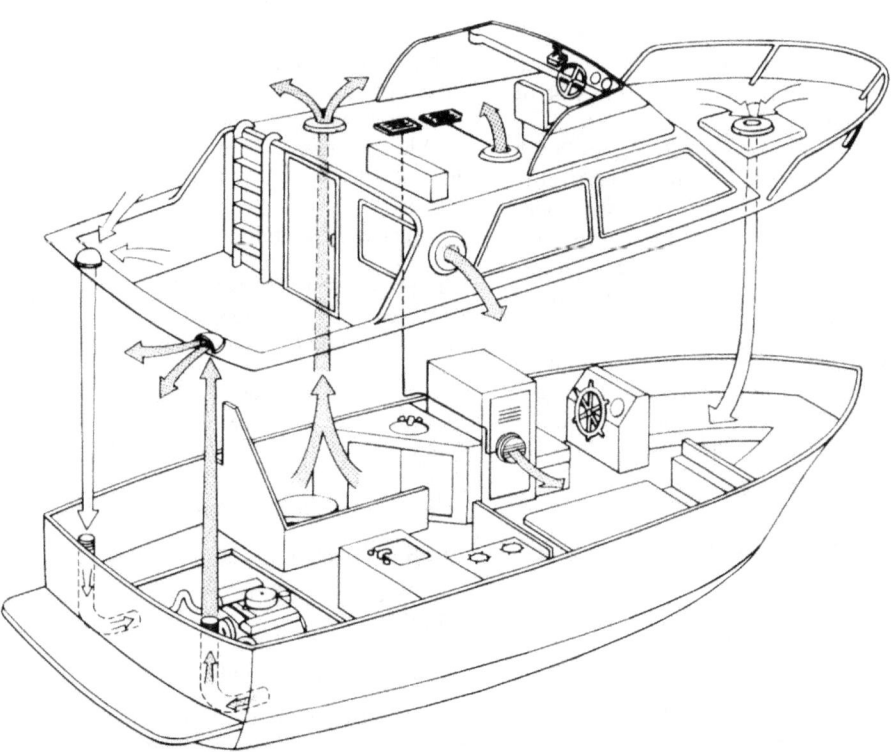

Figure 14-4. Typical vent installations and airflow on a powerboat (Courtesy Marinco/Nicro Ventilation Systems)

PART FIVE: VENTILATION, AIR-CONDITIONING, AND HEATING

Figure 14-5.
Mushroom vent

be left open or partially open in most conditions, you can deduct the area they contribute from the vent requirements, but keep in mind that when you do close these hatches or windows, you'll have only the vents to breathe with.

CHECKING AIR PER PERSON AGAINST THE VCR
We should check the vent-per-person requirement against individual compartments' VCRs as well as against the entire boat.

Example: We found we needed between 46.8 cfm and 62.4 cfm (between 79 m^3/hr. and 106 m^3/hr.) to meet the VCR requirements for the master stateroom earlier.

This stateroom sleeps two people, so based on 15 cfm per person that's just 30 cfm. You should select the larger of the two where possible, so we would go with vents delivering at 46.8 cfm in 4 knots of wind, which—from Table 14-3—would be four 4-inch vents (50.4 sq. in. total).

ROD STEPHENS' VENT RULE If 92 square inches (594 cm^2) of vent area seems like a lot, Sparkman & Stephens' founding designer Rod Stephens' rule of thumb for vent area for a single-deck vessel is as follows.

Formula 14-2.

Formula 14-2. Rod Stephens' Vent Rule

Total vent area, sq. in. = WL, ft. × beam overall, ft.

or

Total vent area, cm^2 = 69.4 × WL, m × beam overall, m

Example: If *Ocean Breeze* were a 38-footer with a 32-foot waterline and an 11-foot, 10-inch beam overall, it would require

32 ft. WL × 11.83 ft. beam overall = 378 sq. in. vent area

Or

If *Ocean Breeze* were an 11.6-meter boat with a 9.75-meter waterline and 3.6-meter beam overall, it would require

69.4 × 9.75 m WL × 3.6 m beam overall = 2,436 cm^2 vent area

This rule assumes that a reasonable portion of the vent area will come from partly open hatches with dodgers over them in most conditions. If you took 25 percent of this (allowing the remaining 75 percent to come from hatches and windows), you would end up with 94 sq. in., which is about the same as the dedicated vent area calculated earlier.

Note that a more complete statement of Rod Stephens' vent rule is that 1 square inch of vent area is required for every square foot of cabin area (not volume) in temperate climates and 1.5 square inches for every square foot of cabin area in tropical climates.

Or

Note that a more complete statement of Rod Stephens' vent rule is that 69.4 cm^2 of vent area is required for every square meter of cabin area (not volume) in temperate climates and 104 cm^2 for every square meter of cabin area in tropical climates.

This can be restated as

Vent area, temperate climates = cabin area ÷ 144

Vent area, tropical climates = cabin area ÷ 96

Example: Our example master stateroom is 9.9 feet long × 8.8 feet wide. It has a head compartment in one corner that is 3.25 feet × 4.67 feet

Net stateroom square footage is

9.9 ft. long × 8.8 ft. wide   = 87.1 sq. ft.
− 3.25 ft. long × 4.67 ft. wide = − 15.2 sq. ft.
Total   = 72 sq. ft.

For temperate climates

72 sq. ft. ÷ 144 = 0.5 sq. ft.
0.5 sq. ft. × 144 in./sq. ft. = 72 sq. in.

This would be six 4-inch ventilators, which is not likely to be practical. You could approach this requirement by using, say, four 5-inch ventilators (78.4 sq. in.) or between two and four 4-inch ventilators combined with hatches, dodgers, or ventilated companionway doors, and arranged so they can be left open in bad weather.

Or

Example: Our example master stateroom is 3.02 meters long × 2.68 meters wide. It has a head compartment in one corner that is 1 meter × 1.43 meters.

Net stateroom square footage is:

3.02 m long × 2.68 m wide = 8.1 m^2
−1.0 m long × 1.43 m wide = − 1.43 m^2
Total = 6.67 m^2

For temperate climates

6.67 m^2 ÷ 144 = 0.0463 m^2 × 10,000 cm^2/m^2 = 463 cm^2
0.0463 m^2 × 10,000 cm^2/m^2 = 463 cm^2

This would be six 10.2 cm ventilators, which is not likely to be practical. You could approach this requirement by using, say, four 12.7 cm ventilators (507 cm^2) or between two and four 10.2 cm ventilators combined with hatches, dodgers, or ventilated companionway doors and arranged so they can be left open in bad weather.

Windows, Hatches, and Skylights

The fact is that properly designed windows, skylights, and hatches can and should contribute to vent area in warm weather. By including these items, you can approach or even exceed Rod Stephens' rule. Figure 14-6 shows a motor cruiser my office designed. This is similar to the vessel we had at the Miami Boat Show. Note that almost every window you see opens. The wheelhouse roof has a huge skylight, and there are large sliding doors. Even when it's raining and unpleasant out, at least a quarter of these windows or hatches can be left partly open without water coming in. (Which ones to open depends on wind and spray direction, obviously.) In most conditions, the total vent area in use—even in bad weather—is greater than Rod Stephens' rule. In fact, the first two of these boats did not have air-conditioning at all, including *Summer Kyle*, based out of Florida. At the same time, with the hot-water cabin-heating system and the windows and hatches buttoned up, this boat is also warm and snug in 30°F (−1°C) weather. Buttoned up like this, the numerous mushroom vents still provide adjustable fresh air, which is vital.

Figure 14-8 shows the inside of *Summer Kyle*, giving the inside view of another of these vessels from my office and showing the amount of both light and air designed in.

Figure 14-6. The 47-foot Peregrine/ Nancy Lankin. *Nearly every window on this boat opens.*

PART FIVE: VENTILATION, AIR-CONDITIONING, AND HEATING

Figure 14-7. Open hatches and skylights provide plenty of vent area

Figure 14-8. Pilothouse of Summer Kyle (Courtesy Starke Jett)

Solar-Powered Air

One of the best solutions for getting air below is the solar-powered mushroom vent (Figure 14-9). Standard 4-inchers (10.2 cm) deliver about 18 cfm (30.6 m³/hr.). What's more, they do it every day the sun shines, whether you're aboard or not, and they don't even drain the batteries. Better still are the day/night solar vents equipped with built-in nicad batteries. These gizmos store enough juice on sunny days to keep them going overnight. Indeed, once fully charged, they can run nearly 48 hours without sun. High-output solar vents are also available. Nicro-Fico's 4-inch (10.2 cm) vent pulls about 26 cfm (44.2 m³/hr.). Although not inexpensive, a few of these nearly add up to a cool mountain breeze. Two or three of these solar-powered vents installed over the galley and the head will keep your *Ocean Breeze* mildew-free and smelling fresh as a daisy. Better still, since these vents aren't tied into the electric system, you can leave them running all the time without fear of draining the batteries, even when you're not aboard. As a result, your boat will be fresh and well ventilated when you open it up for a cruise after a long absence.

For solar-powered vents located where the vent won't get direct sun (such as on the

Figure 14-9. Solar mushroom vent (Courtesy Jack Hovnor)

Vents and Hoods

Before air-conditioning became so common on boats, ventilation was given much higher priority than it seems to get today. Cowl vents came in many sizes and shapes, including beautiful polished-brass cowls made of sheet metal. Screw-in rain and spray hoods were used on round portlights. These permitted the windows to be left wide open even in a heavy rain. A venturi vent was not uncommon. This vent uses the energy in the wind flow to create a suction to exhaust cabin air, and often both an inlet and outlet are included in the same vent. All of these are worth keeping in mind and applying today. For instance, rain and spray hoods could be configured to fit more common rectangular windows. They could be fabricated from plastic and can snap in place rather than screw in.

Sheet metal cowl vent

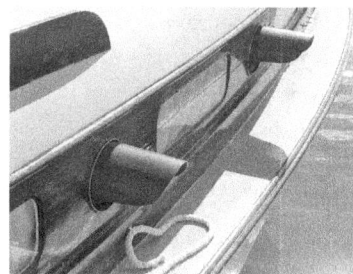

Rain hoods for round portlight

Venturi vent

cabin side), there are remote solar panels available to power each vent.

Electric-Powered Air: Blowers and Ducts

Larger boats may have compartments on a lower deck or inboard, where it isn't convenient or possible to install a vent directly through the cabin roof. On a 180-footer (55 m) with twin lower decks, this gets into full HVAC design with integrated heating and air-conditioning. On vessels under 90 feet (27 m) or so, you can generally provide natural ventilation through relatively short ducts and keep the air-conditioning and heating separate. In fact, this may be the best approach because even if the heating and air-conditioning system go offline, the separate, simple ventilation system will still provide basic comfort.

Again, you can determine the air required by either the VCR for a given compartment or the number of people expected to be in that compartment. But you have to allow for the losses in the ducting system that directs the air to the compartment. Detailed analysis of a

TABLE 14-4. ABYC ESTIMATED EFFECT OF BLOWER SYSTEM COMPONENTS

Item	Percent Loss of Blower Rated Capacity
Ducting	2% per ft. of length, or 6.56% per m of length
Ducting Bends—90°	10% each bend
Clamshell Vent Intake	20%
Louver	20%
Screen—¼-in. (6.35 mm) mesh	10%

Figure 14-10. Squirrel-cage blower (Courtesy Vetus Den Ouden)

ventilation duct is complex, but a simple approximation can be used for small, ducted systems up to about 14 feet (4.3 m) long, as shown in Table 14-4.

Example: In the master stateroom from earlier, we found we needed between 46.8 and 62.4 cfm, say 55 cfm. This stateroom is entirely below the aft saloon. The windows on the hull side are too close to the waterline to open safely. Vent ducts can run down from the cabin roof. They enter from a mushroom vent on the roof and go straight down the cabin side for 9 feet to exit through louver grilles via a 90-degree bend. Percent loss of blower capacity is

$$9 \text{ feet} \times 2\% \text{ per foot} = 18\%$$
$$90\text{-degree bend} = 10\%$$
$$\text{Louver grille} = 20\%$$
$$\text{Total approximate loss} = 58\%$$
$$\text{Effective vent output} = 100\% - 58\% = 42\% \text{ of blower's rated cfm output}$$

Required blower capacity is then

$$55 \text{ cfm} \div 0.42 = 131 \text{ cfm}$$

NOTE: If the approximate loss is over 80 percent, this simple approach is not adequate, and a detailed duct analysis is required.

The 131 cfm could be handled by a standard 3-inch squirrel-cage blower (Figure 14-10), rated at 150 cfm.

Or

Example: In the master stateroom from earlier, we found we needed between 79 m^3/hr. and 106 m^3/hr., say 93 m^3/hr. This stateroom is entirely below the aft saloon. The windows on the hull side are too close to the waterline to open safely. Vent ducts can run down from the cabin roof. They enter from a mushroom vent on the roof and go straight down the cabin side for 2.74 meters to exit through louver grilles via a 90-degree bend. Percent loss of blower capacity is

$$2.74 \text{ m} \times 6.56\% \text{ per m} = 18\%$$
$$90\text{-degree bend} = 10\%$$
$$\text{Louver grille} = 20\%$$
$$\text{Total approximate loss} = 58\%$$
$$\text{Effective vent output} = 100\% - 58\% = 42\% \text{ of blower's rated cfm output}$$

Required blower capacity is then

$$93 \text{ m}^3/\text{hr.} \div 0.42 = 221 \text{ m}^3/\text{hr.}$$
$$221 \text{ m}^3/\text{hr.} \div 60 \text{ sec./hr.} = 3.7 \text{ m}^3/\text{min.}$$

NOTE: If the approximate loss is over 80 percent, this simple approach is not adequate, and a detailed duct analysis is required.

The 3.7 m^3/min. could be handled by a standard 7.6 cm squirrel-cage blower, rated at 255 m^3/hr. or 3.7 m^3/min.

As a rule, avoid long duct runs in simple ventilation systems, particularly horizontal ones, unless a complete, detailed duct analysis is performed. One 110-foot (33.5 m) motoryacht I surveyed had a vent duct running from the crew utility room, with washer and dryer, about 70 feet (21 m) aft to vent into the engine room. No calculations were done on the duct blower, which was so underpowered that airflow was too slow. Not only was this ineffective, the velocity was so low that lint from the dryer collected in the duct, largely clogging it and creating a fire hazard. Long air-duct runs—if used—need to be carefully engineered to ensure proper operation.

BLOWER CONFIGURATIONS OR TYPES As a general rule, the most efficient and most common types of blowers are squirrel-cage blowers (centrifugal blowers). Axial blowers (helicoidal blowers) look like "fans." Though in smaller sizes and less-expensive units, axial blowers aren't usually as effective, in larger sizes they can work quite well.

It can be difficult to locate blowers of any type larger than 4 inches (10.2 cm) in diameter. Two sources for large marine blowers are Delta-T Systems of Jupiter, Florida (www.deltatsystems.com), and Gianneschi & Ramacciotti blowers, available in the United States through Cole Marine Distributing, Ft. Lauderdale, Florida (www.colemarine.com). Figure 14-11 shows an axial blower from Delta-T Systems, which is available from 12 to 36 inches diameter, with capacities ranging from 800 to over 25,000 cfm (1,360 m³/hr. to over 42,500 m³/hr.). Moving this much air takes a great deal of power. Large blowers moving over 1,200 cfm (2,000 m³/hr.) or so need to be powered off the AC electric system. Up to about 1,200 cfm (2,000 m³/hr.), you can find blowers that will run off 12- or 24-volt DC.

CONTROLLING NOISE Air flowing too fast through a duct or louvers causes unacceptable noise. To keep this under control, the cross-section area has to be large enough to keep velocity to under 600 feet per minute (fpm) or 3 m/sec. in sleeping spaces and under 800 fpm (4 m/sec.) in other passenger spaces. Machinery spaces can accept up to about 2,000 fpm (10 m/sec.), since duct noise here isn't a factor. Exceed this air velocity in passenger spaces, and you'll need to line or jacket the air ducts with sound insulation. In fact, some home and industrial systems use just this approach—small-diameter, high-velocity air ducts with heavy sound insulation. This reduces the amount of space such ducting takes up, but few such systems are available for marine use.

Example: We can find the velocity in fpm or m/sec. for our cabin air duct with blower as follows:

From Table 14-3, a 3-inch duct has a section area of 7.1 sq. in.

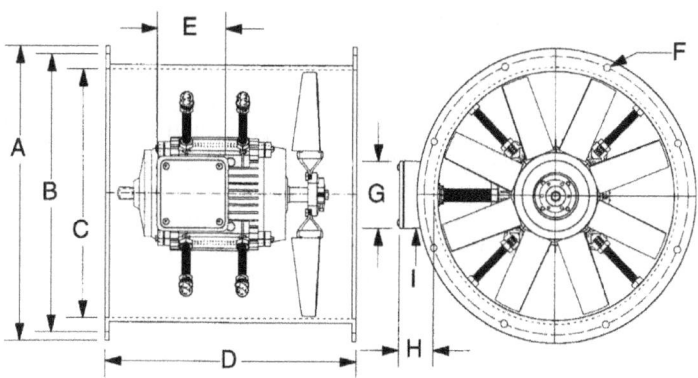

Figure 14-11. Axial blower (Courtesy Delta-T Systems)

7.1 sq in. ÷ 144 sq. in./sq. ft. = 0.049 sq. ft.
131 cfm ÷ 0.049 sq. ft. = 2,673 fpm; this is too fast; need a larger duct

Required duct section for 600 fpm:

131 cfm ÷ 600 fpm max. = 0.218 sq. ft.
0.218 sq. ft. × 144 sq. in./sq. ft. = 31.4 sq. in.

$$\text{Dia.} = 2 \times \sqrt{31.4 \text{ sq. in.} \div \pi} = 6.3 \text{ in.}$$

use a standard 6-in. dia. duct to keep noise down

Or

From Table 14-3, a 7.6-cm duct has a section area of 45.6 cm²:
45.6 cm² ÷ 10,000 cm²/m² = 0.0045 m²
221 m³/hr. ÷ 0.0045 m² = 49,111 m/hr.
49,111 m/hr. ÷ 3,600 sec./hr. = 13.6 m/sec.; too fast; need a larger duct

Required duct section for 3 m/sec.:

221 m³/hr. ÷ 3,600 sec./hr. = 0.0614 m³/sec.
0.0614 m³/sec. ÷ 3 m/sec. max. = 0.02 m²
0.02 m² × 10,000 cm²/m² = 200 cm²

$$\text{Dia.} = 2 \times \sqrt{200 \text{ cm}^2 \div \pi} = 15.9 \text{ cm}$$

use a standard 150 mm dia. duct to keep noise down

The on/off switch ideally would be located next to the main overhead cabin light by the stateroom door and clearly labeled as "Ventilator."

Note that the 3-inch (7.6 cm) squirrel-cage blower we specified for this vent duct is acceptable, but it has a rather high speed and can produce a high-pitched whine. This is not a problem in machinery compartments, but it could be undesirable around cabin areas. Now that we know we'll use a 6-inch (150 mm) duct, we can specify a lower-speed axial blower 6 inches (150 mm) in diameter, as long as it is rated at least the required 131 cfm (221 m³/hr., 3.7 m³/sec.) or somewhat more. This would provide the quietest powered ventilation for our below-deck cabin. In general, try to keep blowers away from passenger areas, though often practical considerations make this difficult.

LARGE DUCTS MAY TAKE UP TOO MUCH SPACE Of course, this 6-inch-diameter (150 mm) duct takes up much more space than the smaller 3-inch (7.6 cm) duct we initially considered. This can be a problem. The duct needs to run where it won't interfere with the accommodations, structure, or machinery. You don't want the duct exposed on the inside of finished accommodations spaces either. Some references allow as much as 1,200 fpm (6 m/sec.) as acceptable with regard to noise. This is on the high side, and at 900 fpm (4.7 m/sec.) noise will be definitely noticeable in quiet spaces like sleeping cabins. Still, you may have no choice in some instances but to go with smaller-diameter ducts and thus higher airflow speeds than is optimal for reducing noise. Such real-world trade-offs may be unavoidable given the limited volume available in some vessels.

PROVIDING AN AIR-INTAKE PATH For most of the cabin ventilation we've been considering, we're assuming that some of the vents are on intake and some are working as exhaust, as shown in the Nicro ventilation schematics in Figures 14-3 and 14-4. In addition, there is free exchange of air between cabins within the boat and to the outside. This is the *permeability* (μ) of the structure. Permeability is generally enough so that cabins can share intake and exhaust air between them. In fact, this permeability to the outside is usually great enough that provisions for additional *make-up air* (in air-conditioning systems) are unnecessary in most boats under 120 feet (36 m) or so. (Make-up air is air taken into the air-conditioning system through a dedicated outside vent to ensure that sufficient fresh air gets into the accommodations.)

For a cabin belowdecks requiring a 9-foot (2.74 m) duct run, intake air due to permeability from another cabin—from a vent located somewhere else on deck—can't be counted on. For this reason, a second passive intake duct should be provided with the same diameter or one size larger than the blower duct. This is assuming that the blower is on the exhaust duct.

INTAKE AIR TRAVELS A STRAIGHT PATH; OUTLET AIR DOES NOT Keep in mind that intake air generally travels a straight path out of the outlet opening in a compartment until it strikes something. Outtake air (suction) tends to be sucked into its inlet from the entire general area nearby. I once made the mistake of installing an engine-air intake and outlet high up on the same aft bulkhead in the engine compartment, one port and the other starboard. The vents were large but the engine room got terribly hot. A quick check using cigarette smoke during sea trials showed that the inlet air was blowing straight across the bulkhead from port to starboard and exiting immediately. Luckily, this was easily corrected by installing an air-duct hose over the outlet opening and running it down to the lower starboard corner of the engine room. This immediately corrected the problem and created a nice diagonal circular rotation of airflow in and around the machinery space.

Apply this principle to any vent system you install. For our below-deck stateroom, the intake air louver grille should be, say, high up and forward on the starboard side, with the outlet (exhaust) air grille low down and aft on the port side.

EXHAUST OR INTAKE? An important thing to keep in mind is that all powered vents for areas with unpleasant smells should be exhaust vents. This sucks the bad air out and draws sweet air in. It's tempting to try to blow fresh air into a head or galley, but don't do it—you'll simply blast the foul air into the rest of the boat. You can blow into sleeping accommodations, salons, or other social gathering areas, however.

Mushroom Vents on Hatches

If a boat has plenty of hatches, often one of the easiest places to install a mushroom vent (solar powered or passive) is in the middle of a hatch. The advantage is that you don't have to cut any of the deck structure or worry about hidden wiring or plumbing when installing the vent. When the hatches are closed, the vents work well. The drawback is that you effectively lose the vents when the hatches are open. I've installed lots of vents in hatches, but wherever possible, I prefer to install them on the deck (or cabin side) proper, so both the open hatches and the vents work with the hatches open.

Staying Alive

Another absolutely vital consideration is carbon monoxide. I can't stress this strongly enough. Be very, very careful not to locate vents where they can suck in exhaust gases from the engine, gen set, cabin heater, or stove. Carbon monoxide and carbon dioxide are silent killers. Every season I read of a family who went to sleep aboard some evening and never woke up because of CO poisoning. This is serious business. You should review a copy of ABYC's standard TH-22, *Educational Information about Carbon Monoxide*.

VENTILATION OF STORAGE SPACES: FOREPEAK, LAZARETTE, LOCKERS

A sure way to gum things up is to neglect ventilation of the storage areas on a boat. Forepeaks and lazarettes are frequently neglected when it comes to ventilation. Table 14-1 gives the VCRs required for the forepeak and lazarette as 5, but 8 for storage compartments. I tend to use 8 for both the forepeak and lazarette as these are really storage areas, but a VCR of 5 is acceptable.

Neglecting to install vents here can be literally sickening. In one case, I was surveying a boat that had no ventilation in a separate forepeak. The durn thing had been sealed closed for months, with soaking wet lines, fenders, and anchor gear festering in the hot sun. The stench that wafted off the greenish, yellow mildew made me ill. It had also ruined the fender covers and life preservers.

Figure 14-12 shows the foredeck of *Imagine*. The forepeak is completely walled off by a watertight bulkhead. It's entered thorough the flush hatch to port. The circular

Figure 14-12. The author on the foredeck of Imagine. *Note the solar vent amidships between the anchor chains. Note the louvre vent on the starboard bulwark.*

object forward of the windlasses and between the chains is a 4-inch (10.2 cm) Nicro solar day/night vent mounted on a 4-inch-high (10.2 cm) riser and set on exhaust. Behind the louvers and behind the fashion plate is a pair of gooseneck pipe vents, which provide the intake air. This peak has stayed pleasant and mildew-free.

Individual lockers should be ventilated as well. Deck lockers, for instance, can have clamshell vents port and starboard angle down and toward midships (Figure. 14-13).

Figure 14-13. Clamshell vent on a locker

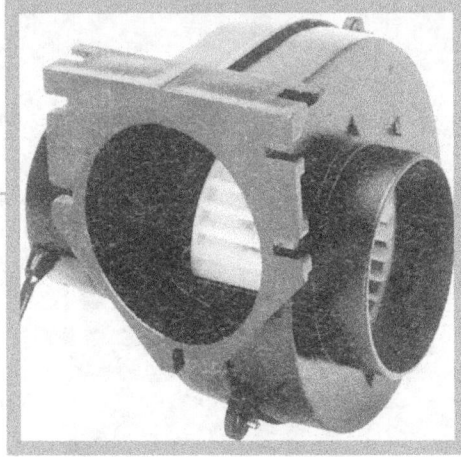

CHAPTER 15

Air-Conditioning and Heating
With Notes on Refrigeration

AIR-CONDITIONING

Though 30 or 40 years ago air-conditioning was primarily a luxury found in large vessels, today more boats and smaller boats have air-conditioning installed. Air-conditioning units, of course, cool the air, but they are called "air-conditioners" rather than "air coolers" because they also condition the air by reducing humidity—a critical component in comfort. (In large home and commercial installations, air-conditioners also further condition the air by filtering it.)

Pumping Heat

Air-conditioning, in fact, does not make cold. Instead, air-conditioning moves heat from place to place. On boats, it pumps the heat from the cabin interior and dispels it into the water outside. Indeed, air-conditioners are really heat pumps. Essentially, they all work similarly. The compressor changes (compresses) the refrigerant into a high-temperature vapor at high pressure. The vapor flows through the heat exchanger where it loses heat to the seawater and condenses into a liquid at high temperature and pressure. From here, the refrigerant travels to the evaporator (in the cabin), where it passes though a small orifice. (The evaporator is in the air handler, which includes an evaporator coil with metal heat-transfer fins and blower.) Passing through this orifice into the evaporator tubes causes the liquid to expand. Thus, it is transformed into a low-temperature vapor at low pressure. Heat from the cabin air blowing over the evaporator is absorbed by the now cold refrigerant, and the cooled air is blown back into the cabin. The refrigerant continues back to the compressor where the cycle repeats.

Freon Anyone?

For years, the refrigerant in more than 90 percent of air-conditioners (and in refrigerators, which operate using the same principle) was Freon. Freon, however, is a chlorofluorocarbon (CFC). CFCs are the chemicals that have been dissolving holes in our ozone layer, so they've been almost entirely banned. New air-conditioners use various alternative refrigerants such as DuPont's HFC-134a (a hydrofluorocarbon), R-12 or R-22 (also hydrofluorocarbons), or OZ Technology's HC-12a (an organic, environmentally compatible hydrocarbon compound).

Air-Conditioner Types

For boats, just two types of air-conditioning are commonly available: direct expansion and chilled water. Chilled-water systems (also termed "tempered-water systems") are intended for larger vessels—over 75 feet (23 m). This is the industrial system found in many commercial buildings and business complexes. When installed in a boat, the chilled-water system uses a compressor and evaporator located in the machinery compartment to cool water (the chilled water), which is then pumped around the boat to air handlers in the cabin spaces. In this case, the air handlers are not evaporators. The evaporator is back in the machinery space, where it chills the water. Unless you're dealing with a 75-footer (23 m) or up, chilled or tempered water is not for you, which is a bit of a shame because it's the quietest air-conditioning available. On the other hand, the plumbing system for a chilled-water air-conditioning system is complex. Initial expense is high, and trained HVAC technicians are required for installation and for any major repairs. Many quite large vessels avoid chilled-water air-conditioning for these reasons.

Direct-expansion systems (which work as described earlier) are also available in two flavors: self-contained direct-expansion and split direct-expansion. Fundamentally, they are exactly the same. Indeed, some self-contained units can be converted to split types simply by, well, splitting them. The split-expansion system (Figure 15-1) is nothing

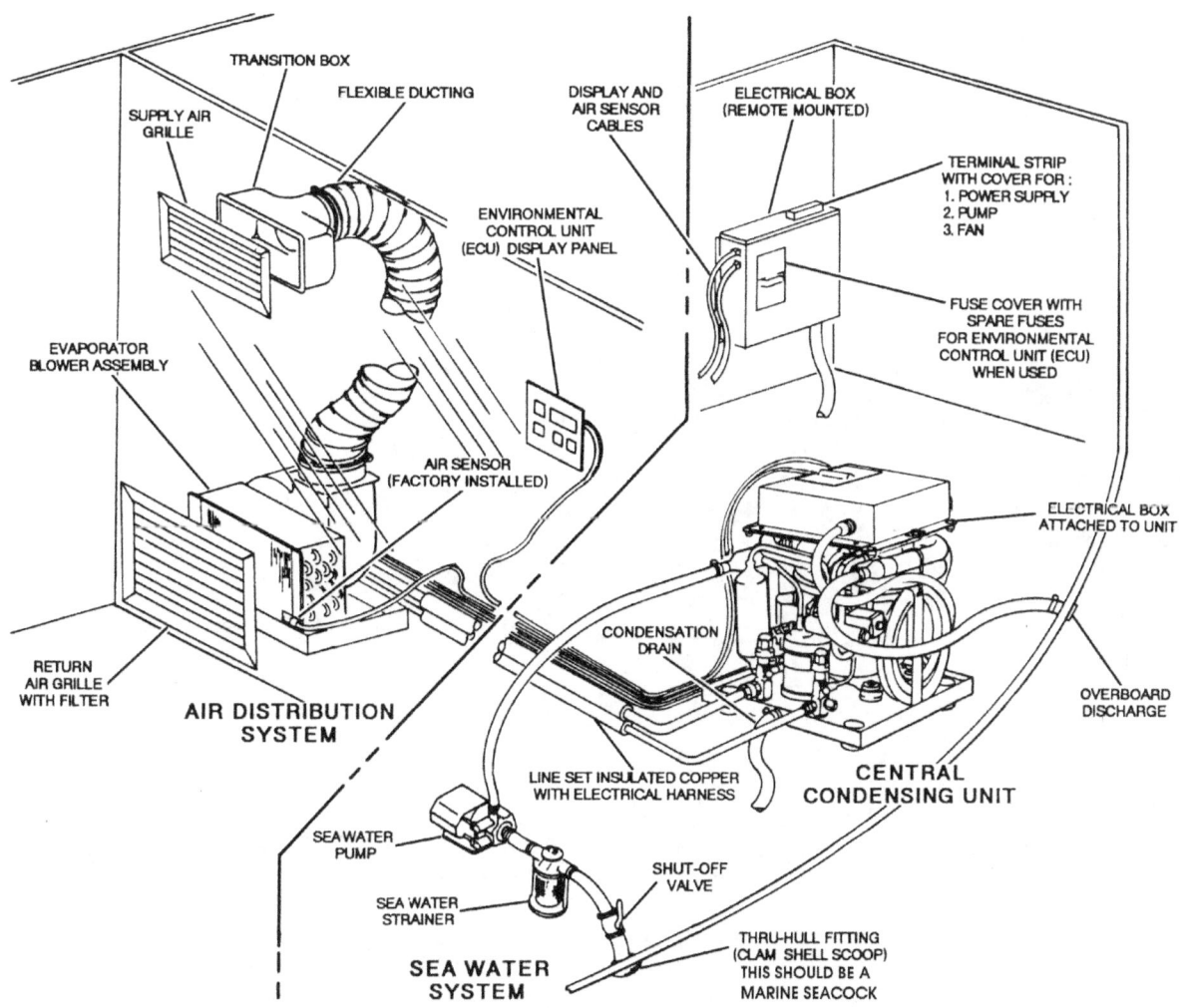

Figure 15-1. Split direct-expansion air-conditioner (Courtesy Marine Air Systems, Inc.)

more than an air-conditioning unit in which the compressor and condenser have been separated from the air handler (the evaporator/heat-exchanger and blower in the cabin). This is sometimes termed the "central-condenser system," because on larger vessels, a single compressor and condenser (properly sized) can service more than one evaporator/heat-exchanger/blower unit (air handler) in the various cabins.

Usually, the compressor/condenser is located in the machinery compartment. The refrigerant travels to and from the cabin evaporators through insulated hoses. There are two nice pluses to split-expansion installations: One is that the noise of the compressor and seawater pump are kept out of the cabin. The other is that the evaporator/air-handler alone is a more compact package to work into tight accommodation spaces. The drawback to split-expansion systems is that, since the refrigerant is transferred in special insulated hose, the system should be installed and charged with refrigerant by professionals.

Self-contained direct-expansion systems (Figure 15-2) are somewhat larger and noisier in the cabin itself, but they can be retrofitted

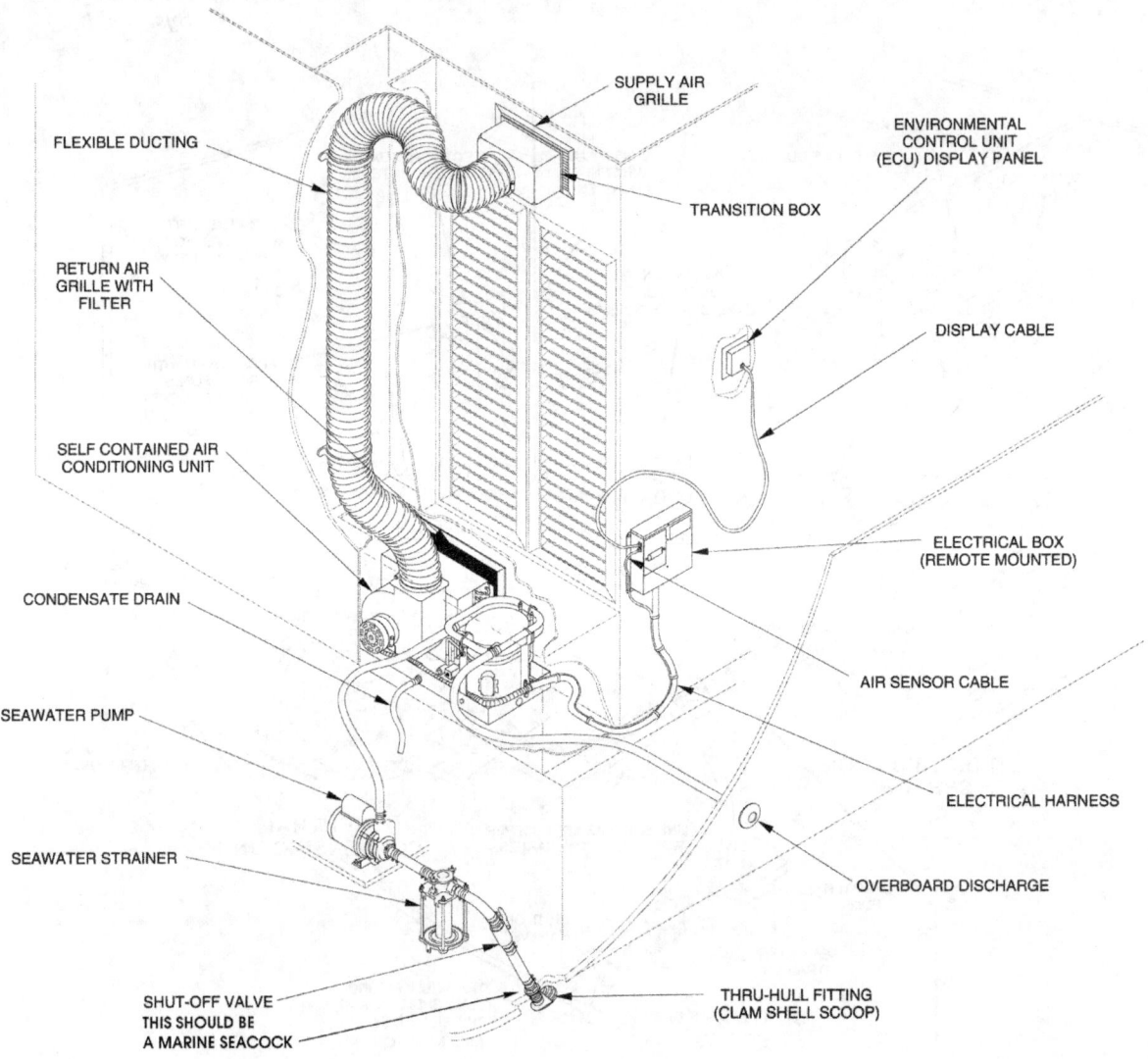

Figure 15-2. Single direct-expansion air-conditioner (Courtesy Marine Air Systems, Inc.)

as a home project (a fairly big one) with pretty much everything in one location. Since they are generally simpler to install, they are usually best for smaller boats—under 45 feet (13.7 m) or so. Sometimes, however, it might make sense to have a split system serving most of the accommodations of a large boat, but install one or two self-contained units in areas far from the main machinery space, such as in a wheelhouse located fairly high up.

How Much Air-Conditioning?

The big question (and usually the first one) is, how big or how much? Air-conditioning capacity (like heating) is measured in British thermal units (BTUs). Interestingly, although you don't want too little capacity, you don't want too much either. More than you need is definitely not better. Not only does this put excess drain on the boat's electric system, but also, such oversize air-conditioners don't work efficiently. Indeed, a principal portion of the air-conditioner's job is not just to remove heat, but also to reduce humidity by taking water out of the air. Air-conditioners do this by condensing the water out. This occurs because warm air can hold more moisture—in the form of vapor—than cool air can. As the warm air cools in the evaporator/air-handler, it reaches its dew point, the temperature at which the water vapor condenses out of the air into liquid water droplets. These droplets are deposited on the outside of the evaporator's coils. Air leaves the evaporator not only cooler but much drier, and the dryness (even more than the coolness) makes for comfort. Oversize systems run too cold and are less effective at removing moisture, because air passes too quickly over the cold evaporator coils, or because it cycles on less often. Oversize systems can also ice up, which makes them almost totally ineffective.

The Condensation Problem

So much moisture condenses out of the air (and then drips off the evaporator coils) that the water absolutely must be collected carefully and routed overboard. It's surprising to me just how often this feature is overlooked. Whether you're installing a new air-conditioning system or inspecting an existing one, make doubly certain that there's a good, large, deep drip-collector pan under the evaporator. Then double-check to see that it has a drain hose that leads to a sump, which then pumps overboard.

It's not uncommon to see the drip-collector drain lead directly into the bilge. This isn't good practice. After all, your goal is to keep water out of the bilge. On a hot, humid day, you could easily accumulate several gallons of fresh water in this way. Such accumulated fresh water leads to disagreeable smells, mildew, fungus, and similar unpleasantness.

Sizing Air-Conditioners

For preliminary design and as a check, you can use Formula 15-1, which I worked up to estimate Btus required based on boat displacement.

Formula 15-1. Preliminary Estimate of Required Btus of Air-Conditioning

Btu = 3,000 + (1,500 × disp. tons)
(for southern waters add 10 percent)

Formula 15-1.

Units for Measuring Air-Conditioning Output

In the United States and Canada, the Btu is the standard measure of heat energy. This is the heat energy needed to increase the temperature of 1 pound of water by 1°F, which is very roughly equal to the heat energy given off by burning one match. I guess you could say that a 16,000 Btu air-conditioner is a 16,000-match cooling system. A Btu is equal to 252 calories per hour.

When quantifying air-conditioner output, BTUs are really Btu per hour (Btu/hr.). One Btu/hr. is 0.293 watts. Or

Btu/hr. × 0.293 = watts
watts ÷ 0.293 = Btu/hr.
1,000 Btu/hr. × 0.293 = kilowatts
kilowatts ÷ 0.293 = 1,000 Btu/hr.

In Europe, air-conditioning units are often sold based on their output in kW (kilowatts). You can use the preceding formulas to convert the required capacity in Btu (really Btu/hr.) to kW.

PART FIVE: VENTILATION, AIR-CONDITIONING, AND HEATING

Where
Btu = British thermal units
Disp. tons = boat displacement in long tons or metric tons

The standard method for determining required air-conditioner capacity more precisely than Formula 15-1 permits is to use the vessel's cabin volumes below deck and above deck as a basis for calculating the required BTUs, as in Formula 15-2.

Formula 15-2.

Formula 15-2. Recommended Air-Conditioner Capacity

Below-Deck Btu = length, ft. × width, ft. × headroom, ft. × 11 Btu/cu. ft.
Mid-deck Btu = length, ft. × width, ft. × headroom, ft. × 15 Btu/cu. ft.
Above-Deck Btu = length, ft. × width, ft. × headroom, ft. × 17 Btu/cu. ft.

or

Below Deck Btu = length, m × width, m × headroom, m × 388 Btu/m^3
Mid-deck Btu = length, m × width, m × headroom, m × 530 Btu/m^3
Above Deck Btu = length, m × width, m × headroom, m × 600 Btu/m^3

Add 600 Btu for each person in a compartment after the first two people, if more than two people will be in it for any length of time.

Add 4,000 Btu for compartments with a fully equipped galley, and add 6,000 Btu for a large galley (or a galley with a diesel stove) as might be found on a yacht or small-passenger vessel over 100 feet (30 m).

Add the requirements for all compartments to get the total Btu for a system for the entire boat, or treat individual or groups of compartments separately if that makes more sense. For instance, you may want separate air-conditioning systems for forward and after accommodations areas, and a third, smaller system for, say, the wheelhouse. This way, you can run the air-conditioner units only in the areas being used by the crew.

Add 10 or 15 percent to the preceding Btu requirements for tropical waters.

Example: If our boat, *Kool Kat*, were, say, a 32-foot (9.7 m) express cruiser, we might find:

Below-Deck Btu = 13.75 ft. × 11 ft. × 6.4 ft. × 11 Btu = 10,648 Btu
Above-Deck Btu = 6.5 ft. × 8.5 ft. × 6.4 ft. × 17 Btu = 6,011 Btu

or

Below-Deck Btu = 4.2 m × 3.35 m × 1.95 m × 388 Btu/m^3 = 10,645 Btu
Above-Deck Btu = 2 m × 2.6 m × 1.95 m × 600 Btu/m^3 = 6,084 Btu

Total = 16,659 or 16,729 Btu

A 16,000 Btu air-conditioner would do the job in temperate climates, while two 12,000 Btu units would be about right for the tropics. You wouldn't want to install much more, because you would end up with an oversized, inefficient system.

Note that if the above-deck area had a table for four and also a full galley, you would add 4,000 Btu for the galley and 1,200 Btu for two additional people. This would bring the above-deck total to 11,200 Btu.

In large compartments requiring 12,000 Btu or more, it's best to have two air handlers on opposite ends (or as close to that as possible). 11,200 Btu is almost 12,000, so it would be a good idea to have a pair of 6,000 Btu air handlers (or a 5,000 and a 6,000 Btu combination) installed at opposite ends.

AC Power for Air-Conditioners

This brings us to the question of where you'll get the juice to power your air-conditioner. Except with small units (7,500 Btu or less), battery banks and inverters simply aren't up to this job. Air-conditioners must be run off AC electric systems. In fact, even a standard 120-volt AC circuit can handle only up to about 20,000 Btu. After that, you have to go to 240-volt AC power. Our *Kool Kat*, with 16,000 Btu, is just under the limit here.

If you have a moderately fast boat and usually anchor at marinas, where you can plug into shore power, you could install an air-conditioning system without a gen set and run it only when you're at the marina overnight. Underway—on all but the hottest days—good natural ventilation should keep you at least reasonably cool. For continuous air-conditioner operation underway and at anchor, however, you simply must have a gen set. Regardless, all air-conditioning systems should be equipped with GFCIs (ground-fault circuit interrupters) to reduce shock hazard.

NOTE: Though you can run air-conditioners under 7,500 Btus off 12 volts DC, I'm not crazy about this arrangement. You will need to add at least a 200-amp high-output alternator and a "smart" voltage regulator in addition to the standard engine alternator. You will also need a generously large house battery bank. The current draw at 12 volts will be so big that running off the batteries only—with the engine off—will quickly draw these down flat. Similarly, at these high currents, thick, heavy, expensive electric cables are required. I feel it's usually best to install a small 2-kilowatt AC gen set to power a 120-volt AC electric air-conditioner; however, these small DC-powered air-conditioners can work acceptably if you are aware of the drawbacks and make allowances for them.

Air-Conditioning Generator Size

How big a generator do you need? The minimum power in kilowatts (kW) required is

$$kW = \text{installed A/C Btu} \div 6{,}000$$

(This includes and allows for the higher starting loads from the compressor motor.)

Accordingly, for good old *Kool Kat*—fitted with 16,000 Btu—we would need 2.7, say, 3 kW (16,000 Btu ÷ 6,000 = 2.7 kW). You really want to install a bit more than the minimum generator capacity, however, because—once you have a gen set—you'll use it to power other things as well. As a rule of thumb, use about 1.5 times the minimum generator size required for the air-conditioner alone. For *Kool Kat*, with 16,000 Btu, a 4-kilowatt gen set would be about perfect. Of course, if you also had a large AC electric fridge, a dishwasher, a microwave, and a washer/dryer, you might very well want a 5- or 6-kilowatt set, but that's an awful lot of gear to cram into our poor old 32-foot (9.7 m) *Kool Kat*.

Don't go overboard on gen-set size. Just as with air-conditioners, excess generator capacity is not good. Not only is such a gen set larger, heavier, and more expensive, but it will be run underloaded for long periods of time, which will cause carbon fouling—bad news.

Reverse Flow Equals Heat

An excellent option for many boats is reverse-cycle air-conditioning. Reverse-cycle means exactly what it says. The refrigerant-flow cycle can be reversed: Rather than pumping warmth from the cabin air and depositing it into the ocean, it takes heat from the seawater and deposits it into the cabin interior. This is surprisingly effective. You can get reliable heating even in water as cold as 40°F (4.5°C) and in outside air temperatures near freezing. In other words—for most boats operating south of Maine during the regular boating season—reverse-cycle air-conditioning will not only cool you in summer but also warm you in the early spring and into the late fall when you haul out. The drawback—and an important one—is that you must have the gen set running whenever you want heat.

If you're going to operate farther north or right into winter, or if you want heat without the gen set on, then reverse-cycle air-conditioning won't do the job. In this case, you'll need an independent diesel-fired heating system.

Compressor Refinements

In the old days, all air-conditioning compressors were piston motors (or in very large units, scroll machines). Over the last 15 years or so, rotary compressors have been introduced, and—after some initial problems—they are now quite reliable. Rotary-compressor air-conditioners have several good qualities: They are smaller, lighter, quieter, and—most important—they use roughly 20 percent less electric power both in continuous operation and for the higher engine-start loads. This is significant. In fact, if you install rotary-compressor air-conditioner(s) in your *Kool Kat*, you can take advantage of this to reduce the minimum required generator size by 15 percent. Indeed, if we'd installed an all-rotary air-conditioning system in *Kool Kat*, we could have used just a 3.5-kilowatt gen set rather than the slightly larger 4-kilowatt, while

PART FIVE: VENTILATION, AIR-CONDITIONING, AND HEATING

preserving the same margin for extra loads. This is even more important on larger vessels with 32,000 Btu air-conditioners or greater.

Pumping Seawater

Another critical component of any marine air-conditioning system is the seawater cooling circuit. Raw seawater is drawn in through a seacock (sea suction, see Chapter 17), filtered through a sea strainer, and passed through the seawater pump (driving this circuit, and drawing about 1 to 2 amps of AC electric power). NOTE: Some boats use a DC electric pump for the seawater cooling circuit. This means that to turn on the air-conditioner, the AC electric breaker must be switched on and the DC breaker must be on for the seawater pump. This needs to be clearly marked at the circuit panel and air-conditioning controls.

From the seawater pump, the water goes to the water-cooled condenser/heat-exchanger. And finally the now-warmed seawater exits overboard via a through-hull. The seawater pump should have at least 200 gallons per hour (757 Lph) of rated flow for every 12,000 Btu. In *Kool Kat*'s case, this is a minimum of 268 gph or 1,015 Lph.

$$16,000 \text{ Btu} \div 12,000 \text{ Btu} = 1.34$$
$$1.34 \times 200 \text{ gph} = 268 \text{ gph}$$

or

$$16,000 \text{ Btu} \div 12,000 \text{ Btu} = 1.34$$
$$1.34 \times 757 \text{ Lph} = 1,014 \text{ Lph}$$

A single pump (with sufficient capacity) can supply two or more air-conditioning-unit heat-exchangers through a T-fitting or a manifold (Figure 15-3).

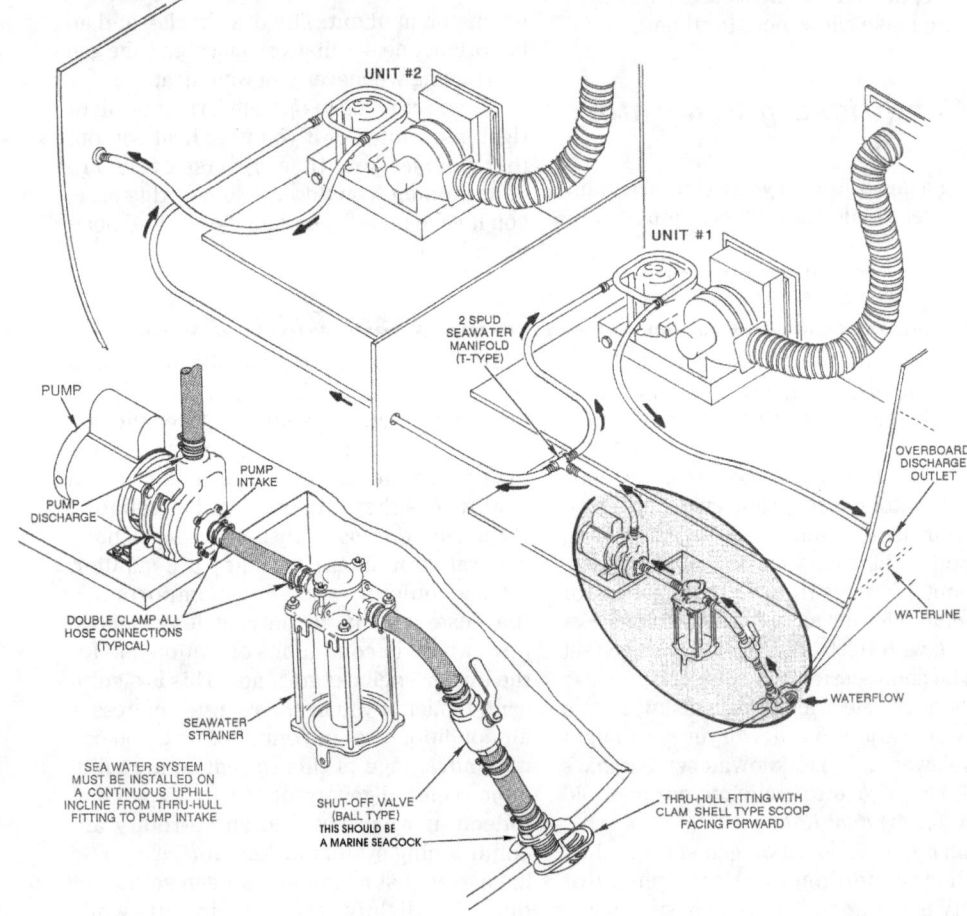

Figure 15-3. Seawater pump serving two self-contained direct-expansion air-conditioning units (Courtesy Marine Air Systems, Inc.)

Almost all air-conditioning seawater pumps are magnetic-drive centrifugal pumps. Such pumps don't have shaft seals to worry about, but they're also not self-priming. Accordingly, the pump must be located below the waterline in the bilge—it must have a positive suction head (see Chapter 19). The seawater circuit must run from the seacock to the pump below the waterline and then gradually and continuously rise to the condenser located above the waterline. From there the water drains through the exit through-hull, which is located below the condenser but a bit above the waterline so you can look to see that there's flow. Don't locate this exit through-hull too high, because the noise of the water will annoy both you and your neighbors. Six inches (15 cm) above the waterline is ideal—8 inches (20 cm) is the maximum, 4 inches (10 cm) the minimum.

Do not try and dump the condensation drain water into this same seawater exit hose or through-hull. If you do, debris in the condensate can block the seawater outlet. Then the seawater will back up and empty into the drip-collector pan, and from there empty into bilge, giving your bilge pump a good workout and possibly sinking the boat! Also, be sure the sea suction follows the recommendations in Chapter 17.

A simple test to see if the heat exchanger is working properly is to put your hand on it after the air-conditioner has been on for a while. If the heat exchanger is too hot to touch, it's not functioning properly.

Recirculating Air to the Air-Conditioning Air Handler

All too often air-conditioners are installed where the return air (the warm air coming back in for cooling) can be sucked in from outside the cooled area. Sucking in air from a crack or hole leading to the bilge is a common mistake. The bilge is humid and not part of the cooled accommodations area.

To remove humidity from the air, the air in the compartment must be recirculated through the air-conditioning air handler on repeated passes. Each successive pass draws out more moisture and further drops the temperature. If you allow outside air into the return-air inlet, you continue to add humidity and thus fail to obtain the decreased temperature and humidity achieved from recirculation. If this air comes from the bilge, it may also disperse foul smells and can potentially suck in deadly carbon monoxide.

The exception to this is make-up air, which may be deliberately added from a dedicated intake duct to a large air-conditioning system to ensure sufficient fresh air in the cabin. As noted earlier, most boats have sufficient permeability (air leaking in) so that make-up air is not required.

Avoiding Carbon Monoxide Dangers

Oh yes, an improperly installed air-conditioner can kill you! How? By causing you to ingest carbon monoxide, carbon dioxide, and other exhaust gases into the air ducts. Do not *ever* run the air ducts through engine spaces, and make very, very sure the ducting can't swallow exhaust gases from the main engine, the generator, or from nearby boats. Do not *ever* install a self-contained air-conditioner unit inside an engine compartment so it can take in warm (return) air from an engine compartment. Check, double-check, and triple-check this. If any of these gases do find their way in, well, you could go to sleep one night and wake up dead.

Smoothing the Flow

A final consideration is that the air ducts themselves should be as large as will fit and should have as few and as gentle bends as possible. Narrow ducts, many tight bends, and tiny outlet grilles can smother your air-conditioner. You'll have all those BTUs installed and wonder where they went to. Keep in mind that cool air sinks and warm air rises. Accordingly, the cool-air outlet grille should be sited as high as possible, and the return-air inlet grille should be as low as possible.

Most air-conditioners come with manufacturer-supplied ducting, distribution and junction boxes, grilles, and such. You can, however, keep in mind that 12,000 Btu of air-conditioning is about equal to 400 cfm (680 m^3/hr.) of airflow. You can use this and the limit of 600 to 800 feet per minute (fpm) or 3 m/sec. to 4 m/sec. (as described in controlling noise in vent ducts) to estimate duct size.

PART FIVE: VENTILATION, AIR-CONDITIONING, AND HEATING

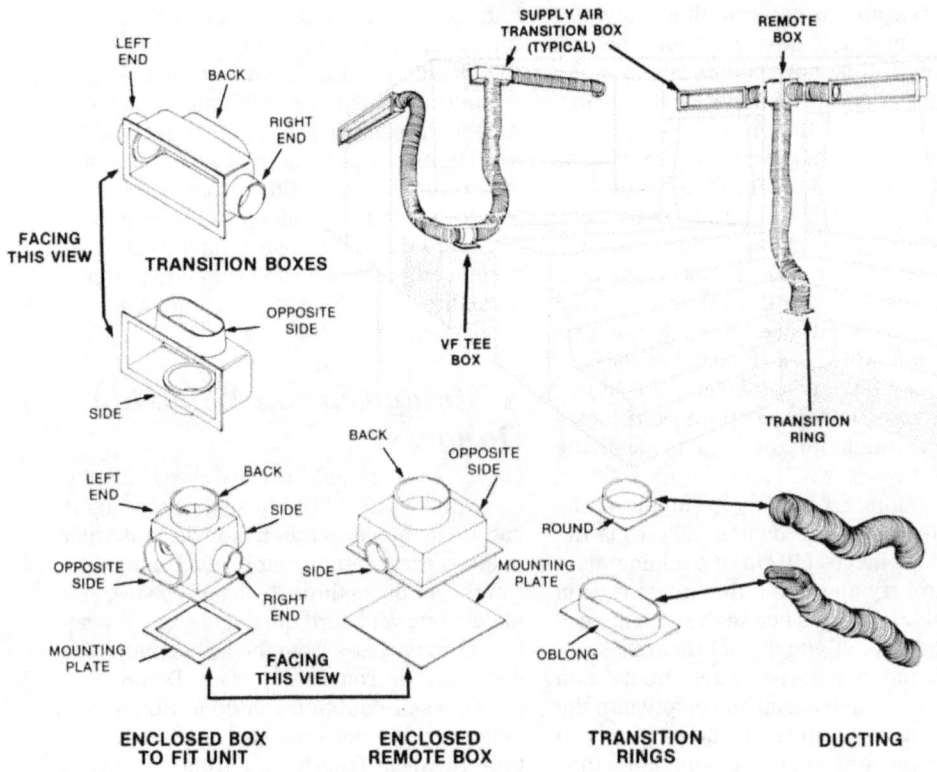

Figure 15-4. Typical air-conditioner ducting (Courtesy Marine Air Systems, Inc.)

Tons of Air-Conditioning

You'll often hear air-conditioning technicians referring to the size of air-conditioning units in *tons*. A ton of air-conditioning is simply another measure of cooling (really heat transfer) capacity. We've seen that the Btu is the British thermal unit, or the quantity of heat required to raise the temperature of 1 pound of water by 1 degree Fahrenheit.

By comparison, a thermodynamic ton (as opposed to weight or mass) is the amount of energy required to melt a 1-ton block of freshwater ice in 24 hours. One ton is roughly equal to 12,000 BTUs or 3.51 kW. Thus, the 16,000 Btus (4.7 kW) installed in *Kool Kat* is a 1.3-ton air-conditioning system.

NOTES ON REFRIGERATION

As with air-conditioning, the widespread installation of refrigeration is a relatively new development. Thirty or forty years ago, almost all boats had only iceboxes. A simple icebox has plenty to recommend it: no moving parts, nothing to go wrong. For many dayboats and small cruisers, using an icebox makes more sense than installing refrigeration. After all, refrigerators basically work the same way air-conditioners do—which is to say they have many moving parts and require power.

Types of Refrigerators

On boats, refrigerators come in four standard types:

1. **Portable cooler-freezers.** These self-contained portable units run on 12 volts DC, 120 volts AC, or both.

250

2. **House-style, front-opening electric refrigerators and freezers.** These are usually powered with 120 volts AC but may be powered to run off 12 volts DC instead of or in addition to 120 volts.
3. **Icebox conversions.** This is a bit of a misnomer, as many of these are designed to fit in purpose-built insulated boxes to form refrigerators. These systems can be thought of as the mechanical "guts" of standard fridges. They may run off 12 or 24 volts DC, 120 volts AC, a compressor clutched directly from the main engine, or some combination of these.
4. **Holding-plate or eutectic-plate systems.** These also fall under the so-called icebox-conversion category; however, they may be the most efficient refrigeration available for boats. They may run off 12 or 24 volts DC, 120 volts AC, a compressor clutched directly from the main engine, or some combination of these.

Portable coolers and freezers are suited to day boats and as extra refrigeration capacity for, say, big parties on larger vessels. The only requirements are a place to stow them properly and a proper electric connection with suitable power.

House-style, front-opening electric refrigerator/freezers are commonly used on small to midsize powerboats. Their advantage is that they function just like the fridge in your home. They are not particularly efficient compared with built-in fridges, however. These self-contained, front-opening units have only modest insulation, and their large, front-opening doors spill out much of the cold air every time they are opened. Also, the boat needs lots of electric power to run these units. A cruising powerboat runs these off 120 volts AC at the dock or when the generator is running. Many of these units have a built-in inverter to allow them to run off DC power under way. Alternatively, you can get a true household unit and run it off the batteries through the shipboard inverter. Both work acceptably. (Note that units with built-in inverters should not be run off shipboard AC from the boat's inverter.)

Another drawback to a front-opening door is that the unit can dump much of its contents if opened in rough weather. I remember spending more than 20 minutes crawling around the saloon floor of one of my office's motor cruisers, collecting all the stuff that sprang out when someone opened the fridge in a 50-knot storm. Not my favorite way to get exercise, though an excellent way to sharpen reflexes!

Because of their easy availability and familiarity, it's becoming increasingly common to find household-type refrigerator/freezers installed on quite large boats. Though they are acceptable, I recommend custom, built-in refrigerators and freezers, run off cold plates—at least as the primary refrigeration. Not only is this more efficient, but these built-in units can have much greater volume to store the large amounts of food such sizable vessels need.

Icebox conversions are ideal for small sailboats. Because sailboats run their engines so infrequently and often don't have a generator, maximizing refrigeration efficiency is paramount. Top-opening fridge compartments are built in with 3 to 6 inches (75 to 150 mm) of foam insulation. The thick insulation and top opening retain the cold air much better than a household-style front-opening fridge. Still, these units may cycle on and off about 30 percent of the time.

Holding-plate or eutectic-plate systems operate the same way as any other refrigeration (Figure 15-5), but they freeze a thin box (the plate) filled with the eutectic solution of an easily melted material that has a freezing point lower than water. The frozen eutectic plate "holds" the cold for several hours. In a well-insulated box, proper temperatures can be maintained with only a couple of hours of compressor operation per day.

Powering Icebox Conversions and Holding-Plate Systems

Both the so-called icebox conversions and the holding-plate systems can be powered off 12 or 24 volts DC or 120 volts AC. Alternatively, their compressor may be clutched right off the main engine. The direct-engine-driven compressor is the most efficient, as there is no loss in converting engine power

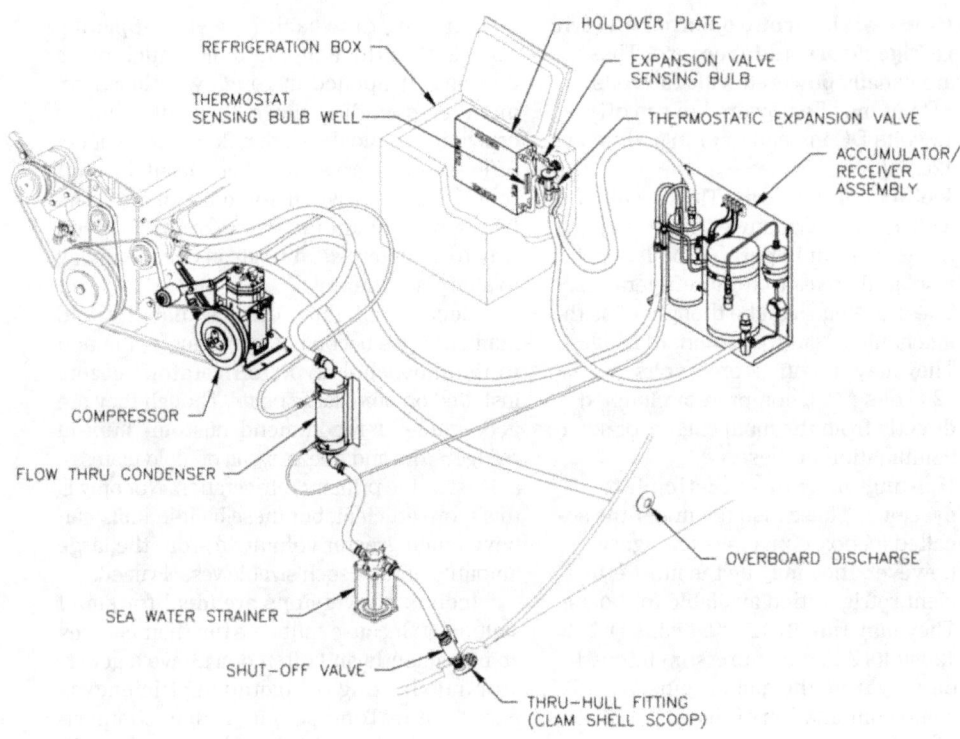

Figure 15-5. Engine-driven holding-plate refrigeration. If this were a 12-volt system the compressor would be driven off a 12-volt motor. (Courtesy Taylor Made Environmental/ Grunert)

to electricity. (Every conversion from one type of energy to another involves losses.) If you are not aboard to run the engine, though, there is no way to keep the icebox cool. This is a problem if—on a cruise—you leave the boat at anchor for two or three days to explore on land. The food in the fridge will go bad.

For this reason, I generally recommend 12- or 24-volt DC power for these systems. If you are careful to top up your batteries, you can leave for several days and the unit will continue to cycle on and off as needed to keep things cool. The 120-volt AC power option enables you to plug these systems in at the dock.

Water-Cooled Heat Exchangers

Another reason household-style fridges are less efficient is that they are air cooled. The heat-exchanger coil on the fridge simply dumps the heat pumped out of the box into the surrounding cabin air. As we saw with air-conditioners, the more efficient way to expel unwanted heat is through a seawater heat exchanger. For either the icebox conversions or the holding-plate systems—though air-cooled units are available—I recommend you go only with seawater heat-exchangers.

CABIN HEATING

With good ventilation, air-conditioning and refrigeration can be considered optional. Both enhance comfort, but sailors have voyaged the globe without either for centuries. Heat is another matter. Without some form of heat, boats can be brutally uncomfortable in cold weather—even deadly. Protracted cold leads to fatigue, poor judgment, and even real danger from hypothermia. There are just seven standard options for cabin heating:

1. Old-time coal or wood stoves and fireplaces
2. Reverse-cycle air-conditioning
3. Direct electric cabin heating

Insulation for Fridges and Freezers

Standard insulation materials for built-in refrigerators and freezers are foams such as pour-in-place polystyrene, urethane, or isocyanate board. They all work by encapsulating bubbles of entrapped air. The efficiency of insulation (its resistance to transmitting heat energy) is measured as its *R-value*. All these standard foam insulations have R-values approximated as follows for a given thickness:

Thickness		
In.	mm	R-Value
3	75	15
4	100	20
5	125	25
6	150	30

The minimum thickness for built-in fridges is 3 inches (75 mm), with 4 inches (100 mm) or more being optimal. The minimum thickness for built-in freezers is 4 inches (100 mm), with 5 inches (125 mm) or more being optimal. The problem here is obvious. After allowing for the structure of the box itself and then adding the insulation and watertight interior liner (usually fiberglass or wood/epoxy), a tremendous amount of volume is lost to insulation. A relatively new development is Dow Chemical's VacuPanel. These are available as 1-inch-thick (25 mm) panels with an incredible R-value of 75. This is equal to 15 inches (380 mm) of standard foam! The drawback to VacuPanel is that it is rigid and cannot be shaped. You must build the box around the flat regular shapes that the VacuPanel comes in.

4. Diesel or kerosene bulkhead heaters
5. Engine-heat heaters
6. Diesel-fired hot-air heaters
7. Diesel-fired hot-water heaters (hydronic heaters)

An eighth option is cabin heaters powered by propane (LPG). These can operate exactly the same as options 4, 6, and 7. There are liquefied petroleum gas (LPG) heating systems manufactured specifically for and installed on boats, but I recommend against this. Though it's perfectly OK for cooking, relying on the large amount of LPG needed for long-term onboard heating is too risky in my opinion. In addition, the heat energy in LPG is notably less per unit volume and per unit weight than diesel. Further, you'll need two sources of fuel aboard rather than just diesel, and finding the larger LPG tanks required is not easy, particularly within a manageable walk from most marinas or fuel docks. If you do install an LPG/propane cabin heater, you must rigorously follow *all* the recommendations of ABYC, NFPA 302, and the CFR.

Wood and Coal Stoves and Heaters

In the old days, of course, boats relied on simple coal or wood stoves and heaters for both cooking and heating. I have fond memories of the Shipmate Skippy cabin heater (Figure 15-6). This little wood and coal stove produced prodigious quantities of heat for its diminutive size, just 19 inches wide, 13¼ inches high, and 14 inches deep (48 by 34 by 35 cm).

Figure 15-6. Shipmate Skippy cabin heater (Courtesy Shipmate Stove Co.)

Even tinier were the old Fatsco Pet and Tiny Tot stoves. The Pet was a bare 11¾ inches high and 10½ inches in diameter (30 cm high by 27 cm dia.). Sitting atop a coal bin, with the chimney running up through the deck ring (a water iron) and to the smoke head, you could warm the cabin of a boat with no machinery—virtually nothing could go wrong, and you could cook some nice meals to boot. Of course, you had to load the wood and coal as needed and dispose of the ash. Learning the proper flue adjustment, and the art of banking the fire overnight just added to the appeal. ("Banking a fire" means getting it good and hot, and then covering it with a thin layer of ash and partly shutting off the flue. This keeps it burning all night at lower output.) Though Shipmate (which also made gas, kerosene, and alcohol stoves) is long out of business, you can still get true marine coal stoves from Fatsco stoves (Mesick, MI) and the Lunenburg Foundry, in Lunenburg, Nova Scotia; smaller units are now available as well from Navigator Stove Works (www.marinestove.com).

As with any cabin-sole or bulkhead-mounted stove, careful protection from heat and fire is needed. The stove should mount on a tile- or stainless-covered platform, with stainless backing behind the stove over insulation, running right up behind the chimney. The legs must raise the stove at least 5 inches (13 cm) above the mounting surface, and everything must be bolted in extra strongly. I can't imagine anything worse than a full-blast coal stove coming adrift at sea. A strong pipe rail around the stove is recommended to keep you from being accidentally thrown against it, as well as an open mesh or grillwork around the chimney.

A good trick is to run the chimney horizontally through a bulkhead and up and out the other side. This way, the heat from the chimney heats two compartments. Remember—the chimney is *hot!* The bulkhead penetration must be very well insulated. (Some manufacturers make special fittings for just this purpose.)

One nice option is a small bulkhead-mounted fireplace. This is a really pleasant, romantic way to take the chill out of the air, though you can't cook on these little fireplaces.

Figure 15-7. Smokehead with water-iron deck ring

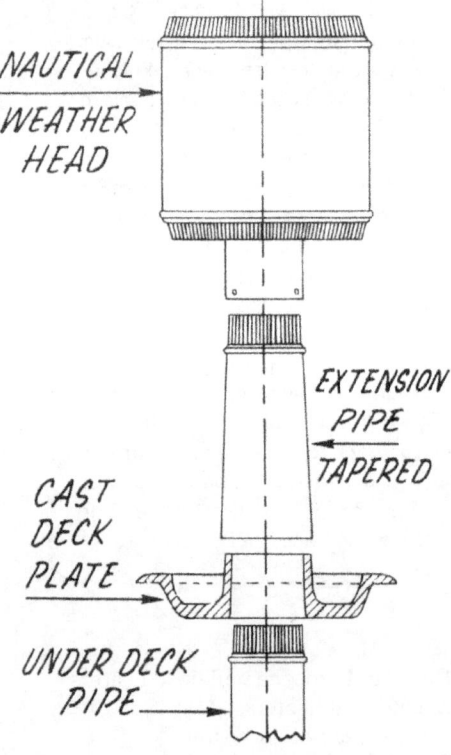

Figure 15-8. Smokehead and water-iron deck ring (Courtesy Fatsco Stoves)

Reverse-Cycle Air-Conditioning

We discussed reverse-cycle air-conditioning previously. Reverse-cycle is simple as part of the A/C system, but it requires a gen set and is limited to delivering heat during moderate temperatures.

Direct Electric Heat

Direct electric heating can make good sense on large yachts or small commercial vessels. It's no different from electric baseboard heating in a home, though because the heater-element size is usually smaller, it often requires a blower. Electric heating is efficient, compact, and easy to install. The drawback is obvious: It takes a lot of electric power. Unless you're running a boat with a couple of generators, one of which will be on almost all the time, it's not for you.

DO NOT USE FREESTANDING ELECTRIC HEATERS Though properly designed and installed marine direct electric heaters are excellent (when the electric power is available), *never* use freestanding electric heaters—that is, the kind you can purchase at a local hardware or home supply store. These heaters are not designed for boats. It can seem a cheap alternative to add one or two of these to keep a boat warm when at the dock, but they are responsible for many boat fires. Beware!

Diesel or Kerosene Bulkhead Heaters

Small bulkhead-mounted heaters fueled by diesel or kerosene can be quite effective and are inexpensive. Usually they can be fed by a gravity tank, so no pump is necessary. But if a gravity tank won't fit, a small electric pump can be installed to take off from the main diesel tanks. (Any tank must meet all the requirements for diesel fuel tanks [Chapter 5], and NFPA 302 limits independent gravity tanks for stoves to a capacity of 2.1 gallons or 8 liters.) Output usually ranges from around 3,000 Btu at low heat on a small unit to as much as 18,000 Btu at high heat on a large unit. This can warm you most effectively in even very cold weather. The drawback is that

Figure 15-9. Diesel cabin heater (Courtesy Dickinson)

as you get farther away from the heater, you get farther away from the heat. A single bulkhead heater in the main saloon may keep this area quite toasty, but it will leave, say, an aft cabin very cold. The trick of running the chimney through the bulkhead (as mentioned for coal stoves) can help here. (Check with the manufacturer for proper fittings and insulation.) Of course, you can install two heaters, one forward and one aft in the boat. This combined with a couple of 12-volt electric fans can distribute the heat moderately well.

Some of these heaters use cabin air for combustion. It is thus vital that there be proper ventilation to the outside. The larger, higher-output models have dedicated combustion-air intake, which is recommended. In addition, ABYC requires an oxygen-depletion sensor, which will automatically turn off the heater should the oxygen content of the air in the cabin be reduced to 95 percent of normal levels. These heaters don't have strong natural draft like old-fashioned wood or coal heaters, which makes arranging the flue tricky. It's necessary to find the right location for the smokehead so downdrafts and backdrafts won't cause problems.

These independent bulkhead heaters make good sense on boats up to about 40 feet (12 m), assuming you can find room for them (they can usually mount on the cabin sole or bulkhead) and you are willing to live with somewhat uneven heat distribution. They are much simpler to install and maintain than diesel-fired hot-air or hot-water heaters (see below). Dickinson, SIG Marine, and Force 10 are three manufacturers of bulkhead heaters.

Engine-Heat Heaters

Engine-heat heaters work by simply circulating engine cooling water through them to generate plenty of hot air in their heat exchanger. This is then ducted throughout the boat with a built-in blower. Since you are using engine heat, there's no extra fuel and (except for some air ducts) virtually no other systems—simple and rugged.

Again, the drawback is obvious. You get heat only when the engine is running. For some commercial boats, engine-heat heaters may serve, particularly if the vessels are not run well into the cold-weather season. Otherwise, having heat only when the engine is running is too much of a limitation.

I actually do install engine-heat heaters on most of my motor cruisers, but for a very specific purpose: windshield defrosting. I specify the smallest of these heaters I can find and duct the hot air in three or four small ducts (about 3 in. or 575 mm) to blow on the inside of the windscreen windows in the pilothouse. This allows you to defrost the windscreen without having to turn on the central hot-air heater. I'm surprised how few boats have a heated windshield defroster system installed. It makes a huge difference in visibility during cold weather.

Electric defrosters available from companies like Heater Craft can also be installed right under the windows. The advantage of these is there's no hose or ducting to run. The disadvantage is the electric load.

Diesel-Fired Hot-Air Heaters

If your home has hot-air heating, it uses basically the same system as diesel-fired hot-air heaters on boats. In a house, the furnace burner heats hot air, which is distributed

Figure 15-10. Typical central hot-air heating system (Courtesy Espar Products, Inc.)

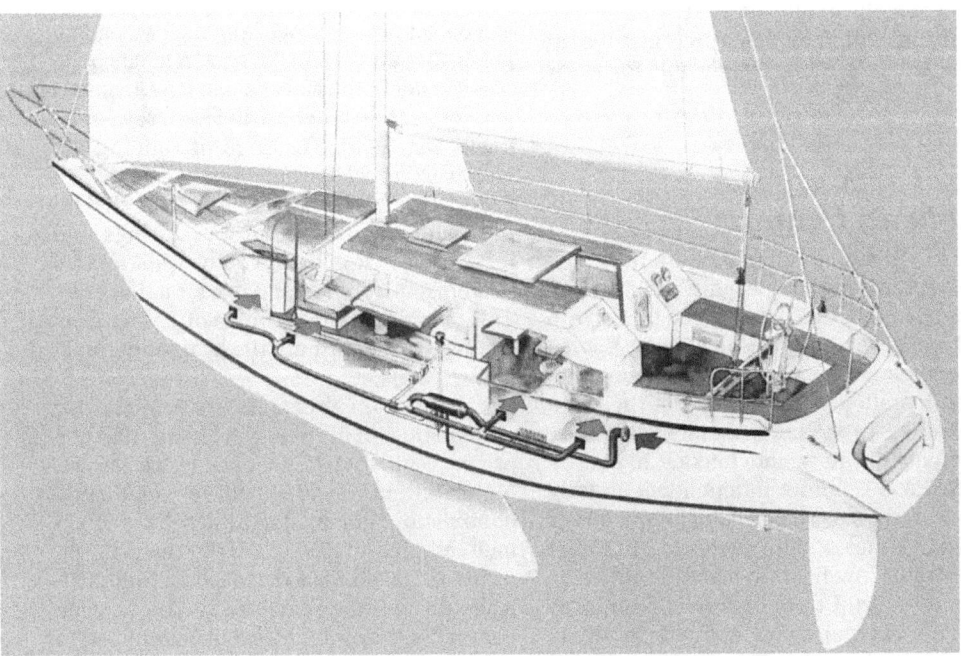

through the house in air ducts. On a boat, a diesel furnace (located in the machinery space, or lazarette, or other compartment well separated from the accommodations) heats the hot air, which is distributed by a blower (usually 12-volt) through the boat via ducts.

Hot-air heaters such as this may be the most common on midsize vessels. There's no need to find space for a bulkhead cabin heater, and because the hot-air ducts are relatively small (4 or 5 in. or 100 to 125 mm dia.) several delivery grilles can be installed throughout the accommodations to ensure even heat distribution. The heater's workings are largely out of sight and out of mind—like your home-heating system. Typical outputs range from around 6,000 Btu for small units to 40,000 Btu for large units.

Hot-air heating is not as efficient as hot-water heating, however, so it's not as satisfactory in really cold weather. Though 4-inch (100 mm) ducts are relatively small, they still take up space and can be awkward to fit in tight spaces. Also, the blower in the heater produces a noticeable dull roar, which can be unpleasant if it's not installed in an insulated compartment far enough from the accommodations. Diesel-fired hot-air systems are a good solution for boats up to about 45 feet (13.7 m) that are not going to be used in extremely cold weather.

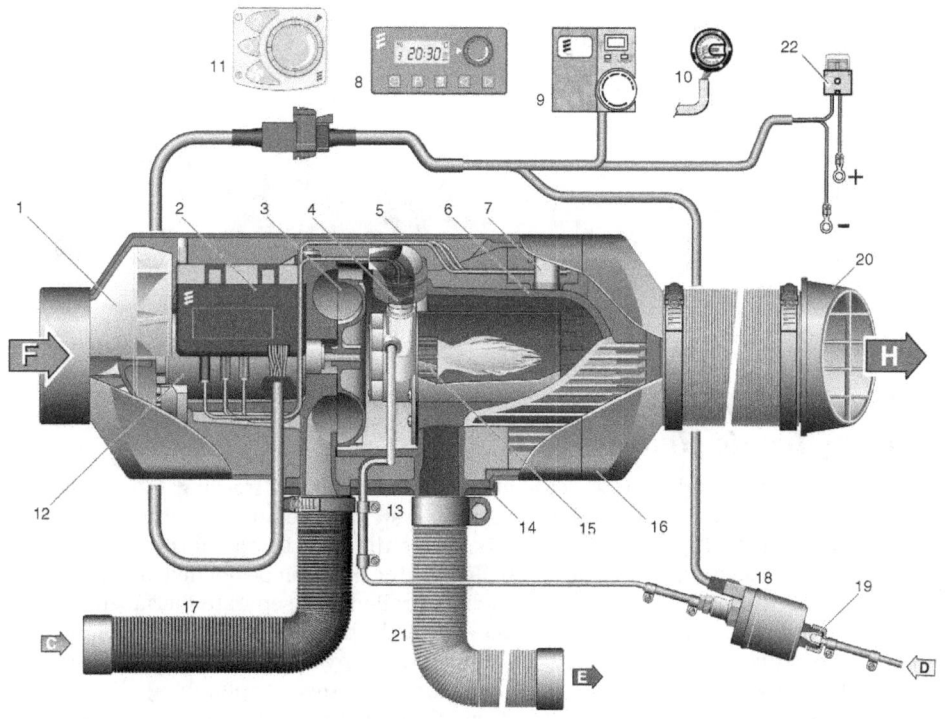

Figure 15-11. Hot-air heater (Courtesy Espar Products, Inc.)

1 Hot Air Blower Wheel
2 Control Unit
3 Combustion Air Blower Wheel
4 Glow Pin
5 Cover
6 Heat Exchanger
7 Overheat/Flame sensor
8 7 Day Timer with Thermostat (optional)
9 Operating Unit (Thermostat)
10 Operating Unit (Rheostat)
11 Mini Controller
12 Blower Motor
13 Fuel Connection
14 Flange Seal
15 Combustion Chamber
16 Hot Air Outlet Hood
17 Combustion Air Intake Hose
18 Fuel Metering Pump
19 Fuel Filter built into FMP
20 Hot Air Output Deflector
21 Flexible Exhaust Pipe
22 Main Fuse: -
   AIRTRONIC D2 - 20 A - 12V
   AIRTRONIC D4 - 20 A - 12V

C = Combustion Air
D = Fuel Intake from Tank
E = Exhaust
F = Fresh Air Intake
H = Hot Air Output

*Figure 15-12.
Typical hot-water
heating system
(Courtesy Espar
Products, Inc.)*

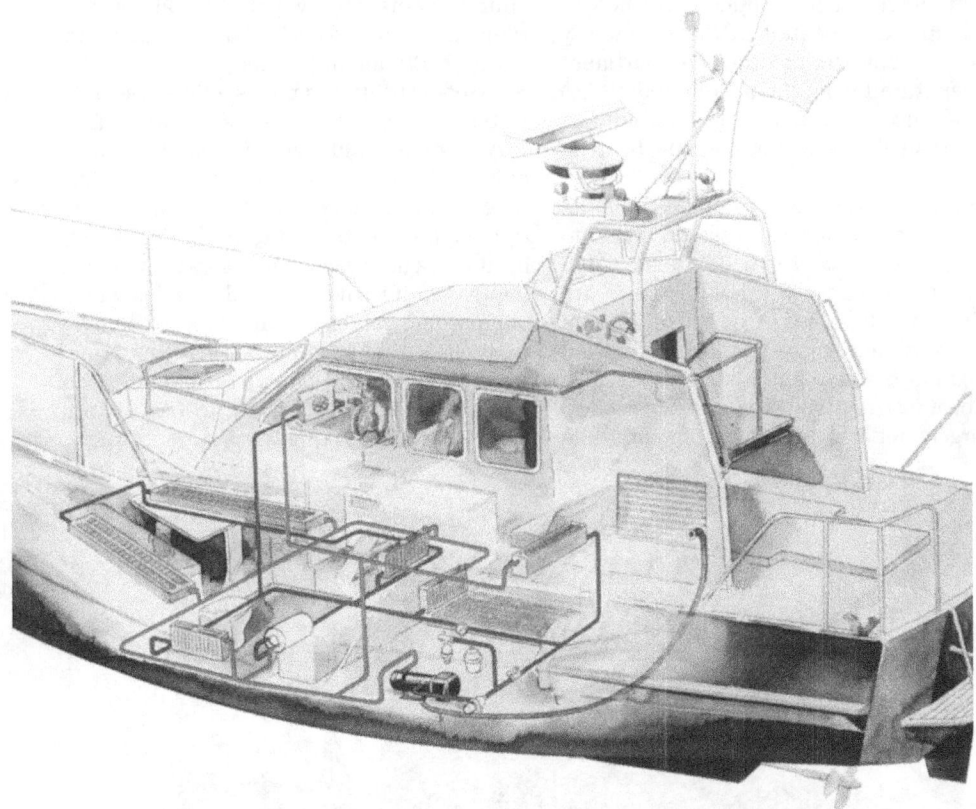

Diesel-Fired Hot-Water Heaters (Hydronic Heaters)

Again, if your home is heated with water circulated through baseboard heaters, this is about the same as diesel-fired hot-water heaters on boats. Like the hot-air system, a diesel furnace heats water, and the water is circulated around the boat to air handlers. Since there is limited room aboard, these air handlers are usually radiators (coils of tubing with hot water running through them) with a blower that more effectively transmits the heat to the surrounding air. Where there is more space, radiators without blowers can be installed. These heater systems are also termed *hydronic heaters*. The blowers at the air handlers should be governed by a thermostat (called an *aquastat* for this use), which prevents the blowers from switching on until the water in the radiator has become hot. Without an aquastat, you will get an unpleasant blast of cold air from the air handler until it warms up properly.

Of course, to increase efficiency and to eliminate the chance of freezing, the "water" in these systems is really a water/antifreeze mix. Since the heat is transferred through plumbing, the boat can be divided into zones, each controlled by a separate thermostat, to get exactly the heat needed in each area. You can also use a hydronic heater to heat hot water for the freshwater plumbing, though I generally prefer to keep the hot-water system separate for simplicity and redundancy. Still, if you're going to live aboard in the winter, this approach gives you virtually unlimited hot water for washing and showers when at the dock. (In the summer, with the heater off, this naturally is not the case.) In arctic or near-arctic conditions, you may also want to preheat the engine. A heat exchanger can be arranged off the hydronic heater to do this. Don't mix the engine coolant and hydronic-heater coolant directly, however.

Chapter 15: Air-Conditioning and Heating

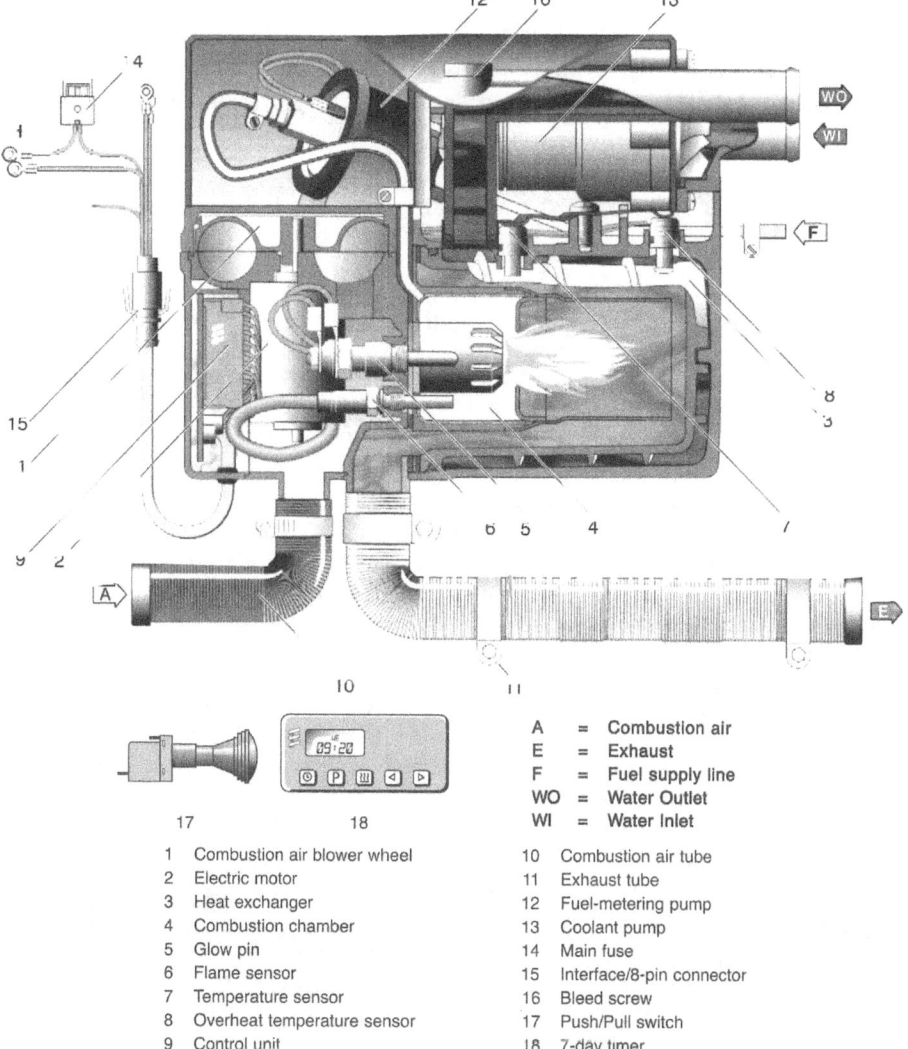

Figure 15-13.
Hydronic heater
(Courtesy Espar
Products, Inc.)

A	=	Combustion air		
E	=	Exhaust		
F	=	Fuel supply line		
WO	=	Water Outlet		
WI	=	Water Inlet		

1 Combustion air blower wheel
2 Electric motor
3 Heat exchanger
4 Combustion chamber
5 Glow pin
6 Flame sensor
7 Temperature sensor
8 Overheat temperature sensor
9 Control unit
10 Combustion air tube
11 Exhaust tube
12 Fuel-metering pump
13 Coolant pump
14 Main fuse
15 Interface/8-pin connector
16 Bleed screw
17 Push/Pull switch
18 7-day timer

Diesel-fired hot-water heaters are the most efficient heating system you can install on a boat. Further, the pipes and hoses to distribute the hot water are quite small, usually ¾ inch (DN 20 mm) or a size smaller. This makes it quite easy to route the heat through all the tight corners on any boat. Typical outputs range from around 10,000 Btu for small units up to 200,000 Btu for very large units. For any serious voyaging cruiser or liveaboard, I almost always specify diesel-fired hot-water heating. Espar and Webasto are two manufacturers of both hot-air and hydronic central heating systems for boats.

Diesel-Fired Heater Exhaust and Intake Air

The diesel exhaust from any diesel central heater is similar to the dry exhaust from a diesel engine (see Chapter 7). It's not quite as hot at around 800°F (1,470°C), but hot enough to cause a serious fire if not properly insulated and to experience cracking without proper allowance for expansion and contraction. Review the discussion on dry exhaust in Chapter 9, and follow the manufacturer's instructions carefully. Unless you are running the exhaust up a stack, the common exits are on the hull side or transom.

TABLE 15-1. REQUIRED HEATING CAPACITY

Cruising Ground	Early Spring Through Late Fall		Winter Cruising		Year-Round Use Liveaboard	
	Btu/cu. ft.	Btu/m³	Btu/cu. ft.	Btu/m³	Btu/cu. ft.	Btu/m³
Warm Climate (Caribbean to South Carolina)	7	247	8	283	9	318
Moderate Climate (North Carolina to Maryland)	9	318	10	353	11	388
Temperate Climate (Delaware to Massachusetts)	11	388	12	424	13	459
Cold Waters (Maine to Nova Scotia)	14	494	15	530	16	565
Arctic	19	671	20	706	21	742

Note that either location can blow hot exhaust onto a dock or a nearby boat, depending on how you are moored. The exhaust is noisy and should be fitted with a silencer provided by the manufacturer. As always, you must *very carefully* consider avoiding any exhaust getting back aboard the boat, since carbon monoxide poisoning can be deadly.

The combustion intake air demand is large for these central-heating systems. They *must* be set up to take their combustion air from outside the boat.

How Much Heat?

To approximate the total heating capacity required, you can use the same formula used to estimate air-conditioning capacity based on boat displacement in tons (Formula 15-1).

To more exactly determine the required heating capacity, measure the net volume in cubic feet or cubic meters of each compartment to be heated. Note the *net* volume, in this case. This is the same concept as the net volume of engine spaces in Chapter 16. In this regard you subtract the volumes of built-in cabinets, bunks, settees, and so on from the total volume of each cabin. Determine your intended cruising ground and type of use, and then multiply the appropriate Btu per cubic foot or per cubic meter factor from Table 15-1.

As with most such things, installing too large a heater is wasteful and inefficient. Don't simply install a huge unit; rather, stick to the recommended output capacity from the Table 15-1. Note that boats intending to cruise cold and arctic waters should also have extensive cabin insulation (not a bad idea for any vessel). Without this, no cabin heater can keep up with the demand. Even worse, the resulting condensation will result in rivers of water running down the cabin walls and into the bilge. The resulting cold, dank, soggy environment can be literally sickening.

THOUGHTS ON HEATING AND AIR-CONDITIONING INSTALLATIONS

A small boat with good natural ventilation and a small bulkhead cabin heater (or a coal stove) has very little in the way of climate control or HVAC (heating, ventilating, and air-conditioning systems). Installing full air-conditioning and central heating is complex and requires a *lot* of ductwork, plumbing, wiring, controls, blowers, distribution boxes, grilles, and more. These all take up space and require maintenance. A large boat that will be fitted with full split direct-expansion air-conditioning and hydronic hot-water heating has two complete and separate systems, plus the required natural ventilation. You must make allowance for the space and weight of all these systems. You must also arrange for all this equipment to be accessed for inspection and maintenance. This is not easy on boats and is overlooked all too often.

Using reverse-cycle air-conditioning for both heating and cooling reduces this to a single system. It's an attractive alternative for powerboats with generators, but you are relying on the generator and won't get sufficient heat for real winter use, except in southern waters. Similarly, a chilled-water (tempered) system can share the piping and air handlers for the air-conditioning with a hydronic (hot-water) heater. This is an excellent approach, but chilled-water systems really are only appropriate for large vessels. Most average craft will end up with the completely separate heating and cooling systems. Be careful to think this through when laying out accommodations or making modifications:

- How and where will ducts and pipes run?
- Where will the central heater be located?
- Where will the air-conditioning units be located?
- Will the air-conditioner be split direct-expansion or self-contained direct-expansion?
- Where will the air handlers and grilles be located?
- Where will the heater radiators be located?
- Where are the thermostats and controls to be installed?
- Are there sufficient breakers on the AC and DC electric panels?

Carefully reviewing all these details in advance will save many headaches down the road.

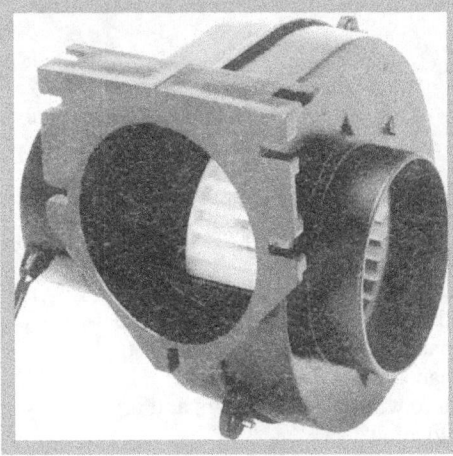

CHAPTER 16

Ventilation of Machinery Spaces

VENTILATION FOR HEATERS

It's often overlooked that cabin heaters that burn fuel need additional ventilation. When a cabin heater is installed in a cabin—a heater that burns fuel (not an electric heater)—you have to allow additional vent area to provide for its combustion and avoid a buildup of carbon monoxide and carbon dioxide.

Formula 16-1.

Formula 16-1. Determining Adequate Ventilation Area for Fuel-Burning Heaters

For unflued heaters

Vent Section Area, sq. in. = Btu/hr. ÷ 1,000
Vent Section Area, cm² = Btu/hr. ÷ 155

For flued heaters

Vent Section Area, sq. in. = Btu/hr. ÷ 5,000
Vent Section Area, cm² = Btu/hr. ÷ 775

Where
Btu/hr. = Btus per hour of heater output
(Btu, British thermal units)
(To convert watts to Btu/hr., multiply watts × 3.415)

The *flue* is a dedicated duct for taking air directly into the heater's combustion chamber from the outside. It is not to be confused with the chimney, which expels the exhaust gases.

Example: Let's say we installed a 6,000 Btu/hr. flued diesel cabin heater mounted on the bulkhead of the main saloon of our example boat, *Ocean Breeze*. We would then need to install

6,000 Btu/hr. ÷ 5,000 = 1.2 sq. in. vent area

or

6,000 Btu/hr. ÷ 775 = 7.74 cm² vent area

Accordingly, add 1.2 to 2 square inches (7.74 to 13 cm²) of vent area to the vents you would install in this area for the occupants only.

If you install a central heating system, say, a diesel-fired hot-water heater system (hydronic heating), the compartment with the furnace or burner would need to be ventilated accordingly. A flued 30,000 Btu unit would require 6 sq. in. (40 cm²) of vent area added to the compartment, above and beyond the vent area determined by either the number of passengers, by the volume change rate (VCR) requirements for that area, or by the vents that are required for an engine.

VENTILATION OF ENGINE SPACES

Engine Vent Requirements

Almost like a living, breathing creature, the engine needs care and consideration. Throttle it with a clogged fuel line or choke it with insufficient air, and performance will falter. Internal combustion engines are much like people doing hard exercise. The perfect conditions for jogging, for instance, are a cool, dry shady day at sea level. This is the environment you should strive for in the engine compartment: low humidity, 50°F or 10°C, and oodles of clean, fresh air. In reality, such engine room conditions are impossible to achieve, but it's the ideal to strive for.

GIVE IT AIR, GIVE IT AIR I'm frequently amazed by the tiny engine vents I see fitted in high-powered craft. On one real 35-foot (10.6 m) twin-diesel sportfisherman—we'll call her *After Burner*—lifting the engine hatch after a hard day's run releases a blast of air almost too hot to bear. In fact, a thermometer placed in *After Burner*'s engine compartment topped out at 135°F (57°C). No wonder this vessel didn't need to turn on its cabin heater until late fall!

The reality is, though, that engine compartment temperatures this high are hot enough to reduce the strength of a wood or fiberglass hull. Further, engines aren't designed to work in this kind of heat any more than you are. Gaskets and hoses soften or crack in prolonged high temperatures, and your engine can't develop its full power. This is because hot air is less dense than cold air. Less weight (mass) of air can be forced into the same space when it's hot than when it's cold. Since the amount of power your engine produces depends on the quantity of air crammed into the combustion chamber during each intake stroke, rarefied, lightweight hot air delivers less oomph per gallon or liter of fuel burned than dense cool air—no matter how much you turbocharge or intercool.

ENGINE VENT SIZING RULE Some of the information I've come across on the subject of engine compartment vents is contradictory and unnecessarily complicated. Some systems base vent area on engine compartment volume, others on boat length or beam, and various other engine manufacturers have specific recommendations for their engines that, needless to say, seldom agree with the engine-compartment or boat-length methods.

Regardless of the method used to size the vents, the goal is not only to supply adequate combustion air but also to keep engine-compartment temperature ideally to no more than 30°F (17°C) above the outside air temperature. I've worked up a pair of simple rules that will allow you to determine proper engine vent area.

Formula 16-2. Minimum Engine Venting for Heat-Exchanger or Raw-Water Cooled Engines with Wet Exhaust

$$\text{Minimum Vent Area (sq. in.)} = \text{hp} \div 3.3$$
$$\text{Minimum Vent Area (cm}^2\text{)} = \text{kW} \times 2.6$$
$$\text{Minimum Airflow (cu. ft./min. or cfm)} = (2.75 \times \text{hp}) - 90$$
$$\text{Minimum Airflow (m}^3\text{/min.)} = (\text{kW} \div 9.5) - 2.5$$

Formula 16-3. Minimum Engine Venting for Keel-Cooled Engines with Drystack Exhaust

Multiply the minimum wet-exhaust engine vent area and airflow by 2.2.

The minimum vent area is the minimum area for natural ventilation without blowers. It makes allowance for standard louvers or grilles over the vent openings and for some short, simple form of baffle box or vent piping. If more extensive baffling or piping is employed, you'll need to increase the minimum area by 20 percent or more. Such more complex configurations are the case with most boats.

Vents sized per the preceding information should provide the airflows indicated by the minimum airflow formulas. However, since you can never have too much air in an engine room, I like to install vents equal to at least 10 percent greater area than recommended, if possible, *plus* forced-air exhaust blowers equal to about one-third the recommended capacity per minute.

As installed power increases, the blowers become more important:

- Above 500 hp (373 kW), blowers are required at a minimum of 33 percent of recommended airflow.
- From 750 to 1,000 hp (560 to 745 kW), blowers are required at a minimum of 50 percent the recommended airflow.
- Over 1,000 hp (745 kW), blowers are required at a minimum of 100 percent the recommended airflow.

NOTE: The power is the power of *all* the machinery in the engine space: all engines, all generators, compressors, heaters, and so on.

As *After Burner* was fitted with twin 325 hp (242 kW) diesels (with the gen set in another compartment), this boat requires a minimum of 197 sq. in. (1,260 cm^2) of vent area.

$$325 \text{ hp} \times 2 = 650 \text{ hp}$$
$$650 \text{ hp} \div 3.3 = 197 \text{ sq. in.}$$

or

$$242 \text{ kW} \times 2 = 484 \text{ kW}$$
$$484 \text{ kW} \times 2.6 = 1,260 \text{ cm}^2$$

The real *After Burner* was fitted with four 4-inch by 5-inch (10 cm by 13 cm) louvered vents, which may seem like plenty but works out to a bare 80 sq. in. (520 cm^2)—less than half the required minimum. What's more, the air had to travel down long, narrow, twisted ducts to reach the engines. No wonder this vessel ran so hot. In fact, it's a wonder it kept running at all.

Due to its complex ducting—the proper venting for *After Burner*'s engines would be 20 percent greater than the minimum of 197 sq. in. (1,260 cm^2), indicated by Formula 16-2, or around 237 sq. in. (1,525 cm^2), plus a pair of 250 cfm (7 m^3/min.) exhaust blowers. (The minimum airflow formula recommends 1,697 cfm, and 1,697 cfm × 0.33 = 560 cu. ft./min., which about equals two 250 cfm blowers—or, minimum flow recommendation is 48 m^3/min., and 48 m^3/min. × 0.33 = 15.8 m^3/min., which about equals two 7 m^3/min. blowers.) These blowers should be wired to run whenever the ignition is turned on for diesel boats, and on gasoline craft should be turned on *at least* 4 minutes before engines start, and left on thereafter. This means the blowers (gasoline or diesel) *must* be rated for continuous duty. It also means that you need to check the electric system to ensure it can handle this modest but continuous additional load—a potential problem on some low-powered sailboats, but seldom a difficulty on powerboats.

Engine compartment blowers should usually be set to exhaust, not as intake. If air is forced into the engine room, it raises the pressure, slightly driving unpleasant engine odors into the rest of the boat.

Two hundred and fifty cfm (7 m^3/min.) blowers are standard 4-inch (10.2 cm) diameter blowers. The exhaust outlets can be led through baffle boxes on the side of the hull. A clamshell vent is installed on the hull exterior over the opening. If the vent runs through the hull side, the clamshell opening should face aft and be angled down about 15 degrees. If the vent is through the transom, the clamshell opening should be angled down and inboard, toward the boat centerline, at about 30 degrees.

Remember that this vent area rule gives a minimum number. You can't have too much engine compartment ventilation! Check the vent area on any boat or design you're dealing with. You'll often find that you have less than the recommended minimum. Even though the boat has the minimum, if at all possible you should add more vent area or powered ventilation. The engine will last longer, fuel consumption will improve, and what's more, the engine compartment will smell sweeter too.

Traditional Half-Cowl Side Vents

Many traditional motorboats have a pair of half-cowl side vents (two each port and starboard, four total) providing most or all of the engine ventilation. These half-cowl side vents (and also clamshell vents) can be useful. You will see, however, that even four of these in any size that will reasonably fit on the side deck will not provide adequate engine vent area on their own.

Comparing to Detroit Diesel Minimum Vent Sizing

The minimum engine vent sizing rule I developed was originally based on exceeding Detroit Diesel's recommended minimum engine vent area. For instance, comparing the minimum vent areas from Detroit Diesel's engine spec sheets with the calculated results for the minimum vent area from the engine vent sizing rule works out as follows:

Model	Power	Detroit Diesel Min. Vent Area		Vent-Sizing Rule Min. Vent Area	
4-71M	180 BHP	55 sq. in.	(353 cm^2)	55 sq. in.	(353 cm^2)
6V-53TI	400 BHP	115 sq. in.	(742 cm^2)	121 sq. in.	(781 cm^2)
6-71TI	485 BHP	110 sq. in.	(712 cm^2)	147 sq. in.	(948 cm^2)
6V-92TA DDEC	565 BHP	134 sq. in.	(867 cm^2)	171 sq. in.	(1,103 cm^2)
8V-92TA DDEC	760 BHP	197 sq. in.	(1,270 cm^2)	230 sq. in.	(1,484 cm^2)
12V-71TA	900 BHP	213 sq. in.	(1,375 cm^2)	273 sq. in.	(1,760 cm^2)
12V-92TA	1,110 BHP	269 sq. in.	(1,735 cm^2)	336 sq. in.	(2,170 cm^2)
16V-97TA DDEC	1,450 BHP	374 sq. in.	(2,415 cm^2)	439 sq. in.	(2,834 cm^2)
16V-149TI	1,800 BHP	480 sq. in.	(3,095 cm^2)	545 sq. in.	(3,520 cm^2)
16V-149TI	2,400 BHP	595 sq. in.	(3,837 cm^2)	727 sq. in.	(4,690 cm^2)

BHP = brake horsepower, the engine manufacturer's full rated engine power

Figure 16-1. Half-cowl side vent

Large-Boat, High-Power Blowers

When installed power increases over about 1,200 hp (895 kW), great blower capacity is required. As noted earlier, companies like Delta-T Systems and Gianneschi & Ramacciotti supply the large blowers needed. In such vessels, it often helps to have both inlet and outlet blowers to achieve the desired airflow. The inlet and outlet blower capacities should match so the engine room is not pressurized over the surrounding air pressure, which would drive unwanted engine smells and gases into other parts of the vessel.

Figure 16-2 shows a Delta-T axial blower—one of four installed, two intake and two exhaust—on a 105-foot (32 m) motoryacht, with twin diesel engines totaling nearly 4,000 hp (2,980 kW). The temperature in the engine compartment was usually under 85°F (30°C).

PART FIVE: VENTILATION, AIR-CONDITIONING, AND HEATING

Figure 16-2. Large axial blower in engine room

Keep Water Out—Solar Vents for Engine Spaces

Of course, there's one very important proviso here. You can never have too much air in the engine room, but you can easily have too much water! You *must* ensure that water can't find its way below through the vents. Keeping vent openings fairly high and including water traps or baffles is critical.

The designer should detail the vent locations and duct runs to ensure that the vent openings are located where they cannot take on water if the boat is knocked down and that all compartments are correctly serviced by a venting system. You can see the basic vent and duct layout in the drawing of a ferry my office designed (Figure 16-3).

A final engine-room vent refinement is to install a solar-powered exhaust vent or two. These vents are independent of the ship's electric system and run whenever the sun is shining. Thus, even when the boat is unoccupied and unused, its engine room is being well ventilated. You'll find a dramatic reduction in mildew and rust, as well as in any buildup of unpleasant oil and fuel smells.

Formula 16-4.

Generator Vent Requirements

Vent requirements for sailboats and motorsailers are exactly the same—an engine is an engine. Remember also to include the total power of all machinery installed in the engine room, including gen sets and compressors.

If you don't have the generator's spec sheet, you can estimate a generator's engine power from Formula 16-4.

Formula 16-4. Approximate Generator Engine Power

Full-Load Gen-Set Engine bhp = 1.7 × max. rated electric kW output

or

Full-Load Gen-Set Engine kW = 1.27 × max. rated electric kW output

If *After Burner* had a 12 kW generator in the engine compartment, you would add 20 hp or 15 kW for its engine when determining total vent requirements.

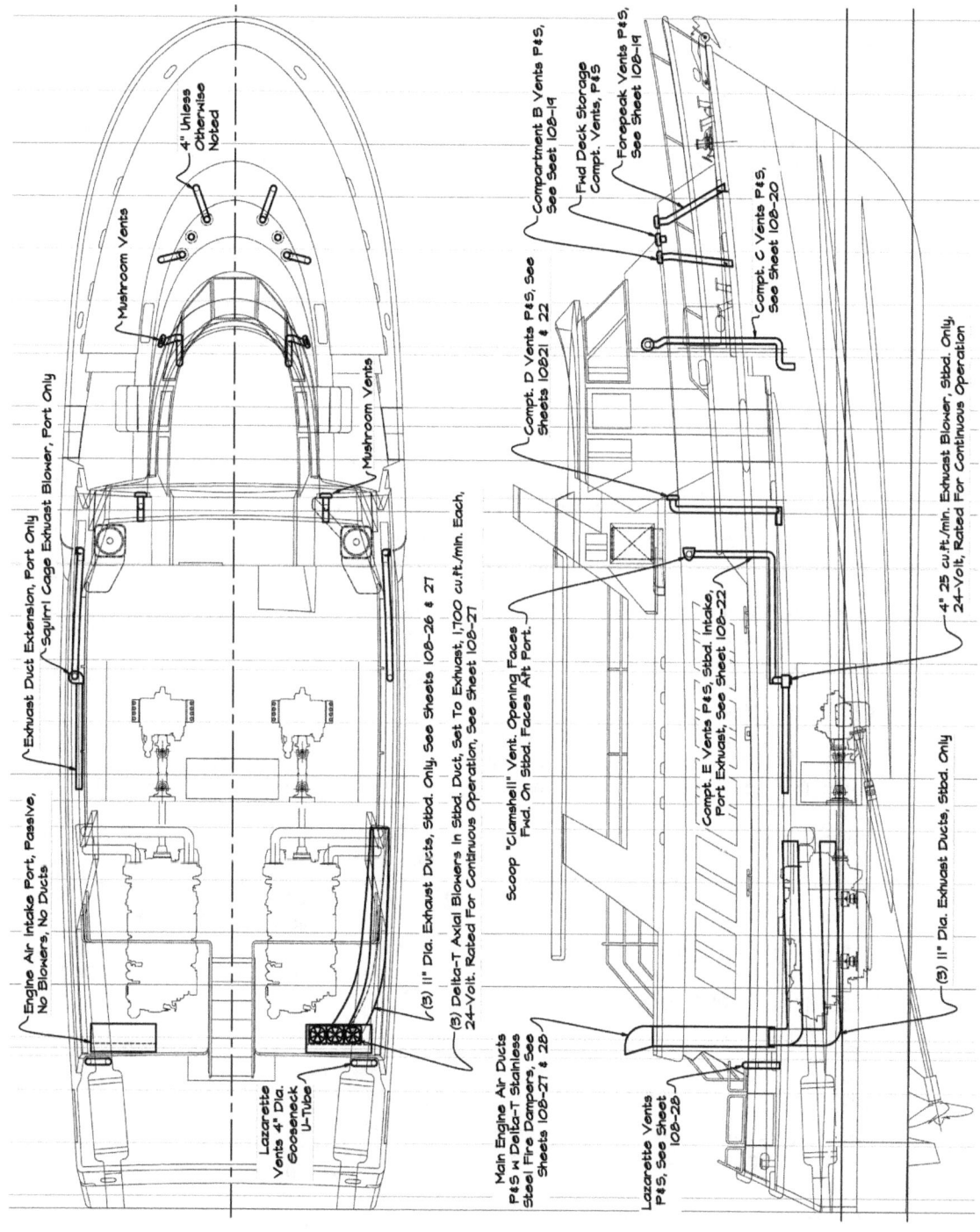

Figure 16-3. Vent plan for a ferry

PART FIVE: VENTILATION, AIR-CONDITIONING, AND HEATING

Engine Vents Based on VCR Requirements

The engine vents can also be sized based on Table 14-1, "Volume Change Rates (VCR) of Various Compartments." It's important to keep in mind that the volume of air in the engine compartment is usually considerably less than the total volume of the engine compartment. This is because the volume of permanent fixtures—the engines, tanks, batteries, generator, and so on—have to be deducted to get the *net volume* of the compartment.

Tank volume can be found from

Tank volume, cu. ft. = 0.134 × tank capacity in U.S. gallons

or

Tank volume, m^3 = 0.001 × tank capacity in liters

Average-size gasoline engines and small diesels, as well as batteries, can be approximated from Table 16-1.

For larger engines and mid-size to large diesels, you should consult the manufacturer.

Let's say that our example boat *After Burner* has an engine compartment that is 8 feet long with 10.5 feet of beam (2.44 m long, 3.2 m beam). Height, from the keel to the underside of the engine compartment overhead, on this V-bottom boat is 4.9 feet (1.5 m), and height from the chine to the overhead is 3.8 feet (1.16 m). We can estimate the average height as

4.9 ft. + 3.8 ft. ÷ 2 = 4.35 ft. average height

or

1.5 m + 1.15 m ÷ 2 = 1.32 m average height

TABLE 16-1. APPROXIMATE MACHINERY VOLUMES

Item	Volume cu. ft.	Volume m^3
4-cylinder, in-line engine	2.5	0.07
6-cylinder, in-line engine	3.5	0.10
6-cylinder, V-6	4.0	0.11
Small V-8	4.5	0.13
Large V-8	5.5	0.16
Batteries	0.5	0.01

Gross engine compartment volume is then

8 ft. long × 10.5 ft. beam × 4.35 ft. average height = 365 cu. ft.

or

2.44 m long × 3.2 m beam × 1.32 m average height = 10.3 m^3

There are, however, five batteries and the two large V-8 engines in the compartment plus a pair of wing tanks, 180 gallons (680 L) each, 360 gallons (1,360 L) total. Also, there's a 15-gallon (57 L) calorifier (water-heater tank), and a 30-gallon (115 L) black-water tank. Finally, there are assorted other small machines mounted, including the forward portion of the exhaust runs.

5 batteries × 0.5 cu. ft./battery	≈ 2.5 cu. ft.
2 large V-8 engines × 5.5 cu. ft./engine	≈ 11 cu. ft.
360 gal. fuel × 0.134	≈ 48 cu. ft.
15 gal. calorifier × 0.134	≈ 2 cu. ft.
30 gal. black water × 0.134	≈ 4 cu. ft.
Other machinery	≈ 8 cu. ft.
Total	75.5 cu. ft.

Net engine compartment volume is

365 cu. ft. − 75.5 cu. ft. = 290 net cu. ft.

VCR should be between 150 and 250 per hour. Use, say, 200, so

290 cu. ft. × 200 changes per hour = 58,000 cu. ft./hr.

58,000 cu. ft./hr. ÷ 60 min./hr. = 967 cfm

or

5 batteries × 0.07 m^3/battery	≈ 0.35 m^3
2 large V-8 engines × 0.16 m^3/engine	≈ 0.32 m^3
1,360 L fuel × 0.001	≈ 1.36 m^3
57 L calorifier × 0.001	≈ 0.05 m^3
115 L black water × 0.001	≈ 0.11 m^3
Other machinery	≈ 0.22 m^3
Total	2.41 m^3

Net engine compartment volume is

$$10.3 \text{ m}^3 - 2.41 \text{ m}^3 = 7.89 \text{ net m}^3$$

VCR should be between 150 and 250 per hour. Use, say, 200, so

$7.89 \text{ m}^3 \times 200$ changes per hour = 1,578 m³/hr.
1,578 m³/hr. ÷ 60 min./hr. = 26.3 m³/min.

The engine vent sizing rule from earlier recommends 1,697 cfm (48 m³/min.), and you should use the higher number; however, it can make sense to use the VCR-calculated flow rate as the minimum size for the powered blower, so long as this is larger than the minimum blower size required from the vent-sizing rule.

The problem with the VCR approach to engine spaces is that it will give rather high airflow rates for large engine compartments with small engines and little else in the space, and proportionately lower airflow rates for smaller engine compartments with large engines and lots of machinery and tanks crammed in.

For instance, had the fuel and blackwater tanks not been located in the engine space, the net volume would have been 342 cu. ft. (9.7 m³). In this case, the engine compartment ventilation would work out to be as follows:

VCR should be between 150 and 250 per hour. Use, say, 200, so

342 cu. ft. × 200 changes per hour
= 68,400 cu. ft./hr.
68,400 cu. ft./hr. ÷ 60 min./hr. = 1,140 cfm

or

9.7 m³ × 200 changes per hour = 1,940 m³/hr.
1,940 m³/hr. ÷ 60 min./hr. = 32.3 m³/min.

The vent airflow found for the less-crowded engine compartment is 18 percent greater, even though we are using the same engines in the same boat.

Venting After Engine Shutdown

Most boats are run for a few hours, brought back to the dock or mooring, and immediately shut down. This is not best practice. Ideally, the engines should be run at idle for 5 or 10 minutes to allow things to cool down evenly and gradually before shutdown. This is an operational consideration, not a ventilation issue, but it is a very good idea to run the engine compartment exhaust blowers anywhere from 15 minutes to an hour after engine shutdown. Naturally, most people don't want to sit around waiting for a quarter of an hour or more just to run an engine blower.

My office has had good results specifying a timer switch at the helm on the blower circuit. This allows you to turn the blower on separately from the standard on/off switch and set the timer for anywhere from 1 to 60 minutes. In hot summer weather, you would usually choose around 30 minutes, and in cold weather, 10 minutes would be adequate. You can thus run the blower and leave the boat, knowing the timer will shut it down shortly.

VENT REQUIREMENTS FOR INVERTERS, CONVERTERS, AND TRANSFORMERS

Inverters, converters, and transformers also generate considerable heat. On one of my office's designs, the inverter would repeatedly shut down for no apparent reason—rather irritating. The engine room was properly vented and was usually only around 85°F (30°C) during routine operation. The problem turned out to be that the inverter was mounted in a corner, and with other machinery and battery boxes nearby, it wasn't getting enough local airflow. When it got too hot, it switched itself off.

We couldn't really relocate the inverter easily, but we remounted it with as much all-around clearance as possible (a few inches), and we set a small, continuous-rated, ignition-protected axial fan to blow on the inverter whenever it was running. This solved the problem. Keep the following in mind:

Allow ample clearance all around inverters, converters (battery chargers), and transformers, and make arrangements to get airflow to them.

It's a good idea to add extra engine compartment vent area for these items as well. For instance, a 4,000-watt inverter is roughly working at 5.3 hp.

$$4{,}000 \text{ watts} = 4 \text{ kW}$$
$$4 \text{ kW} \div 0.7457 \text{ hp/kW} = 5.3 \text{ hp}$$

You could simply add this 5.3 hp (4 kW) to the total engine vent calculation along with any generator. This isn't strictly accurate, as only a modest portion of the 4 kW is lost as heat. However, it is an easy way to make a generous estimate for ventilation purposes.

BATTERY VENTING AND CONSIDERATIONS FOR LPG (PROPANE) AND CNG

The Danger of Hydrogen

Standard marine batteries produce hydrogen gas as a by-product of the charging process. Hydrogen mixed with air is dangerously explosive in mixtures anywhere from 4 to 74 percent by volume—quite a large range. It's critical that battery compartments or the entire engine compartment be well ventilated during charging.

A problem here is that gasoline fumes are heavier than air and sink, while hydrogen gas is the lightest of gases and rises. The layout (particularly on gas-engine boats) of the engine compartment ventilation will often do little to scavenge hydrogen. It is important that there be ventilation at the top of the engine or battery compartment to vent hydrogen gas overboard. The solar vents described earlier for general engine compartment venting will often serve here. Install the vent to take suction as high up in the engine compartment as possible.

In fact—though seldom done—best practice is to locate the batteries in a separate compartment or enclosure. This should be vented directly overboard, with its own dedicated exhaust and intake. The exhaust line should have a standard 3-inch (7.6 cm), 4.2 m³/min., ignition-protected exhaust blower taking suction from the top of the battery enclosure, with a passive inlet leading to the bottom of the battery enclosure. I've probably only seen this done a couple of times in all the boats I've been on, however.

Note that when the boat is left unattended but connected to shore power, the automatic battery charger will be keeping the batteries topped up. The powered blowers on the boat will be shut down and won't remove any hydrogen. Again, this is a good reason for a solar-powered vent—ideally, a solar-powered day/night vent.

LPG and CNG Venting

LPG (liquefied petroleum gas, or propane) and CNG (compressed natural gas) are common stove fuels on many boats. Occasionally, these fuels are also used for flash-type, "instant" hot-water heaters or sometimes for cabin heating. These fuels are even approved for use on passenger vessels. (Be sure to rigorously follow the USCG requirements for installation under the CFR.) As with any such fuels, the potential for a serious fire or explosion is real. Refer to ABYC standards A-22, *Marine Compressed Natural Gas (CNG) Systems* and A-14, *Gasoline and Propane Gas Detection Systems* before making any such installation, and be familiar with them when inspecting or surveying an existing system.

We're only dealing with ventilation here, so the fundamental rule is that LPG and CNG *must* be kept out of the boat. These fuels must be stored in gas-tight (gasket sealed) lockers (Figure 16-4), completely sealed from the interior of the vessel and venting overboard. The overboard vents must be located where the vented gases cannot find their way back into the boat through some other opening such as a hatch, window, or intake vent.

Like gasoline, LPG is heavier than air and will sink to collect in the bilge. CNG is lighter than air and rises. When designing

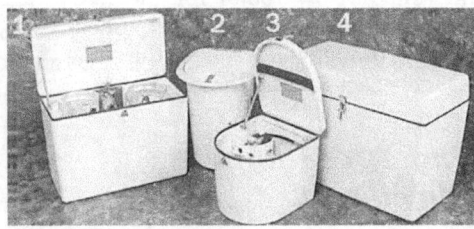

Figure 16-4. LPG lockers (Courtesy Trident)

venting for LPG, you exhaust from the storage area or compartment bottom, but for CNG you need to exhaust from the top. (NOTE: CNG has much less energy per pound or per unit volume than LPG. Some boaters prefer CNG because it rises and thus won't collect in the bilge, but the lower efficiency of CNG combined with the difficulty of locating refill stations makes it a poor choice, in my opinion.)

Fire Dampers

It's often overlooked that in case of fire there needs to be a way to cut off air to the engine compartment. This is done using fire dampers. Many boats have automatic engine compartment fire-suppression systems installed. But for these to work properly, they should also have all the engine vent ducts equipped with fire dampers, which will automatically close off the duct when fire suppression is activated. In addition, an automatic engine shutdown should trigger at the same time. If the vent ducts are not closed off, a fair portion of the fire-suppression foam or gas (FE-241 or CO_2) can blow out of the vents, where it will do no good. Further, air from the open vents will feed the fire, making it stronger. In fact, just closing off well-made fire dampers alone can deprive a fire of enough oxygen to greatly reduce it or even put it out. Note that the engine vent blowers must also be set up to automatically switch off when the fire-suppression system is activated.

Fire dampers are available in stainless steel, galvanized steel (not ideal for marine use), and aluminum. Bearings are often heat-resistant silicone, as are seals. Dampers have mechanical, electric, or pneumatic actuators with manual overrides and are available in round or rectangular shapes to fit the boat's duct system. Delta-T Systems, Inc.; Greenheck Fan Corporation, and Actionair are three of several sources for marine fire dampers.

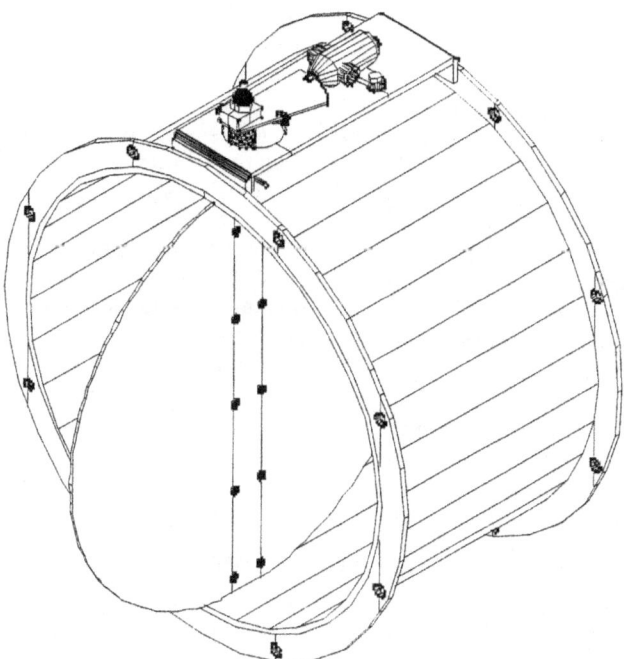

Round fire damper (Courtesy Delta-T Systems, Inc.)

VENTING OF GASOLINE BOATS

In general, the previous engine vent recommendations will serve properly on a gasoline-engine boat. Gasoline vessels, however, must additionally meet specific legal requirements under the Code of Federal Regulations (CFR). Be sure to study and follow ABYC standards H-2, *Ventilation of Boats Using Gasoline*, and H-24, *Gasoline Fuel Systems*. Refer to Chapters 4 through 6 on fuel systems. Ensuring a proper installation minimizes leaks and spills, which is critical with regard to safety and to reducing the loads on the ventilation system. Also see pages 87 through 89 concerning ethanol-gasoline problems in fiberglass fuel tanks.

Note that the requirements for ventilation regarding gasoline apply to any blend of gasoline, including ethanol gasoline such as E-10, E-15, or even E-85 (10%, 15%, or 85% ethyl alcohol by volume).

Basics for Gasoline Ventilation

In the United States, the law requires that every boat with a permanently installed gasoline engine must comply with Subpart K—Ventilation, 33 CFR, sections 183.601 through 183.630. There are no exceptions: main engine, generator, or any other gasoline-driven device that is permanently mounted in the boat. Note that these regulations do not require powered ventilation of engines or tanks that are not permanently mounted. So a small sailboat set up to remove its outboard engine from a bracket and stow it in a locker with a standard 6-gallon (23 L) portable fuel tank stowed in another locker would have to install only passive or natural ventilation for these locker spaces, as we'll discuss later.

In any case, *all* gasoline-engine boats must comply with the CFR and be ventilated accordingly, unless—under the CFR—the engine is installed out in the open—"open to the atmosphere." This is specifically defined as a compartment or space that has 15 square inches directly exposed to the open outside air for every net cubic foot of compartment space (1,041 cm^2 exposed to the open outside air for every net m^3 of compartment space). A small cuddy-cabin boat with a gas engine under the cuddy would likely qualify as "open to the atmosphere" if the cuddy was wide open along its after wall, with no bulkhead closing it off. Critically, if any provision at all is made to seal this open after face of the cuddy with even a canvas cover, it is no longer "open to the atmosphere" and will have to be ventilated according to the CFR.

Net Compartment Volume for Gasoline Ventilation

The net compartment volume is calculated in exactly the same way we calculated the net compartment volume of *After Burner* earlier. To work out the ventilation requirements, you need to calculate the gross and then net compartment volumes for any area containing gasoline engines. As we did for our example *After Burner*, you subtract all permanently installed, built-in machinery or equipment such as

- engines
- tanks: fuel, water, and so on
- generators
- batteries
- accessory equipment and machinery such as water systems, air-conditioning units, compressors, and so on

You *cannot* subtract items that may be stowed in the space but removed, such as

- docking gear: fenders, line, and so on
- anchors and line
- stowed furniture or food
- anything else that may be removed from the compartment

Powered Ventilation Is Required

Every gasoline-engine boat *must* be ventilated by a powered exhaust blower. These *must* be ignition-protected, (nonsparking) exhaust vent blowers. The rate of flow in cfm or m^3/min. is determined based on net compartment volume using the Table 16-2.

TABLE 16-2. GASOLINE BLOWER REQUIREMENT TABLE (CFR 183.610)

English Units

Column 1 Net Compartment Volume (V) cu. ft.	Column 2 Rated Blower Capacity (Fr) cfm	Column 3 Blower System Output (Fo) cfm
less than 34	Fr = 50	Fo = 20
34 to 100	Fr = 1.5V	Fo = 0.6V
over 100	Fr = (V ÷ 2) + 100	Fo = 0.2V + 40

Metric Units

Column 1 Net Compartment Volume (V) m^3	Column 2 Rated Blower Capacity (Fr) m^3/min.	Column 3 Blower System Output (Fo) m^3/min.
less than 0.96	Fr = 1.41	Fo = 0.57
0.96 to 2.83	Fr = 1.5V	Fo = 0.6V
over 2.83	Fr = (V ÷ 2) + 2.83	Fo = 0.2V + 1.13

NOTE: The net compartment volume includes all the volumes of all compartments that open into the compartment that contains the engine, unless the area the engine compartment opens to is "open to the atmosphere," as described above; however, long, narrow compartments need to have openings at both ends or along much of the sides to qualify as "open to the atmosphere."

NOTE: "The 2 Percent Rule": Adjacent compartments do *not* need to be included in the net compartment volume if the openings in the bulkhead or panel between the compartments comprise less than 2 percent of the total surface area of the bulkhead or panel.

Example: If we assume *After Burner* has V-8 gas engines, we would determine the gasoline blower requirements as follows:

Net compartment volume = 290 cu. ft. or 7.89 m^3 (assuming openings on the bulkheads are less than 2 percent of their area)

From column 2 of Table 16-2, we find

Net compartment volume is over 100 cu. ft. or over 2.83 m^3
Blower capacity = Fr = (290 cu. ft. ÷ 2) + 100 = 245 cfm

or

Blower capacity = Fr = (7.89 m^3 ÷ 2) + 2.83 = 6.77 m^3/min.

In this case, the powered-blower requirements would be met with a single 4-inch diameter, 250 cfm (10.2 cm dia., 6 m^3/min.) squirrel-cage exhaust blower. Note, though, that we already specified a pair of these using the engine vent sizing rule earlier. In almost all cases, the blower size from the engine vent sizing rule will exceed the minimum required by the CFR. But you should always check to be sure. Note also that on diesel craft, with installed engine power less than 500 hp (373 kW), the blowers are recommended but optional per the engine vent sizing rule. On gasoline boats, a blower to meet CFR 183.610 is required—*always*.

Of course, if you need extra blower capacity, you can use two or more blowers and duct systems to achieve the required total capacity.

Gasoline Blower System Output

As we saw for our calculation of the required blower size for the below-deck stateroom (Chapter 14), ducting, grilles, and so on reduce the efficiency of the ventilation system and the effective net output of air. Column 3 of Table 16-2 gives the minimum effective blower system output after allowing for duct and other system losses.

Example: Assume that *After Burner*'s engine vents are fitted with louver grilles at the outside and with a 90-degree bend in the water-trap box inside, and then run through 2.5 feet (0.76 m) of duct hose to exhaust from low in the bilge. Referring back to Table 14-4, we would find

$$2.5 \text{ feet} \times 2\% \text{ per foot} = 5\%$$

$$90\text{-degree bend} = 10\%$$

$$\text{Louver grille} = 20\%$$

$$\text{Total approximate loss} = 35\%$$

$$\text{Effective vent output} = 100\% - 35\% = 65\% \text{ of blower's rated cfm output}$$

If we installed a single 250 cfm blower, the net blower system output is then

$$250 \text{ cfm} \times 0.65 = 162.5 \text{ cfm}$$

or

$$7 \text{ m}^3/\text{min.} \times 0.65 = 4.55 \text{ m}^3/\text{min.}$$

Referring to Table 16-2, we find the minimum acceptable blower system output is

$$\text{Net compartment volume} = 290 \text{ cu. ft.}$$
$$(7.89 \text{ m}^3)$$

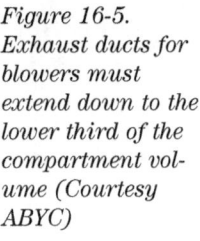

Figure 16-5. Exhaust ducts for blowers must extend down to the lower third of the compartment volume (Courtesy ABYC)

From column 3 of Table 16-2, we find

$$\text{Net compartment volume is over 100 cu. ft.}$$
$$(2.839 \text{ m}^3)$$

$$\text{Blower system output} = F_o =$$
$$(0.2 \times 290 \text{ cu. ft.}) + 40 = 98 \text{ cfm}$$

or

$$\text{Blower system output} = F_o =$$
$$(0.2 \times 7.89 \text{ m}^3) + 1.13 = 2.71 \text{ m}^3/\text{min.}$$

Accordingly, the combination of the 250 cfm (7 m^3/min.) blower we selected with the louvers and ducting planned should meet the CFR requirements. The final system output is subject to test measurement on the actual boat—to prove that the system as installed really does deliver a minimum of 98 cfm (2.71 m^3/min.).

Again, if we would install the twin 250 cfm (7 m^3/min.) blowers, we would find that under the engine vent sizing rule we would meet this blower output requirement with ease.

Exhaust Ducts Located Low Down

Because gasoline vapors are heavier than air and sink to collect in the bilge, the blower exhaust ducts must extend down to the lower third of the compartment volume (Figure 16-5). In some compartments, this can pose a problem because the duct can be so low that the duct intake opening might be

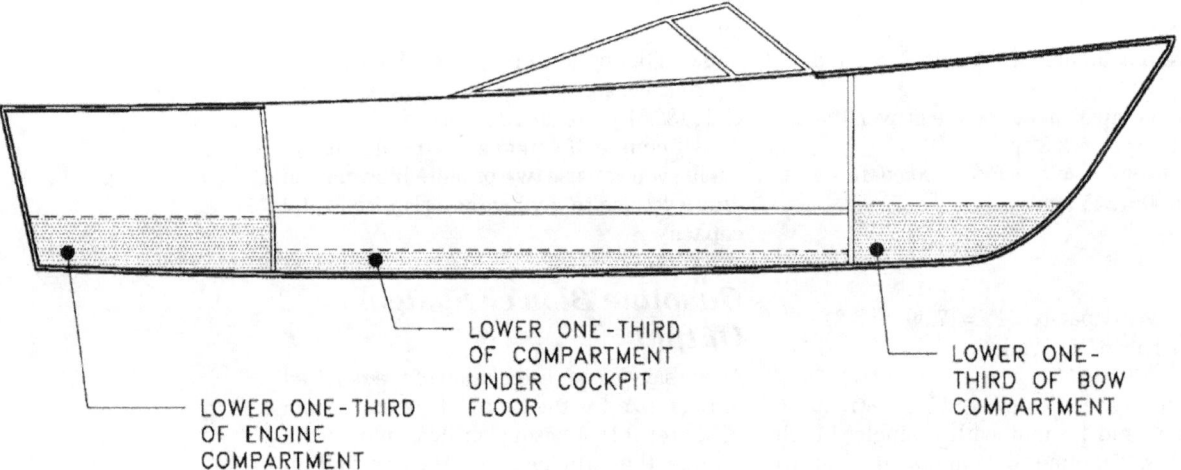

covered at times with bilge water. The CFR makes allowances for this.

You can see in Figure 16-5 that a low, shallow bilge compartment area, in particular, can end up with the exhaust duct very low in the bilge to meet this one-third-height requirement. In such instances where normal bilge-water accumulation could cover or be sucked into the exhaust vent intake, you can and should raise the exhaust intake high enough to avoid this problem.

INLET- AND OUTLET-DUCT SEPARATION The air intake and outlet ducts in a compartment must be separated by a minimum of 24 inches (61 cm) unless the compartment is physically too small to permit this.

Warning Placard Required

It is also a legal requirement that the engine blower (often called a *bilge blower* on gas boats) must be run for a minimum of 4 minutes *before* starting the engine. A warning placard has to be placed near the helm and the engine-ignition switch (with the blower switch clearly labeled and visible nearby) saying

> **WARNING**
> Gasoline Vapors Can Explode, resulting in injury or death.
> Before Starting Engine, Operate Blower for 4 Minutes
> and Check Engine-Compartment Bilge for Gasoline Vapors.
> Verify Blower Operation.

This label must be clearly visible to the operator when he or she is in normal position to turn on the engine or engines. This also applies to the ignition switches of any other gasoline-operated equipment such as generators or compressors.

Natural or Passive Ventilation Required for Gasoline Boats

In addition to the powered blower, all gasoline engine compartments must also be fitted with natural ventilation. The net volume of the compartment and adjoining compartments are determined exactly as done previously for the powered blowers. The 2 percent rule also applies for determining whether an adjoining compartment is considered part of the total net compartment area, and compartments open to the atmosphere aren't included.

NOTE: Natural ventilation is not required for a compartment that contains metal gasoline fuel tanks but doesn't have gasoline engines. The exception is when there is electrical or mechanical equipment in the compartment that is not ignition protected. In that case, such a fuel-tank-only compartment requires the same passive or natural ventilation as a gasoline engine compartment.

Many plastic gasoline fuel tanks have sufficient permeability to require natural ventilation. Check with the tank manufacturer about the tank's permeability with regard to USCG requirements for natural ventilation of the tank compartment. It's generally a good idea to provide natural ventilation for plastic-fuel-tank areas. (Note: As of 2009 or 2010, new EPA regulations may require a vapor barrier built into plastic fuel tanks.)

Natural ventilation is also required for compartments that stow portable gasoline engines (like stowed outboards or portable compressors) or portable fuel tanks (like the standard portable 6-gallon [23 L] outboard fuel tank).

Under the CFR, you can supply fresh air from outside the boat or from another ventilated compartment. You can also exhaust to outside the boat or into another ventilated compartment not connected with the engine compartment. In general, I recommend that all supply and exhaust air be from outside the boat to outside the boat. However, if you have a boat with, say, a bow compartment, a midships bilge compartment, and a stern compartment, it can be both acceptable and sensible to take air in through the bow, direct it aft through the midships bilge, and exhaust it out the stern compartment, as in Figure 16-6. Also, the exhaust duct or opening for the powered blower can double as the exhaust duct for the natural or passive ventilation system if it has sufficient area.

MINIMUM NATURAL-VENTILATION OPENING OR DUCT CROSS-SECTION AREA Formula 16-5 determines minimum allowable cross-section

PART FIVE: VENTILATION, AIR-CONDITIONING, AND HEATING

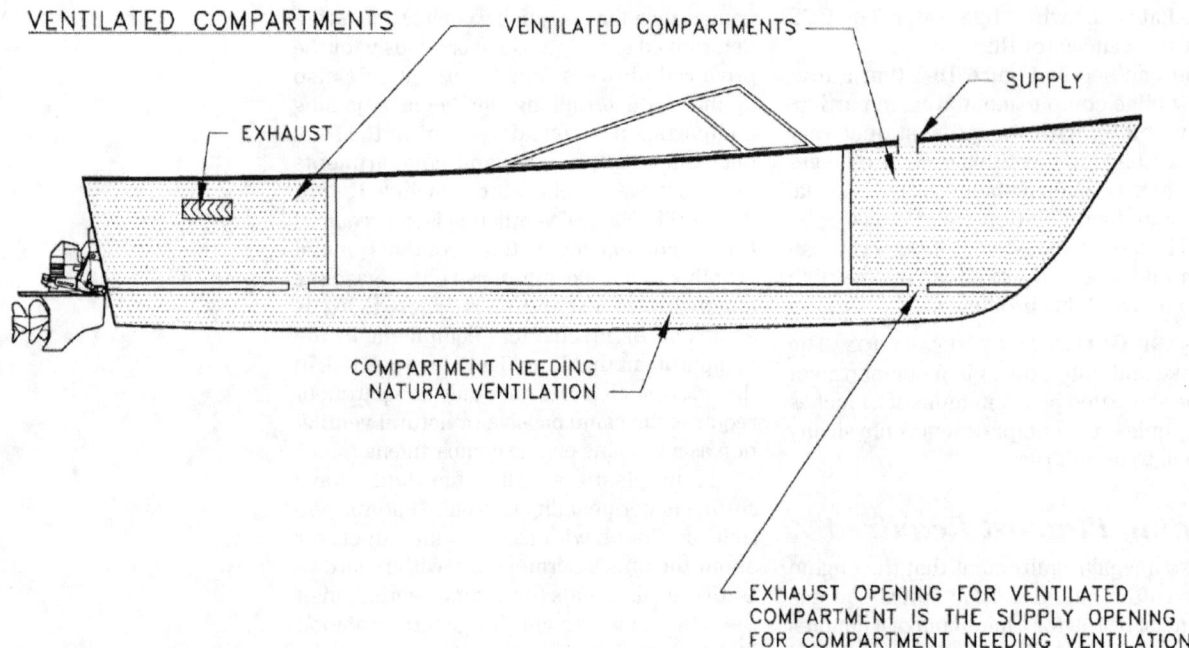

Figure 16-6. Ventilated compartments (Courtesy ABYC)

area for natural or passive ventilation of a gasoline-engine compartment (or for fuel or portable-engine compartments that require ventilation) under CFR 183.630.

Formula 16-5.

Formula 16-5. Minimum Allowable Cross-Section Area for Natural Ventilation

$$A = 5 \times \text{Ln}(V \text{ cu. ft.} \div 5)$$

or

$$A = 63 + [32.3 \times \text{Ln}(V \text{ m}^3)]$$

Where
A = minimum vent cross-section area, in sq. in. or cm²
Ln = the natural logarithm (natural log or log to base e) of the number
V = net compartment volume, in cu. ft. or m³

NOTE: You can find the natural log of any number on an inexpensive scientific calculator. Simply hit the natural-log key (usually "ln"), enter the number you got by dividing volume by 5, and hit Enter. Don't use the "log" key, as that's for the log to the base 10, not the natural log.

This formula is for the area of the intake and outlet vent area combined.

Example: Returning to our *After Burner*, we would find the required natural or passive ventilation area as

Net compartment volume = 290 cu. ft. (7.89 m³)
$5 \times \text{Ln}(290 \text{ cu. ft.} \div 5) = 20.3$ sq. in. minimum cross-section area

or

$63 + [32.3 \times \text{Ln}(7.89 \text{ m}^3)] = 130$ cm² minimum cross-section area

Checking Table 14-3 from Chapter 14, we see that a pair of 4-inch-diameter (10.2 cm) vents would do the job nicely, at 12.6 sq. in. (81.1 cm²) each and 25.2 sq. in. (162.2 cm²) total. Once again, we see that the ventilation area from the engine vent sizing rule greatly exceeds this minimum requirement under the CFR. For *After Burner*, we had found

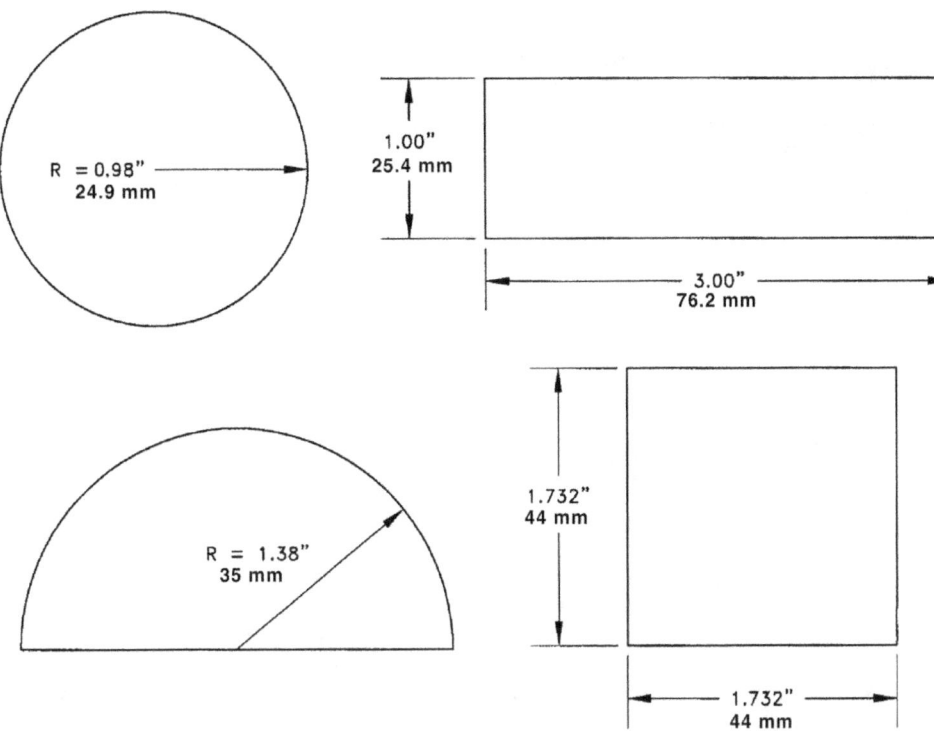

Figure 16-7. Minimum gasoline vent section area for 3 square inches (19.3 cm²) (Courtesy ABYC)

197 sq. in. (1,260 cm²) as bare-minimum vent area with a proper area (allowing for extensive ducting) of 237 sq. in. (1,525 cm²), plus the addition of two 4-inch-diameter, 250 cfm (10.2 cm dia., 7 m³/min.) exhaust blowers.

Minimum Vent Section Area and End Fittings

In all cases, no ventilation duct can be less than 3 sq. in. (19.3 cm²) in cross-section area; this means a pipe or tube must be at least 2 inches (50 mm) ID, a half-circle with a radius greater than 1.38 inches (35 mm), a square larger than 1.732 inches (44 mm) on a side, or a rectangle larger than 1 inch by 3 inches (25.4 mm by 76.2 mm).

The end or terminal fittings (e.g., louver grilles or clamshell vents) must have at least 80 percent of the minimum cross-section area required under any of the preceding requirements.

Part Six

PLUMBING SYSTEMS WITH NOTES ON FIRE SUPPRESSION

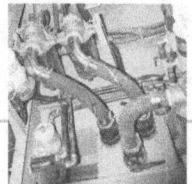

CHAPTER 17 Sea Suction

Almost any boat with an engine (outboards excluded) and virtually every boat with mechanical systems, such as refrigeration or air-conditioning, generators, compressors, deck washdowns, live bait wells, and so on, needs to take in seawater for this equipment to function properly. The piping related to this is called sea suction or seawater intake (even in fresh water), or raw-water intake. This raw-water intake is integral to engine cooling and exhaust, as we saw in Chapter 7.

Fundamentally, sea suction requires an opening in the hull below the waterline. Obviously if something goes wrong here, you have a serious leak. Further, the sea suction has to be set up to provide adequate water supply, to not clog, and to be properly inspected and serviced. The fitting that penetrates the hull is called a through-hull. On aluminum or steel commercial vessels and large yachts, it may be a flanged valve bolted on a metal "spool" instead. Simple through-hulls are adequate well above the waterline, but near or below the waterline, valves must be used to close off any water flow in case of emergencies, as well as for maintenance and repair. These are termed sea valves or, more commonly on boats, seacocks.

SEACOCKS
The Terrible Gate Valve
Perhaps the most inexcusable culprits responsible for boat sinkings are the brass gate valves that, instead of proper seacocks, are fitted to through-hulls. A surprising number of low-cost production boats arrive from the factory so fitted. Often, a do-it-yourselfer will install a gate valve instead of a new seacock because it's a few bucks cheaper. Gate valves are cheaper, occasionally much cheaper, but they corrode and either freeze open or break off—an instant disaster!

ABYC's Seacock Standard: H-27
Under ABYC H-27, seacocks should have a quarter-turn operation in which the handle position gives clear indication of whether the seacock is open or closed. The seacock can be bronze or stainless so long as the alloy is highly resistant to corrosion in seawater. (I recommend bronze over stainless in all applications—except on metal hulls—as stainless is potentially susceptible to pitting corrosion.) Reinforced plastic is also acceptable, but a critical requirement is strength. Any seacock must withstand 500 pounds (227 kg) of static force applied to the end fitting in the direction that the seacock may be weakest. This is like two really hefty men standing on the end of the thing! No ordinary plastic will survive such loads, but this strength is critical to ensure watertight integrity. As far as I'm aware, the only plastic seacocks to meet these requirements are made of Marelon, by Forespar.

Chapter 17: Sea Suction

INCORRECT INSTALLATION

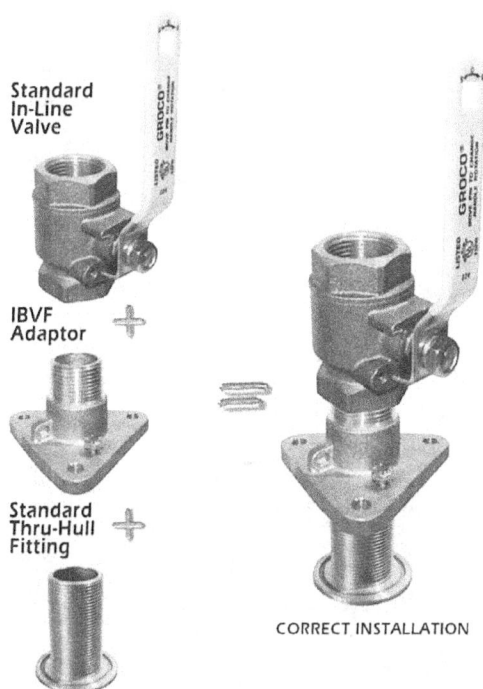

Figure 17-1. Correct and incorrect installation of seacocks (Courtesy Groco)

This strength requirement means that a proper seacock should have a flanged body to mount against the inside of the hull—not simply a bronze or stainless quarter-turn ball valve screwed to the inside tailpiece of the through-hull. This, too, is common, and though vastly better than a brass gate valve, it doesn't meet ABYC strength requirements. In fact, I prefer seacocks with flanges that are through-bolted, as these are strongest. Figure 17-1 illustrates a Groco in-line, quarter-turn ball valve screw mounted on a through-bolted flange base that is screwed to a through-hull. These are the features required for a proper seacock. This happens to be a seacock made up of two components (plus the through-hull), but excellent seacocks from Groco, Wilcox-Crittenden, Conbraco, Forespar, and others are available as single units (plus the through-hull).

I like Marelon seacocks (Figure 17-2) because they are light and completely free from galvanic corrosion problems on metal boats. I use them frequently; however, I tend to use only sizes 1½ inch (38 mm) and up. My concern is that in the smaller sizes, the valve handle-stem (not the seacock itself) is a bit too weak, particularly in cold weather. No plastic seacocks of any type are acceptable under CFR Commercial for passenger vessels. These boats can use only metal for its greater fire resistance.

Seacock Refinements

You can install a T-fitting just above the seacock with a pipe or hose off the T to

Figure 17-2. Marelon seacock (Courtesy Forespar)

279

*Figure 17-3.
Safety seacock
(Courtesy Groco)*

allow two useful things: flushing the engine-cooling system or drawing antifreeze through it, and teeing to a bilge suction so that switching the seacock off uses the engine-cooling water pump as an emergency bilge pump. (Figure 17-4 shows this schematic.) Groco makes an off-the-shelf fitting specifically for this purpose and also the Groco SVB Safety Seacock, which has the side-port inlet built right into the one-piece seacock itself.

When using a metal seacock on a metal hull, the seacock must be galvanically isolated from the hull. Bronze can be used on steel hulls (when isolated) but never on aluminum hulls. Stainless steel seacocks can be used on either steel or aluminum hulls, but still have to be completely galvanically isolated. The isolation must be complete: a pad or gasket at the mating surfaces, bushings around bolts, and washers under bolt heads—no metal part in contact with the seacock can be in contact with the hull, period!

For passenger vessels, the U.S. Coast Guard wants to see a flanged valve through-bolted to a metal "spool" welded to the inside of the hull. You can see this in Figure 17-5. Insulating pads and bushings should be Micarta, or a similar material that has a reasonably high-temperature resistance and moderate fire resistance. This entire assembly, the spool plus through-bolted flanged ball valve, forms the seacock and is not really an off-the-shelf seacock; rather, it has been fabricated by the builder. This is why on commercial boats these are more frequently termed *sea valves*.

Required Seacock Location

ABYC H-27 used to require that seacocks be fitted on all through-hull fittings (sea suction and outlet) which are below the highest heeled waterline. This was arbitrarily defined as 7 degrees of heel for all powerboats (Figure 17-6), but for sailboats, it meant that seacocks were required on all through-hull fittings up most of the topsides. (You can see why this would be by

*Figure 17-4.
Seacock service
port schematic
(Courtesy Groco)*

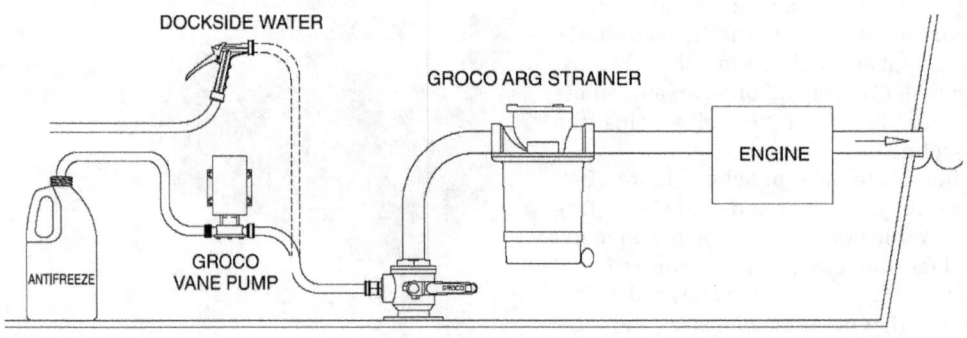

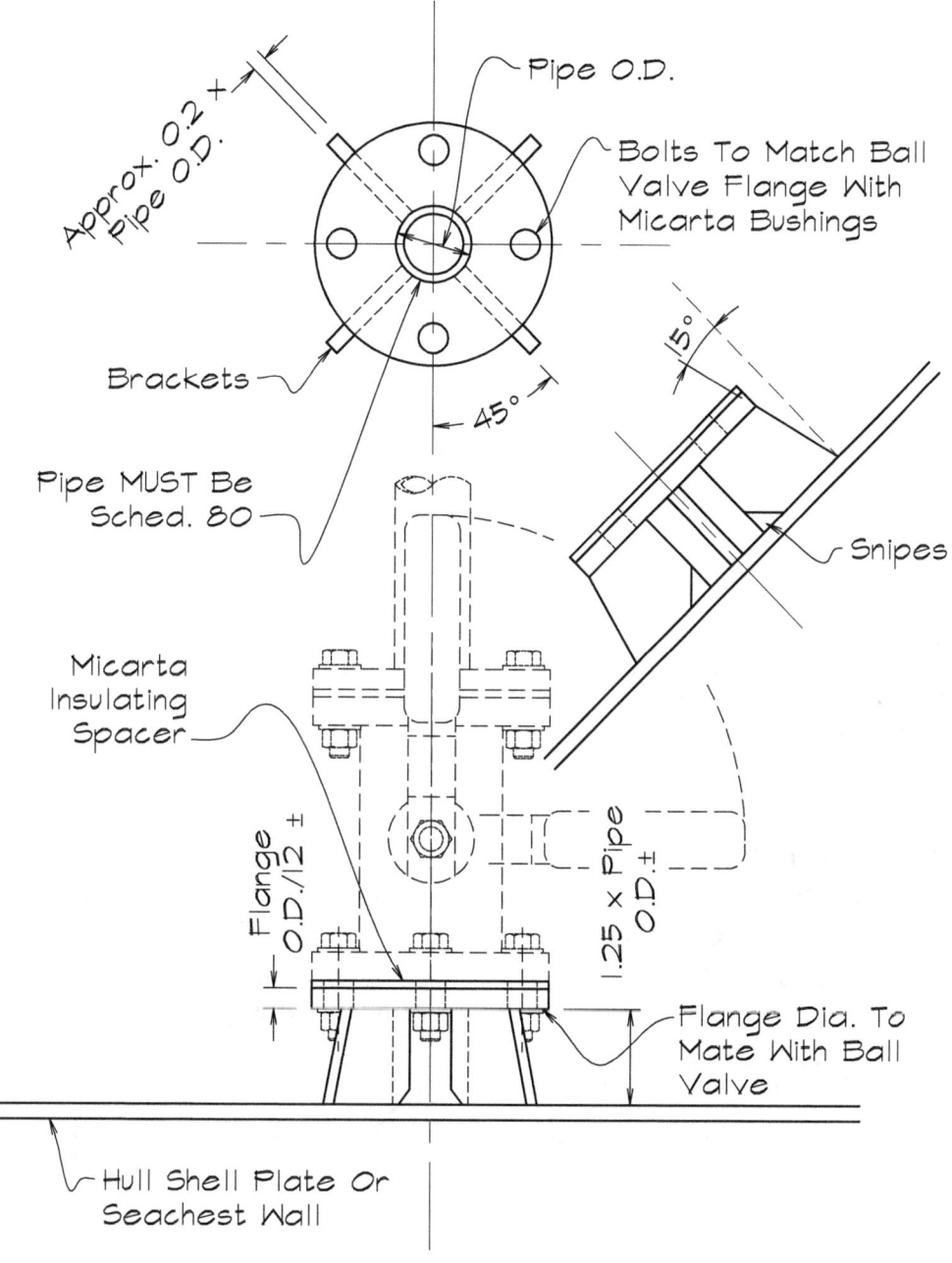

Figure 17-5.
Through-hull spool

looking at Figure 18-3.) In practice most sailboats didn't follow this particular requirement As of 2008, H-27 has been revised to allow through-hulls without seacocks above the static (level) flotation waterline provided reinforced piping or hose that resists kinking and collapse is used. I don't think I've ever surveyed a sailboat that fully complied with the old version of H-27. Still, on really serious offshore voyagers, the old H-27's approach to requiring seacocks to the highest heeled waterline may have merit. ABYC H-27 now simply requires seacocks on all through-hulls below the waterline. My recommendation is

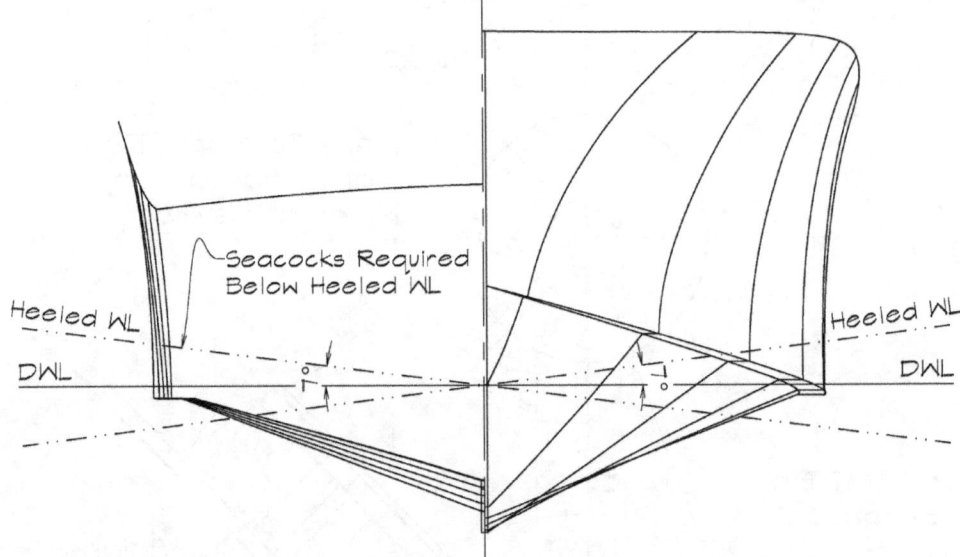

Figure 17-6. Requirements for seacock locations on powerboats per ABYC H-27

that seacocks be fitted on all through-hulls from 12 inches (30 cm) above the waterline and down, or from a height of $1/60$th of the waterline length above the waterline and down, whichever is greater.

HOSE CLAMPS, SEA STRAINERS, AND SHARING SEACOCKS

Double Stainless Hose Clamps

Naturally, as we've discussed several times throughout this book, you don't want the hoses coming loose. The hoses to the seacock or through-hull should all be fastened with two stainless hose clamps at each end, as described in Chapter 4. A hose coming adrift on an open 1½-inch (38 mm) seacock makes a heck of a big leak!

Sea Strainers and Hull Strainers

Seawater is referred to as raw water for good reason. It contains not only salt but also other impurities, from algae and seaweed to plastic bags, sand, mud, fish eggs, grit, and trash. It's important to keep these impurities out of the plumbing system. For this reason, every sea suction should be fitted with a sea strainer (a filter) just inboard of the seacock, before the plumbing is led anywhere else. It's also a good idea to install an external hull strainer or grate over the through-hull opening.

Traditional hull filters or grates are bronze scoops or round filters. (On scoops, the slotted openings face forward.) These work well, but they require you to unscrew or unbolt the grate to access or clean the through-hull proper. Companies like Groco offer hull strainers that hinge open for easy cleaning (Figure 17-7).

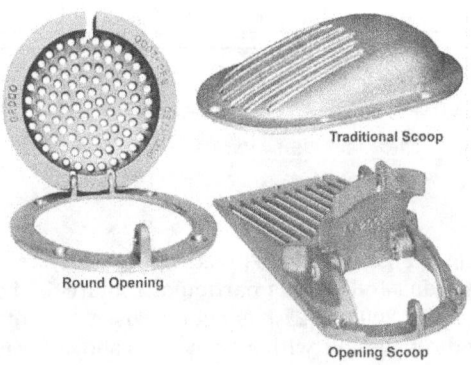

Figure 17-7. Hull strainers (Courtesy Groco)

Sea strainers are simply filters designed to remove sediment, seaweed, and similar impurities from the raw water (Figure 17-8). They should have a clear bowl so you can easily see if there's a buildup of gunk. Though many successful vessels are fitted with single sea strainers on the sea-suction line, it's a good idea to use switchable duplex sea strainers for critical systems such as the main engine (Figure 17-9). As with switchable duplex fuel filters, this allows you to change instantly from a fouled sea strainer to a clear one and then clean the fouled filter without missing a beat.

A relatively new development is self-cleaning sea strainers. These units come with a built-in macerator pump that flushes the filter clean and grinds up any gunk and debris, expelling the waste as a slurry through a smaller dedicated seacock and through-hull. This is a nice feature for a large yacht or commercial vessel, but in general, I prefer duplex sea strainers. The macerator pump, its related fittings, and the necessary wiring involve more systems and more complexity and mean more to maintain.

Figure 17-9. Duplex sea strainer (Courtesy Groco)

You can see how these self-cleaning sea strainers are configured in Figure 17-10. Note that this schematic shows the emergency bilge suction leading to the side port built into this type of seacock. Note also that this sea suction is set up as a common-rail manifold (see Chapter 4). The entire sea-suction intake line—in this configuration—must be large enough in diameter to serve all the water demands of the equipment it serves.

Pumps Sharing a Single Suction or Source

In the reasonable desire to reduce the number of holes in a boat's hull, it's common to arrange a single seacock to serve as sea suction for several functions, as in Figure 17-10. You might have an air-conditioner-condenser pump, a refrigeration-condenser pump, a galley raw-water pump, and a deck-washdown pump all sharing suction (water intake) from a single seacock. This is not a bad idea, but it must be approached with caution. Particularly if one pump is significantly more powerful than others in the group (such as a washdown), it may starve the other pumps of water. This can cause the other pumps to lose prime (especially if they are centrifugal). The resulting problems can be intermittent and hard to track down in service.

If you have multiple pumps sharing a single sea suction, be sure the cross-section area of the through-hull ID is at least 1.1 times the total cross-section area of all the individual takeoff lines to each pump, and there is at least 2 feet (0.6 m) of head at the through-hull

Figure 17-8. Sea strainer (Courtesy Groco)

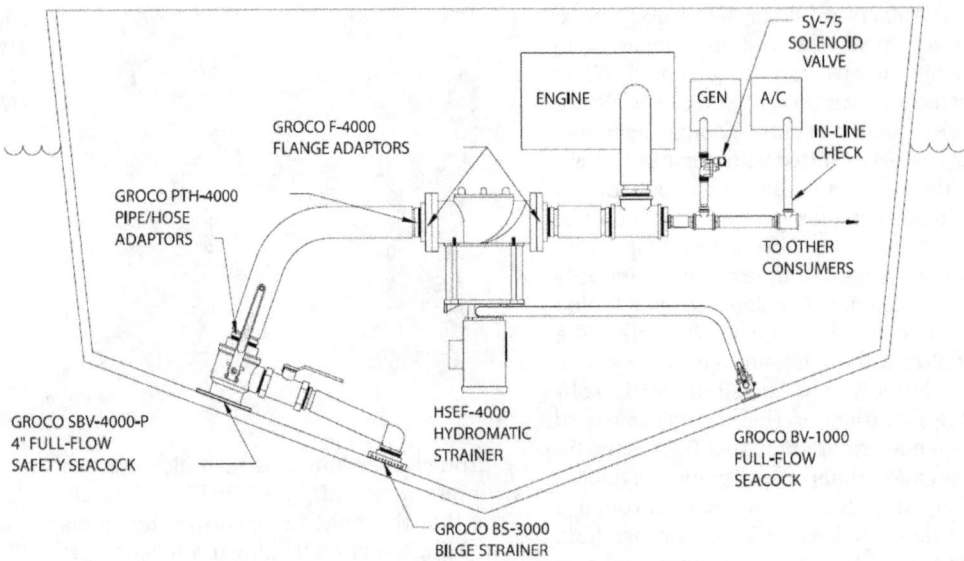

Figure 17-10. Self-cleaning sea strainer (Courtesy Groco)

(locate the through-hull at least 2 feet or 0.6 m below the waterline). Even this can't absolutely ensure that these problems won't occur. The deeper the shared sea suction and the larger its diameter, the better.

Sea Chests

Probably the best way to get a large-diameter inlet opening as deep as possible is by using a sea chest. These are boxes or chambers built onto the inside of the hull, with large openings to the outside water. The openings are covered with grates, and several sea valves or seacocks are installed in the top or side of the sea chest as convenient. Sea chests are not required on any boat, but they offer a number of advantages if used:

- A sea chest gets the water inlet opening as far below the waterline as possible to maximize inlet head and minimize the chance of sucking in air when the boat rolls.
- Its outside opening(s) has a total area far larger than all the suction pipes attached to it.
- The grate at the sea chest's opening (or openings) provides an added coarse filter element to protect internal plumbing.
- With the grates let in flush, water flowing past the boat tends to keep debris from fouling the grate.
- A sea chest in a box keel can be two-sided (open on both sides) and thus ensure full water flow even when a plastic bag is stuck against one side.
- A sea chest centralizes inlet/suction plumbing fittings.

Figures 17-11 through 17-14 illustrate a two-sided sea chest in an aluminum motor

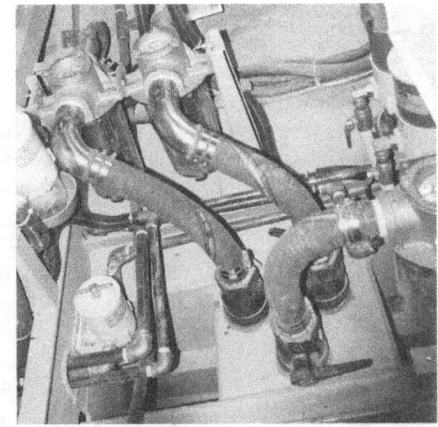

Figure 17-11. Sea chest seen from inside a motor cruiser

Chapter 17: Sea Suction

Figure 17-12. Sea chest seen from outside the motor cruiser (port grate not yet installed)

commercial passenger vessels under the CFR. You can also see the suction-line hoses running immediately to sea strainers.

Many boats do not have a box keel to fit a two-sided sea chest. A one-sided sea chest still offers nearly all the benefits of a two-sided one and can be worked in on most boats. Note the zinc anode (Figure 17-15). This should be installed inside the sea chest on steel and aluminum boats. A sea chest can also be molded into the bottom or keel of a fiberglass boat.

These sea chests are all for intake. It can appear attractive to have an outlet sea chest for many of the same reasons; however, I've never found outlet sea chests to work all that well. Taking water from a deep central point and leading it to where it's necessary makes sense, but there can be quite a few discharge lines. Running them all back to a central location just about doubles the piping complexity and lengths in the boat. Discharge will also contain impurities. These can foul and corrode the interior of an outlet sea chest. This doesn't mean you shouldn't ever use an outlet sea chest, but it hasn't worked out as advantageous in any of my design work to date.

cruiser. It provides all the advantages listed previously. Note the plastic (Marelon) seacocks. I often use these in metal yachts because they eliminate the chance of corrosion, but as we've noted, metal seacocks are required by some class rules and for

Figure 17-13. Sea chest profile

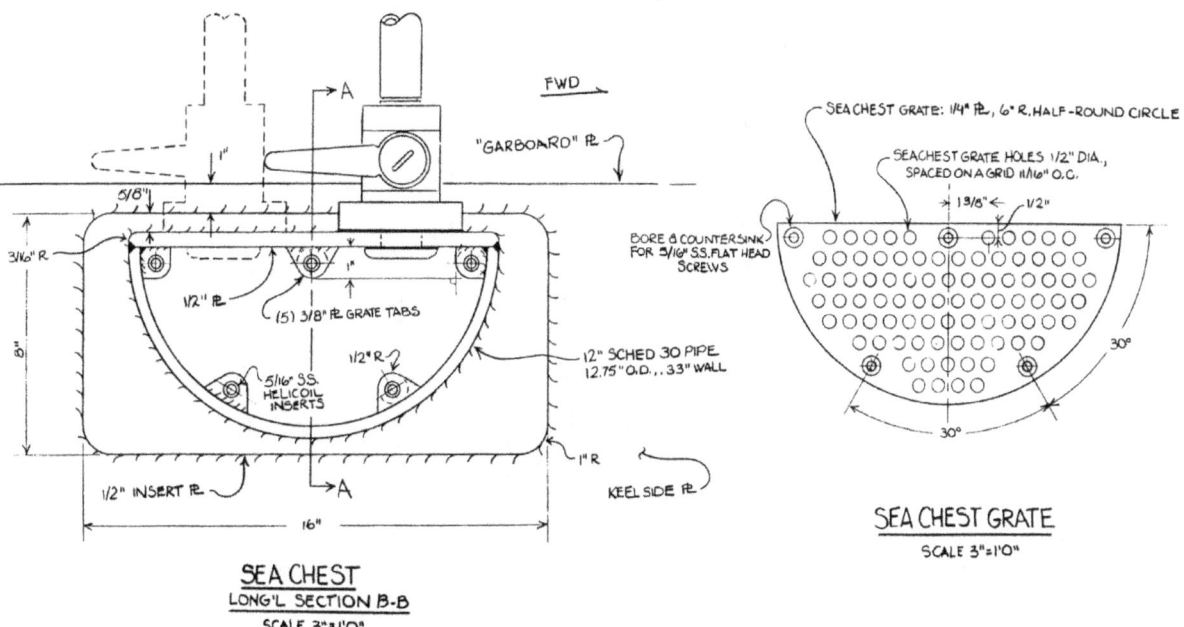

285

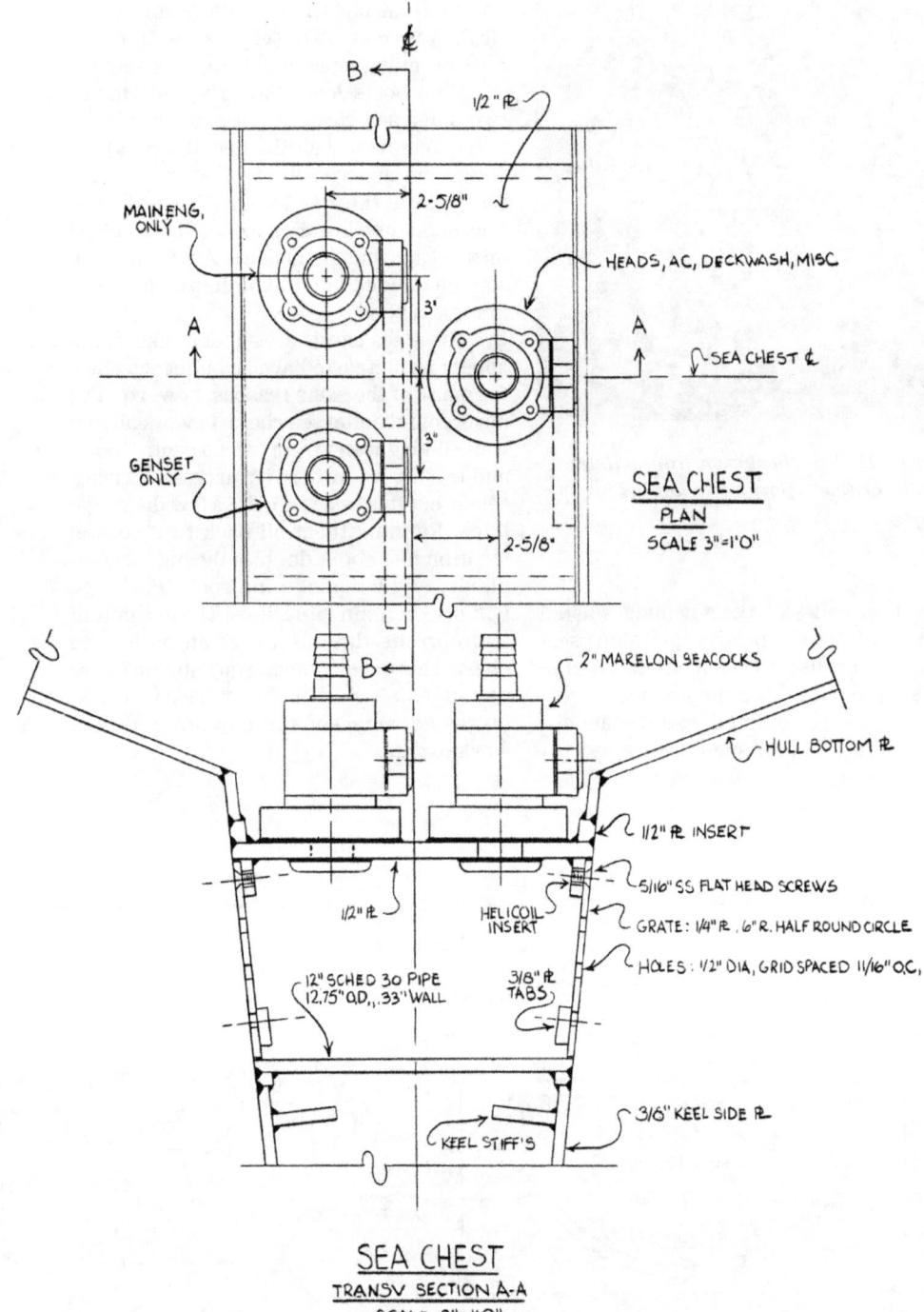

Figure 17-14. Sea chest section

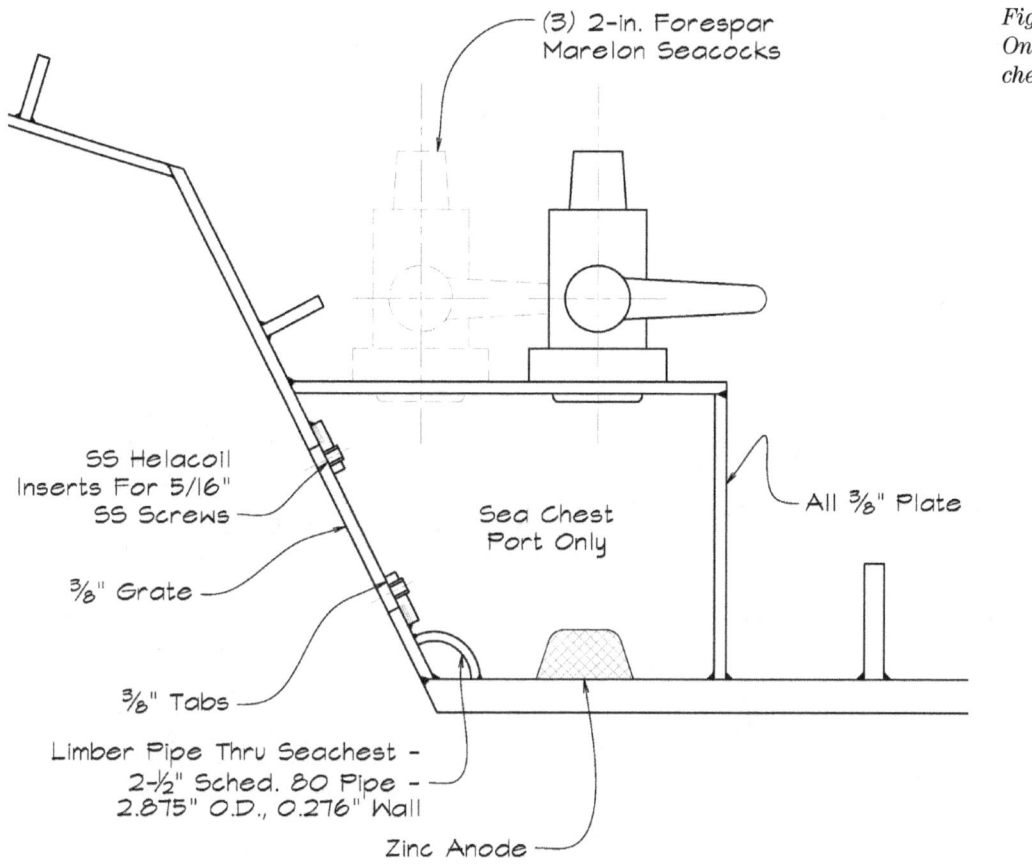

Figure 17-15. One-sided sea chest section

Discharge Aft of Intake

Speaking of impurities, do not forget that the discharge lines—particularly for things like head pumpout (when it's legally permissible to do so)—should be aft of the intake through-hulls or sea chest. You don't want to pump gray or black water back into a deck wash-down or engine-cooling circuit!

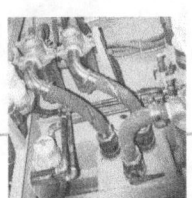

CHAPTER 18

Bilge Systems, Fire Mains, and Fire Extinguishers

BILGE SYSTEMS

It's unquestionable that the first job of any boat hull is to keep water out. Failure in this will result in water damage, loss of stability, and even sinking. Even so, water will find its way aboard through drips in windows, through hatches and ventilators, and through rain and spray entering any opening. In storm conditions, solid water will come on deck. This, too, will find its way below through everything from chain pipes, to hatch gutters, to vents, to a door left open too long. Then of course, there are leaks in the hull itself. These could be small drips from packing glands, more serious inflow from damaged fittings, or—the worst fear—a sizable hole from major impact. As we'll see, even a seemingly quite small hole below the waterline can admit a substantial amount of water and do so quickly!

Accordingly, all boats must be fitted with a bilge system to remove bilge water. A rugged and reliable bilge system is crucial to safe vessel operation. The bilge system primarily consists of

- a pump or pumps
- piping and fittings to transfer water from inside the boat back out to the surrounding sea
- a power source to drive the pumps

Of course, small open skiffs, canoes, and kayaks don't have bilge systems. A hand bailer or a bucket and a sponge do the job. As boats grow somewhat larger, however, a proper bilge pump must be installed.

Under about 20 feet (6 m)—if the boat has no electric system—a manual bilge pump will make up the bilge system. If fixed (bolted in place), it has to be fitted with the appropriate hose and piping to take water from the lowest part of the bilge where water collects (the bilge sump) and discharge it overboard. To prevent clogging, the intake opening should be fitted with a strainer called a strum box (Figure 18-1). (There may be exceptions

Figure 18-1. Strum box (Courtesy Edson International)

Chapter 18: Bilge Systems, Fire Mains, and Fire Extinguishers

for some large-diaphragm pumps, which we'll look at in a bit.) The open area of the grating or mesh in the strum box should be at least 3 times the area of the suction pipe.

A manual bilge pump also can be portable and stowed in a locker, but there needs to be at least a couple of locations you can readily set the pump for operation. Also, the hoses required to reach the sump and discharge overboard must be permanently attached to the pump and ready for immediate use. Again, a hand bailer and a sponge should round out a small-boat bilge system. There's an old saying: "There are few pumps more effective than a frightened sailor with a bucket."

If the boat has an electric system (virtually all modern powerboats and nearly all sailboats large enough to have a cuddy cabin), then it should be equipped with both a manual pump and an electric bilge pump—a true bilge system. On large vessels, the bilge system is often referred to as being used for dewatering, and bilge pumps may be referred to as dewatering pumps.

Required Bilge-Pump Capacity

There aren't many regulations for pleasure-craft pump capacity. We can refer to the CFR for passenger vessels (CFR Commercial) and to American Bureau of Shipping (ABS) Rules for Motor Pleasure Yachts and for High-Speed Craft for some guidance.

Table 18-1 is CFR 182.520's Table 182.520(a), which gives the minimum required pumping capacity for passenger vessels.

Additional Requirements for CFR Commercial (CFR 182.10 and 182.30)

- For vessels under 65 feet (19.8 m), minimum nominal pipe diameter is 1 inch (DN 25 mm).
- For vessels over 65 feet (19.8 m), minimum nominal pipe diameter is 1½ inches (DN 38 mm).
- The bilge suction must be fitted with a suitable strainer with an area not less than 3 times the pipe area.
- If individual pumps are not provided for separate spaces, then the bilge suction lines should lead to a main control station with an on/off valve to control operation and a check valve to prevent back flow (or a combined stop-check valve).
- The portable hand pump must be able to pump water from each compartment (but not necessarily at the same time or from the same location).
- Each bilge pump must be self-priming and permanently connected to the bilge-piping manifold and may also be connected to the fire main.
- Check valves must be installed at the main piping manifold and where needed to ensure that reverse flow cannot take place.
- If there are two power pumps, they must each have a different power source. One may be the main engine, or on a twin-engine boat, each may be off a separate main engine.
- At the forward collision bulkhead, the bilge suction pipe should have a valve

TABLE 18-1. CFR 182.520(A) BILGE-PUMP TABLE

Number of Passengers	Length of Vessel	Bilge Pumps Required	Minimum Capacity Required per Pump
Any number	More than 65 ft. (19.8 m)	2 fixed power pumps	50 gpm (190 lpm)
More than 49 passengers and all ferry vessels	Not more than 65 ft. (19.8 m)	1 fixed power pump and 1 portable hand pump	10 gpm (38 lpm) 10 gpm (38 lpm)
Not more than 49 passengers (other than ferry vessels)	26 ft. (7.9 m) up to 65 ft. (19.8 m)	1 fixed power pump and 1 portable hand pump or 1 fixed hand pump and 1 portable hand pump	10 gpm (38 lpm) 10 gpm (38 lpm) 5 gpm (19 lpm)
	Less than 26 ft. (7.9 m)	1 portable hand pump	5 gpm (19 lpm)

on the front side of the bulkhead that can be operated by a reach rod on deck, or aft of the bulkhead if the valve is easily accessible from inside the boat during normal operation.
- Submersible electric pumps can be used only on vessels up to 65 feet (19.8 m) in length and carrying not more than 49 passengers (other than a ferry), provided that the pump is only used to dewater one watertight compartment and is permanently mounted. Flexible hose may be used on such pumps as long as it does not penetrate a watertight bulkhead. In addition, the submersible pump installation must comply with ABYC H-22, *DC Electric Bilge Pumps Operating Under 50 Volts.*

Figure 18-2 shows the layout of a bilge and fire main system. This is for an aluminum vessel. If the vessel were of any other material, CFR Commercial would require steel or stainless piping.

ABS Bilge-System Requirements

ABS Rules for High-Speed Craft under 150 feet (45.7 m) and Motor Pleasure Yachts require two power-driven bilge pumps on boats 65 feet (19.8 m) in length or more, and one power-driven bilge pump and one manual pump on vessels under that length. Minimum required pump capacity and inside pipe diameter are as presented in Table 18-2.

Under ABS, submersible pumps can be used in individual compartments as long as the boat will remain stable with such a compartment completely flooded, and if—in addition to the submersible pumps—one bilge pump matching the required capacity from Table 18-2 is installed, plus a second bilge pump of at least half this capacity.

ABS Bilge-Piping Diameter

ABS has formulas for determining the minimum internal diameter of the main bilge-suction pipe and also of the branch lines.

Formula 18-1. Minimum Internal Diameter of the Main Bilge-Suction Pipe

$$d = 1 + \sqrt{\frac{L(B+D)}{2,500}} \text{ in.}$$

or

$$d = 25 + 1.68\sqrt{L(B+D)} \text{ mm}$$

Where
d = internal pipe diameter, in. or mm
L = length of vessel on the load waterline, ft. or m
B = beam, ft. or m
D = molded depth, hull fairbody to main deck at sheer at midships, ft. or m
NOTE: Pipe size selected should be within 1/4 inch (6 mm) of the calculated size.

Formula 18-2. Minimum Internal Diameter of Branch or Submersible-Pump Lines

$$d = 1 + \sqrt{\frac{c(B+D)}{1,500}} \text{ in.}$$

or

$$d = 25 + 2.16\sqrt{c(B+D)} \text{ mm}$$

Where
d = internal pipe diameter, in. or mm
c = length of compartment, ft. or m
B = beam, ft. or m
D = molded depth, hull fairbody to main deck at sheer at midships, ft. or m
NOTE: Pipe size selected should be within 1/4 inch (6 mm) of the calculated size.

CHECKING THE REQUIRED BILGE SYSTEM PER CFR COMMERCIAL AND ABS Let's say the dimensions of motor cruiser *Fluky Flooder* are

LOA: 50 ft. (15.2 m)
Waterline: 46.0 ft. (14 m)

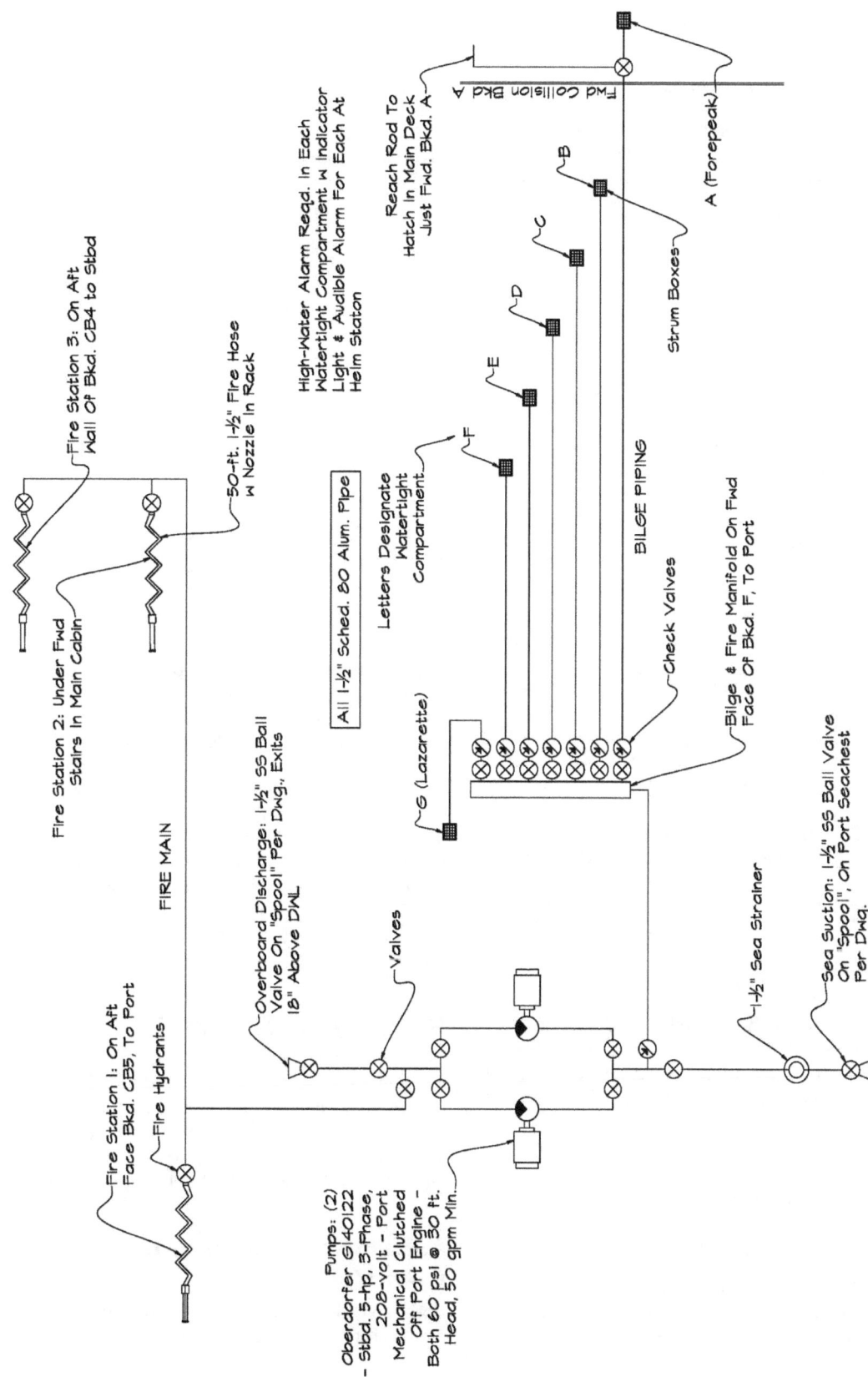

Figure 18-2. Bilge piping and fire main

TABLE 18-2. ABS BILGE-SYSTEM REQUIREMENTS

Vessel Length	Minimum Capacity per Pump	Minimum Pipe Inside Diameter
Below 65 ft. (19.8 m)	25 gpm (240 lpm)	1 in. (25 mm)
65 ft. (19.8 m) or greater but less than 100 ft. (30.5 m)	50 gpm (184 lpm)	1.25 in. (32 mm)
100 ft. (30.5 m) or greater but less than 150 ft (45.7 m)	66.6 gpm (240 lpm)	1.5 in. (38 mm)

Beam: 14.75 ft. (4.5 m)
Molded depth: 7.58 ft. (2.31 m)
Length of longest compartment: 17.6 ft. (5.36 m)
Displacement: 25.2 long tons (25.6 metric tons)

CFR Commercial would require one power-driven pump of 10 gpm (38 lpm) and one portable hand pump, or one fixed hand pump of 10 gpm (38 lpm) and one portable pump of 5 gpm (19 lpm). Minimum bilge pipe diameter is 1 inch (DN 25 mm).

ABS would require one power-driven pump of 25 gpm (95 lpm) with the minimum pipe diameter found by the ABS formulas, but not less than Table 18-2: a 1-inch (DN 25 mm) ID pipe, in this case.

The main suction line for ABS would be

$$1 + \sqrt{\frac{46 \text{ ft. WL } (14.75 \text{ ft. beam} + 7.58 \text{ ft. depth molded})}{2{,}500}}$$

$$= 1.64 \text{ in. ID}$$

Inspecting the pipe tables in Appendix B, we find that 1½-inch schedule 40 pipe has an ID of 1.61 inches. This is within ¼ inch of the calculated pipe ID. Use 1½-inch schedule 40 pipe.

Or

$$25 + 1.68\sqrt{14 \text{ m LOA } (4.5 \text{ m beam} + 2.31 \text{ m depth molded})}$$

$$= 41.4 \text{ mm ID}$$

Inspecting the pipe tables in Appendix B, we find that DN 40 mm schedule 40 pipe has an ID of 40.89 mm. This is within 6 mm of the calculated pipe ID. Use DN 40 mm schedule 40 pipe.

The ABS branch line for the longest compartment would be

$$1 + \sqrt{\frac{17.6 \text{ ft. compartment length}}{(14.75 \text{ ft. beam} + 7.58 \text{ ft. molded depth})} \cdot \frac{1}{1{,}500}}$$

$$= 1.51 \text{ in. ID}$$

Inspecting the pipe tables in Appendix B, we find that 1¼-inch schedule 40 pipe has an ID of 1.38 in. This is within ¼ inch of the calculated pipe ID. Use 1¼-inch schedule 40 pipe.

Or

$$25 + 2.16\sqrt{\frac{5.36 \text{ m compartment length } (4.5 \text{ m}}{\text{beam} + 2.31 \text{ m molded depth})}}$$

$$= 36.78 \text{ mm ID}$$

Inspecting the pipe tables in Appendix B, we find that DN 32 mm schedule 40 pipe has an ID of 35.05 mm. This is within 6 mm of the calculated pipe ID. Use DN 32 mm schedule 40 pipe.

Note that smaller compartments could use smaller branch-line diameters, but not less than 1 inch (25 mm) ID for this vessel. It's usually best, however, to make all branch lines the same diameter (the one required for the largest compartment) to simplify installation, maintenance, and repair.

Bilge-Piping Material

CFR Commercial states that bilge and firemain piping are piping for vital systems. CFR Commercial requires that all such piping be steel or stainless steel. The exception is for aluminum boats, which may use aluminum pipe, schedule 80 wall minimum.

Estimating Flooding Rate from Hull Damage

Both the CFR and ABS minimum recommendations for bilge-pump capacity seem too low

ISO Bilge-Pump Requirements

Under ISO 15083-2003—for categories A, B, and C recreational boats—the requirements for bilge-pump capacity are rather low: a single bilge pump, as shown in the table.

Boat Length	Pump Capacity
Less than 6 m (19.6 ft.)	10 lpm (2.6 gpm)
6 m to 12 m (19.6 ft. to 39.4 ft.)	15 lpm (4 gpm)
12 m to 24 m (19.6 ft. to 78.7 ft.)	30 lpm (8 gpm)

Measured with a pressure of 10 kPa (0.1 m of head), or 1.45 psi (0.34 ft. head), fresh water.

---

to me. We can check the minimum required pump capacity against the approximate flooding rate from a rather small hole in the hull below the waterline. The following is a reasonable approximate formula for flooding rate.

Formula 18-3. Flooding Rate from Hull Damage

$$\text{gpm} = 5.67 \times d^2 \times \sqrt{H}$$

or

$$\text{lpm} = 2.08 \times d^2 \times \sqrt{H}$$

Where
gpm = flooding rate in gallons per minute
lpm = flooding rate in liters per minute
d = approximate opening diameter, in. or cm
H = depth of opening below the waterline (head), in. or cm

Example: Let's assume a simple puncture of approximately 2-inches (50 mm) diameter, located 1.5 ft. (0.46 m) below the waterline. We would find

$$5.67 \times (2 \text{ in.})^2 \times \sqrt{18 \text{ in.}} = 96.2 \text{ gpm}$$

or

$$2.08 \times (5 \text{ cm})^2 \times \sqrt{46 \text{ cm}} = 352 \text{ lpm}$$

You can see that even a hole of modest size (and not all that deep) will quickly exceed the minimum bilge-pump capacity required by CFR Commercial or ABS. There are practical limits to how large a bilge system you can and should install, but I recommend more than the minimum requirements of CFR Commercial or ABS.

Sizing Up a Bilge Pump for the Real World

Many manufacturers' bilge-pump capacity ratings aren't all they ought to be. Most bilge-pump manufacturers rate their pump capacity with no hoses attached, with no lift (head), and with an optimum full-12-volt power source. (Those that do rate for head state this clearly, and it's usually a nominal 10-foot or 3-meter head.) Not a boat in existence operates a bilge pump like this. The friction in the 3 to 6 feet (1 to 2 meters) or more of hose and pipe commonly found in all bilge systems cuts the flow rate, and the batteries are seldom delivering full oomph (not to mention the voltage drop in the wiring). In addition, all bilge systems have some lift (they have to, obviously) usually between 2 and 5 feet (0.6 and 1.5 m) for smaller boats, but as much as 12 feet (3.7 m) or more on larger craft.

Manufacturers rate capacity in gph (gallons per hour) or gpm (gallons per minute); or in metric in lph (liters per hour) or lpm (liters per minute). Unfortunately, that shiny new pump rated at, say, 1,500 gph (5,700 lph) in the catalog will seldom deliver more than half that in a real-service installation. Indeed, 40 percent of rated capacity is about the norm. The real flow out the through-hull outlet from this 1,500-gph (5,700 lph) pump thus will be about 600 gph (2,280 lph).

Gerr's Bilge-Pump Rule

Allowing for this loss in flow rate, what's the minimum pump capacity that should be installed in a given boat? The following formula will give sensible results.

Formula 18-4.

Formula 18-4. Gerr's Bilge-Pump Rule: Minimum Pump Capacity

Pump capacity (gph) = 1,000 + (100 × displacement in long tons)

or

Pump capacity (lph) = 3,785 + (372 × displacement in metric tons)

Where
gph = gallons per hour
lph = liters per hour

Returning to *Fluky Flooder*, we would find

1,000 + (100 × 25.2 long tons) = 3,520 gph
3,520 gph ÷ 60 min./hr. = 58.7 gpm

or

3,785 + (372 × 25.6 metric tons) = 13,308 lph
13,308 lph ÷ 60 min./hr. = 222 lpm

This is almost 6 times more than CFR Commercial for *Fluky Flooder* and more than twice the ABS requirement. This is the minimum power-driven pump capacity (manufacturer's rated capacity; we've allowed for only 40 percent efficiency) that *Fluky* should be fitted with. If you have less capacity installed, go out and get a bigger pump or an additional one. Remember, however, the "minimum"—you can never have too much pump capacity. It wouldn't be unreasonable to install 3 or 4 times this flow rate if you had the space and available power. In addition, every boat should be fitted with at least one manual bilge pump of at least one-third the recommended power-driven pump capacity (up to the maximum that a manual pump can be expected to deliver).

To maximize pump performance, you should do the following:

- Use the smoothest hose you can find.
- Avoid or replace the common corrugated bilge-pump hose completely.
- Minimize the number of kinks and bends.
- Keep the hose run as short as practical.

You also need to make certain all electric connections are tight, sound, and corrosion-free. A loose connection or corrosion buildup will cause a voltage drop that will greatly reduce the pump's discharge rate.

The Vented Loop on Bilge Systems

Keep in mind that when heeled, sailboats can immerse a bilge-pump opening in the topsides that's well above the waterline when the boat is vertical. You must be careful to work out the location of the bilge-pump exit in the worst likely heeled condition. If it will be below the heeled waterline, you must install a vented loop as described in Chapter 7, page 112.

It's best to locate the vented loop as close to the centerline as possible. You can see in Figure 18-3 that moving the vented loop inboard allows you to lower it, while still being above the heeled waterline. Unfortunately, accommodations, machinery, or tanks often take up the middle of the vessel, so you'll frequently have no choice but to locate the vented loop outboard. But see how much you can reduce the static head—if you can move the loop inboard and thus lower it. This either increases bilge-pump output or allows the same output with less power.

Chapter 18: Bilge Systems, Fire Mains, and Fire Extinguishers

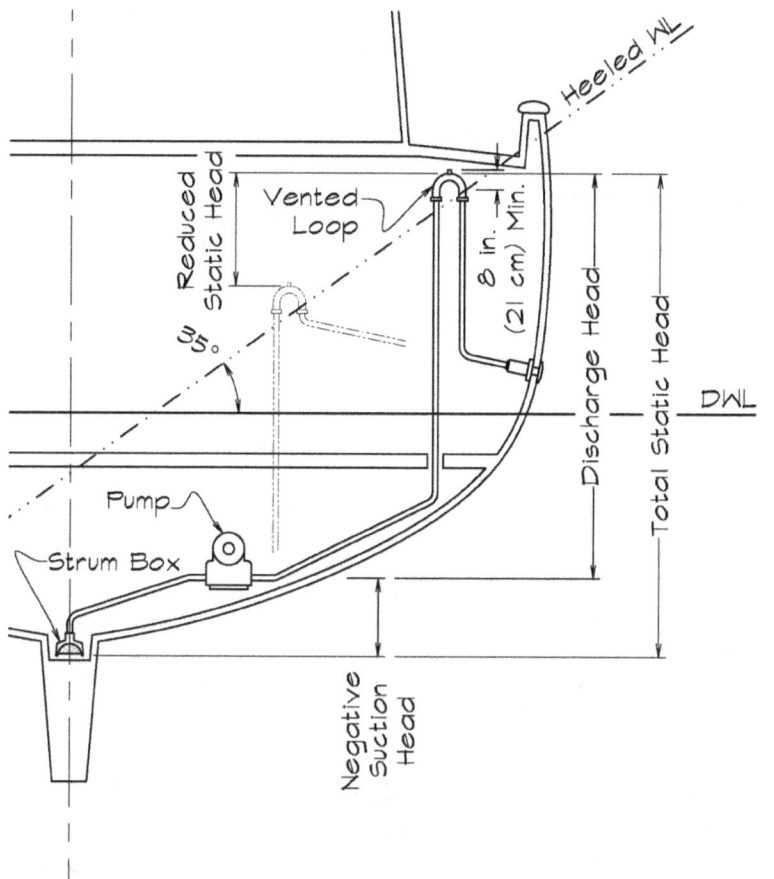

Figure 18-3. Bilge-system vented-loop location

Practical Bilge Piping Diameter

As a general rule, ABS recommendations for bilge-system piping diameter work well; however, keep in mind that the standard inlet/suction and outlet/discharge port on the pump you install is optimized for best pump efficiency. Unless you are building a classed vessel, it's better to use the inlet and outlet size on the pump as your bilge-pipe diameter. The exception is a long or convoluted pipe-exit run. When such a run can't be avoided, it will reduce friction head in the line to increase the bilge-pipe diameter with an expander after the pump-discharge port. Don't do this ahead of the pump suction/inlet port, however, and don't reduce the line diameter on the outlet line after expanding it. The larger diameter must continue through the through-hull outlet.

THOUGHTS AND RECOMMENDATIONS ON BILGE SYSTEMS FOR BOATS

CFR Commercial and ABS, in varying degrees, approach bilge systems as if they were installed on ships. The assumption is that a fairly large professional crew will be intelligently operating the system. Boats are different; most are pleasure craft. As such, they have a small crew, which—by definition—are not professional. Even small passenger vessels and fishing vessels have relatively small crews and tight spaces (at least compared with ships). Though a small passenger vessel must comply with CFR Commercial, my preference is to install automatic submersible bilge pumps in each compartment to meet or

295

exceed my bilge-pump rule in total in addition to the CFR-required bilge system and fire main.

Our example boat *Fluky Flooder* is based on a real yacht my office designed, and it was fitted with four DC submersible bilge pumps rated at 3,700 gph (14,000 lph) each; total 14,800 gph (56,000 lph). These were the primary bilge pumps in each watertight compartment, each with a 1½-inch (31.1 mm) discharge port (Figure 18-4). In addition, we installed four smaller DC submersible bilge pumps of 360 gph (1,360 lph) each, with a ¾-inch (19 mm) discharge port. (As a pleasure craft in this size, she was not fitted with the CFR-required bilge system.)

There are three disadvantages to larger powered bilge pumps. One is that they draw more amperage and thus put greater demand on the battery bank. Another is that the large-diameter discharge line holds a fair amount of water. When the pump is turned off, the water remaining in the discharge line runs back down into the bilge. Assuming about 5 feet (1.52 m) of discharge line on a 1½-inch (30 mm) hose, this is about half a gallon (1.8 L) of water. The third disadvantage is that if there's only a little water in the bilge—even enough to cover the pump inlet opening—there won't be enough pressure (suction head) to create sufficient flow for the pump to work. The pump will just churn the water around without pumping this last bit out (recirculation).

To avoid these disadvantages, larger, high-capacity submersible pumps are installed on pads to lift them about 5 inches (125 mm) above the lowest point in each bilge compartment, with each pump's automatic float switch up on the same level. Small-capacity submersible pumps are located right at the lowest point in the bilge sump of each compartment, with their auto float switches at their level.

In this way the smaller, low-powered pumps handle the vast majority of routine bilge pumping. This reduces battery draw and greatly reduces the amount of water that spills back into the bilge from their smaller discharge lines when the pumps are shut down. In the event of a serious flooding situation, the water rises high enough to trip the upper, large-capacity bilge pumps.

Because the preceding configuration is automatic and high capacity, it's the approach I use on almost all boats. If the boat is to be a passenger vessel, I then add the separate powered bilge and fire-main system to comply with the CFR. This system really would be used only in extreme emergencies, as the automatic, submersible-pump system will handle all ordinary problems.

Bilge-Pipe Material on Pleasure Vessels

On yachts, plastic pipe, hose, and pipe (steel, stainless, or aluminum) can be used for bilge piping. Don't use less than schedule-40-weight pipe. Use heavy hose specifically designed and intended for bilge piping. Use smooth hose, not corrugated hose. Hoses must be fastened with double stainless hose clamps exactly per the specifications in Chapter 4. Remember, the failure of a hose in the bilge system will result at least in loss of that part of the system, and likely cause serious flooding. Plastic pipe must be strong. Most plastic pipe becomes brittle in cold weather and with age. Use only the best grade, and be sure it's properly installed and supported.

Pump Alarms and Counters

When installing small- and high-capacity automatic pumps in the previous dual configuration, you should install a high-water alarm on the upper bilge-pump float switch. Ideally, this should be wired to an indicator board at the helm or at the circuit panel, with

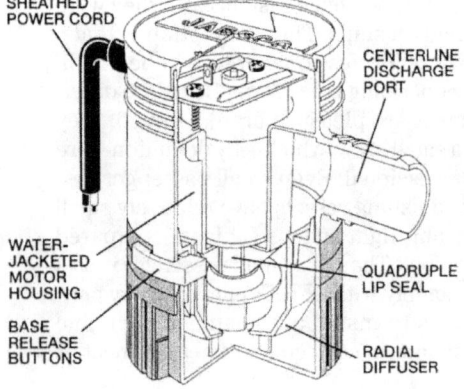

Figure 18-4. Submersible bilge pump (Courtesy Jabsco/ITT Industries)

LED lights to indicate which compartment has tripped the alarm.

On the same indicator board, it's also ideal to set up a run counter for the small-capacity bilge pumps. These can be set up to record the number of times the pump cycles on. If you see that the pump has switched on once or twice in a few weeks or months, no problem. If you notice the frequency increasing, however, you need to find the cause. I slightly prefer a total-hour counter. This gives the total hours the small-capacity pump has run. If you note the hours in the log every time you come aboard, it's a simple matter to divide by the days since the past entry and get the hours per day of operation. (On a new, well-fitted boat it may be close to zero.) In any case, an increase in the number of hours per day is cause for thorough investigation.

Bilge-Discharge Hull-Exit Location

The bilge system should discharge to a through-hull above the waterline—about 12 inches (20 cm) above on boats up to 60 feet (18.2 m) waterline and about 18 inches (45 cm) above on boats over 60 feet (18.2 m) waterline.

Notes on Float Switches

The standard float switch works fine. It's simply a buoyant flapper on a hinge. When the water level rises, it lifts the hinged flap of the float, and a sliding or rolling bead in the flap closes the electric connection, turning on the pump. One drawback is obvious. Debris can jam the float down so it won't lift and activate, or jam under the float and keep it from shutting off. Most manufacturers sell plastic cover guards that surround the float switch to protect it from debris (Figure 18-5). These are so inexpensive that there's no excuse for not installing them.

Another less obvious drawback is that some float switches use a drop of liquid mercury to complete the electric connection. The quantity of mercury is tiny and so really not much of a hazard, but on steel or aluminum boats (especially aluminum), severe corrosion can result if the mercury escapes from a

Figure 18-5. Float switch (right) and cover guard (Courtesy Jabsco/ITT Industries)

cracked float. For metal boats, be sure to specify float switches without mercury. There are modern (and slightly more expensive) automatic switches, such as those that use two Mirus detector cells to sense the presence of water by using a low-impedance electric field. Other standard float switches use a simple ball bearing rather than a drop of mercury.

FIRE MAINS AND FIRE SUPPRESSION

Fire suppression of some form or other is required under law for all boats. Most boats under 75 feet (23 m) or so will rely exclusively on fire extinguishers of various types; however, small commercial vessels are required to have fire mains under CFR Commercial, and this is a good precaution for large yachts too.

Fire Mains

A fire main is nothing more than a powerful pump connected to a piping system to deliver plenty of water to fire hoses at strategically located hydrants throughout the boat. The hydrant connects to a fire hose with a nozzle, usually stored on a rack. Figure 18-6 shows a typical installation on a 110-foot (34 m) motoryacht.

As mentioned earlier, the pump for the fire main can be shared with the bilge system, which usually makes the most sense. You can see the layout in Figure 18-2. As a general rule, I recommend that fire mains be installed on all yachts over 90 feet (27.5 m), though this is not a legal requirement for pleasure

PART SIX: PLUMBING SYSTEMS WITH NOTES ON FIRE SUPPRESSION

Figure 18-6. Fire station with hydrant, hose, and nozzle

Figure 18-7. Pumps suitable for fire mains (Courtesy Oberdorfer)

craft of any type. When installing any fire main, I follow the requirements of the CFR for passenger vessels, with the exception that—on fiberglass boats—I may use aluminum pipe instead of steel.

The fire pump must deliver a hose stream that projects at least 25 feet (7.6 m) out of the nozzle.

The fire pump can be driven off the main engine. It must be capable of operation both from a remote central fire station and from the pump.

Fire hoses and nozzles must be left permanently attached to the hydrant and ready for immediate use, and the hose and fittings must be Underwriters Laboratories (UL)–approved lined fire hose and assemblies or its equivalent, with fittings of brass, bronze, or stainless that won't corrode in the marine environment.

The fire stations and hydrants must be arranged so that hoses from the various fire stations will reach all parts of the boat.

For vessels carrying more than 49 passengers or over 65 feet (19.8 m), the hose and piping must be 1½-inch (40 mm) minimum diameter.

For vessels under 65 feet and carrying 49 passengers or less, the hose may be good-quality garden hose, not less than ⅝-inch (16 mm) diameter.

Since—other than on a small passenger vessel—you usually will install fire mains only on boats well over 65 feet (19.8 m), you can consider 1½-inch (40 mm) fire hose and piping, and 50 gpm (189 lpm) at 60 psi (414 kPa) as measured at the pump outlet as the fire-main standard. If you are using a pair of pumps for combined fire-main and bilge-system operation, they should both be sized to meet these requirements. One pump that meets these requirement is Oberdorfer's N13HDM pump (Figure 18-7). These pumps have 1½-inch (40 mm) ports and meet the required capacity.

TABLE 18-3. CFR FIRE-MAIN POWER-DRIVEN PUMP/CAPACITY REQUIREMENTS

Subchapter T	Description	Capacity and/or PSI
Vessels less than 100 GT carrying 150 or less passengers or having overnight accommodations for 49 or less	Vessels over 65 ft. (19.8 m) and vessels less than 65 ft. carrying more than 49 passengers	1 self-priming, power-driven pump, 50 gpm, 60 psi (189 lpm, 414 kPa) minimum on gauge at outlet of pump
	Ferry vessels not more than 65 ft. (19.8 m) carrying not more than 49 passengers	1 self-priming, power-driven pump, 10 gpm minimum; pressure unspecified

GT = gross tons

Chapter 18: Bilge Systems, Fire Mains, and Fire Extinguishers

Fire Extinguishers

Coast Guard–approved fire extinguishers are required on all boats where a fire hazard can be expected from engines or any fuel. Extinguishers are classified by a letter and a number symbol. The letter indicates the type of fire the unit is designed to extinguish. Type B, for example, is designed to extinguish flammable liquids such as gasoline, oil, and grease fires. The number indicates the relative size of the extinguisher. The higher the number, the larger the extinguisher.

The required extinguishers are either B-I or B-II classification and have specific marine mounting brackets. They should be installed where they are easily accessible in compartments with a possible fire source or just outside such a compartment.

Classes of Fires and Fire Extinguishers

- **A.** (Ash producing) wood, paper, natural fabric, etc.
- **B.** (Boiling/liquid) diesel, gasoline, grease, kerosene, naphtha, paint, etc.
- **C.** (Current/electric) any electrical fire
- **D.** (Deadly) volatile and/or poisonous chemicals, flares, explosives, magnesium, etc.
- **K.** (Kitchen) vegetable oils, animal oils, or fats in cooking appliances. This is primarily for commercial kitchens

Extinguisher markings can be confusing because extinguishers can be approved for several different types of hazards. For instance, an extinguisher marked "Type A, Size II, Type B:C, Size I" is a B-I extinguisher (in addition to being an A and C type). Look for the part of the label that says "Marine Type USCG," and check to see that Type B is indicated. Portable extinguishers of either size I or II are suitable. Size III or larger are too cumbersome for use on most boats. All marine fire extinguishers should be B-type (with any other type listed in addition being just fine).

TABLE 18-4. FIRE-EXTINGUISHER CLASSES AND SIZES

Classes	Foam gal. (L)	CO_2 lb. (kg)	Dry Chemical lb. (kg)	Halon* lb. (kg)	Halocarbon† lb. (kg)
B-I (Type B, Size I)	1.25 (4.7)	5 (2.3)	2 (0.9)	2.5 (1.1)	5 (2.3)
B-I (Type B, Size II)	2.5 (9.5)	15 (6.8)	10 (4.5)	10 (4.5)	15 (6.8)

*Many tables still reference Halon. Halon has been banned to protect the ozone layer. FE 241, FM 200, FE-227, or HFC-227 are the common replacements.
†Halocarbon is either hydrochlorofluorocarbons (HCFCs) or hyrdrofluorocarbons (HFCs).

TABLE 18-5. MINIMUM NUMBER OF REQUIRED HANDHELD EXTINGUISHERS—BOATS UP TO 65 FT. (19.8 M)

Vessel Length	With No Fixed System	With Approved Fixed System
Open boats under 16 ft. (4.9 m)	(1) B-1	None
Open boats over 16 ft. (4.9 m)	(2) B-2	None
All boats less than 26 ft. (7.9 m)	(2) B-I	None
26 ft. to less than 40 ft. (7.9 to 12.2 m)	(3) B-I	(2) B-I
40 ft. to 65 ft. (12.2 to 19.8 m)	(4) B-I	(3) B-I or (2) B-II

(Continued)

(Continued from previous)

TABLE 18-6. ABYC A-4, MINIMUM NUMBER OF REQUIRED HANDHELD EXTINGUISHERS

Boats over 65 ft. (19.8 m)

Gross Tons*	No. of Extinguishers	USCG Type	Location
Not over 50	1†	B-II	Outside engine compartment
	1	B-II	Helmsman's position
	3	B-I	Galley, crew's quarters, and cabin
50–100	1†	B-II	Outside engine compartment
	2	B-II	Helmsman's position and galley
	2	B-I	Crew's quarters and cabin
100–500	1†	B-II	Outside engine compartment
	3	B-II	Helmsman's position, galley, and crew's quarters
	1	B-I	Cabin

*Tons are admeasured gross tons, not displacement.
†Add an additional B-II extinguisher if over 1,000 hp is installed, and for each additional increment of 1,000 hp.

The minimum number is just that, a minimum. It's a good idea to install 2 or 3 times the minimum number as a rule. A typical 44-foot (13.4 m) motor cruiser, for instance, might have an extinguisher in or just outside the galley, in or just outside each stateroom, at or near the helm, in or just outside the main saloon, and in or near the cockpit, as well as in or near the engine compartment. This would be five or six extinguishers. Larger is better—up to B-II size—if you can find the room.

Fixed Fire Extinguishers

As we saw at the beginning of Chapter 4, handheld fire extinguishers are not up to putting out major engine-compartment or fuel fires. For this reason, I recommend that all boats with engine compartments install automatic, fixed fire extinguishers. These usually discharge either CO_2 or FE-241. The manufacturer's recommendation for capacity to serve the compartment's volume should be met or exceeded (see Table 18-7 for capacity/volume). (NOTE: Many references still specify Halon. Halon has been banned to protect the ozone layer.)

An automatic extinguisher should be wired to automatically close the fire dampers, turn off the engine blowers, and turn off the ignition. It should also sound a fire alarm. If a manually operated fixed fire extinguisher is installed without these automatic shutdowns, a warning placard must be located near the fire-suppression controls stating that the engine and blowers must be turned off before discharge. This is acceptable, but arranging these shutdowns as automatic doesn't cost that much more, and the crew will have enough on their minds in such a situation. If toxic chemicals are used, there should also be a placard outside the machinery space warning that the fire-suppression gases are toxic and indicating to use the blower to clear all gas before entering.

TABLE 18-7. ABYC A-4 EXTINGUISHER CAPACITY VERSUS COMPARTMENT VOLUME

Agent		Min. Extinguisher Size lb.	kg	Max. Compartment Volume cu. ft.	m³
CO_2		5	2.3	66	1.9
		10	4.5	133	3.8
		15	6.8	200	5.7
		20	9.1	266	7.5
Halon*		2.5	1.1	108	3.1
		3	1.4	130	3.7
		4	1.8	174	4.9
		5	2.3	217	6.1
		9	4.1	391	11.1
		13	5.9	565	16.0
Halocarbon	USCG B-I	(5.75 lb., 2.6 kg)		108	3.1
	USCG B-II	(10.75 lb., 4.87 kg)		250	7.0

*Halon discontinued. Add at least 50 percent for Halon substitutes.

HALON REPLACEMENTS As noted, Halon has been banned to preserve the ozone layer (though it may still be used on existing installations). The common replacements for Halon are

- **CO_2 (carbon dioxide):** It is good for B- or C-class fires but not so effective on A-class fires. It doesn't leave a residue or damage electric components.
- **FE-241 (chlorotetrafluoroethane):** Probably the most common Halon replacement other than CO_2. It is toxic if inhaled, though it leaves no residue. It is suitable for unoccupied compartments such as engine and machinery spaces. Good for A, B, and C fires.
- **FE-227 and HFC-227 (heptafluoropropanes):** Common Halon replacements for occupied spaces because they are nontoxic. Good for A, B, and C fires.
- **FM-200 (a heptafluoropropane):** A fairly expensive Halon replacement. Unlike FE-241, it is not toxic and is suited to occupied compartments. It is generally a special-order item, however. Good for A, B, and C fires.

NOTE: Most standard tables for required extinguisher capacity give weight in pounds (or kg) of CO_2 and pounds (or kg) of Halon required to protect given compartment volumes. Non-CO_2 Halon replacements, however, are not as effective as Halon. You should allow 50 percent more weight for the Halon replacement and confirm the quantity with the manufacturer.

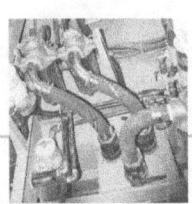

CHAPTER 19

Selecting and Sizing Pumps

So far, we've seen how to determine the required pump size for bilge systems and fire mains using ABS and CFR Commercial rules or Gerr's Bilge-Pump Rule. Pumps are used on boats for all sorts of things. In fact, the more systems there are aboard, the more pumps there likely will be: pressure-water systems, deck washdowns, refrigeration and air-conditioning condensers, bait wells, toilets, engine-cooling water, fuel transfer, bilge systems, fire mains, and more. Each pump, with its associated piping, hoses, and connections, is a potential source of trouble. They must all be accessible for maintenance, and they must all be sized, located, and installed correctly. We'll examine the basic types of pumps used in most boat systems to see which ones are most suited to specific applications and then review a more detailed approach to determining required pump capacity and power.

TYPES OF PUMPS

Pumps are one of the oldest machines in the world. They are available in a bewildering array: jet pumps, centrifugal pumps, mixed-flow pumps, diaphragm pumps, ejector pumps, and many more. Each type has its subtypes. We'll deal specifically with the pumps most commonly found in service aboard boats. These can be divided into two fundamental types based on their mode of operation: positive-displacement pumps and kinetic pumps.

Positive-Displacement Pumps

Positive-displacement pumps work by moving a fixed volume of fluid with each stroke or revolution. They can be divided again into two subcategories: reciprocating-action positive-displacement pumps, and rotary-action positive-displacement pumps.

RECIPROCATING POSITIVE-DISPLACEMENT PUMPS Reciprocating positive-displacement pumps are probably the oldest form of pump in use. They use pistons or plungers in concert with flapper valves, or a diaphragm in concert with flapper valves (check valves). The latter are diaphragm pumps. Figure 19-1 shows the inlet valve opening on the intake stroke and then closing on the outlet stroke, which also opens the outlet valve.

Diaphragm pumps are generally the most effective manual bilge pumps, though they have many uses as powered pumps, as well (Figure 19-2). Reciprocating pumps can be set up to discharge water flow on one stroke (with the handle moving in one direction) or on both strokes (with the handle moving in both directions). The former is a single-action pump and the latter a double-action pump.

Large-inlet-diameter (1 in. [25 mm] or more) diaphragm pumps can handle solid matter mixed with the fluid. This makes them excellent for such applications as pumping bilges (where debris may be mixed in) or pumping out blackwater (sewage). Some of

Chapter 19: Selecting and Sizing Pumps

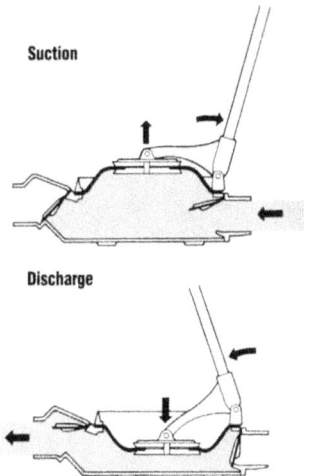

Figure 19-1. Diaphragm pump (Courtesy Edson International)

these pumps (such as the Edson 1½-in., 40 mm diaphragm pump) have pumped an entire shirt (left in the bilge) through the system without clogging. An argument can be made for not using strum boxes on pumps like this,

since the strum box could be blocked by, say, this same shirt. In most instances, however, I recommend a strum box on all bilge-pump intakes.

ROTARY POSITIVE-DISPLACEMENT PUMPS

Rotary positive-displacement pumps may use vanes, lobes, screws, or gears. The most common for use on boats are rotary-vane pumps and flexible-impeller pumps (geared pumps are for high pressure and high output, such as fire pumps).

All positive-displacement pumps share the following characteristics:

- They are self-priming. They can lift fluid to the suction/inlet port, or they can have a negative head at the inlet port—a suction head.
- They act as check valves. Fluid will not flow backward through the pump when the pump is turned off.

In Figure 19-3, the flexible-impeller blades at "a" rotating on the offset cam create a vacuum, causing the pump suction. At "b" the impeller continues to rotate, drawing in more liquid. As the impeller rotates to the outlet port "c," the liquid is expelled. Flexible-impeller pumps can usually handle some solids in the flow, depending on the specific pump and impeller. Check with the manufacturer.

In rotary vane pumps (Figure 19-4), at "a" the liquid is drawn in by the suction created by the vane expanding as it comes off the eccentric portion of the liner. These vanes spring, or squeeze in and out, in their slots in the rotor. Each successive vane "b" draws more liquid into the pump. When the vanes begin to compress again at the eccentric portion of the liner "c," the liquid is expelled from the outlet port. Vane pumps cannot tolerate solids in the fluid flow.

Figure 19-2. Manual diaphragm pump (Courtesy Edson International)

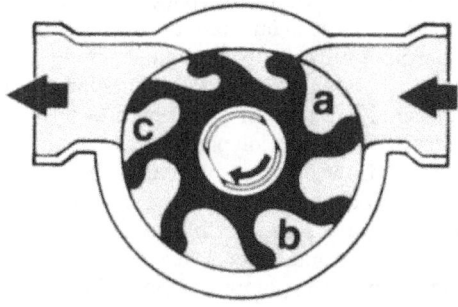

Figure 19-3. Flexible-impeller pump (Courtesy Jabsco/ITT Industries)

303

Figure 19-4. Rotary vane pump (Courtesy Jabsco/ITT Industries)

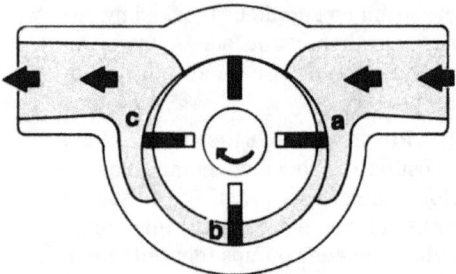

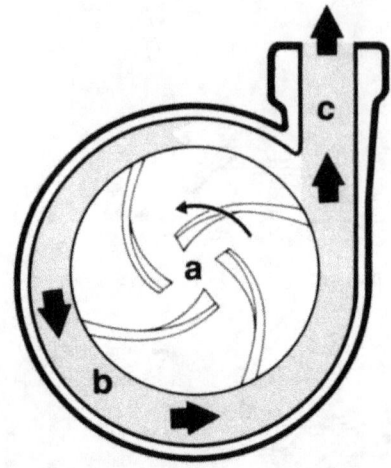

Figure 19-5. Centrifugal pump (Courtesy Jabsco/ITT Industries)

POSITIVE-DISPLACEMENT-PUMP MAXIMUM SUCTION LIFT The maximum theoretical lift (suction head or lift) to the suction/inlet port for positive-displacement pumps is about 30 feet (9 m). In practice, it is commonly around 24 feet (7.3 m). In most applications, you want to keep the suction head to 4 feet (1.2 m) or less if possible; however, it is sometimes necessary to locate a pump far from the fluid source, in which case greater suction heads may be both unavoidable and acceptable. Be sure to check with the pump manufacturer anytime the suction head, particularly the dry suction head, is over 4 feet (1.2 m). Dry suction head is the head (see the discussion to follow) that a pump must self-prime to when there's no water in the pump or intake line. The same pump will lift from a greater suction head once it's wet, but in most boat installations, manually priming a pump is not practical.

Kinetic Pumps

Kinetic pumps use the energy of motion to move the fluid in the pump. For common use on boats, kinetic pumps are essentially centrifugal pumps. Water enters the pump inlet at the center ("a") and is spun by the pump's vanes out to the outside of the pump's volute casing (round housing) by centrifugal force "b," where the water is expelled at the discharge port "c." Since the water is spun outward radially, these are radial pumps. Centrifugal or radial pumps may have a single suction port on one side (a single-suction pump) or a suction port on both sides (a double-suction pump).

An axial-flow pump is basically a propeller. In fact, boat propellers can be analyzed as kinetic pumps. It is possible to have an axial (propeller) pump that also uses centrifugal force as part of its pumping action. This is a combined axial-and-radial or mixed-flow pump. Again, on the majority of boats, standard centrifugal pumps are most common.

Rotary kinetic pumps (centrifugal, axial, or mixed-flow) all share the following characteristics:

- They are not self-priming. They cannot lift fluid up to the suction/inlet port, or they must have a positive head at the inlet port.
- They will not act as check valves. Fluid will flow backward through the pump when the pump is turned off.

Centrifugal pumps are the quietest in operation.

Pump Selection

With the preceding information, you can select a type of pump suited to the intended application. Ask yourself:

- Does the pump need to be self-priming?
- Will backflow be a problem when the pump is off? (A check valve can be used if needed.)
- Does the system require a high flow rate or high pressure?
- Does the pump need to handle solids mixed with the fluid?
- Will the pump be run dry?

We can arrange a selection chart for pump types as in Table 19-1.

TABLE 19-1. PUMP TYPE SELECTION

Pump Type	Engine Cooling		Condenser		Bilge		Gray Water	Toilets		Shower	Water System		Transfer
	Raw Water	Fresh Water	Fridge and Air-Conditioner	Washdown	Electric	Manual	Discharge	Electric	Manual	Dedicated	Pressure	Manual	Fuel and Oil
Flexible Impeller Vane	X		X	X	X			X			X		X
Centrifugal Electrical	X	X	X	X	X		X	X					X
Diaphragm					X		X			X	X		
Manual Diaphragm						X			X			X	
Piston Plunger						X			X			X	

UNDERSTANDING HEAD

Up to now, we've been tossing around the term *head* rather loosely. With regard to pumps, head has a very specific and important meaning. It is based on two interrelated facts:

1. It takes a known amount of power to raise a given quantity of a specific fluid a known distance.
2. Head is equal to pressure in psi, kPa, atmospheres, inches or mm of mercury (Hg), and so on.

It thus becomes convenient to use head, in feet or meters, in determining all the combined resistances a pump has to work against and so find the power required to pump fluid through a given piping system. Since water is the most common fluid pumped, we'll discuss head in terms of feet or meters of fresh water. Then to deal with other fluids, we'll apply adjustments as necessary.

Pumps, plumbing, and piping systems are fantastically complex subjects. The third edition of *Pump Handbook* (2000), edited by Igor Karassik, Joseph Messina, Paul Cooper, and Charles Heald, is about 2,500 pages, and that is just one reference on the subject. Again, what we're doing here is taking a fairly simple look at the basic (and relatively straightforward) pump and piping systems used aboard boats.

Static Head

Lift head or static head is the most obvious type. In Figure 19-6, you can see the total

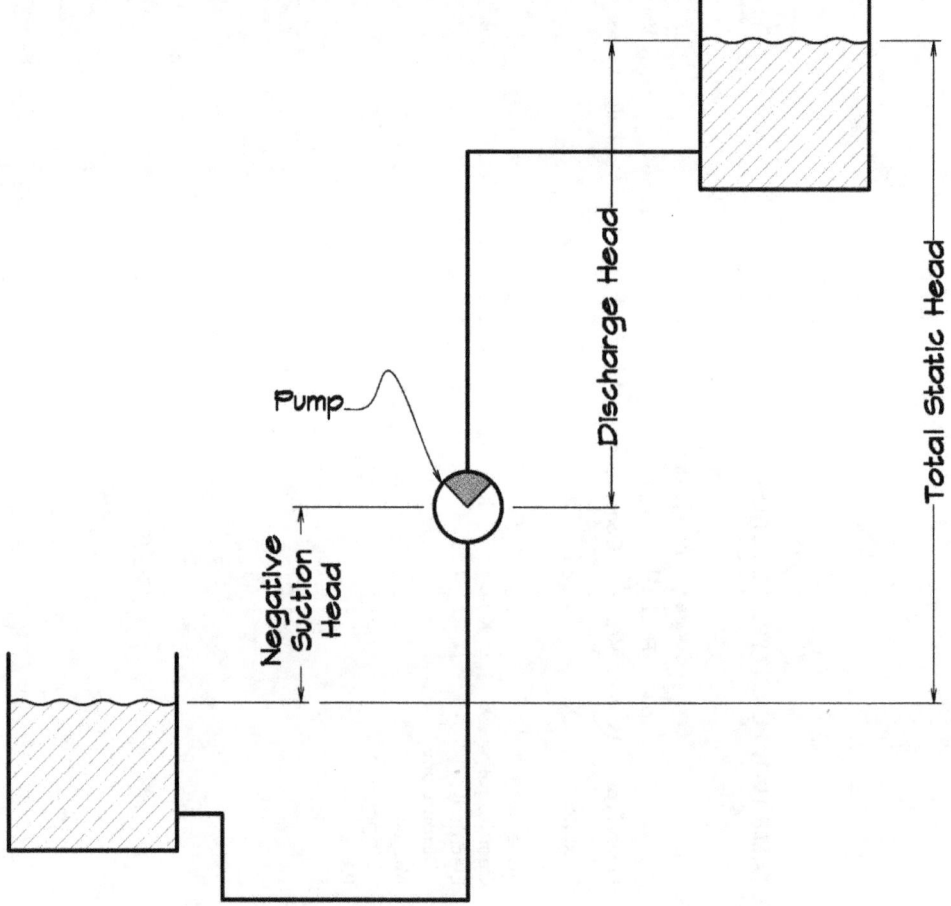

Figure 19-6. Static head with negative suction head

head for the pump in terms of simple lift. This is the static head, which is subdivided into discharge head and suction head. In this drawing, the suction head is negative, so this pump would have to be self-priming to lift water up to the pump.

NOTE: Pumps really don't suck fluid up into them. Positive-displacement pumps create a partial vacuum in their pumping chamber, which allows atmospheric pressure to push the water up into the pump to fill the partial vacuum.

Figure 19-7 shows a configuration with a positive suction head. This means that a non-self-priming pump can be used, such as a centrifugal pump.

Note that the total static head is the discharge head combined with the suction head. If the suction head is negative, this increases the total effective lift height and you add the negative suction head to the discharge head to get total static head. If the suction head is positive, this decreases the total effective lift height and you subtract the suction head from the discharge head to get total static head. You can also see that the head is measured to the top of the fluid being pumped from or into. This is because the column of fluid above the inlet or outlet has a static head (a pressure) that must be overcome to increase the fluid level in the upper container. (If the container didn't empty, the static head would

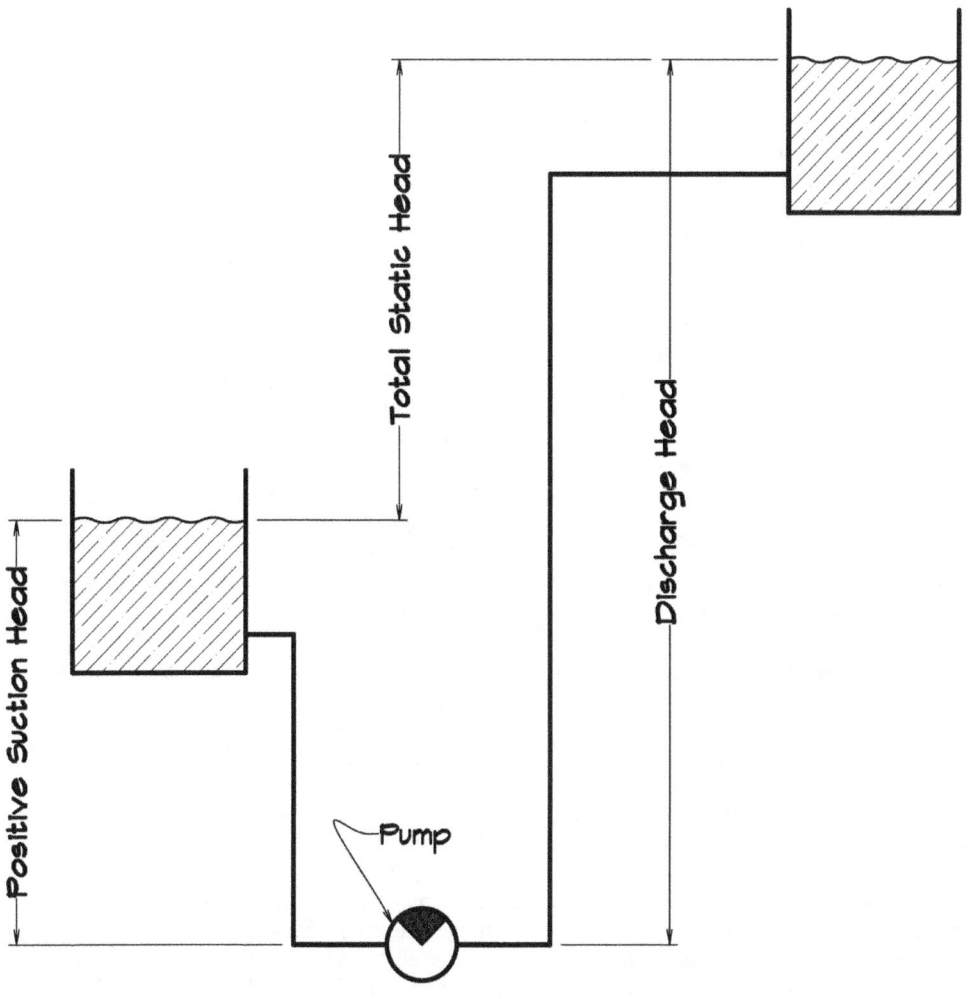

Figure 19-7. Static head with positive suction head

continue to increase.) Static head is found simply by measuring the appropriate vertical distances in feet or meters.

In a system that circulates water, like a closed cooling system, there is no static head. The water begins and ends its travel at the same level—at the pump.

Velocity Head

Velocity head is the head that results from the kinetic energy in the water flow. It is the head (height) the water would have to fall from to reach the velocity it's moving at in the system. Velocity head is important for high-volume systems, but at under 200 gpm or 12,000 gph (760 lpm or 45,600 lph), velocity head is small, usually under 0.4 foot (0.12 m). For our purposes here, we can ignore it.

Pressure Head

Formula 19-1.

In Figures 19-6 and 19-7, we are pumping to and from open containers. The height of the water in the container we're pumping into (above the pipe's inlet) is the pressure head, but it is already taken into account in the height of the discharge head. If you want a given pressure at a nozzle outlet for, say, a fire hose or a deck washdown, you can convert the required pressure in psi or kPa to head in feet or meters and add it to the total required head.

head (fresh water), ft. ÷ 2.31 = psi
psi × 2.31 = head (fresh water), ft.

or

head (fresh water), m × 9.8 = kPa
kPa ÷ 9.8 = head (fresh water), m

Seawater is 1.028 times denser, but for most ordinary pump calculations this can be neglected for static head and pressure head.

A bilge pump simply pumps into the atmosphere. You don't care about the exit pressure, only the flow rate, so the pressure head is zero. However, if you are selecting a pump to fill a tank and the pipe inlet is near the bottom of the tank, you will have to add the pressure head, either by accounting for the total height of water in the tank as static head or by adding it separately as pressure head.

(Note that such a pipe to the bottom of a tank would require a check valve.)

Friction Head

As water flows through pipes and fittings, it loses energy due to the friction of rubbing against the pipe walls. All pumps must overcome this significant component of the head. It has to be taken into account in any piping system. The longer the pipe run and the more fittings or bends, the greater the friction head. Similarly, for a given flow of water, the larger the pipe diameter and the fewer the fittings or bends, the less the friction head.

Calculating Friction Head

Friction head can be calculated as follows.

Formula 19-1. Friction Head

$$hf, ft. = \frac{10.44 \times L, ft. \times gpm^{1.85}}{C^{1.85} \times (ID, in.)^{4.86}}$$

or

$$hf, m = \frac{82.54 \times L, m \times lpm^{1.85}}{C^{1.85} \times (ID, cm)^{4.86}}$$

Where
hf = friction head, ft. or m
L = total length of pipe, ft. or m
gpm = flow, gallons per minute
lpm = flow, liters per minute
ID = inside diameter of pipe, in. or cm
 (NOTE: ID in cm, *not* mm, in this formula)
C = coefficient of roughness for the type of pipe:
 Iron and Steel Pipe = 100
 Plastic, Lead, Copper, and Brass Pipe = 130
 Smooth Hose = 140
 Corrugated Hose = 150

Friction head from fittings can be determined from Table 19-2.

To determine the total friction head in the system, you list all the fittings and then multiply them by their equivalent lengths. For instance, a 90-degree elbow is 30 D; for a 1¼-inch pipe, its equivalent length is 37.5 inches or 3.125 feet; for

TABLE 19-2. EQUIVALENT LENGTH OF PIPE FITTINGS

Fitting	Equivalent Pipe Length
90° Elbow	30D
45° Elbow	20D
T Straight Through	16D
T Through Side	60D
Swept 90° Bend (large radius)	4–8D
Open Gate Valve or Ball Valve	9D
Open Globe Valve	25D
Full-Bore Non-Return/Check Valve	6D
Butterfly Valve	20D
Entrance	12D
Contraction $d/D = 1/4$	16D
Contraction $d/D = 1/2$	12D
Contraction $d/D = 3/4$	8D
Enlargement $d/D = 1/4$	32D
Enlargement $d/D = 1/2$	24D
Enlargement $d/D = 3/4$	8D
Vented Loop	60D
Filter/Strainer	30D
Standard Coupling	2D

NOTE: D = inside diameter of pipe or hose.
NOTE: d = inside diameter of the smaller pipe or hose that follows a reducer coupling. Thus, Contraction d/D = the ratio of contraction in a reducer. Example: 2 inches reduced to 1 inch = 1/2, so multiply effective length by 12D, or 12 × ID.

31.8 mm pipe, its equivalent length is 954 mm, or 0.954 m.

Add the total equivalent lengths of all pipe fittings to the lengths of all the pipe sections, and enter that total length in Formula 19-1.

TOTAL APPARENT HEAD

The total apparent head for our purposes is the sum of all the relevant heads for a given piping system: static, friction, pressure, and so on, as applicable.

Before we can find the pumping power required, we need to determine the total apparent head.

Example: Let's say we want a deck washdown pump as shown in Figure 19-8. This is for a large yacht with 3/4-inch (19 mm) garden hose for the deck washdown and 3/4-inch (19 mm) hose for most of the internal "piping." We want a flow of 12 gpm at 20 psi (45 lpm at 140 kPa) at the nozzle outlet. We convert psi or kPa to feet or meters of head:

20 psi × 2.31 = 46.2 ft. pressure head

or

140 kPa ÷ 9.8 = 14.3 m pressure head

Static head is taken from the total vertical lift. We include the height that the hose nozzle will be held above the deck of about 4 feet (1.2 m), and we subtract the positive suction head as shown to get a static head of 10.25 feet (3.1 m).

To find friction head, we have to list all the fittings in the line and calculate their total equivalent length.

All are 3/4-inch (19 mm) hose (except for the fittings). Count the nozzle as a 90-degree bend and a valve. Table 19-3 lists all the fittings and provides totals.

178.5 in. ÷ 12 in./ft. = 14.87 ft. equivalent length of fittings

or

452 cm ÷ 100 cm/m = 4.52 m equivalent length of fittings

Length of internal hose = 18.25 ft. (5.56 m)

PART SIX: PLUMBING SYSTEMS WITH NOTES ON FIRE SUPPRESSION

Figure 19-8. Deck washdown plumbing

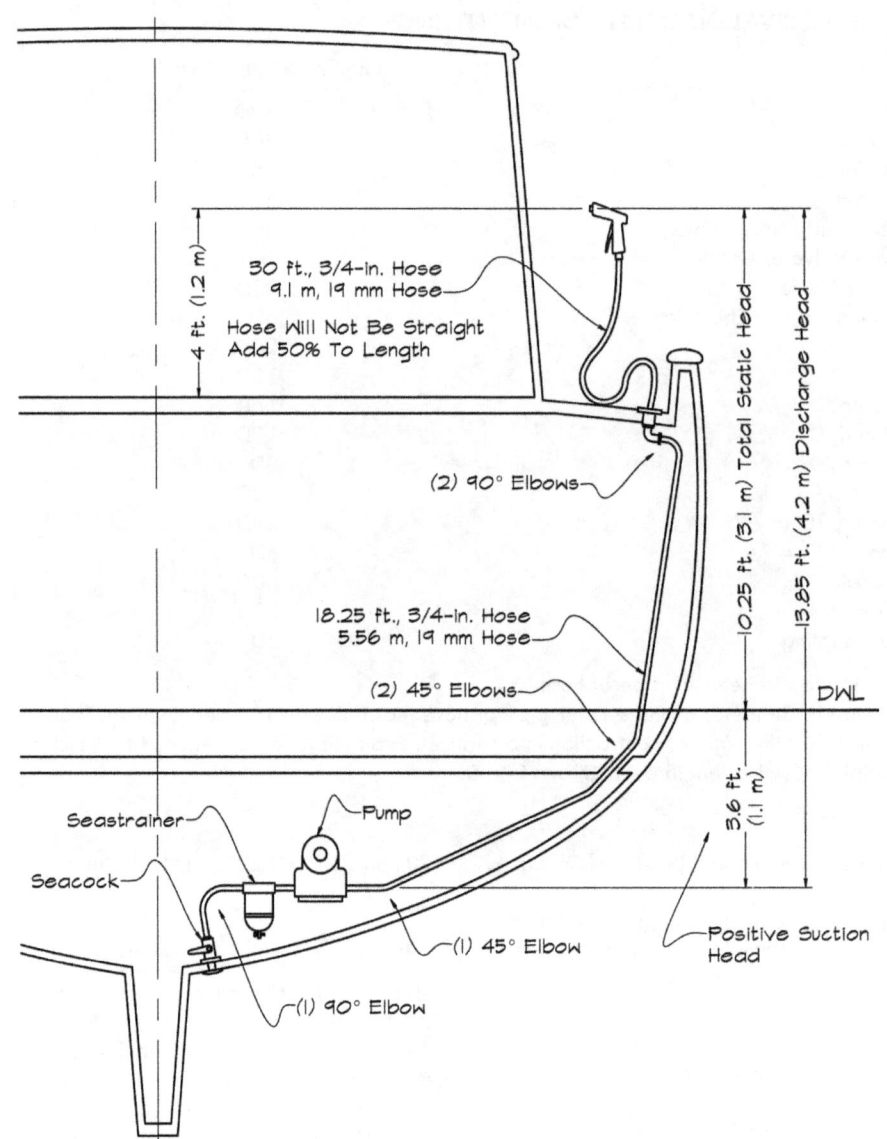

TABLE 19-3. THE TOTAL EQUIVALENT LENGTH OF FITTINGS PER TABLE 19-2 FOR FIGURE 19-8

English Units		Metric Units	
(4) 90° Elbows = 30 × 3/4 in. =	90.00 in.	(4) 90° Elbows = 30 × 1.9 cm =	228 cm
(2) 45° Elbows = 20 × 3/4 in. =	30.00 in.	(2) 45° Elbows = 20 × 1.9 cm =	76 cm
(1) Entrance = 12 × 3/4 in. =	9.00 in.	(1) Entrance = 12 × 1.9 cm =	23 cm
(1) Seacock/Valve = 9 × 3/4 in. =	6.75 in.	(1) Seacock/Valve = 9 × 1.9 cm =	17 cm
(1) Sea Strainer = 30 × 3/4 in. =	22.50 in.	(1) Sea Strainer = 30 × 1.9 cm =	57 cm
(1) Valve at Handle = 25 × 3/4 in. =	18.75 in.	(1) Valve at Handle = 25 × 1.9 cm =	47 cm
(1) Deck Fitting (Coupling) = 2 × 3/4 in. =	1.50 in.	(1) Deck Fitting (Coupling) = 2 × 1.9 cm =	4 cm
Total =	178.50 in.	Total =	452 cm

Washdown garden hose on deck usually lies in serpentine loops; increase effective length by 50 percent.

$$30 \text{ ft. garden hose} \times 1.5 = 45 \text{ ft.}$$

or

$$9.1 \text{ m garden hose} \times 1.5 = 13.6 \text{ m}$$

Total effective length of all hose (pipe) and fittings:

$$14.87 \text{ ft. fittings} + 18.25 \text{ ft. internal hose} + 45 \text{ ft. garden hose} = 78.1 \text{ ft.}$$

or

$$4.52 \text{ m fittings} + 5.56 \text{ m internal hose} + 13.6 \text{ m garden hose} = 23.7 \text{ m}$$

Friction head (hf) is

$$hf, \text{ ft.} = \frac{10.44 \times 78.1 \text{ ft.} \times (12 \text{ gpm})^{1.85}}{140^{1.85} \times (0.75 \text{ in.})^{4.86}} = 35 \text{ ft.}$$

or

$$hf, \text{ m} = \frac{82.54 \times 23.7 \text{ m} \times (45 \text{ lpm})^{1.85}}{140^{1.85} \times (1.9 \text{ cm})^{4.86}} = 10.6 \text{ m}$$

(Note: Used the constant 140 for smooth hose.) Total apparent head is

$$35 \text{ ft. friction} + 46.2 \text{ ft. pressure} + 10.25 \text{ ft. static} = 91.45; \text{ use } 91.5 \text{ ft.}$$

or

$$10.6 \text{ m friction} + 14.3 \text{ m pressure} + 3.1 \text{ m static} = 28 \text{ m}$$

ACCEPTABLE FLOW SPEEDS

If water flows into a pump too slowly, it will cause problems such as recirculation, reduced pump efficiency, and even failure to pump. Similarly, if water flows too fast, it can cause water hammer, noise in the piping, and cavitation in the pump (vibration and reduced output). Flow speeds (fluid velocities) for water pumping systems should be in the ranges shown in Table 19-4.

TABLE 19-4. ACCEPTABLE FLOW SPEEDS, WATER

	ft./sec.	m/sec.
Minimum for proper pump performance	2	0.6
Optimum for continuous domestic operation	3 to 5	0.9 to 1.5
Maximum for high discharge (bilge pump, fire main, washdown)	9	3

Nine feet per second (3 m/sec.) should be the absolute maximum. You want to be a bit under this in all applications. Continuous domestic operation is for items like pressure-water systems or bait-well circulation.

NOTE: Restrictions at the nozzle of a hose (like a fire hose) can be used to increase velocity and pressure at the nozzle. This does not affect the flow speed through the rest of the system, though you would need to include the added head from the nozzle reduction in calculating the system's friction head.

Formula 19-2. Flow Speed (Fluid Velocity)

$$\text{Velocity, ft./sec.} = \frac{\text{gpm}}{2.45 \times (\text{ID, in.})^2}$$

or

$$\text{Velocity, m/sec.} = \frac{21.2 \times \text{lpm}}{(\text{ID, mm})^2}$$

Where
gpm = gallons per minute
lpm = liters per minute
ID = pipe inside diameter, in. or mm (Take from the pipe tables in Appendix B. Hose ID is the nominal ID of the hose.)

You can find the minimum and maximum flow speeds for varying pipe sizes from Table 19-5.

Returning to our deck washdown, we can see that a 12 gpm (45.5 lpm) flow is comfortably under the maximum for a ¾-inch (DN 20 mm) pipe and nowhere near the minimum value. So the flow speed is acceptable. You can calculate the precise flow speed using Formula 19-2 for the exact ID of ¾-inch (19 mm) hose, but inspection of Table 19-5 shows it wouldn't be required here.

TABLE 19-5. FLOW SPEED VERSUS PIPE DIAMETER

Nominal Diameter		Min. Flow		Max. Flow	
Schedule 40 Pipe in.	DN, mm	gpm for 2 ft./sec.	lpm for 0.6 m/sec.	gpm for 9 ft./sec.	lpm for 3 m/sec.
1/8	6	0.4	1.3	1.6	6.0
1/4	8	0.4	1.7	2.0	7.6
3/8	10	1.2	4.5	5.4	20.3
1/2	15	1.9	7.2	8.5	32.3
3/4	20	3.3	12.6	15.0	56.7
1	25	5.4	20.4	24.3	91.8
1 1/4	32	9.3	35.3	42.0	159.0
1 1/2	40	12.7	48.1	57.2	216.4
2	50	20.9	79.2	94.2	356.6
2 1/2	65	29.9	113.1	134.4	508.8
3	80	46.1	174.6	207.5	785.7
3 1/2	90	61.7	233.5	277.6	1,050.7
4	100	79.4	300.6	357.4	1,352.9

FINDING REQUIRED PUMP POWER

The power to drive a pump is determined by the head and flow rate (in gpm or lpm) and the motor and pump efficiency.

Formula 19-3.

Formula 19-3. Required Pump Power

$$hp = \frac{\text{Apparent Head, ft.} \times \text{gpm} \times \text{SG}}{3{,}956 \times \text{Pump e} \times \text{Motor e}}$$

or

$$\text{watts} = \frac{\text{Apparent Head, m} \times \text{lpm} \times \text{SG}}{6.12 \times \text{Pump e} \times \text{Motor e}}$$

Where
Apparent Head = total apparent head, ft. or m
gpm = gallons per minute
lpm = liters per minute
SG = specific gravity of the liquid being pumped
Pump e = pump efficiency—between 55% and 75%, use 60% as average*
Motor e = motor efficiency—for electric motors approximately 75%

NOTE: If you set SG and pump and motor efficiency all to 1, you get what is termed *pure water horsepower*, the theoretical power required to lift fresh water to the head specified at the given flow rate.

*Pump efficiency is actually a function of flow rate and specific pump speed. You can read exact efficiency from manufacturers' pump-performance curves. At flow rates from 100 to 200 gpm (380 to 560 lpm), for instance, efficiency varies from around 50 percent to 75 percent.

Example: For our deck washdown, we find the following:

Referring to Table 6-2 for specific gravities, we see that seawater has an SG of 1.028:

$$hp = \frac{91.5 \text{ ft.} \times 12 \text{ gpm} \times 1.028 \text{ SG}}{3{,}956 \times 0.60 \text{ Pump e} \times 0.75 \text{ Motor e}}$$

$$= 0.63 \text{ hp}$$

To ensure the motor does not run overloaded, add about 15 percent.

0.63 hp × 1.15 = 0.72 hp; use a 3/4 hp motor
hp × 745.7 = watts, so 745.7 × 0.75 hp = 559 watts; use a 560-watt DC motor
amps = watts ÷ volts, so 560 watts ÷ 12 volt DC = 47 amps

or

$$\text{watts} = \frac{28 \text{ m} \times 45 \text{ lpm} \times 1.028 \text{ SG}}{6.12 \times 0.60 \text{ Pump e} \times 0.75 \text{ Motor e}}$$

$$= 470 \text{ watts}$$

To ensure the motor does not run overloaded, add about 15 percent.

470 × 1.15 = 540 watts; use about a 550 watt DC motor
amps = watts ÷ volts, so 550 watts ÷ 12 volt DC = 46 amps

The maximum draw will be about 46 to 47 amps. Assume about 40 to 42 amps continuous at 12 volts. This will take a lot of juice out of the battery bank. A large yacht like this will probably have two generators, and it would make more sense to run this motor off 120 volts AC (240 volts in Europe).

Pump Type

Since this pump has a positive suction head and won't be passing solids, we could use a centrifugal pump driven by a ³/₄ hp (560 watt) electric motor, with ³/₄-inch (19 mm) inlet and outlet and rated at 12 gpm (45.4 lpm). It can also be a positive-displacement pump, however. A close match would be a Jabsco pump 3890-9011 (Figure 19-9), rated at 11.3 gpm (42.7 lpm), with ³/₄-inch (DN 19 mm) IPS ports and a ½-inch-diameter (12.7 mm) motor shaft. This happens to be a flexible-impeller pump.

Figure 19-9. Flexible-impeller pump (Courtesy Jabsco/ITT Industries)

Pumping Other Fluids

Calculations for other fluids, such as diesel and lubricating oil, can be made the same way. Apply the fluid's specific gravity to Formula 19-3. The specific gravity for petroleum products is lower than water, so static head also should be reduced by multiplying it by the specific gravity.

Because diesel and lubricating oil are more viscous than water, the friction head should be increased. For diesel, multiply the friction head by 1.1. For lubricating oil, multiply by 1.5.

PRESSURE DROP

Another way to evaluate losses in a piping system is by pressure drop. For instance, a closed cooling system—such as a keel cooler—may have a pump that is specified as having an allowable pressure drop of no more than, say, 14 psi, or 87 kPa, or 28.5 in. Hg (mercury). All are measures of pressure. Refer to the conversion chart in Appendix C to convert the allowable pressure drop to feet or meter of water to head. The pressure drop in such a system is the total friction resistance we found earlier when determining the friction head. In a closed-loop system, there is no static head and the velocity into and out of the pump is the same, so there is no change in velocity and thus no velocity head.

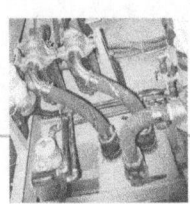

CHAPTER 20 Freshwater Systems

In the days of square-rigged sail, drinking water was served from a wooden barrel, or butt, lashed on deck near a midships hatch (a scuttle). A seaman would grab a ladle with a hook on the end, flip up the lid, dip, and drink deep. Naturally, this nautical "water fountain" became the center of casual conversation, gossip... you know... *scuttlebutt*. These scuttlebutts were filled from buckets with water from the ship's main wooden water casks. Indeed, *butt* was originally the term for wooden barrels specifically of 126-gallon (468 L) capacity. After several weeks at sea, the water casks would contain enough algae and minute beasties to take on the appearance of weak broth. To say the flavor was ripe would be putting it gently. More than one captain proved his mettle to the crew by making a display of drinking the rancid ship's water rather than sticking to his personal stock of fine wine and steward-prepared tea.

As for showers, even the officers seldom took them, and the showers were generally of cold seawater or nothing. Combined with greasy cooking, hot tar, oakum, and gunpowder, the fragrance 'tween decks must have been, ah... interesting.

Things have changed just a bit over the last two hundred years. Today's boaters take clean, fresh water (hot and cold) for granted—instant and at the turn of a tap, if you please. Hot showers at your whim, and on larger boats even Jacuzzis and washer-dryers, are common. Fresh water onboard, though, shouldn't be taken lightly. It's supplied by the vessel's freshwater system. Water is so important to health and safety (as well as to comfort) that careful consideration must be given to ensuring the water system works reliably all the time. We'll take a look now at what makes a good freshwater system.

Figure 20-1. Water casks (Reprinted from The Ways of the Sea, *by Charles G. Davis)*

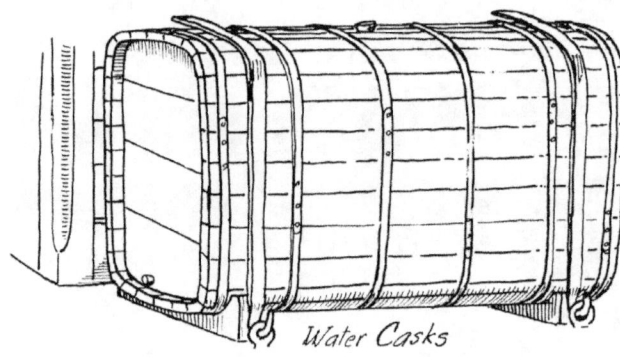
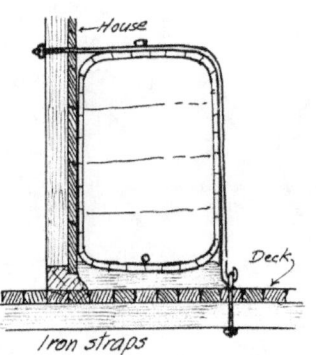

FRESHWATER TANKS AND WATER TANK CAPACITY

We no longer store water in wooden casks; rather, water is stored in purpose-made tanks. This is cleaner and much less prone to algae growth. It also permits a lot more water per person. How much? Well, in the old days the rule of thumb was 1 gallon (3.8 L) per person per day. This still works, but only for drinking and rinsing your hands and face. A survey of long-range cruisers recently came up with an average of 1.9 gallons (7.2 L) per person per day for personal use only. But all together, after adding in cooking, washing dishes, and so on, the total was actually 3.7 gallons (14 L) per person per day.

This is a pretty good guide to the way water is used on modern boats with pressure-water systems. Accordingly, a family of four on a seven-day cruise would need 103.6 gallons (494 L), plus at least a 30 percent reserve, say 135 gallons (510 L). This is still taking some reasonable care—using salt water for primary dish-washing, keeping showers short, and being sure not to leave the taps running. (Yes, if you're frugal, you could still get by on less than a third of this—saltwater showers with a quick fresh rinse, no pressure-water system, all-manual pumps, careful attention to conservation.)

The rule of thumb for tank capacity for average cruising boats is a minimum of 15 gallons (57 L) for each usable berth aboard. This is a bit low, as a typical 36-footer (11 m), might have six berths and thus 90 gallons (342 L) by this rule. As we've seen, this wouldn't really be enough for a week's cruise for a family of four.

Cruisers equipped with watermakers have topped 15 to 16 gallons (57 to 60 L) per person per day or more. You could never carry that much fresh water, but if you can "make" it from the ocean, you're OK. We won't go into watermakers here, but they're generally not as practical for coastwise cruisers as you might think. This is because longshore waters are often muddy, brackish, polluted, or some combination thereof. Without clean, fresh ocean water, watermakers won't work well, or at all. In fact, a megayacht trick is to build in big saltwater tanks. These can be filled offshore and used to make fresh water in harbor. Vessels this big, however, can't pull in just anywhere to fill up the tanks as small to mid-size vessels can.

Tastes in Tanks: Tank Material

So what is the best material for freshwater tanks? Stainless steel. Use only 316L for corrosion resistance; everything else is second best. Of course, second best is perfectly acceptable. I've installed plastic, fiberglass, wood-epoxy, and aluminum freshwater tanks. They all work well enough, but each leaves some taste in the water. Water from a well-cleaned stainless tank—frequently emptied and filled—can taste nearly as good as fresh spring water. (Even better than stainless is Monel. However, this is harder and harder to find these days and quite expensive.)

Tank Details

Check to see that your tanks (regardless of material) are well secured. You don't want them ever coming loose. (Fresh water weighs 8.32 pounds per gallon, so a moderate-size 40-gallon tank would weigh about 360 pounds, not a thing to have rolling around loose in a storm.) Refer to Table 5-1 to make a quick, close estimate of total tank weight. As with the fuel tanks discussed in Chapter 5, water tanks should have one or more clean-out openings where possible (though this isn't practical on smaller tanks). It's a nice plus to have a tank drain at the bottom, ideally with a sediment sump to collect any gunk. This, too, isn't practical on many boats because of access limitations. If you do have a tank drain, it should not only have a shutoff valve, but the end should be threaded. This allows you to install a screw cap so that an accidental opening of the valve won't empty your tank. It also means you can screw on a hose to pump out the tank rather than just emptying it into the bilge.

Baffles are required for both strength and boat stability. In general, water tanks should follow most of the requirements for fuel tanks in Chapter 5. Making water tanks this strong is not a legal requirement, but having a freshwater tank leak or come adrift will certainly ruin your day. Losing your water supply well offshore can be life threatening. Of course, you don't have to worry about fumes or minor drips when dealing with freshwater tanks and plumbing as you do with fuel systems. On the other hand, small leaks have a tendency to get larger. You really want all your freshwater tanks about as tight and rugged as your fuel tanks, though they don't have to be pressure tested over 3 psi (20.7 kPa) or 1 foot (0.3 m) above the maximum head to the highest vent, whichever is greater.

FRESHWATER SUPPLY PIPING

The schematic in Figure 20-2 shows a good standard pressure-water system's supply-side piping. Most of these details are required for safe and reliable operation. Note that the tank vents must be higher than the fills. The sumps and drain cocks on the tank bottom are optional but do help with cleaning.

Immediately downstream of the tank(s) should be a filter to keep silt and other particulate matter out of the rest of the plumbing. Most boats have just a simple mesh filter, but you can add more sophisticated filters right on up to UV filters that come close to sterilizing the water. A good mesh filter (a strainer) is adequate for most installations.

Pressurizing the Accumulator

From the filter, the water travels to the pressure pump, which drives water through the rest of the system. Some small, simple piping arrangements have just this pump with a switch built into the faucets. Turn on a faucet, and you turn on the pump. The better and more sophisticated method is to have an accumulator after the pump. An accumulator is simply a tank with an air bladder inside. As the pump develops pressure, it squeezes the air bladder, and a sensor switches off the pump when the bladder pressure reaches a given pressure, say, 20 psi (2.9 kPa). Now with all your faucets off, the pump will shut

Figure 20-2. Freshwater supply piping

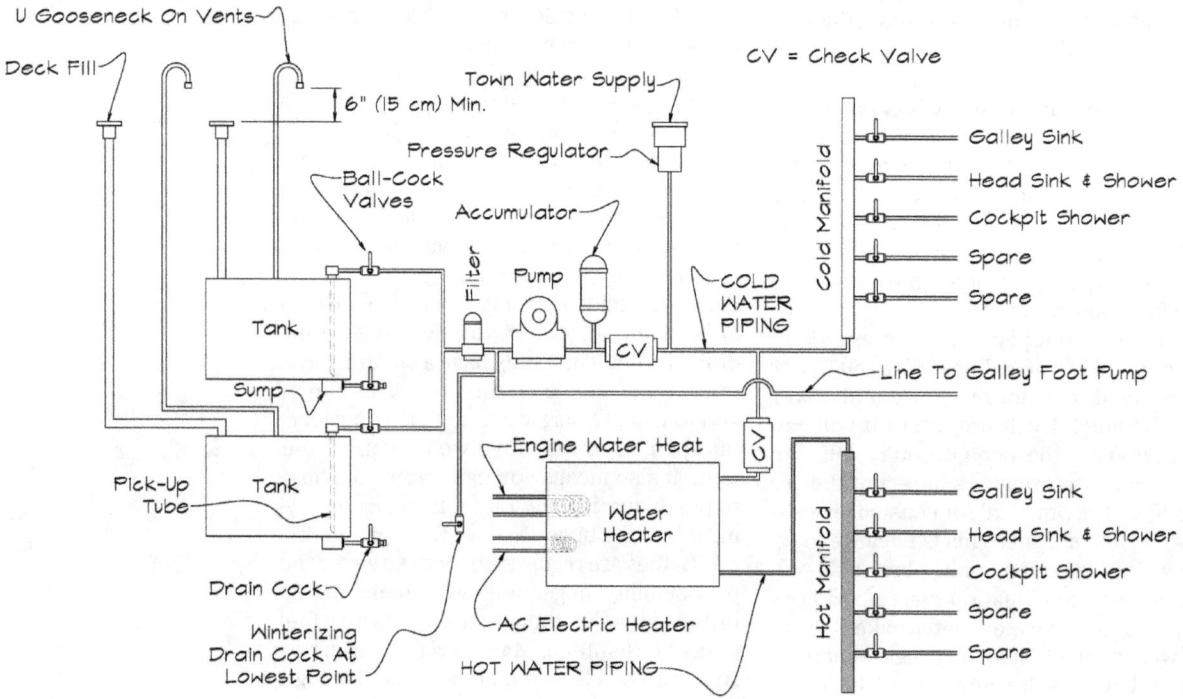

down and the bladder will hold pressure—unavoidably leaking air very gradually. Eventually pressure will drop below, say, 10 psi (1.4 kPa), and the pump will automatically kick back on again. In this way, the pressure-water system is always pumped up. In addition, the accumulator smoothes out pressure pulses and knocks to achieve a continuous, even flow. Of course, when you have water running for a bit, the pump will switch on. Frequent cycling with all water taps off is an indication of a leak or (much less likely) a faulty pressure sensor.

Variable-Speed Water Pumps

Some newer pressure-water pumps are strictly on-demand pumps (as for the very simple system) without an accumulator, but they manage the flow with a variable-speed pump motor. The motor automatically speeds up to deliver more water as more faucets are opened. When designed specifically for larger systems, these can work quite well, though so far, I've most frequently used accumulator systems.

Pressure-Water-Pump Capacity

It's almost as bad an idea to install a pressure-water system that has too much capacity as it is to install one with too little. Water pumps for freshwater systems typically range from 1 to 12 gpm (3.8 to 45 lpm). Installing a 6 gpm (23 lpm) pump on a small boat with two faucets not only adds weight and cost, but won't match the plumbing-service demands. Also, don't size the pump based on maximum demand with every faucet and shower open at full at the same time. This will never happen in real life. Follow Table 20-1 as a good guide.

TABLE 20-1. FRESHWATER-PUMP CAPACITY

Number of Fixtures	Max. Pump Capacity	
	gpm	lpm
1–2	3	11
2–3	4	15
4–6	7	26
7 or more	11	42

Water-Pump Location

You would think you could locate the pressure-water unit—pump, accumulator, and so on—pretty much anywhere that didn't exceed the pump's suction-lift limitations. True, but don't forget these pumps make noise. On one 50-footer (15.2 m) I designed, the builder installed the pressure-water pump under the master-stateroom berth, just about dead under the owner's pillow. To say the owner was ticked off at being woken up five or six times a night as the pump cycled on would be an understatement! I arranged to move the pressure-water pump into the engine room, where it had been originally drawn. Keep all such noisemaking machinery as far away from sleeping accommodations as possible.

Avoiding Overpressure

At the dock, you want to be able to screw right into the town or city water supply. Standard fittings are available, and you can see where this is located in Figure 20-2. The absolutely vital thing is that this attachment be fitted with a pressure regulator. Components of your boat's water system may be rated to only 3 or 4 psi (21 to 27 kPa) maximum. City water systems can have much higher pressures. More than one boat has ruptured some part of its water piping and sunk at the dock because a regulator wasn't installed. Even if nothing is ruptured, without either a check valve or a regulator in place, the water tanks will fill up and spray water out their vents. What an interesting sight! If the vents can't keep up, a tank or some other fitting can rupture.

Tee to Heat and Standard Water Heaters

At this point, we're ready to branch off and make heat (literally). The cold water simply continues on to a distribution manifold, but to get hot, the water is teed off into the heater. Most marine water heaters are insulated tanks. They heat the water from a 120-volt (or 240-volt) AC electric element at dockside (or when the generator is running). Underway, the engine-cooling water circulates through a heat exchanger in the tank, which makes plenty of hot water for free. A good tank will keep the water hot several hours. These water heaters are often called *calorifiers*, because they add calories (energy) to the water. Nevertheless, when you're not underway, not running a generator (or don't have one at all), and not plugged in to shore power, there will come a time when you're plain out of hot. The only answer then is to fire up the engine for twenty minutes or so to make more—noisy and inefficient. Still, this is infrequent and manageable enough that standard hot-water-heater tanks (calorifiers) are the common answer for most boats.

Flash or Instant Hot-Water Heaters

The alternative is *on-demand hot-water heaters*, also called *instant heaters* or *flash heaters*. These are flash-coil devices that heat water almost instantaneously as it passes through. They are small, light, and efficient and have no large tank to take up space. The drawback is that they require either LPG (propane) or a large generator to produce the heat required. LPG is probably the logical choice for small cruisers, though you must take great care with safety precautions in the LPG system. You must also give careful thought to location of the hot combustion exhaust run and exhaust exit, and to making sure carbon monoxide can't get below. In theory, generators are even better as a source of engine-cooling-water heat, but if you have that much generating capacity, you can simply use the generator's electric output to heat a standard hot-water tank (calorifier). In spite of the cautions regarding LPG, some sailors prefer LPG on-demand heaters, as they may go days without running the engine, and many have no gen set.

One problem with instant hot-water heaters is temperature control. On many units, the first rush of water is too hot, but then if the water is flowing steadily, the temperature reduces to tepid and stays there. The best units don't pull these hijinks, but ask around and if possible, test any instant heater you're planing to install.

FRESHWATER DELIVERY PIPING

The delivery-side water piping should be well installed to avoid chafing or leaks. You also need to minimize excess freshwater usage as much as possible. Dishes in particular can be washed just fine in salt water. This means you need a seawater tap at the galley sink. You could put an electric pump on this, but a good-quality foot pump (like the Whale Gusher MK 3) does a fine job and keeps both hands free. (There are good hand pumps too, and we've installed them, but my preference is the foot pump.) Make sure there is a recess that gives plenty of clearance over the foot-pump pedal so you can get your foot on it easily to work it.

Backup Water

An identical foot pump should be installed on the cold-water tap at the galley sink as well. Why? So equipped, you can still pump fresh water for drinking and cooking even with a complete electric outage. This foot pump needs to be supplied from a separate, dedicated pipe from the tank (right after the filter but before the pressure pump) because the foot pump can't take the pressure from the water-pressure pump. The cold pressure-water line tees into the riser to the faucet tap above the foot-pump line, with a check valve (a one-way valve) to further protect the foot pump from excess pressure.

High-Quality Filtering

On most of my office's designs, we install a charcoal filter on the cold-water line at the galley-sink mixer tap. This means that the fresh water you use for cooking, making coffee or tea, and for most drinking is double filtered—first through the mesh filter/strainer right after the tanks, and then through the charcoal filter. The head sinks and the showers aren't used much for drinking, so you really don't need charcoal filters there. On larger boats, you may want to run the cold fresh water to a single common-rail manifold (see Figure 4-9) and have a larger charcoal filter just ahead of the manifold or even a combined charcoal and UV filter. This way,

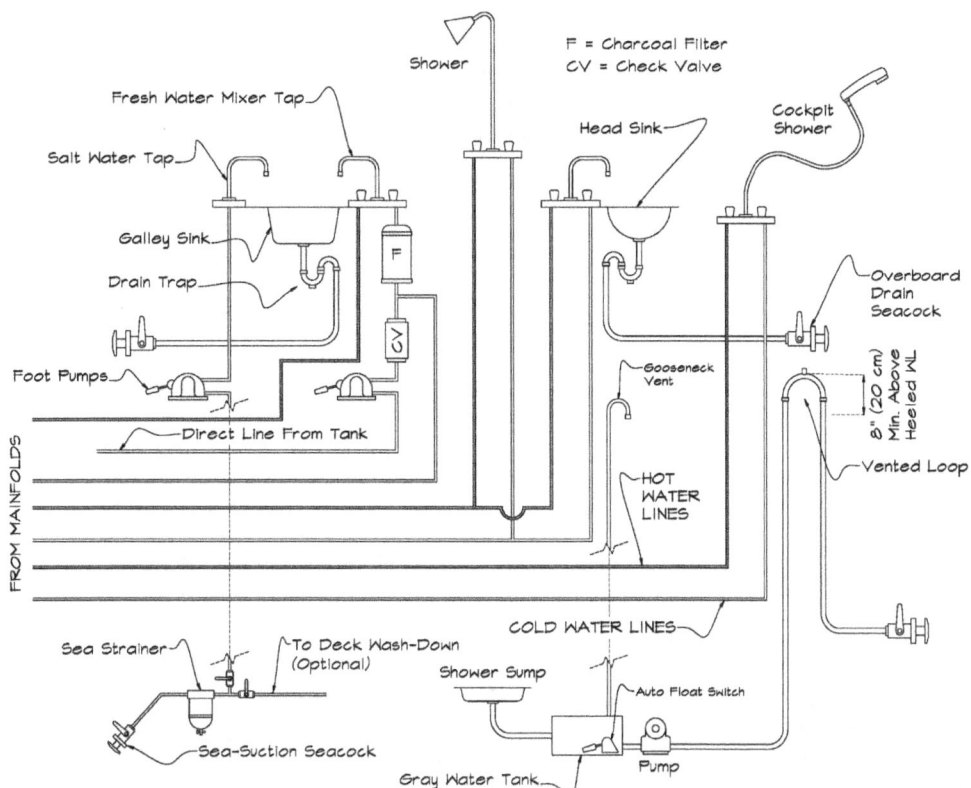

Figure 20-3.
Freshwater
delivery piping

all the cold, freshwater taps will have the same top-quality drinking water. On very large boats, you would have a main hot-water and a cold-water line (or possibly two of each, one leading forward and the other aft). Piping to serve the individual fixtures is teed off these main lines.

DRAINING AWAY—HANDLING GRAY WATER

Naturally, you need to direct all the water you use overboard efficiently. Drains should be at least 1-inch (DN 25 mm) diameter. Larger sinks fit 1¼-inch or 1½-inch (DN 32 or 40 mm) drains. Some small sinks use ¾-inch (DN 20 mm) drains, but that's a bit too small and tends to get plugged up. I'm amazed at how few sinks are fitted with U-traps. There's a good chance any boat you inspect won't have them. Not only do the U-traps help keep things from escaping overboard, but the water in the trap forms an air seal between inside and out, which makes heating and cooling more efficient. The U-trap also minimizes back surges, which can generate small geysers in the sink when a boat plunges deeply. Indeed, though standard U-traps are fine, I prefer a full circle of hose. It is reliable and easy to install. If something such as your wedding ring falls into the drain, you can shut off the seacock and unscrew the hose clamps. Your ring might still be there. All these drains should exit below the waterline and so must have seacocks and double stainless hose clamps (Figure 20-4).

Shower Drainage and Vented Loops

Shower sumps pose additional problems. More than a few boats simply drain the shower into the bilge. This is just awful. All that soapy water, hair, and bits of skin swirl around in the bilge, gunking things up and

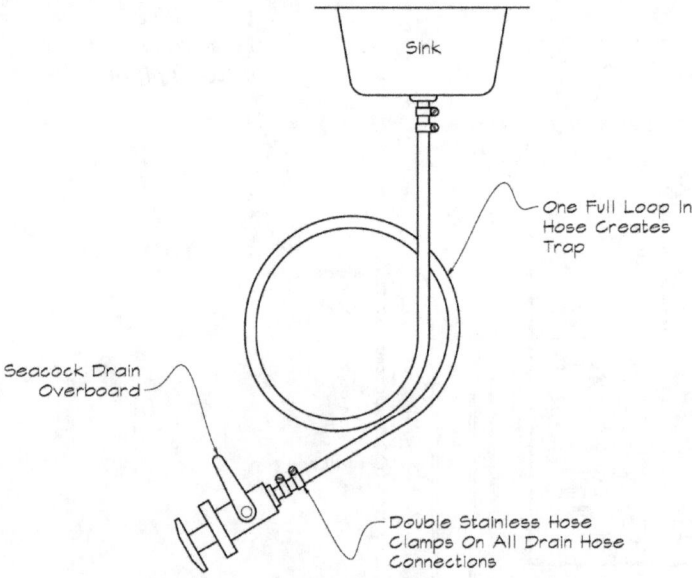

Figure 20-4. Hose drain trap

overboard, all the sink and shower drains must empty into one or more gray-water tanks. These are pumped out from deck fittings at the dock just like a head holding tank, or they can be emptied overboard through a Y-valve when you're no longer in an NDZ.

RUNNING PIPE

Twenty or thirty years ago, almost all this "piping" was made from whatever was handy, frequently from inexpensive hose. Such hoses can crack or tear. They can impart a bad taste to the water and may not be certified as safe for drinking water. Hose is still fine, of course, but be sure that it's good-quality hose certified safe for potable water. Drain hose only needs to be tough and long-lasting, as I doubt you'll be drinking from it. Hose is often the best solution for drain lines.

creating unpleasant smells. Every shower sump should drain into a dedicated and fully enclosed, properly vented gray-water tank. This tank should have its own dedicated pump, with an auto float switch, to empty it. Remember also that the shower sump is usually well below the waterline. If so, the pumpout line must rise well above the waterline to a vented loop and then back down and overboard. Follow the recommendations in Chapter 7 and as discussed in Chapter 18 (see Figure 18-3).

The alternative is that each shower sump be deep enough to hold a fair amount of water under its grate and have a dedicated pump for emptying it directly overboard. Essentially, this makes each shower sump a small, individual gray-water tank.

Gray-Water Tanks

Discharge from sink and shower drains is termed *gray water*. This is different from discharge from heads (sewage), which is *black water*. In most areas, gray water can be discharged overboard, but not in all areas. Be careful; check the local regulations. If a boat will operate in 100 percent no-discharge waters (no-discharge zones or NDZ), then it needs a much larger gray-water tank—as large or even larger than the black-water (sewage) holding tank. In this case, instead of draining

Plastic-Tube Piping

Freshwater plumbing, though, is better made from purpose-manufactured plastic tube (not hose). My personal preference is the standard for plumbing in many homes. It's light, corrosion free, inexpensive, fully approved for use with drinking water, and available off the shelf at Home Depot, Lowe's, and such. It is PEX tubing (cross-linked polyethylene, Figure 20-5) connected with Flair-It connectors. The tubing is easy to cut and bend, and the many Flair-It connectors and valves will meet virtually any need. Attaching the tubing to a Flair-It elbow, tee, valve, and so on is a snap. You just cut the tube to length, slide the crimp ring onto the tube, press the tube on the fitting's tube barb, slide the crimp ring back up to the fitting, and screw it tight. No special tools are required and no sealant, plumber's dope, or plumber's tape is needed. Companies such as Whale, Sea Tech, and others also make a complete line of marine plumbing fittings and tubing. These, too, are designed for quick tool-free and sealant-free connections. My experience with some of these is that the fittings will start to leak after you have disconnected and reconnected them a few times. PEX doesn't have this problem. Of course, you can still use all hose for your

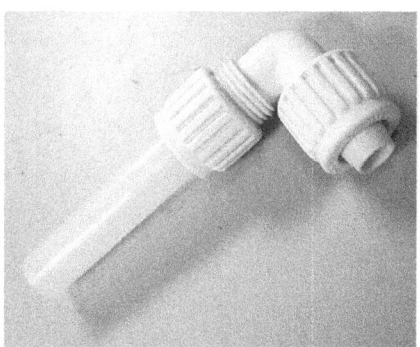 

Figure 20-5. PEX tubing and fittings

water delivery system (as long as it's potable-water certified), but hose installations aren't generally as neat or as chafe-free.

Freshwater Piping Sizes

Half-inch pipe or tube (DN 15 mm) is standard for small to mid-size boats. Larger vessels with more than five fixtures to supply are better off with ¾ inch (DN 20 mm), and this is the standard size for higher-output pressure-water pump systems. Branch lines can be ½ inch (DN 25 mm). Most mixer taps and faucets are ½ inch (DN 25 mm), but smaller ones may be ⅜ inch (10 mm). As we've seen, sink and shower drains should be 1, 1¼, or 1½ inches (DN 25, 32, or 40 mm).

A larger size is better if you can fit it. I recommend against ¾-inch (DN 20 mm) drains.

Fine Faucets

Plenty of excellent marine faucets are available (properly called "mixer taps" when they combine hot and cold water), but I usually prefer to use high-quality home faucets. These come in beautiful designs and in a wide array of shapes and sizes. Delta, Moen, and Grohe are some of the many well-known brands. Easily available at most large home-supply outlets and plumbing-supply stores, they not only are rugged and convenient, but also give a boat an extra touch of class at a reasonable price.

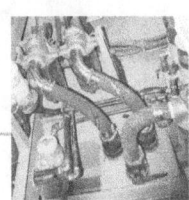

My Favorite Head: Thoughts and Recommendations on Marine Toilets and Installations

CHAPTER 21

Let's face it. The less time you spend thinking about your boat's toilet, the better. Then let's face it again. The less time you spend thinking about your boat's toilet, the better. What this means, of course, is that it's worth spending some time thinking about your boat's toilet. After all, if you can install a complete head/toilet system that is trouble-free to start with, then it won't need thought later. Even better, you or the crew won't have to unclog it either.

Over the last thirty-five or so years of sailing, building, and designing boats, I've finally settled on the marine toilet and the fittings and attachments I prefer. It's simple, inexpensive, and more trouble- and odor-free than any other system that I and my clients have used. Before I get to describing my favorite head, I should say that I've had fine results with many other toilet systems, from Groco to SeaLand, Wilcox, Raritan, Headhunter, and more. Properly engineered and installed, all these manufacturers make excellent products. We'll review the complete assortment of standard marine toilets later, but first let's get a feel for a reliable toilet-plumbing system—a marine sanitation system—by examining my personal ideal.

Figure 21-1. Blakes Lavac head (Courtesy Blakes)

MY FAVORITE HEAD—THE BLAKES LAVAC TOILET

On my own boat, I would install a Blakes Lavac head. Built in Britain (www.blakes-lavac-taylors.co.uk), they are unique in that they have virtually no moving parts and thus nothing to go wrong. In fact, I've installed quite a few of these on boats that are easily topping over 100,000 combined cruising miles, and—to the best of my knowledge—there's been only one clog! Now that's a head you don't have to think about. As I write this (2007), the only U.S. distributor for Blakes Lavac heads appears to be St. Brendan's Isle, Inc., of Green Cove Springs, Florida.

Figure 21-2 shows the plumbing arrangement of the Blakes Lavac. This schematic is based on the old days, when you could discharge overboard. Today, the discharge is into a holding tank. The toilet bowl itself is part of the flushing mechanism. The lid has a gasket all around. When closed, this seals the head and allows you to pump a vacuum in the bowl, which is the secret of its function. To flush, close the lid (#5 in the drawing) and stroke on the pump. This pulls water and air out of the toilet bowl (2) along with anything else that was in the bowl. Everything exits the hull through a seacock (4) or enters the holding tank. Because the bowl is sealed airtight by the lid, the vacuum then sucks in fresh seawater to refill the bowl (1). That's it. There are no valves, flappers, or other obstructions or mechanisms to get plugged.

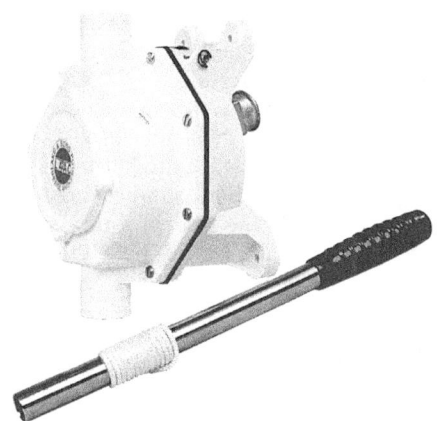

Figure 21-3. Diaphragm pump. (Courtesy Blakes)

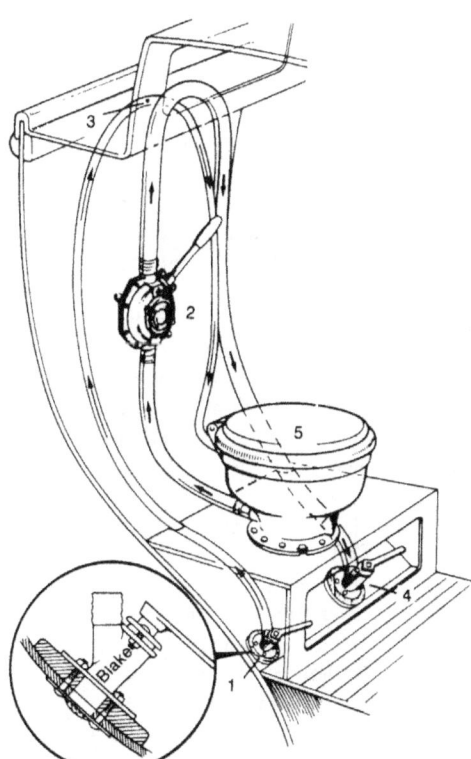

Figure 21-2. Head operation (Courtesy Blakes)

Pumping a Vacuum

The pump is a simple, standard diaphragm bilge pump such as the Henderson or Blakes's own. Any good-quality diaphragm bilge pump of matching inlet diameter will do fine. Pick a rugged one that is easily opened for cleaning or repair, though both will be infrequent.

Water Levels

Another nice feature of the Blakes Lavac toilet is that after you've pumped to a clean bowl, you can open the lid and pump again with the lid open. In this case—with no vacuum formed—you pump to a dry bowl. You can now close the lid, and without stagnant seawater in the bowl, you won't get that vague rotten-egg smell from the toilet. You also won't have water sloshing out in rough seas. Most other toilets allow you to pump to a dry bowl in one way or another. Be sure any toilet you install has this feature.

The level of water remaining in the bowl (during normal flushing with the lid closed) is controlled by a vent-plug fitting on the intake hose—an "air bleed valve," or simply a hole at the highest point in the seawater intake hose (see [3] in Figure 21-2). If this hole is too small, the vacuum won't release soon enough, and the bowl will be too full after flushing. (Note that this forms the vented loop for the Blakes Lavac.) Too large a hole, and you won't get enough vacuum and the bowl won't fill high enough.

Blakes Lavac Drawbacks

Nothing is perfect, and the Blakes Lavac is no exception (though the drawbacks are slight). One drawback is that it takes a good couple of minutes for the vacuum to finish bleeding out of the bowl after a flush. Until this happens, you can't lift the lid to use the toilet again. If you're impatient and force the lid up, you'll likely pull the seal off the underside of the lid. This doesn't hurt the first dozen or so times (you just reseat the seal), but ultimately it can damage the seal.

Another minor drawback is appearance. There's nothing wrong with the look of the Blakes Lavac toilet, but there's nothing stylish about it either. The head looks fine and fits the decor of most ordinary cruising boats. If, however, you have a large, fancy head compartment with fine fittings and custom-color porcelain, the plain white, no-nonsense Lavac looks a bit out of place. (Also, it's available only in white.) This has been one of the most common reasons that my office has installed other heads in larger custom boats—simply to better match the high-style decor of the surroundings.

The Blakes Lavac comes in two models: the lower-cost Popular and the higher-end Zenith. They look nearly identical, but I would use the Zenith on all but the smallest boats. The Zenith model is intended for heavier use. Cost seems to hover around $500 these days (2008), which is a very reasonable price for a quality marine toilet.

High-Volume Flushing

A more serious consideration is that the Blakes Lavac toilet pulls a lot of water through for each flush, or it can. Remember, you're using a true diaphragm bilge pump—really a bilge pump. This is one of the reasons that the pump is so unlikely to clog. You can, however, stroke as many times as you like with the lid closed. This will surely clear all the effluent from the toilet and all the sewage lines, which is a plus if you pump overboard. With no effluent in the hoses, there's no smell. The drawback is that you can quickly pump a holding tank full—something to be wary of.

Toilet Water Usage and Holding Tank Size

The old standard landlubber toilet installed in most homes and offices uses 3.5 gallons (13.2 L) per flush. In most places in the United States, new toilets are required to use less than 1.6 gallons (6 L) per flush. Marine toilets do much better. The thriftiest marine vacuum-flush toilets can average about 1.5 pints (0.7 L) per flush. Most standard marine toilets use between 2 and 3 quarts (1.9 and 2.8 L) per flush. It's been found that an average individual is likely to flush a toilet about 8 times per day. Thus for average toilets, if you assume 2.25 quarts (2.1 L) per flush and 8 flushes per person per day, that's 4.5 gallons (17 L) per person per day. Four crew for five days between tank pumpout would then be 90 gallons (340 L). Switching to toilets that average just 1.5 pints (0.7 L) per flush would reduce the required black-water tank size to only 30 gallons (113 L).

You should size the holding tanks for any boat this way. Determine the type of toilet and the average gallons or liters per flush. Multiply that by the average of 8 flushes per person per day. Then multiply by the number of crew and the days between pumpouts to get minimum holding-tank (black-water tank) size.

Push-Button Flush?

Some folks like push-button toilet operation. You can arrange this with a Blakes Lavac simply by installing an electric-powered bilge pump. (Blakes Lavac makes an electric version of their standard hand pump.) In case of electrical failure, there should be a manual pump installed in series, just ahead of the electric pump. This way you can pump out regardless. So far, I've talked all my clients out of electrifying their Blakes Lavac heads. After all, the whole point is being simple and direct. Why further complicate things? It takes no effort and very little time to pull a few strokes on a hand diaphragm pump.

HEAD INSTALLATION PLUMBING

Odor and Hose

After the toilet itself, you have to consider the hose and the tanks to ensure a completely trouble-free system. The two brands of hose that seem to have given my office the least trouble are SeaLand's OdorSafe Hose (Figure 21-4) and Trident's smooth-wall PVC sanitation hose warranted for 3 years (the longest warranty I'm aware of on marine sanitation hose). Don't scrimp on hose. To avoid odor, use the best; *never* use any corrugated hose in any part of the system. The corrugations reduce flow rate and catch things. Don't use car radiator hose either. Though good and tough, it doesn't seal in odors well enough.

You can check if the hose on a boat is a source of odor by soaking a rag in hot water and wrapping it (while wet) around the hose. (This works best at a low point, where effluent can collect.) When the rag has cooled, pull it off and sniff it. If you smell sewage, odor is coming through the hose.

The T and Y Pitfall

Avoid Ys or Ts in your sewage-line runs. Every such junction is a place for gunk to catch and clog. Y and T valves are even worse than plain Y or T connectors. These can all be avoided by installing the system as shown in Figure 21-5. If you have to have a holding tank (and we almost all do), then run the hose direct from the head to the holding tank. From the holding tank you'll have a pumpout hose leading to the pumpout fitting on deck, and a separate outlet hose from the tank leading to a macerator pump and from there through a seacock overboard. You also need a tank vent as well, of course. There are no valves and no Y or T connections anywhere in this setup except for the sea-suction seacock and the outlet seacock.

Of course, if you're using an off-the-shelf holding tank, it may not have the three

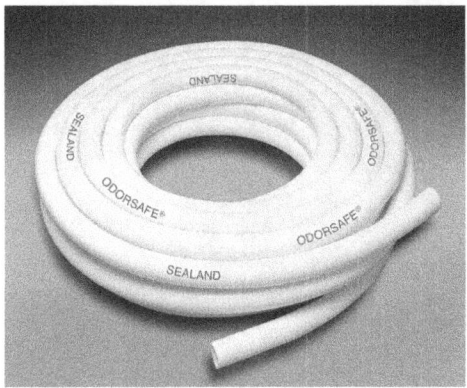

Figure 21-4. OdorSafe hose (Courtesy SeaLand)

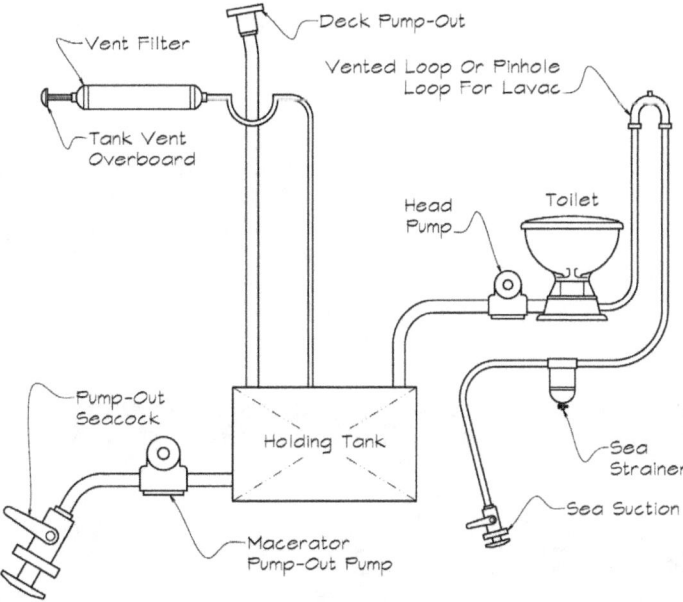

Figure 21-5. Ideal head plumbing

openings required in the preceding description. In this case you have no choice but to Y or T the macerator pumpout off the same pipe that leads to the deck pumpout. Regardless, keep the elimination of valves, Ts, and Ys as one of your primary goals. The fewer there are, the less the chance of clogs. It's not unusual to see "clever" piping arrangements on some boats that have enough valves, connectors, junctions, and loops to serve as the cooling system for a nuclear reactor. They may be clever, but they will give trouble in the long run.

Discharge Considerations

Be sure that the seacock exits below the waterline. For reasons I'll never know, a builder I worked with once installed the discharge seacock on one of my office's designs above the waterline. Even though we stood on the foredeck and the outlet was near the stern, and even though we were going at full cruising speed during pumpout, the smell while emptying was indescribable! Also, be very, very sure that you have quick access to the overboard pumpout seacock. You absolutely must have a padlock that will secure it in the closed position when you're in no-discharge zones (NDZs). There should be a placard posted near or at this seacock stating that overboard discharge of sewage is illegal in coastal waters. If you fail to have these items and are boarded for a routine inspection, you're in for a hefty fine.

Vent Odors

Holding tank vents (Figure 21-6) are another consideration. There's only so much you can do to minimize the odor from these. Locate the vent opening as far from windows, hatches, doors, and cockpits as you can. The next step is to install a vent filter such as made by SeaLand. These work well at decreasing the smell and require that their filter element be replaced only once a year, at the beginning of each season. The only thing to keep in mind is that these filters are rather large (about 14 in. or 36 cm long). You need space to fit them and room to access them once a year to change the filter.

PUMPING SLUDGE—HANDLING SEWAGE

Groco, ITT Jabsco, and others make fine, reliable macerator pumps (electric pumps designed to grind up and pump sewage). My office has used them all successfully, but the SeaLand T-series pump seems to have given us the best overall service (Figure 21-7). For pumping out holding tanks, you have two options: a macerator pump or a pump that will pass solids. I generally lean slightly to macerator pumps, which grind up the effluent into a fine slurry. Whale, however, makes its Gulper electric sanitation pump, which passes unmacerated solids almost as large as the 1½-inch (38 mm) hose diameter. Alternatively, they make a manual, diaphragm waste pump intended for the same use. Powered macerator pumps must be monitored carefully during operation, however, since being run dry will damage them.

Holding Tanks

Finally, you want to consider the holding tank material and manufacturer. Aluminum can be used for holding tanks, but adding chlorine

Figure 21-6. Holding tank vent filter (Courtesy Dometic)

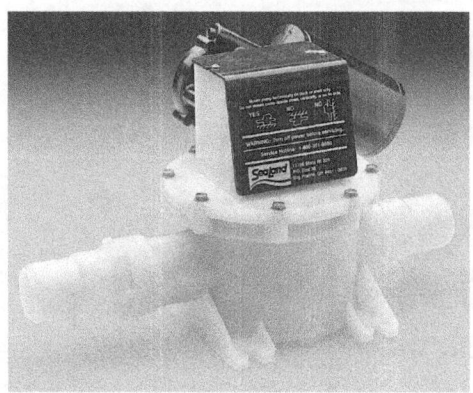

Figure 21-7. T-pump (Courtesy SeaLand)

and other chemicals can then cause corrosion. (That said, many of my aluminum boats have integral aluminum holding tanks with no problems.) Even the black water itself (marine sewage or effluent is termed *black water*) can potentially cause corrosion over time. Top-quality 316L stainless steel holding tanks are excellent if the proper weld filler has been used and proper welding procedures employed. (No other stainless alloy is up to the job.) Such tanks will last a lifetime. Monel is another excellent option. But stainless and Monel tanks are expensive (Monel particularly so), heavy, and almost always a custom order.

Plastic Tanks

The best remaining material is polyethylene. It's light and totally corrosion-proof. It is plastic, however, and can suffer from some odor permeation. The better quality and thicker the poly tank, the less likely there will be odor or leak problems. Once again, SeaLand's polyethylene holding tanks seem about the best available (Figure 21-8). They are fully ³⁄₈ inch (9.5 mm) thick, which is thicker than most others, and so virtually odor-free. Available in an array of shapes, they range from 9 to 52 gallons (34 to 200 L). Remember, though, that whatever tank you install, you can reduce odor and any corrosion by being sure to completely flush the entire tank and sanitation system with fresh water at the end of every season. Even the best PVC hose and poly tanks will eventually absorb some effluent and thus transmit some odor if you leave them year after year with sewage sitting in them for months at a time.

TYPES OF MARINE TOILETS (HEADS)

We've looked at my favorite marine toilet, but there are many other fine choices. The most common marine toilets are

- bucket
- Porta Potti (toilet with self-contained holding tank)
- direct drop (gravity discharge)
- plunger pump with joker valve
- pump with macerator
- water-jet macerator
- manual diaphragm pump vacuum
- powered vacuum

The Cedar Bucket

The bucket is the oldest and simplest, but most of us aren't into that sort of roughing it. True wooden cedar buckets are best. The cedar greatly reduces odor. Of course, you must empty the bucket after every use. The cedar bucket should fit into a recess (often a hole in a plank or ply panel) to ensure it doesn't slide around and should have a seat lid that fits on top, so you can do what's needed in comfort.

Porta Potti

The common term Porta Potti is actually a trademarked name by the Thetford Corporation that's often generically applied to most self-contained, portable toilets with a built-in holding tank and a freshwater flush tank built into and surrounding the seat. The holding tank usually removes to empty at the nearest land-based toilet. These toilets are complete Type-3 sanitation systems and meet all requirements for all waters.

Direct-Drop or Gravity Toilets

Direct-drop or gravity toilets are built-in toilets. They must be located nearly vertically above the holding tank. When the toilet is

Figure 21-8. Plastic holding tanks (Courtesy SeaLand)

flushed, the valve opens to the drainpipe leading straight down to the holding tank below. Water is simultaneously pumped into the bowl to complete the cleansing. These are about as simple an installed unit as you can get, so they are popular with low-end tour and ferry boats and such. They have little to go wrong and are inexpensive, but the smell wafting up through the sewage pipe when the valve is open to flush is pretty strong. I would use at least double the recommended air-change rate from Table 14-1 for any such toilet compartment. Also, install commercial deodorizers and pour deodorant into the holding tank.

Traditional Marine Pump Toilets

The traditional marine toilet uses a simple plunger pump: a standard positive-displacement pump. These have a joker valve (flapper valve) that is subject to clogs, but otherwise they are the old reliable. They do tend to use a lot of water. The best manual joker-valve toilets have very large diameter pumps—as large as 4 inches (100 mm) ID, such as the Wilcox-Crittenden Skipper II. The large diameter makes them less likely to clog. Typical low-cost, plunger-pump toilets will have around 1½- to 2-inch ID (38 to 50 mm) pumps. They will work acceptably but need more care to avoid clogging. The smaller diameter uses somewhat less water per flush, however. These pumps can be motorized, but if you're going to do that, it's better to go with a macerator-pump toilet.

Electric Macerator-Pump Toilets

One way to minimize the chance of clogs in a standard water-pump toilet is to grind up the effluent into a fine slurry. This is done in macerator-pump toilets. These work quite well, though their water usage is only average at about 1 to 2 quarts (0.9 to 1.9 L) per flush (leaning closer to 2 quarts or 1.9 liters for most models). Raritan's Atlantes is a good example of this toilet, and my office has specified this model on larger yachts with luxurious head compartments because it's quite modern and stylish. The drawback over, say, the Blakes Lavac is the extra electric and mechanical systems and parts. Another model is Wilcox-Crittenden's Newport electric macerating toilet. It is quite economical in water use, at around 1.5 pints (0.5 L) per flush.

Vacuum-Flush Toilets (Manual and Powered)

Vacuum-flush toilets draw water through the system via suction rather than pumping a column of water. The Blakes Lavac is an example of a manual vacuum-flush toilet (which can be motorized with an electric pump). SeaLand, Groco, and others make a wide assortment of vacuum-flush toilets. SeaLand calls their models VacuFlush, and this term is often used for all powered vacuum-flush toilets. Most vacuum-flush toilets are quite water thrifty, quiet, and resistant to clogging. SeaLand's VacuFlush models, for example, are around 1.5 pints (0.5 L) per flush. Again, the drawback is the extra complication of the powered pump and its electric demands.

Water-Jet Macerator Toilets

There are also water-jet macerator pumps. These use a powerful jet of water blown into the toilet to flush. Since the pump is before the toilet, it is virtually clog free, and the water jet is arranged to macerate the effluent as it is pumped out. Headhunter is one manufacturer of these pumps, which have passed women's stockings, shirts, and other objects that would clog nearly any other type of head. These pumps can be installed as individual units, but particularly shine on large boats where five, six, or more of these toilets can be driven off a single, central pressure-water pump with a rather large 1-inch (24 mm) delivery pipe. (Often all the toilets share the same holding tank as well.) The pressure-water pump—entirely before the toilets—can be the same pump used for the domestic freshwater system.

Freshwater for Flushing?

This brings us to the refinement of using fresh water for flushing. I've never been enthusiastic about this, because fresh water is a limited commodity aboard, and there's plenty of seawater available at all times.

Types of Marine Sanitation Devices

It used to be that a toilet was a toilet and that a toilet in a boat was simply a head, and that was that. Not anymore. These days, a toilet flushes into a *marine sanitation device* (*MSD*). This is the sort of thing that happens when legislators get involved with practical matters. It's important to know about MSDs, however, because there are only three types approved for use on boats. You must be certain you comply fully with the local regulations for MSDs in the area you're cruising or you can be in for big-time legal trouble.

Peculiarly (this is law after all), there don't appear to be any restrictions that prohibit you from hanging over the side of the boat and . . . ah . . . depositing directly overboard. Similarly, an *unattached* bucket can be used in the vessel and dumped (at least that's my understanding, but you should check your local laws). What you can't do is dump any sewage from any source back into the water from an *installed* system (so don't screw that bucket down). If you're not into this sort of roughing it, then you'll have an *installed MSD system*, and it must comply strictly with all federal and local regulations.

Type-1 MSD

A Type-1 MSD is one that treats sewage before discharge. One of the most common units is Raritan's LectraSan. The LectraSan goes for about $1,000 (2008) and requires salt water and a fair amount of electric current to work. The PuraSan works in fresh water, or salt may be added for freshwater use. Groco offers their Thermopure 2 Type-1 MSD system.

Regardless, all Type-1 MSDs reduce bacteria count to less than 1,000 per 100 milliliters, which is pretty good but not as good as Type-2 systems. Type-1 systems are acceptable for discharge directly overboard on all boats under 65 feet (19.8 m) overall. You can do with no holding tank at all, with one really big exception. There are more and more local (state and city) 100 percent zero-discharge zones (*no-discharge zones* or *NDZ*). In such waters, you can't pump even Type-1 or Type-2 discharge overboard. Thus, if you have no holding tank, you can't cruise such areas, even with an approved Type-1 or Type-2 waste-treatment system on board.

Type-2 MSD

Type-2 MSDs are also waste treatment systems. They meet more stringent requirements, however, allowing less than 1,000 parts per 100 milliliters of suspended particulate matter. This is almost clear. (There may be some color.) Bacteria count must be below 200 per 100 milliliters. Boats over 65 feet (19.8 m) must have Type-2 MSDs if they intend to discharge overboard in territorial waters. It's a good thing that Type-1 MSDs are allowed on smaller boats, because Type-2 systems cost a whole lot more—say, $6,000 or so (2008)—and they take up more room and demand more power. Microphor, Humphries, and Galley Maid are three manufacturers of Type-2 MSDs.

Type-3 MSD

A Type-3 MSD is a holding tank, period. A Porta Potti is a Type-3 MSD. Basically, holding tanks are the only MSDs that are guaranteed to be acceptable on all waters, including all NDZs. The drawbacks are obvious—they take up room, and they get full and have to be pumped out. If you can't find a pumpout station, you can pump out through your overboard discharge using a macerator pump, but if you do so inside the three-mile limit, you're breaking the law.

Nevertheless, seawater does contain impurities. It can deposit salt crusts and can cause unpleasant odors in itself when retained inside the head system's plumbing. The ultimate in luxury is using fresh water to flush toilets. These days, with watermakers and large gen sets aboard even mid-size boats, and with the thriftiest heads using 1.5 pints (0.5 L) per flush, there's no reason not to use fresh water for flushing. Some electric macerator-pump toilets have a selector switch that allows you to use salt water on long passages and fresh water inshore or at the dock. Once again, the drawback is the complication of the added plumbing and the electric and motor systems required. If you have an electric outage or a pressure-water-pump failure, you can't flush!

Evacuation Head or Height Limits

Don't forget that all toilets are basically pumping water (whether a conventional pump or a vacuum). The limit of lift or head for the best toilets is about 19.7 feet (6 m). Be sure to consult the manufacturer if the toilet will have to pump against a head much over 9 feet (3 m). Note that some toilets are rated on evacuation heights of no more than just 3 or 4 feet (1 m).

Part Seven

ANCHORING SYSTEMS

Anchoring Systems, Anchor Types, and Anchor Selection

CHAPTER 22

(NOTE: All anchor dimensions given in this book are approximate and are intended for general reference. Confirm dimensions with manufacturer prior to ordering.)

Several years ago, I was headed out for a cruise on one of my office's 44-foot (13.4 m) sailing-cat designs. While we were still among the finger piers, a fuel-line blockage killed the engine. It was blowing 15 to 18 knots and we were drifting out of control, setting down on the boats at the docks. While most of the crew worked frantically to get the engine running again, I dashed forward and eased the anchor over. It bit, held, and kept us off. Swinging just 18 inches (45 cm) from the nearest boat, we needed another hour to trace and fix the engine fault. Then we went sailing. Had we not gotten the anchor set, we might very likely have spent the rest of the day on insurance claims.

Anchors and their related gear are the *only* thing that really *stop* a boat. Inadequate or improper anchoring systems can lead to serious situations: damage or loss of a vessel, injury to crew and people on other craft or to nearby docks or piers, and even loss of life. Too often, individuals and manufacturers spend time discussing the merits of different types of anchors; however, considering the anchoring system *as a whole* is critical. Whether you're speccing an entire anchor system for a new design, retrofitting parts of an existing system, or surveying an existing boat, you need to be able to evaluate the suitability of the gear and its reliability. Here we'll examine the entire anchoring system: the anchor, the rode, the windlass, chain or rope storage, and deployment and retrieval gear. We'll also take a look at the important and closely related gear of mooring cleats and chocks.

ANCHORING SYSTEMS

Anchoring-System Sizes

Of course, there is a considerable difference between an anchoring system appropriate for a 15-foot (4.5 m) daysailer and one for a 120-foot (37 m) motoryacht. The 15-footer could have an anchor so light even a child could swing it over the side, while the 120-footer's anchor and chain would be so heavy even several strong men would be unable to manage it without mechanical assistance.

We can divide anchor systems into three size categories:

1. Small-boat systems: craft under 25 feet (7.6 m)
2. Medium-boat systems: craft between 25 and 50 feet (7.6 and 15.2 m)
3. Large-boat systems: craft over 50 feet (15.2 m)

Each of these can be further subdivided into systems for lightweight inshore craft and those for heavy cruising vessels. Naturally, there are differences between anchor systems for light use and those for serious cruising, even on boats of roughly the same length.

Anchoring-System Components

We also need to identify the components that make up an anchoring system. Not all of them are applicable to every vessel regardless of size, type, or approach to anchoring. It's important, though, to define what the principal components of an anchoring system are:

- anchor
- rode (chain, shackles, rope, or wire)
- deployment and retrieval gear (anchor roller, hawsepipes, davit, or cathead)
- mechanical retrieval aid (windlass or capstan)
- load-carrying mechanism (cleat, bollard, samson post, snubber, chain stopper)
- chafe protection (protect rope against chafe, protect hull and decks from chain)
- chocks or fairleads
- rode storage
- backup anchors and gear, and anchors for special purposes

Each of these components must be properly selected and sized for the boat and for the anchoring approach employed, or the system is subject to failure.

ANCHOR TYPES

For several centuries, when mariners talked about an anchor for a boat, they were always referring to about the same thing. Today, this standard, traditional anchor is often called a *fisherman* anchor or a *kedge* anchor. Neither term is strictly correct, as we'll see, but fisherman anchor is acceptable. You really shouldn't call them kedge anchors. Kedges are anchors that are taken out from the boat and set to either pull a boat off or hold it off from some location. A kedge can be any type of anchor.

Over the past ninety years or so, a truly bewildering array of new anchor forms have been introduced, each one supposedly better in some way than the previous. Originally, much of the impetus for newfangled, lightweight anchors was due to seaplanes. Between the two World Wars, seaplanes were the only means of fast transoceanic travel. The Pan Am Clippers and their many cousins were the cutting edge of high-tech transport. Traditional fisherman anchors were too unwieldy and much too heavy for use on such planes. The strange new anchors developed to serve on seaplanes were patented inventions, and thus these lightweight anchors were often termed *patent anchors*. Most sailors of those days felt that patent anchors were terrible and considered the term *patent anchor* an epithet. Nevertheless, time has shown that many of these patent anchors hold better, pound for pound, than the traditional fisherman anchor. In fact, so many new types of anchors are now available that we couldn't possibly cover them all. We'll take a look at the more common or so-called standard anchors and then at some of the more recent anchor developments.

Standard Anchors and Their Characteristics

ADMIRALTY-PATTERN OR FISHERMAN ANCHORS
Early anchors—of recognizable form—were used in ancient Rome. In fact, the word *anchor* comes from the ancient Greek word *ankos*, meaning "angle or bend," which describes the hook of an anchor's arms pretty well. Around the 1500s, the form was almost completely standardized. They were cast iron with wooden stocks, and usually back then, they had straight arms.

The traditional Admiralty-pattern anchor is shown in Figure 22-1 with its parts defined.

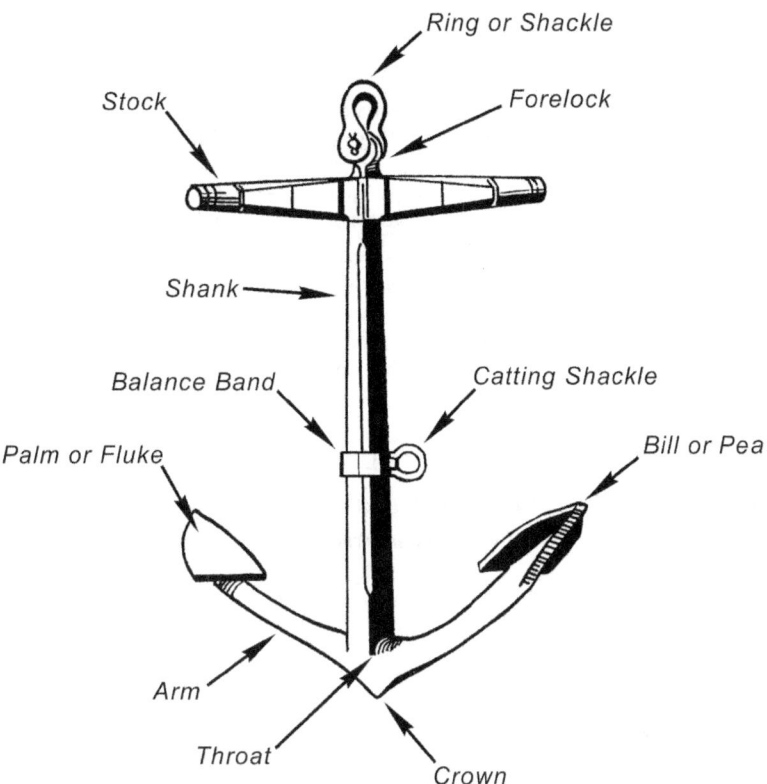

Figure 22-1. Parts of a standard anchor

This was a major development in anchor technology. In fact, when a Captain Hawke requested one for his command in 1804, he was met with scorn. By 1807, however, the new anchor was accepted. It was cast iron with curved arms (as in Figure 22-1) and later had an iron rather than a wooden stock. Though extremely heavy by modern standards, it worked reliably and was standard issue from the British Admiralty throughout the first half of the nineteenth century.

These anchors are hard to stow, but the Admiralty-pattern anchor's biggest drawback is that when set with one fluke and arm fully buried, the opposite fluke stuck straight up. As a boat swung around the anchor, the rode could wrap around the upper arm and catch under the upper palm. This could then yank the anchor out—not good!

TROTMAN'S ANCHOR To correct the fouling problem, John Trotman in the mid-1800s invented an anchor in which the arms and attached flukes pivoted at the crown, as you can see in Figure 22-3.

The Trotman anchor did work and did solve the Admiralty-pattern anchor's problem, but it had a nasty tendency to mash fingers, hands, and arms in the pivot mechanism during retrieval and storage.

YACHTSMAN OR FISHERMAN ANCHORS: HERRESHOFF-, NICHOLSON-, AND LUKE-PATTERN ANCHORS Captains Nat Herreshoff and Charles Nicholson each worked out improved versions

Figure 22-2. Fisherman anchor

PART SEVEN: ANCHORING SYSTEMS

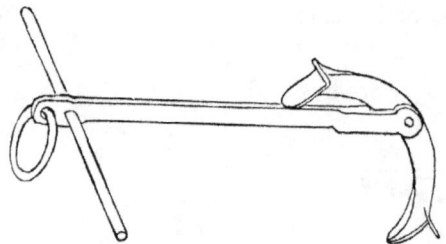

Figure 22-3. The Trotman anchor

of the Admiralty-pattern or fisherman anchor. These are really the *fisherman* anchors of today and are probably best termed *yachtsman* anchors.

These yachtsman anchors incorporate two big improvements. First, the palm or fluke is diamond shaped (Figure 22-6). This means that there is no shoulder or heel on the upturned arm for a line to snag. With yachtsman anchors, fouling the upturned fluke is thus much less likely. The second is that they are fabricated with a metal rather than a wooden stock, and this slides out and lies flat alongside the shank for compact storage.

The Merriman company manufactured a modification of the Herreshoff anchor that came apart in three pieces. A version of this

TABLE 22-1. THREE-PIECE YACHTSMAN ANCHOR DIMENSIONS (USE WITH FIGURE 22-4)

MERRIMAN - HERRESHOFF-PATTERN ANCHOR DIMENSIONS—ENGLISH
Dimensions in Inches

Size Weight lb.	A	B	C	D	E	F	G	H
30	36½	35¾	21¼	4⅜	1¾	¾	⅞	9⅛
40	38	36	23⅜	4⅞	1¾	⅞	1	10
50	39½	37¾	25¼	5¼	2	1	1⅛	10¹³/₁₆
65	43¼	42¼	25½	5¾	2¼	1	1¼	11¾
75	45½	45½	28⅞	6	2¼	1⅛	1¼	12⅜
100	48½	47	31⅞	6⅝	2½	1¼	1⅜	13⅝
125	56	53¼	34⅝	7¹³/₁₆	2¾	1¼	1½	14⅞
150	57¼	53	37¼	7¾	2¾	1½	1½	15¹⁵/₁₆
175	60	61	36¼	8⁵/₁₆	3	1¼	1⅝	16½
200	69	72½	40	8¹⁵/₁₆	3	1½	1⅝	17⅛
260	71	72	43	8¹⁵/₁₆	3½	1¾	1¾	18⁷/₁₆
300	73	76	47	9¾	4	1¾	2¼	20
400	76	76	49	10	4	2	2¼	21

MERRIMAN - HERRESHOFF-PATTERN ANCHOR DIMENSIONS—METRIC
Dimensions in Millimeters

Size Weight kg	A	B	C	D	E	F	G	H
14	927	908	540	111	44	19	22	232
18	965	914	594	124	44	22	25	254
23	1,003	959	641	133	51	25	29	275
29	1,099	1,073	699	146	57	25	32	298
34	1,156	1,156	733	152	57	29	32	314
45	1,232	1,194	810	168	64	32	35	346
57	1,422	1,353	879	183	70	32	38	378
68	1,454	1,346	946	197	70	38	38	405
79	1,524	1,549	921	211	76	32	41	419
91	1,753	1,842	1,016	227	76	38	41	435
118	1,803	1,829	1,092	227	89	44	44	468
136	1,854	1,930	1,194	248	102	44	57	508
181	1,930	1,930	1,245	254	102	51	57	533

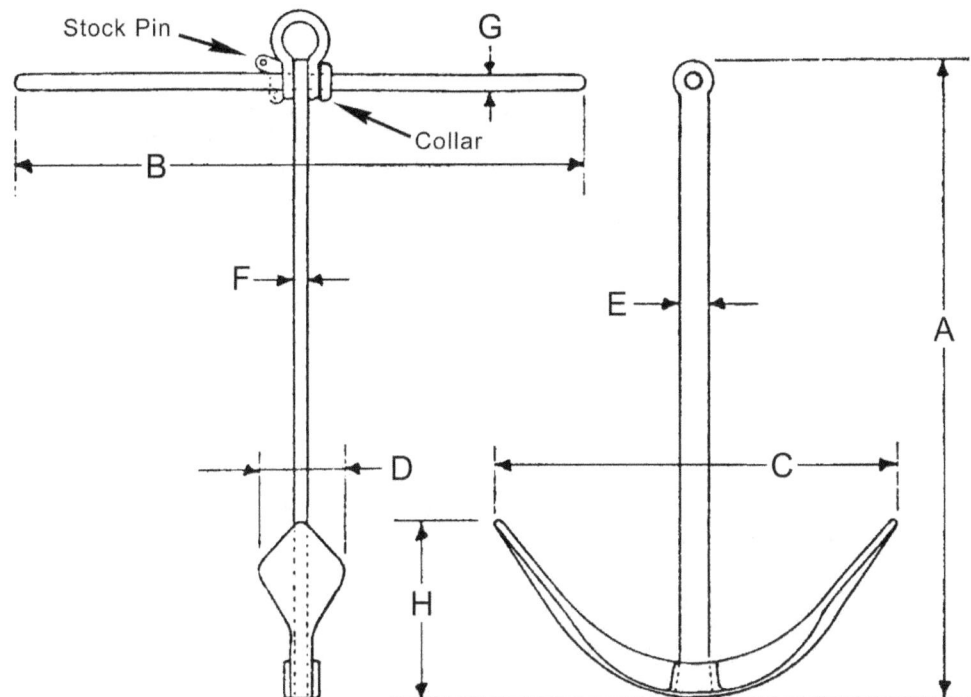

Figure 22-4. Merriman-Herreshoff-type three-piece anchor

is still available from Paul E. Luke, Inc., East Boothbay, Maine, and it makes an excellent storm anchor in the appropriate weight. Whereas the original Herreshoff anchor has the shank, arms, and fluke all cast as one piece, the Luke anchor comes apart into three pieces. This not only makes for compact storage in the bilge, but also makes it easier to bring the individual pieces up on deck to be assembled when needed.

Modern testing and reports on the holding power of yachtsman anchors vary incredibly. Some sources give them high marks, others don't. My recommendation is that yachtsman anchors can make ideal storm anchors. A large Luke stowed in three pieces in the bilge is nice insurance for a major blow. Also, because these anchors have clear hooks as their arms, they can grab in rocky ground where some modern anchor types may not set.

More modern anchors, such as the plow, Danforth, and claw types, give more holding power per pound, and—equally important—are considerably easier to launch and retrieve.

"NAVY" STOCKLESS ANCHORS Speaking of ease of launch and retrieval, one of the most convenient ways to deploy and retrieve an anchor is via hawsepipes on the side of the hull, up at the bow. (We'll look at this in detail later.) Westeney Smith probably invented the first stockless anchor widely accepted for

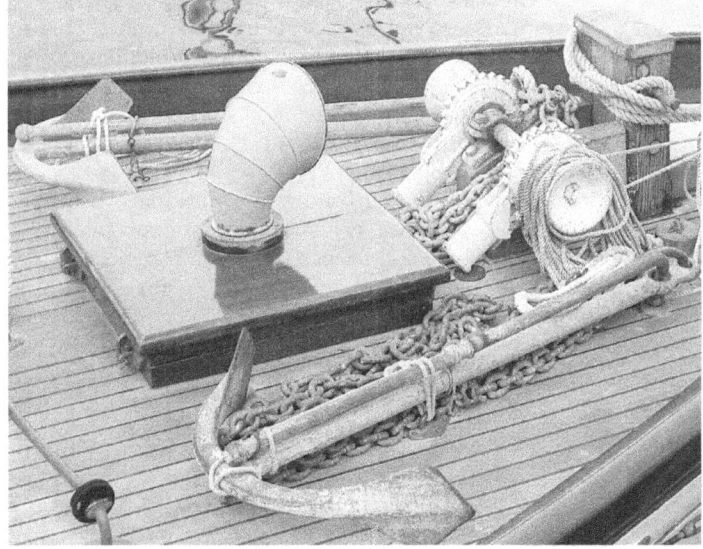

Figure 22-5. Herreshoff anchors stowed on deck

PART SEVEN: ANCHORING SYSTEMS

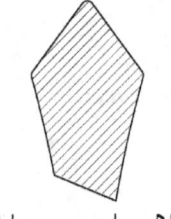
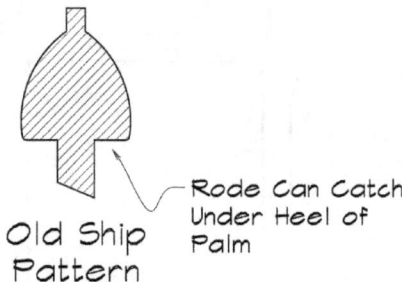

Figure 22-6. Comparison of anchor fluke patterns

commercial use in hawsepipes. For big ships this is an improvement, and this form is usually termed the *navy stockless anchor*, though there are now many types of stockless anchors for ships, such as the Hall and Forfjord, to mention just a couple. Figure 22-8 shows a further assortment of modern stockless ship anchors, improvements over the original Westeney Smith navy stockless.

Nevertheless, most of these anchors have no place on any boat (as opposed to ships). Though easy to deploy and retrieve, navy stockless anchors have abysmal holding power until they weigh at least 200 to 300 hundred pounds (90 to 140 kg) and—in most patterns—over 500 pounds (225 kg). Many really work best at weights over a ton (1,800 kg)! If you see a boat fitted with navy stockless anchors, you're looking at a boat that's likely to drag.

There are a couple of exceptions. On larger yachts (over 90 feet [27 m] or so), a heavy stockless anchor in hawsepipes may make sense. Two stockless anchors that work well in what are lightish weights for stockless anchors are the Manson Anchors kedge anchor (available in sizes as small as 110 lb. [50 kg]) and the G. J. Wortelboer D'Hone Special.

Figure 22-10 shows a traditional Westeney Smith navy stockless anchor in a hawsepipe on a wooden commuter yacht. I would not want to weather a nor'easter

Figure 22-7. Disassembled Luke anchor

aboard while riding on this anchor, or even a pair of them.

DANFORTH-TYPE ANCHORS The original Danforth anchor was invented by Bill Danforth in 1939 as one of those lightweight patent seaplane anchors. It has worked well enough over the years to be used in World War II landing craft and almost to be considered today's "standard" or "traditional" anchor form. There have been several variations of the original Danforth. The company was later purchased by the White Instrument Company and is now part of the ITT (Jabsco, Rule) corporate structure. The three common original Danforth anchors currently sold are the Deepset II, the Hi-Tensile, and the Standard. Only the Deepset II and Hi-Tensile are of drop-forged, heat-treated steel, and these two are recommended for cruising. The standard Danforth is really for small, coastal dayboats. This is close to the original Danforth, though earlier models such as the Danforth Mark III and Mark IV had somewhat different proportions. Figure 22-11 shows a generic Danforth anchor with approximate dimensions. It is important to note that these dimensions vary and are only a general guide (though they should be close enough to size most anchor roller and storage arrangements).

Since the original Danforth patent expired, numerous other manufacturers have offered their own either "improved" or lower-cost versions. Some of these are excellent anchors, some aren't. The quality of manufacturer, the alloy, the sharpness and proportions of the flukes, and the angle of the palms at the crown all contribute to proper anchor holding power and further vary performance for better holding in soft mud, or sand and gravel, and so on.

Regardless, the Danforth-type anchor can be considered one of the standard modern anchors and is probably the most common all-around anchor. Holding tests for well-made and well-proportioned Danforth-type anchors are consistently good to very good in most bottoms, with the exception that these anchors have trouble digging into grassy, rocky, or hard-clay bottoms.

ALUMINUM, LIGHTWEIGHT DANFORTH TYPES (FORTRESS, GUARDIAN) The most recent version of the Danforth-type anchor is the

Chapter 22: Anchoring Systems, Anchor Types, and Anchor Selection

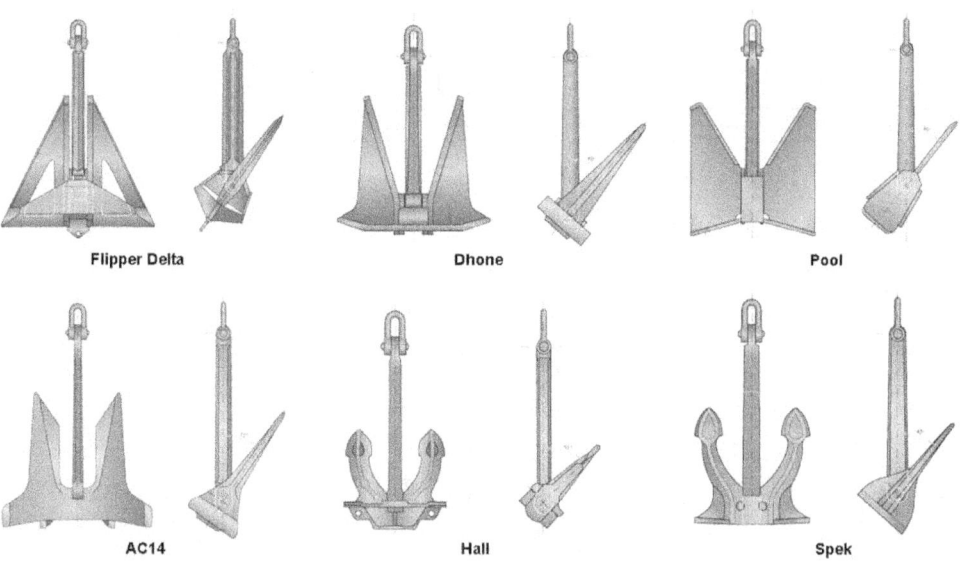

Figure 22-8. Assorted stockless anchors (Courtesy G. J. Wortelboer Jr. B.V.)

lightweight, aluminum Danforth-type typified by the Fortress (Figure 22-12) and Guardian anchors. Made of aluminum, these anchors weigh considerably less than standard steel Danforths of the same dimensions. Since the holding power of this form of anchor—once dug in—is largely determined by the area of the flukes, these aluminum Danforth types can have much greater holding power per pound of anchor weight than steel Danforth types (which were once considered lightweight anchors themselves).

The problem comes with the qualifier "once dug in." Lightweight anchors with large, flat flukes tend to sail or kite and take their time to reach the bottom, and they can take longer to dig in and hold once they reach the bottom. This will apply again should the anchor break out when the boat swings or surges and then has to reset itself. These anchors are even less reliable in grassy, rocky, or hard-clay bottoms than standard steel Danforth types.

In fact, the manufacturers of these anchors will often claim immense holding power (backed up by independent testing)

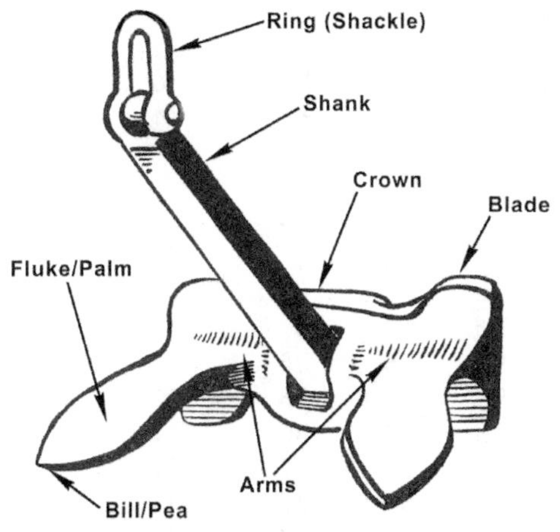

Figure 22-9. Parts of a stockless anchor

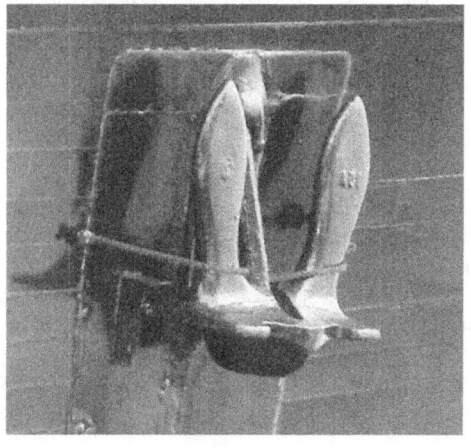

Figure 22-10. A navy stockless anchor in a hawsepipe

PART SEVEN: ANCHORING SYSTEMS

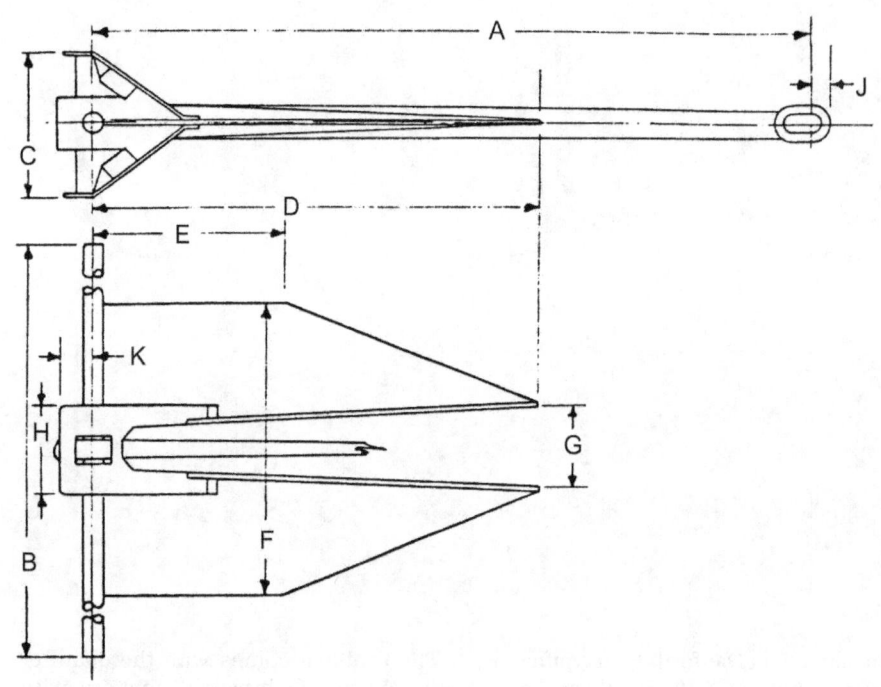

Figure 22-11. Typical Danforth anchor proportions

TABLE 22-2. DANFORTH ANCHOR DIMENSIONS (USE WITH FIGURE 22-11)

Size Weight, lb.	A	B	C	D	E	F	G	H	J	K	Chain Shackle
				APPROXIMATE (ENGLISH) Dimensions, inches							
17	25	21 5/8	4 1/2	15 3/4	6 1/2	9 11/16	3 1/2	3	1/2	1 3/16	3/8
30	31	26 3/4	5 7/8	19 1/2	8 1/16	12	4 1/4	3 3/4	5/8	1 3/8	7/16
43	35 1/2	30 3/4	6 1/8	22	8 7/8	13 7/16	4 5/8	3 13/16	5/8	1 1/2	1/2
50	36	31 1/8	6 3/8	22 3/4	9 3/8	13 5/8	4 3/4	3 7/8	3/4	1 9/16	1/2
75	44	38 1/8	7 7/8	26 11/16	11 7/16	16 7/16	5 3/16	4 3/4	1	1 7/8	5/8
100	47 1/2	41 1/8	8 3/8	30	12 3/8	17 3/4	6	5 1/2	1 3/16	2 1/16	3/4
150	49	42 1/2	8 5/8	31	12 3/4	19	6 1/4	5 5/8	1 1/4	2 1/8	3/4
200	53	45 1/2	9 1/4	32 3/4	13 7/8	20 3/4	6 3/4	6 1/8	1 5/16	2 3/8	7/8

Size Weight, kg	A	B	C	D	E	F	G	H	J	K	Chain Shackle
				APPROXIMATE (METRIC) Dimensions, millimeters							
8	635	549	114	400	165	246	89	76	13	30	10
14	787	679	149	495	205	305	108	95	16	35	11
20	902	781	156	559	225	341	117	97	16	38	13
23	914	791	162	578	238	346	121	98	19	40	13
34	1,118	968	200	678	291	418	132	121	25	48	16
45	1,207	1,045	213	762	314	451	152	140	30	52	19
68	1,245	1,080	219	787	324	483	159	143	32	54	19
91	1,346	1,156	235	832	352	527	171	156	33	60	22

TABLE 22-3. RECOMMENDED SIZES FOR LIGHTWEIGHT DANFORTH ANCHORS

GUARDIAN ANCHOR DIMENSIONS AND SPECS										
Model		G-5	G-7	G-11	G-16	G-23	G-37	G-55	G-85	G-125
Boat Length	ft.	12'–16'	17'–22'	23'–27'	28'–33'	34'–41'	42'–47'	48'–53'	54'–62'	63'–72'
	m	4–5	5–7	7–8	8–10	10–12	12–14	14–16	16–19	19–22
Weight	lb.	2½	4	6	7	13	18	29	42	65
	kg	1.1	1.8	2.7	3.2	5.9	8.1	13.1	19	29.3
Replaces Steel	lb.	4–6	6–9	10–13	14–18	19–20	33–50	50–65	70–90	100–170
Anchors	kg	2–3	3–4	5–6	6–8	9–13	15–23	23–29	32–41	45–77
HOLDING POWER										
Model		G-5	G-7	G-11	G-16	G-23	G-37	G-55	G-85	G-125
Working Load	lb.	350	575	750	1,075	1,625	2,500	3,500	4,625	6,000
	kg	159	261	340	488	737	1,134	1,588	2,098	2,722
32° Hard Sand	lb.	1,050	1,725	2,250	3,225	4,875	7,500	10,500	13,875	18,000
Holding Power	kg	476	782	1,021	1,462	2,211	3,402	4,763	6,294	8,165
32° Soft Mud	lb.	210	345	450	645	975	1,500	2,100	2,775	3,600
Holding Power	kg	95	156	204	293	442	680	953	1,259	1,633
DIMENSIONS (Refer to Danforth Anchor Drawing)										
Model		G-5	G-7	G-11	G-16	G-23	G-37	G-55	G-85	G-125
"A" Shank Length	in.	19"	22"	25"	29"	33"	38"	43"	48"	53"
	mm	483	559	635	737	838	965	1,092	1,219	1,346
"D" Fluke Length	in.	11"	13"	15"	17"	19"	22"	25"	28"	31"
	mm	179	330	381	432	483	559	635	711	787
"B" Stock Length	in.	16"	18"	20"	23"	27"	31"	35"	39"	43"
	mm	406	457	508	584	686	787	889	991	1,092
SUPPORT HARDWARE										
Model		G-5	G-7	G-11	G-16	G-23	G-37	G-55	G-85	G-125
Proof-Coil Chain	in.	3/16"	3/16"	3/16"	1/4"	5/16"	3/8"	3/8"	1/2"	1/2"
	mm	5	5	5	6	8	9	9	13	13
Nylon Rope**	in.	3/8"	3/8"	3/8"	3/8"	1/2"	5/8"	3/4"	7/8"	1"
	mm	9	9	9	9	13	16	19	22	25
Shackle Size	in.	3/16"	3/16"	1/4"	1/4"	5/16"	3/8"	7/16"	1/2"	5/8"
	mm	5	5	6	6	8	10	12	12	16

**Rope size based on 25% of rope's breaking strength

and explain that weight has little to do with holding power. This is true to some degree, but a look at the lightweight-anchor-manufacturer's catalog data will show that their larger, heavier anchors hold more than the smaller, lighter ones.

As we'll discuss in more detail later, I'm a believer in big, heavy anchors where appropriate. Nevertheless, these lightweight, aluminum Danforth-type anchors have proved themselves. Indeed, it was a lightweight Fortress anchor that I deployed to secure my catamaran with the balky engine in the anecdote that began this chapters. A heavy anchor and anchoring system would not be appropriate for a lightweight sailing catamaran or for

PART SEVEN: ANCHORING SYSTEMS

Figure 22-12.
Fortress anchor

many raceboats or performance boats. A Fortress or Guardian anchor is a suitable and sensible selection for such craft.

PLOW-TYPE ANCHORS (CQR, DELTA) The *CQR* in "CQR plow anchor" stands for "secure" . . . clever. This first plow-type anchor was invented by Sir Geoffrey Taylor in 1933 and so predates the Danforth. Taylor was a physicist who, among other things, worked on the original nuclear bomb project at Los Alamos. The plow-type anchor was revolutionary in its day. The idea was that the anchor's plow shape would enable it to, well, plow its way down into the sea bottom. The original CQR plow has a hinged connection from the shank to the plow's flukes, and has lead ballast at the plow's tip to ensure it takes the right angle and digs in. Simpson-Lawrence originally offered the CQR, which was later purchased by Lewmar. After the Danforth, the CQR plow is currently probably the most common "modern" anchor.

Most tests today indicate that the CQR is only average in holding power, not as good as more recent anchor designs. Modern variants of the plow and spade hold more tenaciously in many bottoms. Nevertheless, the CQR has been a reliable performer for many decades and does have the advantage of holding moderately well in nearly every type of seabed. This makes it an excellent all-around anchor. Still, it would no longer be my first choice. These days, I would more likely spec the Delta or a spade type.

DELTA (FIXED-SHANK) PLOW ANCHORS The more modern version of the plow anchor is the Delta anchor (and some other similar plow anchors without a pivot on the shank). The Delta has the additional advantage of being balanced to self-launch from an anchor roller. Deltas in most anchor tests consistently rate with good to very good holding power in most bottoms. Because of its self-launching ability and its good holding power, the Delta happens to be one of my personal picks for a cruising-boat anchor. I've specced it for most of my cruising designs and have yet to hear of a dragging problem or to experience one myself. Of course—as we'll see—I usually spec rather heavy anchors, which is one of the keys to good holding power.

CLAW ANCHORS (BRUCE, CLAW) Originally developed for use on fishing vessels, the Bruce anchor is the original claw-type anchor. By the late 1970s and early 1980s, the Bruce (Figure 22-16) became popular—in huge sizes—for anchoring heavy equipment in the offshore oil industry, including entire oil rigs, particularly in the North Sea where Shell UK made extensive use of it.

The Bruce or claw anchor was a new concept for yachts and boats in the 1980s, but with its track record of commercial use in the North Sea, it was soon widely accepted. Many tests indicate that the Bruce is one of the best anchor types for setting and setting quickly. In fact, on some rocky bottoms, it has been the only pattern of anchor to set nearly 100 percent of the time, according to various trials. Though the Bruce or claw

TABLE 22-4. CQR ANCHOR DIMENSIONS (USE WITH FIGURE 22-13)

CQR—ANCHOR DIMENSIONS

ENGLISH UNITS—Dimensions, inches

Size Weight, Lb.	A	B	C	D	E	F	G	H	I	J	K	L	M	N
15	$13^1/4$	$9^1/4$	$25^1/4$	$10^3/4$	18	$7/8$	$9/16$	$1^5/16$	$2^1/4$	$22^1/4$	2	12	$4^3/4$	$2^5/8$
20	$15^1/4$	$10^5/8$	$31^5/8$	$12^3/8$	21	$1^1/8$	$5/8$	$1^3/4$	$2^3/8$	26	2	$14^1/2$	6	3
25	$16^1/2$	12	$33^3/4$	$13^1/2$	22	$1^1/4$	$5/8$	$1^7/8$	$2^9/16$	$27^7/8$	2	15	$6^1/4$	$3^1/8$
35	$18^1/4$	$13^3/4$	38	14	25	$1^3/8$	$13/16$	$2^1/4$	3	$30^1/5$	2	$7^1/2$	7	$3^1/4$
45	20	15	$41/2$	$14^5/8$	$26^5/8$	$1^1/2$	1	$2^3/8$	$3^1/4$	$32^1/4$	$2^1/2$	$18^1/2$	$7^1/2$	$3^1/2$
60	22	$16^1/2$	$45^1/2$	16	$30^1/8$	$1^5/8$	1	$2^3/4$	$3^1/2$	36	$2^1/4$	21	$8^1/4$	4
75	$23^3/4$	$17^3/4$	$48^5/8$	$17^3/8$	$32^1/4$	$1^3/4$	1	3	$3^3/4$	$38^1/2$	$2^1/4$	$22^1/2$	9	$4^7/16$
105	$27^1/8$	19	$45^3/8$	$15^1/2$	26	$1^7/8$	$13/16$	$4^1/5$	$4^3/4$	33	$2^1/4$	$19^1/2$	9	$2^1/2$
140	30	$21^1/8$	$50^1/8$	$17^1/4$	$28^3/4$	2	$1^1/4$	5	5	$36^1/5$	$2^1/4$	$21^1/2$	9	$2^7/8$
180	$30^1/2$	23	$54^1/4$	$18^5/8$	31	$2^1/4$	$1^1/2$	$5^3/8$	$5^1/2$	$39^1/2$	$2^1/4$	$21^3/8$	$9^3/4$	$3^1/8$
240	$35^3/4$	$25^1/4$	$59^3/4$	$20^1/2$	$34^1/4$	$2^1/2$	$1^1/2$	6	$5^3/4$	$43^1/2$	3	$25^3/4$	$10^3/4$	$4^7/16$
300	$38^3/4$	$27^3/4$	$64^5/8$	$22^1/4$	37	$2^5/8$	$1^5/8$	$6^7/16$	5	47	$3^1/2$	$27^3/4$	$11^5/8$	$3^3/4$
400	$42^1/2$	30	$70^7/8$	$24^3/8$	$40^5/8$	$2^7/8$	$1^7/8$	7	$6^1/2$	$51^1/2$	$3^1/2$	$30^1/2$	$12^3/4$	4
500	$45^1/2$	$32^1/2$	$80^7/8$	$26^1/8$	$43^3/4$	$3^1/8$	2	$7^3/8$	$6^7/8$	56	4	$32^7/8$	$13^3/4$	$4^3/8$
600	$48^5/8$	$43^1/4$	$61^1/4$	$27^7/8$	$46^1/2$	$3^5/16$	$2^1/8$	8	$7^1/4$	59	4	35	$14^5/8$	$4^5/8$

METRIC UNITS—Dimensions, millimeters

Size Weight, kg	A	B	C	D	E	F	G	H	I	J	K	L	M	N
7	337	235	692	273	457	22	14	33	57	565	51	305	121	67
9	387	270	803	314	533	29	16	44	60	660	51	368	152	76
11	419	305	857	343	559	32	16	48	65	689	51	381	159	79
16	464	349	965	356	635	35	21	57	76	775	51	191	178	83
20	508	381	1,029	371	676	38	25	60	83	819	64	470	191	89
27	559	419	1,156	406	765	41	25	70	89	914	64	533	210	102
34	603	451	1,235	441	826	44	25	76	95	972	57	572	229	113
48	689	483	1,153	394	660	48	30	114	121	838	57	495	229	64
64	762	537	1,273	438	730	51	32	127	127	927	57	546	230	73
82	775	584	1,378	474	787	57	38	135	140	1,003	57	542	248	79
109	908	641	1,518	521	870	64	38	152	146	1,105	76	654	273	87
136	984	692	1,642	565	940	67	41	164	127	1,194	89	705	295	95
181	1,080	762	1,800	619	1,032	73	48	178	165	1,308	89	775	324	102
227	1,156	826	2,054	664	1,111	79	51	187	175	1,422	102	835	349	110
272	1,236	870	1,556	708	1,181	84	54	203	184	1,499	102	889	371	117

PART SEVEN: ANCHORING SYSTEMS

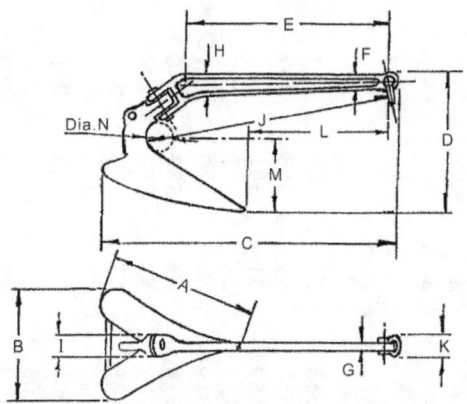

Figure 22-13. CQR anchor proportions (Courtesy Simpson-Lawrence)

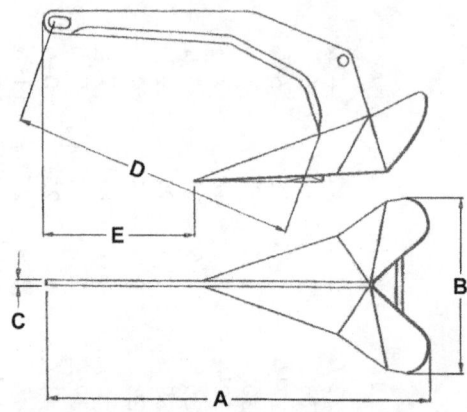

Figure 22-14. Delta anchor proportions

anchor sets very reliably, holding power per pound of anchor weight seems to be only average to good in many experiments.

The original Bruce Anchor Group no longer manufactures or supplies the standard Bruce anchor. This company now specializes in providing large anchors and anchor systems to the offshore-oil industry and other commercial operations, and they fabricate anchors that look quite unusual and rather industrial. What is traditionally known as the Bruce anchor is available from Imtra Corporation, and the Claw anchor is available from Lewmar. Assorted variants from other companies are available, too.

NORTHILL ANCHOR To my knowledge, the Northill anchor is no longer being manufactured. It, too, was one of the original lightweight

TABLE 22-5. DELTA ANCHOR DIMENSIONS (USE WITH FIGURE 22-14)

	ENGLISH UNITS—Dimensions, inches						METRIC UNITS—Dimensions, millimeters				
Size Weight, lb.	A	B	C	D	E	Size Weight, kg	A	B	C	D	E
					Galvanized						
9	20¼	9	5/16	15¼	8¼	4	514	229	8	387	210
14	23⅜	10⅜	⅜	17⅝	9½	6	594	264	10	448	241
22	27⅜	12¼	½	20⅝	11⅛	10	695	311	13	524	283
35	32	14¼	½	24⅛	13	16	813	362	13	613	330
44	34½	15⅜	⅝	26⅛	14	20	876	391	16	664	356
55	37¼	16⅜	⅝	28	15¼	25	946	416	16	711	387
88	43½	19¼	¾	32¾	17¼	40	1,105	489	19	832	438
110	46¼	20½	¾	35	18⅞	50	1,175	521	19	889	479
					Stainless Steel						
14	23⅜	10⅜	⅜	17⅝	9½	6	594	264	10	448	241
22	27⅜	12¼	½	20⅝	11⅛	10	695	311	13	524	283
35	32	14¼	½	24⅛	13	16	813	362	13	613	330
44	34½	15⅜	⅝	26⅛	14	20	876	391	16	664	356
55	37¼	16⅜	⅝	28	15¼	25	946	416	16	711	387
88	43½	19¼	¾	32¾	17¼	40	1,105	489	19	832	438
110	46¼	20½	¾	35	18⅞	50	1,175	521	19	889	479
140	50	22⅜	⅞	38	20	64	1,270	568	22	965	508

Chapter 22: Anchoring Systems, Anchor Types, and Anchor Selection

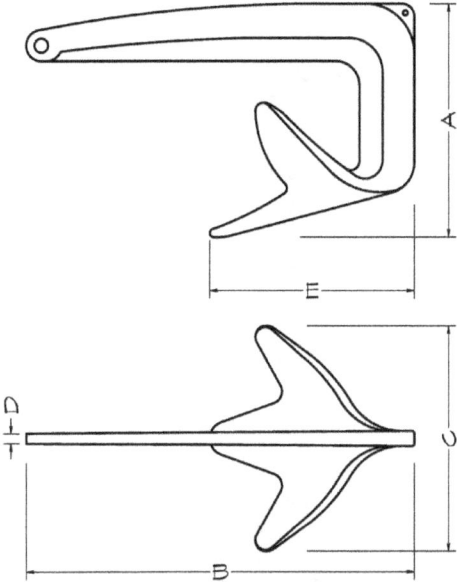

Figure 22-15. Bruce anchor proportions

seaplane patent anchors (Figure 22-17). The stock is located at the crown and folds flat for easier storage. As is often the case, tests of the Northill's holding power vary widely, but many sailors who have used Northills swear by them and claim their boats have never dragged.

A modern variant of the Northill was invented by Robert E. Pekny, and not surprisingly, it is known as the Pekny anchor. This anchor apparently performs as well as the Northill, but I'm not aware of any companies manufacturing the Pekny anchor today.

GRAPNEL ANCHORS For small boats, such as dinghies, the simple grapnel anchor is a common choice (Figure 22-18). The grapnel has superb holding power, but only when it can hook on something, such as buried logs, branches, or rocks. The folding grapnel, though, makes a very compact package and conveniently will set as a lunch hook for most very small boats (Figure 22-19). Grapnel anchors are also useful for dragging the bottom to pick up lost anchor rodes and such.

Because grapnel anchors primarily work by hooking, they are particularly subject to fouling and refusing to release. On any larger grapnel or in any longer-term use, a buoyed trip line to the anchor crown is recommended.

New Anchors

SPADE ANCHORS One of the newer successful developments in anchor design is the spade-anchor form (Figure 22-20 and 22-21). This works almost opposite from a plow, digging down into the sea bottom. As you would expect, the anchor flukes or blades are configured roughly like a spade, usually with a "roll bar" over the anchor to force it to right itself and dig in at the correct attitude.

TABLE 22-6. BRUCE ANCHOR DIMENSIONS (USE WITH FIGURE 22-15)

	Dimensions, inches						Dimensions, millimeters				
Size Weight, lb.	A	B	C	D	E	Size Weight, kg	A	B	C	D	E
4	7.0	14.3	9.7	0.3	4.7	2	178	363	246	8	119
11	9.3	18.5	12.4	0.4	7.0	5	236	470	315	10	178
16	10.6	21.3	14.2	0.4	7.5	7.5	269	541	361	10	191
22	11.4	23.0	15.3	0.5	8.0	10	290	584	389	12	203
33	12.9	25.8	17.6	0.5	8.7	15	328	655	447	12	221
44	14.3	28.1	18.5	0.7	9.5	20	363	714	470	17	241
66	16.0	32.1	21.3	0.8	11.0	30	406	815	541	19	279
110	18.9	38.1	25.3	0.9	13.4	50	480	968	643	23	340
176	21.8	42.9	28.0	1.0	14.8	80	554	1,090	711	25	376
242	24.1	48.4	31.9	1.2	17.3	110	612	1,229	810	30	439
330	27.5	53.4	35.3	1.5	19.5	150	699	1,356	897	37	495
550	33.8	63.7	42.0	1.7	22.8	250	859	1,618	1,067	43	579

Figure 22-16. Bruce anchor (Courtesy Imtra Corporation/Bruce International Ltd.)

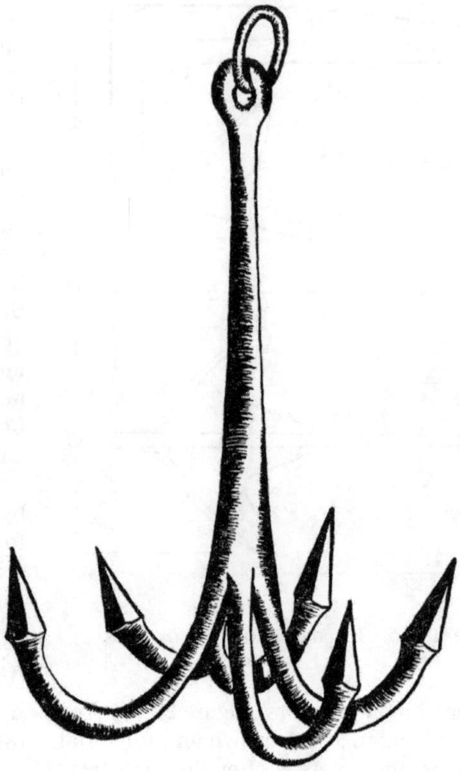

Spade-type anchors are available from an assortment of manufacturers as the spade anchor (Figure 22-21), the Bugel anchor (Figure 22-22), the Sword anchor, the Rocna anchor (Figure 22-20), the Manson Supreme, and others. Each has somewhat different proportions, but they work along generally similar principles. I haven't included dimension drawings of spade anchors here because there are too many varieties to make such drawings practical.

Since the spade anchor type is so new, it hasn't had the many decades the plow and Danforth types have had to prove itself. Nevertheless, over the past several years, spade anchors have tested well and have shown themselves to have generally good holding power in most bottoms, as well as to set reliably. A number of independent trials have given the spade-type anchors the highest holding power per pound among the assortment of anchors examined. Until further data are in, I would recommend sticking with the spade anchors I've mentioned. Some lightweight spade anchors, such as the HydroBubble and XYZ, have shown less reliable holding results in independent tests.

Figure 22-18. Grapnel anchor

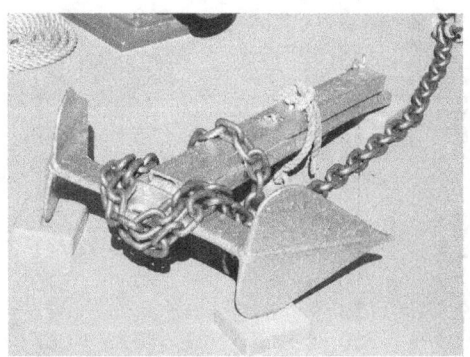

Figure 22-17. A Northill anchor

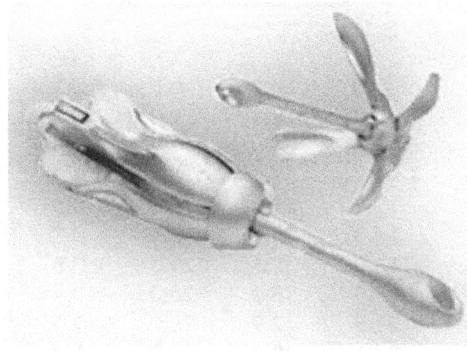

Figure 22-19. A folding grapnel anchor (Courtesy Plastimo)

Chapter 22: Anchoring Systems, Anchor Types, and Anchor Selection

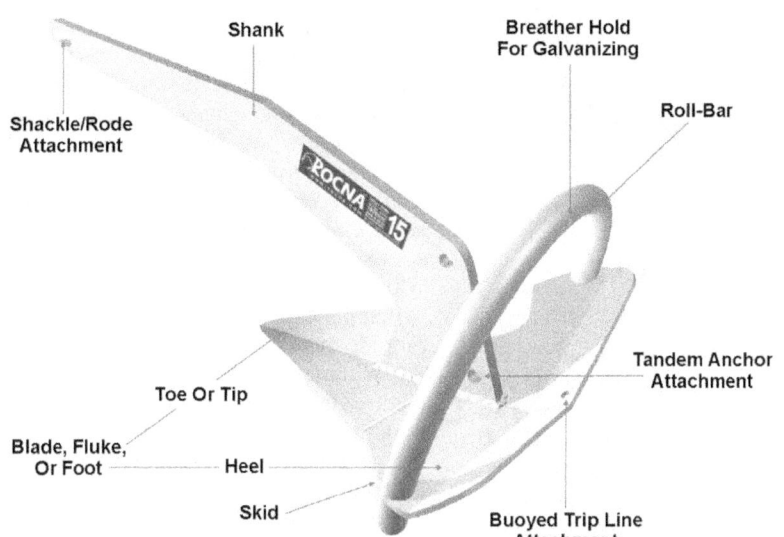

Figure 22-20. Parts of a spade anchor (Courtesy Rocna Anchors)

ODD ANCHORS All the preceding anchors look at least vaguely as you would expect an anchor to look—like an old traditional yachtsman anchor, a plow, a claw, or a spade. There are a few other really oddball anchors. Some of these have received high marks in independent anchor tests. A good example is the Bulwagga anchor, which looks just plain weird but does very well in most anchor tests. Particularly in smaller sizes, where its odd shape won't be too difficult to deal with in storage (it breaks down), an anchor like this is worth considering.

Figure 22-22. Bugel anchor (Courtesy Bugel Anchor)

Figure 22-21. Spade anchor (Courtesy Spade High-performance Anchors)

345

PART SEVEN: ANCHORING SYSTEMS

Figure 22-23. Bulwagga anchor (Courtesy Bulwagga Marine Anchors)

ANCHOR SIZE AND DESIGNATION

Most boats (as we'll see shortly) should carry two or more anchors. Common modern terminology for the primary anchor that is used most of the time is the *working anchor*. The heavy anchor used for anchoring in severe weather is the *storm anchor*; while the light anchor used for short-term anchoring is the *lunch hook*. The lunch hook is usually the anchor carried off to either keep the boat away from something (e.g., shore, dock, or another boat) or to pull a boat off when it has run aground. This is kedging off, and the lunch hook is also properly the *kedge anchor*, though people commonly misuse this term to mean a fisherman or yachtsman anchor type.

More traditional terms for the different anchors are as follows: *Bower anchors* are the standard working anchors, with the "best bower" being the heaviest standard working anchor. The light lunch hook was termed the *stream anchor*, and the storm anchor is the *street anchor*—the heaviest anchor aboard. In the days of wooden, square-rigged sail, the street anchor (also called the *sheet anchor*) was stored ready for instant use, and the term *sheet anchor* became a synonym for safety; something that was your sheet anchor was your security. (The word *bower*, by the way, originally came from *bow*, meaning nothing more than an anchor carried at the bow.)

When an anchor is hanging free on the chain over the bow (ready to drop or to bring up and cat home for storage), it was said to be *cockabill*. Today, when the anchor chain is straight up and down, with the anchor on the bottom and ready to break out, we simply call out "straight up and down," but this is properly termed *apeak*.

ANCHOR SELECTION RECOMMENDATIONS

Having reviewed the assortment of anchors commonly available, the question becomes which type to specify for a particular boat. Table 22-7 is based on the breakdown of boat sizes with which this chapter began.

TABLE 22-7. RECOMMENDED ANCHORS FOR INSHORE AND CRUISING BOATS OF VARIOUS SIZES

Boat Size	Type	1st Working or 1st Bower	2nd Working or 2nd Bower	Lunch Hook or Stream	Storm or Street
Small Boat under 25 ft. (7.6 m)	Inshore, Lightweight	Fortress or Guardian, folding grapnel for dinghy	na	na	na
	Heavy, Cruising	Fortress or Guardian	(optional) Delta, plow, spade	na	(optional) Luke stowed in bilge
Medium Boat 25 to 50 ft. (7.6 to 15.2 m)	Inshore, Lightweight	Fortress or Guardian	Delta or spade	(optional) Fortress or Guardian	(optional) Luke stowed in bilge
	Heavy, Cruising	Delta, spade, plow, claw	Delta, spade, plow, claw (different from 1st bower)	Fortress or Guardian	Luke or very large Fortress stowed in bilge
	Heavy, Cruising with hawsepipe anchor stowage	Danforth hi-tensile, large	Danforth hi-tensile, large	Fortress or Guardian	Luke or very large Fortress stowed in bilge

(Continued)

TABLE 22-7. RECOMMENDED ANCHORS FOR INSHORE AND CRUISING BOATS OF VARUOIS SIZES (CONTINUED)

Boat Size	Type	1st Working or 1st Bower	2nd Working or 2nd Bower	Lunch Hook or Stream	Storm or Street
Large Boat over 50 ft. (15.2 m)	Inshore, Lightweight	Fortress or Guardian	Delta, spade, plow, claw (different from 1st bower)	(optional) Fortress or Guardian	(optional) large Fortress stowed in bilge
	Heavy, Cruising	Delta, spade, plow, claw	Delta, spade, plow, claw (different from 1st bower)	Fortress or Guardian, or Danforth hi-tensile	Luke or very large Fortress stowed in bilge
	Heavy, Cruising with hawsepipe anchor stowage	Danforth hi-tensile; (optional for boats over 90 ft. [27 m]): Manson "kedge anchor" or Wortelboer "D'Hone Special"	Danforth hi-tensile; (optional for boats over 90 ft. [27 m]): Manson "kedge anchor" or Wortelboer "D'Hone Special"	Fortress or Guardian, or Danforth hi-tensile	Luke or very large Fortress stowed in bilge

Table 22-7 presents the minimum recommended number of anchors. It's not unusual for a boat to carry one to three more anchors, depending on how serious their crew is about cruising. In fact, traditional sailing vessels carried as many as eight to ten anchors. Table 22-8 shows HMS *Victory*'s standard anchor complement.

HMS *Victory* was 226 feet long from bowsprit to taffrail and carried 104 guns into the Battle of Trafalgar. Chances are you won't need as many anchors or anchors as large, but more and bigger is often better.

TABLE 22-8. HMS VICTORY'S STANDARD ANCHOR COMPLEMENT

Type	Number	Weight
Best bower anchor	1	4 tonnes/4.54 tons
Small bower anchor	1	4 tonnes/4.51 tons
Sheet anchors	2	4 tonnes/4.31 tons
Stream anchor	1	1 tonne/1.10 tons
Large kedge anchor	1	½ tonne/0.51 ton
Small kedge anchor	1	¼ tonne/0.30 ton

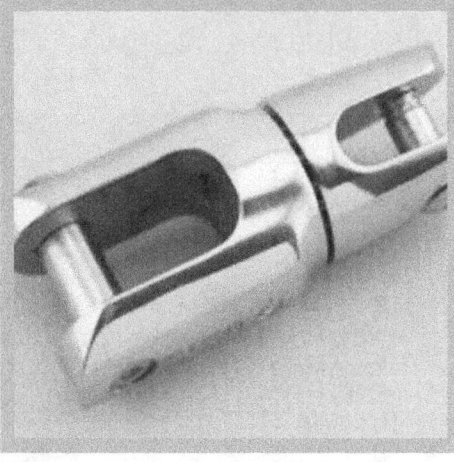

CHAPTER 23 Anchor Rode

CHAIN

Most serious cruisers prefer an all-chain anchor rode. There are a number of reasons for this:

1. The chain doesn't chafe or abrade on rock, coral, or other underwater hazards.
2. The weight of the chain creates a sag (a catenary curve) that absorbs shock when surges lift and straighten it. (The word *chain* can be traced back to the Latin word *catena* for "chain" or "brace," and *catena* is the root for the *catenary curve* a chain makes due to its weight.)
3. With a proper windlass and anchor locker, the entire rode and chain self-stow and self-deploy reliably.
4. The weight of the chain increases anchor holding power by lowering the angle of pull to be more nearly horizontal.

Drawbacks to chain include the following:

1. It is much heavier than rope.
2. It is more expensive than rope.
3. Except in short lengths and small sizes, chain can't be managed by hand and requires a windlass, which adds more weight and more expense.
4. Though chain has the catenary sag to help absorb shocks, once the catenary has been straightened out under load (e.g., in a sustained strong wind) there is no elasticity left to absorb shock. Rope has great elasticity or stretch to absorb shock.

Because rope can chafe (particularly along the seabed) and because the weight of a length of the chain improves the angle the rode pulls on the anchor (makes the load direction more nearly horizontal), even so-called all-rope rodes require some length of chain at the anchor—a *chain leader*:

- For small or lightweight dayboats, use one fathom (6 ft., or 2 m) of chain leader from the anchor to the rope.
- For all other boats, use a chain leader at the anchor at least equal to the LOA of the boat. (For performance boats, where the ultimate in weight saving is required, half of LOA can be used, though this results in some reduction in anchor holding power and some increased risk of chafe damage to the rope rode.)

There are many types of chain, and it's important to spec the correct type as well as size.

Stud-Link Chain

Ships use stud-link chain (Figure 23-1). The studs (crossbars between each link) make the chain both stronger and heavier. The studs also somewhat reduce the tendency of chain

Figure 23-1. Stud-link chain (Courtesy Washington Chain and Supply, Inc.)

links to kink and lock in a bunch (to *hockle*). Stud-link chain isn't welded; rather, the links are forged as a unit. The stud (crossbar), with hollowed ends to mate with the inside of the chain link, is inserted into the red-hot link, which is then hammered tight. When the link cools, the stud is fixed in place with incredible strength. Minimum available size for stud-link chain is usually ⅝ inch (15.8 mm). Breaking strength of standard grade 2, ⅝-inch (15.8 mm) stud-link is 33,200 pounds (15,060 kg), and its weight is 405 lb./100 ft. (6 kg/m), while high-test ⅝-inch (15.8 mm) anchor chain has a breaking strength of 33,000 pounds (14,970 kg), at 382 lb./100 ft. (5.6 kg/m). Stud-link chain should be considered only for vessels over 150 feet (45 m) LOA.

Note that it's *very* important that chain under load be straight and smoothly extended. Any kink or hockle dramatically reduces the strength of the chain and can result in a complete failure.

Chain for Boats

The type of chain suitable for use on boats is short-link open chain of hot-dip galvanized steel or 316 stainless steel. The links need to be short so they will wrap properly around a windlass chain *wildcat* ("chain *gypsy*" in the United Kingdom), and only either true hot-dip galvanized steel or 316 stainless steel have the corrosion resistance required for reliable use in salt water.

Chain Grades

You will find references to chain "grades" (e.g., grade 40, grade 80, etc.). Some of these have other, more common designations such as "proof coil," "BBB," and "high test." This section describes the more common designations.

GRADE 30 "PROOF COIL" OR "COMMON CHAIN" This is general-purpose chain and common anchor chain when hot-dip galvanized. Made from carbon steel with a tensile

TABLE 23-1. GRADE 30—"PROOF-COIL" CHAIN SPECIFICATIONS

Trade Size inches	Wire Diameter mm	Wire Diameter inches	Inside Length inches	Inside Length mm	Inside Width inches	Inside Width mm	Working Load Limit, lb.	Working Load Limit, kg	Wgt. per 100 ft. lbs.	Wgt. kg/m
⅛	4.0	0.162	0.90	22.86	0.29	7.37	400	180	20.4	0.3
3/16	5.5	0.218	0.97	24.64	0.40	10.16	800	360	39.4	0.6
¼	7.0	0.276	1.19	30.23	0.50	12.70	1,300	590	62.5	0.9
¼†	7.0	0.276	1.00	25.40	0.50	12.70	1,300	590	66.8	1.0
5/16	8.4	0.329	1.24	31.50	0.46	11.68	1,900	860	93.0	1.4
5/16†	8.4	0.329	1.12	28.45	0.50	12.70	1,900	860	96.6	1.4
⅜	10.0	0.394	1.33	33.78	0.57	14.48	2,650	1,200	141.3	2.1
⅜†	10.0	0.394	1.23	31.24	0.62	15.75	2,650	1,200	148.2	2.2
½†	13.0	0.519	1.50	38.10	0.81	20.57	4,500	2,040	263.7	3.9
⅝	16.0	0.630	2.12	53.85	0.82	20.83	6,900	3,130	382.4	5.7
⅝†	16.0	0.630	1.90	48.26	1.01	25.65	6,900	3,100	388.0	5.8
¾	20.0	0.781	2.60	66.04	1.02	25.91	10,600	4,810	552.1	8.2
¾†	20.0	0.781	2.20	55.88	1.09	27.69	10,600	4,810	575.8	8.6
⅞	22.0	0.906	2.66	67.56	1.25	31.75	12,800	5,810	776.1	11.6
1	26.0	1.031	2.88	73.15	1.40	35.56	17,900	8,120	1,043.8	15.5

† = to ISO Specifications

PART SEVEN: ANCHORING SYSTEMS

TABLE 23-2. BBB CHAIN SPECIFICATIONS

Trade Size inches	Wire Diameter inches	Wire Diameter mm	Working Load Limit. lb.	Working Load Limit, kg	Nominal Inside Length inches	Nominal Inside Length mm	Nominal Inside Width inches	Nominal Inside Width mm	Maximum Length 100 Links inches	Maximum Length 100 Length cm	Wgt. Per 100 feet lbs.	Wgt. kg/m
3/16	7/32	5.55	800	363	0.78	19.81	0.37	9.40	81	206	43	0.6
1/4	9/32	7.14	1,300	590	0.87	22.10	0.43	10.92	88	224	72	1.1
5/16	11/32	8.73	1,900	862	1.00	25.40	0.50	12.70	104	264	110	1.6
3/8	13/32	10.32	2,650	1,202	1.09	27.69	0.62	15.75	113	287	156	2.3
1/2	17/32	13.48	4,500	2,042	1.34	34.04	0.75	19.05	139	353	277	4.1
9/16	19/32	15.07	5,875	2,666	1.58	40.13	0.73	18.54	162	411	337	5.0
5/8	21/32	16.67	6,900	3,131	1.74	44.20	0.84	21.34	176	447	451	6.7
3/4	25/32	19.84	10,600	4,809	2.20	55.88	1.09	27.69	225	572	598	8.9

strength of 55,000 psi, it is stamped with G3, or G30, or G300, depending on the manufacturer, in sizes from 5/16 inch (8.4 mm) up.

GRADE 30 "BBB" CHAIN This is the shortest link chain available for anchoring. Its short links work best on a windlass's wildcat drums, and BBB (or triple-B) chain weighs somewhat more than proof coil, making a bigger catenary curve when deployed (Figure 23-2). Made from carbon steel with a tensile strength of 55,000 psi (380 MPa), BBB is stamped with 3B or BBB, depending on manufacturer, in sizes from 5/16 inch (8.73 mm wire dia.) up.

GRADE 40 "HIGH TEST" CHAIN Suitable for marine anchor use, this chain is hot-dip galvanized. Grade 40 was originally a designation used exclusively by ACCO Chain. This is somewhat confusing, because the majority of the chain industry uses grade 43 for this chain strength. Grade 40 and grade 43 chain are of high-carbon steel with a tensile strength of 85,000 psi (585 MPa). It is stamped with G4, G40, or G400, depending on the manufacturer, in sizes from 5/16 inch (8.4 mm) up.

GRADE 43 CHAIN This chain is of the same strength as grade 40.

GRADE 63 CHAIN Higher strength than grade 40 high test, this chain is sometimes available in hot-dip galvanized steel for anchor use. It is stamped with G6 or G63, depending on manufacturer, in sizes from 5/16 inch (8.4 mm) up. (Note that these high-strength-steel chains may also be stamped with a proprietary mark such as ACCO's "AS.")

GRADE 70 HIGH-STRENGTH TRANSPORT CHAIN This chain is not suited for anchor systems. It is stamped with G7, G70, or G700, depending on manufacturer, in sizes from 5/16 inch (8.4 mm) up.

GRADE 80 HIGH-STRENGTH CHAIN This chain is specifically designed for Occupational Safety and Health Administration (OSHA) approval for overhead lifting. In short-link size of hot-dip galvanized steel, it could be used as anchor chain; however, grade 80 generally is not available as hot-dip galvanized and also doesn't mate with standard galvanized chain shackles and fittings, so the connections wouldn't be strong enough. It is stamped with G8, G80, or G800, depending on manufacturer, in sizes from 5/16 inch (8.4 mm) up. (Note that these high-strength-steel chains may also be stamped with a proprietary mark such as ACCO's "A8A.")

GRADE 100 VERY-HIGH-STRENGTH CHAIN This is generally available in sizes or coatings suitable for use in anchor systems. It is stamped with G10 or G100, depending on manufacturer, in sizes from 5/16 inch (8.4 mm) up. (Note that these high-strength-steel chains may also be stamped with a proprietary mark such as ACCO's "A10.")

IMPORTANT NOTE: There are other industrial chains not at all suited for use in anchoring. There are also specific marine chains that aren't appropriate for anchor

Figure 23-2. 3B chain (Courtesy ACCO Chain)

TABLE 23-3. GRADE 40 OR 43—"HIGH TEST" CHAIN SPECIFICATIONS

Trade Size inches	Wire Diameter mm	Wire Diameter inches	Inside Length inches	Inside Length mm	Inside Width inches	Inside Width mm	Working Load Limit, lb.	Working Load Limit, kg	Wgt. per 100 ft. lbs.	Wgt. kg/m
1/4†	7.0	0.276	0.84	21.34	0.41	10.41	2,600	1,180	73.3	1.1
1/4	7.0	0.276	1.19	30.23	0.50	12.70	2,600	1,180	62.5	0.9
5/16†	8.4	0.329	1.03	26.16	0.51	12.95	3,900	1,770	103.0	1.5
5/16	8.4	0.329	1.24	31.50	0.46	11.68	3,900	1,770	94.0	1.4
3/8†	10.0	0.394	1.22	30.99	0.59	14.99	5,400	2,450	147.8	2.2
3/8	10.0	0.394	1.33	33.78	0.57	14.48	5,400	2,450	142.6	2.1
7/16†	11.8	0.464	1.40	35.56	0.65	16.51	7,200	3,270	205.6	3.1
1/2†	13.2	0.519	1.59	40.39	0.76	19.30	9,200	4,170	256.8	3.8
1/2	13.2	0.519	1.72	43.69	0.75	19.05	9,200	4,170	255.6	3.8
5/8†	16.0	0.630	1.79	45.47	0.90	22.86	13,000	5,900	421.2	6.3
5/8	16.0	0.630	2.12	53.85	0.82	20.83	13,000	5,900	382.4	5.7
3/4†	19.8	0.781	2.20	55.88	1.09	27.69	20,200	9,160	591.4	8.8
3/4	19.8	0.781	2.60	66.04	1.02	25.91	20,200	9,160	552.1	8.2
7/8	23.0	0.906	2.66	67.56	1.25	31.75	24,500	11,100	804.6	12.0
1	26.2	1.031	2.88	73.15	1.40	35.56	34,000	15,400	1,044.0	15.5

† = to ISO Specifications

systems. For example, ACCO makes a mooring chain (stamped MC) with higher strength than standard proof coil and BBB. The links on a mooring chain are too long to wrap well around a windlass chain wildcat. It is for use in permanent-mooring systems, not for boat anchoring systems. There are also marine chains for lashing deck cargo and for fishing applications such as trawl-door chain and tuna-net chain. None of these are suitable for anchor rodes.

When purchasing or inspecting chain, look for the identifier stamp marks on the chain. If they are not visible in a size of 5/16 inch (8.4 mm) or over, or do not match the previously recommended chain types, you have a potential problem. Note that some manufacturers stamp every link, while others stamp a link every foot (30 cm) or so.

Meaning of the Chain-Grade Number

Chain-grade numbers roughly relate to the tensile strength of the chain alloy and are nominally one-tenth of the actual strength. Thus grade 40 is actually 400—that is, 400 MPa or N/mm². (Newtons per square millimeter are the same as megapascals.) If you know the chain size, this allows you to approximately calculate the ultimate breaking strength of the chain. Say you had a 3/8-inch (10 mm) grade 40 (high test) chain. The ultimate breaking strength would be approximately as follows:

$$3/8 \text{ in.} = 0.375 \text{ in.} = 9.525 \text{ mm dia.}$$
$$\text{Radius} = 9.525 \text{ mm} \div 2 = 4.7625 \text{ mm}$$

Area of a cross section of the chain link is found from:

$$A = \pi r^2 = \pi (4.7625 \text{ mm})^2 = 71.25 \text{ mm}^2$$
$$71.25 \text{ mm}^2 \times 400 \text{ N/mm}^2 = 28,500 \text{ newtons per side}$$
$$28,500 \text{ newtons per side} \times 2 \text{ sides of a chain link} = 57,000 \text{ newtons}$$
$$57,000 \text{ newtons} \times 0.2248 \text{ lb./newton} = 12,800 \text{ lb. ultimate strength}$$

or

$$57,000 \text{ newtons} \div 9.80665 \text{ newtons/kg} = 5,812 \text{ kg ultimate strength}$$

This is good basic information, but you will find that manufacturers' chain tables don't usually match the preceding calculations. Part of the reason for this is that the length of the chain's links and the chain welds also affect the chain's strength.

Chain Strength Designations

For proof coil and BBB chain:

- Ultimate breaking strength is the load at which a chain actually breaks.
- Proof load (not "proof coil," which is a type of chain) is half the ultimate breaking load.
- Working load limit (WLL) is one-quarter of the ultimate breaking load.

For high-test chain:

- Ultimate breaking strength is the load at which a chain actually breaks.
- Proof load (not "proof coil," which is a type of chain) is half the ultimate breaking load.
- Working load limit (WLL) is one-third of the ultimate breaking load.

Standard Chain Lengths

Chain is traditionally handled in lengths called a *shot* (in Europe, a *shackle*). This is very roughly related to the old unit of distance known as a *cable*. Like most older units of measure, this varies from country to country. In the United States, a cable is 120 fathoms (720 feet), or approximately 0.11 nautical mile. In the United Kingdom and Germany, a cable is almost exactly 0.1 nautical mile, or 185 meters. A cable in Holland is 225 meters; in Portugal, 258 meters; and in Russia, 182 meters. (You can see why the unification of the metric system was so attractive in Europe.) You would think that a shot (a shackle) of chain would be 1/10 of a cable, and it can be... well, sort of. But once again, the old units aren't consistent. A shot of chain in the Royal Navy is 12.5 fathoms (22.86 m), while in the U.S. Navy it is 15 fathoms (90 ft. or 27.43 m). In any case, it was traditional to specify chain in units of shot lengths of 90 feet (27.43 m) in the United States.

Common modern practice is to sell chain in leader lengths of either 6 or 20 feet (1.82 or 6.1 m), or—over 100 feet (30.5 m)—in increments of 20 feet or 6.1 meters (100 feet, 120 feet, 140 feet, and so on; or 30.5 m, 36.6 m, 42.7 m). Alternatively, you can purchase entire drums weighing 600 pounds (183 kg) each or just under. This means that a drum of ¾-inch (19.84 mm wire dia.) BBB chain would contain only 100 feet (30.5 m) of chain, while a drum of ¼-inch (7.14 mm wire dia.) BBB would be 800 feet (244 m), though larger-size chain is also available in double-size drums weighing around 1,200 pounds (544 kg).

The best anchor chain can be ordered with oversize links at either end to facilitate the attachment of fittings.

Stainless Steel Chain

Manufacturers produce stainless steel chain from 304 and 316 alloy, but only 316 chain is

TABLE 23-4. ACCO 316 STAINLESS CHAIN SPECIFICATIONS

Trade Size inches	Trade Size mm	Standard Length in drum feet	Standard Length in drum m	Inside Width inches	Inside Width mm	Inside Length inches	Inside Length mm	Lbs. per 100 feet	Wgt. K\kg/m	Links per foot	Links per meter	Working Load Limit lbs.	Working Load Limit kg
7/32	5.55	800	244	0.40	10.16	0.96	24.38	41.1	0.6	12.46	40.88	1,200	544
7/32	5.55	1,600	488	0.40	10.16	0.96	24.38	41.1	0.6	12.46	40.88	1,200	544
9/32	7.14	400	122	0.41	10.41	0.84	21.34	74.9	1.1	14.46	47.44	2,000	907
9/32	7.14	800	244	0.41	10.41	0.84	21.34	74.9	1.1	14.46	47.44	2,000	907
5/16	7.94	275	84	0.51	12.95	1.03	26.16	106.7	1.6	11.65	38.22	2,400	1,089
5/16	7.94	550	168	0.51	12.95	1.03	26.16	106.7	1.6	11.65	38.22	2,400	1,089
3/8	9.52	200	61	0.59	14.99	1.22	30.99	151.1	2.2	9.84	32.28	3,550	1,611
3/8	9.52	400	122	0.59	14.99	1.22	30.99	151.1	2.2	9.84	32.28	3,550	1,611
1/2	12.70	100	30	0.76	19.30	1.59	40.39	265.5	4.0	7.55	24.77	6,500	2,949
1/2	12.70	200	61	0.76	19.30	1.59	40.39	265.5	4.0	7.55	24.77	6,500	2,949
5/8	15.87	75	23	0.90	22.86	1.79	45.47	397.8	5.9	6.70	21.98	9,800	4,446
5/8	15.87	150	46	0.90	22.86	1.79	45.47	397.8	5.9	6.70	21.98	9,800	4,446

Figure 23-3. Anchor or bow shackle (Courtesy Chicago Hardware and Fixture Co.)

acceptable for marine use. 304 suffers from potentially severe pitting corrosion. 316 stainless chain is available from various manufacturers to match standard proof-coil, BBB, and high-test chain dimensions to suit standard windlass chain wildcats.

Stainless chain is only about 30 percent stronger at WLL than proof coil and has a lower WLL than high-test chain of the same size. The advantage of stainless chain is mostly cosmetic—fewer rust stains, shinier chain—though stainless chain should last longer (when considering many years) than hot-dip galvanized steel anchor chain.

CHAIN FITTINGS

The old saying about something being no stronger than its weakest link comes literally from chain. The various connecting fittings at the ends of a chain (or between two lengths) are the potential weak spots.

Shackles

The common anchor shackle is the standard connector. What we usually refer to as an anchor shackle is a *bow shackle* of hot-dip galvanized steel (Figure 23-2 and Table 23-5). For anchor use, it must be stamped with the working load limit (WLL) as in the photo, and the WLL must be equal to or greater than that of the chain that the shackle is attached to. To save space, WLL is usually stamped in tons, and these are landlubber short tons of exactly 2,000 pounds (which is 907 kg), *not* marine long tons of 2,240 pounds (1,016 kg). Clearly you should select an anchor shackle with the same WLL or somewhat higher than the chain. The rule of thumb for proof-coil and BBB chain is that that the anchor shackle should be one standard size larger than the chain. So for $5/16$-inch (8.4 mm) chain, you would use $3/8$-inch (9.52 mm) shackles. For high-test chain to generate its full strength, however, a shackle two sizes larger is generally needed.

Note that there are bronze and stainless steel bow shackles for rigging use. These are not stamped with a WLL and shouldn't be used for anchor gear. Stainless bow shackles with certified breaking and WLL loads should be used on stainless chain. Suncor is one manufacturer of stainless anchor shackles stamped with WLL.

Anchor or bow shackles provide more freedom of movement at the attachment and a larger surface through which to a tie rope rode to an anchor ring shackle (using an anchor bowline or anchor bend). Standard *chain shackles*, however, can be used when connecting chain to chain, or chain parts to swivels or other connectors. (See Table 23-6.) Chain and swivels are best attached directly to the anchor with an anchor shackle rather than a chain shackle, however, so as to improve the range of motion without binding.

Chain shackles are also known as "D-type" or "D-shackles," as they roughly look like the letter D (Figure 23-4).

Stainless anchor shackles are available from several manufacturers including Suncor, and Table 23-7 gives typical dimensions and WLLs.

The pin on an anchor or chain shackle is specially manufactured to generate maximum strength. It can never be replaced with an ordinary bolt. If you see a shackle fitted with an ordinary bolt instead of the proper shackle pin, the shackle must be replaced. Shackle pins come in three standard forms: *round pin, screw pin,* and *safety* (Figure 23-5). The screw pin is most common and easiest to use. To ensure that the pin can't work loose, it must be seized with light Monel wire through the screw pin's hole and around the nearest leg of the shackle. This safety wire

TABLE 23-5. GALVANIZED SCREW-PIN ANCHOR "BOW" SHACKLE SPECIFICATIONS

Nominal Size inches	Nominal Size mm	Inside Width @ Eyes inches	Inside Width @ Eyes mm	Tolerance +/- inches	Tolerance +/- mm	Inside Width @ Bow inches	Inside Width @ Bow mm	Inside Length inches	Inside Length mm	Tolerance +/- inches	Tolerance +/- mm	OD inches	OD mm	Pin or Bolt dia. inches	Pin or Bolt dia. mm	Working Load Limit Tons*	Working Load Limit MTons*
3/16	4.76	3/8	9.52	1/16	1.58	9/16	14.28	7/8	22.22	1/16	1.58	5/8	16.87	1/4	6.35	1/3	0.30
1/4	6.35	15/32	11.91	1/16	1.58	3/4	19.05	1 1/8	28.57	1/16	1.58	3/4	19.05	5/16	7.94	1/2	0.45
5/16	7.94	17/32	13.48	1/16	1.58	15/16	23.81	1 1/4	31.75	1/16	1.58	7/8	22.22	3/8	9.52	3/4	0.68
3/8	9.52	21/32	16.67	1/16	1.58	1 1/8	28.57	1 7/16	36.51	1/8	3.17	1	25.40	7/16	11.11	1	0.91
7/16	11.11	23/32	18.25	1/16	1.58	1 5/16	33.34	1 11/16	42.86	1/8	3.17	1 1/8	28.57	1/2	12.70	1 1/2	1.36
1/2	12.70	13/16	20.64	1/16	1.58	1 1/2	38.10	1 15/16	49.21	1/8	3.17	1 1/4	31.75	5/8	15.87	2	1.81
5/8	15.87	1 1/16	26.98	1/16	1.58	1 7/8	47.62	2 1/2	57.15	1/8	3.17	1 11/16	42.86	3/4	19.05	3 1/4	2.95
3/4	19.05	1 1/4	31.75	1/16	1.58	2	50.80	3	76.20	1/4	6.35	1 7/8	47.62	7/8	22.22	4 3/4	4.31
7/8	22.22	1 7/16	36.51	1/16	1.58	2 5/8	66.67	3 1/4	82.55	1/4	6.35	2 1/8	53.97	1	25.40	6 1/2	5.89
1	25.40	1 11/16	42.86	1/16	1.58	2 3/4	60.32	3 3/4	95.25	1/4	6.35	2 1/2	57.15	1 1/8	28.57	8 1/2	7.71
1 1/8	28.57	1 13/16	46.04	1/16	1.58	2 15/16	74.61	4 1/4	107.95	1/4	6.35	2 5/8	66.67	1 1/4	31.75	9 1/2	8.62
1 1/4	31.75	2	50.80	1/16	1.58	3 1/4	82.55	4 1/2	114.30	1/4	6.35	3	76.20	1 3/8	34.92	12	10.88
1 3/8	34.92	2 1/4	57.15	1/8	3.17	3 1/2	88.90	5 1/4	133.35	1/4	6.35	3 1/4	82.55	1 1/2	38.10	14	12.70
1 1/2	38.10	2 3/8	60.32	1/8	3.17	3 3/4	95.25	5 3/4	145.05	1/4	6.35	3 1/2	88.90	1 5/8	41.27	17	15.42

*Tons = 2,000 lb.; MTons = 2,000 kg

TABLE 23-6. GALVANIZED SCREW-PIN CHAIN OR "D"-SHACKLE SPECIFICATIONS

Nominal Size inches	Nominal Size mm	Inside Width @ Eyes inches	Inside Width @ Eyes mm	Tolerance +/- inches	Tolerance +/- mm	Inside Length inches	Inside Length mm	Tolerance +/- inches	Tolerance +/- mm	Outside Width inches	Outside Width mm	Pin or Bolt dia. inches	Pin or Bolt dia. mm	Working Load Limit Tons*	Working Load Limit MTons*
1/4	6.35	15/32	11.91	1/16	1.58	7/8	22.22	1/16	1.58	3/4	19.05	5/16	7.94	1/2	0.45
5/16	7.94	17/32	13.49	1/16	1.58	1	25.40	1/16	1.58	7/8	22.22	3/8	9.52	3/4	0.68
3/8	9.52	21/32	16.67	1/16	1.58	1 1/4	31.75	1/8	3.17	1	25.40	7/16	11.11	1	0.91
7/16	11.11	23/32	18.25	1/16	1.58	1 1/2	38.10	1/8	3.17	1 1/8	28.57	1/2	12.70	1 1/2	1.36
1/2	12.70	13/16	20.64	1/16	1.58	1 11/16	42.86	1/8	3.17	1 1/4	31.75	5/8	15.87	2	1.81
5/8	15.87	1 1/16	26.98	1/16	1.58	2	50.80	1/8	3.17	1 5/8	41.27	3/4	19.05	3 1/4	2.95
3/4	19.05	1 1/4	31.75	1/16	1.58	2 5/16	58.74	1/4	6.35	1 7/8	47.62	7/8	22.22	4 3/4	4.31
7/8	22.22	1 7/16	36.51	1/16	1.58	2 7/8	73.02	1/4	6.35	2 1/8	53.97	1	25.40	6 1/2	5.89
1	25.40	1 11/16	42.86	1/16	1.58	3 1/4	82.55	1/4	6.35	2 1/2	63.5	1 1/8	28.57	8 1/2	7.71

*Tons = 2,000 lb.; MTons = 2,000 kg

PART SEVEN: ANCHORING SYSTEMS

Figure 23-4. Chain or D-shackle (Courtesy Chicago Hardware and Fixture Co.)

Round Pin　　Screw Pin　　Safety

Figure 23-5. Assorted shackles (Courtesy Chicago Hardware and Fixture Co.)

can corrode and fail, so some recommend the round pin, which uses a standard cotter pin to secure it. The round-pin shackle also has slightly less bulk to catch on things. The safety pin is seldom used in anchor systems, as the excess bulk makes it more likely to snag.

Swivels

Swivels on the anchor rode pose a conundrum. You can see that the strength of a swivel is lower than that of a comparable shackle or chain. Thus, you need to use the largest swivel that will fit in order to match the WLL of the rest of the rode. Further, galvanizing is prone to grind off a swivel, leading to faster corrosion. In general, I recommend that swivels be avoided unless you expect to be anchored for many days at the same location.

Because there is no galvanizing to come off, stainless anchor swivels are generally superior. Suncor makes stainless anchor swivels with and without built-in toggles to fit right on the anchor (Figures 23-6 and 23-7). Note that Tables 23-9 and 23-10 for stainless anchor swivels list their breaking loads, not their working load limits (WLL): half-inch (13 mm) proof coil has a WLL of 4,500 pounds (2,040 kg). Four times that (to get the breaking load) is 18,000 pounds (8,160 kg), which matches well with the stainless swivel's breaking load. However, ¾-inch (19.8 mm) high test is 20,200 pounds (9,160 kg) WLL. Three times that (to get the breaking load for high test) is 60,600 pounds (27,500 kg), which is well over the breaking load of the stainless swivel supposedly for ¾-inch (19.8 mm) chain. So consider the strengths of the various components and the chain carefully.

TABLE 23-7. STAINLESS ANCHOR "BOW" SHACKLE SPECIFICATIONS

Nominal Size inches	Wire Dia. inches	Wire Dia. mm	Pin Dia. inches	Pin Dia., mm	Inside Width @ Eyes inches	Inside Width @ Eyes, mm	Inside Length inches	Inside Length mm	Working Load Limit lbs.	Working Load Limit kg
3/16	3/16	4.76	1/4	6.35	3/8	9.95	7/8	22.22	650	295
1/4	1/4	6.35	5/16	7.94	15/32	11.91	1 1/16	26.98	1,000	454
5/16	5/16	7.94	3/8	9.52	1/2	12.70	1 1/4	31.75	1,500	681
3/8	3/8	9.52	7/16	11.11	5/8	15.87	1 7/16	36.51	2,000	907
7/16	7/16	11.11	1/2	12.70	3/4	19.05	1 5/8	41.27	3,000	1,361
1/2	1/2	12.70	5/8	15.87	7/8	22.22	1 13/16	46.04	4,000	1,815
5/8	5/8	15.87	3/4	19.05	1 1/16	26.98	2 5/16	58.74	6,000	2,722
3/4	3/4	19.05	7/8	22.22	1 3/16	30.16	2 7/8	73.02	8,000	3,630
7/8	7/8	22.22	1	25.40	1 1/2	38.10	3 7/16	87.31	10,000	4,537
1	1	25.40	1 1/8	28.57	1 5/8	41.27	3 3/4	95.25	12,000	5,445

TABLE 23-8. GALVANIZED JAW-EYE CHAIN SWIVEL

Size inches	A	B	C	N	K	P	R	Working Load Limit Tons*
1/4	1 1/4	5/8	3/4	25/32	15/32	1/4	2 1/2	0.43
5/16	1 5/8	3/4	1	27/32	1/2	5/16	2 7/8	0.63
3/8	2	7/8	1 1/4	1 1/16	5/8	7/16	3 1/2	1.10
1/2	2 1/2	1 1/4	1 1/2	1 15/32	7/8	1/2	4 9/16	1.80
5/8	3	1 9/16	1 3/4	1 17/32	1	5/8	5 5/16	2.60
3/4	3 1/2	1 3/4	2	1 3/4	1 1/8	3/4	6	3.50
mm	A	B	C	N	K	P	R	MTons*
6.35	31.75	15.87	19.05	19.84	11.91	6.35	63.5	0.39
7.94	41.27	19.05	25.40	21.43	12.70	7.94	73.02	0.57
9.52	50.80	22.22	31.75	26.98	15.87	11.11	88.90	0.99
12.70	63.5	31.75	38.10	37.31	22.22	12.70	115.88	1.63
15.87	76.20	39.68	44.45	38.89	25.40	15.87	134.94	2.36
19.05	88.90	44.45	50.80	44.45	28.57	19.05	152.50	3.17

*Tons = 2,000 lb.; MTons = 2,000 kg (from Chicago Hardware and Fixture)

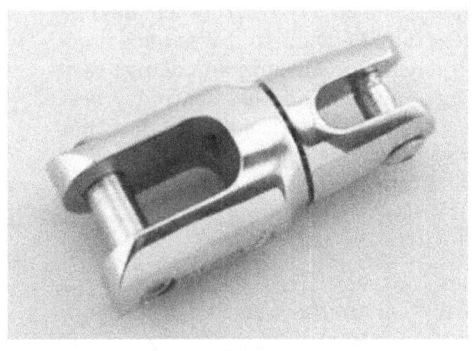

Figure 23-6. Anchor swivel (Courtesy Suncor)

TABLE 23-9. STAINLESS ANCHOR SWIVEL

Chain Size inches	A	B	C	D	Breaking Load lbs.
Dimensions in inches					
1/4"–5/16"	0.39	0.29	0.37	0.66	8,500
3/8"–1/2"	0.60	0.50	0.50	0.87	15,000
1/2"–3/4"	0.80	0.61	0.98	1.52	25,000
Dimensions in millimeters					
Size mm	A	B	C	D	kg
6.35–7.94	9.91	7.37	9.40	16.76	3,860
9.52–12.70	15.24	12.70	12.70	22.10	6,810
12.70–19.05	20.32	15.49	24.89	38.61	11,340

Figure 23-7. Anchor swivel with toggle (Courtesy Suncor)

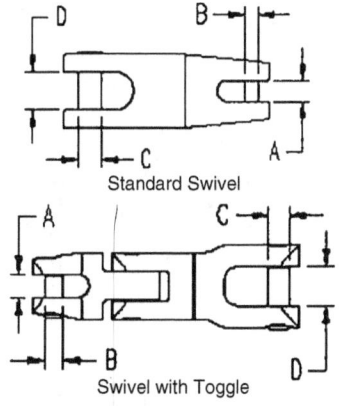

Standard Swivel

Swivel with Toggle

Figure 23-8. Ultra Swivel (Courtesy Quickline USA)

One unusual and compact stainless swivel is the Ultra Swivel, available from Quickline USA. The swivel is a ball-socket arrangement that also allows a toggling action (Figure 23-8).

ROPE

As discussed earlier, one of rope's advantages is that it has stretch, or elasticity, to absorb shock. There are several schools of thought on what makes the best material for anchor rode. What you want is a tough, relatively inexpensive line that has as much stretch as possible. This means nylon, and of the common nylon-line configurations, simple three-strand has the most stretch. Plaited or jacketed construction will work, but I can't see justifying the extra cost or the reduction in stretchiness, except on large boats, where double-braid can be easier to handle, or for Yale Brait line (which we'll consider shortly). Don't use economy three-strand, however; use the best-quality three-strand you can find. The good stuff is softer and more supple, so it stows and handles more easily.

Rope Rode Terms

The terminology for anchor rodes has become rather sloppy. It used to be that the proper name for a rope anchor line less than about ⅝ inch diameter (16 mm) was *anchor warp*. Anchor ropes larger than this were generally termed *anchor cables*. The word *cable* also refers to a measure of distance (as we've seen), and technically, *cable-laid rope* is rope with the strands twisted from right to left (holding the end away from you). Rope twisted in the opposite direction is *hawser-laid rope—right-hand rope*. These distinctions have been largely lost. Hawser-laid rope was generally heavier, so it was once common to generically call any particularly heavy mooring or anchor line a hawser. Today, best practice seems to be to call rope anchor lines either *rope anchor rodes* or simply *anchor warps*. (Warps are also ropes that are trailed

TABLE 23-10. ULTRA SWIVEL SPECIFICATIONS—STAINLESS STEEL

Chain Dia.		Max Anchor Wgt.		Breaking Strength		Case A x B	Anchor Side	Max
mm	inches	kg	lb.	kg	lb.	mm	C × D × E mm	Angle
6	¼"	13	29	2,250	4,960	Ø 35 × 100	Ø 10 × 16 × 31	30°
8	⁵⁄₁₆"	23	51	4,150	9,140	Ø 40 × 120	Ø 12 × 19 × 36.5	30°
10	⅜"	36	80	6,620	14,580	Ø 45 × 136	Ø 14 × 21 × 40	29°
13	½"	60	130	12,000	26,400	Ø 55 × 170	Ø 16 × 26 × 51.5	28°
16	⅝"	100	220	18,200	40,000	Ø 65 × 202	Ø 20 × 30.5 × 59	28°

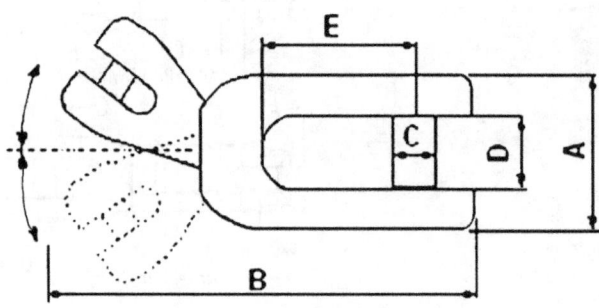

TABLE 23-11. THREE-STRAND NYLON ROPE

Diameter		Weight		Breaking Strength	
inches	mm	lb./100 ft.	kg/m	lb.	kg
3/16	5	1.0	0.015	1,200	544
1/4	6	1.5	0.022	2,000	907
5/16	8	2.5	0.037	3,000	1,361
3/8	9	3.5	0.052	4,400	1,996
7/16	11	5.0	0.074	5,900	2,677
1/2	12	6.5	0.097	7,500	3,403
9/16	14	8.2	0.122	9,400	4,265
5/8	16	10.5	0.156	12,200	5,535
3/4	18	14.5	0.216	16,700	7,577
7/8	22	20.0	0.298	23,500	10,662
1	24	26.4	0.393	29,400	13,339

astern in heavy seas to aid in directional stability underway: "trailing a warp.")

The Problem of Rope Chafe

Rope is lighter and considerably less expensive than chain, but it chafes, abrades, and wears out. It's not well known that sand, salt, and other grit routinely work their way between the strands of rope anchor rodes (warps) and cause internal abrasion, which can lead to failure of the warp. Nylon also absorbs water, and when saturated it loses roughly half its strength.

Figure 23-9 shows the nylon mooring pendant with a polyester chafe jacket that failed in a typical 40-knot nor'easter. Note that the rope was stretched under load, so when it failed, it broke even farther from the chock and the deck edge than it appears in the picture. The surveyor concluded that interfiber abrasion from salt grit was a contributing factor. The combination of interfiber abrasion and loss of strength due to water saturation is usually not taken into account properly. Rope is most definitely good for anchor warps, but keep its weaknesses in mind and check the rope carefully.

Proper Chocks Are Critical

Protection from chafe is paramount. To this end, large, strong, exceptionally well-rounded and strongly fastened chocks are an absolute must. It's an unfortunate thing to note, but many boats have inadequate chocks that are inadequately fastened. There are also many manufacturers of chocks and cleats that seem to make them as angular and sharp as practical (Figure 23-11)! This appears most frequently from some European manufacturers. A few make cleats and chocks that are apparently designed to look "sharp." Possible this is a styling thing (racy?) and possibly it's a cost-saving measure; perhaps it's both. In any case, there are too many inadequately

TABLE 23-12. DOUBLE-BRAID NYLON ROPE

Diameter		Weight		Breaking Strength	
inches	mm	lb./100 ft.	kg/m	lb.	kg
3/16	5	0.9	0.013	1,200	544
1/4	6	1.6	0.024	2,200	998
5/16	8	2.5	0.037	3,400	1,543
3/8	9	3.6	0.054	4,900	2,223
7/16	11	4.9	0.073	6,600	2,995
1/2	12	6.3	0.094	8,500	3,857
9/16	14	8	0.119	10,800	4,900
5/8	16	10	0.149	13,500	6,125
3/4	18	14.3	0.213	19,400	8,802
13/16	18	16.5	0.246	24,400	11,071
7/8	22	19.4	0.289	26,300	11,933
1	24	25.4	0.378	34,000	15,426
1 1/8	28	35	0.521	46,000	20,871
1 1/4	30	40	0.595	52,000	23,593
1 5/16	32	45	0.670	58,000	26,316
1 1/2	36	58	0.863	74,000	33,575
1 5/8	40	71	1.057	90,000	40,835
1 3/4	42	85	1.265	106,000	48,094
2	48	102	1.518	126,000	57,169

PART SEVEN: ANCHORING SYSTEMS

Figure 23-9. A failed rope anchor rode (Courtesy Chris Wentz)

Figure 23-10. A broken chock and a failed anchor roller (Courtesy Chris Wentz)

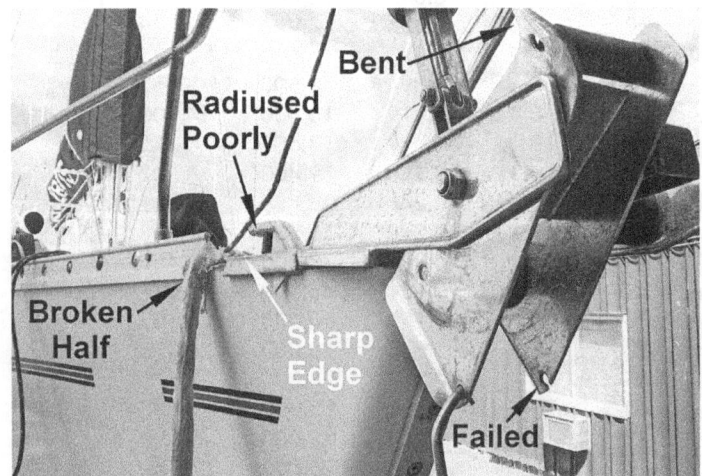

Figure 23-11. A sharp chock

designed and inadequately fastened chocks out there.

Figure 23-10, a closer view of the mooring line failure, shows that the chock is poorly formed with rather industrial sharp edges. It also shows that it was so weak and poorly fastened that it broke in half, with half falling off the boat completely! This is wholly unacceptable. Had the nylon mooring rode not failed due to the interfiber abrasion, it would soon have chafed through and failed at the broken chock. By the way, though Figures 23-9 and 23-10 concentrate on a small area, the damage to this boat was extensive due to running aground after the mooring line parted. The vessel was a total loss. Note also the failures on the anchor roller. We'll review anchor rollers shortly.

Sizing Mooring and Docking Cleats and Chocks

When specifying or inspecting mooring cleats and chocks, be sure they are of a strong, very well-rounded form and are securely through-bolted to strong backing blocks with backing plates. When fastened through cored decks, compression tubes and/or epoxy annuluses must be used, or the core must be locally removed and the resulting solid-glass region considerably built up and reinforced, with large backing blocks and backing plates underneath. Alternatively, the foam or balsa core may be replaced with solid marine ply (well saturated with resin) or, better still, G-10. G-10 can also be used for annuluses.

Give careful thought to avoiding chafe on the mooring and dock lines, and be sure to specify and draw in chocks to accept the line where it goes over the deck edge. Mooring and docking cleats should be of the four-hole pattern for maximum strength and stability.

Size mooring and docking cleats by using the Formula 23-1.

Formula 23-1. Sizing Mooring and Docking Cleats

Bow mooring cleat size (in.) = 4.5 + (0.18 × WL, ft.)

or

Bow mooring cleat size (mm) = 114.3 + (15 × WL, m)

Docking cleats (midships and stern) size (in.) = 2.2 + (0.2 × WL, ft.)

or

Docking cleats (midships and stern) size (mm) = 55.8 + (16.7 × WL, m)

Chocks are specified as one-half the cleat size.

Larger is always better.

Example: For a 32-foot (9.75 m) DWL boat, you would get

Bow mooring cleat size (in.) = 4.5 + (0.18 × 32 ft. WL) = 10.25 in.; use 10-in. cleats

or

Bow mooring cleat size (mm) = 114.3 + (15 × 9.75 m WL) = 260.5 mm; use 280 mm cleats

Docking cleats (midships and stern) size (in.) = 2.2 + (0.2 × 32 ft. WL) = 8.6 in.; use 9- or 10-in. cleats

or

Docking cleats (midships and stern) size (mm) = 55.8 + (16.7 × 9.75 m WL) = 218.6 mm; use 220 or 250 mm cleats

Cleats are measured across their maximum length, end to end. Chocks are measured with reference to the size of their inside opening.

Yale Brait

Though traditional three-strand nylon is excellent and is standard for anchor warps, it does have drawbacks. One is that, particularly after getting wet and drying out repeatedly, nylon three-strand can become stiff and difficult to coil or stow through a pipe into a rope locker. The other is that, good as it is at stretching and absorbing energy, it would be nice to have even more stretch to absorb more shock.

Yale Cordage has a relatively new nylon anchor line called Yale Brait. It is of eight-strand plaited construction, which remains supple and soft and thus compacts easily and into a considerably smaller pile than standard three-strand nylon. You can see in Figure 23-12 that Yale Brait will stow in roughly 45 percent of the volume required for standard three-strand nylon. Yale Brait also has plenty of surface area to work well on windlasses. Further, Yale Brait has 75 percent more energy absorption (shock absorption) than even the already-stretchy standard three-strand nylon.

Attaching Rope to Chain

Since—except for the very smallest dinghies or for temporary kedging—the anchor warp is attached to chain, this attachment must be done properly. There are just three acceptable methods:

1. Tie the rope warp to the chain or anchor at an anchor shackle using an anchor bend or an anchor bowline (Figure 23-13).
2. Put an eye splice with a thimble in the end of the rope to attach to a shackle.
3. Use a rope-to-chain splice.

TABLE 23-13. YALE BRAIT NYLON ROPE

Diameter		Weight		Breaking Strength	
inches	mm	lb./100 ft.	kg/m	lb.	kg
3/8"	9	3.4	0.051	3,700	1,679
1/2"	12	6.2	0.092	6,300	2,858
5/8"	16	10.3	0.153	10,400	4,719
3/4"	18	13.5	0.201	16,200	7,350
7/8"	22	19	0.283	22,000	9,982
1"	24	23.7	0.353	27,000	12,250

PART SEVEN: ANCHORING SYSTEMS

Figure 23-12. Yale Brait rope (right) versus three-strand nylon rope (Courtesy Yale Cordage)

Figure 23-14. Devil's claw used as on-deck chain snubber

All three methods give good results. The anchor bend (also called the fisherman's bend) has proven to give somewhat more strength than the anchor bowline and is preferred. When using an eye splice on an anchor warp, you must use a heavy-duty stainless or galvanized thimble—not nylon or plastic. To ensure that the thimble doesn't twist out sideways, it should be seized to the rope at either side of the thimble's ends and around the throat of the splice. Alternatively, you can use a closed-base thimble with hoops.

Rope-to-chain splices can appear weak but have proven up to the job when properly done. To ensure adequate strength for a rope-to-chain splice, however, you should always increase the rope diameter by one standard size over the rope size that is usually used for the anchor warp. Some sources recommend inserting heat-shrink tubing on the rope splice where it bears on the chain link. I know of no tests that confirm that this is actually stronger, however. Most rope-to-chain splices do not have the heat-shrink tubing and work well. Figure 23-14 shows a devil's claw chain hook attached to a nylon chain snubber, using a rope-to-chain splice.

Storing Long Lengths of Anchor Warp on a Spool

We'll discuss chain and rope lockers in the next chapter, but in addition to a chain or rope locker, there's another way to store long lengths of rope anchor warp neatly: on a rope spool (Figure 23-15). Though you can store

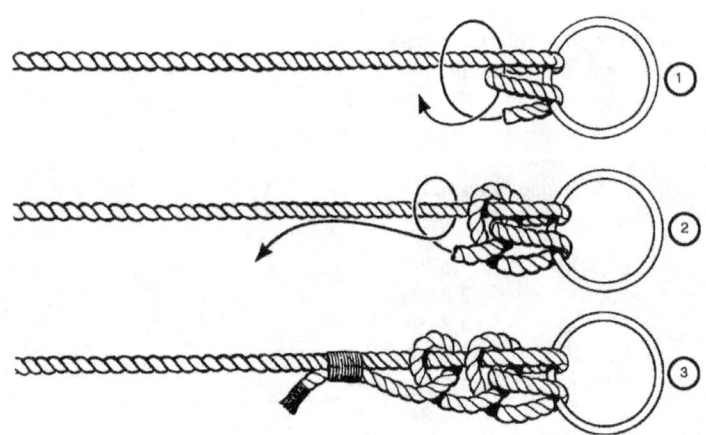

Figure 23-13. Tying an anchor bend (From Field Manual No.5–125 "Rigging Techniques, Procedures, and Applications," Department of the U.S. Army)

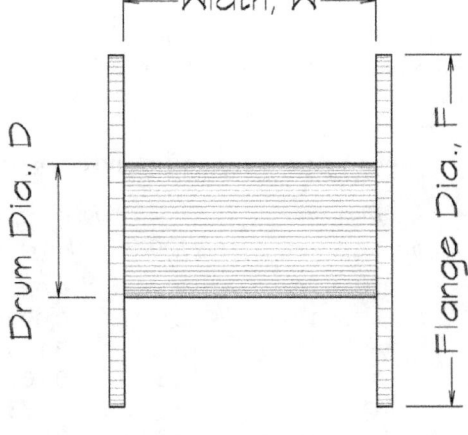

Figure 23-15. Rope spool

362

200 to 300 feet (60 to 90 m) of rope simply fed into a locker, it is much better to store longer lengths wound up on a spool. A serious voyager might want to carry, say, 600 feet (180 m) of ½-inch (12 mm) warp to join to the end of a standard 300-foot (90 m) chain for deepwater emergency anchoring.

You can determine the size of the required spool from the following formula.

Formula 23-2. Rope Spool Size

$$\text{Feet of line} = \frac{W, \text{in.} \times ((F, \text{in.})^2 - (D, \text{in.})^2)}{15.3 \times (\text{rope dia., in.})^2}$$

or

$$\text{Meters of line} = \frac{W, \text{cm} \times ((F, \text{cm})^2 - (D, \text{cm})^2)}{1{,}275 \times (\text{rope dia., mm})^2}$$

Where
Feet of line = spool capacity in feet
Meters of line = spool capacity in meters
W = width of drum, in. or cm
F = outside diameter of flange, in. or cm
D = diameter of central drum, in. or cm
D must be 12 × rope diameter or greater; larger diameters are easier on the line

Example: For 600 feet of ½-inch line, try a 22-inch width, a 16-in. flange, and a 12-inch diameter as follows:

$$\frac{22 \text{ in.} \times ((16 \text{ in.})^2 - (12 \text{ in.})^2)}{15.3 \times (0.5 \text{ in. rope dia.,})^2} = 644 \text{ ft.,}$$

which gives a bit of reserve capacity

Or

For 90 meters of 12 mm line, try a 40 cm width, a 40 cm flange, and a 34 cm diameter as follows:

$$\frac{40 \text{ cm} \times ((40 \text{ cm})^2 - (34 \text{ cm})^2)}{1.275 \times (12 \text{ mm rope dia.})^2} = 96 \text{ m,}$$

which gives a bit of reserve capacity.

WIRE ANCHOR RODE

Wire anchor rode is rare and found in use almost exclusively on some commercial fishing boats in the Pacific Northwest. The advantage of wire-rope anchor rode is that it can be wound up automatically and reliably on a hydraulically operated reel-cable drum winch. This also allows neat and clean stowage of a great length of wire rode. If you need to anchor at a 5:1 scope in 250 feet (75 m) of water, you need 1,250 feet (375 m) of rode. This is prohibitive for routine anchoring, except for wire rope on such a hydraulic drum.

The big disadvantage is that wire rope has virtually no give or shock-absorbing ability. Everything must be sized extra strong and heavy to accept the shock loads, and such repeated large shocks can pull out the anchor as well. Some installations split the wire into 100-foot (30 m) lengths joined with interlocked thimbles. You can use a shackle or claw to fasten a snubber or snatch line to one of these thimbles. Otherwise, you cannot even attach a nylon rope snubbing line to the wire rode. I suppose—using the right gear—it would be possible to run a kellet, or sentinel, down a wire anchor rode, but I've never heard of it being done. You could also attach such a kellet to one of the thimbles. In spite of this drawback, the fishermen who employ wire-rope anchor rode appear to be very satisfied with them.

The only wire rope suitable for use as anchor rode is 7 × 19 flexible wire rope of 316 stainless steel. Kolstrand Marine Supply of Seattle, Washington, makes complete wire-rode reel windlass units of galvanized steel and of aluminum. The larger of these units can handle up to 4,850 feet (1,478 m) of ½ inch (12.7 mm) cable or 2,200 feet (670 m) of ½-inch (12.7 mm) cable with 85 feet (26 m) of ⅝-inch (15.87 mm) chain! Now *this* is

Figure 23-16. Wire-rope windlass (Courtesy Kolstrand)

TABLE 23-14. 7 X 19 316 STAINLESS WIRE ROPE

Diameter		Breaking Strength		WLL	
inches	mm	lb.	kg	lb.	kg
3/64	1.2	83	38	21	9
1/16	1.6	147	67	37	17
5/64	2	230	104	58	26
3/32	2.4	323	147	81	37
1/8	3.2	602	273	151	68
5/32	4	956	434	239	108
3/16	4.8	1,373	623	343	156
7/32	5.5	1,807	820	452	205
1/4	6.4	2,450	1,112	613	278
9/32	7.2	3,031	1,375	758	344
5/16	8	3,820	1,733	955	433
3/8	9.5	5,388	2,445	1,347	611
7/16	11	7,230	3,280	1,808	820
1/2	12.7	9,628	4,368	2,407	1,092
9/16	14.3	12,206	5,538	3,052	1,385
5/8	16	15,300	6,942	3,825	1,735
45/64	18	19,300	8,757	4,825	2,189
3/4	19	21,569	9,786	5,392	2,447
25/32	20	23,900	10,844	5,975	2,711
7/8	22	28,900	13,113	7,225	3,278
1	25.4	38,642	17,533	9,661	4,383
1 1/8	28	46,900	21,279	11,725	5,320

deep-water anchoring capability! Between 40 and 85 feet (12 and 26 m) of chain are usually installed on these rodes between the wire and the anchor.

These reel-drum windlasses are decidedly industrial in appearance; however, they could be installed on a yacht by building the windlasses largely into an enclosed, though fully opening, housing. This wire-rope system is worth keeping in mind for the right application.

Note that stainless 7×19 wire rope of 316 alloy is weaker than 304, but only 316 has the corrosion resistance required.

Sizing the Anchor and Rode and Selecting Anchor-Handling Gear

CHAPTER 24

SIZING THE ANCHOR

Now that we've reviewed the basic anchor components, we can start selecting and sizing the anchor and rode. One of the common methods is using ABYC recommendations per ABYC standard H-40, *Anchoring, Mooring, and Strong Points*. This approach gives the assumed design loads based on boat type (sail or power) and on LOA or beam (whichever is greater). The results have proven themselves, but there are two drawbacks. One is that the table only goes up to 60 feet (18.3 m) LOA. The other is that there is no way to know what the holding power of a given anchor is. Sure, many manufacturers provide tables of holding strengths for their anchors, but the results of independent tests of these same anchors vary widely, both from the manufacturers' data and among independent tests. Also, anchor test results will naturally vary with different bottoms, with boats that have different motions, in different sea conditions, and with different anchor gear. Finally, some manufacturers don't provide anchor holding strengths at all.

Accordingly, I've developed a system to give recommended working anchor weights for standard modern anchors: the CQR plow, Delta, Bruce or Claw, Danforth Hi-Tensile, or spade type. The procedure is as described by Formula 24-1.

As noted earlier, I'm not enthusiastic about lightweight anchors—I like heft. It makes the anchor drop quickly and positively, and it gives you a nice warm feeling of security when it breezes up overnight.

Formula 24-1. Recommended Anchor Weight

Working or bower anchor weight, lb. = $6.8 \times$ (disp. tons)$^{0.75}$

or

Working or bower anchor weight, kg = $3.03 \times$ (disp. tonnes)$^{0.75}$

Storm or street anchor weight, lb. or kg = $1.35 \times$ working anchor

Lunch hook/stream/kedge, lb. or kg = $0.6 \times$ working anchor weight

Where
tons = boat displacement in long tons (2,240 lbs.)
tonnes = boat displacement in metric tons (2,200 lbs.)

For yachtsman anchors (Herreshoff or Luke) intended as storm anchors, use 2.2 times the bower anchor weight above. If you

Formula 24-1.

want to use a yachtsman anchor as the working anchor, use 1.5 times the bower anchor weight above. Do the same for stockless anchors for use in hawsepipes, such as the Manson "kedge anchor" and the G. J. Wortelboer "D'Hone Special."

Keep in mind that displacement is in long tons of 2,240 pounds or metric tons (tonnes) of 1,000 kg (2,200 pounds). Say our trusty *Hold Fast* is 32 feet LOA by 12-foot beam (9.7 m LOA by 3.65 m beam) and displaces 21,000 pounds (9,530 kg). That's 9.37 long tons or 9.5 metric tons. Formula 24-1 says you should use a 36-pound (16.4 kg) anchor: a 35-pound (16 kg) CQR, Delta, spade type (like the Rocna or Manson Supreme), or Danforth Hi-Tensile would fill the bill nicely.

You'll notice lightweight aluminum anchor manufacturers' tables (e.g., Fortress or Guardian) recommend much less weight. Referring to the Guardian anchor table (Table 22-3), we see that Guardian recommends an anchor of just 7 pounds or 3.2 kg (the G-16) to hold a boat this size. The table also says, though, that this replaces a 14- to 18-pound (6 to 8 kg) steel anchor. We've specified a 35-pound (16 kg) steel anchor. Table 22-3 indicates that the G-37, weighing 18 pounds (8.1 kg), replaces a steel anchor of this weight. This is the lightest I would recommend for a bower anchor on a boat this size. This would be the bower anchor of choice to keep weight to a minimum for performance boats, though again, I personally prefer and recommend heft.

Returning to Formula 24-1, we can round out the complement of anchors for a cruising boat with a second working or bower anchor, a lightweight lunch-hook or kedge (stream anchor), and a storm anchor. Remember, it's best to have two different types of bower anchors to ensure you have the best combination for different holding grounds. Thus, if your primary bower is a 35-pound delta, a 33-pound (15 kg) Bruce or Claw, or a spade type around 33 to 38 pounds (15 to 17 kg) would make an ideal second bower. (You wouldn't also specify a CQR, as that's another plow type like the Delta.)

The Guardian 18-pounder (8.1 kg) would do nicely for a lunch-hook or stream anchor.

Using a Luke-pattern yachtsman anchor stowed in the bilge as a storm (street) anchor, we would find

2.2 × 36 lb. = 79 lb.; a 75 lb. (22.8 kg) Luke would work well

Or

2.2 × 16.4 kg = 36 kg; a 75 lb. (22.8 kg) Luke would work well

An alternative to the Luke for a street anchor would be a Guardian or Fortress about equal to a 75- or 80-pound (34 to 37 kg) steel anchor. This would be the Guardian G-85, which weighs only 42 pounds (19 kg). This is physically a big anchor, with a shank fully 48 inches (122 cm) long. It, too, breaks down to stow in the bilge until needed.

If you were setting a pair of anchors in hawsepipes, port and starboard, you would use a pair of Danforth Hi-Tensiles, each 35 pounds (16 kg). This boat is too small to use stockless-type anchors in hawsepipes.

SIZING THE RODE
Chain Diameter

For *Hold Fast*, we'll order a 35-pound (16 kg) Delta and a 33-pound (15 kg) Rocna. Now we have to figure out what size chain to use. Chain size based on anchor weight is calculated in Formula 24.2.

Formula 24-2. Recommended Chain Size

$$\text{BBB or "Proof Coil" Chain Dia., in.} = \frac{\sqrt[3]{\text{Working Anchor Wgt., lb.}}}{10}$$

or

$$\text{BBB or "Proof Coil" Chain Dia., mm} = 3.305 \times \sqrt[3]{\text{Working Anchor Wgt., kg}}$$

NOTE: BBB chain is not metric, and the chain wire diameter is larger than the nominal chain size, so refer to the BBB chain table (Table 23-2). Convert the diameter in mm from Formula 24-2 to inches, and read the nominal size in inches. Then read the BBB wire diameter in mm from the table. For "Proof Coil" (Grade 30) chain, the chain diameter from Formula 24-2 is the nominal chain size. For high test or stainless, find the working load limit (WLL) of the BBB and refer to the high-test chain table (Table 23-3) or the stainless chain table (Table 23-4) to find the high-test chain size with the same or slightly greater WLL.

Use the weight of the standard steel bower anchor, not the weight of a lightweight anchor (if you've gone that route). Returning to *Hold Fast*, we would enter 36 pounds (16.4 kg) as the anchor weight in Formula 24-2, and find that we need to outfit her with 0.33-inch (8.4 mm) chain BBB or proof coil. This falls between 5/16 inch and 3/8 inch (or is closest to 8.73 mm wire dia. BBB). For a no-compromise voyaging world-cruiser, I would go with the 3/8-inch diameter (10.32 mm wire dia.), but most ordinary boats should round down, so we'll get 5/16-inch (0.3125 in. or 8.73 mm wire dia. BBB) chain for *Hold Fast*. Note that I prefer BBB because it functions best of all on a windlass wildcat and is slightly heavier for a more pronounced catenary; however, BBB is not a metric-size chain. Outside the United States and Canada, you would use ISO proof coil or high test.

If saving weight were desirable, then we would use high test. From Table 23-2, we see that the WLL of 5/16 inch (8.73 mm wire dia.) BBB is 1,900 pounds (862 kg). Per Table 23-3, high-test of 1/4 inch (7 mm) has a WLL of 2,600 (1,180 kg). The BBB 5/16 inch weighs 72 pounds/100 feet (1.6 kg/m), while the high-test 1/4 inch (7 mm) weighs 62.5 pounds/100 feet (1.1 kg/m). On 300 feet (90 m) of chain, this is a weight reduction of about 112 pounds (51 kg).

The rule of thumb is that you select high-test chain one standard size smaller than the equivalent BBB or proof coil, which gives the same results here (as would referring to the tables).

Shackle and Swivel Diameter

The galvanized anchor shackle table (Table 23-5) indicates that 5/16-inch (7.94 mm) shackles are too weak, with a WLL of just 3/4 ton (1,500 lb., or 681 kg). Accordingly, we need to specify 3/8-inch (9.52 mm) galvanized anchor shackles, with a working load limit of 1 ton (2,000 lb., or 907 kg). Note that the high-test chain is actually over 1-ton working load limit. Since we've gone to it to save weight and it already exceeds the strength of the BBB required, you don't have to increase the shackle size above 3/8 inch (9.52 mm). However, to use the full strength of the high test, you would need to increase shackle size to 7/16 inch (11.11 mm), with a WLL of 1.5 tons (3,000 lb., or 1,361 kg). Note that this will not fit in 1/4-inch (7 mm) high-test chain, which has an inside width of just 0.41 inch (10.41 mm), while the 7/16-inch (11.11 mm) shackle has a pin diameter of 7/16 inch (0.4375 in., or 11.11 mm). This is the reason that it is best to order anchor chain with oversize end links built in by the manufacturer.

Swivels also need consideration. For our 5/16-inch (8.73 mm wire dia.) BBB chain, we need a swivel with a WLL of 1 ton. Table 23-8 shows that a 3/8-inch (9.52 mm) galvanized jaw-eye swivel will slightly exceed this at 1.1 ton WLL. To match the full strength of 1/4-inch (7 mm) high test, again you would find that the 1/2-inch (12.7 mm) swivel would not fit a standard link.

The stainless swivel would need to have a breaking load of 4 times the WLL of the 5/16-inch (8.73 mm wire dia.) BBB chain; so 1,900 lb. × 4 = 7,600 lb., or 862 kg × 4 = 3,448 kg. This matches the swivel size recommended for this size chain (Table 23-9). Remember not only that high test would need the next size swivel up to develop the full strength of the high test, but also that this full strength isn't required in this application.

Rope Anchor Rode (Warp) Diameter

Of course, most smaller boats and many light performance and inshore boats don't use an all-chain rode, but some combination of chain and rope. The rope rode or warp diameter can be found by using the following formula.

Formula 24-3. Rope Anchor Rode Size

Nylon Anchor Rope Rode (Warp) Diameter, in. = 0.2 + (anchor weight., lb. ÷ 185)

or

Nylon Anchor Rope Rode (Warp) Diameter, mm = 5.08 + (anchor weight., kg ÷ 3.3)

Again, use the bower anchor weight from the formula, not a lightweight anchor's weight.

Formula 24-3.

Example: For *Hold Fast*, we would get

0.2 + (36 lb. ÷ 185) = 0.394 in. diameter

or

5.08 + (16.4 kg ÷ 3.3) = 10 mm diameter

This is close to ⅜ inch (0.375 in.), which is what we could use, or we would use 10 mm nylon three-strand or brait. The one exception is when you're installing a combination rope-chain windlass. To ensure adequate strength in a rope-to-chain splice, you should increase the rope diameter by one standard size. In this case, increase to ½-inch (12 mm) three-strand nylon.

Anchor Rode Length

The total length of the anchor rode is controlled by the scope required. Scope is the length of rode paid out relative to the depth of water. Generally, a 3:1 scope is the bare minimum for any kind of holding, and this is in light weather. Most anchors do best with a 5:1 scope in most weather, going to 7:1 for serious storms or bad holding ground. Even a 10:1 scope is not unheard of in very severe conditions. One way to get this length is by attaching two rodes together. Chain can be connected using shackles or midlinks, while rope can be tied together with 90 percent strength using the Carrick bend (Figure 24-1).

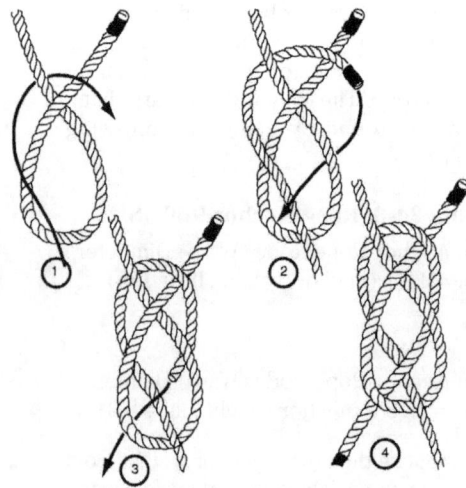

Figure 24-1. Tying the Carrick bend (From Field Manual No. 5–125 "Rigging Techniques, Procedures, and Applications" Department of the U.S. Army)

The standard minimum rode length should be suited to anchoring at 5:1 in 30 feet (9 m) of water for small inshore craft and at 5:1 in 60 feet (20 m) of water for most cruising boats. This is a minimum of 150 feet (45 m) of rode for small craft and 300 feet (100 m) for cruising boats. Larger cruising vessels would do better carrying 400 feet (120 m) of rode.

You often see a distinction made in scope for an all-chain rode versus all-rope or a rope-chain hybrid. My recommendations, however, apply to all rode types.

Keep in mind that when it comes to scope, what we're after is to keep the angle of pull on the anchor as shallow (as close to horizontal) as possible. The real scope is relative to the depth of water plus the freeboard at the bow.

Example: A boat with 5-foot freeboard at the bow in 22 feet of water would need to pay out 135 feet of rode for a true 5:1 scope

22 ft. depth + 5 ft. freeboard = 27 ft.
27 ft. × 5 = 135 ft.

Or

A boat with 1.5 meter freeboard at the bow, in 7 meters of water would need to pay out 42.5 meters of rode for a true 5:1 scope

7 m depth + 1.5 m freeboard = 8.5 m
8.5 m × 5 = 42.5 m

Wire Anchor Rode Diameter

Assuming we had special deep-water anchoring requirements, we might want to go with the wire-rope anchor rode on the hydraulic reel-drum windlass. The WLL for the required BBB chain was 1,900 pounds (862 kg). Referring to the wire-rope table (Table 23-14), we see that this would mean ⁷⁄₁₆-inch (11 mm) 7 × 19 316 stainless wire rope.

Because the wire has no give, it is usual to install a leader of chain *two* standard chain sizes larger than standard BBB or proof coil for a boat of this size with all-chain rode. We found ⁵⁄₁₆-inch (8.73 mm wire dia.) BBB, so this would be ½-inch (13.48 mm wire dia.) BBB. Length of the chain leader should be between 1 and 1.5 times boat LOA. *Hold Fast* is 32 feet (9.7 m), so you would use between 32 and 48 feet

(10 and 15 m) of ½-inch (13.48 mm wire dia.) BBB chain leader.

Checking Rode Specifications Against ABYC Standards

We can check the anchor rode specifications against ABYC standard H-40, *Anchoring, Mooring, and Strong Points*. First we determine the design load for a working anchor from ABYC H-40 Table 1 (Table 24-1). This is based on LOA or beam, whichever is *larger*. *Hold Fast* is a powerboat 32 feet LOA with a 12-foot beam (9.7 m LOA and 3.65 m beam). Referring to Table 24-1, we find a working anchor design load of 900 pounds or 4.0 kN (kilonewtons), or 408 kg. (ABYC tables give forces in kilonewtons. Multiply kN by 101.97 to get kgf—kilograms of force.)

Then referring to ABYC H40 Table AP-1 (Table 24-2), we see that for this design load, the recommend rode is

- ¼-inch (6 mm) BBB or proof-coil chain
- ¼-inch (6 mm) shackles
- 9/16-inch nylon warp

In general, you will find that ABYC recommendations for working-anchor-rode chain and shackles are about a size smaller than from the formulas and recommendations in this chapter. The larger chain size makes sense, as you also want the anchor rode to work in storm conditions. The 5/16-inch (8.73 mm wire dia.) BBB chain specced meets ABYC storm-anchor design loads.

A difficulty occurs with ABYC's rope anchor warp size recommendation. Nine-sixteenth-inch (14 mm) is nearly ⅝ inch (16 mm)—that is huge! Indeed, 9/16-inch (14 mm) nylon can be hard to locate, so you may be forced to go up to ⅝ inch (16 mm), in any case. One of the reasons for using nylon anchor warp is to take advantage of its elasticity. If the warp is too large, that elasticity will not come into play except at extreme loads, which is not what we're after.

ABYC's nylon anchor warp recommendations are much larger than those in *Chapman's Piloting, Seamanship, and Small Boat Handling*, which gives the same ⅜-inch (9.5 mm) nylon warp size recommendation for a working anchor, and ½-inch (12.7 mm) nylon warp for a storm anchor for a boat of *Hold Fast's* dimensions. Nigel Calder, in *Nigel Calder's Cruising Handbook*, also explains why ABYC nylon warp sizes appear to be impractically large.

My recommendation is to use the nylon anchor warp size from Formula 24-3 (or the next size up when using a rope-to-chain splice) and not the ABYC-based size, but you should be aware of ABYC's recommendations under ABYC H-40 and give them due consideration.

TABLE 24-1. ABYC H40 TABLE 1—DESIGN LOADS FOR SIZING DECK HARDWARE

| LOA | | Beam | | | | Permanent Mooring | | Storm Anchor | | Working Anchor | |
| | | Sail | | Power | | | | | | | |
ft.	m	ft.	m	ft.	m	lb.	kN	lb.	kN	lb.	kN
10	3.0	4	1.2	5	1.5	480	2.1	320	1.4	160	0.7
15	4.5	5	1.5	6	1.8	750	3.3	500	2.2	250	1.1
20	6.1	7	2.1	8	2.4	1,080	4.8	720	3.2	360	1.6
25	7.6	8	2.4	9	2.7	1,470	6.5	980	4.4	490	2.2
30	9.1	9	2.7	11	3.4	2,100	9.3	1,400	6.2	700	3.1
35	10.7	10	3.0	13	4.0	2,700	12.0	1,800	8.0	900	4.0
40	12.2	11	3.4	14	4.3	3,600	16.0	2,400	10.7	1,200	5.3
50	15.2	13	4.0	16	4.9	4,800	21.4	3,200	14.2	1,600	7.1
60	18.3	15	4.6	18	5.5	6,000	26.7	4,000	17.8	2,000	8.9

NOTE: Use the greatest of LOA or beam (Courtesy American Boat & Yacht Council, www.abycinc.org)

PART SEVEN: ANCHORING SYSTEMS

TABLE 24-2. ABYC H40 TABLE AP-1—WORKING LOAD LIMIT FOR ANCHOR RODES

Nominal Diameter		Nylon				Galvanized Chain						Shackles—Welded Drop Forged	
		3- and 8-Strand		Double Braided		BBB		Proof Coil		High Test			
in.	mm	lb.	kN	lb.	kN	lb.	kN	lb.	kN	lb.	kN	lb.	kN
1/4	6	186	0.82	208	0.93	1,300	5.8	1,300	5.8	2,600	11.6	1,000	4.4
5/16	8	287	1.3	326	1.5	1,900	8.5	1,900	8.5	3,900	17.3	1,500	6.7
3/8	10	405	1.8	463	2.1	2,650	11.8	2,650	11.8	5,400	24	2,000	8.9
7/16	11	557	2.5	624	2.8	–	–	–	–	–	–	3,000	13.3
1/2	12	709	3.2	816	3.6	4,500	20.0	4,500	20.0	9,200	41	4,000	17.8
9/16	14	888	4.0	1,020	4.5	5,875	26.1	–	–	11,500	51.2	–	–
5/8	16	1,114	5.0	1,275	5.7	6,900	30.7	6,900	30.7	16,200	72	6,500	29
3/4	18	1,598	7.1	1,813	8.1	10,600	47.2	10,600	47.2	–	–	9,500	42.3
7/8	22	2,160	9.6	2,063	9.2	–	–	12,800	57	–	–	12,000	53.4
1	24	2,795	12.4	3,153	14.0	–	–	13,950	62	–	–	15,000	66.7
1 1/4	30	4,345	19.3	4,838	21.5	–	–	–	–	–	–	23,000	102.3
1 1/2	36	6,075	27.0	6,875	30.6	–	–	–	–	–	–	–	–
2	48	10,575	47.0	12,363	55.0	–	–	–	–	–	–	–	–

Only nylon is shown because of its elasticity. Working loads are based on factors of safety, strength loss due to knots and splices, and abrasion and aging. Thimbles shall be designated for the rope size. Check manufacturers' recommendations for all materials. (Courtesy American Boat & Yacht Council, www.abycinc.org)

SELECTING A WINDLASS

Once you know what size anchor and rode you're going to use, you are ready to select the proper windlass. I chose to make *Hold Fast* the size of boat I did because it is on the border of needing a windlass: There could be no windlass if you used, say, the 18-pound (8.1 kg) Guardian with a high-test-chain leader and a rope warp. Alternatively, with high-test chain and anchors around 35 pounds (16 kg), you could use a manual windlass. Most cruisers today would choose a powered windlass on a 32-foot (9.7 m) powerboat. Obviously, as boats get larger and the anchor gear heavier, a powered windlass becomes mandatory, but many smaller vessels—even with anchors as light as the 18-pound (8.1 kg) Guardian—are installing powered windlasses.

We settled on *Hold Fast*'s full anchor and rode specifications as a 35-pound (16 kg) Delta, 5/16-inch (8.73 mm wire dia.) BBB chain, and 1/2-inch (12 mm) three-strand nylon.

We're ready to size the windlass. The rule is that the windlass's rated pull should be 3 times or more the total weight of the chain, rope, and anchor combined. Let's say that we plan to use 100 feet (30 m) of BBB chain and 200 feet (60 m) of nylon.

Chain weight can be found from Table 23-2. A useful formula I developed, which you can put in a spreadsheet to approximate BBB chain weight, follows.

Formula 24-4.

Formula 24-4. BBB Chain Weight

BBB chain weight, lb./ft. $\approx 10.505 \times$ (chain dia., in.)$^{1.858}$

Or

BBB chain weight, kg/m $\approx$ (chain wire dia., mm)$^{2.12} \div 61.1$

NOTE: For BBB chain, refer to the BBB chain table (Table 23-2) for the metric wire diameter to find the nominal English-unit chain size.

Or referring to Table 23-2, we find that *Hold Fast*'s 5/16-inch BBB chain weighs 110 pounds per 100 feet, or 1.1 pounds per foot (the formula gives the approximate weight as 1.2 lb./ft.).

1.1 lb./ft. × 100 feet length = 110 pounds

Or

Or referring to Table 23-2, we find that *Hold Fast*'s 8.73 mm wire diameter BBB chain weighs 1.6 kilograms per meter (the formula gives the approximate weight as 1.61 kg/m).

1.6 kg/m × 30 m length = 48 kg

Total weight of anchor and chain is then 110-pound chain plus 35-pound anchor equal 145 pounds. Half-inch nylon (from Table 23-12)

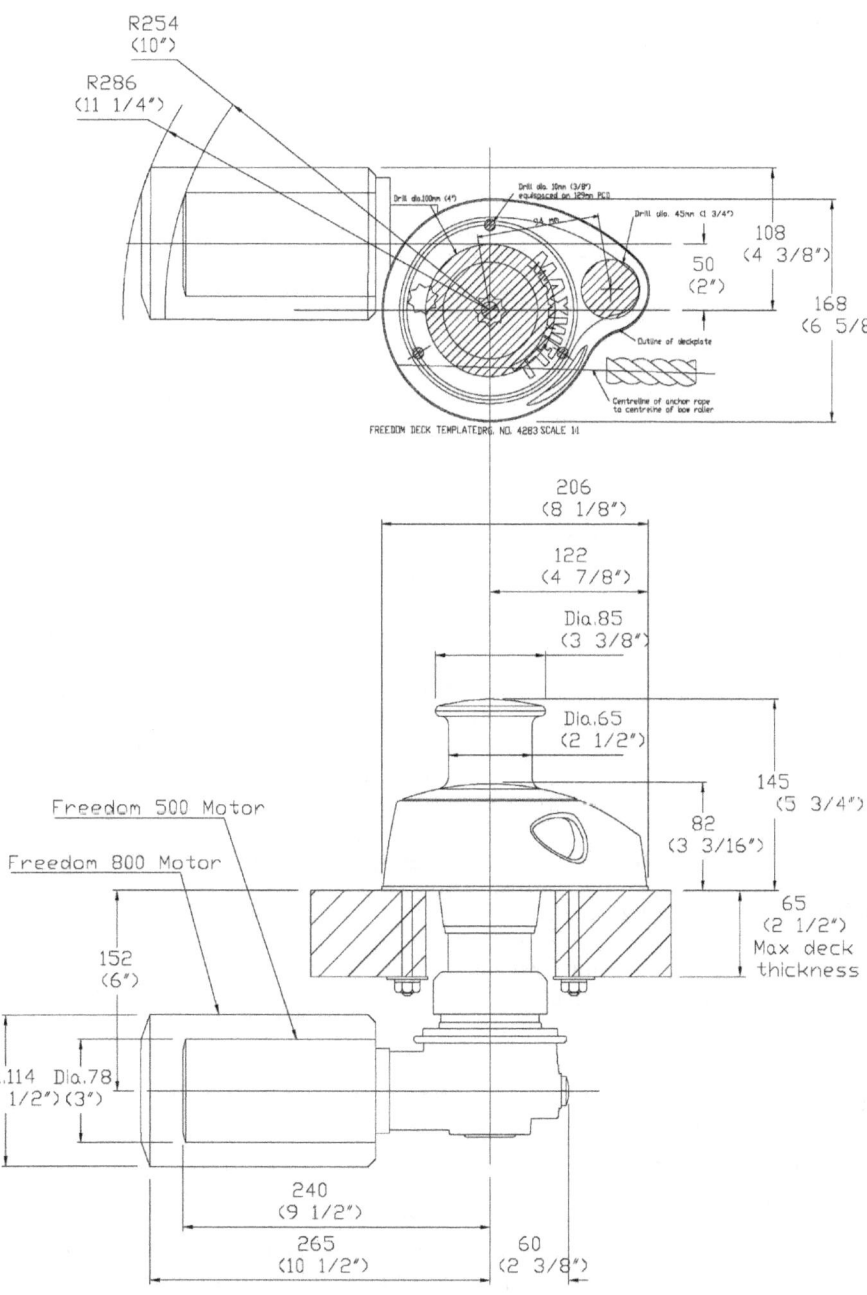

Figure 24-2. Diagram of Maxwell Freedom 500 RC vertical windlass (Courtesy Maxwell Marine)

is 6.3 pounds per 100 feet, so 200 feet is 12.6 pounds. Total anchor and rode weight is 157.6, say 160 pounds, and 3 × 160 pounds gives a windlass-pull rating of 480 pounds. We could safely use any windlass from about 480-pound pull and up, but more is better, within reason.

Or

Total weight of anchor and chain are then 48 kg chain plus 16 kg anchor equal 64 kg. Twelve-millimeter nylon (from Table 23-12) is 0.097 kg/m, so 60 m is 5.82 kg. Total anchor and rode weight is 69.82 kg, say 70 kg, and 3 × 70 kg gives a windlass-pull rating of 210 kg (2 kN). We could safely use any windlass from about 210 kg or 2 kN pull and up, but more is better, within reason.

Several windlass would fill the bill. The Sprint 600 is a vertical unit rated with a 600-pound (272 kg) pull and for ½-inch (12 mm) line and ¼-inch (7 mm) high-test chain. This would work. If we wanted to stick with the ⁵⁄₁₆-inch (8.73 mm wire dia.) BBB, we could ask if a matching chain wildcat was available on special order, or we could simply switch to the ¼-inch (7 mm) high test. The Maxwell Freedom 500 RC (Figure 24-2) has similar specs, as does the Simpson-Lawrence Horizon 600G, but in a horizontal configuration.

If we had an all-chain rode of 300 feet (90 m) and wanted it to be able to haul our 75-pound (23 kg) Luke storm anchor, we would need to increase windlass size as follows:

300 ft. ⁵⁄₁₆-in. BBB chain @ 110 lb./100 ft. = 330 lb.

75-lb. Luke anchor

Total 375 lb.

3 × 375 lb. = 1,125 lb.

A windlass with 1,200 pounds of pull would do. For an ordinary 32-foot motor-yacht, this would be overkill, but not if our *Hold Fast* were a globe-girdling voyager.

Or

90 m 8.73 mm wire dia. BBB chain @ 1.6 kg/m = 144 kg

23 kg Luke anchor

Total 167 kg

3 × 167 kg = 501 kg

A windlass with 500 kg (4.9 kN) of pull would do. For an ordinary 9.7 meter motoryacht, this would be overkill, but not if our *Hold Fast* were a globe-girdling voyager.

Windlass Power Considerations

Electric-powered windlasses draw substantial amperage. This has to be considered carefully. The Maxwell Freedom 500, for instance, is not a large windlass. Nevertheless, it draws 600 watts at full power. Since amps = watts ÷ volts, this means that the windlass is drawing 50 amps at 12 volts (600 watts ÷ 12 volts = 50 amps). This kind of draw will flatten a battery bank fast and requires large electric cables. Assume that the house battery bank is somewhere aft of midships in the engine compartment on our 32-foot (9.7 m) *Hold Fast*. This means that the length of the cable run to the windlass (including all bends—running up and to the side, then forward and back to the windlass on the centerline) will be about 26 feet (8 m). (This distance should be measured accurately on the actual installation or on the boat's drawings.) To size wiring for a given amperage, you need the *total length* to and from *the battery*, so a total of 52 feet (16 m).

Some guides allow heavy equipment, like windlasses and bow thrusters, to experience a 10 percent voltage drop, but this reduces performance and increases heat buildup. Better to stick with 3 percent allowable voltage drop where possible.

The size of copper wire in circular mils for a given length and amperage can be found from Formula 24-5.

Formula 24-5. Copper Wire Size for a Given Voltage Drop

$$cm = \frac{10.75 \times amps \times length, ft.}{allowable\ voltage\ drop}$$

or

$$mm^2 = \frac{amps \times length, m}{55.97 \times allowable\ voltage\ drop}$$

Where
cm = circular mils
mm^2 = wire-conductor cross-section area, nominal metric wire size
amps = current in amps

length, ft. or m = length from power source (usually battery) to equipment *and* back again

allowable voltage drop = allowable drop in volts

NOTE: A circular mil is the equivalent area of a circle whose diameter is 0.001 (10^{-3}) inch, or approximately 0.7854 millionths of a square inch.

In the United States, wire is sized using American Wire Gauge (AWG), which is also the Brown & Sharpe gauge, see Table 24-3. Note that in AWG, the smaller the AWG wire number, the *larger* the wire. The largest wires commonly available are AWG size 0, 00, 000, and 0000. These are also written as 1/0, 2/0, 3/0, and 4/0.

In metric wire size, the wire is called out directly by its total conductor cross-section area. Referring to Table 24-3, you can see that a U.S. no. 6 AWG wire has 26,240 circular mils, and the nearest metric wire size is 16 mm², which has 31,580 equivalent circular mils.

Allowable voltage drop is as follows:

3 percent of 12 volts = 0.36 volt

10 percent of 12 volts = 1.2 volts

3 percent of 24 volts = 0.72 volt

10 percent of 24 volts = 2.4 volts

Example: In our case, the required circular mils for 3 percent voltage drop work out as

$$\frac{10.75 \times 50 \text{ amps} \times 52 \text{ ft.}}{0.36 \text{ volt}} = 77{,}639 \text{ cm}$$

Referring to Table 24-3, we see that we would need 1 gauge wire (AWG). This is a pretty hefty wire at approximately 0.332 in. OD.

Or

In our case, the required circular mils for 3 percent voltage drop work out as

$$\frac{50 \text{ amps} \times 16 \text{ m}}{55.97 \times 0.36 \text{ volts}} = 39.7 \text{ mm}^2$$

Referring to the Table 24-3, we see that 50 mm² wire is the smallest standard metric size with more than this cross-section area. This is a pretty hefty wire at approximately 9.27 mm OD.

This check on wire size has to be done for every electric installation, and breakers *must not* exceed the ampacity of the wire and must meet the manufacturer's spec for the windlass (or other equipment) as well. Equally important is that electric windlasses cannot be run for too long under load. The crew has to be sure to sail up to the anchor and reel the rode in on the windlass under minimum load until the anchor is apeak (straight up and down). At this point, sailing the anchor out is easier on the windlass, but the windlass will be used as well.

This sort of limitation in operation can reduce the windlass's utility. On one occasion, I was cruising on a 60-foot (18.3 m) motor cruiser my office designed. We were anchored off a lee shore in over 50 knots of wind. We motored up to the anchor, reeling in the all-chain rode as we did so. We pulled the hook and sailed out of the harbor with no problem. In such a strong wind and sea, however, the process took a good 15 minutes of nearly continuous windlass operation under varying loads. This would not have been practical with an electric windlass. So what did we use? Hydraulic.

For larger and serious cruising boats, particularly powerboats and motorsailers, I recommend hydraulic windlasses. Hydraulics will allow you to run the windlass virtually as long as you wish under load, making for great flexibility. The catch—there's always a catch—is that the hydraulics are powered off the main engine (occasionally off a gen set). This means that the engine must be running to use the windlass. For powerboats, this will always be the case. For motorsailers, too, this will virtually always be the case. However, smaller sailboats in particular (even larger auxiliaries) will not want to have to turn on their engine (or gen set) every time they set or retrieve the anchor, so electric windlasses are usually the best choice for them.

Power Up and Power Down, and Wildcat Versus Gypsy

Another feature to look for in a windlass is that it has a power-down feature. Small anchors can be allowed to free fall, but over about 20 pounds (9 kg) of anchor and chain, you want

TABLE 24-3. WIRE GAUGES/WIRE SIZE—AWG AND METRIC

Circ. Mils	Equivalent Circ. Mils	AWG Size	Metric Wire Size mm²	Stranding/Wire Dia. per Strand		Approximate Overall Diameter	
				in.	mm	in.	mm
—	937	—	0.5	1/.032	1/.813	0.032	0.81
1,020	—	20	—	7/.0121	7/.030	0.036	0.91
—	1,480	—	0.75	1/.039	1/.991	0.039	0.99
1,620	—	18	—	1/.0403	1/1.02	0.04	1.02
1,620	—	18	—	7/.0152	7/.386	0.046	1.16
—	1,974	—	1	1/.045	1/1.14	0.045	1.14
—	1,974	—	1	7/.017	7/.432	0.051	1.3
2,580	—	16	—	1/.0508	1/1.29	0.051	1.29
2,580	—	16	—	7/.0192	7/.488	0.058	1.46
—	2,960	—	1.5	1/.055	1/1.40	0.055	1.4
—	2,960	—	1.5	7/.021	7/.533	0.063	1.6
4,110	—	14	—	1/.0641	1/1.63	0.064	1.63
4,110	—	14	—	7/.0242	7/.615	0.073	1.84
—	4,934	—	2.5	1/.071	1/1.80	0.071	1.8
—	4,934	—	2.5	7/.027	7/.686	0.081	2.06
6,530	—	12	—	1/.0808	1/2.05	0.081	2.05
6,530	—	12	—	7/.0305	7/.775	0.092	2.32
—	7,894	—	4	1/.089	1/2.26	0.089	2.26
—	7,894	—	4	7/.034	7/.864	0.102	2.59
10,380	—	10	—	1/.1019	1/2.59	0.102	2.59
10,380	—	10	—	7/.0385	7/.978	0.116	2.93
—	11,840	—	6	1/.109	1/2.77	0.109	2.77
—	11,840	—	6	7/.042	7/1.07	0.126	3.21
13,090	—	9	—	1/.1144	1/2.91	0.1144	2.91
13,090	—	9	—	7/.0432	7/1.10	0.13	3.3
16,510	—	8	—	1/.1285	1/3.26	0.128	3.26
16,510	—	8	—	7/.0486	7/1.23	0.146	3.7
—	19,740	—	10	1/.141	1/3.58	0.141	3.58
—	19,740	—	10	7/.054	7/1.37	0.162	4.12
20,820	—	7	—	1/.1443	1/3.67	0.144	3.67
20,820	—	7	—	7/.0545	7/1.38	0.164	4.15
26,240	—	6	—	1/.162	1/4.11	0.162	4.11
26,240	—	6	—	7/.0612	7/1.55	0.184	4.66
—	31,580	—	16	7/.068	7/1.73	0.204	5.18
33,090	—	5	—	7/.0688	7/1.75	0.206	5.24
41,740	—	4	—	7/.0772	7/1.96	0.232	5.88
—	49,340	—	25	7/.085	7/2.16	0.255	6.48

(Continued)

Chapter 24: Sizing the Anchor and Rode and Selecting Anchor-Handling Gear

TABLE 24-3. WIRE GAUGES/WIRE SIZE—AWG AND METRIC (CONTINUED)

Circ. Mils	Equivalent Circ. Mils	AWG Size	Metric Wire Size mm²	Stranding/Wire Dia. per Strand in.	Stranding/Wire Dia. per Strand mm	Approximate Overall Diameter in.	Approximate Overall Diameter mm
—	49,340	—	25	$^{19}/.052$	$^{19}/1.32$	0.26	6.6
52,620	—	3	—	$^{7}/.0867$	$^{7}/2.20$	0.26	6.61
66,360	—	2	—	$^{7}/.0974$	$^{7}/2.47$	0.292	7.42
—	69,070	—	35	$^{7}/.100$	$^{7}/2.54$	0.3	7.62
—	69,070	—	35	$^{19}/.061$	$^{19}/1.55$	0.305	7.75
83,690	—	1	—	$^{19}/.0664$	$^{19}/1.69$	0.332	9.43
—	98,680	—	50	$^{19}/.073$	$^{19}/1.85$	0.365	9.27
105,600	—	0	—	$^{19}/.0745$	$^{19}/1.89$	0.373	9.46
133,100	—	00	—	$^{19}/.0837$	$^{19}/2.13$	0.419	10.6
—	138,100	—	70	$^{19}/.086$	$^{19}/2.18$	0.43	10.9
167,800	—	000	—	$^{19}/.094$	$^{19}/2.39$	0.47	11.9
167,800	—	000	—	$^{37}/.0673$	$^{37}/1.71$	0.471	12
—	187,500	—	95	$^{19}/.101$	$^{19}/2.57$	0.505	12.8
—	187,500	—	95	$^{37}/.072$	$^{37}/1.83$	0.504	12.8
211,600	—	0000	—	$^{19}/.1055$	$^{19}/2.68$	0.528	13.4

(Courtesy Ilsco)

to lower the anchor under control with a power-out or power-down, reel-out mode.

Finally, be sure that the chain wildcat exactly matches the chain size and type as well as the rope (if a rope/chain windlass). If the wildcat doesn't match the chain precisely, the chain can either skip out or jam—neither is good!

Again, in the United States, common terminology is that the chain drum is called a *wildcat* and the rope drum a *gypsy* (a *capstan* in vertical position). In the United Kingdom, it is exactly the opposite—go figure. Keep this terminology difference in mind when ordering and speccing windlasses from or for use in the United Kingdom, Canada, Australia, and so on.

Vertical or Horizontal?

There's very little difference in performance between a horizontal and a vertical windlass. Vertical windlasses, however, take up less space on deck and often fit an optional rope drum or capstan on top, which is useful as a warping winch and for applying pull (using a snatch block or two) for all sorts of odd jobs. (Larger horizontal windlasses usually come with an optional vertical rope capstan on top as well.) It can be less expensive (for a dual anchor system) to install a single horizontal windlass with chain wildcats on both sides than a pair of vertical windlasses. On the other hand, having a pair of windlasses means that if one fails, the other will still work. On yet another hand, the motor and workings of horizontal windlasses are above deck and easy to get at to work on, while vertical windlasses have their motors below deck. Here they are more protected from the elements but harder to reach for maintenance and repairs.

Figure 24-3. Admiralty-pattern anchor lashed to bulwark under the anchor davit

ANCHOR-LAUNCHING CONSIDERATIONS

In the old days, traditional Admiralty-pattern or fisherman anchors were launched over the side from a low, fixed protrusion or arm that projected out over the bulwark—a *cathead*. To begin, the anchor was lashed to the bulwark (Figure 24-3) or inboard with the stock over the edge of the bulwark and an arm lashed around a samson post. To launch the anchor, the lashing was undone and the anchor hoisted from its balance band or balance ring to clear the bulwark. Then it was freed from the tackle to the cathead, whereupon the anchor continued to be lowered to the water where the chain from the hawsepipe finally was engaged. Retrieving the anchor reversed the process, and catching or fishing for the anchor ring to reattach the cathead tackle was always a challenge. More recent boats using Admiralty-pattern or fisherman anchors have often replaced the cathead with a davit or a Spanish-burton tackle from a spreader (Figures 24-3 and 24-4).

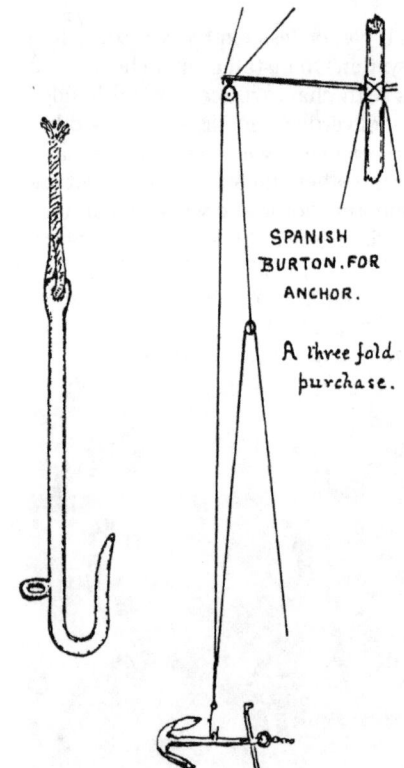

Figure 24-4. Hoisting a yachtsman anchor from a spreader (From Yacht Cruising, by Claud Worth)

Today, modern anchors almost all set from anchor rollers (unless they're small enough to deploy easily by hand). The alternative—particularly for larger craft—is hawsepipes through the side of the boat forward, with the anchors (when stowed) left snugged up in the hawsepipes. We'll examine these two options.

Anchor Rollers

We can look at anchor rollers for our example boat *Hold Fast*. Having squared away the specs for *Hold Fast*'s anchor, rode, and windlass, we have to spec the anchor roller. It should be strong with a large-diameter roller that neatly snugs into the anchor. Most anchors are not balanced such that they'll self-launch off the roller. Even if you have a remote control in the wheelhouse, you still have to go forward and push the anchor uphill and forward enough for it to tip off the roller and then descend. Another alternative is to install the roller at a pronounced down angle so the anchor will be sure to launch off it.

One of the nice things about Delta-pattern anchors is that they've been specifically engineered to self-launch: their center of gravity is farther forward. You really can set and retrieve a Delta without leaving the helm. The other option is to find a pivoting-arm anchor roller. These are more expensive and hard to come by. More often than not, they're custom made. The pivoting-arm action, though, allows any anchor to self-launch.

Larger cruising boat should really have two anchors. This means twin rollers and chain lockers. Horizontal windlasses are available with gypsies on both sides to handle this arrangement. I have a slight preference for installing a pair of vertical windlasses instead. This is more compact on deck, provides two warping winch drums on top, and if one windlass fails, you still have the other.

There are a few common problems with anchor rollers. One of the most frequent is that they are almost never made strong enough. The photo of the failed mooring chock (Figure 23-10) shows a pivoting-arm anchor roller that bent out the aft portion of the articulated roller at the roller pin and pulled the keeper pin clean out of the forward hole. If you study this photo, you'll notice that this anchor roller doesn't appear to be particularly lightly built compared with the gear usually installed.

Figure 24-5 shows yet another anchor roller with common damage. The rolled forward edge of the roller may appear thick in this view, but in fact the stainless steel is relatively thin. This failure occurred in a typical nor'easter, not some hurricane. Note also that, as in most anchor rollers, the roller pin is rather small in diameter. Proper roller pins are large-diameter solid stainless with pipe compression sleeves around them. Tightening up the pin over the compression sleeve, between the roller cheeks, imparts great strength to the assembly. The roller cheeks or sides must be thick and strong. A chain keeper pin should be fitted to keep the chain from jumping out and sawing through the gunwale. Alternatively—and slightly superior—is a chain bail to retain the chain inside the roller, no matter how much the boat jumps around in the seas.

The bent anchor roller in Figure 24-5 also has a black-rubber roller. This is never recommended. The rubber wears away and loses strength. Rollers should be either

Figure 24-5. Bent and broken anchor roller (Courtesy Chris Wentz)

stainless, bronze, or of ultra-high-molecular-weight polyethylene (UHMWPE). UHMWPE is one of my favorite materials for dealing with chafe; for making rollers, slides, and chutes; for lining chain lockers; and even for rudder bearings. UHMWPE is incredibly tough and incredibly slippery. It doesn't corrode or interact chemically with other materials.

Figures 24-6 through 24-8 show a stainless anchor roller for a 47-foot (14.3 m) wood-epoxy motor cruiser my office designed. Note the heavy ½-inch (12.7 mm) stainless cheeks, the extensive through-bolts,

Figure 24-6. Diagram of an anchor roller

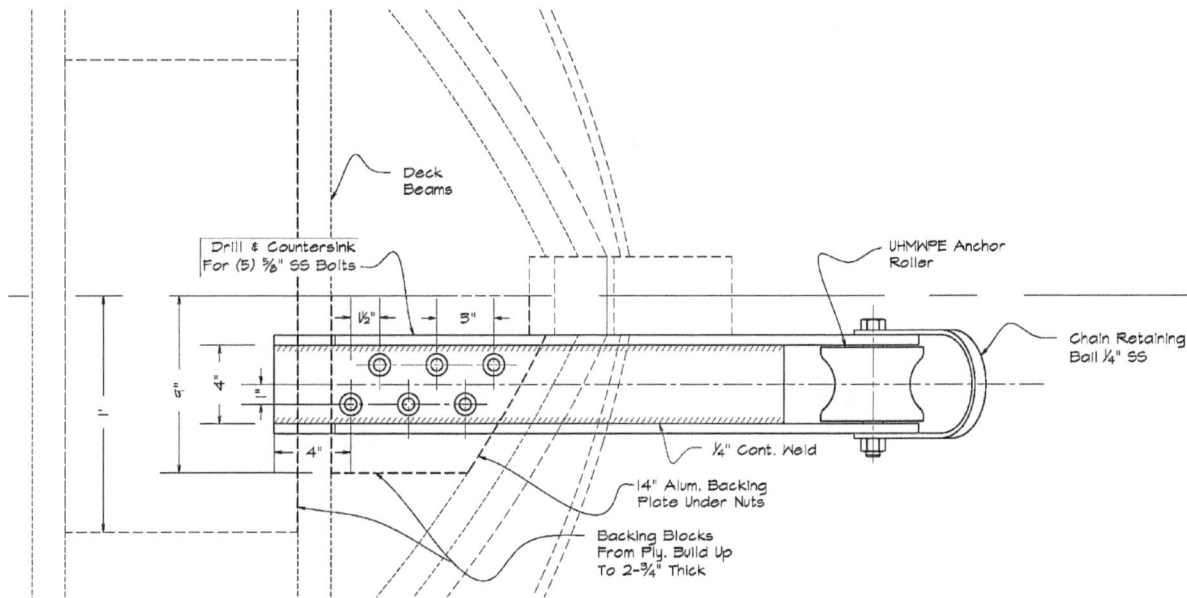

PART SEVEN: ANCHORING SYSTEMS

Figure 24-7. Anchor roller in profile

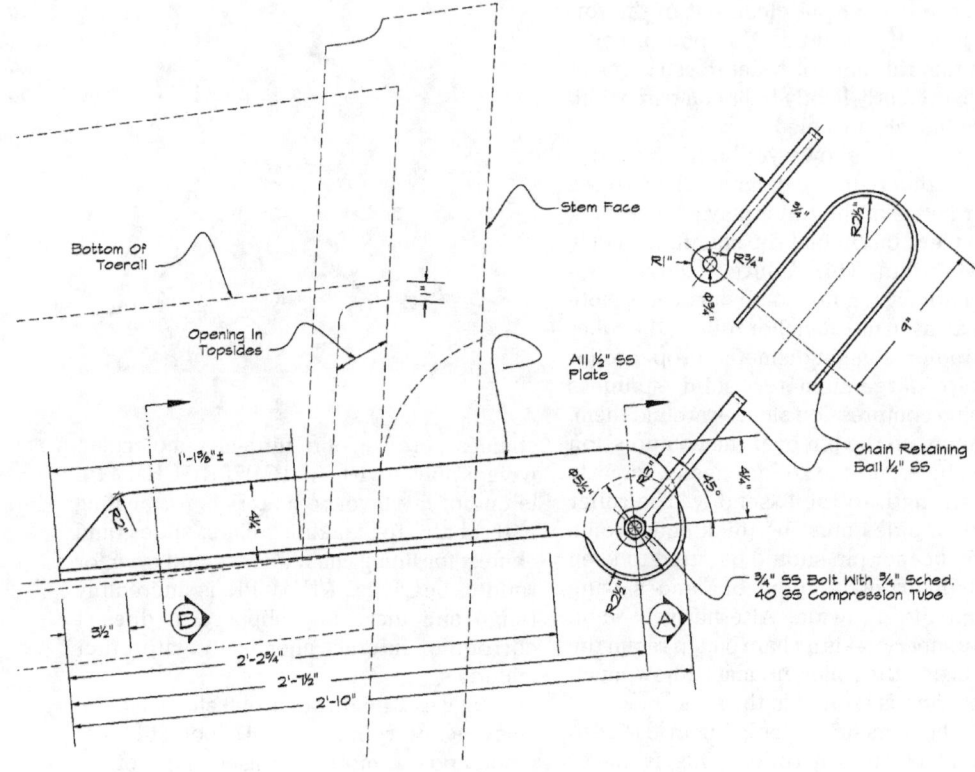

and massive backing block. Similar requirements should be met on FRP construction. On aluminum boats (like *Imagine*), the details are similar, but the rollers are fabricated from heavy aluminum plate welded in place.

Another common problem with anchor rollers is installing double anchor rollers so close side-by-side that only one anchor can fit at a time. See the narrow double roller in Figure 24-9, then look at the bow-on view of this same double roller in Figure 24-10. Notice how the second roller is completely hidden by the one anchor in use. You cannot handle two anchors at the same time in twin rollers such as this.

Figure 24-8. Anchor roller sections. Note the compression tube, a vital component.

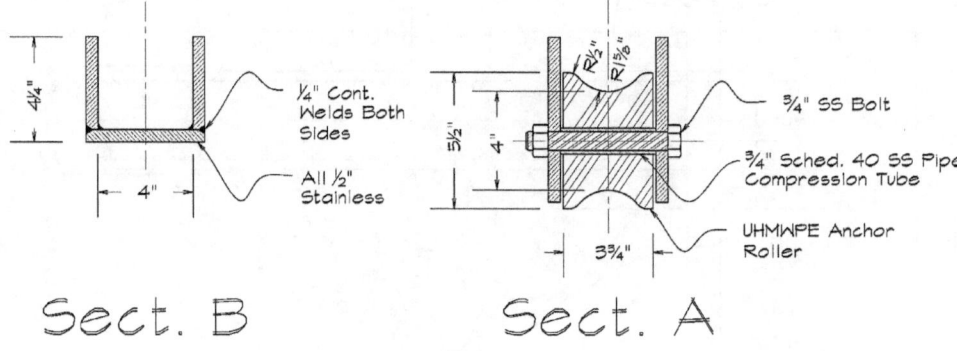

Figure 24-9. Double anchor roller. These rollers are spaced too closely.

The photo of *Imagine*'s foredeck in Figure 24-11 shows the foredeck with the twin windlass and roller arrangement. Note how the rollers are far enough apart to handle both anchors. Both vertical windlasses have warping capstans on top. Also installed are chain stoppers to take the load off the windlasses. You can't really see it in the photo, but from the anchor roller back to the chain stoppers (where the chain can rub on the deck) there is a channel under the chain and the channel is lined with a flat of UHMWPE. This not only keeps the chain from abrading the deck but is quieter too.

The bow-on view of *Imagine* (Figure 24-12) shows these two anchor rollers from outside. One sets a Delta, the other a claw anchor. The line running up to the hawsehole is a nylon snubber, about which more later.

Always remember that the anchor roller and the windlass absorb considerable loads. They must be very securely fastened—through-bolted with heavy backing plates—with compression tubes or annuluses at each fastener. Additional reinforcing in the laminate or a solid core at the fastening is also important. Don't stint here. On an existing boat, inspect to see how this has been done. If

Figure 24-11. Twin vertical windlasses and anchor rollers

Figure 24-12. Bow-on view of Imagine's *double anchor rollers*

Figure 24-10. Bow-on view of the double anchor roller shown in Figure 24-9. The port-side roller is hidden behind the Delta stowed on the starboard roller

you're retrofitting, reinforce the dickens out of everything—you won't be sorry.

Hawsepipes

Though I've designed a number of boats with hawsepipes, none have ever been built that way. In fact, *Imagine* was designed with anchors stowed in hawsepipes, port and starboard on the bow. So far, in every case, the disadvantages of hawsepipes have resulted in changing to anchor rollers when the boat was built. Hawsepipes definitely can work and work well, however. They are particularly appropriate and attractive for larger vessels, over 90 feet (27 m), where the anchors are so heavy that hawsepipes greatly simplify anchor handling. Even so, anchor rollers can be fitted and function nicely on such sizable craft.

Strictly speaking, the pipes that run down from the deck to the hull side are the *hawsepipes*, and the holes exiting the side of the hull are the *hawseholes*. In any case, the geometry here is complex and will need careful thought and design. Among the considerations is that the hawsepipes must be large enough and long enough to accept the full length of the anchor shank with distance to spare, so the anchor and chain will snug up against the hull properly. On deck, the hawsepipe exit must be located where it will provide a clean, fair lead to the windlass, with room for a chain stopper between the windlass and the pipe's deck opening. The hawseholes must be located so the anchor lies flush against the hull and doesn't extend forward of the bow or sit too low to the waterline. The anchor needs to be high enough to be clear of the normal bow wave during routine operation.

Structurally, the hawsepipe must be very rugged (Figure 24-13). If it cracks or breaks free, you will have a serious leak at the bow, which would make for a bad day on the water.

When the anchor is deployed, the chain tends to chafe and cut the bow, marking it badly and potentially even damaging the bow. You can see this in the photo of the Danforth anchor in a hawsepipe (Figure 24-14) where the stock has deeply scarred the hull, the forward fluke's bill has chafed the small pad added for it, and the chain has marred the

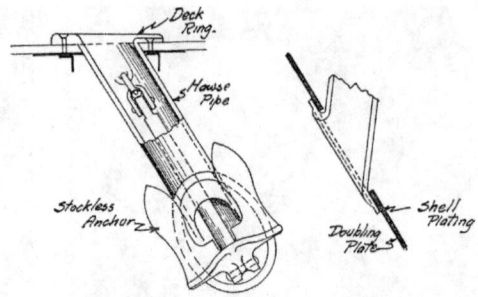

Figure 24-13. Diagram of a hawsepipe (From The Design and Construction of Power Workboats, *by Arthur F. Johnson)*

stem at the waterline. If the boat is a sailboat with bowsprit and bobstay, the chain will foul, chafe, and bend the bobstay even worse than a rode set through chocks on deck or from rollers on a bowsprit; see the bobstay in Figure 24-15. This boat also has navy stockless anchors—not ideal. The anchor will be inclined to bang and scratch against the hull during deployment or retrieval, and the chain can be noisy in the hawsepipe. Finally, you cannot reach down to work on or get at the anchor. If you want to change anchors or otherwise inspect them, you need to drop the

Figure 24-14. Danforth anchor in a hawsepipe. (This bow also has a plastic chafe pad)

Chapter 24: Sizing the Anchor and Rode and Selecting Anchor-Handling Gear

Figure 24-15. Bobstay damaged from anchor chain

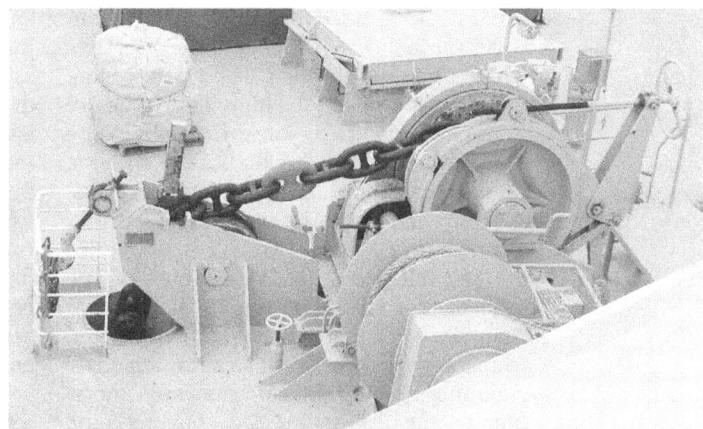

Figure 24-17. Ship windlass and hawsepipe

anchor and hoist it aboard with some sort of tackle rigged to a crane or boom.

For these reasons, almost all yachts fitted with anchors in hawsepipes have substantial chafing pads or plates around the hawsehole for the anchor to rest on and commonly also at the stem by the waterline, where the chain may rub. Usually, these are of stainless steel, but sometimes they are of plastic such as UHMWPE.

Finally, of course there are many fine large yachts with properly fitted and installed anchors in hawsepipes (Figure 24-16). These anchors are often ensconced in recesses in the side of the hull, all lined with stainless, and with stainless chafing built in around the stem. You can see this in the photo of the Jack Hargrave–designed motoryacht *Ilona* (Figure 24-16).

Figure 24-16. Anchors in hawsepipes (Courtesy Hargrave Custom Yachts)

How the Big Fellows Do It

Figure 24-17 shows an anchor windlass, with stud-link chain (navy type in this case) running through a hawsepipe on a 950-foot (290 m) ship. Though it sure is a whole lot bigger, it's really set up the same way as on any boat. The claw extended near the railing on the left is the chain claw for tensioning the anchor chain. The hand wheel at the far right tensions the brake band on the chain wildcat drum. You can get a feel for the scale from the railing on the left. It's about 40 inches (1 m) high.

CHAIN-LOCKER REQUIREMENTS

Of course, as you retrieve your anchor, the rode (rope and chain) has to go somewhere—into the chain locker. This is one of the most common sources of foul-ups (literally) with anchoring systems. Ideally, the chain locker should be as deep and high and narrow as possible and located as directly under the windlass exit pipe as possible. The pipe that leads the chain down into the anchor locker is called either the *spurling pipe* or the *chain pipe*, not the hawsepipe. There should be a minimum of 18 inches (46 cm) clear from the bottom of the spurling pipe to the top of the chain pile (24 inches, or 60 cm, is better) when the locker is full. The spurling pipe should be as vertical as possible, ideally straight up and down, though a small angle is acceptable. The angle can never be more than 45 degrees, however. Each anchor rode must have its

PART SEVEN: ANCHORING SYSTEMS

separate, dedicated locker. Two rodes can never share the same locker. If they do, they will get tangled and jam. The further from these ideals you get, the more likely you are to experience kinks, jams, or fouls in the rode. The ideal chain locker is a tall, narrow, round, vertical drum, though it's not necessary or common to go this far for perfect chain storage.

The minimum inside diameter of the spurling pipe should be 8 times the nominal chain size or 7.5 times the rope warp diameter, whichever is larger. This is to allow adequate clearance for the shackle and any knots. Ideally, the bottom of the spurling pipe should be flared out in a bell mouth. The flare is optional (though always best) if there is 24 or more inches (60 cm) from the top of the full chain pile to the bottom of the spurling pipe and the spurling pipe is less than 10 degrees from vertical.

In the majority of the boats my office draws, the chain lockers are worked in at an early stage in the design. They are located fairly far back from the bow (to get the weight farther aft) and are dead vertical, with the windlass located directly above them. This is exactly the setup on *Imagine*, pictured earlier. It makes for a clean deck and reliable chain stowage and deployment. You can also see this in the drawings of the 75-foot (23 m) cutter (Figures 24-18 and 24-19).

When you're looking at a new boat or a retrofit, consider carefully how the chain/rope locker is arranged. Shallow, flat lockers with long, twisting, or steeply angled spurling-pipe runs are a sign of potential trouble.

Use Formula 24-6 for chain-locker volume.

Figure 24-18. 75-foot (23 m) cutter with double vertical chain lockers

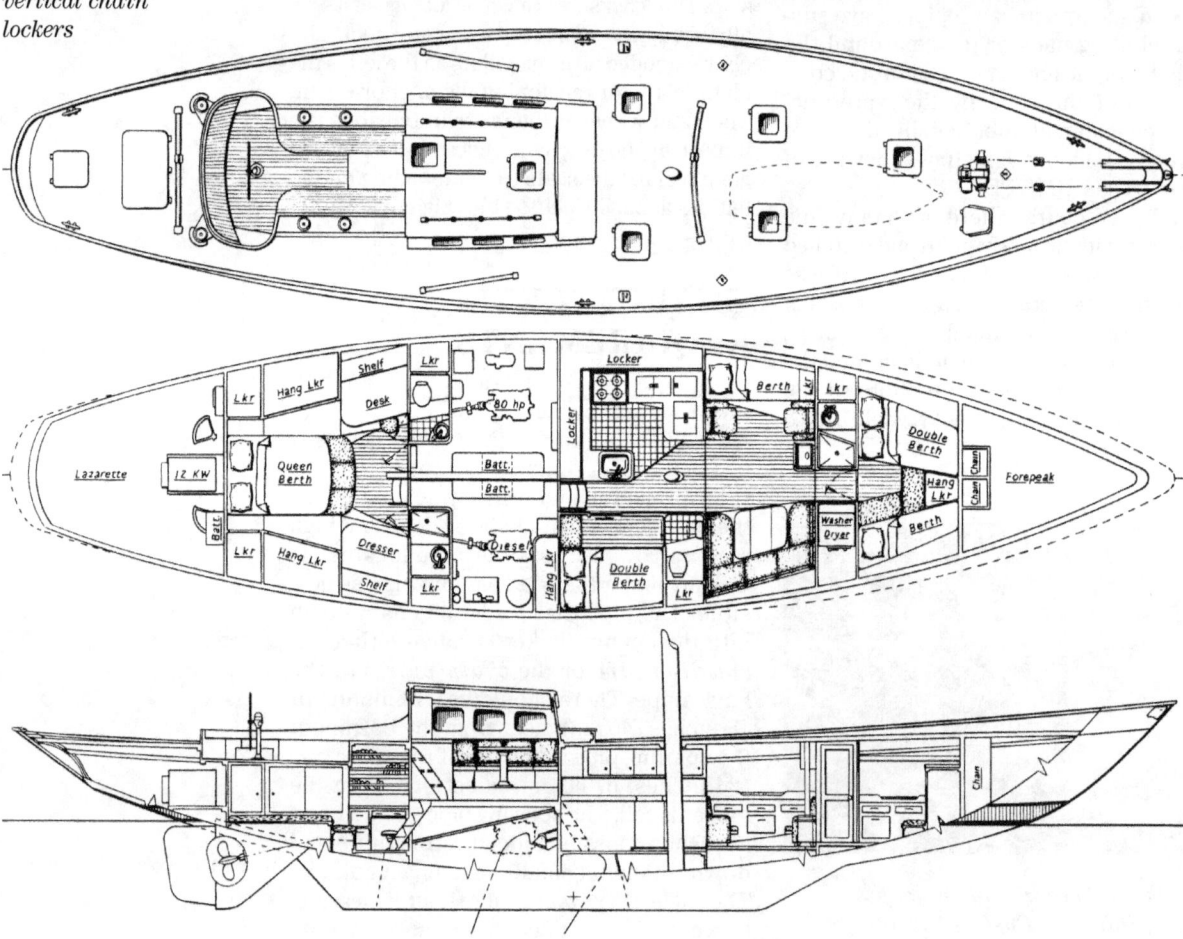

Formula 24-6. Recommended Chain-Locker Volume

Chain-locker volume in cu. ft. = ft. of chain × (chain size, in.)² ÷ 7

or

Chain-locker volume in m³ = m of chain × (chain size, mm)² ÷ 48,612

This is the clear volume measured from 18 inches (46 cm) below the bottom of the spurling pipe down.
Example: Our *Hold Fast* would then require

100 ft. × (¼-in. high-test chain)² ÷ 7 = 0.89 cu. ft. for the chain; say, use 1 cubic foot.

Or

30 m × (7 mm high-test chain)² ÷ 48,612 = 0.03 m³

Rope-locker volume is calculated by using the following formula.

Formula 24-7. Recommended Rope-Locker Volume

Rope-locker volume in cu. ft. = ft. of rope × (rope dia., in.)² ÷ 70

or

Rope-locker volume in m³ = m of rope × (rope dia., mm)² ÷ 481,620

This is the clear volume *below* the bottom of the spurling pipe. (Yale Brait requires only 50 percent of this volume.)
Example: Our *Hold Fast* would then require

200 ft. × (½-in. nylon)² ÷ 70 = 0.71 cu. ft. for the rope; say use 0.8 cu. ft.

or

60 m × (12 mm nylon)² ÷ 481,620 = 0.018 m³

Accordingly, *Hold Fast*'s total chain and rope locker should be at least 1.8 cubic feet—2 cubic feet would be better (0.058 m³—0.06 m³ would be better). The locker ought to be as high, narrow, and vertical as possible, as well as directly under the windlass. Again, keep in mind this volume is only the volume *below* 18 inches (46 cm) beneath the bottom of the spurling pipe.

SNUBBING UP

One of the things I like about all-chain rode is the ability to use a stopper to take the load off the windlass. This should not be done with a rope anchor warp. Such a snubber on rope would be another rope fastened with a rolling hitch, or similar, and these reduce the strength of the warp they attach to by 50 percent! For chain, there are several standard metal stoppers available—all the standard ones work fairly well. You can see chain stoppers on the foredeck photo of *Imagine* (Figure 24-11) and in the drawings of the 75-foot (23 m) cutter's arrangement (Figures 24-18 and 24-19), as well as in the close-up photo (Figure 24-21). This style of chain stopper used to be called a *box chain stopper*.

On many boats, however, there isn't enough room to install chain stoppers. If so, nylon snubbers can do the job.

Chain-Snubbing or Anchor Pendant

In all cases, there's an even better solution to riding on the chain stoppers at anchor (though these are recommended and will do the job adequately). You want to add the elastic snubbing action of rope to an all-chain rode. This is done by attaching a nylon-rope snubber to a cleat on deck, running it through a hawse or chock at the bow, and fastening it to the chain with a rolling hitch or chain claw. The chain is slacked away so the load comes on the nylon snubber. Note that when the nylon snubber is run through a hawse or chock on deck, it should be protected with chafe gear at the chock for any long-term anchoring.

Anchor Pendant or Snubber to Bow Eye

My favorite solution, and one that beats a standard chain stopper hands down, is to use an anchor pendant (pronounced pennant)

PART SEVEN: ANCHORING SYSTEMS

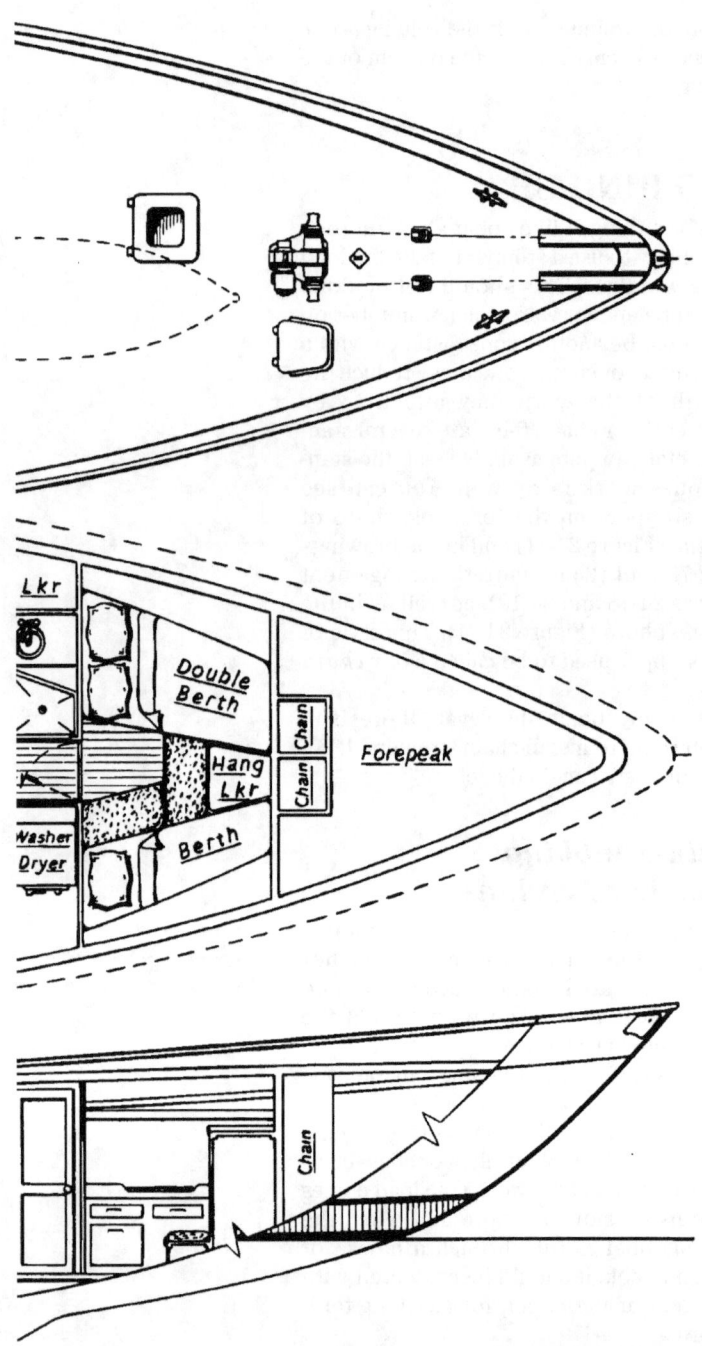

Figure 24-19. Close-up view of chain lockers

Figure 24-20. Chain stopper

Here's what you need to install:

1. Get a length of three-strand nylon line about 3 times as long as the height of the freeboard at the boat's bow. The line should be the same size or one standard size smaller than the anchor rode recommended earlier (not the larger size for a rope-chain splice).
2. Install it on the bow eye with a chain shackle and an eye splice and with a stainless steel thimble in the splice.
3. On the other end, install an eye splice and a stainless steel thimble and a chain claw. Alternatively, leave the free end with no fitting. The free end, in either case, is for attachment to the chain after anchoring. Note that a chain claw is not a chain hook. The proper form of chain claw for this application is known as a *devil's claw*. (See the photo of the devil's claw used on deck in Figure 23-14.)

Devil's claws can be hard to locate these days. One source is www.ropeinc.com (Figure 24-22), which supplies full snubbing pendants with

attached to a strong bow eye installed about 9 to 12 inches (23 to 30 cm) or so above the waterline. This is the line you see in the bow-on photo of *Imagine* in Figure 24-12—the line leading from the eye at the bow up to the hawsehole on deck.

Figure 24-21. Close-up view of chain stopper

Figure 24-22. Devil's claw (Courtesy Rope, Inc.)

chain claw installed. Niro-Peterson (www.niro-petersen.de) also makes stainless devil's claws (Figure 24-23).
4. Leave the chain snubbing pendant permanently in place. When underway, the free end is simply pulled up over the bow, through one of the chocks, and made fast (and held taut) to a bow cleat.

Here's how to use it:

1. Anchor normally, setting the anchor on the all-chain rode.
2. After everything is all set—and at your convenience—go forward and free the chain snubbing pendant from the cleat and fasten it to the chain with the chain claw just forward of the anchor roller (where it's easy to reach).

Alternatively, you can simply tie the chain snubbing pendant to the anchor chain using a rolling hitch. (Be sure to tie the rolling hitch in the right direction to take the load.) Using the rolling hitch, no fitting would be needed. Also, the load is spread across several chain links. (I actually prefer the steeplejack's hitch. This is identical to the rolling hitch, but with an extra round turn made on the side away from the load.)
3. Now pay out anchor chain until the load is taken by the nylon chain-snubbing pendant. Then pay out a little more chain so that the chain hangs a bit loose aft of the pendant's attachment.

What this does:

1. It takes *all* the load off the windlass, off the chain stopper, and off the anchor roller.
2. It lowers the angle of pull so the anchor-chain loads don't tend to depress the bow.
3. Lowering the angle of pull effectively increases the anchoring scope, which increases holding power.
4. The nylon chain-snubbing pendant is stretchy, so it absorbs shock loads, which makes the boat ride easier and reduces the load on the chain and the anchor.
5. It avoids any chance of the chain rubbing against or chafing the stem (or any bowsprit, projecting anchor roller, or bobstay, if one is fitted).
6. If the snubbing pendant parts, you're still riding on the chain.

I'm not sure why this simple and inexpensive solution isn't more commonly installed. If the boat doesn't have room for chain stoppers on deck, this nylon pendant snubber is all that is needed. And even with chain stoppers, this pendant is a great improvement. Note that a nylon chain snubber can also be fastened to a cleat on deck and used to tension the anchor back down on the anchor roller when stowed. This will ensure that the anchor doesn't rattle or come adrift at sea.

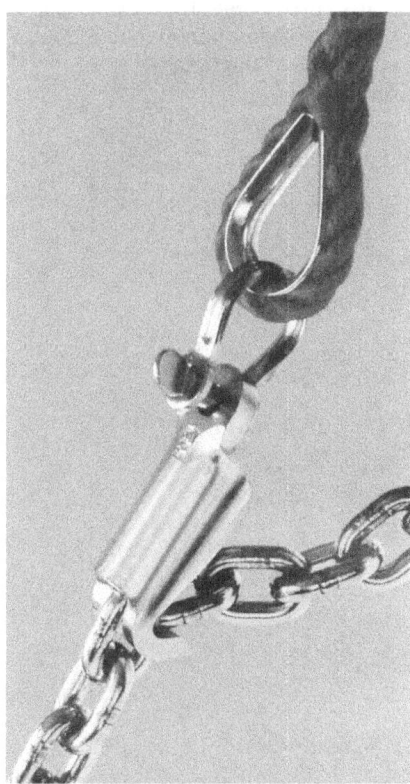

Figure 24-23. Devil's claw (Courtesy Niro Petterson)

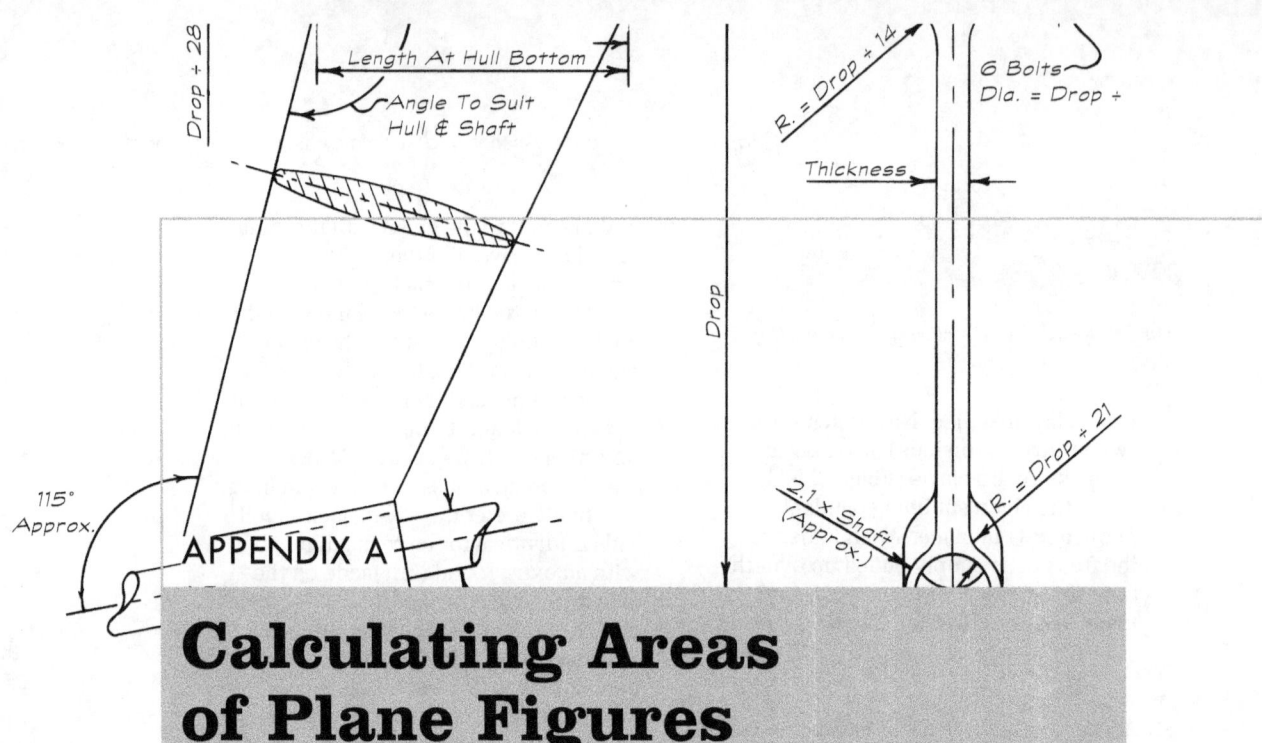

APPENDIX A
Calculating Areas of Plane Figures

Most sections through tanks in boats are some form of regular area—a rectangle, trapezoid, circle, segment of a circle, or some combination of these. Use the following formulas to determine the areas. Remember that complex plane figures can be divided up into combinations of these standard shapes. In such cases, you divide the shape up into these regular areas. Calculate each area, and add them together to get the total area of the figure (i.e., of the tank section).

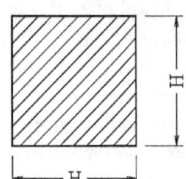

Square

Square:
Area = H^2

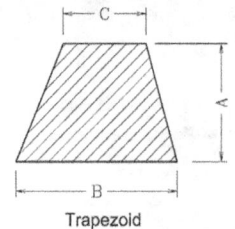

Trapezoid
(Two Sides Parallel)

Trapezoid:
Area = $A \times (B + C) \div 2$

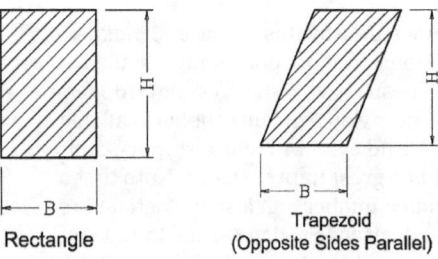

Rectangle

Trapezoid
(Opposite Sides Parallel)

Rectangle and Trapezoid:
Area = $B \times H$

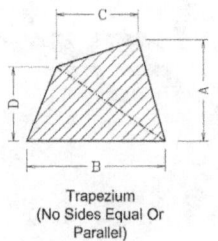

Trapezium
(No Sides Equal Or Parallel)

Trapezium:
Divide into triangles.
Find area of each triangle, and add for total.

Calculating Areas of Plane Figures

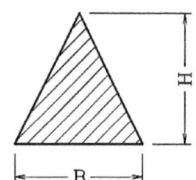

Isosceles Triangle

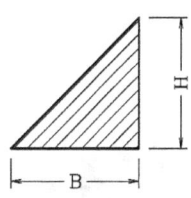

Right Triangle

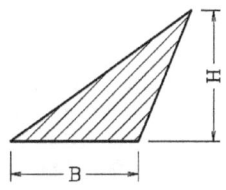

Obtuse Triangle

Triangles:
Area = (B × H) ÷ 2

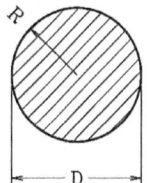

Circle

Circle:
Area = πR^2
Area = $\pi(\tfrac{1}{2}D)^2$

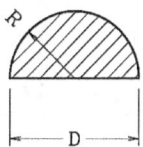

Half Circle

Half Circle:
Area = $\pi R^2 \div 2$
Area = $\pi(\tfrac{1}{2}D)^2 \div 2$

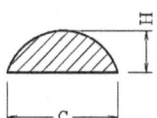

Segment of Circle

Segment of Circle (approximate)
(less than half a circle):

$$\text{Area} \approx 0.82 \times H \times C \times \left(\frac{H}{C}\right)^{0.1}$$

Note: $\pi \approx 3.14$

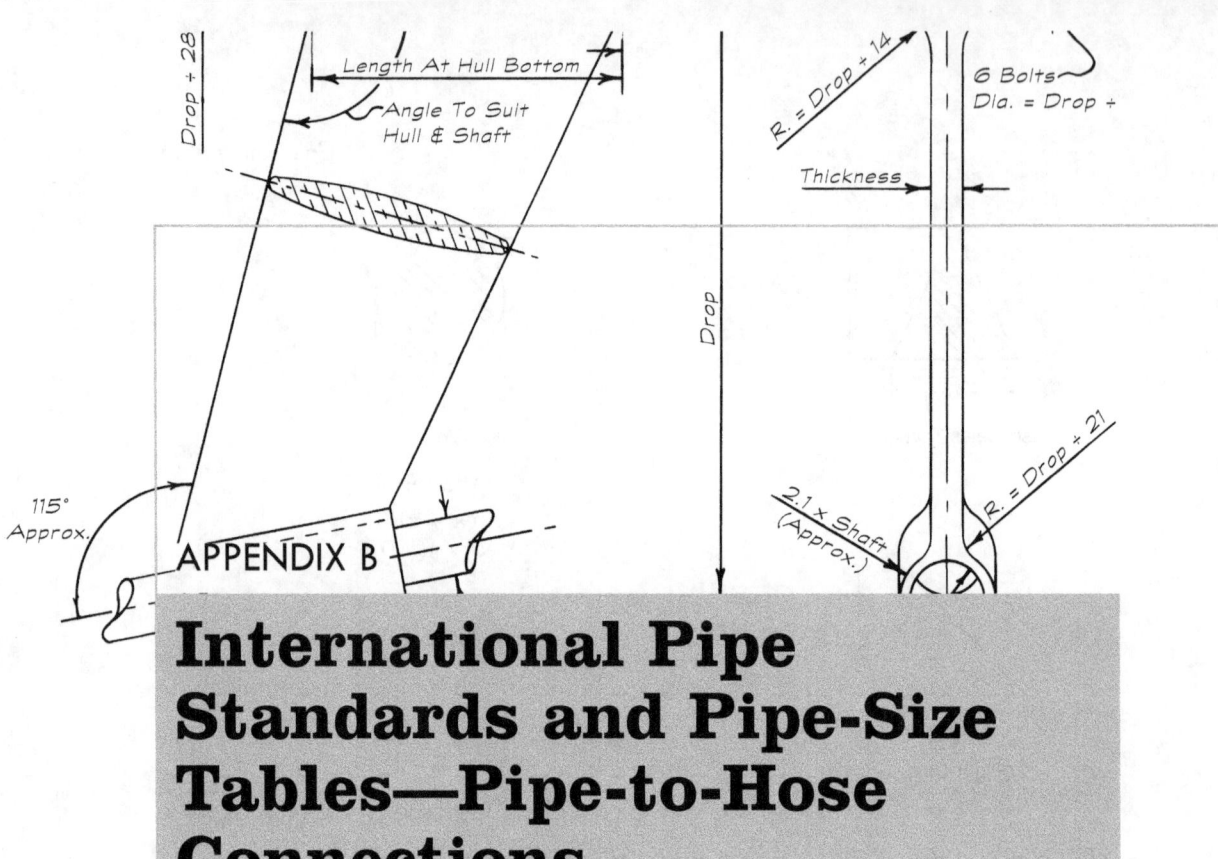

APPENDIX B

International Pipe Standards and Pipe-Size Tables—Pipe-to-Hose Connections

There are several different piping standards in use around the world. This can be a source of potential confusion. Generally, the most widely used standard is IPS schedule pipe size ("iron pipe size") or NPS ("nominal pipe size"). This categorizes pipe by schedule number or "weight." Most metal pipes of other materials, including stainless steel and aluminum, follow the pipe-size standard, but there are important exceptions, particularly for plastic pipe. Note that *tubing*, as opposed to *pipe*, follows completely different size standards.

In the United States, there are eleven schedules ranging from the thinnest wall at 5 through 10, 20, 30, 40, 60, 80, 100, 120, and 140, to schedule 160—the thickest wall. For nominal size piping 6 inches (150 mm) and smaller, schedule 40 (also called "standard weight" in most sizes) is the normal, standard pipe, and—*very* roughly—the dimension or size number of 40-weight pipe approximates the inside diameter. American National Standards Institute (ANSI) pipe standards specify, say, S.40, for steel pipe (as opposed to iron pipe) and 40S for stainless—the *S.* before the schedule number indicating "steel," and the *S* after the number indicating "stainless steel." For the size of pipe used in fuel systems, the dimensions of 40 and 80 pipe are the same for these materials.

Traditional names for U.S. NPS pipe-wall thickness or weight are Standard (Std.), Extra Strong (XS), and Double Extra Strong (XXS). Std. and schedule 40 are the same in sizes up through 10 inches. In sizes above 10 inches, Std. has a constant wall of $3/_8$ inch, and XS has a constant wall thickness of $1/_2$ inch. XXS has no corresponding schedule number, but in sizes through 6 inches, XXS has a wall thickness twice that of XS.

Regardless of the schedule or weight, all pipes of a specified nominal diameter have the same outside diameter whatever the wall thickness. The outside diameter (OD) is larger than the nominal pipe size, as the nominal or schedule diameter roughly relates to the bore, or inside diameter (ID). As the schedule number increases, the OD remains the same and the wall thickness increases, so the ID, or bore, is smaller. For example:

- 4-inch schedule 40 pipe has an OD of 4.5 inches, 0.237-inch wall, for an ID of 4.026 inches.
- 4-inch schedule 80 pipe has an OD of 4.5 inches, 0.337-inch wall, for an ID of 3.826 inches.

Or

- 100 mm schedule 40 pipe has an OD of 114.30 mm, 6.02 mm wall, for an ID of 102.26 mm.
- 100 mm schedule 80 pipe has an OD of 114.30 mm, 8.56 mm wall, for an ID of 97.18 mm.

Only schedules (wall thicknesses) 40 and 80 cover the full range of sizes from $1/8$-inch (3 mm) up to 24-inch (600 mm) nominal sizes and are the most commonly used and available pipe.

In most of the European Union, pipe is manufactured to DIN standards, and DIN 2448 pipe is standard pipe. DIN pipe is specified in millimeters, as OD and wall thickness. So a DIN 2448 pipe 25.4 mm OD and 2.6 mm wall would be specified as "25.4 × 2.6."

In the United Kingdom, piping to EN 10255 (steel tubes appropriate for screwing to BS 21 threads) is also used where the pipe is screwed rather than flanged. These are generally referred to as "Blue Band" and "Red Band," according to their banded identification marks. The different colors refer to the grade or weight of pipe: Red Band, being heavy grade, is commonly used for steam pipe applications. Blue Band, being medium grade, is commonly used for air-distribution systems and low-pressure, low-temperature fluid applications. The colored bands are 50 mm wide, and their positions on the pipe give its length. Pipes less than 4 meters in length only have a colored band at one end, while pipes of 4 to 7 meters in length have a colored band at either end.

TABLE B-1. STANDARD METRIC—U.S. PIPE COMPARISON

Nominal Pipe Size, in.	$1/2$	$3/4$	1	$1 1/4$	$1 1/2$	2	$2 1/2$	3	4	6
Nominal Pipe Size, mm	15	20	25	32	40	50	65	80	100	150
Schedule 40, ID in.	0.622	0.824	1.049	1.380	1.610	2.067	2.469	3.068	4.026	6.065
Schedule 40, ID mm	15.8	21	26.6	35.1	40.9	52.5	62.7	77.9	102.3	154.1
Schedule 80, ID in.	0.546	0.742	0.957	1.278	1.500	1.939	2.323	2.900	3.826	5.761
Schedule 80, ID mm	13.8	18.9	24.3	32.5	38.1	49.2	59	73.7	97.2	146.4
Schedule 160, ID in.	0.466	0.614	0.815	1.160	1.338	1.689	2.125	2.626	3.438	5.189
Schedule 160, ID mm	11.7	15.6	20.7	29.5	34	42.8	53.9	66.6	87.3	131.8
DIN 2448, ID mm	17.3	22.3	28.5	37.2	43.1	60.3	70.3	82.5	107.1	159.3

English-unit/inch sizes in bold

APPENDIX B

U.S. ISO PIPE DESIGNATIONS—DN PIPE SIZES

There's yet another pipe-size naming system. It is ISO pipe-size designations for U.S. IPS or NPS pipe. This is DN pipe size as opposed to DIN pipe standard. *DN* stands for *diameter nominal*. Under this system, U.S. NPS pipe is named for the closest metric dimension to the *nominal* pipe size. For instance, 3/4-inch IPS pipe is DN 20 mm pipe. It's the exact same pipe, with real dimensions from Table B-4. If this were standard weight or schedule 40 pipe, it would be 1.050-inch OD, 0.113-inch wall (26.7 mm OD, 2.87 mm wall). The closest DIN metric pipe would be DIN 2448, 26.9 × 2.9. NOTE: *DN and DIN pipe standards appear the same but they are* different. Table B-2 presents DN pipe sizes and their English-unit equivalents.

U.S. PIPE-THREAD STANDARDS

Just as with the pipe itself there are several standards for the threads on pipe and pipe fittings. In the United States, the most common pipe threads are National Pipe Thread (NPT), which is a tapered pipe thread, and National Standard Free-Fitting Straight Mechanical Pipe Thread (NPSM), which is straight—not tapered. Tapered threads are used for sealed piping, while straight threads are for mechanical connections only. The dry-sealed, taper-thread standard is NPTF. This is tapered thread used for joining pipe to seal liquid tight without using sealants. NOTE: *NPTF is the pipe thread that should be used for fuel-system piping.* The NPTF and NPT threads are interchangable, but only the NPTF is self-sealing. All the other pipe threads are incompatible with each other. Even with NPTF fittings on fuel piping, I recommend using plumber's sealant (dope) on the threads. You will find NPT fittings used in fuel systems in conjunction with plumber's sealant on the threads. This is acceptable, but NPTF is preferable for all fuel-system applications.

Be aware that there are still other pipe-thread standards such as Garden Hose Thread (GHT), Fire Hose Coupling (NST), and British Standard Taper Pipe Thread (BSPT). Don't confuse these with NPTF.

TABLE B-2. NOMINAL U.S. IPS OR NPT PIPE SIZE TO NOMINAL METRIC "DN" CONVERSION CHART

Nominal Pipe Size (Inches/U.S.)	Nominal Pipe Size (Metric)
1/8"	6 mm
3/16"	7 mm
1/4"	8 mm
3/8"	10 mm
1/2"	15 mm
5/8"	18 mm
3/4"	20 mm
1"	25 mm
1 1/4"	32 mm
1 1/2"	40 mm
2"	50 mm
2 1/2"	65 mm
3"	80 mm
3 1/2"	90 mm
4"	100 mm
4 1/2"	115 mm
5"	125 mm
6"	150 mm

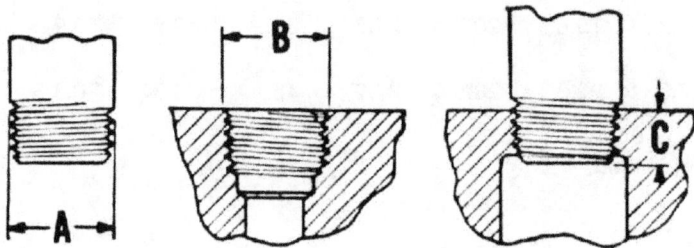

Figure A-B-1. Pipe threads (Courtesy www.plumbing-world.com)

TABLE B-3. U.S. PIPE-THREAD TABLE

OD inches "A" or "B"	NPS or IPS Pipe Size, in.	Engagement for Tight Joint "C," in.	Threads per inch
0.3125	1/16	0.2611	27
0.4050	1/8	0.2639	27
0.5400	1/4	0.4018	18
0.6750	3/8	0.4078	18
0.8400	1/2	0.5337	14
1.0500	3/4	0.5457	14
1.3150	1	0.6828	11.5
1.6600	1 1/4	0.7068	11.5
1.9000	1 1/2	0.7235	11.5
2.3750	2	0.7565	11.5
2.8750	2 1/2	1.1375	8
3.5000	3	1.2000	8
4.0000	3 1/2	1.2500	8
4.5000	4	1.3000	8

Use with Figure A-B-1.

Pipe threads are also male and female. Be sure to specify the gender required for your specific fitting. A barbed hose adapter to fit a 3/4-inch hose to a 3/4-inch NPS male pipe fitting, suited to fuel systems, would be specified as a "female 3/4-inch NPTF pipe to 3/4-inch hose connector."

If you need to determine the size of U.S. pipe thread, measure either dimension A for male fittings or B for female fittings (Figure A-B-1). Enter that in the chart, and read the NPS pipe size. Note the threads per inch (TPI). This changes with the size of pipe. TPI must be matched exactly or the fitting won't work.

HOSE-TO-PIPE SIZE CONSIDERATIONS

While pipe is dimensioned by the preceding various series of standards (and according to the tables that follow), hose is dimensioned by inside diameter, ID. Thus if you were specifying hose for a tank fill to mate with a standard $1^{1}/_{2}$-inch fill pipe, the OD of the pipe would be 1.90 inches and you would use 2-inch ID hose or specify hose to mate with $1^{1}/_{2}$-inch IPS (48.3 × 3.7) pipe. (See Table B-4.)

In smaller sizes, hose must fit over barbed connectors (see Figure A-B-2). These connectors must be carefully selected to match the pipe and hose.

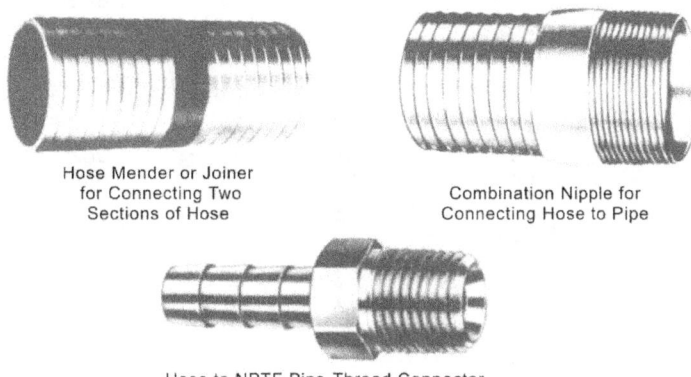

Hose Mender or Joiner for Connecting Two Sections of Hose

Combination Nipple for Connecting Hose to Pipe

Hose to NPTF Pipe-Thread Connector

Hose Connectors

Figure A-B-2. Hose connectors (Courtesy Amazon Hose & Rubber Co.)

TABLE B-4. U.S. IPS (NPS) PIPE-SIZE TABLE

Nominal Pipe Size and Real OD	Schedule No.	Wall Thickness		ID	
		in.	mm	in.	mm
1/8" 0.405" (10.3 mm)	40	0.068	1.73	0.269	6.83
	80	0.095	2.41	0.215	5.46
	—	—	—	—	—
1/4" 0.540" (13.7 mm)	40	0.088	2.24	0.364	9.25
	80	0.119	3.02	0.302	7.67
	—	—	—	—	—
3/8" 0.675" (17.1 mm)	40	0.091	2.31	0.493	12.52
	80	0.126	3.20	0.423	10.74
	—	—	—	—	—
1/2" 0.840" (21.3 mm)	5	0.065	1.65	0.710	18.03
	10	0.083	2.11	0.674	17.12
	40	0.109	2.77	0.622	15.80
	80	0.147	3.73	0.546	13.87
3/4" 1.050" (26.7 mm)	5	0.065	1.65	0.920	23.37
	10	0.083	2.11	0.884	22.45
	40	0.113	2.87	0.824	20.93
	80	0.154	3.91	0.742	18.85
1" 1.315" (33.4 mm)	5	0.065	1.65	1.185	30.10
	10	0.109	2.77	1.097	27.86
	40	0.133	3.38	1.049	26.64
	80	0.179	4.55	0.957	24.31
1 1/4" 1.660" (42.2 mm)	5	0.065	1.65	1.530	36.86
	10	0.109	2.77	1.442	36.63
	40	0.140	3.56	1.380	35.05
	80	0.191	4.85	1.278	32.46
1 1/2" 1.900" (48.3 mm)	5	0.065	1.65	1.770	44.96
	10	0.109	2.77	1.682	42.72
	40	0.145	3.68	1.610	40.89
	80	0.200	5.08	1.500	38.10
2" 2.375" (60.3 mm)	5	0.065	1.65	2.245	57.02
	10	0.109	2.77	2.157	54.79
	40	0.154	3.91	2.067	52.50
	80	0.218	5.54	1.939	49.25
2 1/2" 2.875" (73.0 mm)	5	0.083	2.11	2.709	68.81
	10	0.120	3.05	2.635	66.93
	40	0.203	5.16	2.469	62.71
	80	0.276	7.01	2.323	59.00
3" 3.500" (88.9 mm)	5	0.083	2.11	3.334	84.68
	10	0.120	3.05	3.260	82.80
	40	0.216	5.49	3.068	77.93
	80	0.300	7.62	2.900	73.66
3 1/2" 4.000" (101.6 mm)	5	0.083	2.11	3.834	97.38
	10	0.120	3.05	3.760	95.50
	40	0.226	5.74	3.548	90.12
	80	0.318	8.08	3.364	85.45

TABLE B-4. U.S. IPS (NPS) PIPE-SIZE TABLES (CONTINUED)

Nominal Pipe Size and Real OD	Schedule No.	Wall Thickness in.	Wall Thickness mm	ID in.	ID mm
4" 4.500" (114.3 mm)	5	0.083	2.11	4.334	110.10
	10	0.120	3.05	4.260	108.20
	40	0.237	6.02	4.026	102.30
	80	0.337	8.56	3.826	97.20
5" 5.563" (141.3 mm)	5	0.109	2.77	5.345	135.80
	10	0.134	3.40	5.295	134.50
	40	0.258	6.55	5.047	128.20
	80	0.375	9.53	4.813	122.30
6" 6.625" (168.3 mm)	5	0.109	2.77	6.407	162.70
	10	0.134	3.40	6.357	161.50
	40	0.280	7.11	6.065	154.10
	80	0.432	10.97	5.761	146.30
8" 8.625" (219.1 mm)	5	0.109	2.77	8.407	213.50
	10	0.148	3.76	8.329	211.60
	40	0.322	8.18	7.981	202.70
	80	0.500	12.70	7.625	193.70
10" 10.75" (273.0 mm)	5	0.134	3.40	10.482	266.2
	10	0.165	4.19	10.420	264.7
	40	0.365	9.27	10.020	254.5
	80	0.500	12.70	9.750	247.7
12" 12.75" (323.8 mm)	5	0.156	3.96	12.438	315.9
	10	0.180	4.57	12.390	314.7
	40	0.375	9.53	12.000	304.8
	80	0.500	12.70	11.750	298.5

TABLE B-5. DIN 2448 PIPE TABLE—10.2 to 48.3 mm OD

| OD of pipe, mm Series 1 | 2 | 3 | Normal Wall Thickness mm | \multicolumn{18}{c|}{Other Available Wall Thicknesses (Note: Heavy Walls May Be Special Order)} |

OD Series 1	Series 2	Series 3	Normal Wall Thickness (mm)	1.6	1.8	2	2.3	2.6	2.9	3.2	3.6	4	4.5	5	5.6	6.3	7	8.8	10	11	12.5
10.2			1.6	X	X	X	X	X													
13.5			1.8		X	X	X	X	X	X	X										
	16		1.8		X	X	X	X	X	X	X	X									
17.2			1.8		X	X	X	X	X	X	X	X	X								
	19		2			X	X	X	X	X	X	X	X	X							
	20		2			X	X	X	X	X	X	X	X	X							
21.3			2			X	X	X	X	X	X	X	X	X	X	X					
	25		2			X	X	X	X	X	X	X	X	X	X	X					
		25.4	2			X	X	X	X	X	X	X	X	X	X	X	X				
26.9			2.3			X	X	X	X	X	X	X	X	X	X	X	X				
		30	2.6				X	X	X	X	X	X	X	X	X	X	X				
	31.8		2.6				X	X	X	X	X	X	X	X	X	X	X				
33.7			2.6					X	X	X	X	X	X	X	X	X	X	X			
	38		2.6					X	X	X	X	X	X	X	X	X	X	X	X		
42.4			2.6					X	X	X	X	X	X	X	X	X	X	X	X	X	
		44.5	2.6					X	X	X	X	X	X	X	X	X	X	X	X	X	
48.3			2.6					X	X	X	X	X	X	X	X	X	X	X	X	X	X

TABLE B-6. DIN 2448 PIPE TABLE—51 to 152.4 mm OD

OD of pipe, mm			Normal Wall Thickness mm	Other Available Wall Thicknesses (Note: Heavy Walls May Be Special Order)																		
Series 1	Series 2	Series 3		2.6	2.9	3.2	3.6	4	4.5	5	5.6	6.3	7	8.8	10	11	12.5	14.2	16	17.5	20	22.2	25
	51		2.6	X	X	X	X	X	X	X	X	X	X	X	X	X							
		54	2.6	X	X	X	X	X	X	X	X	X	X	X	X	X	X						
	57		2.9		X	X	X	X	X	X	X	X	X	X	X	X	X	X					
60.3			2.9		X	X	X	X	X	X	X	X	X	X	X	X	X	X	X				
	63.5		2.9		X	X	X	X	X	X	X	X	X	X	X	X	X	X	X				
	70		2.9		X	X	X	X	X	X	X	X	X	X	X	X	X	X	X				
		73	2.9		X	X	X	X	X	X	X	X	X	X	X	X	X	X	X	X			
76.1			2.9		X	X	X	X	X	X	X	X	X	X	X	X	X	X	X	X	X		
		82.5	3.2			X	X	X	X	X	X	X	X	X	X	X	X	X	X	X	X		
88.9			3.2			X	X	X	X	X	X	X	X	X	X	X	X	X	X	X	X	X	
	101.6		3.6				X	X	X	X	X	X	X	X	X	X	X	X	X	X	X	X	X
		108	3.6				X	X	X	X	X	X	X	X	X	X	X	X	X	X	X	X	X
114.3			3.6				X	X	X	X	X	X	X	X	X	X	X	X	X	X	X	X	X
	127		4					X	X	X	X	X	X	X	X	X	X	X	X	X	X	X	X
	133		4					X	X	X	X	X	X	X	X	X	X	X	X	X	X	X	X
139.7			4					X	X	X	X	X	X	X	X	X	X	X	X	X	X	X	X
		152.4	4.5					X	X	X	X	X	X	X	X	X	X	X	X	X	X	X	X

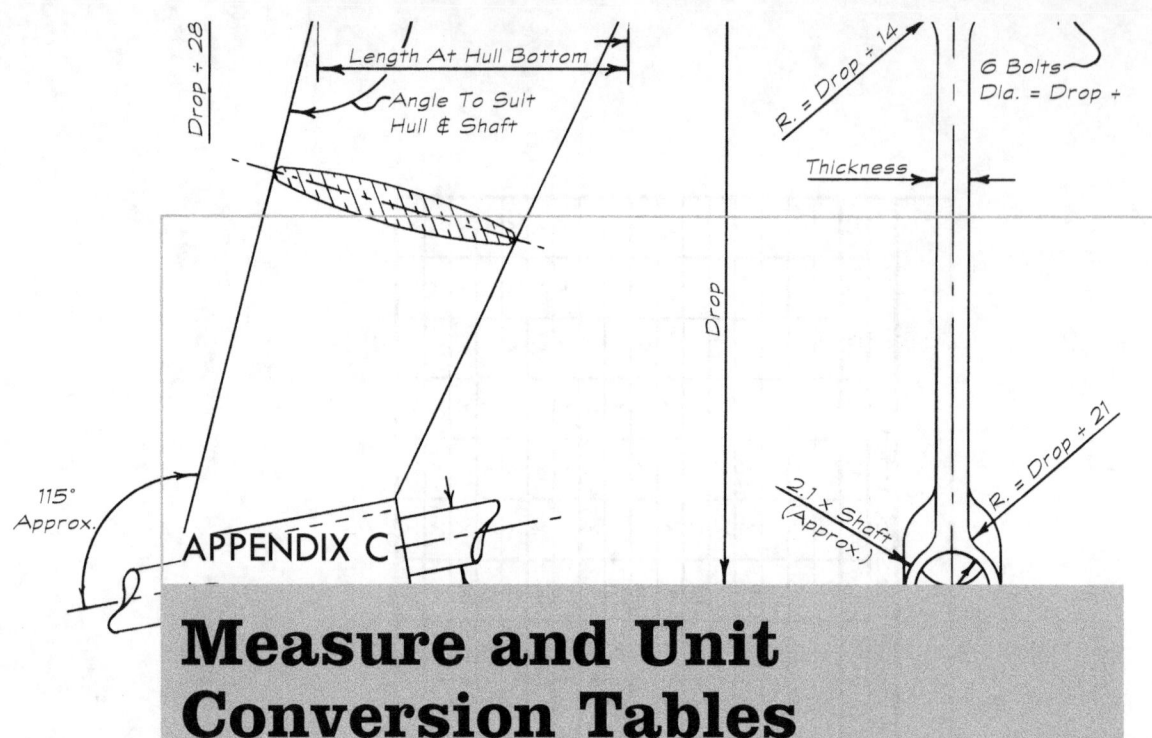

APPENDIX C

Measure and Unit Conversion Tables

LINEAR MEASURE CONVERSIONS

	inches	feet	yards	mm	cm	m	
inches	1	0.08333	0.02778	25.4	2.54	0.0254	inches
feet	12	1	0.33333	304.8	30.48	0.3048	feet
yards	36	3.00000	1	914.4	91.44	0.9144	yards
mm	0.03937	0.00328	0.00109	1	0.1	0.001	mm
cm	0.3937	0.03281	0.01094	10	1	0.01	cm
m	39.37008	3.28084	1.09361	1,000	100	1	m

SQUARE MEASURE (AREA) CONVERSIONS

	sq. in.	sq. ft.	sq. yd	sq. mm	sq. cm	sq. m	
sq. in.	1	0.00694	0.00077	645.16	6.4516	0.000645	sq. in.
sq. ft.	144	1	0.11111	92,903.04	929.0304	0.092903	sq. ft.
sq. yd.	1,296	9.00000	1	836,127.36	8,361.27	0.836127	sq. yd.
sq. mm	0.00155	0.0000108	0.0000012	1	0.01	0.000001	sq. mm
sq. cm	0.155	0.00108	0.00012	100	1	0.0001	sq. cm
sq. m	1,550.00	10.76391	1.19599	1,000,000	10,000	1	sq. m

UNITS OF DENSITY CONVERSIONS

	lb./cu. in.	lb./cu. ft.	g/cu. cm	kg/cu. m	
lb./cu. in.	1	1,728	27.6799	27679.9	lb./cu. in.
lb./cu. ft.	0.0005787	1	0.016018461	16.01846	lb./cu. ft.
g/cu. cm	0.0361273	62.42797	1	1,000	g/cu. cm
kg/cu. m	0.000036127	0.06243	0.001	1	kg/cu. m

CUBIC MEASURE (VOLUME) CONVERSIONS

	cu. in.	cu. ft.	cu. yd.	cu. mm	cu. cm (ml)	cu. m
cu. in.	1	0.00058	0.00002	16,387.10	16.3871	0.0000164
cu. ft.	1,726	1	0.03704	28,316,846.60	28,316.85	0.028317
cu. yd.	46,656	27	1	764,554,858	764,554.86	0.764555
cu. mm	0.000061	0.000000035	0.0000000013	1	0.001	0.000000001
cu. cm (ml)	0.061024	0.00003533	0.00000131	1,000	1	0.000001
cu. m	61,023.74	35.31467	1.30795	1,000,000,000	1,000,000	1
U.S. gal.	231	0.13368	0.00495	3,785,411.784	3,785.41178	0.00379
U.S. oz.	1.80469	0.00104	0.0000387	29,573.5296	29.57353	0.0000296
Imp. gal.	277.41943	0.16054	0.005946	4,546,090	4,546.09	0.00455
Imp. oz.	1.73387	0.001	0.00000372	28,413.0625	28.41306	0.0000284
liters (l)	61.02374	0.03531	0.00131	1,000,000	1,000	0.001
ml (cu. cm)	0.06102	0.0000353	0.000001308	1,000	1	0.000001

	U.S. gal.	U.S. oz.	Imp. gal.	Imp. oz.	liters (l)	ml (cu. cm)
cu. in.	0.00433	0.05541126	0.003605	0.57674	0.01639	16.3871
cu. ft.	7.48052	957.50649	6.228835	996.61367	28.31685	28316.848
cu. yd.	201.97403	25,852.67532	168.178557	26,908.5692	764.55486	764554.858
cu. mm	0.0000002642	0.0000033814	0.0000021997	0.0000351951	0.000001	0.001
cu. cm (ml)	0.000264172	0.03381	0.00021997	0.03520	0.001	1
cu. m	264.17205	33,814.0227	219.96925	35,195.0797	1000	1000000
U.S. gal.	1	128	0.83267	133.22787	3.78541	3785.4118
U.S. oz.	0.007813	1	0.00651	1.04084	0.02957	29.5735
Imp. gal.	1.200950	153.7216	1	160	4.54609	4546.09
Imp. oz.	0.007506	0.96076	0.00625	1	0.02841	28.41306
liters (l)	0.264172	33.81402	0.21997	35.1951	1	1000
ml (cu. cm)	0.000264	0.033814	0.00021997	0.0351951	0.001	1

NOTE: Cubic centimeters (cu. cm) are the same as milliliters (ml)

APPENDIX C

UNITS OF FORCE AND MASS CONVERSIONS

	oz.	lb.	long ton	short ton	metric ton
oz.	1	0.0625	0.000027902	0.00003125	0.0000283495
lb.	16	1	0.000446429	0.0005	0.000453592
long ton	35,840	2,240	1	1.12	1.01605
short ton	32,000	2,000	0.89286	1	0.90718
metric ton	35,273.96	2,204.623	0.98421	1.10231	1
g	0.03527	0.0022046	0.0000009842	0.0000011023	0.000001
Kg	35.27396	2.20462	0.000984207	0.0011023	0.001
N	3.59643	0.22481	0.000100361	0.0001124	0.000101971
kN	3,596.43	224.81	0.100361	0.112405	0.101971
mN	3,596,430	2,24810	100.361	112.405	101.971

	g	Kg	N	kN	mN
oz.	28.34952	0.02835	0.27801	0.000278	0.000000278
lb.	453.59237	0.45359	4.448221	0.004448	0.0000044482
long ton	1,016,046.909	1016.04691	9964.0146	9.964015	0.009964015
short ton	907,184.74	907.18474	8896.4416	8.896442	0.008896442
metric ton	1,000,000	1000	9806.64820	9.806648	0.009806648
g	1	0.001	0.00980665	0.0000098067	0.0000000098
Kg	1000	1	9.80665	0.0098067	0.0000098067
N	101.97	0.10197	1	0.001	0.000001
kN	101971	101.971	1000	1	0.001
mN	101971000	101971	1000000	1000	1

NOTE: Newtons are units of force only. Kilograms, pounds, or ounces of MASS cannot be converted to newtons. Only kilograms, pounds, or ounces of FORCE can be converted to newtons.

UNITS OF PRESSURE AND STRESS CONVERSIONS

	psi	lb./sq. ft.	g/sq. cm (cm water fresh)	kg/sq. cm	kg/sq. m	Pa (N/sq. m)	kPa
psi	1	144	70.307	0.070307	703.0695	6,894.76	6.894757
lb./sq. ft.	0.00694	1	0.4882	0.0004882	4.8824	47.88026	0.04788
g/sq. cm	0.01422	2.0482	1	0.001	10	98.0665	0.0980665
kg/sq. cm	14.22334	2,048.16	1,000	1	10,000	98,066.5	98.0665
kg/sq. m	0.00142	0.2048	0.1	0.0001	1	9.80665	0.009807
Pa (N/sq. m)	0.000145	0.0208854	0.010197	0.000010197	0.10197	1	0.001
kPa	0.14504	20.88543	10.197	0.010197	101.97	1,000	1
mPa (N/sq. mm)	145.03774	20,885.43	10,197	10.197	101,970	1,000,000	1,000
atmosphere	14.69600	2,116.2124	1,033.227	1.033227	10,332.27	101,325	101.325
in. water (fresh)	0.03613	5.2023	2.54	0.00254	25.4	249.079	0.24909
ft. water (fresh)	0.43350	0.0361	30.48	0.03048	304.8	2,989.067	2.98907
m water (fresh)	0.42233	204.8161	100	0.1	1,000	9,806.65	9.80665
hg in.	0.49115	70.7262	34.53155	0.034531	345.3155	3,386.38	3.38638
hg mm	0.01934	2.78446	1.35951	0.00136	13.5951	133.32205	0.13334

UNITS OF PRESSURE AND STRESS CONVERSIONS

	mPa (N/sq. mm)	atmosphere	in. water (fresh)	ft. water (fresh)	m water (fresh)	hg in.	hg mm
psi	0.006895	0.068046	27.679910	2.30666	0.7031	2.0360	51.7149
lb./sq. ft.	0.00004788	0.00047254	0.192221	0.01602	0.0049	0.0141	0.3591
g/sq. cm	0.0000980665	0.00096784	0.393708	0.03281	0.01	0.02896	0.7356
kg/sq. cm	0.0980665	0.967841	393.700790	32.80839	10	28.9591	735.5592
kg/sq. m	0.0000098067	0.0000967841	0.03937	0.00328	0.001	0.002896	0.0736
Pa (N/sq. m)	0.000001	0.000009869	0.004015	0.00033	0.000102	0.0002896	0.00748
kPa	0.001	0.009869	4.014631	0.33455	0.1020	0.294523	7.4809
mPa (N/sq. mm)	1	9.869	4,014.631	334.5526	101.9718	294.523	7,480.88
atmosphere	0.101325	1	406.782	33.8985	10.3323	29.9213	760
in. water (fresh)	0.00024909	0.002458	1	0.083333	0.0254	0.186832	4.4755
ft. water (fresh)	0.002981	0.0294998	12.00000	1	0.3048	0.88267	22.4198
m water (fresh)	0.00981	0.096784	39.37007	3.28084	1	2.8959	73.2229
hg in.	0.00339	13.594	1.132925	0.345323	535.25364	1	25.4
hg mm	0.000133	0.001316	0.53524	0.044603	0.013595	0.03937	1

NOTE: cm water (fresh) is the same as g/sq. cm.

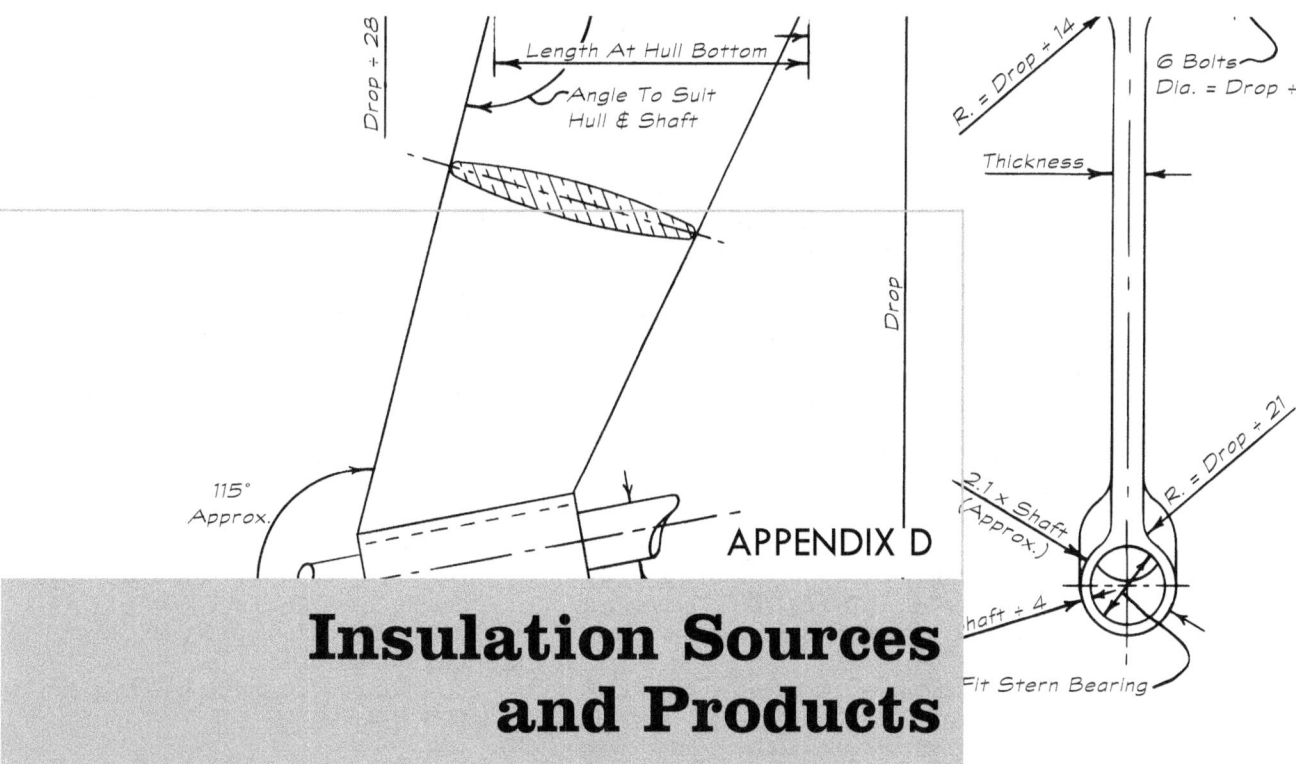

APPENDIX D
Insulation Sources and Products

Some insulation products and sources are

API Distribution www.apidistribution.com

Fiberglass insulation for exhaust piping wrapping, good to 1,000°F (540°C)

GLT Insul-Mat from $\frac{1}{4}$-", $\frac{1}{2}$-", and 1-inch" (6.35, 12.7, and 25.4 mm)

GLT fiberglass cloth, for removable blankets and pipe wraps

Mid-Mountain Materials fiberglass cloth, for lagging and pipe wrapping, turbine blankets

**BNZ Materials, Inc.
www.bnzmaterials.com**

Calcium silicate board and shapes

Marinite P, I, and M BNZ boards (BNZ Tobermorite calcium silicate) to 1,000° F (540°C)

SX85, good to 1,800°F (1,980°C)

Transite HT and Transite 1,000, good to 1,000°F (540°C) (Transite was formerly an asbestos product, but the current product is 100 percent asbestos free.)

**Culimeta Textilglas Technologie GmbH
www.culimeta.com**

Sells complete lagging-wrap kits. Though intended for shoreside installations, these will work on small to midsize marine exhausts.

Foster Products, www.fosterproducts.com

Foster 30-36 and 30-36AF lagging adhesive and coating mastic for sealing the outside of fiberglass and mineral-wool insulation over piping, and so on. It's USCG listed and SOLAS approved.

Figure A-D-1. Wrapping an exhaust pipe (Courtesy Culimeta Textilglas Technologie GmbH & Co.)

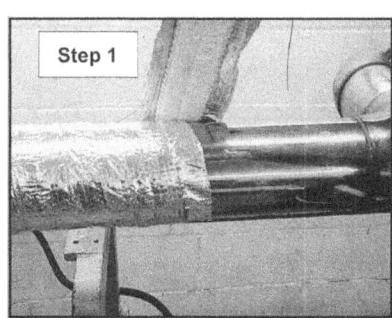

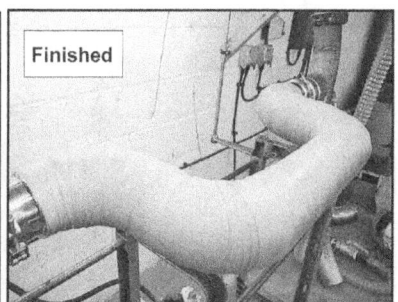

BGF Industries, Inc. www.bgf.com

SilcoSoft, 2,000°F, catalytic converter; heat shields, suitable for exhaust manifold and catalytic converters (2,000°F or 1,090°C)

Techmat 1200F, high-temperature thermal insulation, working temperature 1,000°F (540°C), max 1,200°F (650°C)

Heatshield Products
www.heatshieldproducts.com

Header Wrap

Inferno Wrap, amorphous silica good to a service temperature of about 2,000°F (1,100°C) continuous of 3,000°F (1,650°C) intermittent

Premium exhaust wrap, good to 1,600°F (870°C)

Standard exhaust wrap, good to 1,000°F (540°C)

Truck and automotive exhaust wraps, may be used on smaller diesel engines. Fiberglass, both 1,200°F (650°C) continuous and 2,000°F (1,100°C) intermittent

Firwin Corp. www.firwin.com

Provides a wide assortment of insulation products

Hi-Temp Fabrication
www.hi-tempfab.com

Blankets and wraps

Board and panels

CS-85, good to 1,800°F (980°C)

DuraBoard, high-temperature ceramic fiber boards, good from 2,300° to 3,000°F (1,250° to 1,650°C)

Fiberfrax Durablanket, from 1,400° to 3,000°F (760° to 1650°C)

Mineral wool, from basalt rock and slag, service to 1,500°F (800°C)

Marinite A, good to 1,500°F (800°C)

Marinite I, good to 1,200°F (650°C)

Marinite P, good to 1,700°F (930°C) (and high structural strength)

Super Firetemp, 4-hour fire ratings, good to 2,000°F (1,100°C)

Silex Innovations, Inc.
www.silex.com

Premanufactured insulation blankets and boards; blankets with outer cloth liner, insulation center, and steel-mesh, knitted inner liner, held in place with quilted pins

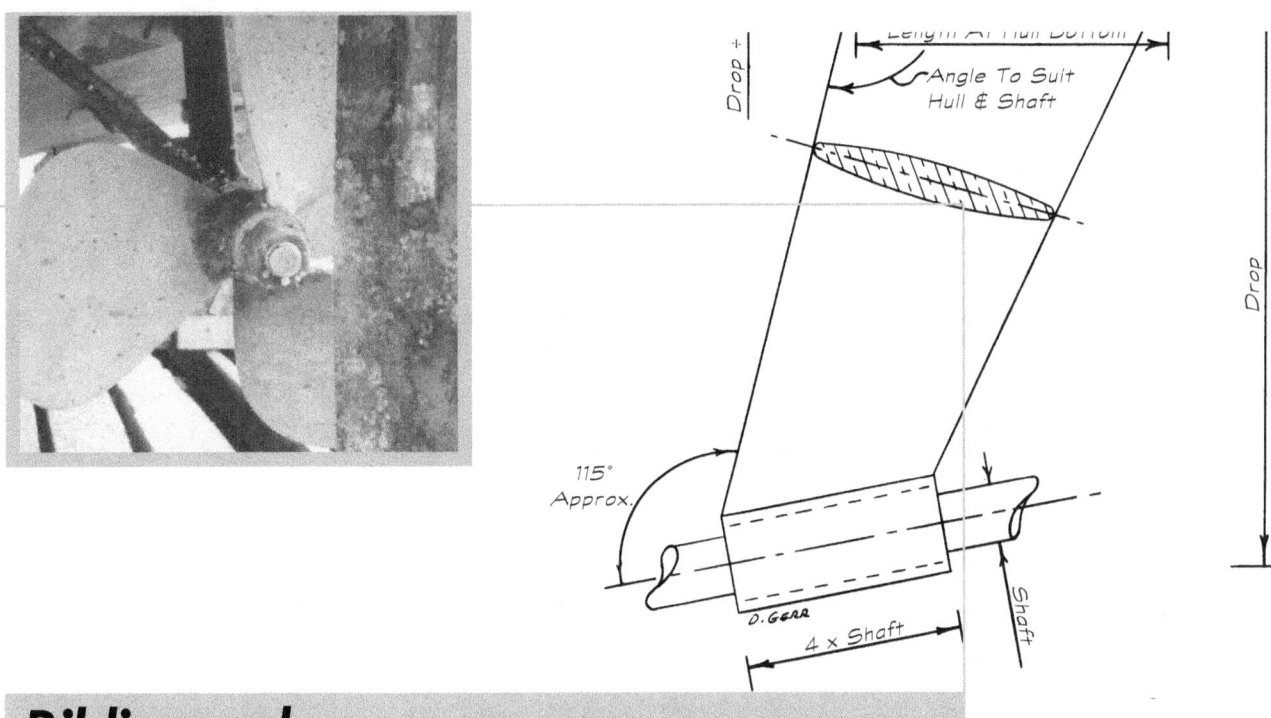

Bibliography

Aluminum Association. *Aluminum Construction Manual: Engineering Data for Aluminum Structures.* New York: Aluminum Association, 1969.

American Boat & Yacht Council (ABYC). *Standards and Recommended Practices for Small Craft.* Annapolis, MD: ABYC, 2007.

American Bureau of Shipping (ABS). *Guide for Building and Classing High-Speed Craft.* Paramus, NJ: ABS, 1991.

———. *Guide for Building and Classing Motor Pleasure Vessels.* Paramus, NJ: ABS, 1986.

———. *Guide for Building and Classing Offshore Racing Yachts.* Paramus, NJ: ABS, 1986.

Breneman, John W. *Strength of Materials.* 3rd ed. New York: McGraw-Hill, 1965.

Brumbugh, James E. *HVAC Fundamentals, Vol. 1. Heating Systems, Furnaces, and Boilers.* 4th ed. Indianapolis, IN: AUDEL, Wiley Publishing, Inc., 2004.

———. *HVAC Fundamentals, Vol. 2. Heating System Components, Gas and Oil Burners, and Automatic Controls.* 4th ed. Indianapolis, IN: AUDEL, Wiley Publishing, Inc., 2004.

———. *HVAC Fundamentals, Vol. 3. Air Conditioning, Heat Pumps, and Distribution Systems.* 4th ed. Indianapolis, IN: AUDEL, Wiley Publishing, Inc., 2004.

Calder, Nigel. *Boatowner's Mechanical and Electrical Manual,* 3rd ed. Camden, ME: International Marine/McGraw-Hill, 2005.

Casey, Don. *Sailboat Electrics Simplified.* Camden, ME: International Marine/McGraw-Hill, 1999.

Caterpillar, Inc. *Marine Engines Application and Installation Guide.* Peoria, IL: Caterpillar, 1998.

———. *Marine Power Systems, Technical.* Peoria, IL: Caterpillar, 1998.

———. *Marine Power Systems, General.* Peoria, IL: Caterpillar, 1998.

Collier, Everett. *The Boatowner's Guide to Corrosion.* Camden, ME: International Marine/McGraw-Hill, 2001.

Cummins Marine. *Naval Architect's Manual.* Charleston, SC: Cummins Marine Division of Cummins Engine Company, Inc., 1997.

Detroit Diesel. *Marine Power, Pleasure Craft.* Detroit, MI: Detroit Diesel, 1994.

DuCane, Peter. *High-Speed Small Craft.* 4th ed., rev. Tuckahoe, NY: J. de Graff, 1973.

Gerr, Dave. *The Nature of Boats: Insights and Esoterica for the Nautically Obsessed.* Camden, ME: International Marine/McGraw-Hill, 1992.

———. *Propeller Handbook: The Complete Reference for Choosing, Installing, and Understanding Boat Propellers.* Camden, ME: International Marine/McGraw-Hill, 1989.

———. *The Elements of Boat Strength for Builders, Designers, and Owners.* Camden, ME: International Marine/McGraw-Hill, 2000.

Goehring, Edward P. *Marine Piping Handbook for Designers-Fitters-Operators.* Cambridge, MD: Cornell Maritime Press, 1944.

BIBLIOGRAPHY

Hatch, G.N. *Creative Naval Architecture*. London: Thomas Reed Publications Limited, 1971.

Fock, Harald. *Fast Fighting Boats 1870–1945: Their Design, Construction, and Use*. Annapolis, MD: Naval Institute Press, 1979.

Fox, Uffa. *Seamanlike Sense in Power Craft*. London: Peter Davies, 1968.

Herreshoff, L. Francis. *Common Sense of Yacht Design*. Jamaica, NY: Caravan-Maritime Books, 1974.

Johnson, Arthur F. *The Design and Construction of Power Workboats*. Cleveland, OH: The Penton Publishing Company, 1920.

Karassik, Igor J., Joseph P. Messina, Paul Cooper, and Charles C. Heald, eds. *Pump Handbook*, 3rd ed. New York: McGraw-Hill, 2001.

Lloyds Register of Shipping. *Rules and Regulations for the Classification of Yachts and Small Craft*. London: Lloyds Register of Shipping, 1983.

Lord, Lindsay. *Naval Architecture of Planing Hulls*. Cambridge, MD: Cornell Maritime Press, 1963.

Lugger/Northern Lights/Alaska Diesel Electric. *Information Binder*, 1997.

Marks, Lionel S. *Marks' Standard Handbook for Mechanical Engineers*, 8th ed. Eugene A. Avallone and Theodore Baumeister III, eds. New York: McGraw-Hill, 1978.

National Fire Protection Association (NFPA). *NFPA 302, Fire Protection Standard for Pleasure and Commercial Motor Craft*, 2004 Edition. Quincy, MA: NFPA, 2004.

Oberg, Erik, Franklin Jones, Henry Ryffel and Holbrook Horton. *Machinery's Handbook*. 24th ed. New York: Industrial Press, 1992.

Osbourne, Alan, ed. *Modern Marine Engineer's Manual, Volumes I and II*. Cambridge, MD: Cornell Maritime Press, 1943.

Pope, J. Edward. *Rules of Thumb for Mechanical Engineers*. Houston, TX: Gulf Publishing Company, 1997.

Sherman, Ed. *Powerboater's Guide to Electrical Systems, Maintenance, Troubleshooting and Improvements*. Camden, ME: International Marine/McGraw-Hill, 2000.

Skene, Norman L. *Elements of Yacht Design*. New York: Kennedy Bros., 1938.

—————. *Skene's Elements of Yacht Design*. 8th ed. Completely rev. and updated by Francis S. Kinney. New York: Dodd, Mead, 1973.

Smith, Carroll. *Caroll Smith's Nuts, Bolts, Fasteners, and Plumbing Handbook*. Osceola, WI: Motorbooks International, 1990.

Traung, Jan-Olan. *Fishing Boats of the World*. Fishing News, 1955.

—————. *Fishing Boats of the Word*. Vol. 2. *Fishing News*, 1960.

—————. *Fishing Boats of the World*. Vol. 3, *Fishing News*, 1967.

U.S. Army. *Operation of Small Boats and Harbor Craft*: Department of the Army Technical Manual TM55-370, June 1950.

Volvo Penta. *Marine Commercial Power, Propulsion, and Auxiliary Engines/Equipment*. Goteborg, Sweden: AB Volvo Penta, 1995/1996.

Warren, Nigel. *Metal Corrosion in Boats*. Camden, ME: International Marine/McGraw-Hill, 1990.

Westerbeke Corporation. *Installation Manual Marine Engines/Generators Diesel and Gasoline, Publication #43268*. Taunton, MA: Westerbeke Corporation, May 2004.

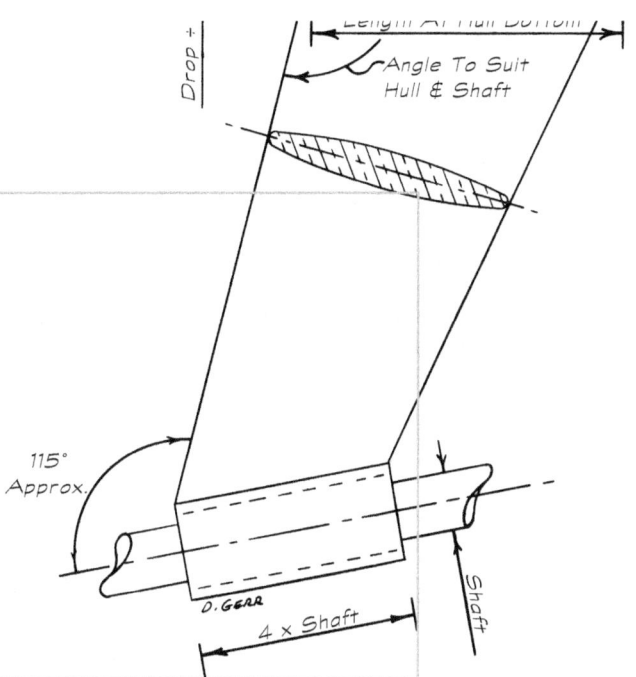

Index

Numbers in **bold** indicate pages with illustrations

ABYC. *See* American Boat & Yacht Council (ABYC) guidelines
accumulator, **316**–17
Actionair, 271
Admiralty-pattern anchor, 332–34, **333**, **375**, 376
aftercoolers, **133**, **136**
air changes per hour, 231–32, 234, 268–69
air-conditioning: capacity, 245; comfort and, 229–30; compressors, 247–48; condensation drain, 245, 249; ducting, 249–**50**; installation, **243**, **244**, 249, 260–61; location of, 249; operation of, 242, 245; power for, 246–47; pump selection, 305; recirculating air, 249; refrigerants, 242; reverse-cycle, 247, 255; seawater cooling circuit, **248**–49; sizing, 245–46, 250; types of air-conditioners, 242–45, **243**, **244**, **248**
air-cooled engines, 128–29
airfoil rudder sections, 170–**72**, 173

air-jacketed dry exhaust system, 153, **158**, 159
Akermann steering, **211**–12
alcohol, 87–88, 93
allowance, 192–93
aluminum bearings, 194
aluminum bronze struts, 21
aluminum fuel piping, 63
aluminum keel cooling components, 133, 134
aluminum rudder stock, 186, 187–88, 195
aluminum sheeting for insulation, 151–**52**
aluminum-strap hold-downs, 66–**68**
aluminum struts, 21, 22
aluminum tanks, **70**–71, 83, 84, **85**, 96, 315, 326–27
American Boat & Yacht Council (ABYC) guidelines, xxiii; anchor and rode selection, 365; anchor rode specifications, 369–70; backfire flame mesh, 74; bilge systems, 290; CNG guidelines, 270; CO information, 126, 241; foam-encapsulated tanks, 71; fuel-hose clamps, 61–62; fuel systems, 46, 47, 50; fuel-system valves, 59, 60; fuel-tank

fill pipes, 50, **77**; fuel-tank labels, 81–82; fuel-tank materials, 83, 84, 87; fuel-tank vents, 50, 73, **77**; gasoline boats, ventilation of, 272; ISO standards compared to, 50; LPG guidelines, 253, 270; oxygen-depletion sensor, 255; propeller shafts, 10–11; rudder palms, 215; seacocks, 278–79, 280–**82**; tank baffles, 80; tank pressure ratings, 82
American Bureau of Shipping (ABS), 289, 290, 202, 203, 294, 295, xxiii
American National Standards Institute (ANSI), 47
American Wire Gauge, 65, 373, 374–75
amorphous silica insulation, 150
anchor bend, **362**
Anchoring, Mooring, and Strong Points (ABYC), 365, 369
anchoring systems: anchor parts, **333**; anchor selection and recommendations, 346–47, 365–66; anchor terminology, 346; anchor types, 332–**46**; components of, 332;

INDEX

evaluation of, 331; launch and retrieval, 335–36, **375**, **376–81**; sizing, 331–32
anchor pendant, 383–84
anchor rode: attaching rope to chain, 361–**62**; chain, 348–53, **349**, **350**; chain fittings, **353–58**, 367, 369; chain leader, 348; length, 368; rope, 348, 358–59, 361, **362**; rope chafe, 359–**60**; scope, 368; sizing, 366–70; snubbing up, **362**, 383–**85**; storage, **362–63**, 381–83, **382**, **384**; wire, 363–64
anchor rollers, 376–80, **377**, **378**, **379**
anchor warp, 358
antifreeze, 129, 130
antisiphon device, **52**
Aquadrive CVs, 37, 39
Aquadrive system, **35**, 40–41
Aqualoy rudder stock, 186, 187, 195
areas of plane figures, calculating, **386–87**
articulated flap rudders, 219, 222, 223–28, **224**, **225**, **226**
aspect ratio, 164, 165, 177–**78**, 187–88
Atlantic Pump and Equipment Company, 17
atmospheric pressure, 102
autopilots, 210
axial-flow pumps, **304**

Babbit: Drivesaver disk, 40
Babbitt: bearing metal, 190
backfire flame mesh, 74
backing blocks and plates, 22–**23**
back pressure, **101**–2, 110, 119
backup steering system, 208–**9**
baffles, tank, **80**, 315
ball valves, **59**, **60**
Barke rudder, 223, 226
barndoor rudder, **176**
barometer, 102
battery compartment, ventilation for, 270

BBB chain, **350**, 366–67, 370–71
Becker rudder, 223, 226
bellows, flexible, 142, **144**, **145**, **147–48**, 149
bending moment, 184–85, 188
bilge blower, 275. *See also* gasoline engines: ventilation of gasoline boats
bilge systems: components of, 288; discharge line, 297; float switches, **297**; hose clamps, 296; layout, 290, **291**; piping diameter, 290, 292, 295; piping material, 292, 296; pump alarms, 296–97; pump capacity, 289–90, 292–94; pump-operation counter, 297; pumps, electric, 289, 290, 305; pumps, manual, 288–89, 290, 302–**3**, 305; pumps, submersible, 290, 295–**96**; pump selection, 305, 308; purpose of, 288; strum box, **288**–89, **295**, 303; vented loop, 294–**95**
black water: discharge lines, 287, 326; no-discharge zones, 320, 326, 329; pumps, 305, **326**; tanks, 320, 324, 326–**27**
bladder tanks, 95–**96**
Blakes Lavac head, **322**–25, 328
blowers and ducts, 237–40, **238**, **239**, 263–64, 265–**66**, 272–75, **274**
blower timer switch, 269
bonding system, **64**–65
bower anchor, 346–47, 365–66
box keel cooler, 139, **140**
brass, 22, 135
Brave Class patrol boat, 183
bronze, 22
Bruce anchor, 340, 342, **343**, **344**, 366
Btu (British thermal unit), 136, 245
Bugel anchor, 344, **345**
bulbous flap rudder, **224**
bulkhead heaters, **255**–56
bulkheads: exhaust lines and, 106, 107; stove and heater installation, 254, 255

Bulwagga anchor, 345, **346**
butt, 314

cabin heating. *See* heating, cabin
cable, 352, 358
cable-and-wheel steering, **200**–202
cable-laid rope, 358
calcium silicate insulation, 150
Calder, Nigel, 369
calorifiers, 318
canoe-sterned boats, 30–**31**
Cape Dory 40, 119, **123**, **124**
carbon composite rudder stock, 186, 187–88, 195
carbon dioxide, 241, 249
carbon dioxide fire extinguishers, 300, 301
carbon monoxide (CO), 125–26, 241, 249
Carbon Monoxide Detection System (ABYC), 126
carburators, 49
Cardan shaft/joints, **37**
Carrick bend, **368**
catamaran, power, 170
cathead, **375**, 376
cavitation, 3, 5–6
cedar bucket, 327, 329
Centek VernaSep muffler, **126**
center of buoyancy, 71–**72**
centrifugal pumps, 249, **304**, 305, **313**
ceramic fiber boards, 150
CFR. *See* Code of Federal Regulations (CFR)
chain: attaching rope to, 361–**62**; characteristics, 348; fittings, **353–58**, 367, 369; lengths, 352; rode sizing, 366–67, 369–70; snubbing up, **362**, 383–**85**; stainless steel, 352–53; types and grades, 348–52, **349**, **350**; weight of, 370–71
chain locker, 381–83, **382**, **384**
chain snubber, **362**, 384–**85**
chain stopper, 383, **384**, 385
Chapman's Piloting, Seamanship, and Small Boat Handling, 369
chilled-water air-conditioner, 243

chlorotetrafluoroethane (FE-241) fire extinguishers, 300–301
chocks, 359–61, **360**
chord, 163, **164**
circle circumference formula, 134
clamshell vent, **241**
claw anchors, 340, 342, **343**, **344**, 346–47, 366
cleats, 359–61, **360**
closed cooling. *See* heat exchangers
CNG (compressed natural gas), **270**–71
coal stoves and heaters, **253–54**
cockabill, 346
Code of Federal Regulations (CFR), xxiii; backfire flame mesh, 74; bilge-system requirements, 289–90, 292, 293, 294; carburetors, 49; CNG, 270; Commercial vs. Yacht, 46; diaphragm tanks, 58; exhaust system materials, 107; fire main system, 298; foam-encapsulated tanks, **70**–71; fuel-fill spill compliance, 79; fuel hose and tubing, 62, 63; fuel-hose clamps, 61–62, **63**; fuel systems, 46, 47; fuel-system valves, 59, 60; fuel-tank labels, 81–82; fuel-tank vents, 73; gasoline boats, ventilation of, 272–75; gasoline fuel pumps, 58; LPG, 253, 270; seacocks, 279, 285; tank baffles, 80; tank materials, 85–86; tank pressure ratings, 82; Yacht vs. Commercial, 46
coefficient of lift, 180, 182, 183
Cole Marine Distributing, 239
commercial bronze struts, 21, 22
common rail manifolds, **55**–57
compressed natural gas (CNG), **270**–71
compressors, 247–48
condensation, **149**, 245, 249
conduit-cable steering, **210**–11

constant-velocity (CV) joints, **35**, 36, 37, 39–40
CON-VEL CV joint, **35**
conversion tables, 93, 396–400
converters, ventilation for, 269–70
cooler-freezers, portable, 250, 251
copper exhaust-system parts, 104
copper keel cooling components, 133, 134, 135, 137
copper-nickle exhaust-system parts, 104
copper-nickle keel cooling components, 133, 134, 135, 137
copper-nickle tanks, 84
copper-silicon tanks, 84
copper tanks, 83, 84
copper tubing, 62, 64
corrosion: dezincification, 22, 135; float switches, 297; fuel tanks, 68–69, 78, 81, 84, 85, 96; raw-water cooling, 129, 130; wet exhaust systems, 104–5, 127; zinc anodes, 22, 127, 285, **287**
couplings and keyways, propeller-shaft, **15–17**
course keeping principles and characteristics, 226–27
cowl vent, **229**, **230**, 232, **237**, 264–**65**
CQR plow anchor, 340, 341, **342**, 366
crewboat exhaust installation, 159–**60**
Cummins engines, 51, 52
Cutless bearing, **12**, 22, 42
CV (constant-velocity) joints, **35**, 36, 37, 39–40

Danforth, Bill, 336
Danforth-type anchors, 336–**40**, 346–47, 366
decimal exponents, xix–xx
deck washdown plumbing system, 309–**13**
Deflector Rudder, **224**, **225**, 226
defrosters, electric, 256
Delta anchor, 340, **342**, 346–47, 366, 376

Delta-T Systems, 239, 265–**66**, 271
density conversion table, 396
Detroit Diesel engine-vent sizing, 265
devil's claw chain hook, **362**, 384–**85**
dezincification, 22, 135
D'Hone Special anchor, 336, 347, 366
diaphragm pumps, 302–**3**, 305, **323**, 324
diesel engines: alcohol fuel and, 88; compartment ventilation, 264, 265, 269; exhaust system metals and corrosion, 104, 105; fuel consumption rate, 58, 83, 90–92, **91**; fuel-line diameter, 60; "loiter" engine, 34; thermostats, 129
diesel fuel: characteristics, 93; filters, 54; fire from, **46**, 60–61; gasoline compared to, 46; hot fuel, 58–**59**; polishing, 54; rubber and, 65; weight of, 68, 69, 71
diesel-fueled heating, **255**–60, 262
diesel fuel systems: bypass feed lines, **54–55**; common-rail manifolds, **55**–57; day-tank piping arrangement, 53–**55**; distribution manifold, **53**; fill pipe, 75–76; filters, 48, 49, **59**; fuel flow rate, 48; fuel heating elements, 59; fuel-line diameter, 60; grounding, **64**–65; oil coolers, 58–**59**; piping arrangements, 50–57, **51**, **53**, **55**, **56**; return lines, 50, **51**, 52, **54–55**, 60; standards and regulations, 46–47; tank materials, 83, 85, 86, 89, 96; tank opening and penetrations, 73; tanks, number of, 47. *See also* fuel systems
direct cooling, 129–**30**

INDEX

direct-drop toilets, 327–28
direct electric heating, 255
direct-expansion air-conditioner, 242–45, **243**, **244**
discharge lines, 287, 297, 326
displacement hulls: boat behavior in turns, **180**–81; helm speed, 201; keel cooling, **139**, 141; measures of, 365, 366; propeller aperture, 25–27, **26**; propeller blade area, 4; reduction gear, 32, 35; rudder, 168–69, 179; standpipe exhaust system, **116–17**; sternway calculation, 188
dorade box, **229**
dory propeller, 37, **38**
double-braid rope, 358, 359
double-ended boats, 30–**31**
double fixed-geometry high-lift rudder, 224–**26**, 228
double-plate rudders, 176
Dow Chemical VacuPanel, 253
down-angle gear, 27–28
Drivesaver disk, **40**
drivetrains, 1. *See also specific components*
drystack exhaust systems: advantages of, 128; air-jacketed, 153, **158**, 159; back pressure, 101; basic system, 142–**44**; bellows, flexible, 142, **144**, **145**, **147–48**, 149; bulkhead clearances, 106; clamps and hangers, 144–**46**; condensation drain, **149**; expansion and contraction, 143–**48**; hose, **148**; keeping water out, **144**, **149**; lagging, **149–52**; mixed-exhaust installations, 119, **120–21**, 155, 159–**60**; multiple-exhaust stacks, 153, **157**; painting, 152–53; pipe specifications, 143–44; schooner exhaust system, 119, **120–21**; slip joint, 143, **144**; support strut, **158**, 159; temperatures around, 127, 142, 144–45,
150–51; trunk, 151–**52**, 153, **154**, **155**, **156**; water-jacketed, 153, 155, **157**, 159; wet vs. dry, 161–62
dry suction head, 304
Du Crane, Peter, 183

Educational Information about Carbon Monoxide (ABYC), 126, 241
ejector ventilation, 153, **154**, **155**, **156**
Electric Bilge Pumps Operating Under 50 Volts (ABYC), 290
electric defrosters, 256
electric heating, 255
electric-powered ventilation, 237–40, **238**, **239**
electric-powered windlasses, 372–73
electric systems, xxii
The Elements of Boat Strength (Gerr), 45
endplate, 166
engine: carburetors, 49; compartment ventilation, 263–69, **265**, **266**, **267**, 270; cooling water, excess, 117–19, **118**; fire dampers for compartment ventilation, **271**; heat from, 128; keeping water out, 103, 105; operating temperatures, 129. *See also* diesel engines; gasoline engines
engine bed, **42**–45
engine cooling systems: air-cooled engines, 128–29; failures, 128; heat exchangers, **130–31**, **132**; heat generated by engine, 128; keel cooling, 131–41, **132**, **133**, **136**, **139**, **140**; operating temperatures, 129; raw-water cooling, 129–**30**; sharing, 129; thermostats, 129
engine-heat heaters, 256
engine installation: angle of, 27–28, 39–40; metal hulls,
36–**37**; mounts, engine, **35–37**, 40; thrust load calculation, 36; transmission geometry, 32–35, **33**, **34**
engine noise, 37, 77
English units, xx
Environmental Protection Agency (EPA), 74
epoxy, G-10 or FR-4, 67
ethanol, 87–89
exhaust gas: danger from, 249, 260; diesel-fueled heating, 259–60; temperatures, 142, 259
exhaust manifolds, 104–5, 151
exhaust riser: back pressure measurement, **101**; dry exhaust, **104**, 127; lagging (insulation), 104, 127; water-injection, **104**; water-jacketed, **103**–4, 127; wet exhaust, **101**, **103**–4, 127
exhaust systems. *See* drystack exhaust systems; wet exhaust systems
exhaust vents, 240, 266
express cruiser design, **72**

Fatso Pet stoves, 254
faucets, 321
FE-227 (heptafluoropropane) fire extinguishers, 301
FE-241 (chlorotetrafluoroethane) fire extinguishers, 300–301
Fernstrum keel coolers, 139
ferry ventilation system, 266, **267**
fiberglass exhaust-line components, 105–6, 107, 127
fiberglass fuel tanks, 70, 85–86, 87–89
fiberglass insulation, **150–51**
fiberglass-reinforced plastic (FRP) hulls: engine bed, **44**, 45; epoxy, G-10 or FR-4, 67; strength of, 22; strut installation and, 22–**23**
fiberglass rudders, 176–**77**
fiberglass water tanks, 315

INDEX

fire dampers, **271**
fire extinguishers, 299–301
fire main system, 290, **291**, 297–**98**
fire-resistant paint, 152
fisherman anchor, 332–**35**, **336**, 376
fishtail rudders, **219**–23, 226–27
fixed-geometry high-lift rudders. *See* fishtail rudders
flanged-corner tank construction, **81**
flapper, **100**, 105, 127
flash heaters, 318
flat-plate rudder, metal, 174–**75**, **222**–23
flexible-impeller pumps, **303**, 305
float switches, **297**
flooding rate from hull damage, 292–93
FloScan fuel-flow meter, 83
flow velocity calculations, 136–38
FM-200 (heptafluoropropane) fire extinguishers, 301
foam-core fiberglass rudders, 176–**77**
foam-encapsulated tanks, **70**–71
foil-thickness form dimensions, 173–74
foot pumps, 318
force and mass conversion table, 398
forepeak, 241
Fortress anchor, 336–37, 339–**40**, 346–47, 366
FR-4 epoxy, 67
free-surface effect, 96–99
freezers, 251, 252–53
frequency testing, 5–6
fresh water, 314
freshwater systems: accumulator, **316**–17; delivery piping, 318–**19**; faucets, 321; filters, 318–**19**; hot-water heaters, 317–18; leaks in, 316; plastic-tube piping, 320–**21**; pressure regulator, 317; pump capacity, 317; pump location, 317; pump selection, 305; requirements, 316; supply piping, **316**–18; tanks, 315–16; watermakers, 315
friction head, 308–9, 313
fuel/air separator, 74, **75**
fuel consumption rate, 58, 83, 90–92, **91**
fuel oil characteristics, 93
fuel spills, 52, 57, 73, 74–**75**, 76, **78**, **79**
fuel systems: access to, **47**, 50; antisiphon protection, **52**; clearances, 50; fill openings, 50; filters, 47–50, **48**, 58, **59**; fuel-line diameter, 60; fuel-line rupture, 57; grounding, **64**–65; hose and tubing, **61**, 62–64; hose connectors and clamps, 61–**62**, **63**; piping arrangements, 47, 50–57, **51**, **53**, **54**, **55**, **56**; pressure testing, 83; pumps, fuel-transfer, 57–58, 305, 313; rubber and, 65; shutoff valves, 60–61; standards and regulations, 46–47; valves, **59**–61. *See also* diesel fuel systems; gasoline fuel systems
fuel tanks: backfire flame mesh, 74; baffles, **80**; bonding system, connection to, **64**–65; capacity calculations, 92–**95**; clean-out openings, 73; common-rail manifold take-off pipe, **56**; construction, 80–**81**; corrosion, 68–69, 78, 81, 84, 85, 96; cushioning and padding, 68–**69**; diaphragm tanks, 58; drains, 73; fill manifold, 58; fill pipes, 50, 75–**78**; foam-encapsulated, **70**–71; grounding, **64**–65; hold-downs, 66–**68**; installation, 66–**68**, 69; installation, twin tanks, **64**; integral tanks, 86; keeping dry, 78; labels, 81–**82**; level sensors and gauges, 57, 58, 83, 96; location, 69, 71–**72**; materials for, 83–89, 95–**96**; multiple tank systems, 58; number of, 47; openings and penetrations, location of, 73; pressure testing and ratings, 82–83; pump for moving fuel between, 58; shared walls with water tanks, 80; sounding stick use, 83, 86; stability and free-surface effect, 96–99; structural support from, 83; take-off pipe, 78; take-off pipe filter, 78; vent collection tank, 74–75, **76**; vents, 50, 73–75, **77**, 275; vent spill prevention, 74–**75**; weight of fuel and tank, 68, 69, 71; welded-on lugs, 69

G-10 epoxy, 67
galvanic isolation, 280
galvanized tanks, 83
gaskets, 65
gasoline: characteristics, 93; diesel compared to, 46; rubber and, 65; weight of, 68, 69
Gasoline and Propane Gas Detection Systems (ABYC), 270
gasoline engines: alcohol fuel and, 88; exhaust system metals and corrosion, 104, 105; fuel consumption rate, 83, 90, 91–92; fuel-line diameter, 60; ventilation of gasoline boats, 264, 269, 270, 272–**77**; waterlift mufflers and, 114
gasoline fuel systems: antisiphon protection, **52**; diaphragm tanks, 58; fill pipe, 75; filters, 48–49; fuel-fill spill compliance, **79**; fuel flow rate, 48–49; fuel-line diameter, 60; grounding, **64**–65; piping arrangements, 50, **51**;

INDEX

pumps, fuel, 58; pumps, fuel-transfer, 58; standards and regulations, 46–47; tank materials, 83, 86, 87–89, 96; tank opening and penetrations, 73; tanks, number of, 47; tank vents, 74, 275; ventilation of gasoline boats, 272–**77**. *See also* fuel systems
Gasoline Fuel Systems (ABYC), 272
gas turbine gear geometry, 34
gate valves, 59
gauge pressure, 102
gear geometry, 32–35, **33**, **34**
gear pumps, 57
generator: cooling systems, sharing, 129; fuel consumption, 92; sizing, 247; ventilation requirements, 266
geometric aspect ratio, 164
Gerr 34 Sportsfisherman, **108**
Gianneschi & Ramacciotti blowers, 239, 265
Globe Drivesaver disk, 40
globe valves, 59–60
GM (metacentric height), 97–99
grapnel anchor, 343, **344**, 346
gravity tanks for stoves, 255
gravity toilets, 327–28
Gray, Lysle, 86
gray water: discharge lines, 287; drains, 319–20; pumps, 305; tanks, 320
Greenheck Fan Corporation, 271
Groco: hull strainers, **282**; seacocks, **279**, **280**
grounding skeg, **25**
Guardian anchor, 336–37, 339–40, 346–47, 366
gudgeons and pintles, 195

Hale, Tom, 87
half-cowl side vents, 264–**65**
Halocarbon fire extinguishers, 301
Halon fire extinguishers, 300, 301
Halyard water-separator exhaust, 124–**25**, 127
Harrison patent rudder, **218**

Hastelloy C exhaust-system parts, 104, 107, 116
hatches, 235–**36**, 240–41
hawseholes, 380
hawsepipes, 335–36, **380–81**
hawser-laid rope, 358
head (marine toilet): Blakes Lavac head, **322**–25, 328; diaphragm pumps, **323**, 324; fresh water for flushing, 328–29; manufacturers, 322; marine sanitation devices (MSDs), 329–30; odor control, 323, 324, **325**, **326**; plumbing installation, **323**, **325**–26; pump to a dry bowl, 323–24; push-button flush, 325; types of, 327–30; water usage, 324
head (pumps), 306; friction, 308–9, 313; pressure, 308; static, **306**–8, 313; total apparent, 309–11, **310**; velocity, 308
heat exchangers: boat speed comparison between keel-cooled and, 141; inspection and maintenance, 127; operation and installation, **130**–**31**, **132**; water-jacketed dry exhaust system and, 155; zinc anodes, 127
heating, cabin: capacity requirements, 260; installation, 260–61; reverse-cycle air-conditioning, 247, 255; types of heaters, 252–**59**; ventilation for, 262
helm limit, 200
helm speed, 201–2
heptafluoropropane fire extinguishers, 301
Herreshoff, Nathanael, 333
Herreshoff anchor, 333–**35**, 365–66
HFC-227 (heptafluoropropane) fire extinguishers, 301
high-lift rudders, **219**–28
High Speed Small Craft (Du Cane), 183
holding-plate refrigeration systems, 251–**52**

holding tanks, 320, 324, 326–**27**
Hooke's joints, **37**
hose, tubing, and pipe: bilge systems, 290, 292, 295, 296; flow speeds, 311–12; freshwater systems, 320–**21**; friction head, 308–9; fuel systems, **61**, 62–64; head installation, **325**–26; pipe thread standards, 390–91; pressure drop, 313; standards and schedules, 388–90, 392–95
hose connectors and clamps: bilge systems, 296; fuel systems, 61–62, **63**; hose-to-pipe connections, **391**; seacocks, 282; wet exhaust systems, **106**, 107–**8**
hot-air heating systems, **256–57**
hot-water heaters, 317–18
hot-water heating systems, **258–59**, 262
hull damage, flooding rate from, 292–93
hull design: boat behavior in turns and, **180–81**; rudder and, 164–**65**. *See also* displacement hulls; planing hulls
hull strainers, **282**
humidity, 242, 245, 249
hydraulic steering, **202**–8
hydraulic windlasses, 373
hydronic heaters, **258–59**, 262

icebox conversions, 251–52
idle bypass line, 119, **123**, **124**
Ilona, 381
Imagine, 221, **241**, 379, 380, 382, 383
impeller pumps, **303**, 305
impellers, 127
imperial units, xx
Imtra bladder tanks, 95
inboard rudder, 165, 166
Inconel exhaust-system parts, 104, 107, 116, 127
indirect cooling. *See* heat exchangers
instant hot-water heaters, 318

410

INDEX

insulation: lagging, 104, 127, **149–52**; materials for, **150–51**, 253; for refrigerators and freezers, 253
intercoolers, 136
intermediate-speed-section rudder, **172**–73
International Paint, International Marine Coatings, 152
International Paint, International Protective Coatings, 152
International Standards Organization (ISO) standards, xxiii; ABYC guidelines compared to, 50; bilge-pump requirements, 293; fuel systems, 46–47, 50; pipe designations, 390
International System of Units (SI units system), xx
Intertherm 50 paint, 152
intumescent paint, 152
inverters, ventilation for, 269–70
iron hose clamps, 107–**8**
iron pipe size (IPS) schedule, 388
iron tanks, 83
ISO. *See* International Standards Organization (ISO) standards
isopropyl alcohol, 87–88

Jabsco pump, **313**
jackshaft, **35**, **37**
Jacuzzi whirlpool, 314, xxi, xxii
Jastram rudders, 226
Jefa Rudder and Steering, 187–88
joker-valve toilets, 328

kedge anchor, 332, 346, 347, 365–66
keel cooling: aftercoolers, **133**, **136**; boat speed comparison between heat exchanger and, 141; box keels, 139, **140**; drag, appendage, **139**, 141; external tubing, 132, 133–35; fairing, **139**; flow speed, increasing, 139; flow velocity and tube length, 136–38; intercoolers, 136; jacket water aftercooled, **133**; length, reducing, 138; manufactured, 139–41, **140**; materials for, 133, 134; operation and installation, 131–**32**, 135–**36**, **139**; required surface area, 133, 134; sea strainers, 141; tank or shell, 132, **133**; water pump, 132
kerosene, 93
kerosene heaters, 255–56
keyways and couplings, propeller-shaft, **15**–**17**
kick-up rudder, **166**, 179
kinetic pumps, **304**, **313**
Kingfisher, 71, **72**, 97
Kitchen, John G. A., 216
Kitchen rudder, 216–18, 219, **219**, 228
Kolstrand Marine Supply, 363
Kool Kat, 246, 247, 248, 250
Kort nozzle rudder, 218–**19**

lagging (insulation): dry exhaust systems, **149–52**; exhaust riser, 104, 127; materials for, **150–51**
lapped-corner tank construction, **81**
lazarettes, 241
LectraSan, 329
Lifeguard fuel/air separator (Racor), 74, **75**
lift coefficient, 180, 182, 183
lignum vitae, 190
Lipsitt, Harry, 84
liquid volume conversion table, 93
liquified petroleum gas. *See* LPG (liquified petroleum gas)
lobsterboats, 25–27, **26**, 107
lockers, **241**
"loiter" engine, 34
longitudinal center of buoyancy, 71–72
LPG (liquified petroleum gas): ABYC guidelines, 270; heating systems, 253; ventilation for storage locker, **270**–71; water heaters, 318

Luke anchor, 335, **336**, 346–47, 365–66
lunch hook, 346–47, 365–66
Lunenburg Foundry, 254

macerator pumps, **326**
macerator-pump toilets, 328
MacLear, Frank, 219–20
MacLear and Harris, Inc., 220, xxi–xxiii
MacLear Thistle rudder, **219**–22, 223, 228
magnetic-drive centrifugal pumps, 249
make-up air, 240, 249
malleable iron hose clamps, 107–**8**
maneuvering principles and characteristics, 227
manganese bronze struts, 21, 22
manifolds: common-rail, **55**–57; exhaust, 104–5, 151
manometer, **101**, 102
Manson anchors, 336, 344, 347, 366
Marelon seacocks, 278, **279**, **284**, 285
Marine Compressed Natural Gas (CNG) Systems (ABYC), 270
marine sanitation devices (MSDs), 329–30
Marinite board, 151–**52**
mass calculation, 183
mass conversion table, 398
mean chord, 163, **164**
measure conversion tables, 396, 397
mechanical systems, xxi–xxiii
mercury, 297
Merriman-Herreshoff anchor, 334–**35**
metacentric height (GM), 97–99
metal hulls: corrosion, 297; engine installation, 36–**37**; engine noise, 37; exhaust piping, 107; galvanic isolation, 280; keel cooling, 132, **133**, 139; sea chest, **284**–**86**; seacocks, 280; strut construction for, 23–**24**; through-hulls, 278

411

INDEX

metal rudders, 174–**75**, 176, 185, **222**–23
metal tanks: construction, 80–**81**; corrosion, 68–69, 78, 81, 84, 85; foam-encapsulated, **70**–71; keeping dry, 78; regulations on, 86; welded-on lugs, 69. *See also specific metals*
methanol, 87–88
metric units, xx
Miami boat show, 229–30
mineral wool, 150
Monel exhaust-system parts, 104
Monel tanks, 83, 84, 315
motoryacht design, **72**
muff coupling, **16**
mufflers: waterlift mufflers, 109–14, **110**, **111**, **115**–16, **125**, 127; water-separator mufflers, 124–**25**, **126**, 128; wet exhaust systems, **100**, 108
multihull sailboats, 173
mushroom vent, 232, **234**, **236**, 240–41

nacelles, underwater, 123, **124**
NASA, 171
National Advisory Committee for Aeronautics (NACA) airfoil sections, **171**
National Fire Protection Agency (NFPA), xxiii; fuel system regulations, 46; fuel-system valves, 60; gravity tanks for stoves, 255; LPG heating systems, 253
Nauta bladder tanks, 95
Navigator Stove, 254
navy stockless anchors, 335–36, **337**, 366
Neoprene, 65, 68–**69**
Neville, Charles, 223
NFPA. *See* National Fire Protection Agency (NFPA)
Nicholson, Charles, 333
nickle-copper exhaust-system parts, 104
nickle-copper tanks, 84
Nicro-Fico vents, 236, **241**

Nigel Calder's Cruising Handbook (Calder), 369
no-discharge zones, 320, 326, 329
nominal pipe size (NPS) schedule, 388
Northill anchor, 342–43, **344**
North Sea exhaust system, 114–16, **115**

Oberdorfer pumps, **298**
oil, 93, 128
oil coolers, 58–**59**
outboard rudder, 165, **166**, **176**, 179
oxygen-depletion sensor, 255

packing material, 40, 41, 193
paint: for drystack exhaust systems, 152–53; keel cooling and, 133, 134
parabolic-section rudder, **172**–73
passenger compartments: air conditioning. *see* air-conditioning; ventilation of, 231–41, **233**, **234**, **235**, **236**, **237**
patent anchors, 332
Pekney, Robert E., 343
Pekney anchor, 343
Pennel bladder tanks, 95
permeability, 240, 249, 275
PEX tubing, 320–**21**
phosphor bronze struts, 21
Pilgrim nut, 17
pillow blocks, **14**
pintles and gudgeons, 195
pipe. *See* hose, tubing, and pipe
pipe thread standards, 390–91
piston pumps, 302, 305
planing hulls: boat behavior in turns, **180**–81; coefficient of lift, 183; engine and shaft installation, 27–28; fuel tank hold-downs, 66; fuel tank location, 71, **72**; helm speed, 201; keel cooling, 141; propeller blade area, 4; rudder, 165, **179**, **198**; rudder safety factor, 185; rudder sizing, 168, 169–70; rudder stock

angle, **198**; sternway calculation, 188
plastic bearing material, 190, **191**, 192–93, 194, 196
plastic pipe, 296
plastic tanks, 315, **327**
plastic-tube piping, 320–**21**
plow-type anchors, 340, 341, **342**, 346–47
plunger pumps, 302, 305
plunger-pump toilets, 328
polyethylene tanks, 86–87
POR-15, Inc., 152
Porta Potti, 327, 330
positive-displacement pumps, 302–**4**, 307, 313
powerboats: exhaust tubing glassed to transom, **107**; helm speed, 201; low-engine exhaust installation, 109; rudder, **179**–80, **184**; rudder safety factor, 185; rudder sizing, 168–69, 170; rudder stock angle, 197, **198**; seacocks, 280, **282**; vent installation, **233**. *See also* planing hulls
power steering, 203, 206–8, **207**
pressure and stress conversion table, 399–400
pressure drop, 313
pressure head, 308
prismoidal formula, 92
propeller: 3-bladed, 2, **3**, 6, 25; 4-bladed, 6, 25; 5-bladed, 2, **3**, 6, 25; 6-bladed, 4, 25; action and operation of, 3, 5; aperture, 25–27, **26**, **214**–15; blade area, 2–4; cavitation, 3, 5–6; clearances, **5**; disc area ratio, 2, 4; fuel consumption rate calculation, 91–92; hub, 16–**17**; induced drag, 5; interference fit with shaft, 16–17; number of blades, 6; overhang, propeller-shaft, 12; pitch, 6; pocket, 6–**9**; removal of, rudder and, 212–15; **213**, **214**; retracting dory, 37, **38**; rotation direction, **28**–29; sizing of, 2;

412

INDEX

tunnel, 6–**9**; water inflow to, 24–28, **26**
Propeller Handbook (Gerr), 215
propeller nuts, 1–**2**, **3**
propeller shaft: alignment, 12; angle and placement, **27–31**; bearings, **12**, 22, 42; bearings, intermediate, 13–15, **14**; bent, 13; collar, 17; diameter, 9–11; divided, 16; failures, 16; interference fit with hub, 16–17; intermediate section, 16; materials for, 11, 12; overhang, propeller-shaft, 12; removal of, rudder and, 212–15, **213**, **214**; shaft-bearing spacing, 11–12; tail section, 16; whirling vibration, 13
propeller-shaft couplings and keyways, **15–17**
propeller slipstream diverters. *See* high-lift rudders
propeller strut: aperture, propeller, 25–27, **26**; bearings, intermediate, **14**, 15; dimensions, 18–21, **19**, **20**, 22; fastening and mounting, 22–**24**; grounding skeg, **25**; importance of, 18; I-struts, 8, 18, **19**, 25; leg angles and water inflow, 24–25; materials, 21–22; P-struts, 8; purpose of, 18; section shape, **20**, 24; V-struts, 8, 18, **19**, 24–25
propeller vibration and noise: cavitation, 3, 5–6; frequency testing, 5–6; number of blades and, 6, 8; overhang, propeller-shaft, 12; shaft noise, 6; strut installation and, 22; tip noise, 5, 6; tunnel and pocket noise, 6–**9**; whirling vibration, 13
PSS Shaft Seal, 40–**41**
Pugh, David, 172–73
pull-pull steering, **210**–11
Pump Handbook (Karassik, Messina, Cooper, and Heald), 306

pumps: access to, 302; dry suction head, 304; fire main, **291**, 297–**98**; flow speeds, 311–12; fuel-transfer, 57–58, 305, 313; gasoline fuel pumps, 58; head, 306; head, friction, 308–9, 313; head, pressure, 308; head, static, **306**–8, 313; head, total apparent, 309–11, **310**; head, velocity, 308; power requirements, 312; pressure drop, 313; pump selection, 308; selection, 304–5, 312–13; sizing, 302; suction head, 304; suction vs. pressure, 58; systems that use, 302; types of, 302–**4**. *See also* raw-water pump
pump toilets, 328
PYI: flexible shaft coupling, 40; Python-Drive, 35
pyrometer, 104
Python-Drive, 35

rack-and-pinion steering, 210
Racor: fuel filter, **59**; Lifeguard fuel/air separator, 74, **75**
radial pumps, 304
radiators, 130, **131**
radius-corner tank construction, **81**
rain and spray hoods, **237**
range, fuel consumption rate and, 90–**91**
Raritan LectraSan, 329
raw-water cooling: cooling circuit for air-conditioning, **248**–49; engine cooling, 129–**30**; excess water, bypass line for, 117–19, **118**; pump selection, 305
raw-water intake. *See* sea suction
raw-water pump: access to, 127; for cooling circuit for air-conditioning, 249; failures, 105–6, 127; heat-exchanger cooling, 131, **132**; pump selection, 305; sharing seacocks, 283–84;

water-jacketed dry exhaust system, 153, 155
reciprocating positive-displacement pumps, 302–**3**
reduction gear coolers, 136
reduction gear geometry, 32–35, **33**, **34**
refrigeration, 250–53, **252**
refrigerators, 251, 252–53
resources, 401–2
reticulated-foam bladder tanks, **96**
retracting dory propeller, 37, **38**
reverse-cycle air-conditioning, 247, 255
right-hand rope, 358
ring-form rudders, 216–**19**
rock wool, 150
Rocna anchor, 344, **345**, 366
roller bearings, 190, **194**
Rolls Royce/Ulstein rudder, 223, **224**
root and root chord, 163, **164**
rope: attaching chain to, 361–**62**; chafe, 359–**60**; characteristics, 348, 358; rode sizing, 367–68, 369–70; storage, **362**–63, 381–83, **382**, **384**; types of, 358, 359, 361, **362**
rope locker, 381–83, **382**, **384**
rope spool, **362**–63
rotary positive-displacement pumps, **303**–4
rotary sliding-vane pumps, 57
rotary vane pump, 303, **304**, 305
Rotor-Rudder, 226, 228
rubber, 65
Rubber Design B.V. exhaust pipe hangers, 145–**46**
rubbing alcohol, 87–88
rudder: allowance, 192–93; angle indicator, 210; aspect ratio, 164, 165, 177–**78**; axial loads, 195–96; balance, 165–**68**, 222, 223; boat behavior in turns and, **180–81**; center of water force, 167, 188; course keeping principles and characteristics, 226–27; free-trailing angles, **212**; gudgeons and pintles, 195; hull

413

INDEX

design and, 164–**65**; installation and removal, 212–**15**; maneuvering principles and characteristics, 227; materials for, 174–77, **175**, **176**; principle of, 163; profile (planform), 177–80, **178**, **179**; propeller aperatures, **214**–15; safety factors, 185; section offsets table, 173–74; section shape, 170–**73**; sizing of, 168–70, 222; terminology to describe, 163–64; water force on, 182–**84**

rudder, types of: articulated flap, 219, 222, 223–28, **224**, **225**, **226**; Barke, 223, 226; Becker, 223, 226; bulbous flap, **224**; Deflector Rudder, **224**, **225**, 226; double fixed-geometry high-lift, 224–**26**, 228; fishtail, **219**–23, 226–27; flat-plate, 174–**75**, **222**–23; Harrison patent, **218**; high-lift, **219**–28; inboard, 165, 166; Kitchen, 216–18, 219, **219**, 228; MacLear Thistle, **219**–22, 223, 228; outboard, 165, **166**, **176**, 179; ring-form, 216–**19**; Rotor-Rudder, 226, 228; Schilling, 222, 228; spade, 166, **167**, 177–79, **178**, 183–**84**, 185; steerable Kort nozzle, 218–**19**; T-rudder, 226, 228

rudder bearings: clearance, 192; loads on, 189–90, 194–95; location, **184**, **189**, **191**; materials for, 190, **194**; self-aligning, **194**

rudder palms, **215**

rudder port: allowance, 192–93; compression tube, **191**, 193–94; location, **184**, **191**; packing gland, **191**, 193; tube wall thickness, 193

rudder stock: angle of, 197–98; bearings above and below blade, 188–89; diameter, 182–87; materials for, 186, 187–88, 189, 195; section modulus, 186–87; strength going astern, 188; weight of, 186; weight-saving strategies, 187–88; welded, 187

rudder stops, **209**–10
rumrunner covers, 105
R. W. Fernstrum keel coolers, 139

safety factors, 185
safety seacock, **280**
sailboats: bilge systems, vented loop on, 294–**95**; exhaust system installation, **107**, 109, 119, **120**–**21**; fuel tank location, 71; helm speed, 201; mechanical systems, xxii; propeller aperatures in rudder, **214**–15; propeller shafts angle, 29, **30**; rudder, **166**, 167, **176**, 177–79, **178**; rudder aspect ratio, 164, 177–**78**, 187–88; rudder safety factor, 185; rudder selection, 173; rudder sizing, 168, 170; rudder stock, 187–88; rudder stock angle, 197; seacocks, 280–81; shaft collars, **196**; vent installation, **233**

Schilling rudder, 222, 228
Schnell boat, 119, **122**, 123, **124**
schooner exhaust system, 119, **120**–**21**
scope, 368
scuttlebutt, 314
Seabreeze, xxi–xxii
sea chest, 126, **284**–**87**
seacocks, 126, 278–**82**
SeaLand: holding tanks, **327**; OdorSafe Hose, **325**; T-series pump, **326**; VacuFlush toilet, 328
seaplanes, 332
sea strainers, **59**, 126, 141, 282–**83**, **284**
sea suction: hose clamps, 282; hull strainers, **282**; pumps sharing seacocks, 283–84; sea chest, 126, **284**–**87**; seacocks, 126, 278–**82**; sea strainers, **59**, 126, 282–**83**, **284**; systems that use, 278

sea valves, 280, **281**
seawater: characteristics, 93; flushing head with, 328–29; washing dishes with, 315, 318
Securefill, 76, **78**
semidisplacement hulls: keel cooling, 141; rudder sizing, 168–69
Sen-Dure oil cooler, **59**
Separ fuel filter, **48**
shackles, **353**–**56**, 367, 369
shaft collars, 195–**96**
sheet anchor, 346
sheet-metal tanks, 80–**81**, 83, 84
Shipmate Skippy heater, **253**–54
showers, 314, 315
shower sumps, 319–20
silicon bronze rudder stock, 186, 187, 189, 195
silicon bronze struts, 18–22
silting, 129, 130
single-screw boats: propeller rotation, **28**–29; propeller shaft removal, **213**; propeller shafts angle, 29, **30**; rudder, 179
siphon break, 110, **112**, 294–**95**, 320
SI units system (International System of Units), xx
skegs: antifouling, **178**, 179; grounding skeg, **25**; rudder section shape and, **173**; rudder sizing and, 170
skid fin, **165**
skylights, 235–**36**
slag wool, 150
slip-ring shaft seals, 40–**41**
slug units, 183, xx
Smith, Westeney, 335
Smokehead, **254**
solar-powered ventilation, **236**–37, **241**, 266, 270
sounding stick, 83, 86
source information, 401–2
spade anchor, 343–44, **345**, 346–47, 366

INDEX

spade rudder, 166, **167**, 177–79, **178**, 183–84, 185
span, 163, **164**
Splash-Stop unit (Vetus), 76, **78**
sportsfisherman designs, **72, 108**
spurling pipe, 381, 382
stability: fuel tanks and free-surface effect, 96–99; GM (metacentric height), 97–99; righting arm (GZ), 97–99
stainless steel bearings, 194
stainless steel chain, 352–53
stainless steel exhaust-system parts, 104, 107
stainless steel rudder stock, 186, 187, 195
stainless steel struts, 21–22
stainless steel tanks, 83, 84, 315
stainless wire rope, 363–64
standpipe exhaust system, **116–17**
static head, **306**–8, 313
steam hose, 105
steel keel cooling components, 133, 134
steel sheeting for insulation, 151–**52**
steel tanks, 83
steerable Kort nozzle rudder, 218–**19**
steering systems: Akermann, **211**–12; backup, 208–**9**; design of, 198–99; free-trailing angles, **212**; helm limit, 200; hydraulic, **202**–8; power steering, 203, 206–8, **207**; pull-pull, **210**–11; rack-and-pinion, 210; responsiveness of, 163; rudder angle indicator, 210; rudder stops, **209**–10; tiller, 199–200, 208, **209**; wheel-and-cable steering, **200**–202; worm-gear, 210
steering torque, 198, 203
Stephens, Rod, 234
stockless anchors, 335–36, **337**, 366
storage areas, ventilation of, **241**
storm anchor, 346–47, 365–66

stoves and heaters, wood and coal, **253–54**
stream anchor, 346–47, 365–66
street anchor, 346–47, 365–66
stress conversion table, 399–400
strum box, **288**–89, **295**, 303
struts. *See* propeller strut
stud-link chain, 348–**49**
stuffing box: flexible (self-aligning) hose-type, **41**–42; operation of, 40; packing material, 40, 41; rigid, 14, 15, **40**; slip-ring-type PSS Shaft Seal, 40–**41**; water injection, 42
suction head, 304
Summer Kyle, **115**, 235–**36**
Summer Moon II, 71–**72**
supply boats, 159–**60**, 162
surge chamber, **100**, 105, 127
swivels, 356–**58**, 367, 369
systems on boats, xxi–xxiii

tanks: areas of plane figures, calculating, **386**–87; capacity calculations, 92–**95**. *See also* fuel tanks; metal tanks
Taylor, Geoffrey, 340
Te Kouma, 223
tempered-water air-conditioner, 243
terneplate steel tanks, 83
Theory of Wing Sections (Abbott and Doenhoff), 171
Thermo-12/Blue insulation, 150
thermodynamic ton, 250
thermostats, 129
Thordon bearings, 22
three-strand rope, 358, 359, 361
through-hulls, **112**, 278
through-hull spool, 278, 280, **281**
thrust bearing, **35**, 36, 37, **39**, 196
thrust load calculation, 36
tiller steering, 199–200, 208, **209**
tinned copper tanks, 83
Tiny Tot stoves, 254
tip and tip chord, 163, **164**
toilet. *See* head (marine toilet)
tolerance, 192

ton of air-conditioning, 250
transformers, ventilation for, 269–70
Transite board, 151–**52**
transmission geometry, 32–35, **33, 34**
transoms, **107**
Trident sanitation hose, 325
Trotman, John, 333
Trotman anchor, 333, **334**
T-rudder, 226, 228
tubing. *See* hose, tubing, and pipe
turbochargers, 106
twin-screw boats: Akermann steering, **211**–12; backup steering system, 208; propeller rotation, **29**; propeller shaft removal, 212–**13**; propeller shafts angle, 29–**31**; rudder, 179–80
twisting moment, 184–85, 188
Twombly, 6, **7**

Ulstein rudder, 223, **224**
ultra-high-molecular-weight polyethylene (UHMW-PE): anchor rollers, 377; bearings, 190, **191**, 192–93, 194, 196; characteristics, 377
underwater exhaust systems, 119, **122–24**
United States customary units, xx
universal joints, 36, **37–39**
U.S. Coast Guard regulations: CNG, 270; fire extinguishers, 299–300; fuel filters, 49; fuel-line hose, **61**, 63; fuel tank materials, 87; fuel tank vents, 275; insulation, 151; LPG, 270; through-hull spool, 280, **281**

VacuPanel, 253
vacuum-flush toilets, 328
valves, fuel-line, **59**–61
vane pumps, 57, 303, **304**, 305
velocity head, 308
vented loop, 110, **112**, 294–**95**, 320

INDEX

ventilation: for battery compartment, 270; blowers and ducts, 237–40, **238**, **239**, 263–64, 265–**66**, 272–75, **274**; blower timer switch, 269; for converters, 269–70; ejector ventilation, 153, **154**, **155**, **156**; electric-powered, 237–40, **238**, **239**; of engine spaces, 263–69, **265**, **266**, **267**, 270; exhaust vents, 240, 266; fire dampers for, **271**; hatches, 235–**36**, 240–41; for heaters, 262; for inverters, 269–70; make-up air, 240, 249; of passenger compartments, 231–41, **233**, **234**, **235**, **236**, **237**; permeability, 240, 249, 275; purpose of, 230; skylights, 235–**36**; solar-powered, **236**–37, **241**, 266, 270; of storage areas, **241**; for transformers, 269–70; vent area requirements, 232, 234–35, 263–64; vent installation, **233**, 266, **267**; vent types, **229**, **230**, 232, **234**, **236**, **237**, 240–**41**; volume change rate, 231–32, 234, 268–69; windows, **235**, **237**
Ventilation of Boats Using Gasoline (ABYC), 272
ventilation plate, 166
venturi vent, **237**
Vetus den Ouden: bladder tanks, 95; Splash-Stop unit, 76, **78**
VHT Paints, 152–53
Victory, HMS, 347
volume calculations, 92–**95**
volume change rate, 231–32, 234, 268–69

Walter Machine Co. keel coolers, 139, **140**, 141
warps, 358–59
water: characteristics, 93; flushing head with, 324, 328–29; use per person per day, 315; weight of, 68, 315. *See also* freshwater systems; raw-water cooling; sea suction
water casks, **314**
water-flow sensor, 104
water heaters, 317–18
water-jacketed dry exhaust system, 153, 155, **157**, 159
waterlift mufflers, 109–14, **110**, **111**, **115**–16, **125**, 127
watermakers, 315
water pump: access to, 127; failures, 105–6, 127; freshwater systems, 305, **316**–17; heat-exchanger cooling, 131, **132**; keel cooling, 132. *See also* raw-water pump
water-separator mufflers, 124–**25**, **126**, 128
water tanks: baffles, 315; capacity, 315; materials for, 315; requirements, 315–16; shared walls with fuel tanks, 80; weight of water and tank, 68, 315
wedge-section rudder, **172**–73
weight calculation, 183
wet exhaust systems: access to, 107; backflow protection, 105, 127; back pressure, **101**–2, 110, 119; basic system, **100**; bulkhead clearances, 106; connectors and clamps, **106–8**; corrosion, 104–5, 127; cracks in, 106; drystack vs. wet, 161–62; exhaust life-line volume, 113; exhaust line diameter, **102**, 113–14; exhaust riser, **101**, **103–4**, 127; flapper, **100**, 105, 127; hose and tubing, 105–6, 127; hose clamps, **106**, 107–**8**; keeping water out, 103, 105; leaks in, 103, 105–6, 107; maintenance of, 100; manifolds, 104–5; materials for, 104–5, 107, 127; mixed-exhaust installations, 119, **120–21**, 155, 159–**60**; mufflers, **100**, 108; North Sea exhaust system, 114–16, **115**; principle of, 102, 128; pyrometer, 104; requirements for reliable systems, 126–27; sharing, 109; space requirements, **108**–9; standpipe exhaust system, **116–17**; support for, 106–**7**; surge chamber, **100**, 105, 127; underwater exhaust systems, 119, **122–24**; water-flow sensor, 104; water injection location, 105; waterlift mufflers, 109–14, **110**, **111**, **115**–16, **125**, 127; water-separator mufflers, 124–**25**, **126**, 128; water volume calculation, 102–3
wheel-and-cable steering, **200**–202
whirlpool, 314, xxi, xxii
Wilcox-Crittenden Skipper II toilet, 328
windlasses: electric-powered, 372–73; horizontal, 375; hydraulic, 373; selection, 370–75; vertical, **371**, 375; wildcat vs. gypsy, 375; wire-rope, **363**–64
windows, **235**, **237**
wire gauges/wire size, 373, 374–75
wire-rope anchor rode, 363–64, 368–69
wire-rope windlass, **363**–64
wood alcohol, 88
wooden rudders, **176**
wood-epoxy tanks, 315
wood stoves and heaters, **253–54**
workboats, 25–27, **26**, 107, 159–**60**, 162, 174–**75**
working anchor, 346–47, 365–66
worm-gear steering, 210

yachtsman anchors, 333–**35**, **336**, 365–66, 376
Yale Brait line, 358, 361, **362**
Yanmar engine curves, 90–**91**

zinc anodes, 22, 127, 285, **287**